Compensation

Compensation

Third Edition

George T. Milkovich
Cornell University

Jerry M. Newman
State University of New York—Buffalo

**BPI
IRWIN**

Homewood, IL 60430
Boston, MA 02116

Sponsoring editor: *Craig S. Beytien*
Project editor: *Rita McMullen*
Production manager: *Bette K. Ittersagen*
Cover Designer: *Image House, Inc.*
Interior designer: *David Corona Design*
Compositor: *J. M. Post Graphics, Corp.*
Typeface: *10/12 Times Roman*
Printer: *R. R. Donnelley & Sons Company*

Library of Congress Cataloging-in-Publications Data

Milkovich, George T.
    Compensation / George T. Milkovich, Jerry M. Newman.—3rd ed.
      p. cm.
    ISBN 0-256-07671-5
    1. Compensation management. I. Newman, Jerry M. II. Title.
HF5549.5.C67M54 1990   89–37682
658.3′2—dc20   CIP

Printed in the United States of America
1 2 3 4 5 6 7 8 9 0 DO 7 6 5 4 3 2 1 0

Preface

Managing compensation is a challenge. Everyone suspects that pay, particularly one's own, is determined without apparent justice. In addition, we are in a period when traditional approaches to pay determination are being increasingly questioned and scrutinized.

Managers face serious economic pressures to improve productivity, boost the quality of products and services, and control labor costs. Social pressures stem from shifting employee expectations and continued government regulations. In light of these pressures, managers seek to better understand how to design and manage the compensation their employees receive. Traditional, often bureaucratic, approaches to pay are being reexamined. Different approaches—some new, some simply old goods in new wrappings—are being tried. Current approaches may be retained but are frequently better understood and managed after reexamination.

This process of creative reexamination is both a boon and a source of frustration for managers. On the positive side, managers have the opportunity to make decisions that dramatically affect their organizations. Pay decisions can be integrated into the entire strategic management process. Compensation policies can facilitate effective work behaviors, support equitable treatment of employees, and accomplish organization objectives.

These opportunities can also be a source of frustration. Very simply, compensation can no longer be managed from a limited approach. Pursuit of the single, correct technique is futile. Viewing problems exclusively from a compensation perspective is also futile. Coordinating compensation decisions with other areas of human resource management will yield better corporate outcomes.

When all is said and done, managing compensation remains an art. Like any art, not everything that can be learned can be taught. Not everything that is learned is done so consciously. Some managers of compensation seem more intuitive than others. They seem to be "naturals"; like Wayne Gretsky. He knows how to put the hockey puck into the net, but cannot always explain what he did right. Often what gets included in textbooks are the beliefs, examples, and tricks of the trade. Some of these are supported by related theory and research, many are not. Systematic knowledge is valued, and we have tried mightily to formalize it in this book. But please remember that compensation management is not a science. The more we learn about this field, the more we sense that the less teachable parts of managing compensation are also valuable.

ABOUT THIS BOOK

The design of this book is largely based on four strategic choices involved in managing compensation systems. As the compensation model in Chapter 1 illustrates, these strategic choices include concerns for internal consistency (internal equity), external competitiveness (external equity), employee contributions (employee equity), and the process of administration. Four sections in this book examine each of these strategic decisions and discuss the major compensation issues requiring resolution. These discussions are placed in the context of related theories, research, and state-of-the-art practices that can guide compensation decision making.

Additional chapters of this book cover employee benefits, government's influence on compensation, pay discrimination, compensation of special groups, and unions' role in pay administration. These are topics of continuing importance. First, costs of employee benefits are escalating rapidly, and employers are taking significant steps to contain those costs by modifying benefit programs. Employees are also increasingly able to choose various benefits tailored to their individual circumstances. Next, the government's role is considered in terms of its direct and indirect effects on pay. Directly, government is a regulator of pay decisions through legislation and the courts (e.g., minimum wage, pay discrimination, and comparable worth). Indirectly, through its fiscal and monetary policies (e.g., tax laws and stimulating the economy), the government affects the supply and demand for labor and, hence, compensation decisions. The changing yet critical role unions and special groups assume in compensation management is also examined in separate chapters and throughout the book.

This book undertakes three central tasks. The first is to examine the current theory and research related to managing compensation. This analysis is supported by extensive up-to-date references in each chapter.

The second task is to examine the changing state of compensation practice. Here we draw upon practices actually used by a wide variety of employers and consulting firms. These practices illustrate new developments as well as established approaches to compensation decisions.

Finally, this book provides an opportunity for you to develop your own decision-making skills through a series of exercises based on actual experiences. These exercises apply concepts and techniques discussed in the chapters. A workbook with more extensive cases and computer applications is also available. Completing these exercises will help you develop skills readily transferable to future jobs and assignments.

ACKNOWLEDGMENTS

We relied on the contributions of many people in the preparation of this book. We owe a special, continuing debt of gratitude to our students. In the classroom they motivate and challenge us, and as returning managers with compensation experience, they try mightily to keep our work relevant.

We appreciate the contributions of the many compensation professionals who shared their ideas and practices with us for this third edition. Some commented on early drafts of chapters; others shared details about particular problems and projects. While we cannot hope to recognize all of them, a few who went beyond the call of duty include:

Jeanie Adkins	Mercer Meidinger Hansen
Lance Berger	Hay
John Bronson	Pepsico
Jim Curnow	3M
Shirley Currey	TRW
Bill Evans	General Electric
Joel Goldberg	RJR—Nabisco
Michael Guthman	Hewitt
Lester Jackson	Compensation Consultants, Inc.
Luiz Kahl	Sohio-Carborundum
Steve O'Byrne	TPF&C
Bob Ochsner	Hay
Ray Olsen	TRW
Larry Phillips	General Electric
Walt Read	IBM
Ken Ross	AT&T
Laura Schoeneman	Chase—Lincoln Bank
Jim Urbas	Borg Warner
Dave Wessinger	Organization Resource Counselors

Several academic colleagues were also very helpful in the preparation of this edition. The comments of the following were especially appreciated.

Eric Cousineau	York University
John Delaney	University of Iowa
Donald Drost	California State—San Bernardino
Barry Gerhart	Cornell University
Luis Gomez-Mejia	Arizona State University
John Kilgour	California State—Hayward
Thomas Mahoney	Vanderbilt University
Robert Risley	Cornell University
Sara Rynes	Cornell University
Glenn R. Thiel	Robert Morris College

We would also like to acknowledge those who helped us with the first and second editions. Detailed comments by Ronald A. Ash (University of Kansas), David B. Balkin (University of Colorado, Boulder), Harold Bell (J.C. Penney), Chris Berger (Purdue University), George Bohlander (Arizona State University), Renae Broderick (Cornell University), Robert Cardy (Arizona State University), William Chew (General Motors), Michael D. Crino (Clemson University), Don Finn (J.C. Penney), John Fossum (University of Minnesota), Cynthia Fukami (University of Denver), Michael Gold (Cornell University), James C. Hodgetts (Memphis State University), Gregory S. Hundley (University of Oregon), John G. Kilgour (California State University), Frank Krzystofiak (State University of New York—Buffalo), Steve Kumagai (IDS-American Express), David Ness (Medtronics), Ronald Page (Hay), Bonnie Rabin (Ithaca College), Vida Scarpello (University of Florida), Donald P. Schwab (University of Wisconsin), Susan Schwochau (State University of New York—Buffalo), Thomas H. Stone (Oklahoma State University), Nathan Winstanley (Rochester Institute of Technology), and Steve Wolf (Kerr-McGee) were particularly useful. David Belcher (San Diego State) influenced the thinking of many compensation professionals, including us.

Several graduate students also offered crisp and cutting commentary, for which they will pay; John Hannon, Caroline Weber, Rochelle Gesoff, Fumi Urashima, Sandhya Narayanan, Melissa Barringer, and Tom Friedrich.

Our deans, David Lipsky (Cornell) and Joe Alutto (SUNY—Buffalo), continue to provide supportive work climates, for which we thank them. Manuscript preparation by Josephine Churey and Hilde Rogers was always thorough and timely.

Contributions of Sarah, Mike, and Matt Milkovich and Terrie, Erinn, and Kelly Newman to the authors' quality of life are unparalleled.

We owe a continuing and special debt to Carolyn Milkovich. Her administrative, editing, and motivational talents continue to be of inestimable value.

George T. Milkovich and Jerry M. Newman

Contents

Chapter **5**   **Job Evaluation: Administration   145**

Part **3**   **Employee Contributions: Determining Individual Pay** **242**

Chapter **8**   **Employee Contributions: Pay and Performance** **244**

Chapter **9**   **Subjective Performance Evaluation and Merit Pay**   **277**

Chapter **10**   **Alternatives to Traditional Reward Systems**   **323**

Part **4**   **Employee Benefits   362**

Chapter **11**   **The Benefits Determination Process   364**

Chapter **12**   **Benefits Options   391**

Part **5**   **Government's Role and Compliance   424**

Chapter **13**   **The Government's Role in Compensation   426**

Chapter **14** **Pay Discrimination**   **444**

Part 6   Managing the System   492

Chapter 15   Budgets and Administration   494

Chapter **16**   **Compensation of Special Groups   522**

Compensation

Chapter

1 Strategic Perspective and the Pay Model

Think of an employer, any employer—from Burlington Northern Railroad to Ralph's Pretty Good Groceries—and consider the array of wages paid. Burlington Northern's wages differ for different jobs ranging from locomotive engineers, to laborers on main-tenance-of-way gangs, accountants, traffic clerks, and nurses. Similarly, Ralph's pays checkout clerks, produce department managers, and butchers.[1]

Why do some employers pay more (or less) than other employers? Why are different jobs within the same organization paid differently? And why do different workers doing

---

[1]Garrison Keillor, *Lake Wobegon Days* (New York: Viking Press, 1985).

1

the same job for the same employer receive different pay? How are these decisions made and who is involved in making them? What are the consequences of these decisions for both the employer and the employee? These questions were so interesting to Mary Lemons, a Denver nurse, that she took her employer, the city of Denver, to court, alleging that it was illegal to pay Denver's tree trimmers (all men) more than its nurses (mostly women).[2] Compensation, whether it's your own or someone else's, is a fascinating topic.

Compensation managers are immersed in one of society's greatest challenges: the efficient and equitable distribution of the returns for work. As already noted, compensation decisions are many and varied. They include how much to pay people who perform both similar and different types of work; whether to use pay to recognize variations in individual employees' experience and/or performance; and how to allocate pay among cash and benefits and services. Such basic decisions must be made by every employer, no matter how large or small. Further, these decisions must be consistent both with society's changing values about what constitutes fair and equitable pay and with government legislation and regulations. Consequently, decisions about compensating people for the work they perform are increasingly complex, as are the skills required to make those decisions.

This book is about the management of compensation—the decisions that go into paying employees; the concepts and research underlying those decisions; the alternative techniques used to help make decisions; and the objectives obtained. Its purpose is to give you the background required to make these pay decisions.

COMPENSATION IN CONTEMPORARY SOCIETY

Perceptions of compensation vary. Some in *society* may see it as a measure of equity and justice. Others may see high pay as a cause of U.S. firms' inability to meet foreign competition. Still others may see it as an underlying cause of tax increases. For example, a comparison of 1988 median weekly earnings of fully employed women ($315, or 70 percent) with that of men ($449) highlights apparent inequities in pay decisions, which many consider an indication of discrimination against women.[3] To consumers, the fact that production workers in South Korea earn, on average, 18 percent ($5.46) of their U.S. counterparts' hourly pay ($13.90) is the root of U.S. manufacturing competitive problems.[4] Some voters also see compensation as the cause of increased taxes (wages for teachers and public employees) and inflation (wage settlements negotiated by unions). Public policymakers and legislators may view income differences as guides for adjusting entitlements and transfer payments (social security, aid to dependent children, and the like).

In contrast to the societal perspective, *employees* may see compensation as a return

---

[2]*Lemons* v. *City and County of Denver,* 620 F.2d 228 (1980).

[3]Labor force statistics derived from *Current Population Survey,* U.S. Dept. of Labor, Bureau of Labor Statistics, August 1988, Bulletin 2307. Also see Chapter 14 on Pay Discrimination.

[4]*International Comparisons of Hourly Compensation Costs for Production Workers in Manufacturing, 1988,* U.S. Department of Labor, Bureau of Labor Statistics, 1989, Report 766.

for services rendered or as a reward for satisfactory or meritorious work. Compensation to some reflects the value of their personal skills and abilities, or the return for the education and training they have acquired. The pay individuals receive for the work they perform is usually the major source of personal income and hence a vital determinant of an individual's economic and social well-being.

Managers also have a stake in compensation; they view it from two perspectives. First, it is a *major expense*. Competitive pressures, both internationally and domestically, force managers to consider the affordability of their compensation decisions. Studies show that in many enterprises labor costs account for more than 50 percent of total costs.[5] Among some industries, such as service or public employment, this figure is even higher. Recent studies report that labor costs as a percent of total costs vary even among individual firms within one industry. This has led some to conclude that compensation practices can offer some firms a competitive advantage in their industry.[6]

In addition to viewing compensation as an expense, a manager also views it as a possible *influence on employee work attitudes and behaviors*.[7] Compensation may affect an individual's decision to apply for a job, to work productively, to organize a union, to take the employer to court, or even to undertake training to acquire new skills or additional responsibilities. This potential to influence employees' work attitudes and behaviors, and subsequently the productivity and effectiveness of the organization, is an important rationale for ensuring that compensation is managed fairly and equitably. These contrasting perspectives of compensation—societal, individual, and managerial, each with different stakes in compensation decisions—can account for the relevance of the topic. But these perspectives can also cause confusion if not everyone is talking about the same thing. So let's define what we mean by compensation.

FORMS OF PAY

Compensation, or pay (the words are used interchangeably in this book), is defined in the following terms:

> **Compensation refers to all forms of financial returns and tangible services and benefits employees receive as part of an employment relationship.**

Exhibit 1.1 shows the variety of forms of compensation. Pay may be received directly in the form of cash (e.g., wages, merit increases, incentives, cost-of-living adjustments)

---

[5]Ira T. Kay and Martin Leshner, *Human Resource Costs and Business Strategy: Striving for Competitive Advantage in the Pharmaceutical Industry* (New York: The Hay Group, 1986).

[6]Ibid.

[7]Edward E. Lawler III, *Pay and Organizational Development* (Reading, MA: Addison-Wesley Publishing, 1981); and George Milkovich and Renae Broderick, "Developing Compensation Strategies," in *Handbook of Wage and Salary Administration*, 3rd ed. M. Rock (New York: McGraw-Hill, 1990).

EXHIBIT 1.1
Forms of Compensation

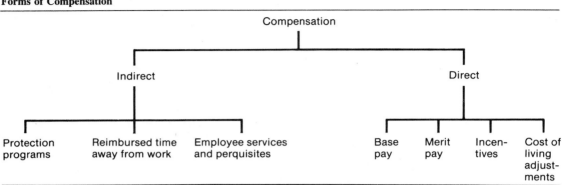

---

or indirectly through benefits and services (e.g., pensions, health insurance, paid time off). This definition excludes other forms of rewards or returns that employees may receive, such as promotions, verbal recognition for outstanding work behaviors, feelings of accomplishment, and the like. Such factors may be thought of as part of an organization's "total reward system" and are often coordinated with compensation.[8]

Programs that distribute compensation to employees can be designed in an unlimited number of ways, and a single employer typically will use more than one program. These pay delivery programs typically fall into four forms: base wage, merit pay, incentives, and employee services and benefits.

Base wage is the basic cash compensation that an employer pays for the work performed. Base wage tends to reflect the value of the work itself and generally ignores differences in contribution attributable to individual employees. For example, the base wage for a word processor's work may be $12 an hour, but some individual operators may receive more because of their experience and/or performance. Some pay systems set base wage as a function of the skill or education an employee possesses; examples include engineers, scientists, and craft workers. Periodic adjustments to base wages may be made on the basis of changes in the overall cost of living or inflation, changes in what other employers are paying for the same jobs, or changes in experience/performance/skill of employees.

A distinction is often made between salary and wage, with *salary* referring to pay for those workers who are exempt from regulations of the Fair Labor Standards Act, and hence do not receive overtime pay.[9] Managers and professionals usually fit this category.

---

[8]Readers interested in a broader perspective of reward systems in organization can turn to M. A. Von Glinow, "Reward Strategies for Attracting, Evaluating and Retaining Professionals," *Human Resource Management,* Summer 1985, pp. 191–206; or L. L. Cummings, "Compensation, Culture, and Motivation: A Systems Perspective," *Organizational Dynamics,* Winter 1984, pp. 33–44.

[9]The Fair Labor Standards Act is discussed in Chapter 13.

We refer to such employees as "exempts." Their pay would be calculated at an annual or monthly rate rather than hourly, because hours worked do not need to be recorded. In contrast, workers who are covered by overtime and reporting provisions of the Fair Labor Standards Act—"nonexempts"—usually have their pay calculated at an hourly rate referred to as a *wage.* Some employers, such as Hewlett-Packard and IBM, label all base pay as salary in an attempt to support a management philosophy that all employees are working as a team, rather than being divided into salaried and wage earners.[10]

Merit pay rewards past work behaviors and accomplishments. It is often given as lump-sum payments or as increments to the base pay. Merit programs are commonly designed to pay different amounts (often at different times) depending on the level of performance. Thus, outstanding performers may receive a 10 to 12 percent merit increase nine months after their last increase, whereas a satisfactory performer may receive, say, a 6 to 8 percent increase after 12 or 15 months. According to a survey of 500 U.S. firms, 90 percent reported pay for performance.[11]

Note that merit pay is defined as *rewards.* A reward is given for meritorious performance. A *return* is given in exchange for something of value. Students of compensation do not always make a distinction between rewards and returns. Some refer to all pay as "rewards." Yet few employees would see all of their compensation as a "reward." Rather, they are more likely to describe it as a *return* received in exchange for labor and services given to an employer.

What difference does the distinction between reward and return make? As we will see later, differences in employee and employer perceptions about pay and pay increases may influence the effectiveness of the pay program. These differences in perception are one reason for the ineffectiveness of many "merit pay" programs.

Incentives also tie pay directly to performance. Incentives may be long or short terms, and can be tied to the performance of an individual employee, a team of employees, a total business unit, or even some combination of individual, team, and unit. Usually very specific performance standards are used in short-term incentive programs. For example, at Union Carbide's Chemicals and Plastics Division, for every quarter that an 8 percent return on capital target is met or exceeded, bonus days of pay are awarded. A 9.6 percent return on capital means two extra days of pay for every participating employee for that quarter. Twenty percent return on capital means $8\frac{1}{2}$ extra days of pay. Performance results may be defined as cost savings, volume produced, quality standards met, revenues, return on investments, or increased profits; the possibilities are endless.

Long-term incentives are intended to focus employee efforts on longer range (multiyear) results. Top managers or professionals are often offered long-term incentives (e.g., stock ownership, bonuses) to focus on long-term organizational objectives such as return

---

[10]All-salaried workforce is discussed in Chapter 10.

[11]Charles Peck, "Pay and Performance: The Interaction of Compensation and Performance Appraisal," Research Bulletin #155, The Conference Board, New York, 1984.

on investment, market share, return on net assets, and the like.[12] Some firms, such as Honeywell, grant shares of stock to selected "Key Contributors" who make outstanding contributions to the firm's success. And employee stock ownership (ESOP) plans in which all employees own shares of their employer are believed by some to motivate performance.[13]

Incentives and merit pay differ. While both may influence performance, incentives do so by offering pay as an inducement. Merit, on the other hand, is a reward that recognizes outstanding past performance. The distinction is a matter of timing. Incentive systems are offered prior to the actual performance. Sales commissions are an example; an auto sales agent knows the commission on a Cadillac versus that on a Chevy prior to making the sale. Merit pay, on the other hand, typically is not communicated beforehand, and the amount of money to fund merit increases is usually not known very far in advance.

Merit and incentives are clearly related. Insofar as employees begin to anticipate their merit pay, it acts as an incentive to induce performance. Thus, anticipated rewards become incentives. Merit is typically based on individual performance; incentives may be based on the performance of an individual, team, or unit.

Another important distinction is that merit pay usually "rolls into" base pay—they increase base pay whereas incentives are one-time payments. Hence incentives have to be reearned and do not have a permanent effect on labor costs.

Employee services and benefits are the programs that include a wide array of alternative pay forms ranging from time away from work (vacations, jury duty), services (drug counseling, financial planning, cafeteria support), and protection (medical care, life insurance, and pensions). Because the cost of providing these services and benefits has been rising (for example, employers pay nearly half the nation's health care bills, and health care expenditures have been increasing at rates in excess of 16 percent), they are an increasingly important form of pay.[14] Many employers now manage benefits as closely as they manage direct compensation.[15]

---

[12]Bruce R. Ellig, *Executive Compensation—A Total Pay Perspective* (New York: McGraw Hill, 1982), pp. 219–66; Jude T. Rich and John A. Larson, "Why Some Long-Term Incentives Fail," *Compensation Review,* First Quarter 1984, pp. 26–38; Frederic W. Cook, "SEC Proposed Major Changes That Would Impact Stock Plans," F. W. Cook Newsletter, Feb. 14, 1989; George Paulin, "The Use and Misuse of Restricted Stock," *Compensation and Benefit Review,* May-June 1989, 51–60; George P. Baker, Michael C. Jensen, and Kevin J. Murphy, "Compensation and Incentives: Practice vs. Theory," *Journal of Finance,* July 1988, pp. 593–616; and Frederic W. Cook, "What the Corporate Raiders Have Taught Us About Executive Compensation Principles," December 1, 1986 newsletter, New York: Frederic W. Cook & Co., Inc.

[13]ESOPs are discussed in Chapter 12. While some believe greater stock ownership motivates performance, others argue that the link between individual job behaviors and the vagaries of the stock market are tenuous at best. See "Stuffing Nest Eggs with ESOPs", *Business Week,* April 24, 1989; and Chapter 11, Employee Stock Ownership Plans, EBRI p. 103–108 in *Fundamentals of Employee Benefit Programs,* 2nd edition (1985), Washington, DC.

[14]R. E. Johnson, "Establishing a Successful Approach to Health Plan Cost Management," Employee Benefit News, April 1989, pp. 27–79; and *Fundamentals of Employee Benefit Plans.*

[15]R. E. Herzlinger, "How Companies Tackle Health Care Costs, Parts I, II, & III," *Harvard Business Review,* July-August 1985, pp. 68–81, September-October 1985, pp. 108–20, and November-December 1985, pp. 72–87.

These four pay forms make up the total compensation package paid to employees. The compensation professional is responsible for designing and managing all elements of pay—total compensation.

Expected Costs and Stream of Earnings

Up to this point compensation has been static, something paid or received at a moment in time. But compensation decisions have a temporal quality. Think about the manager who decides to make you a job offer—say $30,000. Look at that decision over time. Assume new hires stay with the firm an average of 5 years and can expect to receive 7 percent annual increases in each of those 5 years. You will be earning $39,324 in 5 years. The expected cost commitment of the decision to hire you turns out to be $224,279.00 ($30,000 base compounded by 7 percent for 5 years, plus benefits equal to 30 percent of base). But lest you rush out to purchase a BMW, it will cost $30,388 in 5 years, presuming 5 percent inflation.

The point is that compensation can be both simple and involved. It is pay. It can be treated as a stream of future earnings, costs, or investment. It can include nonfinancial and psychological returns as in a total reward system. And it can be defined as cash, benefits, and services. In this book we will usually use the latter definition. We turn now to a pay model that will serve as both a framework for examining current pay systems and a guide for much of this work.

A PAY MODEL

The pay model shown in Exhibit 1.2 contains three basic components: (1) the policies that form the foundation of the compensation system; (2) the techniques that make up much of the mechanics or technology of compensation management; and (3) the compensation objectives. Each of these components and the relationships among them are discussed in turn.

Compensation Objectives

Pay systems are designed and managed to achieve certain objectives. The basic objectives, shown at the right side of the model, include efficiency, equity, and compliance with laws and regulations. These objectives in the model are broadly conceived. The *efficiency* objective is typically stated more specifically: (1) improving productivity and (2) controlling labor costs. Often these two can be found in an employer's statement of pay objectives, such as "to facilitate organization performance, to cost effectively attract and retain competent employees and to reward employee contributions and performance."[16]

---

[16]Some writers distinguish between efficiency and effectiveness in organizations. Efficiency focuses on operational concerns such as improving productivity in operations, whereas effectiveness focuses on overall organization performance. The terms are used interchangeably in this text.

EXHIBIT 1.2
A Pay Model

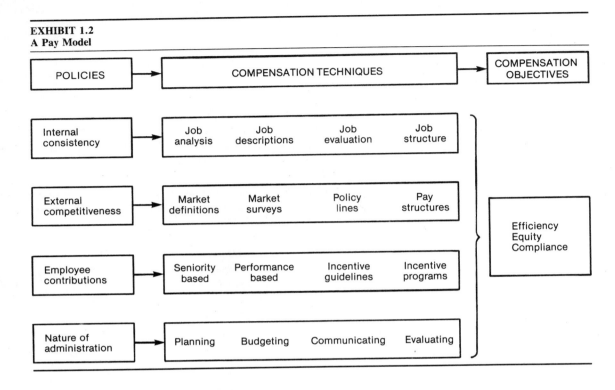

Equity is a fundamental theme in pay systems. Statements such as "fair treatment for all employees" or "a fair day's pay for a fair day's work" reflect a concern for equity. Thus, the equity objective attempts to ensure fair pay treatment for all participants in the employment relationships. The equity objective focuses on designing pay systems that recognize both employee *contributions* (e.g., offering higher pay for greater performance or greater experience or training) and employee *needs* (e.g., providing a "living wage," or health care insurance).

Procedural equity, often overlooked by compensation researchers, is concerned with the processes used to make decisions about pay.[17] It suggests that the way a pay decision is made may be as important to employees as are the results of the decision. As an objective for a pay system, procedural equity helps ensure that employees, managers, and other relevant parties have a voice in the design of pay plans and an opportunity to voice any dissatisfaction with the pay received.

Compliance, as a pay objective, involves conforming to various federal and state

---

[17]Jerald Greenberg "Looking Fair vs. Being Fair: Managing Impressions of Organizational Justice," in B. M. Staw and L. L. Cummings, eds., *Research in Organizational Behavior* 12 (Greenwich, CT: JAI Press, 1990).

compensation laws and regulations. As these laws and regulations change, pay systems often need to be adjusted to ensure continued compliance.

There are probably as many statements of pay objectives as there are employers. In fact, some highly diversified firms, such as TRW and General Electric, which compete in multiple lines of businesses, have different pay objectives for different business units. Examples of Honeywell's and Hewlett-Packard's pay objectives are shown in Exhibit 1.3. Both sets of objectives emphasize high-quality and innovative performance (productivity), competitiveness (costs), ability to attract and retain quality people (productivity), and equity (employee communications, openness, and understanding).

Establishing pay objectives involves several important decisions because these objectives serve several purposes. First, objectives shape the design of the pay system. Consider the employer whose objective is to reward outstanding individual performance. That objective will determine the pay policy (e.g., pay for performance) as well as the elements of pay plans (e.g., merit and/or incentives). Another employer may decide the primary objective of the pay system is to attract and retain competent, highly skilled employees. This employer may decide that performance is best influenced through other personnel practices such as job enrichment or team building techniques. A pay system with these objectives may stress market competitiveness with salaries that at least equal competitors and increases in pay that recognize increased skills or knowledge. The point is that different objectives may result in the design of different pay systems.

Besides affecting the mechanics of pay systems, objectives serve as the standards against which the success of the pay system is evaluated. If the pay objective is to attract and retain a highly competent staff, yet skilled employees are leaving to take higher paying jobs at other employers, the pay system may not be performing effectively. While there may be many nonpay reasons for turnover (or even if there is a desirable level of turnover), objectives serve as a standard for evaluating the effectiveness of a pay system.

EXHIBIT 1.3
Comparisons of Pay System Objectives

Hewlett-Packard

At Hewlett-Packard, our pay program is designed to be innovative, competitive, and equitable so that H-P will continue to attract and retain creative and enthusiastic people who will contribute to H-P's continuing success.

> Your pay has been established to reflect the company's policy of "paying among the leaders."
> Your pay will accurately reflect your sustained relative contribution to your unit, division, and H-P.
> Your pay system will be open and understandable. You are encouraged to discuss the pay process with your supervisor.

Honeywell

To attract the best person available for each Honeywell job.

To encourage growth both on an individual basis and as a participant on a work team.

To recognize the importance of high-quality work performance and to reward it accordingly.

To encourage a career-long commitment to Honeywell.

The Four Basic Policy Decisions

The pay model in Exhibit 1.2 rests on four basic policies that any employer must consider in compensation management. The four policy decisions shown on the left side of the pay model include (1) internal consistency, (2) external competitiveness, (3) employee contributions, and (4) the nature of the administration of the pay system. These policies form the four building blocks, the foundation on which pay systems are designed and administered. These policies also serve as guidelines within which pay is managed to accomplish the system's objectives.

Internal consistency. Internal consistency, often called internal equity, refers to comparisons among jobs or skill levels *inside* a single organization. The focus is on comparing jobs and skills in terms of their relative contributions to the organization's objectives. How, for example, does the work of the word processor compare with the work of the computer operator, the programmer, and the systems analyst? Does one job require more skill or experience than another? Is the output from one job valued more than the output from another? Internal consistency becomes a factor in determining the pay rates both for employees doing equal work and for those doing dissimilar work. In fact, determining what is an equitable difference in pay for people performing different work is one of the key issues in compensation management.

Determining equitable pay focuses on two dimensions:

1. The relative similarities and differences in the content of the work or skills required.
2. The relative contribution of the work or skills to the organization's objectives.

The content of one set of tasks and behaviors (a job) is either equal to or different from another set of tasks and behaviors. A job's relative worth is based on its differing work content and its differing contribution to achieving the objectives of the organization. For example, the contribution of a systems analyst who designs a new inventory or production control system is typically considered to be greater than that of the programmer of the system.

A policy that emphasizes internal consistency may affect all three basic compensation objectives. Equity and compliance with legislation are directly affected, while efficiency is affected more indirectly. As we shall see in Part 1 of the text, equitable pay relationships within the organization affect employee decisions to stay (retention), to invest in additional training, or to seek greater responsibility. By motivating increased training and greater responsibility, pay relationships indirectly affect the efficiency of the work force and hence the effectiveness of the total organization.

External competitiveness. External competitiveness refers to how an employer positions its pay relative to what competitors are paying. How much do other employers pay accountants, and how much do we wish to pay accountants in comparison to what other employers would pay them? Employers have several policy options. Some employers may set their pay levels higher than their competition, hoping to attract the best applicants. Of course, this assumes that someone is able to identify and hire the "best" from the pool of applicants. Another employer may offer lower base pay but greater opportunity to work overtime or better benefits than those offered by other employers. Or pay and benefits may be lower, but job security may be higher. The policy regarding external competitiveness has a twofold effect on objectives: (1) to ensure that the pay rates are sufficient to attract and retain employees—if employees do not perceive their pay as equitable in comparison to what other organizations are offering for similar work, they may be more likely to leave—and (2) to control labor costs so that the organization's prices of products or services can remain competitive. So external competitiveness directly affects both the efficiency and equity objectives. And it must do so in a way that complies with relevant legislation.

Employee contributions. The policy on employee contributions refers to the relative emphasis placed on the performance and/or seniority of people doing the same job or possessing the same job skills. Should all such employees receive the same pay? Or should one programmer be paid differently from another if one has better performance and/or greater seniority? Or should a more productive team of employees be paid more than less productive teams? The degree of emphasis to be placed on performance and/or seniority is an important policy in the design and administration of pay since it may have a direct effect on employees' attitudes and work behaviors and hence on improving efficiency and achieving equity. Employers with strong pay for performance policies are more likely to design more elaborate incentive and merit schemes as part of their pay systems.

Nature of administration. Policies regarding the nature of the administration of the pay system is the last building block in our model. While it is possible to design a system that incorporates internal consistency, external competitiveness, and employee contributions, the system will not achieve its objectives unless it is administered properly. The greatest system design in the world is useless without competent administration. Administration involves planning the elements of pay that should be included in the pay system (e.g., base pay, short-term and long-term incentives), evaluating how the pay system is operating, communicating with employees, and judging whether the system is achieving its objectives. Are we able to attract skilled workers? Can we keep them? Do our employees feel our system is fair? Do they understand what factors are considered in setting their pay? Do they agree that these factors are important? Do employees have channels for raising questions and voicing complaints about their pay? How do the better performing firms, with better financial returns and a larger share of the market, pay their employees? Are the systems used by these firms different from those used by less successful firms? How does our labor cost per unit produced compare to that of our competitors? Such information is necessary to tune or redesign the system, to adjust to changes, and to highlight potential areas for further investigation.

Balancing Consistency, Competitiveness, Contributions, and Administration

The balance or relative emphasis among the four basic policies is a key decision to be made in any employer's compensation strategy. Does it ever make sense to emphasize one policy concern over another? For example, some firms emphasize an integrated approach to all human resource management, and internal consistency of pay becomes part of that strategy. Other firms tend to emphasize external competitiveness of pay and to place less emphasis on internal consistency. Sometimes it makes sense to emphasize external competitiveness because the relationship of an employer's pay level to a competitor's pay level directly affects the ability to attract a competent work force, to control labor costs, and hence to compete with products or services. Yet, ignoring internal consistency and employee contributions may increase an employer's vulnerability to lawsuits and may decrease employee satisfaction. If the person next to me is paid more than I am, there had better be a good reason for this differential. Internal pay differences can affect employees' willingness to accept a promotion, pay satisfaction, absenteeism, turnover, and interest in unionization.

Thus, all four—internal consistency, external competitiveness, employee contributions, and the nature of administration—are critical in the management of pay systems; achieving the desired balance among them is an important part of compensation management. The policies determined for compensation should be consistent and reinforce the overall approach taken to managing human resources.

Pay Techniques

The remaining portion of the model in Exhibit 1.2 shows the pay techniques. The exhibit provides only an overview since techniques are the topic of much of the rest of the book. Techniques tie the four basic policies to the pay objectives. Internal consistency is typically established through a sequence of techniques starting with job analysis. Job analysis collects and then evaluates information about jobs. Based on these evaluations, a job structure is built. A job structure depicts relationships among jobs inside an organization, based on work content and the jobs' relative contributions to achieving the organization's objectives. The goal is to establish a job structure that is internally equitable, because this is related to the equity of the pay system and will affect employee attitudes and behaviors as well as the organization's regulatory compliance.

External competitiveness is established by setting the organization's pay level in comparison with what the competition pays for similar work. But who precisely is the "competition"? The pay level is determined by defining the relevant labor markets in which the employer competes, conducting surveys to find out what other employers pay, and using that information in conjunction with the organization's policy decisions to generate a pay structure. The pay structure influences how efficiently the organization is able to attract and retain a competent work force and to control its labor costs.

The relative emphasis on employee contributions is established through performance and/or seniority based increases, incentive plans, and salary increase guidelines. If an organization decides to pay employees on the basis of performance, it must have some way to evaluate employee performance, and must adjust pay on the basis of that evaluation. Many organizations (and union agreements) decide to pay on the basis of years of service, and so attempt to retain an experienced work force. These practices are all intended to have a significant effect on employee attitudes and behaviors, in particular the decisions to join, to stay, and to perform effectively.

Uncounted variations of these pay techniques exist; many are examined in this book. Such variations arise from the multitude of strategies organizations adopt to accomplish their objectives. Surveys have studied differences in compensation policies and techniques among firms.[18] While no single comprehensive analysis of the four major policy decisions has been reported, it seems clear that the variations in compensation approaches arise from differences in the environments and natures of organizations and in the objectives they are trying to achieve with pay. Such variations may also be derived from the various strategies organizations adopt to accomplish their objectives.

STRATEGIC PERSPECTIVES

So far our discussion has highlighted the major views of compensation and the basic components of the pay model. Upcoming chapters will discuss the particulars of various techniques. But examining and dissecting techniques is so seductive that the mechanics of doing so become the focus, the ends in themselves for some compensation specialists. All too often, traditional pay systems seem to have been designed in response to some historical but long-forgotten situation or purpose. Questions such as "So what does this technique do for (to) us?" "How does this help achieve pay objectives?" and "Why bother with this technique?" are not asked.

So before proceeding to the particulars of pay systems, let us pause to consider some major strategic issues related to pay. The issues to which we will pay special attention include matching compensation to the organization's strategic and environmental conditions, its culture and values, the needs of its employees, and its union/management relationship.

The Pay System and the Organization's Strategies

All pay systems have a purpose. Answer the question, "For what do we want to pay?" and you'll begin to specify the objectives of the pay system. Some are clearly identified, as in our pay model; others must be inferred from the actions of employers. A currently popular prescription found in almost every professor's textbook and consultant's report

---

[18]David B. Balkin and Luis R. Gomez-Mejia, "Compensation Practices in the High Technology Industry," *Personnel Administrator* 30, no. 6 (June 1985), pp. 111–23. Several of the leading consulting firms also survey pay practices of firms. For example, see Peat, Marwick, Main & Co., *Compensation Strategies in the New England High Technology Industry 1989;* Hay Associates, *1989 Hay Compensation Conference Proceedings* (New York: The Hay Group, 1989); Howard W. Risher, *Report on the 1987 Survey of Salary Management Practices* (Scottsdale, AZ: American Compensation Association, 1988); and Peck, *Pay and Performance.*

is for compensation managers to tailor their systems to support the organization's strategic conditions.[19]

The notion is seductive; the reasons offered seem persuasive. They are based on contingency notions. That is, differences in a firm's strategies should be supported by corresponding differences in personnel policies, including compensation policies. The underlying premise is that the greater the congruency, or "fit," between the organization conditions and the compensation system, the more effective the organization. Further, different pay system designs should be aligned with changes in strategic conditions.

Strategy refers to the fundamental direction of the organization. Strategies guide the deployment of all resources, including compensation. USX's $6 billion acquisition of Marathon Oil reflects a new strategic direction for that company. After the acquisition, less than 40 percent of USX's total revenues come from basic steel operations. Another example is Pepsico's decision to acquire the independently owned and operated bottlers of Pepsi Cola. Until the early 1980s Pepsico, the overall corporation, was organized into several business units: Pizza Hut, Frito Lay, Taco Bell, and the soft drink unit Pepsi Cola. Pepsi Cola was manufactured and bottled by local, independently owned facilities throughout the United States and the world. The Pepsi Cola unit focused on marketing the soft drink worldwide. Pepsico shifted its business strategy and began to acquire these independent operators, thereby transforming the Pepsi Cola unit into a manufacturing as well as marketing organizations.

These decisions by USX and Pepsico reflect fundamental changes in direction. Organization resources—financial, capital, and human—will need to be deployed in a manner consistent with these new directions.

---

[19]George T. Milkovich, "A Strategic Perspective on Compensation Strategy," in K. Rowland and G. Ferris, eds., *Research in Human Resource Management* (Greenwich, CT: JAI Press, 1988); George T. Milkovich and Renae Broderick, "Developing Compensation Strategies," in M. Rock, ed., *Handbook of Wage and Salary Administration,* 3rd ed. (New York: McGraw Hill, 1990); Marc J. Wallace, Jr. "Driving Competitive Advantage through Reward Design," paper presented to Jacksonville Compensation Association, 1988; Jerry M. Newman, "Environment, Strategy and Internal Control Systems: Motivating Behavior in Boundary Occupations" (working paper SUNY Buffalo 1989); Michael E. Porter, "From Competitive Advantage to Corporate Strategy," *Harvard Business Review,* May-June 1987, pp. 43–59; Jay Schuster, *Management Compensation in High Technology Companies* (Lexington, MA: Lexington Books, 1984); Jay Schuster, "Compensation Plan Design," *Management Review,* May 1985, pp. 21–25; Ellig, *Executive Compensation—A Total Pay Perspective,* see especially chap. 2 and pp. 14–15; Jude T. Rich, "Strategic Incentives," *1980 National Conference Proceedings* (Scottsdale, AZ: American Compensation Association, 1981), pp. 90–96; D. Balkin and L. Gomez-Mejia, "Toward a Contingency Theory of Compensation Strategy" (University of Florida, Gainesville, FL, working paper, 1986); Steven J. Carroll, "Business Strategies and Compensation Systems," in D. Balkin and L. Gomez-Mejia, *New Perspectives on Compensation* (Englewood Cliffs, NJ: Prentice-Hall, 1987); G. Milkovich, "Compensation Systems in High Technology Companies," in D. Balkin and L. Gomez-Mejia, *New Perspectives on Compensation* (Englewood Cliffs, NJ: Prentice-Hall, 1987); R. Broderick, "Report to the American Compensation Association: Study of Pay Policies and Business Strategies" (Scottsdale, AZ: American Compensation Association, 1985); and James Salscheider, "Devising Pay Strategies for Diversified Companies," *Compensation Review,* Second Quarter 1981, pp. 15–24. Two older references that raise still-relevant issues include Malcolm S. Salter, "Tailor Incentive Compensation to Strategy," *Harvard Business Review,* March-April 1973, pp. 94–102; and J. R. Galbraith and D.A. Nathanson, *Strategy Implementation: The Role of Structure and Process* (St. Paul, MN: West Publishing, 1978).

EXHIBIT 1.4
Strategic Perspective: An Illustration

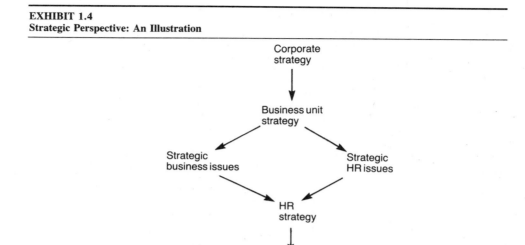

As Exhibit 1.4 depicts, compensation systems can be designed to reinforce the business strategies adopted by these organizations and to adapt to the competitive and regulatory pressure faced in the environment.

Reinforce Business Strategies

In the example above Pepsico corporate strategy for its Pepsi Cola business unit shifted from marketing to manufacturing and marketing when it began to acquire the major bottling plants. As depicted in Exhibit 1.4 this shift to manufacturing has strategic human resources above and beyond compensation. Managers in the Pepsi Cola business, for example, faced decisions about running bottling plants that included negotiating with unions, hiring and supervising production workers, learning how to design and manage employee teams, and the like. None of these decisions were faced when the unit's business focused on marketing. In sum, this overall strategy for managing human resources involves decisions about staffing, organization design, development, employee relations, and compensation. The critical compensation decisions facing managers can be considered in terms of the four basic policies in our pay model.

Consistency. How should different levels of work be paid within each bottling plant? Should employee wages be based on the jobs performed or their abilities or skills to perform many different jobs?

Competitiveness. How should each bottling plant pay in comparison to local wage rates? Should Pepsi Cola have one nation wide set of rates, like AT&T pays its operators and technicians or General Motors pays its assemblers, or should rates be based on local comparable jobs?

Employee contributions. Should Pepsi Cola employee pay increases be based on individual or team performance, on experience and seniority, on changes in cost of living, on the facilities', or on Pepsi Cola's performance?

Administration. What should the policy be toward the employee unions? How involved should employees be in the design of these pay systems? What role will each plant manager play in the design and management of pay systems? Will it be centralized at the business unit or decentralized to each plant?

Note in Exhibit 1.4 that the results of these decisions translate into the compensation system. Our point is that the techniques that make up the compensation system really translate the strategic policy choices into practice. And these strategic choices are critical to the business strategy for the particular business unit and the corporation.

The Pay System and Environmental and Regulatory Pressures

Note in Exhibit 1.4 that the compensation environment also affects the compensation choices. Environment refers to a wide range of pressures, including competitive pressures from product and labor markets, pressures springing from changes in work force demographics, values and expectations, regulatory changes, and the like. In the case of Pepsi Cola, their bottling business is very people-intensive. Consequently, Pepsi Cola managers expect that increasing work force diversity (e.g., with 52 percent of new entrants being women, and increasingly single parents) will affect the forms of pay (child care, educational reimbursements, employee assistance programs) that will be necessary to attract and retain new workers.[20] And Pepsi managers probably do not expect to sit by passively while the Congress considers whether to impose taxes on benefits paid to employees. All to say, the environmental pressures, along with business strategies, probably affect choices about compensation policies and techniques.[21]

Public not-for-profit sector. Strategic decisions are also evident in governmental and public not-for-profit organizations. Examples include a university's desire for a winning football team, or a regional symphony orchestra's attempt to gain national recognition. Pay programs should also be tailored to facilitate the strategic directions of these organizations. The orchestra can offer a renowned conductor a share of the revenues gained from recording sales, or the university may increase funding for the coaching staff through a cut of the gate for that particular sport.

---

[20]William B. Johnston, *Work Force 2000* (Washington, DC: U.S. Department of Labor, 1986).

[21]J. S. Bronson presentation at the 1989 Annual Meeting, Center for Advanced Human Resource Studies, Ithaca, New York.

The common view is that business strategy and anticipated environmental pressures should affect the design of pay systems. But it can also be argued that historical pay decisions can affect subsequent business strategies. In some cases, efforts to adapt pay systems to shifts in strategic conditions are hindered by existing traditional pay policies and technologies.

Compensation managers should recognize that pay systems can be tailored to an organization's strategic conditions. In highly decentralized organizations such as Pepsico, this can even mean that different subunits (e.g., Taco Bell, Frito Lay, Pizza Hut) may adopt different pay systems. It is also important to recognize that existing pay systems can affect the success of shifts in an organization strategy.

The Pay System and the Organization's Culture and Values

Not only are pay programs related to strategic conditions and environment, they are also related to the organization's culture and values. The notions of culture and values are complex.[22] But the values underlying an employer's treatment of its employees can be reflected in its pay system. Some employers articulate their philosophies regarding pay, such as those for Hewlett-Packard and Honeywell, which are shown in Exhibit 1.5. These philosophies give us a sense of how these two firms treat employees and serve as guides for their pay systems. Note that Honeywell's philosophic principles (number 4) reflect its decentralized approach in which each business unit is responsible for its own pay system.

Pay is just one of many systems that make up an organization; its design is also partially influenced by how it fits with the other structures and systems in the organization.[23] A highly centralized and confidential pay system, controlled by a few people in a corporate unit, will not, according to this view, operate effectively in a highly decentralized and open organization.[24] Unfortunately, little research has been done directly on the relationship between pay systems and the culture and values of an organization. This may be because culture and values are ambiguous terms.[25]

The importance of congruency between pay programs and other HR management processes can be illustrated with examples of recruiting, hiring, and promoting. The pay linked with a job offer or a promotion must be sufficient to induce acceptance. Some employers do not maintain significant pay differences between manufacturing workers (such as assemblers or inspectors) and their first-line supervisors. Lack of an adequate pay increase diminishes the incentive for employees to take the training required to be a supervisor or to accept the promotion to supervisor. The situation is reversed for many

---

[22]Harrison M. Trice and Janice M. Beyer, "Studying Organizational Cultures through Rites and Ceremonials," *Academy of Management Review,* October 1984, pp. 653–69.

[23]Lawler, *Pay and Organizational Development.*

[24]Ibid.

[25]Sam Gould and Larry E. Penley, "Career Strategies and Salary Progression: A Study of Their Relationships in a Municipal Bureaucracy," *Organizational Behavior and Human Performance 34* (1984), pp. 244–65.

EXHIBIT 1.5
Comparisons of Pay System Philosophies

Hewlett-Packard's Pay Philosophy

Philosophy of Leadership

Hewlett-Packard's pay philosophy serves as a base for its pay objectives. The major elements of H-P's pay philosophy can be summarized as follows:

"At Hewlett-Packard, we believe in paying people at rates that place us among the leading companies in the country or region from which we attract our people. Our merit pay system uses salary curves derived from these competitive data.

"Your salary position within these curves is determined by your sustained contribution to the company, its customers and shareholders relative to the contributions of others at H-P doing the same or a similar job."

Honeywell's Pay Philosophy

Honeywell is one company, made up of many different businesses. These businesses are united by a common set of values and by common technologies. Yet they differ in respect to their products and services, size, customers, locations, and competitors.

The company's pay philosophy reflects who Honeywell is—both its diversity and its unit. It allows each individual business to design pay systems responding to that business's own requirements. It also means that each system must contain certain assurances of Honeywell employment. These assurances are expressed in four basic pay principles.

Pay Principles

In support of these objectives, four basic pay principles also apply to all Honeywell pay systems.

First, pay must be fully competitive in the market, as defined by each business.

Second, each individual's pay must be fair in relationship to the pay other employees receive within the same Honeywell business.

Third, pay must be communicated. That communication must explain general pay principles, the specific pay system applicable, and the process used to determine individual pay levels under that system.

Fourth, each Honeywell business has the basic responsibility for establishing and maintaining its own pay system.

---

engineering and research jobs, where the pay for managerial positions induces people to leave engineering and research positions.

For managers of compensation, the key point to remember is that pay coexists with other structures in the organization. An effective pay system cannot be designed without taking into account the nature of the organization, its business strategies, and other management systems.

The Pay System and Employee Needs

Within some legally imposed limits, compensation can be delivered to employees in various forms already identified. The allocation of compensation among these pay forms to emphasize performance, seniority, entitlements, or the long versus short term can be tailored to the pay objectives of the organization. It can also be tailored to the needs of the individual employees.

The simple fact that employees differ is too easily and too often overlooked in designing pay systems. Individual employees join the organization, make investment decisions, design new products, assemble components, and judge the quality of results. Individual employees receive the pay. Opsahl and Dunnette were among the first to observe that a major limitation of contemporary pay systems is the degree to which individual attitudes and preferences are ignored.[26] Other researchers agree.[27] Older, highly paid workers may wish to defer taxes by putting their pay into retirement funds, while younger employees may have high cash needs to buy a house, support a family, or finance an education. Dual career couples who are overinsured medically may prefer to use more of their combined pay for child care, automobile insurance, financial counseling, or other benefits. Employees who have young children or dependent parents may desire dependent care coverage.

Short of letting all employees specify their own pay form (a choice that would meet with Internal Revenue Service disapproval and be a headache to administer), pay systems can be designed to permit employee choices. Flexible benefit plans are examples, and many employers have adopted them.[28]

The Pay System and Unions

Pay systems also need to be adapted to the nature of the union-management relationship. Strategies for dealing with unions vary widely. The federal government declared a strike by the air traffic controllers illegal and dissolved their union. The governor of Minnesota sent troops to Austin, Minnesota, to restore order when a strike involving Hormel and local meat-packers threatened to turn violent. Eastern Air Lines' lack of accord with its unions was its rationale for seeking protection under bankruptcy laws. In spite of these highly publicized events, hundreds of union contracts are negotiated each year with little fanfare or rancor.

Union influence on the design and administration of pay systems is significant. Not only do unions affect pay rates and pay forms, they appear to affect the way compensation decisions are made. Freedman and Kochan conclude that a high degree of centralization of decision making exists in collective bargaining.[29] Even where the bargaining was conducted at plant level, only 20 percent of the firms gave responsibility to formulate

---

[26]R. L. Opsahl and M. D. Dunnette, "The Role of Financial Compensation in Industrial Motivation," *Psychological Bulletin 66* (1966), pp. 94–118; Edward E. Lawler III, *Pay and Organizational Effectiveness* (New York: McGraw-Hill, 1971).

[27]Research on this topic dates to the 1970s. See, for example, Lawler, *Pay and Organizational Effectiveness;* George T. Milkovich and Michael Delaney, "A Note on Cafeteria Pay Plans," *Industrial Relations,* February 1975, pp. 112–16; B. N. Fragner, "Employees' 'Cafeteria' Offers Insurance Options," *Harvard Business Review 53* (1975), pp. 2–4; E. E. Lawler and J. R. Hackman, "The Impact of Employee Participation in the Development of Pay Incentive Plans: A Field Experiment," *Journal of Applied Psychology 53* (1969), pp. 467–71.

[28]For an extensive discussion of flexible benefit programs, see Chapters 11 and 12.

[29]Audrey Freedman, *Managing Labor Relations: Organization, Objectives, and Results* (New York: The Conference Board, 1979); Thomas A. Kochan, *Collective Bargaining and Industrial Relations* (Homewood, IL: Richard D. Irwin, 1980).

EXHIBIT 1.6
Hourly Compensation Costs in U.S. Dollars for Production Workers in manufacturing, 1975–88

Country	1975		1980		1983		1985		1987		1988	
		%		%		%		%		%		%
U.S.	$6.36	100	$9.84	100	$12.10	100	$12.96	100	$13.46	100	$13.90	100
Canada	$5.79	91	$8.37	85	$10.85	90	$10.81	83	$11.97	89	$13.58	98
Germany	$6.35	100	$12.33	125	$10.23	85	$9.56	74	$16.87	125	$18.07	130
U.K.	$3.32	52	$7.43	76	$6.39	53	$6.19	48	$8.97	67	$10.56	76
Japan	$3.05	48	$5.61	57	$6.13	51	$6.47	50	$11.14	83	$13.14	95
Singapore	$0.84	13	$1.49	15	$2.21	18	$2.47	19	$2.31	17	$2.67	19
Korea	$0.35	6	$1.02	10	$1.23	10	$1.36	10	$1.79	13	$2.46	18
Taiwan	$0.39	6	$0.98	10	$1.27	10	$1.46	11	$2.19	16	$2.71	19
Brazil	$0.86	14	$1.39	14	$1.26	10	$1.22	9	$1.49	11	—	—
Mexico	$2.00	31	$2.96	30	$1.85	15	$2.09	16	$1.57	12	—	—

Source: U.S. Department of Labor, Bureau of Labor Statistics March 1989, Report 766

pay proposals to plant level management. Corporate staffs typically undertook the drafting and submission of pay proposals. Consequently the very existence of a union seems to affect the degree of centralization that management adopts.

Union preferences for different forms of pay (e.g., cost-of-living adjustments, improved health care) and their concern with job security also affect pay system design. Historically, the allocation between wages and benefits was greatly affected by unions.[30] Unionized workers still have a greater percentage of their total compensation allocated to benefits than do nonunion workers. Solnick found unionization associated with 24 percent higher levels of pension expenditures and 46 percent higher insurance expenditures.[31] More recent evidence suggests that the differentials are declining.[32]

Competitive pressure, particularly from foreign manufacturers, affects the pay rate that unions seem willing to negotiate.[33] During the mid 1980s employers pointed to data, such as those shown in Exhibit 1.6, to argue for changes in existing pay systems. In 1985, hourly compensation for production workers in West Germany was 74 percent of that for the U.S. worker, while a South Korean received only 10 percent of the U.S. average wage. Responding to the pressures, employees and unions accepted wage concessions, wage cuts, smaller pay increases, and one-time lump sum increases which are not

[30]John A. Fossum, *Labor Relations* (Plano, Tex.: Business Publications, 1985); Richard B. Freeman and James Medoff, *What Do Unions Do?* (New York: Basic Books, 1984).

[31]Loren Solnick, "Unionism and Fringe Benefit Expenditures," *Industrial Relations 17,* no. 1 (1978), pp. 102–7.

[32]William T. Dickens and Kevin Lang, *Labor Market Segmentation and the Union Wage Premium* (Cambridge, MA: NBER working paper 1883), April 1986.

[33]Daniel J. B. Mitchell, *Union versus Nonunion Wage Norm Shifts* (Los Angeles: UCLA working paper 91), September 1985; Daniel J. B. Mitchell, "Shifting Norms in Wage Determination," *Brookings Papers on Economic Activity 2,* 1985; and Thomas A. Kochan, Robert B. McKersie, and Harry C. Katz, "U.S. Industrial Relations in Transition: A Summary Report," in *Proceedings of the Thirty-Seventh Annual Meeting,* ed. Barbara Dennis (Madison, WI: Industrial Relations Research Association, 1985), pp. 261–76.

rolled into base pay and health care deductibles. Note the change that occurred by 1988. West Germany's hourly compensation exceeded that of the U.S. worker by 30 percent ($18.07 vs. $13.90). Koreans were up to 18 percent of U.S. workers, and Japanese and Canadian wages were on a par with the United States.[34] Caution should be exercised in interpreting these data, because government-provided benefits (e.g., health care and large layoff awards in West Germany) are not included. International wage comparisons also seem to vary considerably. Currency fluctuations play a substantial role here, too.

In addition to affecting forms of pay, unions also pay a role in administering pay. Most negotiated contracts specify pay intervals, minimum rates, and the basis for movement through a wage range. Some employers adopt the maintenance of union-free status as an objective of its pay system. Such systems usually are based on policies that include strong external competitiveness, internally consistent pay treatment to avoid feelings of inequitable treatment, emphasis on performance, and a fair and open administration of the compensation system. These policies often translate into rates that are at or above those for the market, merit pay or an all-salaried work force, and great emphasis on communicating pay and benefit programs and on attitude surveys to monitor employee reactions.

The basic underlying premise of any strategic perspective is that if managers make pay decisions consistent with the organization strategy, responsive to its employees and its union relations—then the organization is more likely to be successful. Exhibit 1.7 depicts this relationship. It would be nice to be able to say that this presumption has research as well as practical support. Unfortunately we cannot. Little research has been conducted into the types of pay systems that fit different conditions and are related to performance. We do have some evidence beyond the promise and belief. Research on executive pay reveals that firms with higher accounting profits paid their executives more. And top executive pay has also been linked to stockholder returns. Similarly there is evidence that gain-sharing plans for manufacturing employees are related to improved employee work behaviors (e.g., reduced absenteeism, increased suggestions for productivity improvements, and lower unit costs). And the use of bonuses and stock options for managers, engineers, and other professional employees are also related to firm performance. But more evidence and caution are required in interpreting these results. It may be, for example, that organizations that are successful (higher profits, sales, or appreciating stock values) are better able to afford to pay higher wages, offer incentives and stock options. Rather than the pay system affecting employee behaviors and organization performance, the reverse occurs: Employees' behaviors and organization performance cause changes in the pay system. In all likelihood, both happen.

At this point you may be reminded of the definition of an academic—someone who takes something that works in practice (pay systems) and tries to make them work in theory. But the corollary is that if we can find out why some pay systems work in practice, then we can apply them in other settings, too.

---

[34]"International Comparisons of Hourly Compensation Costs for Production Workers in Manufacturing, 1988," U.S. Department of Labor Statistics, March 1989; and Randall Poe, "U.S. Exports are Getting a Boost from Lower Labor Costs," *The Conference Board,* December 1988, p. 4.

EXHIBIT 1.7
Compensation System "Fit" Payoffs

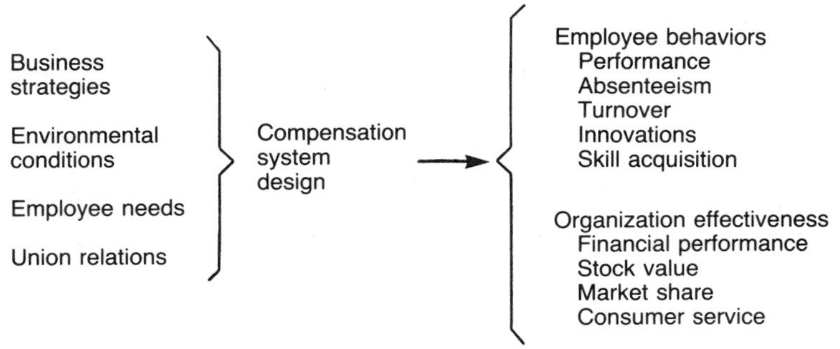

Business
strategies

Environmental
conditions

Employee needs

Union relations

Compensation
system
design

Employee behaviors
Performance
Absenteeism
Turnover
Innovations
Skill acquisition

Organization effectiveness
Financial performance
Stock value
Market share
Consumer service

BOOK PLAN

Compensation is such a broad and compelling topic that several books could be devoted to it. The focus of this book will be on the design and management of compensation systems. To aid in understanding how and why pay systems work, a pay model has been presented. This model, which emphasizes the key policies, techniques, and objectives of pay systems, also provides the structure for much of the book.

Policy decisions form the crucial foundation of any pay systems. The pay model identifies four basic policy decisions; the first three sections of the book examine each in detail. The first, internal consistency (Part I, Chapters 2 through 5), examines pay relationships among jobs within a single organization. What are the pay relationships among jobs and skills within the organization? What are the relative contributions of each job toward achieving the organization's goals? The linkage of pay decisions with the strategic and operating objectives of the organization, the need to establish internal equity, and the importance of ensuring the work relatedness of pay decisions are examined. Job analysis and job evaluation are the main techniques for achieving internally consistent pay. Developments and innovations in these techniques, some of them flowing from research efforts and some from organizations' responses to challenges they face, are discussed.

Part 2 (Chapters 6 and 7) examines external competitiveness—the competitive pay relationships among organizations—and analyzes the influence of market conditions, setting pay policies to reflect these conditions, and tailoring those pay policies to strategic objectives. Techniques include conducting pay surveys; updating survey data; establishing pay policy lines; and determining pay rates, ranges, and structures. Once again, related theoretical, research, and programmatic developments are reviewed.

Once the compensation rates and structures are established, other issues emerge. How much should we pay each individual employee? How much and how often should a person's pay be increased and on what basis? Should employees be paid based on experience, seniority, or performance? Should pay increases be contingent on the unit's or the employee's performance? These are examples of employee contributions, the third building block in the model (Part 3, Chapters 8, 9, and 10). Approaches that deliver pay to individual employees are designed with employee knowledge, skills, abilities, needs, preferences, performance, and seniority, as well as the presence or absence of unions, in mind. Recent theoretical and research developments related to motivational effects of pay, goal setting, and performance evaluation are examined in the light of the pay decisions which must be made by employers and in light of the current state of pay practices.

Part 4 covers employee services and benefits (Chapters 11 and 12). While only two chapters are devoted to employee benefits, this does not imply that the design and management of benefits is unimportant. The opposite is true. Benefits have become so critical that a separate book is required. All we do here is discuss the major benefit forms, the issues involved in designing and administering the benefit program, and how to tie benefits to the organization's strategic directions.

The government's role in compensation is examined in Part 5, Chapters 13 and 14. The government affects compensation through its purchase of goods and services and its employment of a sizable segment of the work force. Additionally, pay practices must comply with legislation and court interpretations.

Managing the compensation system (Part 6, Chapters 15 through 17) includes planning, budgeting, evaluating, communicating, and providing for the special needs of certain groups (e.g., sales representatives, executives, unions).

Even though the book is divided into sections that are reflected in the pay model, that does not mean that pay policies and decisions are necessarily so discrete. All the basic policy decisions are interrelated, and together they form a major system designed to influence organization performance and employee behaviors. Throughout the book our intention is to examine alternative approaches. Rarely is there a single "correct" approach; rather, alternative approaches exist or can be designed. The one most likely to be effective depends on the circumstances.[35] We hope that this book will help you become better informed about these options and how to design new ones. Whether as an employee, a manager, or an interested member of society, you should be able to assess effectiveness of compensation approaches and equity of pay systems.

SUMMARY

The model presented in this chapter provides a structure for understanding compensation systems. The three main components of the model include the objectives of the pay system, the policy decisions that provide the system's foundation, and the techniques that link policies and objectives. The following sections of the book examine in turn each of the four policy decisions—internal consistency, external competitiveness, employee contributions, and the nature of administration—as well as the techniques, new directions, and related research.

---

[35]Barry Gerhart and George T. Milkovich, "Organizational Differences in Managerial Compensation Practices," Working Paper #88-19, Center for Advanced Human Resource Studies, Cornell University, Ithaca, New York, 1988; and Baker, Jensen, and Murphy, "Compensation and Incentives: Practice vs. Theory."

Two questions should constantly be in the minds of compensation professionals and readers of this text. First, "Why do it this way?" There is rarely one "correct" way to design a system or pay an individual. Organizations, people, and circumstances are too varied. But a well-trained compensation specialist can select or design a suitable approach.

Second, "So What?" What does this technique do for us? How does it help achieve our organization goals? If good answers are not apparent, there is no point to the technique. Adapting the pay system to meet the needs of the employees and to help achieve the goals of the organization is what this book is all about.

The basic premise of this book is that compensation systems can have a profound impact on a variety of individuals and objectives. Yet too often, traditional pay systems seem to have been designed in response to some historical but long-forgotten problem. The practices continue, but the logic underlying them is not always clear or even relevant.

REVIEW QUESTIONS

1. How do differing perspectives affect our perceptions of compensation?
2. What rewards can an employer provide that are not part of the compensation system?
3. How does the pay model help organize one's thinking about compensation?
4. What can a pay system do for an organization? For an employee?
5. How may the pay system be tied to organization strategy?
6. Under what circumstances would one of the three basic pay policies be emphasized relative to the other two? Try to think of a separate example for each basic pay policy.

Compensation Application
Paying Graduate Students

Just two weeks before final exam begins, students at a California campus had to cross picket lines to attend class during a two-day strike by graduate students.

Demanding that the university recognize them as employees, the students, most of them members of the Association of Graduate Student Employees, blocked or picketed at all the main entrances to the campus for two days. The association estimated that 2,000 people joined the blockade each day, including some full-time faculty members and undergraduate students.

The strike prompted many faculty members to cancel classes on the two days, and an informal survey of classes that were held indicated a marked drop in attendance.

Graduate students walking picket lines said they wanted the university to recognize their association as the official union of graduate student employees so that wage increases, tuition waivers and other demands could be negotiated.

About 3,200 of the school's 9,000 graduate students are working for the university this semester. Most are either teaching assistants or research assistants.

Teaching assistants, working 20 hours a week, make between $1,063 and $1,265 a month, while research assistants working the same number of hours earn $917 a month. Striking graduate students said inflation, changes in the tax code and the area's high cost of living make it difficult to live on these wages.

The state labor relations board ruled two weeks ago that teaching assistants and research assistants are not university employees for the purposes of collective bargaining. The decision reversed an earlier ruling by the board that the university must recognize the graduate student workers as employees who receive wages, not as students who receive financial aid. In a report issued with the ruling, the board said, "In cases of conflict between academic and employment considerations, academic considerations ultimately prevail."

A spokesman for the school said that although the university recognized the contributions of graduate student employees—who teach 38 percent of undergraduate courses—it would not recognize their association as a union.

"The collective-bargaining process is not the best way to deal with an educational program," a school spokesman said, adding that the university would explore other ways to negotiate with the students.[1]

DISCUSSION QUESTIONS

1. Take the role of the students. Persuade your classmates that you are underpaid. Use the ideas and concepts discussed in this first chapter. What part of the pay model

---

[1]Adapted from an article in *The New York Times*, April 16, 1989, p. 43.

would you point to to buttress your argument? What strategic issue could you raise to counter the University's position?

2. Take the role of an university administrator. Persuade the students that your pay practices are appropriate. Frame your argument using the concepts in this chapter. State your objectives in setting rates for graduate students.

3. How would the above arguments differ if the university were a profit-making institution, that is, the only source of income was tuition from students?

Part

1

Exxon employs a chief executive officer, chemical engineers, plant managers, nurses, market analysts, laboratory technicians, financial planners, hydraulic mechanics, accountants, guards, oil tanker captains, sailors, word processors, and so on. How is pay determined for these different jobs? This question and the techniques employed to answer it lie at the heart of compensation management. Is the financial planner worth more than the accountant, or the mechanic more than the word processor? How much more? What procedures are used to set pay rates and who does it? Should the potential consequences of errors in the job, like the disastrous 1989 Alaskan oil spill blamed on the captain of the Exxon Valdez, be considered in setting pay? How important are the characteristics of the employee—knowledge, skills, abilities, or experience? How important are the characteristics of the work, the conditions under which it is done, or the value of what is produced? What about the employer's financial condition, or employee and union preferences?

These questions can be examined within the framework introduced in Chapter 1 and shown again in Exhibit I.1. This part of the book examines the first basic policy issue (internal consistency) and the pay structure. In Chapter 2, the policy of internal consistency is considered. Chapter 3 discussed various approaches to assess the similarities and differences in work content (job and skill analysis). Chapters 4 and 5 scrutinize job evaluation, which assesses the relative content or value of the work performed.

Internal Consistency: Determining the Structure

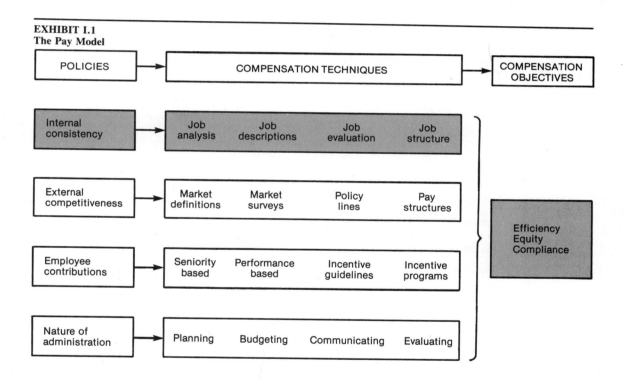

EXHIBIT I.1
The Pay Model

POLICIES	COMPENSATION TECHNIQUES	COMPENSATION OBJECTIVES

Internal consistency	Job analysis	Job descriptions	Job evaluation	Job structure	
External competitiveness	Market definitions	Market surveys	Policy lines	Pay structures	Efficiency Equity Compliance
Employee contributions	Seniority based	Performance based	Incentive guidelines	Incentive programs	
Nature of administration	Planning	Budgeting	Communicating	Evaluating	

2 Internal Consistency and the Structure

For the kingdom of heaven is like a householder who went out early in the morning to hire laborers for his vineyard. And having agreed with the laborers for a denarius a day, he sent them into his vineyard. And about the third hour, he went out and saw others standing . . . idle; and he said to them, "Go you also into the vineyard, and I will give you whatever is just." And again he went out about the vineyard, and about the ninth hour, and did as before. . . . But about the eleventh hour he went out and found others . . . and he said to them, "Go you also into the vineyard." When evening came, the owner said to his steward, "Call the laborers, and pay them their wages, beginning from the last even to the first." When they of the eleventh hour came, they received each a denarius. . . . When the first in their turn came . . . they also received each his denarius. . . . They began to murmur against the householder, saying, "These last have worked a single hour, and thou hast put them on a level with us, who have borne the burden of the day's heat." But answering them, he said, "Friend, I do thee no injustice; take what is thine and go."[1]

Matthew's parable raises age-old questions about internal consistency and pay structures within a single organization.[2] Clearly the laborers in the vineyard felt that those "who have borne the burden of the day's heat" should be paid more, perhaps because they had contributed more to the householder's economic benefit. According to the laborers, the criteria on which to base "fair pay" are two: the value of contributions and the time worked. But perhaps the householder was using a third criterion: an individual's needs, without regard to differences in the work performed.[3] Contemporary compensation practices, reflecting prevalent opinion in Western society, typically include the value of the work performed and the knowledge or skills required, when determining pay structures. Consequently, designers of pay structures must recognize similarities and differences in the value of various kinds of work and contributions and must do so through procedures acceptable to the parties involved. This chapter examines the policy of internal consistency in pay structures and its consequences.

INTERNAL CONSISTENCY AND THE PAY MODEL

Two basic concepts—internal consistency and pay structures—need to be clarified.

> **Internal consistency refers to the pay relationship among jobs or skill levels within a *single* organization. It focuses attention on the importance of the relationships and pressures internal to the organization.**

> **Pay structure refers to the array of pay rates for different work within a single organization. It focuses attention on the levels, differentials, and criteria used to determine those pay rates.**

Internal consistency is one of the basic compensation policies any employer must decide when managing employee compensation. It involves establishing equal pay for

---

[1]Matthew, chap. 20, verses 1–16, of the New Testament.

[2]For an excellent history of the different standards for pay, see N. Arnold Tolles, *Origins of Modern Wage Theories* (Englewood Cliffs, NJ: Prentice-Hall, 1964).

[3]Several Japanese firms, Toshiba and Nissan for example, base a small portion of a worker's pay on the number of dependents. In the early 1900s, workers who were "family men" received a pay supplement in some U.S. firms as well.

jobs of equal worth and acceptable pay differentials for work of unequal worth. But internal consistency involves more than the pay structure. Often called internal equity, a policy that emphasizes internal consistency places importance on the inner workings, the relationships and pressures found within an organization. Consequently it includes concerns for the fairness of the procedures used to establish the pay structure, as well as the structure itself.[4] Thus, compensation managers must design procedures and establish pay structures that (1) assist managers to achieve their organizational objectives, (2) are acceptable to employees, and (3) are in compliance with laws and regulations.

PAY STRUCTURES AND THE PAY MODEL

Pay structures can be described on three dimensions, (1) number of levels, (2) pay differentials among levels, and (3) the criteria used to support the structure.

Levels. The essence of any pay structure is its hierarchical nature: the number of levels and reporting relationships. Pay structures typically reflect the organization structure in which they reside. Some are more hierarchical with multiple levels; others are flat with few levels. For example, General Electric's Aerospace Division has its managerial, engineering, and scientific jobs arrayed into 14 levels. Another GE division, Chemicals and Plastics, uses the 5 broad basic levels described in Exhibit 2.1 to array its jobs. These levels, labeled career bands, range from professional to executive. Obviously, managers in Aerospace have chosen to define their work more specifically than those in Chemicals and Plastics.

Differentials. Pay structures typically pay more for work that requires greater qualifications to perform, performed under less desirable working conditions, and/or whose input is more valued. The pay differences among levels are referred to as differentials. The differentials between a new hire ($5.00) and the hamburger flipper at McDonalds ($6.50) can be expressed as an absolute ($6.50 − $5.00 = 1.50) or as a percent ($\frac{6.50 - 5.00}{5.00} = 30\%$). Pay differentials of interest in managing compensation include those between adjacent levels in a career path, between supervisors and subordinates, between union and nonunion employees, and between executives and regular employees. For example, Michael Eisner, the CEO of Disney, was paid $7,506,000 in salary and annual bonus for his work in 1988.[5] (He also exercised long term incentive stock options for an additional $32,588,000!) How the average employee at Disney feels about this

---

[4]Joanne Martin and Joseph Harder, "Bread and Roses: Justice and the Distribution of Financial and Socio-emotional Rewards in Organizations," Stanford University Research paper no. 1010, August 1988; and Jerald Greenberg, "Looking Fair vs. Being Fair: Managing Impressions of Organizational Justice," in B. M. Staw and L. L. Cummings, eds., *Research in Organizational Behavior*, vol. 12. (Greenwich, CT: JAI Press, 1990).

[5]John A. Byrne, Ronald Grover, and Todd Vogel, "Is the Boss Getting Paid Too Much?" *Business Week*, May 1, 1989, pp. 46–53.

EXHIBIT 2.1
Managerial/Professional Job Levels at a General Electric Division

Career Band	Band Description	Developmental Objectives
Executive	Provides vision, leadership, and innovation to major business segments or functions of GEP	Ability to provide strategic direction and judgment that results in the global objectives of GEP being achieved
Director	Directs a significant functional area or smaller business segment	Management: Ability to provide direction and a global perspective to the management of a small business segment or significant functional area Individual Contributors: Direct a project with broad business impact, drawing on others for completion of business objectives while holding accountability for end results
Leadership	Individual contributors leading projects or programs with broad scope and impact, or managers leading functional components with broad scope and impact	Management: Ability to effectively manage diverse activities within a function and the resolution of decisions in the balanced best interests of the business Individual Contributors: Ability to leverage in-depth technical knowledge in the achievement of business objectives
Technical/ managerial	Individual contributors managing projects or programs with defined scope and responsibility, or first tier management of a specialty area	Management: Develop management skills and business perspective to effectively resolve cross-functional challenges Individual Contributors: Ability to leverage specialized technical knowledge to achieve project or program results
Professional	Supervisors and individual contributors working on tasks, activities, and/or less complex, shorter duration projects	Ability to work independently on well-defined assignments or shorter term projects

33

may be affected by the fact that Mr. Eisner's cash pay alone (the $7.5 million base plus annual bonus) in one year is 10 times more than ride operators in Disney's theme park can expect to earn in a lifetime. Such differentials may affect employees' sense of fair treatment and subsequently their work behaviors.

Criteria. Three criteria may be used to support the number, levels, and size of the differentials that make up structures: the value or content of the work performed, the skills and knowledge required, and/or the performance or outcomes of the work.

Chapters 4 and 5 describe how to use these criteria in the actual design of structures. At this point it is useful to recognize that different criteria may be used to support a pay structure. And the criterion used is presumed to influence employee behaviors by describing what is required (increased work responsibilities, skills, and/or performance) to get a higher paying position.

Why bother with a policy that emphasizes internal consistency? How do internally equitable rates help operating managers achieve these objectives? And what are potential consequences of pay structures that are not internally equitable? A policy that emphasizes the internal consistency of a pay structure focuses attention on the link between employee perceptions and work behaviors. Recall the typical objectives of pay systems shown in Exhibit 1.3. Important among them are employee decisions to join, to stay, or to leave the organization, and to invest in additional training. Pay differences among different jobs influence some of these decisions. Properly designed pay structures may facilitate employee decisions to stay with an organization, to undertake the necessary training, and to gain the required experience to obtain promotions and the accompanying higher pay. Consequently, pay structures can be an important management tool.

Considering their importance, it is surprising that so little is known about employee perceptions of the equity of pay differentials among jobs. Equity, like beauty, may be in the eye of the beholder. For example, little research has been reported on whether different employee groups (older versus younger, line versus staff, men versus women, engineers versus personnel specialists, crafts versus office and clerical) hold different ideas about what constitutes fair pay differences among jobs.[6] Mahoney asked business students and compensation administrators to assign pay levels to organization charts (Exhibit 2.2). One of the jobs was already assigned a pay rate to anchor the responses. The object of the study was to determine if different groups would assign similar pay differentials. He found that business students and administrators did assign similar differentials. On the basis of his findings, Mahoney suggests that a compensation differential of approximately 30 percent is considered appropriate for the higher of two managerial

---

[6]David W. Belcher, "Pay Equity or Pay Fairness?" *Compensation Review,* Second Quarter 1979, pp. 31–37; Jerald Greenberg and Suzy N. Ornstein, "High Status Job Title as Compensation for Underpayment: A Test of Equity Theory," *Journal of Applied Psychology* 68, no. 2 (1983), pp. 285–97.

[7]Thomas A. Mahoney, "Organizational Hierarchy and Position Worth," *Academy of Management Journal,* December 1979, pp. 726–37; and Thomas A. Mahoney, *Compensation and Reward Perspectives* (Homewood, IL: Richard D. Irwin, 1979), p. 171.

EXHIBIT 2.2
Simple Organization Chart

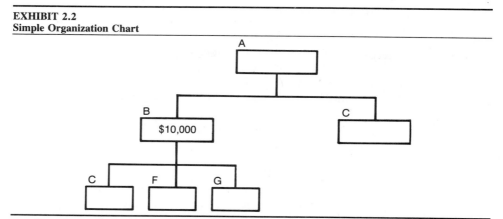

Illustrative organizational configuration from questionnaire, J. L. Kuethe and Bernard Levenson, "Conceptions of Organizational Worth," *The American Journal of Sociology*, November 1964, pp. 342–88. © The University of Chicago Press, 1964.

organization levels and that the hierarchical level in the organization is the key determinant of judgments of equitable pay for managers.[7]

Some research suggests that women have lower pay expectations and lower expectations about future pay than similarly qualified men. For example, two studies have reported substantial differences in the pay expectations of male and female M.B.A. students, with women reporting lower career entry and career peak pay expectations than similarly qualified men.[8]

But judgments about equitable differentials are probably a function of a lot of things, including, apparently, the organization culture. For example, Rosow reports that as work is made more democratic, and as more employees are involved in decision making, salaries and benefits are made more equal; that is, the size of differentials narrows.[9] Jaques asserts the existence of *societal-wide norms* of equitable pay.[10] He believes that most people would assign approximately the same pay differentials to various levels of work, based on commonly held feelings of fairness in pay. While research, limited though it is, lends support to the existence of pay norms among *similar* groups of employees (such as business students and administrators), little evidence supports Jaques's idea of universally held norms across a highly complex society. And the number of lawsuits over what constitutes pay equity would seem to indicate that substantial disagreement exists in contemporary society.

[8]S. M. Freedman, "The Effects of Subordinate Sex, Pay Equity and Strength of Demand on Compensation Decisions," *Sex Roles* 5 (1979), p. 649–58; B. Major, V. Vanderslie, and D. McFarlein, "Effects of Pay Expected on Pay Received: The Conformatory Nature of Initial Expectations," *Journal of Applied Social Psychology* 14, no. 5 (1984), pp. 399–412.

[9]Jerome M. Rosow, *The Organization in the Decade Ahead*, conference sponsored by Work in America Institute, Scarsdale, NY, March 3–5, 1986.

[10]Elliot Jaques, *Equitable Payment* (New York: John Wiley & Sons, 1961).

Egalitarian vs. Hierarchical Structures

An egalitarian philosophy implies a belief that all workers should be treated equally. Some hold this belief as a matter of principle; others also believe that more equal treatment will improve employee satisfaction, aid work team unity, and subsequently affect workers' performance.[11] As applied to pay structures, more egalitarian structures would have fewer levels and smaller differentials between adjacent levels and between the highest (CEO) and lowest paid workers.

By contrast, less egalitarian structures are consistent with a belief in the value of recognizing differences in individual contributions, differences in responsibilities, and greater contributions to the organization. Pay structures would be more hierarchical, have more levels and greater differentials among them. Rather than more equal treatment leading to employee satisfaction, some believe that equal treatment will result in the more competent performers being unrecognized and therefore leaving the organization, thus lowering overall performance.

Note that all pay structures by definition have some degree of hierarchy (levels and differentials); it is just that some have more than others.

How egalitarian or hierarchical should pay structures be? Theory and research do not yet provide much help in answering the question. Lawler and others make a strong argument in support of more egalitarian pay to support work teams and cooperative work environments.[12] Unions make similar arguments. Others argue that individual contributors also need to be recognized, and a compressed structure rewards regression to the mean rather than outstanding contributions and efforts. They also argue that equality offers no incentives to obtain training, take risks, and to excel. In practice the answer probably lies in how the work is organized. It can be organized around teams and cells or around more individual performers. The nature of the pay structure should support the underlying organization structure. Obviously it is not that simple. Think of any professional team sport—baseball, football, hockey—versus individual sports such as golf or bowling. Even in team sports some positions are more valuable than others—a football team's quarterback, a basketball team's point guard and center. Consequently, these positions are paid more on average based on their value to the team's overall performance.[13]

---

[11]E. E. Lawler III, "The New Pay," in *Current Issues in Human Resource Management*, ed. S. Rynes and G. Milkovich (Homewood, IL: Richard D. Irwin, Inc. 1986); Richard E. Walton and Gerald J. Susman, "People Policies for the New Machines," *Harvard Business Review*, March-April 1987, pp. 98–106; and Eric Cousineau and George T. Milkovich, "Pay Structures and the Effects on Firm Performance," (Ithaca: Center for Advanced Human Resource Studies, Cornell University, working paper 89–15).

[12]Lawler, "The New Pay."

[13]Ronald G. Ehrenberg and Michael L. Bognanno, "The Incentive Effects of Tournaments Revisited: Evidence from the European PGA Tour," ILR-Cornell Research Conference on "Do Compensation Policies Matter?" Ithaca, NY: May 24, 1989; Edward Lazear and Sherwin Rosen, "Rank Order Tournaments as an Optimum Labor Contract," *Journal of Political Economy*, October 1981, pp. 841–64; Edward Lazear, "Pay Equality and Industrial Politics," *Journal of Political Economy*, June 1989, pp. 561–80; Sherwin Rosen, "Prizes and Incentives in Elimination Tournaments," *American Economic Review*, September 1986, pp. 701–15; and Charles O'Reilly and Brian S. Main, "Comparisons: A Tale of Two Theories," *Administrative Science Quarterly*, June 1988, pp. 257–74.

Distinction between Employee Contributions and Internal Consistency Policy

Note the distinction between employee contribution (what *I* am worth in this job) and internal consistency (what this *job* is worth to the organization, no matter who does it). Internal consistency refers primarily to the relationships among *jobs* rather than among *individuals*. The comparison is *not* over pay differences between two individuals; the worth of the work itself is determined with little regard to the individuals who are doing it. For example, a word processor may be paid $10.50 per hour whether the employee doing the job holds a Ph.D. or is a vocational school graduate.

Separating internal consistency concerns from employee contribution and individual pay clearly oversimplifies the real world. In some jobs, particularly those with great responsibility and discretion, distinguishing the worth of the job from the individual does not make sense. A vice president whose job is designed around the qualifications and experiences of the individual performing it is one example.

Some organizations have extended this concept to manufacturing and assembly work. In these firms the criteria used to design pay structures are the employees' skills, rather than the job performed. TRW and Digital Equipment Company, for example, have applied such skill-based approaches in several plants. So while a policy of internal consistency deals primarily with *job relationships, irrespective of who is in the job,* equitable pay structures can also be based directly on the skills of employees, irrespective of the jobs to which they may be assigned.[14]

Comparisons of pay structures across organizations reveal significant differences. Mahoney points out that in some organizations the highest paid jobs may receive 100 times the compensation of the lowest paid job.[15] In other organizations the differences are considerably less (9 or 10 times). These observed differences raise questions about the design of internal pay structures. What factors influence or determine these structures? What are the consequences of different structures? Each of these is considered in turn.

FACTORS INFLUENCING INTERNAL PAY STRUCTURES

A variety of factors influence the internal structures within a single organization. Some of the major ones are shown in Exhibit 2.3. They include societal norms and customs; the culture, technology, policies, and objectives of particular organization; the economic conditions in which the organization operates; and the particular characteristics of the jobs and the employees involved. The confluence of these pressures influences the design of pay structures.

---

[14]E. E. Lawler III and G. E. Ledford, Jr., "Skill-Based Pay: A Concept That's Catching On," *Compensation and Benefits Review,* September 1985, pp. 54–61; and Fred Luthans and Marilyn L. Fox, "Update on Skill-Based Pay," *Personnel,* March 1989, pp. 26–32.

[15]Mahoney, *Compensation and Reward Perspectives*; Eric Cousineau, "Pay Structures and Organization Performance" (PhD Thesis, Cornell University, Ithaca, NY 1990); and Bonnie Rabin, "Executive Pay Dispersion: Measurement Issues and Evidence" (paper presented at the 1989 Academy of Management Meetings, Washington, DC: August1989).

EXHIBIT 2.3
Factors Influencing Pay Structures

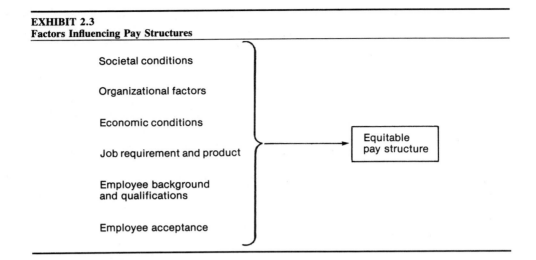

Societal conditions

Organizational factors

Economic conditions

Job requirement and product

Employee background
and qualifications

Employee acceptance

Equitable
pay structure

Societal Factors

The role that societal conditions have played historically can be traced in various theories rationalizing pay differences.[16] These theories draw upon concepts from philosophy, sociology, economics, and psychology. Matthew's parable, for example, reveals an egalitarian policy: "the last even to the first," regardless of employee qualifications, working conditions, or hours worked. Apparently such a policy was less acceptable to the workers, since they are reported to have murmured against it.

Another approach to pay structures, the *just wage doctrine,* is attributed to attempts by 13th-century artisans and craftsmen to take advantage of economic pressures. Nobles and landholders had bid up the prevailing wages of skilled artisans, who were in relatively short supply. The church and state responded by proclaiming a schedule of "just wages." "Just" wages tended to reflect that society's class structure and were consistent with the prevailing notions of birth rights. Economic and market forces were explicitly denied as appropriate determinants of pay structures. Hence, some early "compensation specialists" employed concepts such as *societal norms, customs,* and *tradition* to design and justify pay structures. Present day manifestation of the just wage doctrine can be seen in debates over minimum wage legislation and comparable worth, which also argue against the appropriateness of market forces for determining pay structures.

Economic Factors

"Just wage" may have been a useful theory when the majority of people lived in feudal societies in which wages played little role. But by the end of the 19th century, for the

---

[16]See Tolles, *Origins of Wage Theory*; also see Greenberg and Cohen, eds., *Equity and Justice in Social Behavior*.

first time, the majority of people came to depend on wages for their livelihood. Clearly, the just wage concept preserved a privileged position in society for landowners and other small groups, including some skilled craftsmen. But the new commercial system developing in the 18th century, in Adam Smith's view, had the potential to make nations wealthy and also improve the welfare of the ordinary workers—if it would be allowed to operate unfettered by the customs and regulations of the past, including just wage. Smith advocated allowing supply and demand to be the main factors in setting wages. He ascribed to labor both exchange and use values. *Exchange value* is the price of labor (the wage) determined in a competitive market; in other words, labor's worth (price) is whatever the buyer and seller agree on. *Use value,* on the other hand, is the value or price ascribed to the use or consumption of labor in the production of goods or services. Exchange value is analogous to external competitiveness, whereas use value is related to internal equity.

But Smith did not address the issue of *how* supply and demand regulate wages. Ricardo, a 19th century businessman-turned-economist, addressed the issue of labor supply. Accompanying the Industrial Revolution was a tremendous population surge and widespread poverty as people left the countryside for city life; this poverty contrasted sharply with the rising profits of employers. Observing these trends, theorists assumed the supply of labor would constantly expand until there was just a bare minimum of subsistence for everyone. Ricardo theorized that the wages of labor would always just equal the amount necessary to buy the goods the worker needed in order to live at a subsistence level. Any deviation from this equilibrium, for example, a wage increase, would bring about population changes that would reestablish the equilibrium, again at the subsistence level. This became known as the "iron law of wages."

On this foundation, Karl Marx built his theory of surplus value.[17] Under capitalism, he said, wages will always be based on exchange value and will provide only a subsistent wage. But labor's use value is higher than its exchange value. The difference between exchange and use value produces a surplus which is being pocketed by the employer, when it should be paid to the worker, according to Marx.

These early theorists concentrated on the supply of labor to explain wages. But by the last half of the 19th century, wages began to rise, and so new theories were required. Emphasis shifted to the demand for labor, and theorists argued that employers will pay a wage to a unit of labor that equals that unit's use value.[18] Unless a worker can produce a value equal to the value received in wages, it will not be worthwhile for the employer to hire that worker. This is the marginal productivity theory of wages. It says that work is compensated proportionally to its contribution to satisfying desires or the organization's production objectives. Accordingly, differences in compensation reflect differences in contributions associated with different jobs. In this view, jobs are compensated on the basis of worth to the employing organization, the volume of production or output associated with the job, and the net revenue accruing to the organization from sale of the

---

[17]R. C. Tucker, ed., *The Marx-Engels Reader,* 2nd ed. (New York: W. W. Norton, 1978).

[18]Allan M. Cartter, *Theory of Wages and Employment* (Homewood, IL: Richard D. Irwin, 1959).

output. The marginalist theories assert that one job is paid more or less than another because of differences in productivity of the job and/or differences in consumer valuation of the output. Differences in productivity may be attributed to three factors: (1) *the employee* (e.g., knowledge, skill, abilities, effort); (2) *the job* (e.g., technology, capital investment); and (3) *the match* between the employee's qualifications and the job requirements. Hence, differences in productivity may provide a rationale for the internal job structure. These views underlie many contemporary compensation practices.

The internal structure is also affected by other economic factors. Pay differences may reflect difficulties in recruiting and retaining employees for different jobs. University professors of accounting and engineering who command higher salaries than do professors of history or Serbo-Croatian are examples.

Some explanations of differences in pay among jobs within a single organization combine both sociological and economic factors. Relative pay differences at one particular time may be attributed to temporary economic conditions, such as a shortage of electrical engineers or computer specialists. These differences may become accepted as "just" or customary, and any restructuring of them may be resisted as disruptive of the relationships with the organization. Examples can be found in the auto and steel companies where certain craft jobs receive relatively higher pay than other work, or within municipalities where fire fighters' pay is tied to that of police officers.

Organizational Factors

The effects of many economic and organizational factors are combined in the notion of *internal labor markets*.[19] As depicted in Exhibit 2.4, internal labor markets refer to the rules and procedures that serve to regulate the allocation of employees among different jobs within a single organization. Individuals tend to be recruited and hired only for specific "entry jobs" and are later allocated (promoted or transferred) to other jobs. Because the employer competes in the external market for people to fill these jobs, pay for entry jobs tends to be tied to the external market. It must be set high enough to attract a qualified pool of job applicants. In contrast, pay for nonentry jobs (those staffed internally via transfer and promotions) tends to be more influenced by the organization's culture and norms and less by external economic conditions.[20] In other words, external economic factors are dominant influences on pay for entry jobs, but the differentials for nonentry jobs tend to reflect the organization's culture and traditions.

---

[19]Mark Granovetter, "Labor Mobility, Internal Markets, and Job Matching: A Comparison of the Sociological and the Economic Approaches," *Research in Social Stratification and Mobility* 5 (1986), pp. 222–27; Peter Doeringer and Michael J. Piore, *Internal Labor Markets and Manpower Analysis* (Lexington, Mass.: Heath-Lexington Books, 1971); and ed. Paul Osterman, *Internal Labor Markets* (Cambridge, MA: MIT Press, 1984).

[20]David Pierson, "Labor Market Influences on Entry vs. Non-Entry Wages," *Nebraska Journal of Economics and Business,* Summer 1983, pp. 7–18; and Marc Wallace and Charles Fay, "Job Evaluation and Comparable Worth: Compensation Theory Basis for Modeling Job Worth," *Proceedings, Academy of Management,* 1981, pp. 296–300.

EXHIBIT 2.4
Illustration of an Internal Labor Market

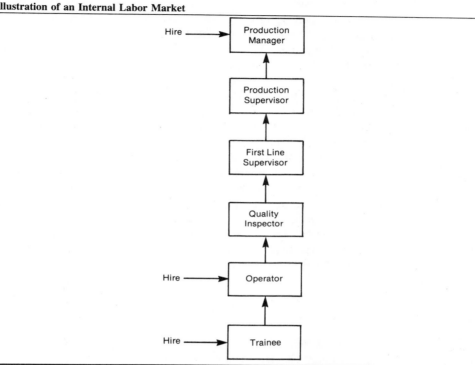

Expanding on this theme, Thurow asserts that internally equitable pay structures must also be designed to be congruent with the progression of jobs, or *career paths,* within an organization.[21] Greater pay is required for higher level jobs in order to encourage employees to undertake the necessary training and gain the required experience to attain these jobs.

Other organizational factors also influence the design of pay structures. The technology employed is one of the factors.[22] Technology used in producing goods and services influences organizational structures, functional specialties, work teams, and departments. Technology influences the work to be performed and the skills required to perform it.

A case in point is the difference in the number of levels in GE Aerospace (14 levels)

---

[21]Lester C. Thurow, *Generating Inequality: Mechanisms of Distribution in the U.S. Economy* (New York: Basic Books, 1975).

[22]M. Roznowski and C. Hulin, "Influences of Functional Speciality and Job Technology on Employees' Perceptual and Affective Responses to their Jobs," *Organizational Behavior and Human Decision Processes 36* (1985), pp. 196–208; Jay Turk, "Determination of Job Characteristics of Automated Process Operators as a Function of Technology and Managerial Choice," Ph.D. thesis, Cornell University, Ithaca, N.Y., June 1986.

and Chemicals and Plastics (5 levels) manager pay structures. Clearly the technology required to produce military hardware differs from that used to manufacture chemicals. Aerospace is more labor intensive (over 50%) than Chemicals and Plastics (less than 20%); hence, different structures emerge.

The organization's human resource policy is another influence. A policy in some organizations dictates using pay as an incentive to induce employees to apply for higher level positions (e.g., machinists to first-line supervisors), while in other organizations, offering "management status" is considered a sufficient inducement, and little or no pay differential is offered. If pay differentials are designated as a key mechanism to encourage employees to accept greater responsibilities, then the pay structure must be designed to facilitate those decisions.

Mahoney points out that all of these explanations of pay structures have some validity and "in fact, likely are interrelated in the explanation of any specific pay structure."[23] In other words, some pay differentials may have been initiated in response to economic factors such as shortages of qualified persons. Over time, the differential associated with the skill became accepted as equitable and customary; efforts to change it were resisted as inequitable and destructive of social relationships within the organization. Thus, the compensation structures within organizations established for economic reasons may be maintained for other reasons.

EMPLOYEE ACCEPTANCE: A KEY TEST

In a classic article on pay structures, Livernash asserts that employees desire "fair" compensation.[24] He states that employees judge the fairness of their pay through comparisons with the compensation paid other jobs related in some fashion to their own jobs. Such interrelated jobs he called *job clusters*. Accordingly, the central criterion for assessing the internal pay structure is its *acceptability to the employees involved*. Effectiveness of the pay structure depends on employee acceptance. Other factors (societal and organizational) also influence employee acceptance; but "workers' views about what constitutes an 'equitable' wage structure have an important role to play in the determination of wages."[25]

Distributive Justice

Since employee judgments about pay structures are so important, we need to understand how employees make these judgments.

---

[23]Mahoney, *Compensation and Reward Perspectives*.

[24]E. Robert Livernash, "The Internal Wage Structure," in *New Concepts in Wage Determination*, ed. George W. Taylor and Frank C. Pierson (New York, McGraw-Hill, 1957), pp. 143–72.

[25]Thurow, *Generating Inequality*.

Procedural Justice

The fairness of the procedures used to design and administer the pay structure is its procedural justice. Note the distinction between procedural and distributive justice.

Suppose you are given a ticket for speeding. Procedural justice refers to the process by which a decision is reached—the right to an attorney, the right to an impartial judge, and the right to receive a copy of the arresting officer's statement. Distributive justice refers to the fairness of the decision—guilty.

Researchers have recently found that employees' perceptions of procedural fairness significantly influences their acceptance of the results; that employees and managers are more willing to accept low pay if they feel the way these results were obtained was fair.[26] This research also strongly suggests that pay procedures are more likely to be perceived as fair (1) if they are consistently applied to all employees involved; (2) if employee participation and/or representative is included; (3) if appeals procedures are available; and (4) if the data used are accurate.

Since employee judgments about pay structures are so important, we need to understand how employees make these judgments. Exhibit 2.5 shows the main determinants of whether an employee is likely to perceive pay as being equitable. The model, adapted from the distributive justice and inequity models, shows that employees' judgments about equity are based on comparisons.[27] A pay structure will be perceived as equitable or inequitable depending on whether the pay for Job A compared to its requirements (education, experience), the work performed (task, behaviors, working conditions), and the value of contributions (to organization objectives and/or consumers) is congruent with the pay for Job B relative to its requirements, work performed, contribution, and so on, through all jobs in the structure.

However, very little research addresses the question of what factors influence employee perceptions of the equity or fairness of pay structures per se.[28] Most of the research examines perceptions of individual pay relative to pay received by other individuals on the same job (a topic discussed in Part 3, Employee Contributions). But the emphasis in this chapter is on factors influencing differential payment for the work itself rather than the attributes of individuals. The distinction is an important one. It assumes that a job's worth is derived from the value of the work performed. Hence, procedures to establish

---

[26]Robert Folger and Mary Konovsky, "Effects of Procedural and Distributive Justice on Reactions to Pay Raise Decisions," *Academy of Management Journal,* March 1989, pp. 115–30.

[27]The first three references listed are classics on this topic. G. C. Homans, *Social Behavior: Its Elementary Forms* (New York: Harcourt Brace Jovanovich, 1961); M. Patchen, *The Choice of Wage Comparisons* (Englewood Cliffs, N.J.: Prentice-Hall, 1961); J. S. Adams, "Inequity in Social Exchange," in *Advances in Experimental Social Psychology,* Vol. 2, ed. L. Berkowitz (New York: Academic Press, 1965), pp. 267–99. Also see Alan Nash, *Managerial Compensation* (Scarsdale, N.Y.: Work in America Institute, 1980); F. S. Hills, "The Relevant Other in Pay Comparisons," *Industrial Relations 19* (1980), pp. 345–51; and P. S. Goodman, "An Examination of Referents Used in the Evaluation of Pay," *Organizational Behavior and Human Performance 12* (1974), pp. 170–95.

[28]Jane Giacobbe, "Examination of Relationship between Perceived Justice of State Impasse Procedures and Perceived Equity of Teacher Pay," Ph.D. Thesis, Cornell University, Ithaca, NY, 1986.

EXHIBIT 2.5
Perceived Equity of a Pay Structure

$$\frac{\text{Pay}_A}{Q_A, W_A, P_A} \quad \begin{matrix}\text{compared}\\ \text{to}\end{matrix} \quad \frac{\text{Pay}_B}{Q_B, W_B, P_B} \quad \begin{matrix}\text{compared}\\ \text{to}\end{matrix} \quad \frac{\text{Pay}_C}{Q_C, W_C, P_C} \text{ etc.}$$

where

Q = Qualifications.
W = Work performed.
P = Product value.

---

internal pay structures focus on the actual content of the work and its requirements (assessed through job analysis) and the work's value to the organization (assessed through job or skill evaluation).

Managing Impressions—"Looking" vs. "Being" Fair

Based on the research on perceptions of procedural and distributive justice, Greenberg argues that employees' impressions can be managed.[29] In effect, he develops a case for marketing the pay structure and the procedures used to design it as one would market products or services to consumers. A campaign of public announcements by executives, well crafted brochures, videos, and articles in the company newsletter should be aimed at managing the belief that the pay structures and procedures are fair. Greenberg is careful to note that he does not mean manipulation—trying to sell an inequitable system; rather, the emphasis is to consider employee perceptions. And these perceptions should not be left to chance. Rather, if fair procedures and structures have been designed, part of administering them involves insuring employees believe they are fair.

CONSEQUENCES OF INTERNAL PAY STRUCTURES

But why worry about the internal pay structure at all? Why not simply pay employees what it takes to get them to take a job and to stay? Why not simply let external market forces determine wages? The answers can be found in several situations. One is the presence of unique jobs that reflect organizational idiosyncrasies. For example, the School of Veterinary Medicine at Cornell University has installed "windows" in the stomachs of several cows to study the animals' digestive processes. Laboratory technicians help install and maintain these windows and perform other exotic duties. Without similar jobs at other employers, it is difficult to determine the appropriate wage for such jobs. Other, more common illustrations of unique jobs may be found under titles such as "administrative assistant" or "research associate." The specific content of these jobs will vary with the technologies employed, the manner in which a supervisor has designed the job, the skills and experiences of the particular incumbent, and so on. The pay for these unique jobs is typically set through comparison of the work with other internal jobs. So the existing internal wage structure provides a basis for arriving at a wage for unique jobs.

---

[29]Greenberg, "Looking Fair vs. Being Fair."

It is also possible that some jobs or skills are valued by a specific organization more or less than the rates reflected for that job in the market. For example, top-notch compensation specialists or accountants may have greater value to a compensation or accounting consulting firm than to heavy manufacturing companies. The consulting firm may pay greater-than-market rates for the greater contribution of the particular job to organization goals. Some finance professors are leaving academia to design strategies for brokerage firms—and become part of lucrative bonus and profit sharing pools that universities cannot match. Other examples of policies that emphasize internal consistency over market-determined external competitiveness can be found among public employers that have granted salary increases to clerical jobs held predominantly by women. The city of San Jose's agreement with the American Federation of State, County, and Municipal Employees to raise the pay for office and clerical jobs relative to the pay for other city jobs is a case in point.[30]

Pay Structures and Work Behaviors

In the compensation literature, the pay structure is said to be related to everything from employee performance to strikes. Exhibit 2.6 suggests some of the consequences of pay structures. Several writers argue that employees' judgments about the fairness of the pay structure affect their work behaviors. Some of those views have been discussed already. Livernash, for example, asserts that departures from an acceptable wage structure will occasion turnover, grievances, and diminished motivation of workers.[31] Jaques argues that if fair differentials among jobs are not paid, individuals may harbor ill will toward the employer, resist change, change employment if possible, become depressed, and "lack that zest and enthusiasm which makes for high efficiency and personal satisfaction in work."[32]

Whyte, Lawler, and others, including labor unions, have long held the belief that more egalitarian pay structures support team workers, high commitment to the organization and improved performance.[33]

Frank argues that pay structures have value in themselves and hence influence employee behaviors.[34] Employees, according to Frank, value the status attached to their relative position in a pay structure. Consequently, they make trade-offs between the value of the status in their current pay structure and the value of pay for a new job and its status in the pay structure. Using the analogy of a big fish in a little pond, Frank argues that pay structures can influence employees "choosing the right pond." Employees may forgo changing ponds (organizations with new pay structures) if their status (relative

---

[30]*Background Material on the San Jose Situation,* available from Comparable Worth Project, 488 41st Street, Oakland, CA 94609; and *Pay Equity: A Union Issue for the 1980's,* American Federation of State, County, and Municipal Employees, 1625 L Street N.W., Washington, DC 20036.

[31]Livernash, "Internal Wage Structure."

[32]Jaques, *Equitable Payment,* p. 123.

[33]Lawler, "The New Pay"; William Foote Whyte, *Money and Motivation* (New York: Harper and Row, 1955).

[34]Robert H. Frank, *Choosing the Right Pond* (New York: Oxford University Press, 1985).

EXHIBIT 2.6
Some Consequences of Pay Structure

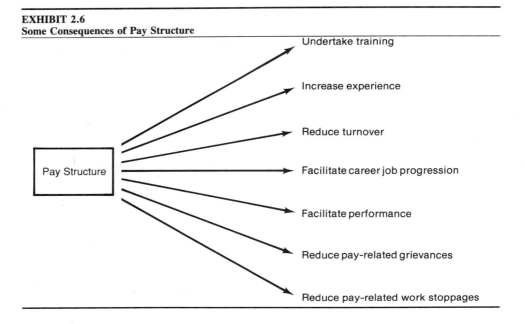

position) in the current pay structure has greater value than the increased pay for the new job and its status.

Pay structures also imply future rewards in a career, and hence influence both the attractiveness of current employment and decisions to stay or leave. Pay structures may induce employees to increase their human capital by undertaking the training and obtaining the experience required for promotions. Human capital theorists suggest that pay differentials serve as inducements for employees to invest in acquiring added knowledge, skills, and experience. Workers do not bring fully developed job skills into the labor market. After obtaining an entry job, skills are acquired either formally or informally through on-the-job training. The incentive to acquire these skills is the pay differential among jobs requiring varying skill levels. According to this view, a computer design engineering job should pay more than a programming job. Without that pay difference, individuals are less likely to go through the education (and forgone earnings while in school) required. Similar logic can be applied to differentials to encourage employees to undertake more responsibilities (pay differentials between supervisors and production workers). Wage differentials within organizations induce employees to remain with the organization and increase their experience and training.[35]

Mahoney observes, "The structure of compensation differentials within the organization influences dissatisfaction and the desire to leave but does not appear to be particularly relevant in the motivation of desired behavior within the organization . . . [*it*] is

---

[35]Edward P. Lazear, "Severance Pay, Pensions, and Efficient Mobility," Working Paper No. 854, National Bureau of Economic Research, Cambridge, MA, February 1982.

a necessary but not sufficient, condition for the motivation of task performance."[36] He asserts that equity of the structure does not appear to contribute to *job* satisfaction, but it contributes to *pay* satisfaction. Let us examine the question of pay satisfaction and its relationship to pay structures in greater detail.

Pay Structures and Pay Satisfaction

Pay satisfaction, as defined by Lawler, is a function of the discrepancy between two perceptions.[37] The first is how much pay employees feel they *should receive* and the second is how much pay they feel they *do receive*. If these two perceptions are equal, an employee is said to experience pay satisfaction; if a discrepancy exists, then the employee feels dissatisfaction with pay.

Heneman states that "use of term 'pay satisfaction' is a bit of a misnomer."[38] He argues that pay satisfaction needs to be considered in terms similar to the four basic policy areas used in the pay model: satisfaction with the pay structure (internal consistency), with the pay level (external competitiveness), with individual pay (employee contribution), and with the administration of the pay system. Another study found that perceived adequacy of pay administration was an important aspect of pay satisfaction.[39]

Recognizing that satisfaction may be linked to each of the basic pay model components permits better analysis of specific aspects of the compensation system and employee attitudes toward them. Lowering the external competitive position of pay may affect the satisfaction with the pay level, but should leave attitudes toward the pay structure unchanged.

Despite the fact that a great deal of research has been conducted relating to pay satisfaction and dissatisfaction, very little research has been directed toward understanding the consequences of *pay differences for different jobs*. Consequently, there are few theories of views that relate employees' judgments about the *equity of pay structures* to their work behaviors.

Based on reviews of the pay satisfaction research, we can glean the following general findings:

1. Pay satisfaction is related to both absenteeism and turnover, though the strength of the relationships is moderate.
2. The greater the pay dissatisfaction, the greater the likelihood of voting for a union, going on strike, and filing grievances.
3. Pay satisfaction is a function of how much pay is received, how much others are

---

[36]Mahoney, *Compensation and Reward Perspectives*, p. 202.

[37]E. E. Lawler, III., *Pay and Organization Development* (Reading, MA: Addison-Wesley Publishing, 1981).

[38]Herbert G. Heneman III, "Pay Satisfaction," *Research in Personnel and Human Resources Management*, Vol. 3, eds. K. M. Rowland and G. R. Ferris (Greenwich, CO: JAI Press, 1985), pp. 115–39.

[39]L. Dyer and R. Theriault, "The Determinants of Pay Satisfaction," *Journal of Applied Psychology 61* (1976), pp. 596–604; and Nan Weiner, "Determinants and Behavioral Consequence of Pay Satisfaction: A Comparison of Two Models," *Personnel Psychology 33* (Winter 1980), pp. 741–57.

perceived to receive (e.g., perceived pay structures), and perceptions of what should have been received.

4. Pay satisfaction can influence job satisfaction.
5. The stronger causal tendency is that of *performance causing pay satisfaction, rather than pay satisfaction causing performance*. Interestingly, pay satisfaction will be related to performance only when pay is based on performance—an issue to which we will return in our discussion of performance-based pay systems in later chapters.

What does the pay satisfaction/dissatisfaction literature tell us about designing pay structures? The answer is not much. Most of the studies fail to distinguish among internal pay structures, external market comparisons, individual pay, and how the pay is administered. Consequently, few of them offer much guidance in designing compensation systems.

SUMMARY

This chapter discusses what is meant by a pay policy that emphasizes internal consistency and how it affects employees, managers, and employers. Internal consistency refers to the pay relationships among jobs within a single organization. While the potential consequences of internal pay structures are vital to organizations and individuals, little guidance has emerged from research concerning employee perceptions of internal pay structure. Jaques posits the existence of society-wide norms of equitable pay structures ("divine" differentials?), but little research supports this.

Pay structures—the array of pay rates for different jobs within an organization—are shaped by societal, economic, and organizational factors. Employees judge a structure to be equitable on the basis of comparisons. The "ratio" of a job's relative pay to its relative requirements, work performed, and value of that performance is compared to the "ratio" for other jobs in the structure. Congruent ratios are felt to be equitable. Acceptance by employees of the relative pay differentials is the key test of an equitable pay structure.

Keep in mind that these comparisons focus on the jobs themselves, and not on the individuals doing the jobs. Thus, personal characteristics such as seniority or experience do not enter into the judgment here and are not discussed until a later section of this book. The emphasis here is on jobs, and the next chapter discusses the analysis of jobs with an eye toward determining an equitable structure.

REVIEW QUESTIONS

1. Why is internal consistency an important policy issue for the compensation system?
2. Discuss the factors that influence internal equity and pay structures. Based on your own experience, which ones do you think are the most important?
3. How would you go about trying to manage employees' impressions of the pay structure? Isn't this sheer manipulation and potentially destructive?
4. What is the "just wage" doctrine? Can you think of any present-day applications?
5. Explain how internal labor markets work.
6. What are pay structures most likely to affect?

Compensation Application
Parcel Plus

Parcel Plus is a rapidly growing service that handles all a consumer's mailing needs. Bring in an item, and Parcel Plus will prepare it for shipping and make arrangements with UPS, air freight services, or overnight delivery services. They will advise you of your options and costs.

As more and more people are working out of their own homes, the owner of Parcel Plus, Joan Bauman, has investigated the possibility of expanding its service by offering pickups and delivery. Buying its own trucks would also allow handling larger packages that are outside the size and weight limitation set by UPS. Parcel Plus could pick up heavy shipments and take them to nearby larger cities for transfer to one of the nationwide trucking lines. This would help people who do not ship things on a regular basis and do not want to be bothered making the necessary shipping arrangements.

At present, Parcel Plus employs 10 people: 8 customer service representatives, an assistant manager, and a manager. The customer service representatives are paid between $5.50 and $6.50 per hour, depending on how long they have been employed. Both the assistant manager and the manager are former customer service representatives, and they are paid $8.50 and $10.00 per hour, respectively. Joan intends to create a new position, driver/customer service representatives, and hire two new employees for this position. The job would consist of driving truck as needed, and doing regular customer service-representatives duties when not driving. Since the pickup and delivery is a new service, Joan isn't sure what amount of time will be spent driving versus customer service work. The proportion spent driving will increase as the demand for this service increases. She decided that $6.50 per hour would be a fair wage. But the first person who applied for the job, Carlos Sherman, said $6.50 was too low. "No self-respecting trucker would start at less than $8.50 an hour." Joan suspects that if she offers $7.50 per hour, Carlos will take the job. Carlos seems physically strong enough to handle the job, even though he's had no trucking experience. When she told this to Corrianne Nation, the manager, Corrianne became quite upset. "If you hire someone off the street and pay him $7.50 an hour, you better be sure no one else hears about it." Joanie thought about this, but when no other job applicants seemed suitable, she decided to renegotiate with Mr. Sherman. She was just about to call him, when two customer service representatives came into her office. They were upset. "Mrs. Bauman," they began, getting right to the point, "we think we all deserve a raise."

DISCUSSION QUESTIONS

1. Select three students to play the role of the two customer representatives and Mrs. Bauman. Make your case, using the issues discussed in this chapter.
2. Have two new students take the role of Mrs. Bauman and Mr. Sherman. Should she hire him?
3. Is the amount of time on the job spent driving an important factor?
4. How can Mrs. Bauman salvage the situation?

Chapter

3 Job Analysis

Three workers sit in front of computer display terminals, all of them nimbly pushing keys. But each of them is doing a different job. Modern technology has made it possible for a stockbroker, a word processor, and a telephone operator to all perform very different jobs using the same tool, the computer terminal. If pay is to be based on work performed, some way is needed to discover the differences and similarities among jobs. Observation is not enough.

What is required is information that will help ensure that compensation decisions are firmly based on identifiable similarities and differences in the work. Collecting and interpreting information about jobs is known as job analysis, which can be defined as:

> **The systematic process of collecting and making certain judgments about all of the important information related to the nature of a specific job.**

Internal consistency is one of the building blocks in our compensation model. Recognizing similarities and differences among jobs is an important aspect of achieving internal

EXHIBIT 3.1
Determining the Internal Job Structure

Internal relationships among jobs within the organization	→	Job Analysis	→	Job Descriptions	→	Job Evaluation	→	Job Structure
		Collecting information and making judgments about the nature of a specific job		Summary reports that identify, define, and describe the job as it is actually performed		Comparison of jobs within an organization		An ordering of jobs based on their content or relative value

Some Major Issues in Job Analysis
- Analysis for what purpose
- What information to collect
- How to collect information
- Who should be involved
- Usefulness of results

consistency. The basic premise underlying job analysis is that jobs are more likely to be described, differentiated, and valued fairly if accurate information about them is available. Exhibit 3.1 shows that job analysis provides the underlying information for preparing job descriptions and evaluating jobs; it is a prerequisite for describing and valuing work and therefore is highly related to the equity and efficiency of the pay system.

Exhibit 3.1 also calls out the major decisions in designing a job analysis: (1) For what purpose are we collecting job information? (2) What information should be collected? (3) What methods should be used? (4) To what extent should the various parties be involved? (5) How useful for compensation purposes are the results?

WHY PERFORM JOB ANALYSIS?

There are a number of reasons why an organization may perform job analysis.[1] They range from concerns for consistent treatment of employees to more specific uses in compensation and other personnel systems.[2]

Internal Consistency

For most people, the pay attached to their job is a matter of stunning importance. Pay decisions must be shown to be based on work-related logic and administered fairly. If an employer is not consistent in its treatment of employees across all business units in the organization or cannot demonstrate the work-related logic of its pay, then it will be hard-pressed to explain its actions to employees or as a defendant in lawsuits. While job analysis is not legally required, the data collected helps managers construct a work-related rationale to defend their decisions and assists their efforts to communicate that rationale.[3]

Compensation

There are two critical uses for job analysis in compensation: (1) to establish job similarities and differences in the content of the jobs and (2) to help establish an internally equitable job structure. If jobs have equal content, then in all likelihood the pay established for them will be equal. If, on the other hand, the job contents differ, then those differences

---

[1]Particularly valuable sources of information on job analysis definitions and methods are U.S. Department of Labor, Manpower Administration, *Handbook for Analyzing Jobs* (Washington, D.C.: U.S. Government Printing Office, 1972); S. A. Fine and W. W. Wiley, *An Introduction to Functional Job Analysis,* monograph no. 4 (Kalamazoo, Mich.: W. E. Upjohn Institute for Employment Research, 1971); E. J. McCormick, "Job and Task Analysis," in *Handbook of Industrial and Organizational Psychology,* ed. M. D. Dunnette (Chicago: Rand McNally, 1976), pp. 651–96; E. J. McCormick, *Job Analysis: Methods and Applications* (New York: AMACOM, 1979); Stephen E. Bemis, Ann Holt Belenky, and Dee Ann Soder, *Job Analysis: An Effective Management Tool* (Washington, D.C.: Bureau of National Affairs, 1983); Jai V. Ghorpade, *Job Analysis: A Handbook for the Human Resource Director* (Englewood Cliffs, N.J.: Prentice Hall, 1988) and *Job Analysis* (n.a.) (Winnipeg, Manitoba: Pay Equity Bureau, Manitoba Labour, 1989).

[2]J. R. Hackman and G. R. Oldham, *Work Redesign* (Reading, Mass.: Addison-Wesley Publishing, 1980).

[3]John Lacy, "Job Evaluation and EEO," *Employee Relations Law Journal* 7, no. 3 (1979), pp. 210–17.

are part of the rationale for paying them differently. Additional data, such as market rates and skills required to perform the jobs, are also considered before any pay structure is determined.

Any process designed to collect job data for determining pay rates needs to ensure that sufficient detail about the actual work performed is collected and that the methods employed can withstand challenges from both inside and outside the organization. The data collected through job analysis becomes one of the key supports of an equitable pay structure. If the support is weak, the structure is vulnerable to challenge.

Additional Applications of Job Analysis Data

Pay decisions are only one of many possible uses of job analysis data. Potential applications are found in every major personnel function.[4] Often the type of job analysis data needed varies by function, as shown in Exhibit 3.2. For example, job analysis is used to identify the skills and experience required to perform a job, thereby clarifying hiring and promotion standards.[5] Training programs may be designed with job analysis data;

EXHIBIT 3.2
Personnel Functions, Job Analysis Information, and Results

Function	Job Analysis		
	Information		Result
Recruitment and selection	Required skills, abilities, and experience	→	Selection and promotion standards
Training and development	Tasks, behaviors	→	Training programs
Performance appraisal	Behavior standards or expected results	→	Performance appraisal criteria
Job design and organization development	Tasks, expected results	→	Organization structure
Compensation	Tasks, abilities, skills, behaviors	→	Similarities and differences in the work; job descriptions

---

[4]R. A. Ash, E. L. Levine, and F. Sistrunk, "The Role of Jobs and Job-Based Methods in Personnel and Human Resources Management," *Research in Personnel and Human Resources Management* 1 (1983), pp. 45–84; Duane Thompson and Toni Thompson, "Court Standards for Job Analysis in Test Validation," *Personnel Psychology* 35 (1982), pp. 865–74; also see George T. Milkovich and John Boudreau, *Personnel/Human Resource Management: A Diagnostic Approach*, 5th ed., chap. 4. (Homewood, Ill.: Richard D. Irwin, 1988).

[5]Robert M. Guion, "Recruiting, Selection, and Job Placement," in *Handbook of Industrial and Organizational Psychology*, ed. Marvin D. Dunnette (Chicago: Rand McNally, 1976); and D. P. Schwab, "Recruiting and Organization Participation," in *Personnel Management*, ed. K. M. Rowland and G. R. Ferris (Boston: Allyn & Bacon, 1982), pp. 105–30.

jobs may be redesigned based on it.[6] In performance evaluation, both employees and supervisors look to the required behaviors and results expected in a job to help assess performance.

Rather than conducting a separate analysis for each application, some writers argue that a single, omnibus method can be designed to capture sufficient data for all (or most) uses.[7] Several employers, including J.C. Penney, Hewlett-Packard, 3M, and Nationwide Insurance, have attempted to design such methods.[8] To date, their implementation focuses on one or two uses (e.g., compensation and training); wider application seems to be limited by lack of acceptance of the results by employees and managers, questions about the usefulness of the data collected, and the significant expense involved. J.C. Penney discontinued the use of their plan. After investing over $300,000 to design an omnibus job analysis, they discovered that the data collected did not yield the pay structure they had expected. The multiple uses simply did not materialize, maintenance costs exceeded expectations, and use of the analysis imposed too great a burden on line managers.

Employee and manager acceptance of data collected is important and easily overlooked.[9] For example, the analyst may feel behavioral descriptions adequately describe a job (e.g., coordinate advertising campaigns with marketing group plans), while the jobholders may feel that greater emphasis on the scope of contacts (e.g., works with outside clients, prepares reports for vice president of marketing) or the financial responsibility (e.g., budgetary control and approvals) more accurately describes the job. No matter how well the rest of the compensation system is designed and administered, if jobholders are dissatisfied with the initial data collected, they are less likely to feel satisfied with the resulting structure.

The key issue for compensation professionals is still to ensure that the data collected serve the purpose of the compensation decision makers and are acceptable to the employees involved. As the flowchart in Exhibit 3.1 indicates, collecting job information is only an interim step, not an end in itself.

---

[6]Hackman and Oldham, *Work Redesign;* R. W. Griffen, A. Welsh, and G. Moorhead, "Perceived Task Characteristics and Employee Performance: A Literature Review," *Academy of Management Review* 6 (1981), pp. 655–64; J. M. Nicholas, "The Comparative Impact of Organizational Developments on Hard Criteria Measures," *Academy of Management Review* 7 (1982), pp. 531–42; R. W. Griffen, *Task Design, an Integrative Approach* (Glenview, Ill.: Scott, Foresman, 1982), pp. 14–24; C. Pinder, *Work Motivation: Theory, Issues, and Application* (Glenview, Ill.: Scott, Foresman, 1984); and Ramon J. Aldag, Steve H. Barr, and Arthur P. Brief, "Measurement of Perceived Task Characteristics," *Psychological Bulletin* 90, no. 3 (1981), pp. 413–31.

[7]Ronald C. Page, "The Use of Job Content Information for Compensation and Reward Systems," paper presented at Academy of Management Meetings, August 1982; and Debra Suhadolnik, Clark Miller, Ronald Page, *FOCUS Job Analysis/Evaluation System* (Minneapolis, Minn.: Control Data Business Advisors, 1986).

[8]J. C. Penney General Management Position Questionnaire (New York: J. C. Penney Company, 1985); Management Position Description (Palo Alto, Calif.: Hewlett-Packard, 1983); 3M Management Position Description Questionnaire (St. Paul, Minn.: 3M, 1985); and Superior Oil Job Analysis Questionnaire (Houston, Tex.: Superior Oil Company, 1982).

[9]Luis R. Gomez-Mejia, Ronald C. Page, and Walter W. Tornow, "A Comparison of the Practical Utility of Traditional, Statistical, and Hybrid Job Evaluation Approaches," *Academy of Management Journal* 25, no. 4 (1982), pp. 790–809.

WHAT DATA TO COLLECT?

Recommendations on the types of data to collect can range from the job title (clerk typist I, administrative assistant) to the frequency with which specific tasks (i.e., answer the phone or open the mail) are performed. Generally, a good job analysis must collect sufficient information to adequately identify, define, and describe a job.[10]

Identifying a job. Data that identify a job include its title, the number of people in the organization who hold this job, and the department where the job is located. Good job titles will provide information and will not obfuscate. Job families may have similar titles, but titles should be consistent with work level; similar sounding titles at different levels can be confusing. The job may be further identified by number of incumbents, whether or not it is exempt from the Fair Labor Standards Act, where it is located (department, work site), and job number, if any is used.

Defining a job. Data here reflects the purpose of the job, why the job exists, and how it fits in with other jobs and with overall organization objectives. End results that flow from the satisfactory performance of this job are typically included.

For managerial jobs, statistics on the size of the budget under the control of this job, the number (and job titles) of people supervised, and reporting relationships with other managers at both higher and lower organization levels are frequently included, also. Financial and organizational data are needed in order to locate a job in the hierarchy. So "defining" may have two aspects, one including information on what positions and departments are supervised and what functions are the responsibility of this position; and another including the number of people directly and indirectly supervised, the department budget, and payroll.

Describing a job. There are lists upon lists of suggested data to be gathered to describe a job. Exhibit 3.3 is typical. Notice that there are two main categories of data to describe jobs: those that are a function of the job (content and work characteristics), and those that are a function of the employee (knowledge, prior experience). These two categories are clearly delineated in some of the earliest work on job analysis. This work, done by the U.S. Department of Labor (DOL) in the 1930s, has been refined into Functional Job Analysis.

Functional Job Analysis

The U.S. Department of Labor's work on job analysis may be the strongest single influence on job analysis practice in the United States.[11] Certainly anyone contemplating undertaking

---

[10]Sidney Gael, *Job Analysis* (San Francisco: Jossey-Bass, 1983); Bemis, Belenky, and Soder, *Job Analysis: An Effective Management Tool;* and Jesse T. Cantrill, "Collecting Job Content Information through Questionnaires," and Thomas S. Roy, Jr., "Collecting Data through Interviews and Observations," both in *Handbook of Wage and Salary Administration,* 2nd ed., ed. Milton L. Rock (New York: McGraw-Hill, 1984).

[11]U.S. Department of Labor, *Handbook for Analyzing Jobs.*

EXHIBIT 3.3
Typical Data Collected for Job Analysis

Data Related to Job

Job content/context factors

Duties	Communications network
Functions	Output (e.g., reports, analyses)
Tasks	Working conditions
Activities	Time allocation
Performance criteria	Roles (e.g., negotiator, monitor, leader)
Critical incidents	

Work characteristics

Risk or exposure	Dependence/independence
Constraints	Pattern or cycle
Choices	Time pressure
Conflicting demands	Fragmentation
Origin of activities	Sustained attention
Expected/unexpected	Time orientation (short or long)

Data Related to Employee

Employee characteristics

Professional/technical knowledge	Managerial skills
Prior experience	Bargaining skills
Manual skills	Leadership skills
Verbal skills	Consulting skills
Written skills	Human relations skills
Quantitative skills	Aptitudes
Mechanical skills	Values
Conceptual skills	Style

Interpersonal relationships

Internal	External
Boss	Suppliers
Other superiors	Customers
Peers	Regulatory
Subordinates	Consultants
Other juniors	Professional/industry
	Community
	Union/employee group

---

job analysis for the first time would be well advised to consult the *Handbook for Analyzing Jobs*.

The original Department of Labor (DOL) methodology categorized data to be collected as (1) actual work performed (job data) and (2) worker traits or characteristics (employee data). It further refined work performed into three categories.[12]

1. Worker functions: What the worker does in relationship to *data, people,* and *things.*
2. Work fields: The methods and techniques employed.

---

[12]U.S. Civil Service Commission, *Job Analysis: Developing and Documenting Data* (Washington, D.C.: Bureau of Intergovernmental Personnel Programs, 1973).

3. Products and services: The materials, products, subject matter, and/or services that result.

For each of these three categories of data, a list of classes was developed. For example, data, people, and things were further refined into 24 worker functions (e.g., computing data differs from copying it). Work fields, defined into 39 subfields, include both "method" verbs (e.g., pouring) and the equipment used to carry out the action (e.g., steel cauldron). An analyst is trained to distinguish the two types of verbs: Method verbs are all action verbs, while the verbs in worker functions are descriptive and encompass a broader activity. Products and services include 375 different categories of results from the job. Finally, worker traits were refined into (1) training time, (2) aptitudes, (3) temperament, (4) interests, and (5) physical demands and environmental conditions.

In the 1970s, Fine modified the DOL's methodology to place greater emphasis on the worker functions and relate those functions to the goals and objectives of the organization.[13] His work resulted in Functional Job Analysis (FJA), which is widely used in the public sector. While few private-sector employers use it, their practices reflect FJA's influence.

The DOL's two basic categories, actual work performed and worker traits, provide the basis for much of current research on quantifying the job analysis process. However, most researchers subdivide worker traits into two groups, one concerned with the worker's behavior on the job, and the other with the underlying abilities required to make such behavior possible.

So we essentially have three categories of information to consider: work data (what tasks are done), worker data (what behaviors occur), and ability data (what abilities underlie the behaviors and task performance).[14] These categories can be confusing because they all look at the same thing—a worker doing a job—and take different approaches to describe what is happening. Perhaps some examples will clarify the differences.

Task Data

Task data involve the elemental units of work, subparts of a job, with emphasis on the purpose of each task. An excerpt from a job analysis questionnaire that collects task data is shown in Exhibit 3.4. Note how the inventory describes communication in terms of actual tasks; for example, "read technical publications" and "consult with co-workers." The other distinguishing characteristic is the emphasis on output, or objective of the task; for example, "read technical publications to keep current on industry" and "consult with

---

[13]Sidney Fine, *Functional Job Analysis Scales: A Desk Aid* (Kalamazoo, Mich.: Upjohn Institute for Employment Research, 1973); Fine and Wiley, *Introduction to Functional Job Analysis.*

[14]Ron Ash, "Job Elements for Task Clusters: Arguments for Using Multi-Methodological Approaches to Job Analysis and a Demonstration of their Utility," *Public Personnel Management Journal,* June 1982, pp. 80–90.

EXHIBIT 3.4
Job Analysis Questionnaire (*excerpt*)

	Do This	Time spent in current position
1. Mark the circle in the "Do This" column for tasks that you currently perform. 2. At the end of the task list, write in any unlisted tasks that you currently perform. 3. Rate each task that you perform for relative time spent by marking the appropriate circle in the "Time Spent" column. Please use a No. 2 pencil only and fill all circles completely		Very small amount / Much below average / Below average / Slightly below average / About average / Slightly above average / Above average / Much above average / Very large amount
PERFORM COMMUNICATIONS ACTIVITIES		
Obtain technical information.		
421. Read technical publications about competitive products.	○	① ② ③ ④ ⑤ ⑥ ⑦ ⑧ ⑨
422. Read technical publications to keep current on industry.	○	① ② ③ ④ ⑤ ⑥ ⑦ ⑧ ⑨
423. Attend required, recommended, or job-related courses and/or seminars.	○	① ② ③ ④ ⑤ ⑥ ⑦ ⑧ ⑨
424. Study existing operating systems/programs to gain maintain familiarity with them.	○	① ② ③ ④ ⑤ ⑥ ⑦ ⑧ ⑨
425. Perform literature searches necessary to the development of products.	○	① ② ③ ④ ⑤ ⑥ ⑦ ⑧ ⑨
426. Communicate with system software group to see how their recent changes impact current projects.	○	① ② ③ ④ ⑤ ⑥ ⑦ ⑧ ⑨
427. Study and evaluate state-of-the-art techniques to remain competitive and/or lead the field.	○	① ② ③ ④ ⑤ ⑥ ⑦ ⑧ ⑨
428. Attend industry standards meetings.	○	① ② ③ ④ ⑤ ⑥ ⑦ ⑧ ⑨
Exchange technical information.		
429. Interface with coders to verify that the software design is being implemented as specified.	○	① ② ③ ④ ⑤ ⑥ ⑦ ⑧ ⑨
430. Consult with co-workers to exchange ideas and techniques.	○	① ② ③ ④ ⑤ ⑥ ⑦ ⑧ ⑨
431. Consult with members of other technical groups within the company to exchange new ideas and techniques.	○	① ② ③ ④ ⑤ ⑥ ⑦ ⑧ ⑨
432. Interface with support consultants or organizations to clarify software design or courseware content.	○	① ② ③ ④ ⑤ ⑥ ⑦ ⑧ ⑨
433. Attend meetings to review project status.	○	① ② ③ ④ ⑤ ⑥ ⑦ ⑧ ⑨
434. Attend team meetings to review implementation strategies.	○	① ② ③ ④ ⑤ ⑥ ⑦ ⑧ ⑨
435. Discuss department plans and objectives with manager.	○	① ② ③ ④ ⑤ ⑥ ⑦ ⑧ ⑨

co-workers to exchange ideas and techniques." Task data reveal the actual work performed and its purpose or outcome.[15]

Behavioral Data

This data approach describes jobs in terms of the behaviors that occur. Exhibit 3.5 shows such behavioral observations, again concerned with "communications." This time, the questions focus on verbs that describe the human behavior (e.g., advising, negotiating,

---

[15]Ramon J. Aldag, Steve H. Barr, and Arthur P. Brief, "Measurement of Perceived Task Characteristics," *Psychological Bulletin* 90, no. 3 (1981), pp. 415–31; and Page, "The Use of Job Content Information."

EXHIBIT 3.5
Job Analysis Questionnaire (*excerpt*)

Section 4   Relationships with Other Persons

This section deals with different aspects of interaction between people involved in various kinds of work.

Code Importance to this Job (1)	
N	Does not apply
1	Very minor
2	Low
3	Average
4	High
5	Extreme

4.1   Communications

Rate the following in terms of how *important* the activity is to the completion of the job. Some jobs may involve several or all of the items in this section.

4.1.1   Oral (communicating by speaking)

99 ____ Advising (dealing with individuals in order to counsel and/or guide them with regard to problems that may be resolved by legal, financial, scientific, technical, clinical, spiritual, and/or other professional principles)

100 ____ Negotiating (dealing with others in order to reach an agreement or solution, for example, labor bargaining, diplomatic relations, etc.)

101 ____ Persuading (dealing with others in order to influence them toward some action or point of view, for example, selling, political campaigning, etc.)

102 ____ Instructing (the teaching of knowledge or skills, in either an informal or a formal manner, to others, for example, a public school teacher, a machinist teaching an apprentice, etc.)

103 ____ Interviewing (conducting interviews directed toward some specific objective, for example, interviewing job applicants, census taking, etc.)

104 ____ Routine information exchange: job related (the giving and/or receiving of *job-related* information of a routine nature, for example, ticket agent, taxicab dispatcher, receptionist, etc.)

105 ____ Nonroutine information exchange (the giving and/or receiving of *job-related* information of a nonroutine or unusual nature, for example, professional committee meetings, engineers discussing new product design, etc.)

106 ____ Public speaking (making speeches or formal presentations before relatively large audiences, for example, political addresses, radio/TV broadcasting, delivering a sermon, etc.)

4.1.2   Written (communicating by written/printed material)

107 ____ Writing (for example, writing or dictating letters, reports, etc., writing copy for ads, writing newspaper articles, etc.; do *not* include transcribing activities described in item 4.3, but only activities in which the incumbent creates the written material)

4.1.3   Other Communications

108 ____ Signaling (communicating by some type of signal, for example, hand signals, semaphore, whistles, horns, bells, lights, etc.)

109 ____ Code communications (telegraph, cryptography, etc.)

persuading). Exhibit 3.5 is from the Position Analysis Questionnaire (PAQ), developed by McCormick and his associates.[16] The PAQ groups work information into seven basic factors: information input, mental processes, work output, relationships with other persons, job context, other job characteristics, and general dimensions. With the PAQ, similarities and differences among jobs are described in terms of these seven general processes, rather than in terms of specific aspects unique to each job.[17] The communications behavior in Exhibit 3.5 is part of the "relationships with other persons" factor. Let us compare the PAQ's approach to communications to the task inventory's approach in Exhibit 3.4. Item 105 on the PAQ: "nonroutine information exchange (the giving and/ or receiving of *job-related* information of a nonroutine or unusual nature, for example, professional committee meetings, engineers discussing new product design, etc.)" is probably similar to item 430 on the task inventory: "consult with co-workers to exchange ideas and techniques." Both are getting at the same aspect of work, by different approaches. But lest you think the previous task inventory (Exhibit 3.4) offers the beauty of simplicity, note that item 431 lists "consult with members of other technical groups . . . to exchange new ideas and techniques" and item 432 lists "interface with support consultants to clarify . . . design." In fact, the task inventory from which Exhibit 3.4 is excerpted contains 250 items and covers only systems analyst jobs, whereas the work behavior data in Exhibit 3.5 is from an inventory of 194 items, whose developers claim it can be used to analyze *all* jobs. Consequently, new task-based questions need to be designed for each new set of jobs, whereas behaviors, at least as defined in the PAQ, may be applied across all jobs. However, some evidence suggests that the PAQ's seven functions are simply

---

[16]Much of the developmental and early applications of the PAQ was done in the 1960s and 1970s. See, for example, Ernest J. McCormick, "Job Information: Its Development and Applications," in *Handbook of Personnel and Industrial Relations*, ed. D. Yoder and H. G. Heneman, Jr. (Washington, D.C.: Bureau of National Affairs, 1979); McCormick, *Job Analysis* (New York: AMACOM, 1979); McCormick, "Job and Task Analysis," in *Handbook of Industrial and Organizational Psychology*, ed. M. D. Dunnette (Chicago: Rand McNally, 1979); McCormick, *The Development, Analysis, and Experimental Application of Worker-Oriented Job Variables* (Washington, D.C.: Office of Naval Research Report, Department of the Navy, 1964); E. J. McCormick, J. W. Cunningham, and G. C. Gordon, "Job Dimensions Based on Factorial Analyses of Worker-Oriented Job Variables," *Personnel Psychology* 20 (1967), pp. 417–30; E. J. McCormick, R. H. Finn, and C. D. Scheips, "Patterns of Job Requirements," *Journal of Applied Psychology* 41 (1957), pp. 358–65; E. J. McCormick, P. R. Jeanneret, and R. C. Mecham, *The Development and Background of the Position Analysis Questionnaire (PAQ)* (West Lafayette, Ind.: Occupational Research Center, Purdue University, 1969); McCormick et al., *A Study of Job Characteristics and Job Dimensions as Based on the Position Analysis Questionnaire* (West Lafayette, Ind.: Occupational Research Center, Purdue University, 1969); P. R. Jeanneret and R. C. Meacham, "A Study of Job Characteristics and Job Dimensions as Based on the Position Analysis Questionnaire (PAQ)," *Journal of Applied Psychology* 56 (1972), pp. 347–68; R. C. Mecham and E. J. McCormick, *The Rated Attribute Requirements of Job Elements in the Position Analysis Questionnaire* (West Lafayette, Ind.: Occupational Research Center, Purdue University, 1969); and Mecham et al., *The Use of Data Based on the Position Analysis Questionnaire* (West Lafayette, Ind.: Occupational Research Center, Purdue University, 1969). The PAQ is distributed by the University Book Store, 360 West State St., West Lafayette, Ind. 47906.

[17]R. C. Mecham, E. J. McCormick, and P. R. Jeanneret, *Technical Manual for the Position Analysis Questionnaire (PAQ) System* (Logan, Utah: PAQ Services, 1977).

too generally defined for pay purposes.[18] These functions seem to emphasize similarities in the jobs and are less sensitive to differences. Nevertheless, employers do use the PAQ to analyze jobs and establish pay structures.

Abilities Data

Abilities data capture the knowledge and skills a worker must possess for satisfactory job performance. A taxonomy developed by Fleishman includes (1) psychomotor abilities, (2) physical proficiency abilities, and (3) cognitive abilities, and forms the foundation for ability-based job analysis.[19] Ross and others at AT&T, in conjunction with the Communication Workers of America and other unions, have developed a set of 16 abilities required in nonmanagerial work at AT&T, shown in Exhibit 3.6.[20] "Expression" and "comprehension," their first two factors, probably correspond most closely to the communication aspect we looked at with task and behavior data. Exhibit 3.7 AT&T excerpts the measurement of comprehension abilities required on the job. Note that the behavioral descriptors used to anchor the scales for oral comprehension (e.g., "understand a McDonald's hamburger commercial," "understand instructions for a sport," and "understand a lecture on navigating in space") are not work-specific but are drawn from daily life outside of the job. Work-specific illustrations could also be used to anchor these scales. In addition to Oral Comprehension, there is the additional factor of Written Comprehension, measured on a separate scale.

While "communication" scales, shown in Exhibits 3.4, 3.5, and 3.7, were used to illustrate the shades of differences in task, behavior, and ability data, these three represent different views of work. They vary in the way they describe a job. Thus, it is not surprising that varying approaches to job analysis may yield different results. Cornelius, Carron, and Collins examined seven foreman jobs in a chemical processing plant using all three types of job analysis data.[21] Using the same statistical procedures on all three data sets,

---

[18]E. T. Cornelius III, T. J. Carron, and M. M. Collins, "Job Analysis Models and Job Classification," *Personnel Psychology* 32 (1979), pp. 693–708; also see R. W. Lissitz, J. L. Mendoza, C. J. Huberty, and V. H. Markos, "Some Ideas on a Methodology for Determining Job Similarities/Differences," *Personnel Psychology* 32 (1979); and JoAnn Lee and Jorge L. Mendoza, "A Comparison of Techniques which Test for Job Difference," *Personnel Psychology* 34 (1981), pp. 731–48.

[19]E. A. Fleishman, *Structure and Measurement of Physical Fitness* (Englewood Cliffs, N.J.: Prentice-Hall, 1964); Fleishman, "Toward a Taxonomy of Human Performance," *American Psychologist* 30 (1975), pp. 1017–32; Fleishman, "Evaluating Physical Abilities Required by Jobs," *The Personal Administrator* 24 (1979), pp. 82–92; and Fleishman, "On the Relation between Abilities, Learning, and Human Performance," *American Psychologist* 27 (1972), pp. 1017–32.

[20]Ken Ross, "Occupational Job Evaluation Study," unpublished report (Basking Ridge, N.J., AT&T, 1983); and Ronnie J. Straw and Lorel E. Foged, "The Limits of Job Evaluation to Achieve Comparable Worth," paper presented at Atlantic Economic Conference, Montreal, Canada, October 11–14, 1984.

[21]Cornelius, Carron, and Collins, "Job Analysis Models;" and Jack E. Smith and Milton D. Hakel, "Convergence among Data Sources, Response Bias, and Reliability and Validity of a Structured Job Analysis Questionnaire," *Personnel Psychology* 32, no. 4 (1979), pp. 677–92.

EXHIBIT 3.6
CWA Job Analysis Factors: Knowledge/Abilities/Skill-Based

1. *Expression* is speaking and/or writing in words, sentences, or numbers so others will understand. It is measured in terms of the complexity of the information being expressed as well as the comprehension ability of the receiver of the information.

2. *Comprehension* is understanding spoken and/or written words, sentences, or numbers. It is measured in terms of the complexity of the information being received as well as the quality of the information being received.

3. *Fact Finding* is obtaining or selecting pertinent information through observation, research, or questioning. It includes organizing and combining different pieces of information into meaningful order to identify a problem. It does not include the application of this information to solve the problem. An unknown is the key element in fact finding.

4. *Systems Reasoning* is making decisions that involve the selection and application of appropriate business resources or usage of relevant facts to solve identified problems or to achieve a desired result. This is based on knowledge and understanding of products and services, materials, policies, practices, and procedures.

5. *Mathematics* is the selection and application of mathematical methods or procedures to solve problems or to achieve desired results. These systems range from basic arithmetic computations to the most complex statistical techniques or other applications such as occur in physics or engineering problems.

6. *Adaptability* is the need to adapt one's behavior to changing or unusual circumstances to achieve a desired result. This includes changes in personal interactions or work situations.

7. *Persuasion* is influencing the behaviors or actions of others. The changes in others' behaviors or actions may not be observed immediately.

8. *Mental Demand* is mental effort associated with attending to or performing a task in the presence of distractions or work frustrations. Distractions and work frustrations arise from boredom, overlapping demands, exacting deadlines and output standards, lack of latitude to adapt behavior, discouraging circumstances, repeated unsuccessful attempts, and nonemployee controlled work flow.

9. *Physical Demand* is physical effort associated with activities such as handling weights, repetition of work motions, maintenance of difficult work positions, or exposure to unpleasant surroundings.

10. *Safety Skills* measures the adherence to prescribed safety and personal security practices in the performance of tasks involving exposure to hazard or risk in the work environment.

11. *Electrical/Electronic Knowledge* is the knowledge and application of the principles of electricity, electronics, electronic logic, and integrated transmission technologies such as lasers and fiber optics. This includes understanding of circuits, their component parts and how they work together, and understanding the output from devices or meters that register or display information related to these systems.

12. *Mechanical Knowledge* is the knowledge and application of principles of how mechanical equipment such as gears, pulleys, motors, and hydraulics works. It includes the operation, repair or maintenance of systems. It *does not* include knowledge of tools and their uses.

13. *Tools and Uses* is the knowledge, appropriate selection and application of hand tools, office machines, mechanical and electrical tools (test sets). This does not include keyboard devices.

14. *Graphics* is reading, interpreting and/or preparing graphic representations of information such as maps, plans, drawings, blueprints, diagrams, and timing/flow charts. It includes the preparation of visual artwork.

15. *Coding* is reading and/or writing and interpreting coded information. Codes may be identified by the fact that the ideas or concepts they represent may be translated, expanded, or expressed in English.

16. *Keyboard Skills* is the operation of keyboard devices such as typewriters, data terminals, calculators, and operator equipment.

EXHIBIT 3.7
Sample Measurement of AT&T-CWA Job Analysis Factor

ORAL COMPREHENSION

This is the ability to understand spoken English words and sentences.

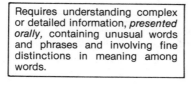

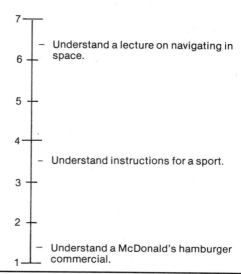

Source: AT&T

they found that different data sets yielded different results. In other words, the type of data collected will affect the results. Their research provides sound advice for the compensation professional: The purpose of the analysis dictates the nature of the data to collect. Thus, if you intend to design training programs, according to Exhibit 3.2, you'll need to collect task and behavioral data. If developing a pay structure, then all three types of data may be useful. Other research has identified another factor that affects the results of job analysis: the level of analysis.

Level of Analysis

The nature of the data collected can be considered in terms of a hierarchy, shown in Exhibit 3.8. Some of the levels in the hierarchy are the same as the types of data we just discussed. Employee attributes (abilities) and task elements are examples. In the hierarchy, tasks represent a grouping of elements or behaviors into a basic accomplishment or duty. For example, elements such as "gathering time cards and using calculators to multiply hours worked by hourly wage" are combined into a task called "calculating employee wages for time cards." Moving up the hierarchy, tasks are grouped into positions, which

EXHIBIT 3.8
Levels of Analysis

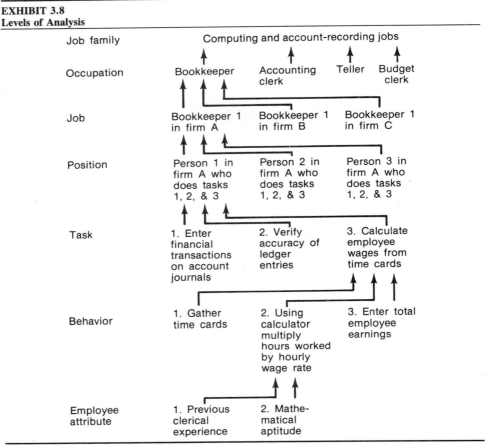

Job family	Computing and account-recording jobs
Occupation	Bookkeeper	Accounting clerk	Teller	Budget clerk
Job	Bookkeeper 1 in firm A	Bookkeeper 1 in firm B	Bookkeeper 1 in firm C
Position	Person 1 in firm A who does tasks 1, 2, & 3	Person 2 in firm A who does tasks 1, 2, & 3	Person 3 in firm A who does tasks 1, 2, & 3
Task	1. Enter financial transactions on account journals	2. Verify accuracy of ledger entries	3. Calculate employee wages from time cards
Behavior	1. Gather time cards	2. Using calculator multiply hours worked by hourly wage rate	3. Enter total employee earnings
Employee attribute	1. Previous clerical experience	2. Mathematical aptitude

Source: Adapted from K. Pearlman, "Job Families: A Review and Discussion of their Implications for Personnel Selection," *Psychological Bulletin 87* (1980), pp. 1–28. Copyright 1980 by the American Psychological Association. Adapted by permission of the author.

constitute different individuals performing the same group of tasks in a particular organization. In the illustration in Exhibit 3.8 there are three positions (individuals) as Bookkeeper I (job in firm A). Jobs similar across several firms (Bookkeeper, Accounting Clerk, Teller) are in turn considered to belong to an occupation. The occupation, at the most general level of analysis, could be grouped with other occupations into a job family. Such a family would involve computing, classifying, and recording numerical data, and may form a "computing and account/recording job family."

What does all this have to do with making pay decisions? The level or unit of analysis chosen may influence the decision of whether the work is similar to dissimilar. At the occupation level, bookkeepers, tellers, and accounting clerks are considered to be similar; yet at levels below occupation (the job level, for example) these three are considered dissimilar. Hence, a critical decision in the design of job analysis is the level of analysis, which determines the specificity of the work information to be collected. An analogy might be looking at two grains of salt under a microscope versus looking at them as part of a serving of french fries. This is important because if job data suggest that jobs are similar, then the jobs must be paid equally; if jobs are different, they can be paid differently. The issue of whether or not jobs are substantially similar has been a main focus of a lot of discrimination litigation and thus takes on financial meaning beyond concerns for internal consistency.

Generic Jobs

In practice, the level of analysis, and therefore the amount and detail of information collected for job analysis, varies considerably. Most employers use more general levels (position or job) and ignore specific tasks and employee behavior, arguing that all the detailed data on tasks and behaviors get combined when determining wages. They argue that the time and expense to collect data is unjustified. Increasingly, employers are using more general levels in order to increase flexibility. Thus, many firms are reducing the number of separate job classifications used. New United Motors Manufacturing, Inc. (NUMMI), a joint venture between General Motors and Toyota, went from 120 separate jobs to four levels of technicians needed to perform all the tasks necessary to assemble automobiles.[22] The result is broad, generic descriptions that cover a large number of related tasks akin to the occupation level in Exhibit 3.8. Two employees working in the same broadly defined jobs may be doing entirely different sets of related tasks. But for pay purposes, they are doing the same job. Employees working in very broadly defined jobs can easily be switched to other tasks that fall within the broad range of the same job, without the bureaucratic burden of making job transfer requests and wage adjustments. Thus, employees can more easily be matched to changes in the work flow.

So where does this leave us? What data should be collected and what level of analysis should be used? There is no clear-cut answer. It depends on the situation, the resources available. But the more specific and detailed the data, the more likely it is to capture job differences and adequately describe the job content. Whether such detailed information is worth the expense involved depends on the circumstances in the organization. Clearly, detailed data may justify pay differences to a skeptical judge presiding over a pay discrimination suit. Yet, more broadly defined jobs with generic titles and descriptions can increase flexibility in work assignments.

HOW CAN THE DATA BE COLLECTED?

After having decided on the purpose, level, and the nature of the data, the next major decision is the method(s) of collecting it. A wide variety of methods exists; the most common ones are described in Exhibit 3.9. In this section we will combine these methods into two basic types: conventional and quantitative.

---

[22]John F. Krafcik, "High Performance Manufacturing: An International Study of Auto Assembly Practice," Working paper, International Motor Vehicle Program, Cambridge, Mass.: MIT, January 1988; Haruo Shimada, "The Perceptions and the Reality of Japanese Industrial Relations," in *The Management Challenge: Japanese Views,* ed. L. Thurow (Cambridge, Mass.: MIT Press, 1985); and John Paul MacDuffie, "The Japanese Auto Transplants: Challenges to Conventional Wisdom," ILR Report, Fall 1988, pp. 12–18.

EXHIBIT 3.9
Data Collection Methods

Method	Descriptions	Characteristics
Questionnaire	Using standardized form, jobholders and/or supervisors describe the work. Data can be gathered either through mailed survey or through individual interview.	Variations include combining questionnaire with individual or group interview. As with all questionnaires, responses may be incomplete or difficult to interpret, a limitation minimized by combining with interviews. Standard format eases mathematical analysis. Interviews, however, may be time consuming, and become more difficult with workers at multiple locations.
Checklist	Jobholders and/or supervisors check items on a task inventory that apply to their particular job. Check list can be tailor-made or purchased.	Depends on recognition rather than recall. Cheap, easy to administer and analyze. However, care must be taken that all significant aspects of work are included in the list.
Diary	Jobholders record activities as they are performed.	Has the advantage of collecting data as events occur, but it is often difficult to obtain continuous and consistent entries. Obtained data is not in a standardized format.
Observation	Analyst records perceptions formed watching the work being done by one or more jobholders.	The absence of preconceived structures or artificial constraints can lead to richer data. Each job can be studied in any depth desired. However, validity and reliability of data can be a problem, and the relative emphasis of certain work aspects is dependent on the acuteness of the analyst's perceptions. Also, the observation of employee behavior by an analyst influences it.
Activity sampling	Observations are made at random intervals.	
Activity matrix	Respondents identify time spent in relation to tasks and products or services.	Data collected is amenable to quantitative analysis, and is highly adaptable to other human resource management needs; however, another job analysis procedure must be used initially to develop the matrix.
Critical incidents	Behaviorally oriented incidents describe key job behaviors. Analyst determines degree of each type of behavior present or absent in each job.	Analysis clearly based on concrete behavior. Scales require some expertise to develop.

Conventional Methods

A common data collection method involves an analyst using a questionnaire to conduct a structured interview of job incumbents and supervisors. The questionnaires and interviews are structured to achieve a uniform response format. The approach requires considerable involvement of employees and supervisors, which increases their understanding of the process, provides an opportunity to clarify their work relationships and expectations, and increases the likelihood that they will accept the results. Usually, an analyst translates the data collected to a summary job description sheet. Often, both incumbents and supervisors are given an opportunity to modify and approve the job description; this helps assure its acceptance. In some cases the preparation of these description sheets is left to the supervisors and incumbents, while the analyst role becomes one of trainer/facilitator. The analysts are trained (either formally or through trial and error) in verbal style and form to ensure that description sheets are uniform. Some trainers go so far as to specify "correct" verbs and adjectives to use.[23] A step-by-step procedure for conducting a conventional job analysis is shown in Exhibit 3.10, and Appendix A in this chapter contains a conventional job analysis questionnaire.

Conventional methods place considerable reliance on the analyst's abilities to understand the work performed and to translate it. Certain safeguards, such as multiple approvals (by supervisors and incumbents), may help minimize the difficulties inherent in translating the results of questionnaires and personal discussions into an accurate representation of the job.

In a review of job analysis, McCormick points out that "of the various deficiencies of conventional job analysis procedures, probably the sharpest criticism is that the typical essays of job activities *are not* adequately descriptive of the jobs in question." After granting the positive contribution of obtaining work-related data through conventional methods, he observes in an artful understatement, "They probably ha[ve] not generally benefited from . . . systematic, scientific approaches."[24]

Reducing subjectivity in job analysis is the primary goal of quantitative job analysis. The critical advantage of quantitative job analysis over conventional approaches is that quantitative analysis lends itself to statistical analysis, is documentable and quantifiable, and *may* be more objective. Additionally, a computerized job analysis may relieve much of the drudgery of collecting and translating job data.

Quantitative Methods

Inventories are the core of all quantitative job analysis. Inventories, illustrated in Exhibits 3.4, 3.5, and 3.7, are questionnaires in which tasks, behaviors, and abilities are listed. Each item is assessed, usually by both job incumbents and supervisors, in terms of time spent, importance to the overall job, and/or learning time.[25] Systematic assessment documents decisions and results, and the resulting data can be subjected to further statistical analysis.

Usually a compensation professional must decide whether to buy a commercially available, predeveloped inventory or to develop a quantitative inventory tailored for a specific organization. Not surprisingly, consulting firms stand at the ready to offer prede-

---

[23]R. T. Henderson, *Compensation Management*, 4th ed. (Reston, Va.: Reston Publishing, 1985).

[24]McCormick, "Job and Task Analysis."

[25]J. E. Morsh, "Job Analysis in the United States Air Force," *Personnel Psychology* 17, no. 17 (1964), pp. 7–17; J. E. Morsh, M. Joyce Giorgia, and J. M. Madden, "A Job Analysis of a Complex Utilization Field—The R&D Management Officer," Personnel Research Laboratory, Aerospace Medical Division, Air Force Systems Command, 1965; J. N. Mosel, "The Domain of Worker Functions as a Partially Ordered Set," Paper presented at American Psychological Association Meetings, Philadelphia, 1963; and A. I. Siegel and D. G. Shultz, "Post-Training Performance Criterion Development and Application: A Comparative Multidimensional Scaling Analysis of the Task Performed by Naval Aviation Electronics Technicians at Two Job Levels" (Wayne, Pa.: Applied Psychological Services, 1964).

EXHIBIT 3.10
General Procedures for Conventional Job Analysis

Step	Things to Remember or Do
1. Develop preliminary job information	*a.* Review existing documents in order to develop an initial "big-picture" familiarity with the job: its main mission, its major duties or functions, work flow patterns.
	b. Prepare a preliminary list of duties which will serve as a framework for conducting the interviews.
	c. Make a note of major items which are unclear, or ambiguous or that need to be clarified during the data-gathering process.
2. Conduct initial tour of work site	*a.* The initial tour is designed to familiarize the job analyst with the work layout, the tools and equipment that are used, the general conditions of the workplace, and the mechanics associated with the end-to-end performance of major duties.
	b. The initial tour is particularly helpful in those jobs where a first-hand view of a complicated or unfamiliar piece of equipment saves the interviewee the thousand words required to describe the unfamiliar or technical.
	c. For continuity, it is recommended that the first level supervisor-interviewee be designated the guide for the job-site observations.
3. Conduct interviews	*a.* It is recommended that the first interview be conducted with the first-level supervisor who is considered to be in a better position than the jobholders to provide an overview of the job and how the major duties fit together.
	b. For scheduling purposes, it is recommended that no more than two interviews be conducted per day, each interview lasting no more than three hours.
Notes on selection of interviewees	*a.* The interviewees are considered subject matter experts by virtue of the fact that they perform the job (in the case of job incumbents) or are responsible for getting the job done (in the case of first-level supervisors).
	b. The job incumbent to be interviewed should represent the *typical* employee who is knowledgeable about the job (*not* the trainee who is just learning the ropes *nor* the outstanding member of the work unit).
	c. Whenever feasible, the interviewees should be selected with a view towards obtaining an appropriate race/sex mix.
4. Conduct second tour of work site	*a.* The second tour of the work site is designed to clarify, confirm, and otherwise refine the information developed in the interviews.
	b. As in the initial tour, it is recommended that the same first-level supervisor-interviewee conduct the second walk-through.
5. Consolidate job information	*a.* The consolidation phase of the job study involves piecing together into one coherent and comprehensive job description the data obtained from several sources: supervisor, jobholders, on-site tours, and written materials about the job.
	b. Past experience indicates that one minute of consolidation is required for every minute of interviewing. For planning purposes, at least 5 hours should be set aside for the consolidation phase.
	c. A subject matter expert should be accessible as a resource person to the job analyst during the consolidation phase. The supervisor-interviewee fills this role.
	d. Check your initial preliminary list of duties and questions—all must be answered or confirmed.
6. Verify job description	*a.* The verification phase involves bringing all the interviewees together for the purpose of determining if the consolidated job description is accurate and complete.
	b. The verification process is conducted in a group setting. Typed or legibly written copies of the job description (narrative description of the work setting *and* list of task statements) are distributed to the first-level supervisor and the job incumbent interviewees.
	c. Line by line, the job analyst goes through the entire job description and makes notes of any omissions, ambiguities, or needed clarifications.
	d. Collect all materials at the end of the verification meeting.

veloped plans as well as the experience and analytical skills necessary to design a tailored one.[26]

Predeveloped Quantitative Inventories

Several quantitative inventories are available. Three are briefly discussed here; more details and other options may be found through the references.

Comprehension Occupational Data Analysis Program (CODAP). Originally developed to aid the U.S. Air Force to design training programs, CODAP is perhaps the earliest attempt to quantify job analysis.[27] The data are task oriented and cover over 200 Air Force specialties. The items are scaled in terms of the "average time spent" on each. While its use for pay administration is limited, the CODAP computer software, developed to analyze job analysis data, is available free to nonprofit organizations and can be used on pay-related job data.[28]

FOCUS. Personnel Decisions Research developed an approach that is task based.[29] However, it differs from other quantitative job analysis inventories in that separate questionnaires have been developed for several occupations (e.g., management, systems analysis, manufacturing, personnel, and others). All these questionnaires share a common core of task-based items; the approach is flexible, since unique items are added to the core for each unique occupation. Hewlett-Packard, 3M, and Nationwide Insurance are among the employers using some variation of FOCUS to help determine their pay structures.

Position Analysis Questionnaire. Without question the PAQ is the best-known and most generally used quantitative job analysis.[30] The PAQ has 194 items (Exhibit 3.5 is an example). As noted earlier, these items form seven basic factors and are scaled according to how important each item is in the total job. According to its developers, the PAQ can be used to analyze virtually any job or position, and can be completed by

---

[26]Information on custom designed quantitative job analysis plans can be obtained from Control Data Business Advisors, 8200 34th Avenue South, Minneapolis, Minn.: Personnel Decisions Research Institute, Foshay Tower, Minneapolis, Minn.: Sibson & Co., Chicago, Ill., (and other locations); and Wyatt & Company, New York, Detroit, San Francisco (and other locations).

[27]R. E. Christal and J. J. Weissmuller, *New Comprehensive Occupational Data Analysis Programs (CODAP) for Analyzing Task Factor Information,* AHFRL Interim Professional Paper No. 7R-76-3 (Lackland Air Force Base, Tex.: Air Force Human Resources Laboratory, 1976); and M. H. Trattner, "Task Analysis in the Design of Three Concurrent Validity Studies of the Professional and Administrative Career Examination," *Personnel Psychology* 32 (1979), pp. 109–19.

[28]Contact the Personnel Research Division of the Human Resources Laboratory, Lackland Air Force Base, Texas.

[29]The address for Personnel Decisions Research Institute is included in Note 26.

[30]Information on the PAQ is available from PAQ Services, P.O. Box 3337, Logan, UT 84321, (801) 752-5698.

a typical employee without much special training.[31] However, its reading comprehension level is quite high and the instructions complex, making it difficult for some employees to complete it on their own.[32] Mecham and McCormick suggest that an analyst trained in its use could be used to assist employees in completing the inventory.[33] Compensation analysts may want to obtain a copy and try completing it themselves to get a feel for the questionnaire before they adopt it.[34]

Predeveloped inventories such as the CODAP, FOCUS, or PAQ offer the advantage of having been pretested, which avoids substantial expense and lead time required in inventory design. But a major limitation of most of these predeveloped plans is that they are not tailored to particular job families or organizations. Rather, most were developed to be applied across a wide variety of work in different organizations. Consequently, their questions may be too general to be useful in identifying differences in specific jobs.

Tailoring a Plan

Rather than adopting an existing inventory, some employers opt to tailor one to its specific work and conditions. Several consulting organizations market technical expertise to assist these employers. So the choice is whether to purchase a predeveloped inventory or to custom-design one. While specific processes through which inventories are developed vary somewhat among consultants, all involve four basic steps.

Step 1: Generate items. An exhaustive list of tasks or worker traits relevant to the work is generated, typically through interviews with small groups of job incumbents and supervisors.

Tornow suggests that the following factors be considered when developing items.[35] Try to ensure:

- Item content covers the entire domain of tasks/activities/behaviors of the jobs under analysis.
- Items are able to discriminate among jobs that are known to be different.
- Items are not so general as to apply to all positions equally, yet not so specific as to apply to only one job.
- Items permit a quantifiable response format.

Once a preliminary list of items is generated, it is culled for duplicate or overlapping items. Usually this process yields between 200 and 300. Several consulting firms have

---

[31]See Mecham, McCormick, and Jeanneret, *Technical Manual*.

[32]Ronald A. Ash and S. L. Edgell, "A Note on the Readability of the Position Analysis Questionnaire (PAQ)," *Journal of Applied Psychology* 60 (1975), pp. 765–66; John R. Roark and John H. Burnett, "Objective Methods of Job Analysis," in *Handbook of Wage and Salary Administration,* ed. Milton L. Rock (New York: McGraw-Hill, 1984).

[33]PAQ *Technical Manual*.

[34]See address for the PAQ given in Note 16.

[35]Walter W. Tornow, "An Integrated Personnel Approach to Job Analysis and Job Evaluation," Paper presented at Conference on Job Analysis, Institute of Industrial Relations, University of California, Berkeley, February 1979.

developed shortened versions. TPF&C's Weighted Job Questionnaire has 65 items. Other compensation consulting firms offer similar products.

Step 2: Determine the scaling format. Scaling formats usually include the frequency, importance, and learning time required. Other scales could include consequences of errors, and difficulty. For some jobs, a three-interval scale is sufficient, e.g., In my job, I do this task:

a lot   ☐

some   ☐

never   ☐

Greater number of intervals obviously permit more distinctions. The inventory in Exhibit 3.4 uses a 9-interval scale to measure Time Spent on a Task. The PAQ in Exhibit 3.5 uses five intervals to measure Importance of an activity.

Step 3: Pilot the preliminary inventory. Once the inventory is generated and scaled, it is administered to a group of jobs whose contents and requirements are relatively unambiguous and accepted by all the parties involved. The purpose of the pilot is to determine if the inventory does identify similarities and differences in work of known characteristics. The pilot also provides feedback on how "user friendly" it is, the time required to complete it, and the reactions of incumbents to how adequately the items capture all the aspects of the work. Most pilots include provisions for open-ended responses to write in information that may have been omitted in the item list.

Step 4: Analyze and feed back results. A primary advantage of quantitative job analysis over conventional methods is that the data are amenable to statistical analysis. The increased availability of statistical software packages capable of analyzing such data has led to new techniques for determining similarities and differences in work. Examples are noted in references in this chapter.

Results of analysis are usually fed back to supervisors and jobholders in profiles and narrative descriptions. Exhibit 3.11 shows a format used by a major consulting firm to compare results of analysis of managerial jobs at two different locations within the same organization. The exhibit shows that managers at Facility A spent more time collecting and analyzing information, and less time dealing with crises, than did managers at Facility B. It also appears that managers at Facility B were more inclined to communicate orally rather than in writing. The exhibit shows some of the information and comparisons possible from job analysis results.

Computerized Analysis

Computer assisted job analysis ranges from using optical scanners to enter data, to scoring responses, to generating generic job descriptions. The promise of computerized job analysis is that it reduces the demands of a highly labor intensive activity—job analysis—and permits employees and line managers to complete job analysis and descriptions. For example, Pdwriter, a software package, permits a worker to select among a set of duties and tasks, choose among an array of skills and knowledge required to perform duties,

EXHIBIT 3.11
Sample Format for Feedback of Job Analysis Results

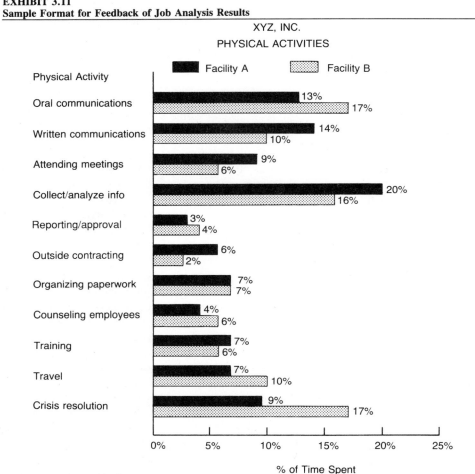

XYZ, INC.

PHYSICAL ACTIVITIES

and generates a position/job description in 10 to 25 minutes.[36] Most major consulting firms have job description software. However, the promise of automated systems has yet to be fully realized. Some managers are not sufficiently computer literate to handle the "friendly" software. And we seem to rediscover that automation often requires more highly trained employees to achieve its full advantage.

---

[36]Information on Pdwriter is available from the Office of Civilian Personnel Management, Ballston Towers, No. 1, Room 1219, 800 N. Quincy Street, Arlington, Va. 22203.

WHO IS INVOLVED IN JOB ANALYSIS?

New York State employs approximately 175,000 people, 30 of whom are job analysts. These analysts receive about 4,500 requests for job analysis and reclassification annually. IBM includes job analysis tasks as part of its personnel specialist job, while TRW deemphasizes job analysis altogether. Some employers view the job analyst as an entry-level position and adopt the "learn by doing" approach: Analyzing work provides a thorough introduction to the company, and after 6 to 12 months the analyst is ready for a new job assignment. In spite of real world practice, most textbook writers continue to insist that the analysis should be done by someone who is thoroughly familiar with the organization, its work flow, and its policies and objectives.

Who Collects the Data?

The choice of who collects the data is usually among an analyst, the supervisors, and/or the jobholders. Some firms require the supervisor to perform the analysis, since supervisors are assumed to be knowledgeable, and their involvement may help increase their understanding of exactly what their subordinates do and help them gain acceptance of subordinates. Obvious shortcomings of this arrangement include the possibility of limited knowledge of the actual tasks, skills, and behaviors required on the job. The writers' experience suggests that the employees actually performing the work need to be involved in the analysis process as a way to ensure accuracy and acceptability of any pay structures based on it. But not everyone agrees; Brandt says job descriptions written by job incumbents are unsatisfactory because they don't use the proper words to facilitate comparisons among jobs.[37] He even argues against incumbent approval of a proposed job description, saying this is a prerogative of management. But research results suggest that the involvement of multiple parties as well as mutual "sign-offs" by the supervisor and jobholders are likely to increase the usefulness of the data.

Regardless of who collects the data, some training in the process seems to be a requirement. In the absence of more research, publicly available materials from the Department of Labor may be of value in developing training programs.

Who Provides the Data?

The decision on the source of the data (jobholders, the supervisors, and/or an analyst) hinges on how to ensure consistent, accurate, and acceptable data. Expertise about the work resides with the jobholders and the supervisors; hence they are the principle sources. For key managerial/professional jobs, supervisors "two levels above" have also been suggested as valuable sources since they may have a more cosmic view on how jobs fit into the overall organization. In other instances, subordinates and coordinates (employees

---

[37] Alfred R. Brandt, "Describing Hourly Jobs," in *Handbook of Wage and Salary Administration,* ed. Milton L. Rock (New York: McGraw-Hill, 1984).

in other jobs that interface with the job under study) are also involved if disagreements over reporting relationships or work domain occur. The number of incumbents per job from which to collect data probably varies with the stability of the job. An ill-defined or changing job will require either the involvement of a greater number of respondents, or a more careful selection of respondents.[38] Obviously the greater the number of people involved, the more time-consuming and expensive the process.

Finally, Henderson points out the need for the support of top management. They must also be alerted to the cost and time-consuming nature of job analysis.[39]

- Does top management understand what is involved in performing job analysis?
- Have all time and cost considerations been explored? Are they understood and approved?
- Is it understood that changes may be recommended as a result of the analysis? Has the potential nature of these changes been discussed prior to undertaking job analysis?

The vital importance of employee and operating management involvement has been repeatedly emphasized. This involvement may take several forms, ranging from active participation in describing their own and/or subordinates' work to serving on compensation task forces or committees directly responsible for the design and development of job analysis procedures. Even those employees not directly involved need to be kept informed as to the purposes and progress of all the activity. Employees will guess at the purpose of this work, and it seems only sound compensation practice to help make it an educated guess.

IS JOB ANALYSIS USEFUL?

Job analysis procedures, whether conventional or quantitative, involve a high degree of judgment. It is important to consider the comparative usefulness of job analysis methods, particularly in terms of their reliability, validity, acceptability, and costs.

Reliability

Reliability is the consistency of the results obtained. Are the results (whether the work is similar or dissimilar) the same regardless of who is involved (supervisors, incumbents, analysts, consultants) and what methods are used?

Several studies have compared employee-supervisor agreement to work content.[40]

---

[38]Samuel B. Green and Thomas Stutzman, "An Evaluation of Methods to Select Respondents to Structured Job-Analysis Questionnaires," *Personnel Psychology,* Autumn 1986, pp. 543–64; and Edwin T. Cornelius III, Angelo S. DeNisi, and Allyn Blencoe, "Expert and Naive Raters Using the PAQ? Does it Matter?" *Personnel Psychology* 37 (June 1984), pp. 453–64.

[39]Henderson, *Compensation Management.*

They present a mixed picture of the reliability of job analysis. Employees and supervisors often differ in how they view the distribution of time among tasks, the skills required to perform the work, and the difficulties of the tasks performed. Different analysts using the same quantitative methods on the same jobs tend to get the same results. However, even job incumbents may have different perceptions and definitions of the same work.[41] For example, employees who have been on the job a long time may change it by adopting shortcuts and new routines. All these differences may influence the job analysis results.

Conventional job analysis does not usually lend itself to formal reliability analysis because of the narrative and unstructured output.[42] This imprecision and obscure structure makes reliability a serious issue for conventional methods. But even quantitative methods have problems. The high reliability measures attributed to the PAQ, for example, are probably the result of inadequate statistical analysis.[43] The high number of "does not exist (as part of this job)" responses may yield false statistics that paint an overly optimistic picture of the questionnaire's reliability. With such mixed results, it is important that whatever method is adopted it should be used independently by several people (analysts, supervisors, subordinates), and any differences should be investigated and resolved.[44]

Consistent (reliable) job information does not necessarily mean that it is accurate,

[40]Paul R. Sackett, Edwin T. Cornelius III, and Theodore J. Carron, "A Comparison of Global Judgment vs. Task-Oriented Approaches to Job Classification," *Personnel Psychology* 34 (1981), pp. 791–804. Other examples of earlier studies include H. H. Meyer, "Comparison of Foreman and General Foreman Conceptions of the Foreman's Job Responsibility," *Personnel Psychology* 12 (1959), pp. 445–52; A. P. O'Reilly, "Skill Requirements: Supervisor-Subordinate Conflict," *Personnel Psychology* 26 (1973), pp. 75–80; J. T. Hazel, J. M. Madden, and R. E. Christal, "Agreement between Worker-Supervisor Descriptions of the Worker's Job," *Journal of Industrial Psychology* 2 (1964), pp. 71–79; and R. Likert, *New Patterns of Management* (New York: McGraw-Hill, 1961).

[41]Charles A. O'Reilly III and David F. Caldwell, "The Impact of Normative Social Influence and Cohesiveness on Task Perceptions and Attitudes: A Social Information Processing Approach," *Journal of Occupational Psychology* (September 1985), pp. 193–206; D. Caldwell and C. A. O'Reilly III, "Task Perceptions and Job Satisfaction: A Question of Causality," *Journal of Applied Psychology* 67, no 3 (1982), pp. 361–69; Kenneth N. Wexley and Stanley B. Silverman, "An Examination of Differences between Managerial Effectiveness and Response Patterns on a Structured Job Analysis Questionnaire," *Journal of Applied Psychology* 63, no. 5 (1978), pp. 646–49; Charles O'Reilly, G. N. Parlette, and J. Blum, "Perceptual Measures of Task Characteristics: The Biasing Effects of Differing Frames of Reference and Job Attitudes," *Academy of Management Journal* 123, no. 1 (1980), pp. 118–31; Dunham, "The Measurement of Dimensionality"; and C. O'Reilly and D. Caldwell, "Informational Influence as a Determinant of Task Characteristics and Job Satisfaction," *Journal of Applied Psychology* 64 (1979), pp. 157–65.

[42]George T. Milkovich and Charles J. Cogill, "Measurement as an Issue in Analysis and Evaluation of Jobs," in *Handbook of Wage and Salary Administration,* ed. Milton L. Rock (New York: McGraw-Hill, 1984).

[43]Roark and Burnett, "Objective Methods of Job Analysis"; and Cornelius, DeNisi, and Blencoe, "Expert and Naive Raters Using the PAQ?" For an example of the statistical analysis on PAQ results, see R. D. Arvey, S. E. Maxwell, R. L. Gutenberg, and C. Camp, "Detecting Job Differences: A Monte Carlo Study," *Personnel Psychology* 34 (1981), pp. 709–30.

[44]Ash, "Job Elements for Task Clusters."

comprehensive, or free from bias. To find out if the results are accurate, we need to consider its validity.

Validity

Research on how to estimate the validity of job analysis is particularly difficult, since there is almost no way of showing the extent to which the results are accurate portraits of the work. The most promising approach may be to examine the convergence of results among multiple sources of job data (analysts, incumbents, supervisors) and multiple methods. A common approach to attempt to increase accuracy of job analysis is to require the job holder and the manager to mutually "sign off" on the results. While getting the parties to mutually sign off on the results may reflect their acceptance, it may also reflect their desire to get rid of the analyst and get back to performing the job rather than analyzing it.

Acceptability

Employee acceptability of data collected is important and easily overlooked. No matter how well the rest of the compensation system is administered, if jobholders are dissatisfied with the initial data collected and the process for collecting it, they are not likely to feel the results are internally equitable.

Conventional job analysis is not always well accepted by the parties involved because of its potential for subjectivity. One writer says, "We all know the classic procedures. One (worker) watched and noted the actions of another . . . at work on (the) job. The actions of both are biased, and the resulting information varied with the wind, especially the political wind."[45] But the acceptability of quantitative job analysis is also mixed. Gomez-Mejia reported that Control Data's Executive Position Questionnaire, developed over a four-year period, ran into several problems, which led most managers to refuse to use it.[46] Among the problems faced were:

1. Employee/manager understanding. The statistical methods used were difficult to understand, so many managers were unable to communicate the results to employees. Consequently, an antagonistic climate was created and the credibility of the system deteriorated.
2. Behaviorally oriented versus "scope" data. Analyzing work in terms of work behaviors, omitting "scope" data (e.g., size of budgets, total payroll, contribution to organization objectives) caused managers to feel that the questionnaire did not accurately analyze their jobs.

---

[45]E. M. Ramras, "Discussion," in *Proceedings of 19, Division of Military Psychology Symposium: Collecting, Analyzing, and Reporting Information Describing Jobs and Occupations,* 77th Annual Convention of the American Psychological Association, Lackland Air Force Base, Tex., September 1969, pp. 75–76.

[46]Gomez-Mejia, Page, and Tornow, "A Comparison of the Practical Utility of Traditional, Statistical, and Hybrid Job Evaluation Approaches."

3. Abstract and ambiguous factors. The data collected (e.g., analyze subordinates' weaknesses and strengths) were perceived to be too abstract and ambiguous. Results were considered too subjective and open to personal interpretation.

Practicality

Researchers recognize the necessity of judging the usefulness of job analysis methods according to the purpose of the analysis.[47] A group of researchers asked 93 experienced job analysts to compare a number of job analysis methods on their utility for 11 different organization purposes.[48] They concluded that the different methods were rated differently for effectiveness and practicality across all purposes. The PAQ and CODAP were among those rated highest for the purpose of job evaluation (i.e., job structures), in spite of CODAP's original development for training needs analysis. While this study is based only on perception of analysts rather than on evaluation of the actual uses of different methods, the authors concluded that combining methods is preferable to using one method alone. Reliance on a combination of methods is a common theme in the research literature on job analysis. The usefulness of the results obtained is probably the most important criterion on which to judge alternative approaches to job analysis.

There is very little data publicly available on costs of various approaches to job analysis.[49] Our own experience with custom designed quantitative job analysis plans suggests direct costs of between $350,000 and $500,000 for consulting and development expertise, at least one personnel professional's time for one year, about 24 months from design through installation, plus significant time commitments from participating managers who serve on task forces. So considerable time and money are required for any job analysis, with or without computer assistance.[50] By comparison, predeveloped (e.g., PAQ) or conventional job analysis is relatively inexpensive.

The practical utility of quantitative job analysis, with its relatively complex procedures and analysis, remains in doubt for many organizations. Some advocates get so taken with their statistics and computers that they ignore the role that human judgment must continue to play in job analysis. As Dunnette states,

> I wish to emphasize the central role played in all these procedures by human judgment. I know of no methodology, statistical technique or objective measurement that can negate the

---

[47]Ronald A. Ash and Edward L. Levine, "A Framework for Evaluating Job Analysis Methods," *Personnel* 57, no. 6 (November-December 1980), pp. 53–59; E. L. Levine, R. A. Ash, and N. Bennett, "Exploratory Comparative Study of Four Job Analysis Methods," *Journal of Applied Psychology* 65 (1980), pp. 524–35; and R. A. Ash, E. L. Levine, and F. Sistrunk, "The Role of Jobs and Job Based Methods in Personnel and Human Resources Management," *Research in Personnel and Human Resources Management* 1 (1983), pp. 45–84.

[48]Edward L. Levine, Ronald A. Ash, Hardy Hall, and Frank Sistrunk, "Evaluation of Job Analysis Methods by Experienced Job Analysts," *Academy of Management Journal* 26, No. 2 (1983), pp. 339–48.

[49]Frank Krzystofiak, Jerry M. Newman, and Gary Anderson, "A Quantified Approach to Measurement of Job Content: Procedures and Payoffs," *Personnel Psychology,* Summer 1979, pp. 341–57.

[50]J. J. N. Gambardella and W. G. Alvord, "Ti-CODAP: A Computerized Method of Job Analysis for Personnel Management," Prince Georges County, Maryland, April 1980.

importance of, nor supplement, rational judgment as an important element in the process of deriving behavior and task information about jobs and of using that information to develop or justify human resources programs.[51]

Quantitative and more systematic approaches to job analysis do not remove the judgment; they only permit us to become more systematic in the way we make it.

JOB DESCRIPTIONS

The data collected in job analysis must be in a form that is usable to people other than the analyst. That form is the job description. A job description identifies, defines, and describes the job as it is being performed. As with job analysis, textbooks extol the multiple uses of job descriptions—in career development, replacement charting, performance evaluation, and employment planning, among others. However, one study reports that over 40 percent of the respondents in a 77-company survey made little use of job descriptions for purposes other than wage administration.[52] That study also found little or no apparent correlation between the character of the job description and its intended usage or the size or type of company involved.

The job description typically contains three sections, which roughly correspond with the purposes of identifying, defining, and describing the job. Recall that these were the purposes delineated in deciding what data to collect in job analysis. Exhibit 3.12 is a typical job description of a nurse's position.

1. *Identification.* This section may contain the job title, number of incumbents, whether or not the job is exempt from coverage of the Fair Labor Standards Act that regulates hours of work and overtime pay (see Chapter 13), where it is located (department work site), and job number, if any is used. Its purpose is to clearly identify the job and distinguish it from those with similar job titles or duties. The date of the analysis is also important. Comparing Exhibits 3.12 and 3.13 should indicate why.

2. *Definition.* This summary section reflects the purpose of the job: why the job exists, and how it fits in with other jobs and with the organization and its overall objectives. End results that flow from the satisfactory performance of this job are typically included. It ought to provide an accurate "word picture" of the job. The "word picture" of the nurse position in Exhibit 3.13, making the 5 cent per day raise contingent on a debt-free employer, reflects a century of change.

3. *Description.* This section is an elaboration of items in the definition, or summary section. It indicates what, why, and how tasks are done to carry out the responsibilities of the job. The description section should indicate the major duties of this jobholder, the specific work performed, how closely supervised this job is, and what controls

---

[51]M. D. Dunnette, L. M. Hough, and R. L. Rosse, "Task and Job Taxonomies as a Basis for Identifying Labor Supply Sources and Evaluating Employment Qualifications," in *Affirmative Action Planning,* ed. George T. Milkovich and Lee Dyer (New York: Human Resource Planning Society, 1979), pp. 37–51.

[52]Brandt, "Describing Hourly Jobs."

EXHIBIT 3.12
Midway Hospital Nursing Department Job Description

JOB TITLE   Date: July 1989
Registered Nurse

JOB SUMMARY
Accountable for the complete spectrum of patient care from admission through transfer or discharge through the nursing process of assessment, planning, implementation, and evaluation. Each R.N. has primary authority to fulfill responsibility for the nursing process on the assigned shift and for projecting future needs of the patient/family. Directs and guides patient teaching and activities of ancillary personnel while maintaining standard of professional nursing.

RELATIONSHIPS
Reports to: Head Nurse or Charge Nurse.
Supervises: Responsible for the care delivered by L.P.N.'s. nursing assistants, orderlies, and transcribers.
Works with: Ancillary Care Departments.
External relationships: Physicians, patients, patient's families.

QUALIFICATIONS
Education: Graduate of an accredited school of nursing.
Work experience: Critical care requires one year of recent medical/surgical experience (special care nursing preferred), medical/surgical experience (new graduates may be considered for non-charge positions).
License or registration requirements: Current R.N. license or permit in the State of Minnesota.
Physical requirements: A. Ability to bend, reach, or assist to transfer up to 50 pounds.
                       B. Ability to stand and/or walk 80 percent to 90 percent of 8 hour shift.
                       C. Visual and hearing acuity to perform job related functions.

RESPONSIBILITIES
1. Assesses physical, emotional, and psycho-social dimensions of patients.
    Standard: Provides a written assessment of patient within one hour of admission and at least once a shift. Communicates this assessment to other patient care providers in accordance with hospital policies.
2. Formulates a written plan of care for patients from admission through discharge.
    Standard: Develops short and long term goals within 24 hours of admission. Reviews and updates care plans each shift based on ongoing assessment.
3. Implements plan of care.
    Standard: Demonstrates skill in performing common nursing procedures in accordance with but not limited to the established written R.N. skills inventory specific to assigned area. Completes patient care activities in an organized and timely fashion, reassessing priorities appropriately.

(Additional responsibilities omitted from exhibit.)

---

limit the actions of the jobholder. In addition to describing the tasks performed, the training and experience required to perform them may also be included here, or in a separate section called Job Specifications.

Managerial Jobs

Describing managerial jobs poses special problems. Managers frequently do not perform a prescribed set of duties. Instead of specific tasks with specific outcomes, they have broad accountability for the accomplishment of results that help the organization attain its objectives. For example, a marketing vice president is broadly responsible for moving goods from their site of manufacture to the consumer in a profitable manner. A further

---

EXHIBIT 3.13
Partial Description of Job of Nurse, Cleveland Lutheran Hospital, 1887

In addition to caring for your 50 patients each nurse will follow these regulations:

1. Daily sweep and mop the floors of your ward, dust the patient's furniture and window sills.
2. Maintain an even temperature in your ward by bringing in a scuttle of coal for the day's business.
3. Light is important to observe the patient's condition. Therefore, each day, fill kerosene lamps, clean chimneys, and trim wicks. Wash the windows once a week.
4. The nurse's notes are important in aiding the physician's work. Make your pens carefully, you may whittle nibs to your individual taste.
5. Each nurse on day duty will report every day at 7 A.M. and leave at 8 P.M. except on the Sabbath on which day you will be off from 12:00 noon to 2:00 P.M.
6. Graduate nurses in good standing with the director of nurses will be given an evening off each week for courting purposes, or two evenings a week if you go regularly to church.
7. Each nurse should lay aside from each pay day a goodly sum of her earnings for her benefits during her declining years, so that she will not become a burden. For example, if you earn $30 a month you should set aside $15.
8. Any nurse who smokes, uses liquor in any form, gets her hair done at a beauty shop, or frequents dance halls will give the director good reason to suspect her worth, intentions, and integrity.
9. The nurse who performs her labors and serves her patients and doctors faithfully and without fault for a period of five years will be given an increase by the hospital administration of five cents a day, provided there are no hospital debts that are outstanding.

---

difficulty in describing managerial jobs is the expectation that the individual will change the jobs. Therefore, the format for describing these jobs must be adjusted to adequately describe such work. The following additions are usually made to managerial job descriptions, in a format similar to the one used in Exhibit 3.14.

1. *Dimensions.* Provides statistics on the size of payroll, budget, and number of people supervised. This is an expanded version of the Identification section in the previous job description.
2. *Nature and Scope.* Identifies how the position fits into the organization, the composition of the supporting staff (e.g., assistant director of personnel, director of development, etc.) and the key issues to be handled by the person in this job. This is similar to the Definition Section in the previous description.
3. *Accountabilities.* Delineates the broad end results this position seeks to attain. Our personnel vice president in Exhibit 3.14 has listed for Principal Accountabilities, for example, final responsibility for providing "a wage, salary and benefits program which is both internally equitable and externally competitive." Yet the job description does not list a compensation director reporting to this position. We have taken the liberty of sending the vice president a copy of this book to help overcome the oversight.

Writing the Job Description

Great detail exists on how to write job descriptions, including specific definitions of verbs. Vague terms (e.g., "many" or "relatively easy"), or those with a variety of meanings

---

EXHIBIT 3.14
Sample Position Description for a Manager

TITLE:	Vice president personnel	**DATE:**	
INCUMBENT:		**ANALYST:**	
REPORTS TO:	Chairman and CEO	**APPROVALS:**	

ACCOUNTABILITY OBJECTIVE

This position is accountable for assuring the continuing availability of acceptable levels of human resources (both quantity and quality) for the company. This is accomplished by selecting, training, and compensating the employees in a manner which helps to create a positive working environment.

DIMENSIONS

Personnel budget: $3MM
Personnel dept. payroll: $350M

Total co. payroll: $12–14MM
Personnel supervised: 3 direct
                                        51 indirect

NATURE AND SCOPE

This position along with the VP Control, VP Branches and VP Operations reports to the chairman and CEO. Reporting to the incumbent is a staff of three: the assistant director of personnel, the director of training, and the director of development.

The personnel department's subdivisions include employment, training, compensation and benefits, and record keeping, covering approximately 6,000 hourly rated employees and 250 senior executives.

Labor relations and contract negotiations with the seven unions working at the store are a significant responsibility for the incumbent. Although the actual time involved in contract negotiations may appear minimal, the implications and consequences of the contracts themselves are felt throughout the year. The incumbent also directs personnel activities which ensure the company's compliance with EEOC, and department of labor regulations.

The Vice President assures the completion of his acountabilities through his direction of the following functions:

Assistant director of personnel – Supervises all branch personnel directors, the record room and benefits. Administers the employment and record keeping function for the downtown store. Assures the proper functioning of the wage and salary program and the publication of the in-house newspaper.

Director of development – Responsible for recruiting, placement and career ladder movement of all junior executives (generally assistant, buyer, and above). This includes maintaining and developing an effective college relations program as well as administering the storewide executive training program.

Director of training – In addition to the rank and file orientation program, initial and retraining programs, the director administers the training programs run by the branch store training managers and the five downtown training representatives.

In addition to ensuring coordinated personnel effort, company-wide, the vice president works closely with the division level organization on matters concerning executive recruiting, placement, and compensation and the participation of corporate executives on intrastore committees. This position is also personally in charge of senior executive training and aids in productivity reviews.

Because of the wide corporate scope of this position, the incumbent finds a portion of time must be devoted to working with various racial or ethnic groups, fund raising, community service, and participating on external committees such as the State Retail Merchants Association, College Advisory Boards, etc.

PRINCIPAL ACCOUNTABILITIES

1. A wage, salary and benefits program which is both internally equitable and externally competitive.
2. Union contracts which fairly and equitably reflect the desires of company management, while maintaining effective working relationships with union personnel.
3. A trained and motivated personnel department staff capable of carrying out the objectives assigned.
4. Identified and available executive and junior executive talent sufficient for corporate growth and maintenance of current operations.

(Additional accountabilities omitted from exhibit.)

(e.g., "takes care of," or "handles") are frowned upon. This is not the place for polished prose, or even complete sentences. English majors need not apply, since a smooth-flowing writing style may make the crucial information harder to pick out, thus discouraging use of the description.

To ensure equitable comparisons of content across jobs, jobs are typically described in a standardized manner, not only in format but also in choice of words. For example, "supervises" is not the same as "directs," "facilitates," or even "leads."

While it is necessary to be brief, the description also needs to be accurate. One organization goes so far as to suggest writing a first draft of unlimited length, ensuring inclusion of all necessary detail. The first draft then is reviewed to eliminate all words and sentences that do not contribute to meaning. A length of two to three pages for managerial jobs, less for nonmanagerial jobs, is usually considered long enough to be accurate without being unwieldy. The attractiveness of computer-generated job descriptions should be obvious to all readers!

Accuracy of job descriptions can have effects beyond the compensation system. Accurate job descriptions can also affect union/management relations. For example, disputes may arise if workers feel they are performing work that belongs to a higher level, higher paid job. Problems can also arise if job descriptions are not kept current or are not changed if the jobs change. Changes in technology, physical location, product line, strategic direction, and even key personnel can precipitate job changes.

ALTERNATIVE CRITERIA FOR STRUCTURES

As we have seen, traditional pay systems begin by building a job structure that reflects relationships among jobs within an organization. Later chapters will discuss how prices are then attached to this structure. The focus of the underlying structure is on the *job* rather than the *person* doing the job. But as Exhibit 3.15 shows, there are alternatives. Structures can be based on the skills, knowledge, abilities possessed by individuals, the behaviors or results of their work, as well as the job content. Just as the data collected for job analysis can focus on the job, the individual, or some combination of these two extremes, so can the pay structure. Alternatives to conventional job content are increasingly being considered, and we will illustrate some of these options.

Managerial and Professional Work

John Scully was a highly regarded marketing executive at PepsiCo when Apple Computer hired him. The price of Apple's stock immediately rose as a result of Scully's joining the firm. No one expected Mr. Scully to perform exactly the same marketing tasks that his predecessor had done; indeed, everyone assumed Scully would use his unique skills in whatever way he felt was to Apple's advantage. Mr. Scully did just that: He soon became Apple's chief executive officer. The point is that in certain jobs, particularly at the managerial level, the person's unique abilities and knowledge may shape the job.

EXHIBIT 3.15
Possible Criteria for a Job Structure

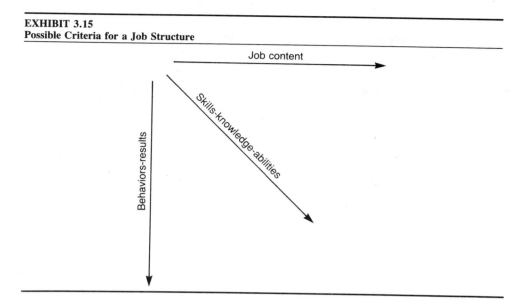

The top jobs in almost any organization seem to be designed more around the talents and experience of the individuals involved, rather than any rigidly defined duties and responsibilities. This is not to say that internal consistency is not important in executive compensation; the pecking order gets pretty intense. But job analysis plays a smaller role in establishing internal structures.

The work structure for scientists and engineers is often based on the individual rather than the job, too. The nature of their work may not lend itself to a job structure if it varies as a function of the project on which they are working. Typically, a team of professionals will be assembled based on their complementary expertise. The projects to which they are assigned usually require a great deal of interaction and cooperation among team members. Pay for scientists and engineers assigned to team projects is initially set according to the type of degree (e.g., B.S. in computer science, Ph.D. in chemistry). The nature of the work done by scientists and engineers makes traditional job analysis less relevant because the tasks may change with every project. The focus is more profitably on the person doing the job, rather than the job. Only broadly-defined or generic job descriptions may be needed. (Professional and executive pay is discussed in greater detail in Chapter 16, Compensation of Special Groups.)

Knowledge-Based Pay Approaches

Knowledge is one of the alternative criteria for an internal structure shown in Exhibit 3.15. Knowledge-based pay systems (KBP) pay employees based on what they *know* rather than what particular *job* they are doing.[53] Generally, KBP systems can be grouped into two types:

> *knowledge systems,* which link pay to depth of knowledge related to *one job,* e.g., scientists and teachers; and
> *multi-skill systems,* which link pay to the number of *different jobs* (breadth) an employee is certified to do, e.g., related production jobs.[54]

Knowledge systems: depth. Basing pay structures on knowledge possessed by individual employees is not new. The pay structures for your elementary or high school teachers have long been based on their knowledge (education level). A typical teachers contract specifies a series of steps, with each step corresponding to a level of education. A bachelor's degree in education is step one, and is the minimum required for hiring. To advance a step to higher pay requires additional education. For example, an additional 9 semester hours of coursework earns an increase of $225 in Ithaca, New York. The result can be that two teachers may receive different pay rates for doing essentially the same job—teaching English to high school juniors. The pay is based on the knowledge of the individual doing the job (measured by number of college credits) rather than job content. The presumption is that teachers with more knowledge are more effective and more flexible—able to teach seniors, too.

Multi-skill systems. A survey published in 1986 found that about 8 percent of large U.S. employers used a KBP system in at least one of their plants.[55] Approximately 40 percent of the applications were in manufacturing industries, and 75 percent of the plants were new ones that had adopted a KBP system at startup (called "greenfield" settings). KBP replaced an existing pay system in only 25 percent of its applications.

As with the teachers, employees in a multi-skill system earn pay increases by acquiring new knowledge, but the knowledge is specific to a range of related jobs. An example from Borg Warner illustrates the system. Borg Warner assembles drive chains for automobile transmissions. Exhibit 3.16 shows their job hierarchy. Previously, 10 different jobs were involved in the assembly process, starting with riveters, and moving up through oilers, testers, and measurers. When Borg Warner switched to a knowledge-based pay system, these 10 jobs were reorganized into three broad categories: Cell Operators A, B, and C. Cell Operator A is an entry level position. Once Operator As are able to

[53]E. E. Lawler III and G. E. Ledford, Jr., *Skill-Based Pay* (Los Angeles: Center for Effective Organizations, University of Southern California Working Paper #84-18); Nina Gupta, G. Douglas Jenkins, Jr., and William Curington, "Paying for Knowledge: Myths and Realities," *National Productivity Review,* Spring 1986, pp. 107–23; T. P. Schweizer, "Pay-for-Knowledge Systems: An Alternative Approach to Compensation," *Proceedings of the Southwest Academy of Management,* 1986, pp. 159–63; and H. Tosi and L. Tosi, "What Managers Need to Know About Knowledge-Based Pay," *Organization Dynamics* 14, 3 (1986), pp. 52–64.

[54]Fred Luthans and Marilyn L. Fox, "Update on Skill-Based Pay," *Personnel,* March 1989, pp. 26–32.

[55]Nina Gupta, et al. *Exploratory Investigations of Pay-for-Knowledge Systems* (U.S. Department of Labor, Bureau of Labor-Management Relations and Cooperative Programs, Washington, D.C., 1986).

EXHIBIT 3.16
Borg Warner Automotive Assembly Classifications

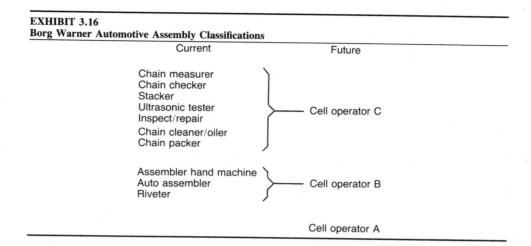

satisfactorily demonstrate that they have mastered the riveter, auto assembler, and assembler hand machine jobs, they become Operator Bs, and they receive a pay raise. Operator Bs can be rotated among any of the jobs for which they have demonstrated mastery, including A level jobs. It is the same process to become an Operator C. An Operator C can do all the jobs required, including riveting, and still receive Operator C pay. The advantage to Borg Warner is work force flexibility (Cs do all jobs), and hence lower staffing levels.

The multi-skill system differs from the knowledge system of engineers or teachers in that the job responsibilities assigned to an employee in a multi-skill system can change drastically over a short period of time. Whereas teachers and engineers increase the *depth* of their skills on the same basic job, multi-skill systems emphasize increased *breadth* of skills so that employees can perform a variety of jobs. Pay is based on the highest level of individual skill mastery. Typically, training and evaluation systems are established to ensure that individuals have adequately mastered the skills for which they are being paid, and that those skills are maintained.

There are a number of variations on knowledge-based systems. FMC has a slightly different approach from Borg Warner. Their KBP plan for shop technicians contains three types of qualifications and parallels many college degree requirements (mandatory core, mandatory electives, and electives). An Appendix to this chapter lists all the qualifications and their point value.

Advantages of Knowledge-Based Systems

Clearly, the flexibility in scheduling and the leaner staffing that results is the overwhelming advantage of knowledge-based pay. For example, a Topeka, Kansas, dog food plant hired just 70 employees, rather than the 110 it had originally estimated would be needed for a given production level when it adopted KBP.[56] It also required fewer supervisors. Advocates of the system also claim it benefits employees: job satisfaction increases because employees get a sense of having an impact on the organization, and motivation increases because pay and performance are strongly linked. Chapter 10 expands this discussion of KBP as an alternative reward system.

Disadvantages of Knowledge-Based Systems

Exhibit 3.17 contrasts job- versus knowledge-based systems. It points out that no system is perfect. The knowledge-based system has potential limitations, in addition to its advantages. The most important one is that they can become expensive if not properly managed. As you might expect, the majority of employees whose pay is based on skill mastery want the necessary training to move to the top of the pay ladder as fast as possible. But if all employees are earning top pay rates, e.g., all are Operator Cs, an employer may have higher labor costs than its competitors', and will therefore be at a price disadvantage in marketing its products. There are several ways to avoid this situation: set starting pay slightly below competitors; or control the rate at which employees can move up in skill mastery. But higher wage rates must be offset by a smaller work force or greater productivity, or the organization's labor costs will become a significant competitive disadvantage.

In addition to higher pay rates and training costs, maintaining records and managing an equitable job rotation schedule can become an administrative burden. To date, little

EXHIBIT 3.17
Knowledge-Based Compared to Job-Based Plans

	Job Based	*Knowledge Based*
Pay structure	Based on job performed	Based on skills possessed by the employee
Managers' focus	Job carries wage Employee linked to job	Employee carries wage Employee linked to skill
Employee focus	Job promotion to earn greater pay	Skill acquisition to earn greater pay
Procedures required	Assess job content Value jobs	Assess skills Value skills
Advantages	Pay based on value of work performed	Flexibility Reduced work force
Limitations	Potential personnel bureaucracy Inflexibilities	Potential personnel bureaucracy Cost controls

---

[56]R. E. Walton, "Work Innovations at Topeka: After Six Years," *Journal of Applied Behavioral Science* 13 (1977), pp. 422–33.

research on the effectiveness of KBP exists. Most accounts are written by advocates and describe applications.

Additionally, questions still remain about the system's compliance with the Equal Pay Act. If a member of a protected group is doing the same job as a white male, and being paid less for it (because of a difference in skill mastery), does this violate the equal pay—equal work standard specified in the legislation? Later chapters (13 and 14) discuss this and other pay legislation at length.

SUMMARY

Fairness of the pay structure within an organization is one of the hallmarks of a sound compensation system. The compensation professional faces several decisions during the process of designing an equitable pay structure. One of the first is a policy decision—how much to emphasize the importance of an internally consistent and equitable pay structure. Some emphasize market pricing over internal consistency. Whatever the choice, it needs to support the organization's overall human resource strategy.

Next, managers must decide whether job and/or individual employee characteristics will be the basic unit of analysis supporting the pay structure. This is followed by deciding what data need to be collected, what method(s) will be used to collect it, and who should be involved in the process.

A key test of an equitable pay structure is acceptance of results by managers and employees. The best way to ensure acceptance of job analysis results is to involve employees as well as supervisors in the process. At the minimum, all employees should be informed of purposes and progress of the activity.

If almost everyone agrees about the importance of job analysis for equitable compensation, does that mean everyone does it? Of course not. Unfortunately, job analysis can be tedious and time-consuming. Often the job is given to newly hired compensation analysts, ostensibly to help them learn the organization, but perhaps there's also a hint of "rites of passage" in such assignments.

Alternatives to job content-based structures such as knowledge-based systems are being experimented within many firms. The premise is that basing structures on the knowledge required will encourage employees to become more flexible, and fewer of them will be required for the same level of output. Nevertheless, job content remains the conventional criterion for structures.

This completes our discussion of job analysis. The next step is to take the resulting job descriptions and evaluate the jobs according to their contributions to the organization goals. This is the subject of the next chapters.

REVIEW QUESTIONS

1. What does job analysis have to do with internal consistency?
2. Describe the major decisions in designing job analysis.
3. Distinguish between task data and worker data.

4. What is the critical advantage of quantitative job analysis over conventional approaches? Why is this important?

5. What are some noncompensation uses of job analysis information? Would the same data serve all needs?

6. How would you decide whether to use job based, knowledge based or results based pay structures?

Appendix 3–A

**Conventional Job Analysis Questionnaire
(next three pages)**

Job Analysis Report

Date___2-23-90___

Job Analyst___C. Davis___

1. Job Title___Executive Secretary___

2. Department___General Headquarters___

3. No. incumbents___2___   Interviewed___2___

4. Relation to other jobs:

   Promotion: From___Secretary-D___   To___Executive Secretary___

   Transfer: From___Administrative Assistant___   To___Executive Secretary___

   Supervision received___From President and/or Chairman of the Board.___

   ___Works under minimal supervision.___

   Supervision given___Regularly to other clerical personnel.___

5. Summary of Job:

   Personal Secretary to President and/or Chairman of the Board. Performs variety of secretarial and clerical duties including transcribing dictation, filing, routing mail, as well as answering telephone and written inquiries. Exercises discretion in handling confidential and specialized information, screening telephone calls and letters, arranging meetings, and handling inquiries during superior's absence.

6. Equipment used: Typewriter, word processor, dictaphone and telephone.

Working conditions:

   Hazards (list): N/A

   Work space and quarters: Office environment

Noise exposure: None

Lighting: Good

Temperature: Regulated office environment

Miscellaneous: —

Job training:

A. Required experience: (include other jobs)
Four years of secretarial-stenographic experience or the equivalent.

B. Outside educational courses:

	Time in semesters/quarters
Vocational courses: Typing, stenography	2 semesters
High school courses: Graduate	6-8 semesters
College courses:	None
Continuing education required:	None

C. In-house training courses:

	Time in months
Courses: Basic and Advanced Word Processing	1/2 month

Task Statement Worksheet

Task Statement: Opens and organizes mail addressed to superior.

1. Equipment used —

2. Knowledge required Must be well versed on superior's responsibilities, how superior's job fits into overall organization.

3. Skills required —

4. Abilities required Discretion. Organization skills.

5. Time spent and frequency of task performance (hourly, daily, monthly)
   `Time varies by assignment. Weekly frequency.`

6. Level of difficulty/consequence of error
   `Relatively difficult, little effect of error.`

Task Statement: `Establishes, maintains, and revises files.`

1. Equipment used `Typewriter, word processor.`

2. Knowledge required `Understanding of organization and responsibilities of superior.`

3. Skills required `Typing and word processing, filing.`

4. Abilities required `Ability to organize and categorize information.`

5. Time spent and frequency of task performance (hourly, daily, monthly)
   `One hour spent daily.`

6. Level of difficulty/consequence of error `Relatively easy, but moderate to serious consequences if information mishandled.`

Appendix 3–B

Skill Based Pay Progression Plan for Shop Technician

The shop technician pay progression system is based on a current pay range of $7.73 to $8.76. A shop technician's proficiency is quantified by that person's progress in completing *qualification standards*. The qualification standards are classified into three major groups: *mandatory qualifications, mandatory elective qualifications,* and *optional elective qualifications*. Exhibit 3.18 shows the criteria for pay progression, and time expectations for advancement.

Mandatory qualifications: safety, material handling, and general work procedures. All mandatory qualifications must be mastered to reach the first step of the pay scale.

Mandatory electives: necessary to production operations, e.g., fabrication, finishing, machining. Each qualification is assigned a point value. A total of 40 points (out of 370) must be mastered, in addition to the mandatory qualifications, to reach the first step of the pay scale.

Optional electives: computer usage, working in groups, and administration. Optional electives are required for pay steps beyond step one.

EXHIBIT 3.18
Shop Technician Pay Increase Criteria

$7.73 SHOP TECH→Step 1 ⟶	$7.98	$8.24 Step 2 ⟶	$8.50 Step 3 ⟶	$8.76 Step 4 ⟶
(New hire)	—all mandatory qualifications	—100 additional points mandatory electives	—100 additional points mandatory electives	—125 additional points mandatory electives
	—40 points mandatory electives	—1 optional elective	—2 additional optional electives	—2 additional optional electives
	—Time expectation: 3 to 12 months after hire	—team consensus	—team consensus	—team consensus
		—Time expectation: 6 to 24 months after hire		

MANDATORY QUALIFICATIONS:

These qualifications are necessary to be a safe and effective shop technician. These are:

Quality Program
Shop Floor Control System
Material Handling

Hazardous Material
Safety
Employee Orientation

NOTE: Mandatory qualifications are not assigned point values but must be completed as part of the first shop technician pay progression step.

MANDATORY ELECTIVE QUALIFICATIONS:

These qualifications are necessary to production operations and are assigned weighting point values for pay progression purposes. The point values are shown below.

Qualification	Points	Qualification	Points
Longeron Fabrication	10	Leak Check/Patch Weld	5
Panel Fabrication	15	Final Acceptance Test	10
Shell Fabrication	15	Welding Inspection	15
End Casting Welding	20	Flame Spraying	15
Finishing—Paint	20	Assembly Inspection	5
Finishing—Ablative/Autoclave	20	Safe & Arm Assembly	15
Finishing—Surface Prep	10	MK13 Machining	25
MK13 Assembly	15	MK14 Machining	25
MK14 Assembly	15	Tool Set Up	10
Finishing Inspection	5	NC1 Inspection	30
Machining Inspection	20	Degrease	10
Pad Welding	15	Guide Rail Assembly	5
		Receiving Inspection	5

OPTIONAL ELECTIVES:

These qualifications enhance a shop technician's personal development. These are:

Maintenance
Logistics—JIT
Plant First Aid
Geometric Tolerancing
Computer-Lotus

Career Development
Group Decision Making
Public Relations
Group Facilitator
Training

Computer-DEBASE III
Computer-Word Processing
Assessment Center
Consensus Building

Group Problem Solving
Administration
Plant Security

NOTE: Optional elective qualifications are not assigned point values. Optional qualifications must be completed for the second, third, and fourth pay progression steps.

Compensation Application
Job Analysis

1. Use the job analysis questionnaire in Appendix 3–A to describe a specific job you presently hold or have held in the past. This can be a part-time job or volunteer work for which you were not paid. Be sure to put your name on the questionnaire.
2. After you have completed the questionnaire, pick a teammate (or the instructor will assign one) and exchange completed questionnaires with your teammate.
3. Write a job description for your teammate's job. Does the questionnaire give you sufficient information? Is there additional information that would be helpful?
4. Exchange descriptions. Critique the job descriptions written by your teammate. Does it adequately capture all the important job aspects? Does it indicate which aspects are most important?
5. Save the description. We will examine it again in a later case.

Job Evaluation: Perspectives and Design

> "When I use a word," Humpty Dumpty said in rather a scornful tone, "it means just what I choose it to mean—nothing more or less."
>
> "The question is," said Alice, "whether you *can* make words mean so many different things."
>
> "The question is," said Humpty Dumpty, "which is to be master—that is all."[1]

Were Humpty Dumpty and Alice discussing job evaluation? Some managers may think so. People have differing perspectives on the purpose of job evaluation and differing opinions about its value. This chapter discusses these various perspectives on job evaluation and some of the key decisions in the process. Chapter 5 continues the discussion. Establishing the purposes and choosing among alternative methods of job evaluation are discussed here. Evaluating the process and involving affected managers and employees are discussed in the next chapter.

Designing a pay structure involves setting the pay for each job relative to other jobs within a single employer. By law, pay must be equal for equal work; pay differentials may be established for dissimilar work. Job evaluation helps develop and maintain pay structures by comparing the similarities and differences in the content and value of jobs. When properly designed and administered, job evaluation can help ensure that pay structures are internally consistent and acceptable to the parties involved.

JOB EVALUATION AND THE PAY MODEL

Recall from our model on page 29 the techniques used to design internal pay structures. The results of job analysis serve as input for evaluating jobs and establishing a job structure. Job evaluation involves the systematic evaluation of the job descriptions that result from job analysis. The evaluation is based on many factors: content of the work, value of the work to the organization, the culture of the workplace, and external market forces. This potential to blend internal and external market forces represents both a major contribution of job evaluation and a source of controversy. This will become evident as we discuss the variety of definitions and decisions that surround job evaluation.

DIFFERING PERSPECTIVES

Perspectives on job evaluation are as diverse as the blind men's elephants. The differences in perspectives revolve around three basic issues: (1) the distinction between classifications and hierarchies, (2) the distinction between a job's content and its value, and (3) the view that job evaluation may simultaneously include aspects of measurement as well as negotiation and rationalization.

---

[1]Lewis Carroll, *Through the Looking Glass* (Chicago: Classic Press, 1969).

Classifications and Hierarchies

Historically, job evaluation was conceived in the public sector as a device for classifying rather than valuing jobs. As part of attempts in the 1880s to reform abuses in government hiring and pay practices, jobs were classified according to their work content. As early as 1912, the city of Chicago adopted a system of job classification.[2] Personnel decisions were to be based on the content of the work as assessed through job evaluation, rather than on who you voted for or who you knew. While job evaluation was not a cure for such practices, it did help group jobs according to similarities and differences in their content.

In addition to classifying jobs, job evaluation may be used to design pay structures. Structure refers to a hierarchy of jobs ordered, according to their relative content and/or value, whereas classification refers to grouping jobs in terms of their similarities and differences. Thus, you could classify jobs into groups without arranging them in a hierarchy.

Content and Value

Usually the end result of job evaluation is a structure—a hierarchy of jobs or groups of jobs in the organization. Perspectives vary on whether structures are based on comparing the jobs' content, on their value, or on some combination of both. Job content refers to the skills required, the degree of responsibilities assumed, and so on. The relative value of jobs can refer to their relative contributions to organization goals, to their external market rates, or to some other agreed upon rates set through collective bargaining or other processes.[3]

Note the various shadings of perspectives on job evaluation in Exhibit 4.1. Some say that job evaluation "considers only the inherent characteristics and data of jobs" or "the real object of comparison is the content of jobs, not the rather imprecise notion of

---

[2]E. Lanham, *Job Evaluation* (New York: McGraw-Hill, 1955). Also see Charles Walter Lytle, *Job Evaluation Methods* (New York: Ronald Press Company, 1954); Theodore R. Lawson, "How Much Is a Job Worth?" *Personnel* 43, no. 5 (September-October 1965), pp. 16–21; Bryan Livy, *Job Evaluation: A Critical Review* (London, England: George Allen & Union Ltd., 1975); George Thomason, *Job Evaluation: Objectives and Methods* (London: Institute of Personnel Management, 1980); R. C. Smyth and M. J. Murphy, "Job Evaluation by the Point Plan," *Factory Management and Maintenance,* June 1946; Paul T. Stimmler, "The Job Evaluation Myth," *Personnel Journal,* November 1966, pp. 594–96; Douglas S. Sherwin, "The Job of Job Evaluation," *Harvard Business Review* 35 (1957), pp. 63–71; M. S. Viteles, "A Psychologist Looks at Job Evaluation," *Personnel,* May 1941; Herbert G. Zollitsch and Adolph Langsner, *Wage and Salary Administration* (Cincinnati, Ohio: South-Western Publishing Co., 1970); Howard Risher, *Job Evaluation Revisited* (New York: William M. Mercer, Inc., 1982); and R. F. Milkey, "Job Evaluation after 50 Years," *Public Personnel Review,* January 1960.

[3]Thomas A. Mahoney, *Compensation and Reward Perspectives* (Homewood, Ill.: Richard D. Irwin, 1979); Lester Thurow, *Generating Inequality* (New York: Basic Books, 1975); E. Robert Livernash, "Internal Wage Structure," in *New Concepts in Wage Determination,* ed. George W. Taylor and Frank C. Pierson (New York: McGraw-Hill, 1957); also see C. Kerr and L. Fisher, "Effect of Environment and Administration on Job Evaluation," *Harvard Business Review,* May 1950, pp. 77–96.

EXHIBIT 4.1
Perspectives on Job Evaluation

"the comparison of jobs by the use of formal and systematic procedures in order to determine the relative position of one job to another in a wage or salary hierarchy. The real object of comparison is the content of the job, not the rather imprecise notion of its 'value' to the organization."[a]

"We are not talking about worth in a metaphysical sense. Instead, we are talking about worth as defined in classification systems that already operate in large bureaucratic organizations."[b]

"should consider only the inherent characteristics and data of the job and *exclude extraneous factors* such as supply and demand of labor, local wage rates and geographic location"[c]

"the process in which the organization *finally assigns a worth to the job* and decides the related importance of one job to another"[d]

"the fundamental purpose is to establish a *mutually acceptable criterion of equity.*"[e]

"statistically establishing the relationships between wages paid for jobs and the content of these jobs. This is the specification of worth"[f]

"There is no single measure of job worth."[g]

"Job evaluation can and typically does accomplish a reasonable adaptation to internal and external forces."[h]

"is a method which helps to establish a justified rank order of jobs . . . it is *only one of the starting points for establishing the relative differentiation of wage rates*"[i]

[a]David W. Belcher, *Compensation Administration,* 3rd ed. (Englewood Cliffs, N.J.: Prentice-Hall, 1974), p. 88.
[b]Ronnie J. Steinberg, "Identifying Wage Discrimination and Implementing Pay Equity Adjustments," in *Comparable Worth: Issue for the 80*'s, vol. 1 (Washington, D.C.: U.S. Civil Rights Commission, 1985).
[c]J. D. Dunn and Frank M. Rachel, *Wage and Salary Administration: Total Compensation Systems* (New York: McGraw-Hill, 1971).
[d]Richard I. Henderson, *Compensation Management: Rewarding Performance in the Modern Organization* (Reston, Va.: Reston Publishing, 1976), p. 149
[e]William Gombert, *A Trade Union Analysis of Time Study,* 2nd ed. (Englewood Cliffs, N.J.: Prentice-Hall, 1955).
[f]Steinberg, "Identifying Wage Discrimination."
[g]Harold D. Janes, "Union Views on Job Evaluation, 1971 vs. 1978," *Personnel Journal,* February 1979, pp. 80–85; and John Zalusky, "Job Evaluation: An Uneven World," *AFL–CIO American Federationist,* April 1981, pp. 13–18.
[h]E. Robert Livernash, "Internal Wage Structure," in *New Concepts in Wage Determination,* ed. George W. Taylor and Frank C. Pierson (New York: McGraw-Hill, 1957).
[i]Eugene J. Benge, *Job Evaluation and Merit Rating* (New York: National Foremen's Institute, Inc., 1946).

'value'." Others see job evaluation as "the process in which the organization finally assigns worth to the job" or "there is general agreement that the objective of job evaluation is to produce an acceptable pay structure."[4]

When the structure is based on the comparison of job content, some argue that it reflects relative value.[5] In this view, there is no practical difference between content and

---

[4]F. Munson, "Four Fallacies for Wage and Salary Administrators," *Personnel* 40, no. 4 (1963), pp. 57–64.

[5]Alvin O. Bellak, "Comparable Worth: A Practitioner's View," in *Comparable Worth: Issue for the 80's,* vol. 1 (Washington, D.C.: U.S. Civil Rights Commission, 1985); and Ronnie J. Steinberg, "Identifying Wage Discrimination and Implementing Pay Equity Adjustments," in *Comparable Worth: Issue for the 80's,* vol. 1.

value. The job structure derived from comparing the content of different jobs becomes the structure for determining the pay differences among the jobs. Thus: "The value of the jobs may be inferred by examining the variety and complexity of behaviors required by the job. The higher the variety and complexity the greater the 'contribution' of the job to the firm's viability and the more it should be compensated."[6]

This perspective of job evaluation overlooks the possibility that a structure based on comparing the relative content of jobs may differ from one based on relative value. This occurs, for example, when the relative value of the work performed is greater (or less) in one organization than in another. The value of a compensation specialist to a firm whose earnings are generated through sales of manufactured goods or engineering expertise may differ from the value of that specialist to a consulting firm whose revenues come through the sale of compensation expertise. The skills are similar, yet their relative value differs for each organization.

Linking Content with the External Labor Market

Some see job evaluation as a mechanism that links job content with the external market rates. Livernash observed, "The fundamental character of job evaluation is the integration of market wage rates and job content factors."[7] Schwab concurs: "As practiced, it [job evaluation] serves the important administrative function of linking external and internal labor markets. . . . No alternative procedure has been proposed that better performs this function."[8]

In this view, the structure resulting from job evaluation does not completely reflect the job's relative value unless it incorporates external market influences. Consequently, certain aspects of job content (e.g., skills required, magnitude of responsibilities) take on value based on their relationship to market wages. Because higher skill levels or willingness to undertake greater responsibility usually command higher wages in the labor market, then skill level and degree of responsibility become useful criteria in job evaluation for establishing differences in pay among jobs. If some aspect of job content, such as working conditions, were not related to wages paid in the external labor markets, then it would not be included in the job evaluation. Accordingly, since job content obtains value through the external market, it makes little sense to assert that content has an intrinsic value outside of its worth in the external market. It is job evaluation's role to integrate job content with external market forces.

But as you probably expect, another perspective on our elephant exists. Not everyone agrees that job evaluation's purpose is to link internal and external markets. Bellak, in describing the Hay job evaluation plan, states that the "measures are independent of the

---

[6]David A. Pierson, Karen S. Koziara, and Russell E. Johannesson, "Equal Pay for Jobs of Comparable Worth: A Quantified Job Content Approach" (Philadelphia: Department of Industrial Relations and Organizational Behavior, Temple University, 1981).

[7]E. Robert Livernash, *Comparable Worth Issues and Alternatives* (Washington, D.C.: Equal Employment Advisory Council, 1980).

[8]Donald P. Schwab, "Job Evaluation and Pay Setting: Concepts and Practices," in *Comparable Worth: Issues and Alternatives,* ed. E. Robert Livernash (Washington, D.C.: Equal Employment Advisory Council, 1980), pp. 49–77.

market and encourage rational determination of the basis for pricing of job content rather than automatic reaction to the forces that drove pay in the past."[9] For Bellak, job evaluation establishes the relative values of jobs based on their content and without reference to the external market. In this view, structure (pay differences) among jobs can be established with job evaluation independent of a link to the market.

As you can see, job evaluation takes on many forms. In some cases it only classifies jobs, in others it helps establish a hierarchy. On the one hand it is a mechanism used to compare the relative content of jobs without reference to current or market-based rates. On the other hand, it serves as the link between market rates and the content of jobs. Various job evaluation plans have been designed based on all these perspectives.

Measurement and Rationalization

Job evaluation can take on the trappings of measurement (objective, numerical, generalizable, documented, and reliable). If it is viewed as a measurement instrument, then job evaluation can be judged according to technical standards. Just as with employment tests, the reliability and validity of job evaluation plans should be reported. And presumably every consulting firm would publish reliability and validity data on plans they sold.[10] Yet such data typically are not reported and may not even be available in some cases.

Consequently, job evaluation may be viewed by consultants and practitioners as a process to help gain acceptance of pay differences among jobs. It is an administrative procedure through which the parties can haggle over the relative worth of jobs—"the rules of the game."[11] As in sports contests, we are more willing to accept the results if we believe the rules of the game, in this case job evaluation, are fair.[12]

As an administrative procedure, job evaluation invites give and take. Consensus building often requires active participation by all those involved. Employees, union representatives, and managers may be included in discussions about the pay differences among various jobs. Job evaluation even involves negotiations among managers of different units or functions within a single organization. So viewed as an administrative

---

[9]Bellak, "Comparable Worth."

[10]Howard W. Risher, "Job Evaluation: Validity and Reliability," *Compensation and Benefits Review,* January-February 1989, pp. 22–36.

[11]George T. Milkovich, "Compensation, Equity, and Job Evaluation in the 1980's," *Proceedings of the Symposium on Job Evaluation and Equal Employment Opportunity* (New York: Industrial Relations Counselors, 1979); and George T. Milkovich and Charles J. Cogill, "Measurement as an Issue in Job Analysis and Job Evaluation," in *Handbook of Wage and Salary Management,* ed. Milton Rock (New York: McGraw-Hill, 1984). Also see Howard Risher, "Job Evaluation: Mystical or Statistical?" *Personnel* 55, no. 5 (September/October 1978), pp. 23–36; John Gaito, "Measurement Scales and Statistics: Resurgence of an Old Misconception," *Psychological Bulletin* 87, no. 3 (1980), pp. 564–67.

[12]Robert Folger and Mary Konovsky, "Effects of Procedural and Distributive Justice on Reactions to Pay Raise Decisions," *Academy of Management Journal,* March 1989, pp. 115–30; Jerald Greenburg, "A Taxonomy of Organizational Justice Theories," *Academy of Management Review* 12 (1987), pp. 9–22; and E. A. Lind and T. R. Tyler, *The Social Psychology of Procedural Justice* (New York: Plenum Press, 1988).

procedure, job evaluation is used for working out conflicts that inevitably arise about pay differences over time.

Some readers may conclude that job evaluation is no more than rationalization of a pay structure that is either negotiated by the parties or reflected in the external markets. Livernash comments on this view:

> Job evaluation is not a rigid, objective, analytical procedure. Neither is it a meaningless process of rationalization. If a group of people with reasonable knowledge of certain jobs rate (evaluate) them, there will be frequent small differences of opinion, some major differences as well, but also a high degree of general agreement. The application of group judgment through the rating process normally produces an *improved pay structure, but extreme attitudes as to the accuracy of ratings are difficult to defend.*[13]

Culling through all of this, the following definition seems to include the nuances attributed to job evaluation.

Job evaluation is a systematic procedure designed to aid in establishing pay differentials among jobs within a single employer.

MAJOR DECISIONS

The major decisions involved in the design and administration of job evaluation are depicted in Exhibit 4.2. They include: (1) determine the purpose(s) of job evaluation, (2) decide whether to use single or multiple plans, (3) choose among alternative approaches, (4) obtain the involvement of relevant parties, and (5) evaluate its usefulness. The first three of these decisions are discussed in this chapter; the remaining two are covered in the next. Examples of actual job evaluation plans are found on pages 574–85.

EXHIBIT 4.2
Determining an Internally Consistent Job Structure

| Internal Consistency: Relationships among jobs within the organization | → | Job analysis | → | Job descriptions | → | Job evaluation | → | Job structure |

Some Major Decisions in Job Evaluation
- Establish purpose of evaluation
- Decide whether to use single or multiple plans
- Choose among alternative approaches
- Obtain involvement of relevant parties
- Evaluate plan's usefulness

---

[13]E. Robert Livernash, "The Internal Wage Structure," pp. 143–72.

Establish the Purpose

Why bother with job evaluation? Because it aids in establishing a pay structure that is internally equitable to employees and consistent with the goals of the organization. The results of job evaluation should be relevant to managers who will use them to help make pay decisions, and to employees whose pay rates they influence.

More specific purposes of job evaluation often include:

- Help foster equity by integrating pay with a job's contributions to the organization.
- Assist employees to adapt to organization changes by improving their understanding of job content and what is valued in their work.
- Establish a workable, agreed-upon pay structure.
- Simplify and rationalize the pay relationships among jobs, and reduce the role that chance, favoritism, and bias may play.
- Aid in setting pay for new, unique, or changing jobs.
- Provide an agreed-upon device to reduce and resolve disputes and grievances.
- Help ensure that the pay structure is consistent with the relationships among jobs, thereby supporting other human resource programs such as career planning, staffing, and training.

However, little empirical evidence exists that demonstrates the effects of formal job evaluation on these objectives.

Since they guide the design and administration of job evaluation, objectives need to be specified. But initially established objectives too often get lost in statistical procedures and in the bureaucracy which tends to sprout around the administration of job evaluation. Job evaluation sometimes seems to exist for its own sake, rather than as an aid to achieving the goals listed above.[14] So an organization is best served by initially establishing its objectives for the process, and using these objectives as a constant guide for its decisions.

Job evaluation emphasizes a systematic, rational assessment of jobs as a part of pay determination. Yet managers seem interested in job evaluation only when a pay problem exists—employee dissatisfaction, grievances, threats of unionization, or lawsuits. A more productive strategy is to anticipate or avoid potential challenges by ensuring an equitable and work-related pay structure.

Single versus Multiple Plans

Once the objectives of job evaluation are selected, then it is necessary to decide which jobs or job groups are going to be evaluated. Rarely will an employer evaluate all jobs in the organization at one time.[15] More typically, related groups of jobs, for example production, engineering, or marketing, will be concentrated on. Even when introducing job evaluation for the first time, it is usually applied to one occupation or subunit of the organization.

---

[14]Mike Burns, *Understanding Job Evaluation* (London: Institute of Personnel Management, 1978); Edwin F. Beal, "In Praise of Job Evaluation," *California Management Review,* Summer 1963, pp. 9–15.

[15]Bellak, "Comparable Worth."

Most employers design different job evaluation plans for different job families. They do so because they believe that the work content of various job families is too diverse to be adequately evaluated using the same plan. For example, production jobs may vary in terms of working conditions and the physical, manipulative skills required. But engineering and marketing jobs do not vary on these factors, nor are those factors particularly important in engineering or marketing work. Rather, other factors such as technical knowledge and skills and the degree of contacts with external customers may be relevant. These *compensable factors* are aspects of work that vary among jobs and may play an important role in establishing pay differences among jobs.

The point is that separate plans are typically used for production, engineering, marketing, managerial, office and clerical, and executive jobs within a single employer. The most common criteria for determining different job families include similar knowledge/skill/ability requirements, common licensing requirements, union jurisdictions, and career paths. Those who argue for multiple plans, each with unique compensable factors, claim that different job families have different and unique work characteristics. To design a single set of compensable factors capable of universal application, while technically feasible, risks emphasizing generalized commonalities among jobs and minimizing uniqueness and dissimilarities. Accurately gauging the similarities and dissimilarities in jobs is critical to establish and justify pay differentials. Therefore, more than one plan is often used for adequate evaluation.

The decision about single versus multiple plans is important in the comparable worth controversy. The National Academy of Sciences' study committee on job evaluation and wage discrimination was divided on whether the jobs usually found within a single firm can be adequately evaluated by a single job evaluation or whether several plans are required to measure job characteristics adequately.[16] Remick argues that an operational definition of comparable worth hinges on the application of a single evaluation system across job families, both to rank order jobs and to set salaries.[17] Yet to define universal factors in such a way that they accurately evaluate all jobs within a single employer and at the same time remain acceptable to all parties imposes a burden on a single job evaluation plan.[18] The issue of comparable worth is examined in detail in the chapter on pay discrimination.

Rather than either universal factors or entirely unique factors for each job family, some employers, notably Hewett-Packard, use a core set of common factors and another

---

[16]Donald J. Treiman and Heidi J. Hartmann, eds., *Women, Work and Wages: Equal Pay for Jobs of Equal Value* (Washington, D.C.: National Academy Press, 1981); and D. Treiman, ed., *Job Evaluation: An Analytic Review*, Interim Report to the Equal Employment Opportunity Commission (Washington, D.C.: National Academy Press, 1981).

[17]Helen Remick, *Comparable Worth and Wage Discrimination* (Philadelphia: Temple University Press, 1984). See also Karin Allport, "Equal Pay for Equal Work? Of Course," *Across the Board* 17, no. 10 (October 1980); and James T. Brinks, "The Comparable Worth Issue: A Salary Administration Bombshell," *Personnel Administrator,* November 1981, pp. 37–40.

[18]Legislation in Ontario, Canada, requires single plans for each bargaining unit with an employer. Thus a single employer could have three plans if the Teamsters Union represented one occupation, and the Sheetmetal Workers Union another. An additional plan is required for employees who are not in a bargaining unit. *Pay Equity Implementation Series* (Toronto, Ontario, Canada: The Pay Equity Commission, 1989).

EXHIBIT 4.3
Methods Used in Job Evaluation

	Executive/ Managers	Scientists/ Engineers	Customer Reps	Exempt Staff	Clerical Employees	Hourly Employees
Whole job ranking	22.6	14.0	15.6	20.3	20.8	16.3
Point	49.9	37.8	44.6	55.6	56.2	36.4
Factor comparison	11.5	9.3	10.1	12.1	11.3	7.4
Other	6.4	3.8	4.7	5.4	6.1	9.9

Source: Reprinted by permission of the American Compensation Association from *Report on the 1987 Survey of Salary Management Practices,* 1988.

set of factors unique to particular occupational or functional areas (finance, manufacturing, software and systems, sales). These companies' experiences suggest that unique factors tailored to different job families are more likely to be both acceptable to employees and managers and easier to verify as work related than are generalized universal factors.

Choose among Job Evaluation Methods

Four fundamental job evaluation methods are in use: ranking, classification, factor comparisons, and point plan.

Uncounted variations of these methods exist. According to a survey of job evaluation practices, shown in Exhibit 4.3, point plans are the most commonly used. The following sections examine each of the methods and provide examples of some adaptations. All of the methods assume that the results of an accurate, thorough job analysis have been translated into readable, useful job descriptions and that the job families to be evaluated have been identified.

RANKING

Ranking simply involves ordering the job descriptions from highest to lowest based on a definition of value or contribution. In Exhibit 4.3 whole job ranking is reportedly used across all job families. Our experience suggests that it is common in small to medium size firms. It is the simplest, fastest, easiest to understand and explain to employees, and the least expensive job evaluation method, at least initially.

Two ways of ranking are usually considered: alternation ranking and paired comparison. Alternation ranking involves ordering the job descriptions alternately at each extreme. Exhibit 4.4 illustrates the method. Agreement is reached among evaluators on which job is the most valuable, then the least valuable. Evaluators alternate between the next most valued and next least valued, and so on, until all the jobs have been ordered. For example, evaluators agreed that the job of master welder was the most valued of the six jobs listed in the exhibit, and receiving clerk the least valued. Then they selected most and least valued from the four remaining jobs on the list.

The paired comparison method involves comparing all possible pairs of jobs under study. A simple way to do paired comparison is to set up a matrix, as shown in Exhibit

EXHIBIT 4.4
Alternation Ranking

Jobs		Rank
Number	Title	Most Valued
1	Shear operator	Master welder
2	Electrician	Electrician
3	Punch press operator	
4	Master welder	
5	Grinder	
6	Receiving clerk	Receiving clerk
		Least Valued

4.5. The higher ranked job is entered in the cell. For example, of the shear operator and the electrician, the electrician is ranked higher. Of the shear operator and the punch press operator, the shear operator is ranked higher. When all comparisons have been completed, the job with the highest total number of "most valuable" rankings becomes the highest ranked job, and so on. Some evidence suggests that the alternation ranking and paired comparison methods are more reliable (produce similar results consistently) than simple ranking.[19]

Caution is required if ranking is chosen. The criteria or factors on which the jobs are ranked are usually so poorly defined (if they are specified at all) that the evaluations become subjective opinions that are difficult if not impossible to explain and justify in work-related terms. Further, evaluator(s) using this method must be knowledgeable about every single job under study. The numbers alone turn what should be a simple task into a formidable one—50 jobs require 1,225 comparisons $[(n) (n - 1)/2]$; and as organizations change, it is difficult to remain knowledgeable about all jobs. Some organizations try to overcome this difficulty by ranking jobs within single departments and merging the results. However, without greater specification of the factors on which the rankings are based, merging ranks is a major problem. Even though ranking appears simple, fast, and inexpensive, in the long term it may be more costly. The results are difficult to defend, and costly solutions are often required to overcome the problems created. However, in simplified structures, with fewer, broad generic jobs (e.g., Nummi's four types of technicians) ranking is appealing.

CLASSIFICATION

The classification method is not even listed in the survey data shown in Exhibit 4.3. In spite of this omission, classification methods are widely used by public sector em-

---

[19]David J. Chesler, "Reliabilility and Comparability of Different Job Evaluation Systems," *Journal of Applied Psychology*, October 1948, pp. 465–75.

EXHIBIT 4.5
Paired Comparison Ranking

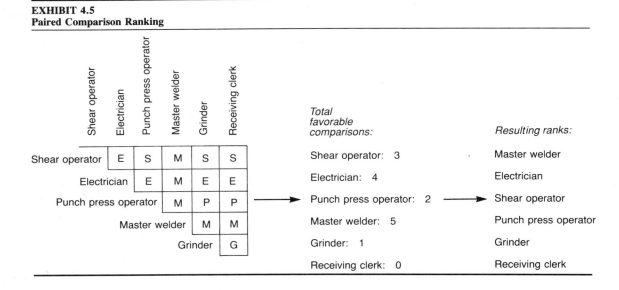

ployers. The classification method involves slotting job descriptions into a series of classes that cover the range of jobs. Classes can be conceived as a series of carefully labeled shelves on a bookshelf. The labels are the class descriptions which serve as the standard against which the job descriptions are compared. Exhibit 4.6 lists the typical steps in the classification approach. Each class is described in such a way that it captures sufficient work detail and yet is general enough to cause little difficulty in slotting jobs.

Writing class descriptions can be troublesome when jobs from several occupations or job families are covered by a single plan. While greater specificity of class definition improves the reliability of evaluation, it also limits the variety of jobs that can easily be classified. For example, class definitions written with sales jobs in mind may make it difficult to slot office or administrative jobs and vice versa. You can see the difficulty by examining the class definitions from the federal government's 18-class evaluation system, Exhibit 4.7.

The classes may further be labeled by the inclusion of benchmark jobs that fall into each class. Benchmark jobs are defined as reference points having the following characteristics:

- The contents are well known, relatively stable over time, and agreed upon by the employees involved.
- The jobs are common across a number of different employers. They are not unique to a particular employer.
- They represent the entire range of jobs being evaluated.
- They are accepted in the external labor market for setting wages.

EXHIBIT 4.6
Typical Steps in Classification System

1. Define classes.
2. Identify and slot benchmarks.
3. Prepare classification manual.
4. Apply system to nonbenchmark jobs.

EXHIBIT 4.7
Examples of General Schedule Descriptions for the Federal Government Job Classification Method

Grade General Schedule 1 includes all classes of positions the duties of which are to be performed, under immediate supervision, with little or no latitude for the exercise of independent judgment, (1) the simplest routine work in office, business, or fiscal operations, or (2) elementary work of a subordinate technical character in a professional, scientific, or technical field.

Grade-General Schedule 5 includes all classes of positions the duties of which are (1) to perform, under general supervision, difficult and responsible work in office, business, or fiscal administration, or comparable subordinate technical work in a professional, scientific, or technical field, requiring in either case (A) considerable training and supervisory or other experience, (B) broad working knowledge of a special subject matter or of office, laboratory, engineering, scientific, or other procedure and practice, and (C) the exercise of independent judgment in a limited field; (2) to perform, under immediate supervision, and with little opportunity for the exercise of independent judgment, simple and elementary work requiring professional, scientific, or technical training equivalent to that represented by graduation from a college or university of recognized standing but requiring little or no experience; or (3) to perform other work of equal importance, difficulty, and responsibility, and requiring comparable qualifications.

Grade-General Schedule 9 includes all classes of positions the duties of which are (1) to perform, under general supervision, very difficult and responsible work along special technical, supervisory, or administrative experience which has (A) demonstrated capacity for sound independent work, (B) thorough and fundamental knowledge of a special and complex subject matter, or of the profession, art, or science involved, and (C) considerable latitude for the exercise of independent judgment; (2) with considerable latitude for the exercise of independent judgment, to perform moderately difficult and responsible work, requiring (A) professional, scientific, or technical training equivalent to that represented by graduation from a college or university of recognized standing, and (B) considerable additional professional, scientific, or technical training or experience which has demonstrated capacity for sound independent work; or (3) to perform other work of equal importance, difficulty, and responsibility, and requiring comparable qualifications.

Grade-General Schedule 13 includes all classes of positions the duties of which are (1) to perform, under administrative direction, with wide latitude for the exercise of independent judgment work of unusual difficulty and responsibility along special technical, supervisory, or administrative lines, requiring extended specialized, supervisory, or administrative training and experience which has demonstrated leadership and marked attainments; (2) to serve as assistant head of a major organization involving work of comparable level within a bureau; (3) to perform, under administrative direction, with wide latitude for the exercise of independent judgment, work of unusual difficulty and responsibility requiring extended professional, scientific, or technical training and experience which has demonstrated leadership and marked attainments in professional, scientific, or technical research, practice, or administration; or (4) to perform other work of equal importance, difficulty, and responsibility, and requiring comparable qualifications.

The point of using benchmark jobs is to anchor the comparisons for each job class. Anchoring the classes in this way has the advantage of illustrating the typical job in a class.

In practice, the job descriptions not only are compared to the standard class descriptions and benchmark jobs but also to each other, to insure that jobs within each class are more similar to each other than to adjacent classes. The final result is a series of classes with a number of jobs in each. The jobs within each class are considered to be equal (similar) work and will be paid equally. Jobs in different classes should be dissimilar and may have different pay rates.

How Many Classes?

Class descriptions and the number of classes depend on tradition, range, and diversity of the job involved and on the career and promotion paths of the organization. A common "rule of thumb" is that 7 to 14 classes will meet the needs of most organizations.[20] Some organizations have expanded their classes from 10 to 20; others have collapsed classes from 40 to 20; all seemed pleased with the results. Those adopting greater number of classes argue that employees favor frequent upgrading or promotions, and a larger number of classes facilitates such moves. Those collapsing the number of classes argue that a proliferation of classes is difficult to explain or defend and become needless bureaucracy.

What is the appropriate number of classes? It depends. Variability and diversity in the work may call for many classes. Comparisons in the external market may be easier if the same number of classes as similar employers is adopted. The class descriptions, like job descriptions, are useful only when they are embedded in the actual work performed and when they capture meaningful similarities and differences among jobs and help ensure a workable and defensible pay structure.

The Federal Government's General Schedule

While classification is more complex than ranking, it still is relatively inexpensive to develop and simple to install and understand. Probably the best known example is the Office of Personnel Management's General Schedule (GS), with 18 "grades" (classes).[21] Several grade descriptions are given in Exhibit 4.7. The GS system is *not* based on related subject matter of work (e.g., accounting jobs); rather, level of difficulty distinguishes the various classes. Most jobs are in 15 grades; the top three have been combined with a "supergrade" that covers senior executives. Employees in these top three grades are eligible

---

[20]Belcher, *Compensation*, pp. 151–52. See also Paul A. Katz, "There IS Something New in Position Classification," *Defense Management Journal*, September 1978, pp. 16–19.

[21]The federal system utilizes the terms grades and classes differently than does this book. We have previously avoided referring to *job grades* because of possible confusion with *pay grades*, discussed in Chapter 7. However, the federal government refers to the results of its classification as grades, rather than classes. In the GS system a series of *classes* links jobs of similar work (e.g., clerk typist class I, clerk typist class II).

EXHIBIT 4.8
Career Paths and Pay Bands Compared to General Schedule

Career Path

Professional	GS	1-4	5-8	9-11	12-13	14-15	16-18
	Pay band	A	I	II	III	IV	V

Technician	GS	1-4	5-8	9-10	11-12
	Pay band	A	I	II	III

Technical specialist	GS	1-4	5-8	9-10	11-12
	Pay band	A	I	II	III

Administrative specialist	GS	1-4	5-8	9-10	11-12
	Pay band	A	I	II	III

General	GS	1-3	4-5	6-7	8-9	10-11
	Pay band	A	I	II	III	IV

for bonuses and special stipends based on performance. Collapsing the top three classes into one "supergrade" provides flexibility by making it easier to move people at this level among different agencies, in order to best utilize these particular employees' skills, and meet different agency needs. The Naval Ocean Systems Center in San Diego went even further in combining classes. There, the 18 separate GS classifications were combined into broad pay bands.[22] In lieu of GS classes, five separate career paths, depicted in Exhibit 4.8 were created. Within each path employees are assigned to one of the several pay bands, each of which includes at least two of the conventional GS grades. Under the traditional GS approaches, "managers lacked flexibility when assigning work to their employees because the GS process required too much paper work and time. (Managers) expressed concern that the classification process was in the hands of personnel specialists rather than line managers."[23] So the original rational structure became an inflexible structure bureaucracy run amok.

The Federal Classification Act of 1923 provided an early impetus for job classification in the federal government. Classification and the job descriptions provided the basis for internal consistency and a uniform job terminology, which allowed centralized financial

---

[22]GAO Report to the Chairman, Subcommittee on Federal Services, Post Office, and Civil Service, *Observations on the Navy's Personnel Management Demonstration Project* (May 1988).

[23]Ibid, p. 10.

EXHIBIT 4.9
Factor Evaluation System: Nine Factors, with Subfactors

Knowledge required by the position
1. Nature or kind of knowledge and skills needed
2. How the knowledge and skills are used in doing the work

Supervisory controls
1. How the work is assigned
2. The employee's responsibility for carrying out the work
3. How the work is reviewed

Guidelines
1. The nature of guidelines for performing the work
2. The judgment needed to apply the guidelines or develop new guides

Complexity
1. The nature of the assignment
2. The difficulty in identifying what needs to be done
3. The difficulty and originality involved in performing the work

Scope and effect
1. The purpose of the work
2. The impact of the work product or service

Personal contacts

Purpose of contacts

Physical demands

Work environment

---

control.[24] The argument at the time was that it made better, more efficient government a possibility. (Not a reality, only a possibility.) It also specified a standard of equal pay for equal work, over 40 years before legislation required such a standard in the private sector.

Subsequent classification acts further refined and expanded the use of the classification method at the federal level. A Factor Evaluation System (FES) was installed in 1977, which uses nine factors to classify approximately 1 million nonsupervisory general schedule positions. These factors are listed in Exhibit 4.9. Using the plan, jobs as diverse as work unit conservationist in the Agriculture Department, border patrol officer in Immigration, and account auditor in the Internal Revenue Service were placed in the same GS level. Each factor also receives point values that reflect the factor's importance in a job. The sum of the factor ratings equals the job's total worth.

The Factor Evaluation System changes the original classification system to a hybrid of classification and point system evaluation. Under its use, managers have three potential comparisons to guide their evaluation of a job: the general class description, the factor comparisons, and the benchmark jobs that anchor each class.

The Factor Evaluation System is not the only job evaluation system within the federal government. The government's approach seems to be similar to that of private industry: pick and choose and adapt, according to specific needs. Many states and other govern-

---

[24]Paul A. Katz, "Specific Job Evaluation Systems: White Collar Jobs in the Federal Civil Service," in *Handbook of Wage and Salary Administration*, ed. Milton Rock (New York: McGraw-Hill, 1984), pp. 14/1-14/10; and Steven W. Hays and T. Zane Reeves, *Personnel Management in the Public Sector* (Boston: Allyn and Bacon, 1984).

mental units use variations of the classification system, too. The references contain additional sources of information on public sector pay practices.[25]

In addition to public sector jobs, our experience is that classification is applied to a wide variety of private sector jobs. High-technology and defense-related businesses have frequently developed four to six job classes for engineers.[26] However, the differences among classes in this setting are often more related to experience or "years-since-degree" than to differences in work done by the engineers.

Inherent Flexibility

Sufficient vagueness exists in many classification plans to permit what Patten calls "aggrandizing language" in the job descriptions.[27] A potential problem with the classification method is that it may degenerate into a title game. Usually each class has a title associated with it, often as part of the benchmark job. Managers may decide the classes to which they want the jobs assigned prior to any analysis, and then try to influence the classification by assigning an inflated title to the job. The potential for manipulating the results is inherent in the flexible nature of the classification system.

While not as vulnerable to legal and employee challenges as a ranking approach, some classification plans do not offer much detailed, work-related rationale to justify pay differentials. This lack of work-related rationale may not be very compelling to a line manager whose immediate problem is getting a salary increase for a subordinate, but it takes on importance in an equal pay lawsuit or in reassuring disgruntled employees who feel their jobs are misvalued.

Finally, many employers are currently slashing the number of classes in their plans. At Colgate Palmolive's Ohio facilities, all plant jobs are grouped into only four job classes. Rather than use diverse job titles, all workers are known as technicians or associates. The logic behind reducing classes and using generic titles is increased flexibility to overcome inefficient work rules. Yet some balance between complete flexibility and control is required. Prior to the widespread use of job evaluation, employers in the 1930s and 1940s had complex and irrational pay structures—the legacy of decentralized and uncoordinated wage setting practices.[28] Pay differences were a major source of unrest among workers. American Steel and Wire, for example, had over 100,000 pay classi-

---

[25]Edward B. Shils, "A Perspective on Job Measurement," in *Handbook of Wage and Salary Administration*, ed. Milton Rock (New York: McGraw-Hill, 1984), pp. 8/1-8/14; Katz, "Specific Job Evaluation Systems," in *Job Evaluation and Pay Administration in the Public Sector*, ed. Harold Suskin, (Chicago: International Personnel Management Association, 1977); and Hays and Reeves, *Personnel Management in the Public Sector*.

[26]Robert B. Pursell, "R&D Job Evaluation and Compensation," *Compensation Review*, Second Quarter 1972, pp. 21–31; T. Atchinson and W. French, "Pay Systems for Scientists and Engineers," *Industrial Relations* 7 (1967), pp. 44–56.

[27]Thomas H. Pattern, Jr., *Pay Employee Compensation and Incentive Plans* (New York: Free Press, 1977).

[28]Livernash, "Internal Wage Structure."

fications. According to Jacoby, employment and wage records were rarely kept before 1900; only the foreman knew with any accuracy how many workers were employed in his department and the rates they received. Foremen jealously guarded wage information and used it to play favorites by varying the day rate or assigning favored workers to jobs where piece rates were loose.[29] Where complete flexibility was given to supervisors, uncoordinated and irrational pay structures were too frequently the result. Removing inefficient bureaucracy is important, but some of the rules are necessary to help ensure that pay accomplishes the system's objectives.

FACTOR COMPARISON

In the factor comparison method, jobs are evaluated based on two criteria: (1) a set of compensable factors and (2) wages for benchmark jobs. The two criteria are combined to form a job comparison scale, which is then applied to nonbenchmark jobs. However, the method's complexity often limits its usefulness.[30] It is the least popular of the conventional methods listed in the survey in Exhibit 4.3.[31]

While several versions of factor comparison exist, the basic approach involves the following steps:

1. *Conduct job analysis.* As with all job evaluation methods, information about the jobs must be collected and job descriptions prepared. However, the factor comparison method differs from others in that it requires that jobs be analyzed and described in terms of the compensable factors used in the plan. Benge, Burk, and Hay prescribed five factors: mental requirements, skill requirements, physical factors, responsibility, and working conditions. Exhibit 4.10 contains definitions of these five factors. The developers consider these factors to be universal—able to evaluate all jobs in all organizations. However, there is some latitude in the specific definition of each factor among organizations.

    Conducting job analysis on the basis of predetermined factors raises some questions. Should compensable factors be selected prior to job analysis? Or, should job analysis and job descriptions be done, and then factors selected based on information gleaned in the analysis? If every job must be defined in terms of the five factors, then the *content* of the job analysis and job descriptions is controlled by these "universal"

[29]Sanford M. Jacoby, "Development of Internal Labor Markets," in *Internal Labor Markets,* ed. P. Osterman (Cambridge, Mass.: MIT Press, 1984), pp. 23–70.

[30]Eugene J. Benge, Samuel L. H. Burk, and Edward N. Hay, *Manual of Job Evaluation* (New York: Harper & Row, 1941). See also Eugene J. Benge, "Using Factor Methods to Measure Jobs," in *Handbook of Wage and Salary Administration,* ed. Milton R. Rock (New York: McGraw-Hill, 1972); Edward N. Hay, "Four Methods of Establishing Factor Scales in Factor Comparison Job Evaluation," *Personnel,* September 1946, pp. 115–24; and Edward N. Hay, "Characteristics of Factor Comparison Job Evaluation," *Personnel* 22, no. 6 (1946), pp. 370–75.

[31]American Compensation Association, *Survey of Salary Management Practices in the Private Sector* (Scottsdale, Ariz.: American Compensation Association, 1988).

EXHIBIT 4.10
Universal Factor Definitions Used in Factor Comparison Method

1. Mental requirements—either the possession of and/or the active application of the following:
    A.   (Inherent) mental traits, such as intelligence, memory, reasoning, facility in verbal expression, ability to get along with people, and imagination.
    B.   (Acquired) general education, such as grammar and arithmetic; or general information as to sports, world events, etc.
    C.   (Acquired) specialized knowledge such as chemistry, engineering, accounting, advertising, etc.

2. Skill:
    A.   (Acquired) facility in muscular coordination, as in operating machines, repetitive movements, careful coordinations, dexterity, assembling, sorting, etc.
    B.   (Acquired) specific job knowledge necessary to the muscular coordination only; acquired by performance of the work and not to be confused with general education or specialized knowledge. It is very largely training in the interpretation of sensory impressions. Examples:
        (*1*)   In operating an adding machine, the knowledge of *which key* to depress for a subtotal would be skill.
        (*2*)   In automobile repair, the ability to determine the significance of a certain knock in the motor would be skill.
        (*3*)   In hand-firing a boiler, the ability to determine from the appearance of the firebed how coal should be shoveled over the surface would be skill.

3. Physical requirements:
    A.   Physical effort, as sitting, standing walking, climbing, pulling, lifting, etc.; both the amount exercised and the degree of the continuity should be taken into account.
    B.   Physical status, as height, weight, strength and eyesight.

4. Responsibilities:
    A.   For raw materials, processed materials, tools, equipment, and property.
    B.   For money or negotiable securities.
    C.   For profits or loss, savings or methods' improvement.
    D.   For public contact.
    E.   For records.
    F.   For supervision.
        (*1*)   Primarily the complexity of supervising *given* to subordinates; the number of subordinates is a secondary feature. Planning, direction, coordination, instruction, control, and approval characterize this kind of supervision.
        (*2*)   Also, the degree of supervision *received*. If jobs A and B gave no supervision to subordinates, but A received much closer immediate supervision than B, then B would be entitled to a higher rating than A in the supervision factor.
        To summarize the four degrees of supervision:
            Highest degree—gives much—gets little
            High degree—gives much—gets much
            Low degree—gives none—gets little
            Lowest degree—gives none—gets much

5. Working conditions:
    A.   Environmental influences, such as atmosphere, ventilation, illumination, noise, congestion, fellow workers, etc.
    B.   Hazards—from the work or its surroundings.
    C.   Hours.

factors, and the decision on which factors to use necessarily comes before job analysis. But such an approach risks omitting aspects of the work unique to an organization and important to employees and managers. These five factors may not adequately capture the nature of the work. This risk can be reduced by first developing factors based on analysis of a representative sample of jobs, then applying the factors to all other jobs. In this way the factors are custom-tailored to particular occupations and organizations. Exhibit 4.10 is an example of a job description prepared for factor comparison evaluation.

2. *Select benchmark jobs.* The selection of benchmark jobs is critical since the entire method is based on them. Benchmark jobs (also called key jobs) serve as reference points. Earlier, we specified the following characteristics for a benchmark job:

- The contents are well known and agreed upon by the parties involved.
- The contents change very little over time.
- The current pay rates are generally acceptable and the differentials among the jobs are relatively stable.
- They are accepted in the external labor market for setting wages.

Another criterion is that the sample of benchmark jobs cover the entire range of jobs being evaluated (i.e., some from the top, middle, and low end of the range). If more than one job family is being evaluated, benchmarks are drawn from the top, middle, and low end of every included job family. But for factor comparison, the requirements for a benchmark job are even more specific: they must cover the entire range of each factor. For example, if a compensable factor is mental requirements, benchmark jobs must cover the full range of mental requirements that exists in the job group being evaluated. The exact number of benchmarks required varies; some rules of thumb have been suggested (15 to 25), but the number depends on the range and diversity of the work to be evaluated.

3. *Rank benchmark jobs on each factor.* Each benchmark job is ranked on each compensable factor (Exhibit 4.11). In our example, a job family consisting of six jobs is first ranked on mental requirements, then on experience, and so on. The approach differs from the ranking plan in that each job is ranked on *each factor* rather than as a "whole" job.

EXHIBIT 4.11
Factor Comparison Method: Ranking Benchmark Jobs by Compensable Factor

Benchmark Jobs	Mental Requirements	Experience/ Skills	Physical Factors	Supervision	Other Responsibilities
A. Punch press operator	6	5	2	4	4
B. Parts attendant	5	3	3	6	1
C. Riveter	4	6	1	1	3
D. Truck operator	3	1	6	5	6
E. Machine operator	2	2	4	2	5
F. Parts inspector	1	3	5	3	2

Note: Rank of 1 is high.

EXHIBIT 4.12
Factor Comparison Methods: Allocation of Benchmark Job Wages Across Factors

	Benchmark Jobs	Current Wage Rate ($/hour)		Mental Requirements $		Experience/ Skills $		Physical Factors $		Supervision $		Other Responsibilities $
							Factors					
A.	Punch press operator	5.80	=	.80	+	.80	+	2.40	+	1.10	+	.70
B.	Parts attendant	9.60	=	2.15	+	2.35	+	1.90	+	.60	+	2.60
C.	Riveter	13.30	=	2.50	+	3.10	+	2.45	+	4.50	+	.75
D.	Truck operator	8.50	=	3.40	+	3.20	+	.60	+	.80	+	.50
E.	Machine operator	11.80	=	3.60	+	2.90	+	1.75	+	2.90	+	.65
F.	Parts inspector	11.40	=	4.50	+	2.20	+	1.20	+	2.50	+	1.10

4. *Allocate benchmark wages across factors.* Once each benchmark is ranked on each factor, the next step is to allocate the wages paid for each benchmark to each factor. Essentially this is done by deciding how much of the wage rate for each benchmark job is associated with mental demand, how much with physical requirements, and so on across all compensable factors. This is done for each benchmark job and is usually based on the judgment of a compensation committee. For example, in Exhibit 4.12, of the $5.80 per hour paid to the punch press operator, the committee has decided that the job's mental requirements equal $.80, experience/skill is worth $.80, physical factors account for $2.40, supervision accounts for $1.10, and other responsibilities are worth $.70 an hour in this job. The total $5.80 is allocated among the compensable factors. This process is repeated for each of the benchmark jobs.

After the wage for each job is allocated among that job's compensable factors, the dollar amounts for each factor are ranked as shown in Exhibit 4.13. The job that has the highest wage allocation for mental requirements is ranked 1 on that factor, next highest is 2, and so on. Separate rankings are done for the wage allocated to each compensable factor. In the example in Exhibit 4.13, parts inspector has more of its wages allocated to mental demands than does any other job, and so it receives the highest rank for that factor.

EXHIBIT 4.13
Ranking Wage Allocations

	Benchmark Jobs	Mental Requirements $	Mental Requirements Rank	Experience/ Skills $	Experience/ Skills Rank	Physical Factors $	Physical Factors Rank	Supervision $	Supervision Rank	Other Responsibilities $	Other Responsibilities Rank
A.	Punch press operator	.80	6	.80	6	2.40	2	1.10	4	.70	4
B.	Parts attendant	2.15	5	2.35	4	1.90	3	.60	6	2.60	1
C.	Riveter	2.50	4	3.10	2	2.45	1	4.50	1	.75	3
D.	Truck operator	3.40	3	3.20	1	.60	6	.80	5	.50	6
E.	Machine operator	3.60	2	2.90	3	1.75	4	2.90	2	.65	5
F.	Parts inspector	4.50	1	2.20	5	1.20	5	2.50	3	1.10	2

Note: Rank of 1 is high.

EXHIBIT 4.14
Comparison of Factor and Wage Allocation Ranks

Benchmark Jobs	Mental Requirements		Experience/ Skills		Physical Factors		Supervision		Other Responsibilities	
	Factor Rank	Wage Rank	Factor Rank	Wage Rank	Factor Rank	Wage Rank	Factor Rank	Wage Rank	Factor Rank	Wage Rank
A. Punch press	6	6	5	6	2	2	4	4	4	4
B. Parts attendant	5	5	3	4	3	3	6	6	1	1
C. Riveter	4	4	6	2	1	1	1	1	3	3
D. Truck operator	3	3	1	1	6	6	5	5	6	6
E. Machine operator	2	2	2	3	4	4	2	2	5	5
F. Parts inspector	1	1	3	5	5	5	3	3	2	2

We now have two sets of rankings, which are shown in Exhibit 4.14; the first ranking is based on comparisons of each benchmark job on each compensable factor (Exhibit 4.11). It reflects the relative presence of each factor among the benchmark jobs. The second ranking is based on the proportion of each job's wages that is attributed to each factor (Exhibit 4.13). The next step is to see how well the two rankings agree.

5. *Compare factor and wage allocation ranks.* The two rankings are judgments based on comparisons of compensable factors and wage distributions. They agree when each benchmark is assigned the same location in both ranks. If there is disagreement, the rationale for the wage allocations and factor rankings is reexamined. Both are judgments, so some slight "tuning" or adjustments may bring the rankings into line. The comparison of the two rankings is simply a cross-checking of judgments. If agreement cannot be achieved, then the job is no longer considered a benchmark and is removed. Exhibit 4.14 reveals that the two rankings of benchmarks agree on all factors except experience/skills, and so the decisions that went into ranking this factor need to be reexamined. Perhaps the allocation of wages requires adjustment to bring the ranks into agreement.

6. *Construct the job comparison scale.* Constructing a job comparison scale involves slotting benchmark jobs into a scale for each factor based on the amount of pay assigned to each factor. Such a scale is illustrated in Exhibit 4.15. Under mental requirements, the punch press operator is slotted at $.80, the parts attendant at $2.15, and so on. These slottings correspond to the wage allocations shown in Exhibit 4.12.

7. *Apply the scale.* The job comparison scale is the mechanism used to evaluate the remaining jobs. All the nonbenchmark jobs are now slotted into the scales under each factor at the dollar value thought to be appropriate. This is done by comparing the factors in the job descriptions of nonbenchmark jobs with the factors in the reference points. Consider nonbenchmark job parts stocker. The evaluator reads the stocker job description, examines the first compensable factor on the job comparison scale (mental requirements), and locates two benchmark jobs between which the mental requirements of the stocker job ranks. After examining the job descriptions for punch press operator and parts attendant, the stocker job might be judged to require greater mental demands than those required for the punch press operator but less than those for the parts attendant, and might be slotted at a rate of $1.40 for mental requirements.

EXHIBIT 4.15
Job Comparison Scale

$ Value	Mental requirements	Experience/ skills	Physical demands	Supervision	Other responsibilities
.00					
.20					
.40					Truck operator
.60			Truck operator	Parts attendant	Machine operator
					Punch press operator
					Riveter
.80	Punch press operator	Punch press operator		Truck operator	
1.00	— — — — — —	— — — — —	STOCKER — —	— — — — —	STOCKER — —
.20			Parts inspector	Punch press operator	Parts inspector
.40	STOCKER			STOCKER	
				Parts inspector	
.60			Machine operator		
.80			Parts attendant		
2.00	— — — — — —	— — — — —	— — — — —	— — — — —	— — — — —
	Parts attendant				
.20		Parts inspector			
		Parts attendant			
.40			Punch press operator		
	Riveter		Riveter		
.60		STOCKER			Parts attendant
.80					
		Machine operator		Machine operator	
3.00	— — — — —	Riveter — — —	— — — — —	— — — — +	— — — — —
.20		Truck operator			
.40	Truck operator				
.60	Machine operator				
.80					
4.00	— — — — —	— — — — —	— — — — —	— — — — +	— — — — —
.20					
.40					
	Parts inspector			Riveter	
.60					
.80					
5.00					

The same procedure is carried out for each of the other factors. To calculate the wage rate for each job, the dollar values assigned on the job comparison scale for all the factors are simply added. For the stocker job, the rate is $7.40 (mental requirements = $1.40, experience = $2.60, physical demands = $1.00, supervision = $1.40, and other responsibilities = $1.00).

Only about 10 percent of employers using formal job evaluations use the factor comparison approach.[32] The method is complex and difficult to explain to dissatisfied employees and managers, or anyone assessing the "fairness" of pay rates.

In addition, as the agreed-upon wage rates of the benchmark jobs change, the relationships among the jobs may change, and the allocation of the wages among the factors must be readjusted. So continuous updating is required.

In spite of these difficulties, the factor comparison approach represents a significant change from simple ranking and classification. First, the criteria for evaluating jobs, the compensable factors, are made explicit. Second, the use of existing wage rates of benchmark jobs as one of the criteria for designing and explaining the pay structure is unique. In a sense, factor comparison more systematically links external market forces with internal, work-related factors. Finally, in the factor comparison approach we see the use of a scale of degrees of worth (dollars) for each compensable factor in the job comparison scale. These three features—defining compensable factors, scaling the factors, and linking an agreed-upon wage structure with the compensable factors—are the basic building blocks on which point plans are based. We turn to point plans next.

POINT METHOD

Like factor comparison, designing a point system is rather complex and often requires outside assistance by consultants. But once designed, the plan is relatively simple to understand and administer. Point methods have three common characteristics: (1) compensable factors, with (2) factor degrees numerically scaled, and (3) weights reflecting the relative importance of each factor. Appendix B provides factor definitions and weights for a plan used for manufacturing jobs.

In point methods, each job's relative value, and hence its location in the pay structure, is determined by the total points assigned to it. A job's total point value is the sum of the numerical values for each degree of compensable factor that the job possesses. In the illustration in Exhibit 4.16 the point plan has four factors: skills required, effort required,

---

EXHIBIT 4.16
Characteristics of the Point Method of Job Evaluation: Factors, Scaled Degrees, Weights

(3) Weights	(1) Factors	(2) Degrees				
40%	Skills required	1	2	3	4	5
30%	Effort required	1	2	3	4	5
20%	Responsibility	1	2	3	4	5
10%	Working conditions	1	2	3	4	5

---

[32]Allan N. Nash and Stephen J. Carroll, Jr., *The Management of Compensation* (Belmont, Calif.: Wadsworth Publishing, 1975).

responsibility, and working conditions. There are five degrees of each factor. In addition to factor definitions, the evaluator will be guided by benchmark jobs and/or written descriptions that illustrate each degree of every factor. Thus, the evaluator chooses a degree for each factor according to the correspondence between the job being evaluated and the benchmark jobs or descriptions for each factor scale.

Additionally, factors may be weighted. For example, in Exhibit 4.16, skills required carries a greater weight (40 percent of the total points) for this employer than does working conditions (10 percent of the total points). Thus a job's 240 total points may result from two degrees of skills required (2 × 40 = 80), three each of effort required (3 × 30 = 90) and responsibility (3 × 20 = 60), and one of working conditions (1 × 10 = 10); (80 + 90 + 60 + 10 = 240). Weighting reflects the relative value of a factor to an employer.

Once the total points for all jobs are computed and a hierarchy based on points established, then jobs are compared to each other to ensure that their relative locations in the hierarchy are acceptable.

DESIGNING THE POINT PLAN

Exhibit 4.17 illustrates the steps in the design of a point plan. As with all job evaluation plans, the first step is job analysis. The next steps are to choose the factors, scale them, and establish the factor weights. The end product of the design phase is a job evaluation plan that can be used to evaluate all other jobs.

Conduct Job Analysis

Information about the jobs to be evaluated is the cornerstone of all job evaluation. While ideally, all jobs will be analyzed, the relevant work content—the behaviors, tasks performed, abilities/skills required, and so on—of a representative sample of jobs forms the basis for deriving compensable factors.

Choosing Compensable Factors

Compensable factors play a pivotal role in the point method. In choosing factors, an organization must decide: "What factors are valued in these jobs? What factors will be

---

EXHIBIT 4.17
Steps in Design of Point Job Evaluation

1. Conduct job analysis.
2. Choose compensable factors.
3. Establish factor scales.
4. Derive factor weights.
5. Prepare evaluation manual.
6. Apply to nonbenchmark jobs.

EXHIBIT 4.18
Example of a Compensable Factor Definition: Decision Making

Compensable Factor Definition: Evaluates the extent of required decision-making and the beneficial or detrimental effect such decisions would have on the profitability of the organization. Consideration is given to the:
• Risk and complexity of required decision-making
• Impact such action would have on the company

What type of guidelines are available for making decisions?

_____1. Few decisions are required; work is performed according to standard procedures and/or detailed instructions.

_____2. Decisions are made within an established framework of clearly defined procedures. Incumbent is only required to recognize and follow the prescribed course of action.

_____3. Guidelines are available in the form of clearly defined procedures and standard practices. Incumbent must exercise some judgment in selecting the appropriate procedure.

_____4. Guidelines are available in the form of some standard practices, well-established precedent and reference materials and company policy. Decisions require a moderate level of judgment and analysis of the appropriate course of action.

_____5. Some guidelines are available in the form of broad precedent, related practices and general methods of the field. Decisions require a high level of judgment and/or modification of a standard course of action to address the issue at hand.

_____6. Few guidelines are available. The incumbent may consult with technical experts and review relevant professional publications. Decisions require innovation and creativity. The only limitation on course of action is company strategy and policy.

What is the impact of decisions made by the position?

_____1. Inappropriate decisions, recommendations or errors would normally cause minor delays and cost increments. Deficiencies will not affect the completion of programs or projects important to the organization.

_____2. Inappropriate decisions, recommendations or errors will normally cause moderate delays and additional allocation of funds and resources within the immediate work unit. Deficiencies will not affect the attainment of the organization's objectives.

_____3. Inappropriate decisions, recommendations or errors would normally cause considerable delays and reallocation of funds and resources. Deficiencies will affect scheduling and project completion in other work units and, unless adjustments are made, could affect attainment of objectives of a major business segment of the company.

_____4. Inappropriate decisions, recommendations or errors would normally affect critical programs or attainment of short-term goals for a major business segment of the company.

_____5. Inappropriate decisions, recommendations or errors would affect attainment of objectives for the company and would normally affect long-term growth and public image.

The effectiveness of the majority of the position's decisions can be measured within:

_____1. One day.
_____2. One week.
_____3. One month.

_____4. Six months.
_____5. One year.
_____6. More than a year.

Source: Jill Kanin-Lovers, "The Role of Computers in Job Evaluations: A Case in Point," *Journal of Compensation and Benefits* (Warren Gorham and Lamont, New York, N.Y.), Nov–Dec 1985.

paid for in this work?" To illustrate, a scale for measuring the factor "Decision Making" is shown in Exhibit 4.18. Note that it has 3 dimensions: (1) the risk and complexity (hence the guidelines available to assist in making decisions) and (2) the impact of the decisions and (3) the time that must pass before the impact is evident.

Compensable factors should possess the following characteristics:

Work related. They must be demonstrably derived from the actual work performed. Some form of documentation (i.e., job descriptions, job analysis, employee and/or supervisory interviews) must support the factors. Factors that are embedded in a work-related logic can help withstand a variety of challenges to the pay structure. For example, managers often argue that the salaries of their subordinates are too low in comparison to other employees or that the salary offered to a job candidate is too low for the job. Union members may question their leaders about why one job is paid differently from another. Allegations of illegal pay discrimination may be raised. Line managers, union leaders, and compensation specialists must be able to explain differences in pay among jobs. Hence, differences in factors that are work related help provide that rationale. Properly selected factors may even diminish the likelihood of the challenges arising.

Business related. Compensable factors need to be consistent with the organization's culture and values, its business directions, and the nature of the work. Any changes in the organization or its directions may necessitate changing factors. For example, both 3M and TRW recently considered including "Multinational Responsibilities," as shown in Exhibit 4.19, as a factor in their managerial job evaluation plans. Note it is defined in terms of the type of responsibility, the percent of time devoted to international issues, and the number of countries covered. In both firms, strategic business plans call for increased emphasis on international operations, which already account for over 30% of revenues. Consequently, the business related logic is to insure that the compensable factors include international responsibilities in the work. Another example: Burlington Northern revised its job evaluation plan to omit the factor "number of subordinates supervised." While many plans include a similar factor, Burlington Northern decided that a factor that values increases to staff runs counter to the organization's objective of

---

EXHIBIT 4.19
Compensable Factor Definition: Multinational Responsibilities

This factor concerns the multinational scope of the job. Multinational responsibilities are defined as line or functional managerial activities in one or several countries.

1. The multinational responsibilities of the job can best be described as:
    A Approving major policy and strategic plans.
    B Formulating, proposing, and monitoring implementation of policy and plans.
    C Acting as a consultant in project design and implementation phases.
    D Providing procedural guidance and information on well-defined topics.
    E Not applicable.

2. Indicate the percentage of time spent on multinational issues:
    A >50%
    B 25–49%
    C 10–24%
    D <10%

3. The number of countries (other than your unit location) for which the position currently has operational or functional responsibility:
    A More than 10 countries
    B 5 to 10 countries
    C 1 to 4 countries
    D Not applicable

reducing work force size. While major changes in organizations are not daily occurrences, when they do occur the factors need to be reexamined to ensure that they are consistent with the new circumstances.

Acceptable to the parties. Acceptance of the pay structure by managers and employees is critical. This is also true of compensable factors used to slot jobs into the pay structure. To achieve acceptance of the factors, all the relevant parties' viewpoints need to be considered.

An example illustrates the point. A senior manager refused to accept a job evaluation plan unless the factor "working conditions" was included. The compensation specialist, a recent college graduate, demonstrated through statistical analysis that working conditions did not vary enough among 90 percent of the jobs under study to have a meaningful effect on the resulting pay structure; therefore the compensation specialist did not want "working conditions" included. The manager rejected this data, pointing out that the compensation professional had never seen the other 10 percent of the jobs (in the plant's foundry). The manager knew that working conditions were important to the foundry employees. To get the plan and pay decisions based on it accepted, the compensation specialist redesigned the plan to include working conditions.

In addition to being work related, business related, and acceptable, compensable factors should have the ability to differentiate among jobs. As part of differentiating among jobs, each factor must be unique from other factors. If two factors overlap in what they assess in jobs, then that area of overlap will contribute disproportionately to total job points, which may bias the results. Factor descriptions must also possess clarity of terminology so that all concerned can understand and relate to them.

Approaches to Choosing Factors

There are two basic ways to select and define factors: Adapt factors from an existing standard plan, or custom design a plan. In practice most applications fall between these two. Standard plans often are adjusted to meet the unique needs of a particular organization, and many custom-designed plans rely heavily on existing factors.

Adapting factors from existing plans. Although a wide variety of factors are used in standard existing plans, they tend to fall into four generic groups: skills required, effort required, responsibility, and working conditions. These four were used originally in the National Electrical Manufacturers Association (NEMA) plan in the 1930s and are also included in the Equal Pay Act (1963) to define equal work.[33]

Many of the early point plans, such as National Metal Trades Association (NMTA), NEMA, and the Steel Plan, were developed for nonexempt manufacturing and/or office

---

[33]William Gomberg, *A Labor Union Manual on Job Evaluation* (Chicago: Roosevelt College, Labor Education Division, 1947).

jobs.[34] Since then, point plans have also been applied to managerial and professional jobs. The Hay Guide Chart—Profile Method, used by 5,000 employers worldwide (130 of the 500 largest U.S. corporations), is perhaps the most widely used.[35] The three Hay factors—know-how, problem solving, and accountability—and an example of the guide charts are included in Appendix A on pages 574–79. Hay Associates does not define their guide chart–profile method as a variation of the point method. Whether it is a point or factor comparison is less important than recognizing that it is a widely used plan that combines characteristics of both methods. In light of the Hay plan's wide acceptance, the three factors may have implicitly become "universally accepted" descriptors of managerial work.

Adapting factors from existing plans usually involves relying on the judgment of a task force or job evaluation committee. More often than not the committee is made up of key decision makers (or their representatives) from various functions (or units, such as finance, operations, engineering, and marketing).

In the early 1940s, union-management task forces were commonly used to jointly develop job evaluation plans. The Cooperative Wage Study (CWS) undertaken by 12 steel companies and the United Steel Workers designed an industry-wide point plan (the Steel Plan). Joint union-management development of compensable factors has recently resurfaced; AT&T and the CWA, and Borg Warner and the machinists' union are two examples. Not only is increased employee acceptance of a jointly developed plan likely, but employees provide valuable expertise since they are usually the most knowledgeable about the actual work performed.

Custom designed factors. While modifying factors borrowed from standard plans remains a common approach to choosing factors, several employers have custom designed their own plans. Approaches vary, but typically it begins with a task force or committee representing key figures from management. To identify compensable factors involves getting answers to two basic questions:

1. What in the nature of these jobs (work) should we value and pay for?
2. Based on our operating and strategic objections, what should we value and pay for in these jobs?

---

[34]Helen Baker and John M. True, *The Operation of Job Evaluation Plans* (Princeton, N.J.: Princeton University, Industrial Relations Section, 1947); William Gomberg, "A Collective Bargaining Approach to Job Evaluation," *Labor and Nation,* November-December 1946, pp. 46–53; L. Cohen, "Union and Job Evaluation," *Personnel Journal,* May 1948, pp. 7–12; and Boris Shiskin, "Job Evaluation: What It Is and How It Works," *American Federationist,* July-September 1947, p. 213–22.

[35]Hay Associates, *The Guide Chart—Profile Method of Job Evaluation,* 1981. See also The Hay Group Annual Report, 1982; Edward N. Hay and Dale Purves, "A New Method of Job Evaluation," *Personnel,* July 1954, pp. 72–80; Edward N. Hay and Dale Purves, "The Profile Method of High-Level Job Evaluation," *Personnel,* September 1951, pp. 162–70; Edward N. Hay, "The Application of Weber's Law to Job Evaluation Estimates," *Journal of Applied Psychology* 34 (1950), pp. 102–4; Edward N. Hay, "Setting Salary Standards for Executive Jobs," *Personnel,* January/February 1958, pp. 18–21; Edward N. Hay, "Any Job Can be Measured by Its Know, Think, Do Elements," *Personnel Journal,* April 1958, pp. 24–30. See also *Management Job Evaluation Plan,* Human Resources Department, AT&T, July 1979.

Two approaches to soliciting factors seems to have emerged: extensive coverage of managers and employees through focus groups; or selective executive and key manager interviews.

An example illustrates the extensive process. J. C. Penney designed a new managerial job evaluation plan. The process used to generate compensable factors involved over 5,000 of the 15,000 managers whose jobs would eventually be covered by the plan in meetings. A compensation committee combined the lists of factors, refined the factor definitions, and eliminated duplicates and overlapping factors. In the end, six compensable factors were approved by top management (decision making, impact on the company's objectives, communications, supervision and management, knowledge requirements, and internal and external contacts). Two additional factors (stress and employee development) were eliminated because after further discussions with the top executive management, Penney's decided that these two factors were difficult to quantify and tended to be a function of the person, not the job (i.e., what I find "stressful," you may find "energizing"). Since the compensable factors were suggested by such a cross section of the managers, there's little question of their acceptability to those same managers when used to determine pay structures.

Obviously, custom designing factors is time-consuming and expensive. The argument in favor of it rests on the premise that these factors are more likely to be work related, business related, and acceptable to the employees involved.

Several consulting firms adopt a more selective approach to soliciting factors. Early in the design of the point plan, key executives and senior managers are interviewed to collect information on a variety of issues.[36] Questions can cover what the executives see as inequities in current practices, their views on the firm's value system, and future business directions.

Establish Factor Scales

Once the factors to be included in the plan are chosen, scales reflecting the different degrees within each factor are constructed. Each degree may also be anchored by the typical skills, tasks, and behaviors taken from benchmark jobs that illustrate each factor degree. Exhibit 4.20 shows NMTA's scaling for the factor of knowledge.

A major problem in determining degrees is to make each degree equidistant from the adjacent degrees (interval scaling). Belcher suggests the following criteria for determining degrees: (1) limit to the number necessary to distinguish among jobs; (2) use understandable terminology; (3) anchor degree definition with benchmark job titles; and (4) make it apparent how the degree applies to the job.[37] Using too many degrees makes

---

[36]Jill Kanin-Lovers and Michael L. Davis, "Selecting and Defining Job Evaluation Factors," *Journal of Compensation and Benefits,* January–February 1988, pp. 1–38.

[37]Belcher, *Compensation Administration.*

EXHIBIT 4.20
Illustration of a Compensable Factor from National Metal Trades Association

---

1. Knowledge

This factor measures the knowledge or equivalent training required to perform the position duties.

1st Degree

Use of reading and writing, adding and subtracting of whole numbers; following of instructions; use of fixed gauges, direct reading instruments and similar devices; where interpretation is not required.

2nd Degree

Use of addition, subtraction, multiplication and division of numbers including decimals and fractions; simple use of formulas, charts, tables, drawings, specifications, schedules, wiring diagrams; use of adjustable measuring instruments; checking of reports, forms, records and comparable data; where interpretation is required.

3rd Degree

Use of mathematics together with the use of complicated drawings, specifications, charts, tables; various types of precision measuring instruments. Equivalent to 1 to 3 years applied trades training in a particular or specialized occupation.

4th Degree

Use of advanced trades mathematics, together with the use of complicated drawings, specifications, charts, tables, handbook formulas; all varieties of precision measuring instruments. Equivalent to complete accredited apprenticeship in a recognized trade, craft or occupation; or equivalent to a 2-year technical college education.

5th Degree

Use of higher mathematics involved in the application of engineering principles and the performance of related practical operations, together with a comprehensive knowledge of the theories and practices of mechanical, electrical, chemical, civil or like engineering field. Equivalent to complete 4 years of technical college or university education.

---

it difficult for evaluators to accurately choose the appropriate degree and may result in a wide variance in total points assigned by different evaluators, which reduces the acceptability of the system.[38]

Some plans employ two-dimensional grids to define degrees. For example, in the Hay Plan, degrees of the factor know-how are described by four levels of managerial know-how (limited, related, diverse, and comprehensive) and eight levels of technical know-how (ranging from professional mastery through elementary vocational). An evaluator may select among at least 32 (= 4 × 8) different combinations of managerial and technical know-how to evaluate a job.

---

[38]Scaling has emerged as an issue in recent disputes in the State of Minnesota, where comparable worth legislation requires the use of job evaluation by all governmental units. There are several views of how to construct scales. Those who see job evaluation as measurement of value akin to employment tests argue that factor scales should be derived like test scales. Others who see job evaluation as an administrative process to establish acceptable job structures seem to follow more conventional linear or geometric scaling. Finally, some derive the scales empirically by scaling each factor so it best captures a predetermined criteria.

Establish Factor Weights

Once the degrees have been assigned, the factor weights must be determined. Different point plans may assign different weights to factors. For example, the National Electrical Manufacturers Association plans weights education at 17.5 percent; another employer's association weights it at 10.6 percent; a consultants' plan recommends 15.0 percent; and a trade association weights the same factor at 10.1 percent.

Factor weights are important since different weights reflect differences in importance attached to each factor by the employer.

There are two basic methods used to establish factor weights: *committee judgment* and *statistical analysis*. In the first, members of the compensation committee or, in some rare cases, groups of employees are asked to allocate 100 percent of value among the factors. Some structured decision process such as delphi or other nominal group technique may be used to facilitate consensus.[39]

Statistical Approach

In the statistical approach, the weights are empirically derived in such a way as to correlate as closely as possible to a set of pay rates that is agreed upon by the parties involved.[40] Typically those rates are the agreed-upon pay structure for benchmark jobs. By statistically analyzing an agreed-upon pay structure for benchmark jobs on the factor degrees assigned to each job, a set of weights is derived that will produce total job evaluation scores that will closely match the agreed-upon pay structure.

This statistical approach is not new. Edwards, and Otis and Leukart both used it in the 1940s.[41] More recently this approach is being used to establish further weights and scales by most major consulting firms. While each firm's model and computer software are proprietary, at best we can judge the basic approaches that are similar statistically.

Choosing the criterion. The relative weights can reflect whatever criterion is specified. The choice of the criteria is a critical decision since the factor weights and degrees are modeled to reproduce it. Several criteria are available: (1) Current wage rates paid by the firm for benchmarks when these rates are acceptable and the firm simply wants a

[39]Dov Elizur, *Job Evaluation: A Systematic Approach* (London: Gower Press, 1980); Dov Elizur, "The Scaling Method of Job Evaluation," *Compensation Review,* Third Quarter 1978, pp. 34–46; Dov Elizur and Louis Guttman, "The Structure of Attitudes toward Work and Technological Change within an Organization," *Administrative Science Quarterly* 21 (December 1976), pp. 611–21.

[40]Andre L. Delbecq, Andrew H. Van de Ven, and David H. Gustafson, *Group Techniques for Program Planning: A Guide to Nominal Group and Delphi Processes* (Glenview, Ill.: Scott, Foresman, 1975); and D. D. Robinson, O. W. Wahlstrom, and R. C. Mecham, "Comparison of Job Evaluation Methods: A 'Policy-Capturing' Approach Using the PAQ," *Journal of Applied Psychology* 59, no. 5 (1974), pp. 633–37.

[41]Paul M. Edwards, "Statistical Methods in Job Evaluation," *Advanced Management,* December 1948, pp. 158–63; and J. L. Otis and R. H. Leukart, *Job Evaluation: A Basis for Sound Wage Administration* (Englewood Cliffs, N.J.: Prentice-Hall, 1954). See also Eugene J. Benge, "Statistical Study of a Job Evaluation Point System," *Modern Management,* April 1947, pp. 17–23.

job evaluation plan that will reproduce the current structure, or (2) competitive rates paid in the labor market for benchmark jobs. The premise in this case is that the firm wants to set its pay structure to match the structure found in the labor market at a particular time. These two are probably the most common criteria used. But many people object to both of them, because they believe wage rates for some jobs, i.e., those held predominantly by women, are artificially depressed due to historical gender discrimination. Duplicating the existing pay structure, whether within the firm or in the market, perpetuates this discrimination, they say.[42] Other possible criteria include (3) the rates for jobs held predominantly by men (on the grounds that they are the best nonbiased estimates of bias free rates); and (4) wage rates that have been negotiated with employees through collective bargaining. So the criterion for deriving the factor weights and degrees is crucial—it serves as the standard for all pay rates set through job evaluation. Note that the same statistical procedure could be used to capture any pay structure agreeable to the parties involved. For example, the American Federation of State, County, and Municipal Employees negotiated equity pay adjustments for jobs held predominantly by women with the city of San Jose to satisfy a concern about comparable worth.[43] This new pay structure can be described statistically with an adjusted set of factor degrees and weights, and an adjusted job evaluation plan would be capable of reproducing the new pay structure.

The statistical approach is often labeled as *policy capturing* to contrast it with the committee judgment approach. Both approaches are "policy capturing"; only the policy or criterion captured may vary and the method used to capture that policy may vary (statistical versus judgmental).

Are factor weights even required? Studies at AT&T and J. C. Penney suggest that if the comparable factors are richly defined and the factor degrees empirically derived, then weights are empirically unnecessary. Evaluations yielded an agreed-upon pay structure without the use of factor weights. However, the results of job evaluation seem to be more intuitively acceptable to managers and employees if factor weights are included.[44]

Initial results of either the committee judgment or statistical approach for deriving factor weights may not lead to completely satisfactory results. The correspondence between the job evaluation results and the agreed-upon pay structure may not be sufficiently high. Several procedures are commonly used to increase this correspondence. First, the sample of benchmark jobs is often changed through adding or deleting jobs. Second, the factor degree assigned to each benchmark job may be adjusted. Third, the pay structure

---

[42]Donald J. Treiman, "Effect of Choice of Factors and Factor Weights in Job Evaluation," in *Comparable Worth and Wage Discrimination,* ed. H. Remick (Philadelphia: Temple University Press, 1984), pp. 79–89.

[43]Susan L. Josephs, "Equal Pay and Comparable Worth: Collective Bargaining Approaches," unpublished paper, Columbus: Ohio State University; Winn Newman, "Pay Equity Emerges as a Top Labor Issue in the 1980's," *Monthly Labor Review,* April 1982, pp. 49–51; and the MacNeill/Lehrer Report, "Wage Discrimination," Library #1287, Show #6047, New York: Educational Broadcasting Corporation, September 2, 1980.

[44]Richard Arvey, Sex Bias in Job Evaluation Procedures, *Personnel Psychology* 39, 1986, pp. 315–335; and Steve O'Byrne, *TPF&C Report on Statistical Methodology for the Weighted Job Questionnaire* (N.Y.: TPF&C, 1988); and J. E. Laughlin, "Comment on 'Estimating Coefficients in Linear Models: It Don't Make No Never Mind'," *Psychological Bulletin* 8, 1978, pp. 247–53.

serving as criterion may be adjusted. And finally, the weighting scheme may be adjusted. Thus, a task force beginning with exactly the same factors and degrees could end up with very different job evaluation plans, depending on the specific benchmark jobs, the pay structure chosen as the criterion, and the method used to establish the weights.

How many factors? A remaining issue to consider is how many factors should be included. We have already noted that factors must often be included to ensure the plan's acceptance. About 40 years ago Lawshe and others demonstrated that a few factors will yield practically the same results as many factors.[45] Some factors may have overlapping definitions and may fail to account for anything unique in the criterion chosen. In multifactor plans, three to five factors explained most of the variation in the job hierarchy. In a study conducted over 20 years ago, a 21-factor plan produced the same job structure that could be generated using only seven of the factors. Further, the jobs could be correctly slotted into classes using only three factors. Yet the company decided to keep the 21-factor plan because it was "accepted and doing the job."

Combining factor scales and weights. To translate weights and factor scales into actual job points, the maximum number of points to be used in the system is first divided among the factors according to their weights. The points for each factor are then attached to that factor's scale. For example, if the Knowledge factor scaled in Exhibit 4.20 is weighted 20 percent in a 500-point system, then a total of 100 points are assigned to this factor, and each degree of knowledge is worth 20 points.

Single Factor Systems

Single factor job evaluation systems have been proposed by some researchers. They all appear to focus on measuring the amount of discretion an employee has in a job. The two most widely known are Jaques's Time Span of Discretion (TSD) and Arthur Young's Decision Banding.[46] In Time Span of Discretion, each job is comprised of tasks, and each task has an implicit or explicit time before its consequences become evident. Jaques defines TSD as "the longest period of time in completing an assigned task that employees are expected to exercise discretion with regard to the pace and quality of the work without

---

[45]C. H. Lawshe, Jr., "Studies in Job Evaluation. 2. The Adequacy of Abbreviated Point Ratings for Hourly-Paid Jobs in Three Industrial Plants," *Journal of Applied Psychology,* June 1945, pp. 177–84; C. H. Lawshe, Jr., and R. F. Wilson, "Studies in Job Evaluation. 6. The Reliability of Two Point Rating Systems," *Journal of Applied Psychology,* August 1947, pp. 355–65.

[46]Elliott Jaques, *Equitable Payment* (London: Heinemann, 1970); T. T. Paterson, *Job Evaluation,* Vol. 1 (London: Business Books Ltd., 1972); A. W. Charles, "Installing Single-Factor Job Evaluation," *Compensation Review,* First Quarter 1971, pp. 9–21; Jay R. Schuster, "Job Evaluation at Xerox: A Single Scale Replaces Four," *Personnel,* May/June 1966, pp. 15–23; Lee A. Chambliss, "Our Employees Evaluate Their Own Jobs," *Personnel Journal* 29, no. 4 (September 1950), pp. 141–42; Thomas J. Atchison, *A Comparison of the Time-Span of Discretion, A Classification Method of Job Evaluation and a Maturity Curve Plan as Methods of Establishing Pay Differentials for Scientists and Engineers Using Perceived Equity as a Criterion,* unpublished Doctoral Dissertation, Graduate School, University of Washington, Seattle, 1965; and T. T. Paterson, *Job Evaluation,* Vol. 2 (London: Camelot Press Ltd., 1972).

managerial review."[47] According to Jaques, TSD is distinct from job evaluation in that it represents measurement (of time units) rather than subjective judgment.

The single factor used in the Decision Banding method is the decision making required on the job.[48]

The premise underlying these single factor approaches is that the job content or value construct is unidimensional. Elizur, for example, argues that job worth should be measured on the one dimension—freedom of action—which appears to be similar to both the discretion factor used by Jaques and the Decision Banding concept.[49] Perhaps the major complaint about single factor plans is from employees who are not convinced that one factor can adequately represent the entire domain of their jobs.

MARKET PRICING

Another approach, one that differs markedly from the four fundamental job evaluation methods already discussed, is market pricing. Basically, this involves setting pay structures almost exclusively through reliance on rates paid in the external market.

Employers following such an approach typically match a large percentage of their jobs with market data and collect as much market data as possible. Opting for market pricing may reflect an emphasis on external competitiveness and a deemphasis on internal consistency, the relationships among jobs within the firm. Organizations that fill large proportions of their job vacancies with new hires from the outside may become market pricers. The potential problems with market pricing stem from giving up internal relationships among jobs to the vagaries of the external market and therefore your competitors' decisions.

Market pricers often use the ranking method to determine the pay for jobs unique to their firms. Often called "Rank to Market," it involves first determining the competitive

---

[47]Elliott Jaques, *Time Span Handbook* (London: Heinemann, 1964); Elliott Jaques, *Measurement of Responsibility* (London: Heinemann, 1972); and Elliott Jaques, "Taking Time Seriously in Evaluating Jobs," *Harvard Business Review,* September/October 1979, pp. 124–32. See also Michael E. Gordon, "An Evaluation of Jaques' Studies of Pay in the Light of Current Compensation Research," *Personnel Psychology* 4 (1969), pp. 369–89; Paul S. Goodman, "An Empirical Examination of Elliott Jaques' Concept of Time Span," *Human Relations* 20 (1967), pp. 155–70; T. O. Kvalseth and E. R. Crossman, "The Jaquesian Level-of-Work Estimators: A Systematic Formulation," *Organizational Human Performance* 11 (1974), pp. 303–15; J. M. M. Hill, "A Note on Time-Span and Economic Theory," *Human Relations,* November 1958, pp. 373–80.

[48]T. T. Paterson and T. M. Husband, "Decision-Making Responsibilities: Yardstick for Job Evaluation," *Compensation Review,* Second Quarter 1970, pp. 21–31; T. T. Paterson, "The Link between Pay and Decision-Making," *International Management,* December 1977, pp. 14–16; and N. H. Cuthbert and J. M. Paterson, "Job Evaluation: Some Recent Thinking and Its Place in an Investigation," *Personnel Management,* September 1966, pp. 152–62.

[49]Dov Elizur, *Job Evaluation* (Hants, England: Gower Publishing, 1980) (Distributed in North America by Renouf/USA, Brookfield, Vt.); and Dov Elizur, "Facets of Work Values: A Structural Analysis of Work Outcomes," *Journal of Applied Psychology* 69, no. 3 (1984), pp. 379–89.

EXHIBIT 4.21
Market Pricing at Pfizer

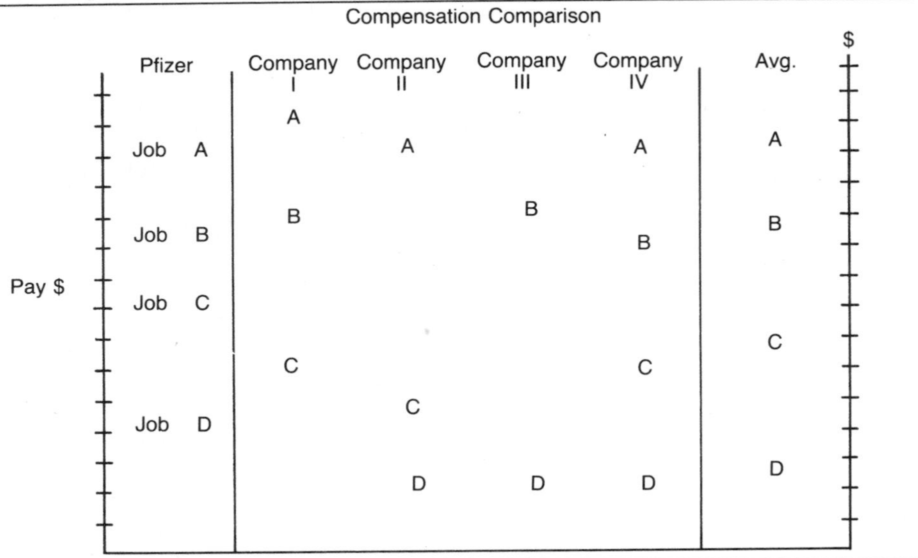

Compensation Comparison

rates for positions for which external market data is available and then blending the remaining (nonbenchmark) jobs into the pay hierarchy.

At Pfizer, for example, job analysis results in written job descriptions. This is immediately followed by labor market analysis and market pricing for as many jobs as possible. Exhibit 4.21 shows Pfizer's pay comparisons with comparable jobs at surveyed companies. After that, the internal job relationships are reviewed to be sure they are "reasonable in light of organization needs." The final step is pricing those jobs not included in the survey. These remaining jobs are compared to the survey positions "in terms of their total value to Pfizer." This internal evaluation seeks to ensure consistency with promotion opportunities and to properly reflect "cross-functional job values," e.g., production versus clerical jobs.

SUMMARY

The differences in pay among jobs within a single organization affect the ability of managers to achieve the objectives of the pay system. Together with job analysis, job evaluation techniques seek to ensure that the job structure is based on the content and relative contributions of the work.

Since its widespread use in the mid-1940s, job evaluation has evolved into many different forms and methods. Consequently, wide variations exist in its use and how it is perceived. This chapter discussed some of the many perceptions of job evaluation's role. No matter how job evaluation is designed, it should be tailored to the unique circumstances in each application.

At this point we have examined the alternative purposes of evaluation, whether to use single or multiple plans, and alternative job evaluation methods. In the next chapter we turn to ensuring the involvement of relevant parties, how to administer the plan once it has been designed, and evaluating its usefulness.

REVIEW QUESTIONS

1. What does job evaluation have to do with internal consistency?
2. What does job evaluation have to do with efficiency and equity?
3. Why do you think the federal government's general schedule plan is not more widely used in private industry?
4. Why are there so many definitions of job evaluation? What would you emphasize in a definition? Why?
5. What are the pros and cons of using multiple evaluation plans within an organization?
6. You are the manager of ten employees. Everyone becomes very suspicious and upset when they get a memo from the personnel deaprtment saying their jobs are going to be evaluated. How will you reassure them?

Compensation Application
Sun State

Sun State is enjoying economic growth. Tax revenues are up, but so is the work load for government employees. Recently there have been increasing complaints about pay. Some employees feel their salary is out of line in comparison to the amount received by other employees. As a first step, Sun State personnel director hired a summer intern to perform job analysis and write job descriptions. The results are shown below. Now, a job structure is needed.

1. Divide into teams of four to six students each. Each team should evaluate the eight jobs and prepare a job structure based on their evaluation.
2. Each team should describe the process the group went through to arrive at that job structure. Job evaluation techniques and compensable factors used should be described, and the reasons for selecting them should be stated.
3. Each team should give each job a title and put its job structure on the board. Comparisons can then be made among job structures of the various teams. Does the job evaluation method used appear to affect the results? Do compensable factors chosen affect the results? Does the process affect the results?
4. Evaluate the job descriptions. What parts of them were most useful? How could they be improved?

JOB A

Kind of Work

Highly responsible administrative work in directing a fiscal management program.

Difficulty and Responsibility of Work

Directs a large and complex fiscal management program in a large state department, agency, or institution. Provides technical and supervisory financial support to carry out policies and programs established by the department head. Serves as the chief liaison to activity managers to ensure coordination of their activities in planning with the accounting division. Maintains a close working relationship with the finance agency controller to ensure compliance with budgetary and financial planning requirements of the Department of Finance. Considerable latitude is granted employee in this class for developing, implementing, and administering financial methods and procedures. Typically reports to a high level department manager with work reviewed through periodic conferences and reports.

Principal Responsibilities

*   Directs all accounting functions of the department, agency, or institution so that adequate financial records and fiscal controls are maintained.

- Provides supervisory and high professional skills for the financial operations of the department consistent with the appropriate state and federal laws and regulations so that state and federal funds are utilized and expanded in the most efficient and effective manner.
- Provides coordination with other state and federal agencies relating to financial matters so that the department head and agency controller are informed as to matters pertaining to policies, procedures, and programs which may have an effect on the financial operation of the department.
- Develops authorized department budgets and financial plans, goals, and objectives for review and approval by the agency controller and the department head so that maximum use will be made of financial resources.
- Consults with and advises the department head, managers, supervisors, and the agency controller on financial policies and procedures, organizational changes, and interpretation of financial data and reports to ensure efficient and effective fiscal management.

Essential Requirements of Work

Knowledge, skills, and *abilities* necessary for functioning at full productivity. (Those asterisked are also essential at entry.)

   Extensive knowledge of the department's accounting structure.
* Extensive knowledge of accounting principles and practices.
* Extensive knowledge of federal government accounting, auditing, and reporting requirements.
* Thorough knowledge of the state's appropriation, budgetary, and accounting systems.
* Ability to direct a large fiscal program involving a considerable number of accounting professionals and technicians.
* Ability to develop and implement procedures to increase the efficiency and effectiveness of the fiscal program.
* Ability to independently carry out department objectives with only limited supervision.
* Ability to prepare and interpret complex fiscal records and reports, recognize problems, and effect solutions.
* Ability to coordinate the fiscal management program with the overall functions of the department.
* Ability to speak and write effectively.
* Ability to establish and maintain effective working relationships with managers, public, and other employees.

JOB B

Kind of Work

Difficult bookkeeping and clerical work in the maintenance of financial records.

Difficulty and Responsibility of Work

Keeps financial records where the accounts are relatively complex or assists higher level accountants and accounting technicians where the accounts are complex and extensive. Differentiated from the account clerk by the difficulty and complexity of the work, the greater use of initiative and independent judgment, and the greater specialized training required.

Receives direction from higher level accounting personnel in the form of a review of work for accuracy and completeness. In some cases, may provide lead work direction to account clerks or clerical personnel engaged in the bookkeeping operation. Prepares relatively simple reports, makes preliminary analyses of financial conditions for use by other employees, and implements minor procedural and transactional changes in the fiscal operation. As opposed to the accounting technician, however, emphasis is on bookkeeping procedures and the smooth transition of fiscal operations.

Principal Responsibilities

- Assists accountants or accounting technicians in a major department in a specific segment of the fiscal operation.
- Maintains the financial records of a moderate size department according to established procedures and makes adjustments to the records as directed.
- Prepares special analytical data for use by other accountants in preparing budget requests or other reports.
- Approves and processes travel, account, invoice, and claim documents for payment.
- Codes and records all receipts and disbursement of funds.
- Reviews encumbrance or liquidation documents for accuracy and conformity with procedures and expedites financial transactions.
- Accesses or inputs information to the statewide accounting system.
- Investigates errors or problems in the processing of fiscal transactions and recommends changes in procedures.
- Issues purchase orders.
- Provides lead work direction to other bookkeeping and clerical employees.
- Performs related work as required.

Essential Requirements of Work

Knowledge, skills, and *abilities* necessary for functioning at full productivity. (Those asterisked are also essential at entry.)

- * Considerable knowledge of office procedures, methods, and equipment.
- * Working knowledge of modern bookkeeping practices.
- * Working knowledge of the State's appropriation, budgeting, and accounting system.
- * Some knowledge of arithmetic and simple mathematics.
- * Ability to do detailed and repetitive work with speed and accuracy.
- * Ability to use a variety of office equipment.

* Ability to establish effective working relationships with the public and other employees.
* Ability to interpret bookkeeping records and documents and prepare information in summary form.
* Ability to understand fiscal procedural and transactional practices.

JOB C

Kind of Work

Highly difficult and responsible fiscal management and supervisory accounting work.

Difficulty and Responsibility of Work

Serves as section chief or top assistant to an accounting director or other high level fiscal management officer in a moderate or large size state department. Directs the activities of an accounting or fiscal management section consisting of several subsections or assists the supervisor with the supervision of a very large and complex accounting operation. Works closely with the chief fiscal officer in formulating fiscal policies and independently establishes new accounts in payroll procedures to accomplish the department's program. Considerable independence of action is granted the employee, with work reviewed through reports and conferences.

Principal Responsibilities

* Prepares and administers the department budget, confers with operating officials on projected needs, and devises methods of adjusting budgets so that agency programs may be carried on efficiently and effectively.
* Provides technical accounting assistance and guidance to operational accounting units within a large or medium size agency so that operating procedures and staff skills will be upgraded on a continuing basis with resultant improvement in quality and reduction in cost.
* Produces special accounting plans, reports, and analyses involving complex accounting methods and principles as a basis for decision making by the chief fiscal officer and the department head.
* Constructs and maintains the department's accounting structure and cost accounting capabilities so the department can conform to legislative intent, meet state and federal regulatory requirements, and provide the department with reporting capabilities.
* Provides coordination and assistance in the revision of present systems and implementation of new systems and procedures that affect the fiscal division so that controls, services, and maximum utilization of available facilities may be maintained.
* Assists in the coordination and ongoing analysis and control of fiscal matters relevant to satellite institutions under departmental supervision.

Essential Requirements of Work

Knowledge, skills, and *abilities* necessary for functioning at full productivity. (Those asterisked are also essential at entry.)

* * Extensive knowledge of accounting principles and practices.
  Thorough knowledge of the department's accounting structure.
  Thorough knowledge of the state's appropriation, budgetary, and accounting systems.
  Thorough knowledge of federal government accounting, auditing, and reporting requirements.
  Considerable knowledge of statutes pertaining to an individual's agency.
* * Ability to plan, assign, and direct the work of a large number of professional and semiprofessional accounting employees.
* * Ability to implement procedures to increase effectiveness and efficiency of employees.
* * Ability to carry out departmental objectives with limited and infrequent supervisory conferences.
* * Ability to prepare and interpret complex fiscal records and reports, recognize problems, and effect solutions.
* * Ability to relate accounting to overall functions of the department.
* * Ability to write and speak effectively.
* * Ability to establish and maintain effective working relationships with managers, public, and other employees.

JOB D

Kind of Work

Difficult and responsible fiscal management and supervisory accounting work.

Difficulty and Responsibility of Work

Maintains a large and complex system of accounts. Serves as a section chief in the finance division of a very large department, maintains large state-federal or state-county accounts, and oversees a major statewide accounting function in the Department of Finance. Responsible for coordinating and supervising the various phases of the accounting function. Responsibility extends to the development of procedure and policies for the work involved. Supervises a staff of account clerks, accounting technicians, and accounting officers.

Principal Responsibilities

* Provides regular budget review so that program managers have adequate funds to be effective.
* Conducts financial analysis for economical and equitable distribution or redistribution of agency resource.
* Prepares long- and short-range program recommendations for fiscal action so that agency policies are consistent.

- Plans and directs the computerization of systems applied to fiscal services to ensure efficient operation.
- Develops and defines accounting office procedures to ensure the efficient delivery of fiscal services.
- Reviews and analyzes cost accounting computer output to ensure proper documentation of projected cost as required by federal policy and procedures.
- Prepares and supervises the preparation of federal budgets and grant requests, financial plans, and expenditure reports so that they accurately reflect needs and intent of the agency.
- Develops accounting and documentation procedures for county welfare departments so that state and federal auditing and reporting requirements are met.
- Establishes and maintains a financial reporting system for all federal and other nonstate funding sources so that all fiscal reporting requirements are adhered to on a timely and accurate basis.
- Assists grantee agencies in proper reporting procedures under federal grant programs so that requirements for reimbursement may be made on a timely basis.
- Determines the statewide indirect costs so that all state agencies are allocated their proportionate share of indirect costs.
- Supervises the review and processing of all encumbrance documents submitted to the Department of Finance so that necessary accounting information is recorded accurately and promptly in the accounting system.

Essential Requirements of Work

Knowledge, skills, and *abilities* necessary for functioning at full productivity. (Those asterisked are also essential at entry.)

    Thorough knowledge of the department's accounting structure.
*   Thorough knowledge of accounting principles and practices.
    Considerable knowledge of the state's appropriation, budgetary, and accounting systems.
    Working knowledge of statutes pertaining to an individual's agency.
*   Ability to supervise clerical and accounting support staff.
*   Ability to prepare and interpret complex fiscal records and reports, recognize problems, and effect solutions.
*   Ability to relate accounting to overall functions of the department.
*   Ability to write and speak effectively.
*   Ability to establish and maintain effective working relationships with managers, public, and other employees.

JOB E

Kind of Work

Specialized bookkeeping and clerical work in the maintenance of financial records.

Difficulty and Responsibility of Work

Keeps financial records where the accounts are relatively simple, or assists accountants and accounting technicians in assigned work of greater difficulty where accounting operations are more complex and extensive. The work involves a combination of clerical and bookkeeping responsibilities requiring specialized training or experience. Receives direction from higher level accounting personnel in the form of detailed instructions and close review for accuracy and conformance with law, rules, or policy. Once oriented to the work, employee may exercise independent judgment in assigned duties.

Principal Responsibilities

- Maintains complete bookkeeping records independently where scope, volume, or complexity is limited or maintains a difficult part of an extensive bookkeeping operation.
- Codes and records all receipts and disbursement of funds.
- Prepares travel, account, invoice, and claim documents for payment.
- Reviews encumbrance or liquidation documents for accuracy and conformity with procedures and expedites financial transactions.
- Prepares financial information for reports and audits, invoices, and expenditure reports.
- Keeps general, control, or subsidiary books of accounts such as cash book appropriation and disbursement ledgers and encumbrance records.
- Accesses or inputs information to the statewide accounting system as directed.
- Performs related tasks as required.

Essential Requirements of Work

Knowledge, skills, and *abilities* necessary for functioning at full productivity. (Those asterisked are also essential at entry.)

- * Working knowledge of office procedures, methods, and equipment.
- * Working knowledge of modern bookkeeping practices.
- * Some knowledge of arithmetic and simple mathematics.
  Some knowledge of the state's appropriation, budgeting, and accounting system.
- * Ability to do detailed and repetitive work with speed and accuracy.
- * Ability to follow detailed instructions.
- * Ability to use a variety of office equipment.

JOB F

Kind of Work

Difficult semiprofessional accounting work.

Difficulty and Responsibility of Work

Performs varied and difficult semiprofessional accounting work within an established accounting system. Maintains a complex set of accounts and works with higher management outside of the accounting unit in planning and controlling expenditures. Works with higher level employees in providing technical fiscal advice and service to functional activities. This class is differentiated from the Accounting Technician level by the difficulty and complexity of work, considerably greater fiscal analysis, evaluation and planning responsibilities, and independence of action. Receives supervision from higher level management or accounting personnel. May provide lead work to lower level accounting, bookkeeping or clerical personnel.

Principal Responsibilities

- Assists the chief accounting officer in the preparation of all budgets to assure continuity in financial operations.
- Prepares and assembles the biennial budget and coordinates all accounting functions for a small department according to overall plan of department head and needs expressed by activity managers.
- Maintains cost coding and allocation system for a major department to serve as a basis for reimbursement.
- Provides accounting and budgetary controls for federal, state, and private grants including reconciling bank statements and the preparation of reports on the status of the budget and accounts.
- Evaluates the spending progress of budget activities, ensures that budgetary limits are not exceeded, and recommends or effects changes in spending plans.
- Provides technical services to divisions of an agency in the supervision of deposits, accounts payable, procurement, and other business management areas.
- Performs related work as required.

Essential Requirements of Work

Knowledge, skills, and *abilities* necessary for functioning at full productivity. (Those asterisked are also essential at entry.)

* Thorough knowledge of bookkeeping procedures and the ability to apply them to accounting transactions.
* Considerable knowledge of the state's appropriation, budgeting, and accounting system.
* Working knowledge of accounting and public financial administration.
* Some knowledge of arithmetic and simple mathematics.
  Some knowledge of federal grant accounting and auditing and reporting requirements.
* Ability to use a variety of office equipment.
* Ability to write and speak effectively.
* Ability to establish and maintain effective working relationships with managers, the public, and other employees.

JOB G

Kind of Work

Entry level professional accounting work.

Difficulty and Responsibility of Work

Performs professional accounting work as the fiscal officer of a small department, institution, or major division, or as an assistant to a higher level accountant in a large fiscal operation. Work involves providing a wide range of accounting services to professional and managerial employees. Assists in the development and maintenance of broad fiscal programs. Regularly performs complex fiscal analysis, prepares fiscal reports for management, and recommends alternative solutions to accounting problems. May supervise account clerks, accounting technicians, or clerical employees engaged in the fiscal operation. Receives supervision from a higher level accountant, business manager, or other administrative employee.

Principal Responsibilities

- Helps administrative employees develop budgets to ensure sufficient funds are available for operating needs.
- Monitors cash flow to ensure minimum adequate operating balance.
- Produces reports so that management has proper fiscal information.
- Submits reports to federal and state agencies to ensure financial reporting requirements are met.
- Analyzes and interprets fiscal reports so that information is available in useful form.
- Instructs technicians and clerks in proper procedures to ensure smooth operation of accounting functions.
- Investigates fiscal accounting problems so that adequate solutions may be developed.
- Recommends and implements new procedures to ensure the efficient operation of the accounting section.
- Interprets state laws and department policies to ensure the legality of fiscal transactions.

Essential Requirements of Work

Knowledge, skills, and *abilities* necessary for functioning at full productivity. (Those asterisked are also essential at entry.)

* Considerable knowledge of accounting principles and practices.
  Considerable knowledge of the state's appropriation, budgetary, and accounting systems.
  Working knowledge of fiscal analysis methods.
  Working knowledge of federal government accounting, auditing, and reporting requirements.

* Ability to prepare and interpret complex fiscal records and reports, recognize problems, and effect solutions.
* Ability to write and speak effectively.
* Ability to establish and maintain effective working relationships with managers, public, and other employees.

JOB H

Kind of Work

Semiprofessional accounting work.

Difficulty and Responsibility of Work

Performs semiprofessional accounting work within an established accounting system. Responsible for maintaining accounting records on a major set of accounts, preauditing of transactions in a major activity, or handling cash receipts in a major facility, and for classifying transactions, substantiating source documents, balancing accounts, and preparing reports as prescribed. Responsible for recognizing errors or problems in the fiscal transactions of an agency and recommending alternative solutions for consideration by other staff. This level is differentiated from the account clerk, senior class, by the semiprofessional accounting work, less emphasis on transactional matters, and greater responsibility for the analysis and preparation of accounting records and reports. Must regularly exercise initiative and independent judgment and may provide lead-work direction to account clerks or clerical employees engaged in the fiscal operation. Receives supervision from an accounting technician, senior business manager, or professional accountant.

Principal Responsibilities

* Controls expenditures so they do not exceed budget totals and prepares allotment requests in the agency's budgetary accounts.
* Processes encumbrance changes of expenditures authorization and adjusts budget as necessary and desired.
* Reconciles department accounting records with the statewide accounting system records documents so that funds may be appropriated, allotted, encumbered, and transferred.
* Authorizes reimbursement for goods and services received by a major department.
* Develops and maintains a system of accounts receivable, including issuance of guidelines for participants and the preparation of state and federal reports.
* Provides daily accounting on loans receivable or financial aids for a major college.
* Audits cost vendor statements for conformity within departmental guidelines.
* Reconciles the payroll disbursements by payroll period for a major organization and prepares spending reports by AID.
* Supervises cash accounting unit and prepares reports on receipts and deposits.
* Performs related work as required.

Essential Requirements of Work

Knowledge, skills, and *abilities* necessary for functioning at full productivity. (Those asterisked are also essential at entry.)

* Considerable knowledge of bookkeeping procedures and the ability to apply them to accounting transactions.
  Considerable knowledge of the state's appropriation, budget, and accounting system.
* Some knowledge of accounting and public financial administration.
* Some knowledge of arithmetic and simple mathematics.
* Ability to use a variety of office equipment.
* Ability to analyze financial records and reports, locate errors, and recommend solutions to procedural or other problems.
* Ability to establish effective working relationships with the public and other employees.

Job Evaluation: Administration

Chapter Outline	**The Parties Involved in Job Evaluation** Compensation/Job Evaluation Committees Employee/Manager Participation **Administering the Plan** Appeals/Review Procedures Training Approve and Communicate Results Final Result: Structure **Evaluate Job Evaluation's Usefulness** Reliability: Consistency of Results Validity: Which Method Does the Job? Costs Gender Effects in Job Evaluation **A Look at Job Evaluation Practices** **Summary**

American Telephone & Telegraph Co. for years had little competition in its business. Their local operating companies petitioned state commissions for rate changes which more often than not were granted. Prices for phone services were calculated on some sense of "adequate return on investment." Profits generated by improved technology in long distance lines were used to hold down charges for local service. But antitrust lawsuits led to the breakup of AT&T. AT&T kept its long distance lines unit, its manufacturing unit (Western Electric), and its research arm (Bell Labs). They were integrated into two major business sections—regulated (long distance calls) and unregulated (information technologies, such as computers or switching equipment). Other subsidiaries and operating companies became completely separate business entities. For the first time, AT&T faced direct competition in both its regulated and unregulated businesses. The company became free to compete in the communications/information industry, and it transformed its basic business directions. Its objectives changed, and as a result, its compensation system also changed. For example, the management job evaluation plan at AT&T was redesigned to include compensable factors which more accurately reflect the new competitive environment. The company asked, "What is it we want to pay for?" and it got a different set of answers than it did under its previous totally regulated environment. As a result of the changing business strategies and technological improvements, the work at nonmanagerial levels also has changed. More work involves information processing. Phones and other equipment are no longer owned, installed, and maintained by AT&T. Rather, the consumers now purchase and install such equipment. Even the telephone is changing. Has anyone not had the experience of calling a business whose phone is answered by a computer that delivers the message, "If you wish to place an order, press 1. If you wish to inquire about an order, press 3. If you wish, etc., etc., etc.," to be finally greeted at the end by a dial tone?

For AT&T managers, the balance shifted from emphasis on government and public relations to increasing market share and profitability. While the job evaluation plans may retain a "skills required" factor, the nature of the required skills is being redefined and reweighted to reflect more accurately the changing environment, technologies, and strategies. At one newly created regional phone company, Bell South, the job evaluation plan was modified to reflect movement into new business ventures such as Hispanic yellow pages, cellular phones, and building services. So it is with other employers: the job evaluation system must be designed and administered in a manner consistent with the organization's strategies and objectives.

We began our discussion of job evaluation in the previous chapter. Recall the major decisions already discussed: (1) determine the purpose of job evaluation, (2) decide whether to use single or multiple plans and (3) choose among job evaluation methods. The remaining decisions include: (4) ensure the involvement of relevant parties and (5) evaluate the plan's usefulness.

THE PARTIES INVOLVED IN JOB EVALUATION

Who should be involved in designing job evaluation? The choice is usually among compensation professionals, managers, and/or jobholders. If job evaluation is to be an aid to managers and if maximizing employee understanding and acceptance is an important objective, then all these groups need to be included.

Compensation/Job Evaluation Committees

A common approach to gaining acceptance and understanding of pay decisions is through use of a compensation (job evaluation) committee. Membership on these committees seem to vary among firms. All include representatives from key operating functions, and some even include nonmanagerial employees. In some cases the committee's role is only advisory; in others its approval may be required for all major changes. Some go so far

EXHIBIT 5.1
Roles of Job Evaluation Committee Members

Leader	Committee Members	Facilitator	Job Expert
• Understand evaluation plan	• Understand evaluation plan	• Understand evaluation plan	• Clarify job analysis data
• Listen	• Listen	• Listen	• Provide additional job content information
• Keep the group moving	• Discuss facts and assumptions	• Ask questions to facilitate objectives	• Serve as an advisor
• Encourage participation	• Analyze information objectively	• Make suggestions on group process	• Can be a temporary "voting" member
• Prevent individuals from dominating	• Ask questions	• Help group reach a consensus	
• Express own opinion	• Formulate and express opinion	• Can be a full committee member	
• Encourage consensus	• Encourage and reach consensus	• Maintain documentation	
	• Commit to participation and timetable		

Source: Jill Kanin-Lovers, "Using Committees to Evaluate Jobs," *Journal of Compensation and Benefits* (Warren Gorham and Lamont, New York, N.Y.), July–Aug., 1986.

as to prescribe roles, similar to those shown in Exhibit 5.1, for members. Very little information is available on the composition of committees, their roles, or even whether their use makes any difference in the results obtained and their acceptance by employees and managers.

Employee/Manager Participation

Participation in the design and administration of compensation plans seems related to increased trust and commitment on the part of employees and managers. Procedural equity, discussed in Chapter 2, is related to participation.

Research strongly suggests that attending to the equity of the procedures (e.g., job evaluation) rather than to the results alone (e.g., job structures) is likely to sustain employee and managers' commitment, trust and acceptance of the results.[1] And achieving procedural equity is related to employee participation. One study, for example, examined

---

[1] R. Folger and M. A. Konovsky, "Effects of Procedural and Distributive Justice on Reactions to Pay Raise Decisions," *Academy of Management Journal* (in press); J. Greenberg, "Reactions to Procedural Injustice in Payment Distributions: Do the Ends Justify the Means?" *Journal of Applied Psychology* 72 (1987), pp. 55–61; and R. Folger and J. Greenberg, "Procedural Justice: An Interpretative Analysis of Personnel Systems," in *Human Resources Management,* eds. K. M. Rowland and G. R. Ferris, vol. 3 (Greenwich, Conn.: JAI Press, 1985), pp. 141–83.

a pay plan designed by a committee of employees and managers.[2] Within six months after the plan went into effect, significant improvements occurred in turnover and satisfaction with pay and administration. These improvements were attributed to employee participation.

The absence of participation may make it easier for employees and managers to imagine ways the structure might have been rearranged to their personal liking. Crepanzano and Folger observed ". . . if people do not participate in decisions, there is little to prevent them from assuming that things would have been better, if I'd have been in charge."[3] Additional research is needed to ascertain if the payoffs from increased participation offset potential costs (time involved to reach consensus, potential problems caused by disrupting current perceptions, etc.).

For example, the involvement of both operating managers and compensation professionals raises the potential for conflict due to their differing perspectives. Operating managers may wish to adjust the job title for a star performer, in order to exceed the maximum pay permitted for the present job title. The compensation specialist wishes to ensure the policy of consistent treatment across the entire organization and is aware of the difficulty caused by a title and pay change unconnected to a change in the actual work performed. Note the differences in focus. The manager has operating objectives to achieve, does not want to lose a key performer, and views compensation as a mechanism to help accomplish this. The compensation specialist on the other hand adopts an organization-wide perspective and focuses on ensuring that the system is managed consistently and fairly throughout the organization.

To what extent should unions be involved? Management probably will find it advantageous to include union representation as a source of ideas and to help promote acceptance of the results. For example, both at AT&T and at a Borg-Warner facility, union-management task forces participated in the design of new job evaluation systems. Their roles involved mutual problem solving. Other union leaders feel that philosophical differences prevent their active participation in job evaluation.[4] They take the position that collective bargaining yields more equitable results than does job evaluation. In other

---

[2]Edward E. Lawler III and J. Richard Hackman, "Impact of Employee Participation in the Development of Pay Incentive Plans: A Field Experiment," *Journal of Applied Psychology* 53, no. 6 (December 1969), pp. 467–71; D. E. Ewing, *Freedom Inside the Organization* (New York: E. P. Dutton, 1978); Carl F. Frost, John W. Wakely, and Robert A. Ruh, *The Scanlon Plan for Organization Development: Identity, Participation, and Equity* (East Lansing: Michigan State Press, 1974); E. E. Lawler, "Creating High Involvement Work Organizations," in *Perspectives on Organizational Behavior*, 2nd ed., ed. J. R. Hackman, E. E. Lawler, and L. W. Porter (New York: McGraw-Hill, 1982); K. C. Sheflen, E. E. Lawler, and J. R. Hackman, "Long-Term Impact of Employee Participation in the Development of Pay Incentive Plans: A Field Experiment Revisited," *Journal of Applied Psychology* 55 (1971), pp. 182–86; E. A. Locke and D. M. Schweiger, "Participation in Decision Making: One More Look," *Research in Organization Behavior* (Greenwich, Conn.: JAI Press, 1979); J. F. Carey, "Participative Job Evaluation," *Compensation Review*, Fourth Quarter 1977, pp. 29–38; and G. J. Jenkins, Jr., and E. E. Lawler III, "Impact of Employee Participation in Pay Plan Development," *Organizational Behavior and Human Performance* 28 (1981), pp. 111–28.

[3]R. Crepanzano and R. Folger, "Referent Cognitions and Task Decision Autonomy: Beyond Equity Theory," *Journal of Applied Psychology* (in press).

[4]Mike Burns, *Understanding Job Evaluation* (London: Institute of Personnel Management, 1978).

cases, jobs are jointly evaluated by union and management representatives, and disagreements are submitted to an arbitrator. So the extent of union participation varies.

In 1971 and again in 1978, Janes surveyed the leaders of 38 unions representing over 7.2 million members.[5] While in 1971 the leadership viewed job evaluation as a threat to collective bargaining, by 1978 Janes identified a trend toward its acceptance. Leaders who oppose evaluation do so because they feel it is not understood by their members or because job descriptions on which evaluation is based may be poorly written. More recently a few leaders have advocated the adoption of job evaluation as a means of assessing comparable worth.[6] It appears that no single union perspective exists on the value of job evaluation, just as no single management perspective exists.

ADMINISTERING THE PLAN

Our previous chapter led us through the design of a job evaluation plan. The output of the design phase is typically a manual to assist in applying the plan. The manual becomes the "yardstick" for the plan. It contains information on the job evaluation plan, including a description of the method used. If there are compensable factors, these are defined in the manual, along with enough information to allow the user to recognize varying degrees of compensable factors. Information needs to be detailed enough to permit accurate and rapid evaluation of the bulk of jobs.

Appeals/Review Procedures

No plan anticipates all situations. It is inevitable that some jobs will be incorrectly evaluated, or at least employees and managers may suspect incorrect evaluation. Consequently, the manual needs to contain review procedures to handle such cases and to help ensure procedural equity. Often the compensation specialist can handle most reviews, but sometimes the assistance of the compensation committee is required. Very occasionally these take on the trappings of formal grievance procedures (e.g., documented complaints and responses, levels of approval, and so on). More often problems are handled by managers and the compensation professional through "open door" arrangements.

Training

Once the job evaluation manual is complete, those who will be applying the job evaluation methodology require training in its proper use, especially those evaluators who come from outside the personnel department. These employees may also need background

---

[5]Harold D. Janes, "Union Views on Job Evaluation, 1971 vs. 1978," *Personnel Journal,* February 1979, pp. 80–85; "Job Evaluation Plans," *Collective Bargaining Report,* June 1957, pp. 33–39.

[6]Winn Newman, "Pay Equity Emerges as a Top Labor Issue in the 1980s," *Monthly Labor Review,* April 1982, pp. 49–51; Lisa Portman, Joy Ann Grune, and Eve Johnson, "The Role of Labor," in *Comparable Worth and Wage Discrimination,* ed. H. Remick (Philadelphia: Temple University Press, 1984); and K. S. Koziara, "Comparable Worth: Organizational Dilemmas," *Monthly Labor Review,* December 1985, pp. 13–16.

information on the entire pay system and how it is related to the overall strategies for managing human resources and the organization's objectives.

Approve and Communicate Results

When the evaluations are completed, approval by higher levels in the organization (e.g., vice president of human resources) is usually required. The particular approval process differs among organizations; Exhibit 5.2 is one example. The approval process serves as a control. It helps ensure that any changes that result from job evaluation are consistent with the rest of the organization's operations and directions.

The emphasis on employee and manager understanding and acceptance of the job evaluation requires that communications occur during the entire process. The goals of the system, the parties' roles in it, and the final results need to be explained.

Final Result: Structure

The final result of the administration phase is a hierarchy of jobs. This hierarchy translates the employers' internal consistency policy into practice. Exhibit 5.3 shows four hypothetical job structures within a single evaluation. These structures were obtained via different approaches to job evaluation. The jobs are arrayed in hierarchies within four basic functions: managerial, technical, manufacturing, and administration. The managerial structure was obtained via a point plan, technical and administrative jobs via two different classification plans, and the manufacturing hierarchy via a point system that was negotiated with the union. The point of Exhibit 5.3 is to illustrate the results of job evaluation: a job structure that should be consistent with the policy of internal consistency. The exhibit also illustrates that it is common for organizations to have multiple structures derived through multiple procedures. Consistency in such cases may be interpreted as consistency within each functional group or unit. While some employees in one job structure may wish to compare the procedures used in another structure versus their own, the underlying premise in the illustration and in practice is that internal equity (consistency) is most influenced by fair and equitable treatment of employees doing similar work (other jobs

EXHIBIT 5.2
Job Evaluation Approval Process

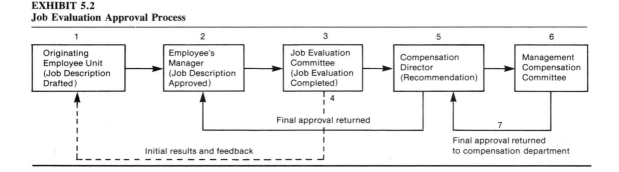

EXHIBIT 5.3
Resulting Job Structures

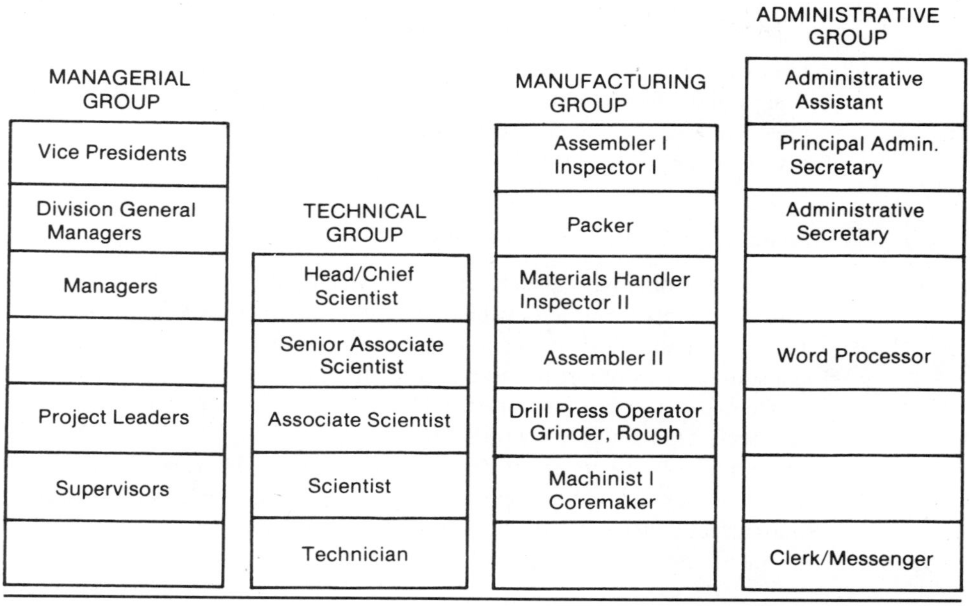

MANAGERIAL GROUP	TECHNICAL GROUP	MANUFACTURING GROUP	ADMINISTRATIVE GROUP
Vice Presidents		Assembler I Inspector I	Administrative Assistant
Division General Managers	Head/Chief Scientist	Packer	Principal Admin. Secretary
Managers	Senior Associate Scientist	Materials Handler Inspector II	Administrative Secretary
	Associate Scientist	Assembler II	Word Processor
Project Leaders	Scientist	Drill Press Operator Grinder, Rough	
Supervisors	Technician	Machinist I Coremaker	
			Clerk/Messenger

in the same skill group) rather than dissimilar work. Some evidence supports this premise; however, little is known about the stability of such comparisons under different conditions.

Once the structure or structures are established, compensation managers must ensure that they remain equitable. This requires seeing that jobs which employees feel are incorrectly evaluated are reanalyzed and reevaluated (e.g., appeals/review procedures) and that new jobs or those that experience significant changes get submitted for evaluation.

EVALUATE JOB EVALUATION'S USEFULNESS

The usefulness of any management system is a function of how well it accomplishes its objectives.[7] Job evaluation is no different; it needs to be judged in terms of its objectives. In the previous chapter we noted that pay structures are intended to influence a wide variety of employee behaviors, ranging from staying with an employer to investing in additional training and willingness to take on new assignments. Consequently, the structures obtained through job evaluation ought to be evaluated in terms of their ability to affect such decisions. Unfortunately, little of this type of evaluation seems to be done.

---

[7]Edward E. Lawler III, "What's Wrong with Point-Factor Job Evaluation," *Compensation and Benefits Review,* March–April 1986, pp. 20–28 (also reprinted in *Personnel,* January 1987).

More often than not, job structures are compared to what other employers are doing rather than to whether they aid employees and the organization.

On the other hand, the job evaluation procedures per se, rather than the structure obtained, have been subjected to extensive evaluation. In general, these efforts focus on job evaluation as a measurement device: its reliability, its validity, the costs included in design and implementation, and its compliance with laws and regulations. Ignored in these analyses has been research on the procedural equity of job evaluation. But let us review some of the work that has been reported.

Reliability: Consistency of Results

Job evaluation involves substantial judgment. Reliability refers to the consistency of results obtained from job evaluation conducted under different conditions. For example, to what extent do different job evaluators produce similar results? Few employers or consulting firms report the results of their studies. However, several research studies by academics have been reported.[8] These studies present a mixed picture; some report relatively high consistency (different evaluators assign the same jobs the same total point scores), while others report lower agreement on the values assigned to each specific compensable factor. Some evidence also reports that evaluators' background and training may affect consistency of the evaluations. An evaluator's affiliation with union or management appears to have little effect on the consistency of the results.[9]

---

[8]Several studies on the reliability of job evaluation plans have been reported. Four reviews provide useful overviews: R. Arvey, "Sex Bias in Job Evaluation Procedures," *Personnel Psychology,* Summer 1986, pp. 315–35; D. P. Schwab, "Job Evaluation and Pay Setting: Concepts and Practices," in *Comparable Worth: Issues and Alternatives,* ed. E. R. Livernash (Washington, D.C.: Equal Employment Advisory Council, 1980), pp. 49–78; R. J. Snelgar, "The Comparability of Job Evaluation Methods," *Personnel Psychology* 36 (1983), pp. 371–80; and R. M. Madigan, "Comparable Worth Judgments: A Measurement Properties Analysis," *Journal of Applied Psychology* 70 (1985), pp. 137–47. Other references include: G. Satter, "Method of Paired Comparisons and a Specification Scoring Key in the Evaluation of Jobs," *Journal of Applied Psychology* 33 (1949), 212–21; R. Richardson, *Fair Pay and Work: An Empirical Study of Fair Pay Perception and Time Span of Discretion* (Carbondale: Southern Illinois University Press, 1971); D. Doverspike and G. Barrett, "An Internal Bias Analysis of a Job Evaluation Instrument," *Journal of Applied Psychology* 69, no. 4 (1984), pp. 648–62; P. Ash, "The Reliability of Job Evaluation Rankings," *Journal of Applied Psychology* 32 (1948), pp. 313–20; D. J. Chesler, "Reliability and Comparability of Different Job Evaluation Systems," *Journal of Applied Psychology* 32 (1948), pp. 465–75; D. Doverspike, A. M. Carlisi, G. V. Barrett, and R. A. Alexander, "Generalizability Analysis of a Point-Method Job Evaluation Instrument," *Journal of Applied Psychology* 68 (1983), pp. 476–83; C. H. Anderson and D. B. Corts, *Development of a Framework for a Factor Ranking Benchmark System of Job Evaluation,* TS-73-3 (Washington, D.C.: U.S. Civil Service Commission, Personnel Research and Development Center, 1973); R. D. Arvey, S. E. Maxwell, and L. M. Abraham, "Reliability Artifacts in Comparable Worth Procedures," *Journal of Applied Psychology* 70, no. 4 (1985), pp. 695–705; and T. Naughton, "Effects of Female-Linked Job Titles on Job Evaluation Ratings," *Journal of Management* 14, 4 (1988), pp. 567–78.

[9]C. H. Lawshe, Jr., and P. C. Farbo, "Studies in Job Evaluation: 8. The Reliability of an Abbreviated Job Evaluation System," *Journal of Applied Psychology* 33 (1949), pp. 158–66; Francis D. Harding, Joseph M. Madden, and Kenneth Colson, "Analysis of a Job Evaluation System," *Journal of Applied Psychology,* no. 5 (1960), pp. 354–57; F. G. Moore, "Statistical Problems in Job Evaluation," *Personnel,* September 1946, pp. 125–36; Marvin G. Dertien, "The Accuracy of Job Evaluation Plans," *Personnel Journal,* July 1981, pp. 566–70.

Using evaluators who are familiar with the jobs appears to enhance reliability.[10] This result lends support to the practice of involving employees in the evaluation process. One study reports that the job evaluation results obtained through a group consensus process were similar to those obtained by independent evaluators or an average of individual evaluator's results.[11] The group consensus process, a device widely used in practice, has each evaluator make a preliminary independent evaluation. Then, meeting as a job evaluation committee, they discuss their results until consensus emerges.

While all this research is interesting, it fails to address a key issue—to what extent does the degree of reliability of job evaluation influence pay decisions and employees' attitudes and work behaviors? Only one study has directly addressed this issue. In it, Madigan examined three different job evaluation plans: a guide chart method similar to the Hay Guide Charts presented in Appendix A on page 574, the Position Analysis Questionnaire discussed in Chapter 3, and a custom-designed point plan using six factors (knowledge, experience, interpersonal skill, supervisory, decision making, and fiscal responsibilities).[12] He found that interrater evaluations (consistency among raters) was high and compared favorably to results of studies discussed above. However, when he examined the impact of the results from different plans on actual pay decisions, he found significant differences. For example, when different evaluators used the custom-designed point plan (the most reliable one), Madigan found that their pay recommendations for the jobs agreed in only 51 percent of jobs. The differences in results translated into a range of ± 160 evaluation points, which meant significant differences in the pay for employees. Madigan points out that by traditional academic standards, the reliability of these three methods was acceptable. However, from a manager's perspective, it is not. Madigan observes, "The assessment of potential error . . . in job evaluation must go beyond reliability estimates to include the estimates of impact of pay decisions."[13]

Validity: Which Method Does the Job?

The choice among ranking, classification, factor comparison, and point methods depends on the circumstances and objectives faced. Does it make any difference? Do the results obtained differ?

Validity refers to the degree to which a job evaluation method yields the desired results. The desired results can be measured several ways: (1) the hit rate (percentage of correct decisions it makes), (2) convergence (agreement with results obtained from other

---

[10]J. M. Madden, "The Effect of Varying the Degree of Rater Familiarity in Job Evaluation," *Personnel Administrator* 25 (1962), pp. 42–45; R. E. Cristal and J. M. Madden, *Effect of Degree of Familiarity in Job Evaluation* (Lackland Air Force Base, Tex.: Personnel Laboratory, Wright Air Development Division, 1960).

[11]D. P. Schwab and H. G. Heneman III, "Assessment of a Consensus-Based Multiple Information Source Job Evaluation System," *Journal of Applied Psychology,* in press.

[12]Madigan, "Comparable Worth Judgments."

[13]Ibid.

job evaluation plans), and (3) employee acceptance (employee and manager attitudes about the job evaluation process and the results).[14]

Hit rates: agreement with predetermined benchmark structures. The hit rate approach focuses on the ability of the job evaluation plan to replicate a predetermined, agreed-upon job structure. The agreed-upon structure, as we discussed in the last chapter, can be based on several criteria. The jobs' market rates, or a structure negotiated with a union or a management committee, or rates for jobs held predominately by men or some combination of these are all examples. Exhibit 5.4 shows the hit rates for a hypothetical job evaluation plan. The agreed-upon structure has 49 benchmark jobs in it. This structure was derived through negotiation among managers serving on the job evaluation committee along with market rates for these jobs. The job evaluation plan placed only 14 or 29 percent of the jobs into their current (agreed-upon) pay classes and comes within ± one pay class for 82 percent of the jobs in the agreed-upon structure. In a study conducted at Control Data Corporation, the reported hit rates for six different plans ranged from 49 to 73 percent of the jobs classified with ± 1 class of their current, agreed-upon classes.[15] In another validation study Madigan and Hoover applied two job evaluation plans (a modification of the federal government's Factor Evaluation System and the Position Analysis Questionnaire discussed in Chapters 3 and 4) to 206 job classes for the State of Michigan.[16] They reported rates ranging from 27 to 73 percent, depending on the scoring method used for the job evaluation plans.

Is a job evaluation plan valid (i.e., useful) if it can correctly place only one third of the jobs? As with so many questions in compensation, the answer is "it depends." It depends on the alternative approaches available, on the costs involved in designing and implementing these plans, and on the magnitude of errors involved in missing a "direct hit." If, for example, being within ± 1 pay class translates into several hundred dollars in pay, then employees probably aren't going to express much confidence in the "validity" of this plan. If, on the other hand, the pay difference between ± 1 class is not great *or* the plan's results are treated only as an estimate to be adjusted in the job evaluation committee, then its "validity" (usefulness) is more likely.

Convergence of results. Job evaluation plans can also be judged by the degree to which different plans yield similar results. The premise is that convergence of the results

---

[14]Validity can also be reflected in the R^2 and standard error of estimate generated via regressing benchmark job's wages on compensable factors. R^2 alone is insufficient because it only reflects the strength of the relationship. The error terms are also important, since they reflect the precision with which job grade and pay decisions can be made. Hit rates, in a general sense, capture the R^2 and standard error information. For an early discussion of validation and job evaluation, see William M. Fox, "Purpose and Validity in Job Evaluation," *Personnel Journal* 41 (1962), pp. 432–37.

[15]L. R. Gomez-Mejia, R. C. Page, and W. W. Tornow, "A Comparison of the Practical Utility of Traditional, Statistical, and Hybrid Job Evaluation Approaches," *Academy of Management Journal* 25 (1982), pp. 790–809.

[16]R. M. Madigan and D. J. Hoover, "Effects of Alternative Job Evaluation Methods on Decisions Involving Pay Equity," *Academy of Management Journal,* March 1986, pp. 84–100.

EXHIBIT 5.4
Illustration of Plan's Hit Rate as a Method to Judge the Validity of Job Evaluation Results

Total Jobs: 49

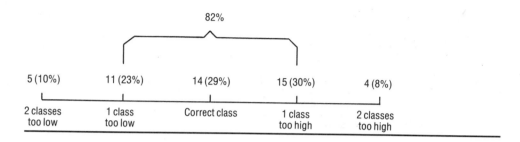

from independent methods increases the chances that the results, and hence the methods, are valid. Different results, on the other hand, point to lack of validity. For the best study to date on this issue, we again turn to Madigan's report on the results of three job evaluation plans (guide chart, PAQ, and point plan).[17] He concludes that the three methods generate different and inconsistent job structures. Further, he states that the measurement adequacy of these three methods is open to serious question. An employee could have received up to $427 per month more (or less), depending on the job evaluation method used.

These results are provocative. They are consistent with the proposition that job evaluation, as traditionally practiced and described in this and other textbooks, is not a measurement procedure. This is so because it fails to consistently exhibit properties of reliability and validity. However, it is important to maintain a proper perspective in interpreting these results. To date, the research has been limited to only a few employers. Further, few compensation professionals seem to consider job evaluation a measurement tool in the strict sense of that term. More often, it is viewed as a procedure to help rationalize an agreed-upon pay structure in terms of job and business-related factors. As such, it becomes a process of give and take, not some immutable yardstick. This perspective leads us to a third criteria used to judge the validity of a job evaluation plan: acceptance among the parties involved.

Acceptability. Acceptance by the employees and managers involved remains a key test of job evaluation. A recurring theme in this book is that the usefulness of pay techniques must include assessing employee and manager acceptance.

Several devices are used to assess and improve acceptability of job evaluation. An obvious one is the inclusion of a *formal appeals process,* discussed earlier. Employees

---

[17]Madigan, "Comparable Worth Judgments"; also see Doverspike and Barrett, "Internal Bias Analysis," and Richardson, *Fair Pay.*

EXHIBIT 5.5
Illustrations of Audit Indexes

A. Overall indicators.
   1. Ratio of numbers of current descriptions to numbers of employees.
   2. Number of job descriptions evaluated last year and previous year.
   3. Number of jobs evaluated per unit.
      (a) Newly created jobs.
      (b) Reevaluation of existing jobs.
B. Timeliness of job descriptions and evaluations.
   1. Percent of total jobs with current descriptions.
   2. Percentage of evaluation requests returned within 7 working days, within 14 working days.
   3. Percentage of reevaluation requests returned with changed (unchanged) evaluations.
C. Workability and acceptability of job evaluation.
   1. Percentage of employees (managers) surveyed who know the purposes of job evaluation.
   2. The numbers of employees who appeal their job's evaluation rating.
   3. The number of employees who receive explanations of the results of their reevaluation requests.

---

who feel their jobs are incorrectly evaluated should be able to request reanalysis and reevaluation. Most firms respond to such requests from managers, but few extend the process to all employees, unless those employees are represented by unions who have negotiated a grievance process. They often justify this differential treatment on the basis of fears of being inundated with requests. Employers who open the appeals process to all employees theorize that jobholders are the ones most familiar with the work performed and the most sensitive to significant changes or misrepresentations. No matter what the outcome from the appeal, the results need to be explained in detail to anyone who requests reevaluation.

A second method of assessing acceptability is to include questions about it in *employee attitude surveys*. Questions can assess perceptions of how useful job evaluation is as a management tool. Another method is to *audit* how the plan is being used based on a series of measures of use. Exhibit 5.5 lists examples of indexes used by various employers. These indexes range from the percentage of employees who understand the reasons for job evaluation to the percentage of jobs with current descriptions, to the rate of requests for reevaluation.

As noted earlier, stakeholders of job evaluations extend beyond employees and managers, to include unions and, some argue, comparable worth advocates. The point is that acceptability is a somewhat vague test of the job evaluation—acceptable to whom is an open issue. Clearly managers and employees are important constituents because acceptance makes it a useful device. But as we will discuss in the chapter on pay discrimination (Chapter 14), others have a stake in job evaluation and the pay structure.

Costs

How costly is job evaluation? Two types of costs associated with job evaluation can be identified: (1) design and administration costs and (2) labor costs that result from pay structure changes occasioned by job evaluation. The labor cost effects will be unique for each application. Little recent data has been published on design and administration costs.

Winstanley offers a rule of thumb of 1 to 3 percent of covered payroll.[18] Recent experience suggests that costs can range from a few thousand dollars for a small organization to over $300,000 in consultant fees alone for major projects in firms like Digital Equipment, 3M, TRW, or Bank of America.

Gender Effects in Job Evaluation

Much attention has been directed at job evaluation as both a potential source of bias against women and as a mechanism to reduce bias.[19] Chapter 14 presents an extended discussion of pay discrimination and the use of job evaluation to establish a pay structure based on a policy of comparable worth. At this point we will discuss some of the studies of the effects of gender in job evaluation and then consider some recommendations offered to ensure bias-free job evaluation.

It has been widely speculated that job evaluation is susceptible to gender bias. To date, three ways that job evaluation can be biased against women have been studied.[20]

Jobholder's gender. Direct bias occurs if jobs held predominantly by women are undervalued relative to jobs held predominantly by men, simply because of the jobholder's gender. The evidence to date does not support the proposition that the gender of the jobholder influences the evaluation of the job. This evidence is drawn from several studies. Arvey, Passino, and Lounsbury found no effects when they varied the gender of jobholders using photographs and recorded voices.[21] They used the PAQ to evaluate the jobs. One study even reported a slight point bias in favor of female-linked *job titles* (e.g., orderly vs. nurses aide). The evaluators received extensive training in potential gender bias; hence, they may have "bent over backwards" to avoid it.[22] In another study, Grams and Schwab found no effects when they varied the gender of jobholders by simply telling

---

[18]Based on one of N. Winstanley's many welcome notes to us about the real world of compensation management.

[19]D. J. Treiman and H. I. Hartmann, eds., *Women, Work and Wages: Equal Pay for Jobs of Equal Value* (Washington, D.C.: National Academy of Sciences, 1981); H. Remick, *Comparable Worth and Wage Discrimination* (Philadelphia: Temple University Press, 1984); and R. G. Blumrosen, "Wage Discrimination, Job Segregation, and Title VII of the Civil Rights Act of 1964," *University of Michigan Journal of Law Reform* 12, no. 3 (1979), pp. 397–502.

[20]This discussion is adapted from D. Schwab and R. Grams, "Sex-Related Errors in Job Evaluation: A 'Real-World' Test," *Journal of Applied Psychology* 70, no. 3 (1985), pp. 533–59; and R. D. Arvey, "Sex Bias in Job Evaluation Procedures."

[21]Richard D. Arvey, Emily M. Passino, and John W. Lounsbury, "Job Analysis Results as Influenced by Sex of Incumbent and Sex of Analyst," *Journal of Applied Psychology* 62, no. 4 (1977), pp. 411–16; Carol T. Schreiber, "Job Evaluation and the Minority Issue." Paper presented at Industrial Relations Counselors Symposium, Atlanta, Georgia, September 1978, pp. 14–15; J. Goodman and J. Morgan, "Job Evaluation Without Sex Discrimination," *Personnel Management* 11, no. 10, October 1979, pp. 158–67; Catherine M. Meek, "Auditing Your Job Evaluation Plan—A Case Study," *EEO Today,* Spring 1979, pp. 21–27.

[22]Michael K. Mount and Rebecca A. Ellis, "Investigation of Bias in Job Evaluation Ratings of Comparable Worth Study Participants," *Personnel Psychology,* Spring 1987, pp. 85–96.

evaluators that varying proportions of men and women performed the jobs.[23] They also used 103 compensation specialists as evaluators in another study and again found no evidence that the gender of the jobholder influenced the results of job evaluation.[24] This conclusion must be tempered by the evidence of gender effects in other studies.[25] For example, Barrett and Doverspike report that while jobholders' gender had no effects on the job's total evaluation, it appears that specific compensable factors may be biased for or against gender-segregated jobs.[26]

Another study found those factors related to job content (e.g., contact with others and error in judgment) did reflect bias while others pertaining to employee requirements, (e.g., education and experience required) did not.[27] Two job descriptions, executive secretary and associate professor of nursing, were evaluated. The female-linked title, executive secretary was reportedly undervalued on the job content factors. However the author concludes "that the job evaluation procedures appear to perform their intended purpose; to array jobs in a hierarchy based on job requirements.[28]

The psychological literature identifies a common tendency to make stereotypical assumptions, usually to the detriment of women when compared to men. Perhaps by calling out the job-related criteria for making judgments, job evaluation is able to avoid this bias.

Wages criteria bias. The second potential source of bias affects job evaluation indirectly, through the current wages paid for jobs. In this case, job evaluation results may be biased if the jobs held predominantly by women are incorrectly underpaid. Treiman and Hartmann argue that women's jobs are unfairly underpaid simply because women hold them.[29] If this is the case and if job evaluation is based on the current wages paid, then the job evaluation results simply mirror any bias in the current pay rates. Considering that many job evaluation plans are purposely structured to mirror the existing pay structure, it should not be surprising that the current wages for jobs influence the results of job evaluation. In one study, 400 experienced compensation administrators were sent information on current pay, market, and job evaluation results. They were asked to use this information to make pay decisions for a set of nine jobs. Half of the administrators received jobs linked to men (e.g., over 70 percent of job holders were men—security

---

[23]R. Grams and D. Schwab, "An Investigation of Systematic Gender-Related Error in Job Evaluation," *Academy of Management Journal* 28, no. 2 (1985), pp. 279–90.

[24]Schwab and Grams, "Sex-Related Errors."

[25]L. A. Krefting, P. K. Berger, and M. J. Wallace, Jr., "The Contribution of Sex Distribution, Job Content, and Occupational Classification to Job Sextyping," *Journal of Vocational Behavior* 13 (1978), pp. 181–91; and L. A. Krefting, P. K. Berger, and M. J. Wallace, Jr., "Sextyping by Personnel Practitioners," Paper presented at Academy of Management national meetings, San Francisco, 1978.

[26]Gerald V. Barrett and Dennis Doverspike, "Another Defense of Point-Factor Job Evaluation," *Personnel*, March 1989, p. 33–36.

[27]R. Arvey, "Sex Bias in Job Evaluation Procedures."

[28]T. Naughton, "Effect of Female-Linked Job Titles on Job Evaluation Ratings."

[29]Treiman and Hartmann, *Women, Work and Wages.*

guards) and the jobs given the other half were held predominately by women (e.g., over 70 percent of job holders were women—secretary II). The results revealed several things: (1) Market data had a substantially larger effect on pay decisions than did job evaluations on current pay data. (2) The jobs' gender had no effects. (3) There was a hint of possible bias against physical, nonoffice jobs over white-collar office jobs. This study is a unique look at several factors that may affect pay structures. Other factors, such as union pressures, turnover of high performers, and so on which also affect the decisions were not included. The implications of this evidence are important.[30] If, as some argue, market rates and current pay already reflect gender bias, then these biased pay rates could work indirectly through the job evaluation process to deflate the evaluation of jobs held primarily by women.[31] Clearly the criteria used in the design of job evaluation plans are crucial and need to be business and work related.

Evaluator's gender. The third possible source of gender bias in job evaluation flows from the gender of the individual evaluators. Some argue that male evaluators may be less favorably disposed toward jobs held predominantly by women. To date the research finds no evidence that the job evaluator's gender affects the results.

Several recommendations ensure that job evaluation plans are bias free.[32] Among them are:

1. Ensuring that the compensable factors and scales are defined to include the content of jobs held predominantly by women. For example, working conditions should include the noise and stress of office machines and the working conditions surrounding word processors.
2. Ensuring that factor weights are not consistently biased against jobs held predominantly by women. Are factors usually associated with these jobs always given less weight?
3. Ensuring that the plan is applied in as bias-free a manner as feasible. This includes ensuring that the job descriptions are bias free, that incumbent names are excluded from the job evaluation process, and that women are trained as evaluators.

Some writers see job evaluation as the best friend of those who wish to combat pay discrimination. Bates and Vail argue that without a properly designed and applied system, "employers will face an almost insurmountable task in persuading the government that

---

[30]S. Rynes, C. Weber, and G. Milkovich, "The Effects of Market Survey Rates, Job Evaluation, and Job Gender on Job Pay," *Journal of Psychology* (in press); and D. Doverspike and G. Barrett, "An Internal Bias Analysis of a Job Evaluation Instrument," *Journal of Applied Psychology* 69 (1984), pp. 648–62.

[31]Grams and Schwab, "Investigation of Systematic Gender-Related Error in Job Evaluation."

[32]Remick, *Comparable Worth and Wage Discrimination;* Helen Remick, "Strategies for Creating Sound, Bias-Free Job Evaluation Plans," Paper presented at Industrial Relations Counselors, Inc., Symposium on Job Evaluation and EEO, September 15 and 17, 1978, Atlanta, Georgia. Also see David J. Thomsen, "Eliminating Pay Discrimination Caused by Job Evaluation," *Personnel,* September–October 1978, pp. 11–22; John Lacy, "Job Evaluation and EEO," *Employee Relations Law Journal* 7, no. 3 (1979), pp. 210–17; and Pay Equity Bureau, *Pay Equity: Equality at Work, Book 3: Interpretation and Wage Adjustments* (Winnipeg, Manitoba: Pay Equity Bureau, 1989).

ill-defined or whimsical methods of determining differences in job content and pay are a business necessity."[33] On the other hand, some lawyers recommend that employers avoid job evaluation on the grounds that the results will lead to lawsuits.

A LOOK AT JOB EVALUATION PRACTICES

A recent survey of job evaluation practices reports the following results.[34]

> Eight-six percent of respondents reported using formal job evaluations for wage determination. A little more than half of the evaluation systems were developed with assistance from outside consultants, while 43 percent were developed by compensation specialists themselves.

On the average, 87 percent of the work force in each firm was covered by a job evaluation program. The use of multiple job evaluation programs was common (59 percent), especially in larger firms. The majority of job evaluation plans relied upon a judgmental weighting of compensable factors (59 percent), as opposed to weighting derived from statistical analysis (40 percent).

Microcomputers and job evaluation. Several compensation consulting firms offer computer-based job evaluation plans. Their software does everything from analyze the job analysis questions, provide computer-generated job descriptions, to predict the pay classes for each job. Some caution is required because "computer assisted" does not equate with more efficient, more acceptable, or cheaper. In a survey of over 1,000 U.S. organizations, 76 percent of respondents currently are not using computer assistance in the job evaluation process.[35] However, approximately 30 percent said they are considering using some form of computer assistance. Complaints about job evaluation voiced by compensation professionals in the survey are that it takes too much time, it's a burdensome bureaucracy, it involves too many people to assure perceived equity, and the accuracy, objectivity, and usefulness of the results remain in question. The primary advantages seen for computer aided job evaluation according to its advocates include:

- Alleviation of the heavy paperwork and tremendous time saving.
- Marked increase in the accuracy of results.
- Creation of more detailed databases.
- Opportunity to conduct improved analysis.[36]

But even with the assistance of computers, job evaluation remains a subjective process that involves substantial judgment. Computers may help reduce the bureaucratic burden

---

[33]Marsh W. Bates and Richard G. Vail, "Job Evaluation and Equal Employment Opportunity: A Tool for Compliance—A Weapon for Defense," *Employee Relations Law Journal* 1, no. 4 (1984), pp. 535–46.

[34]Thomas Mahoney, Sara Rynes, and Benson Rosen, "Where Do Compensation Specialists Stand on Comparable Worth?" *Compensation Review* 16, no. 4 (1984), pp. 27–40.

[35]Fred Crandall, "Micro Computer Use on the Rise in Job Evaluation," *American Compensation Association News,* February 1986, p. 6. A full copy of the report is available from Sibson & Company, 101 N. Wacker Drive, Suite 705, Chicago, IL 60606.

[36]Robert A. Rheaume and Warren W. Jones, "Automated Job Evaluations That Consolidate What Employees Do," *Computers in Personnel,* Summer 1988, pp. 39–45.

that job evaluation often becomes, and it may even help make the process more systematic—but judgment remains.

SUMMARY

This section of the book started by examining pay structures within an organization. The importance placed on internal consistency in the pay structures was the basic policy issue addressed. We pointed out that the basic premise underlying a policy which emphasizes internal consistency is that equitable pay structures and the procedures used to manage them can influence employee attitudes and behaviors. Internal equity, the relationships among jobs within a single organization, is an important part of a policy of internal consistency. Equitable structures, acceptable to the parties involved, affect satisfaction with pay, the willingness to seek and accept promotions to more responsible jobs, and the propensity to remain with the employer, and they also reduce the incidence of pay-related grievances.

The techniques used to help establish internally consistent (equitable) structures typically include job analysis, job descriptions, and job evaluation. Although viewed by some as bureaucratic burdens, these techniques can aid in achieving the objectives of the pay system when they are properly designed and administered. Without them, our pay objective of equity is more difficult to achieve.

In response to challenges to traditional techniques, other approaches such as knowledge or skill-based systems and computer-assisted plans are being implemented. But no matter what mechanism is ultimately used, the purpose remains—to achieve pay structures that will help employees and employers achieve their objectives.

We have now finished the first part of the book. In it, you were introduced to compensation management, and the model that provides a framework for the book. Compensation management requires adapting the pay system to support the organization strategies, its culture, and the needs of individual employees. We examined the first basic policy issue—internal consistency of the pay structures. We discussed the techniques used to establish consistency, and its effects on compensation objectives. The next section of the book focuses on the second major policy issue in our pay model, external competitiveness.

REVIEW QUESTIONS

1. What are the pros and cons of having employees involved in compensation decisions?
2. Thinking back on the earlier chapters of job analysis and job evaluation, what forms can employee involvement take?
3. Where would such involvement be most effective? Easiest to attain?
4. If you were a compensation specialist, how would you recommend your company evaluate the usefulness of its job evaluation systems?
5. What are the sources of possible gender bias in job evaluation?
6. How can compensation specialists and employees insure that job evaluation plans are bias free?

Compensation Application
Hit Rates at Sun State

This case should be done as a follow-up to the Sun State case. Have each team prepare a brief summary of their results of the Sun State job evaluation. The summary should include:

a. The structure that resulted.
b. The job evaluation method used.
c. Compensable factors and weights (if used).

Copies of the summaries from all the teams will be given to all students. Use these summaries and the material in Chapter 5 to answer the discussion questions.

DISCUSSION QUESTIONS

1. Are there any major differences in the proposed structure? Any minor differences? How would you account for these discrepancies (e.g., do the job evaluation method, compensable factors, or weights assigned to factors account for these discrepancies)?
2. How would you resolve these differences?
3. Based on your classmates' results, what conclusions can you draw about the usefulness of various job evaluation techniques?

Compensation Application
Discriminatory Job Factors

The chart below is taken from a United Kingdom Equal Opportunities Commission report. It deals with gender bias in job factors and describes some factors that, in their opinion, strongly favor males or females, weakly favor males or females, or are neutral.

1. Use this chart to analyze the job descriptions in Exhibits 3.12, 3.13, and 3.14 (nurse and personnel vice president). For each description, list any factors that appear to

   a. Strongly favor males.
   b. Weakly favor males.
   c. Are neutral.
   d. Weakly favor females.
   e. Strongly favor females.

What is your overall assessment of the possibility of gender bias in these descriptions?

2. In the same way, analyze the job description you and your teammate prepared in the Compensation Application that followed Chapter 3. Is there gender bias?

EXHIBIT 1
Gender-Biased and Gender-Neutral Job Factors Cited by United Kingdom Equal Opportunities Commission

	Favors Male Jobs			Favors Female Jobs	
	Strongly	*Weakly*	*Neutral*	*Weakly*	*Strongly*
Factors with a time dimension	*Length of service *Experience	*Age *Qualifications *Education *Knowledge *Breadth of know-how *Depth of know-how	*Training period *Level of skill		
Factors with a seniority dimension		*Responsibility for cash or assets *Discretion *Responsibility *Effect of decisions *Supervision of subordinates *Accountability *Decision-making *Planning	*Confidential data/ information		
Factors with a relationship dimension			*Safety of others *Cooperation *Supervising *Creating new business *Communication *Coordination *Personal appearance *Expression	*Contacts: internal/ external *Human relations responsibility *Public relations responsibility *Accuracy	*Caring

(continued)

EXHIBIT 1
Gender-Biased and Gender-Neutral Job Factors Cited by United Kingdom Equal Opportunities Commission

	Favors Male Jobs		Neutral	Favors Female Jobs	
	Strongly	*Weakly*	*Neutral*	*Weakly*	*Strongly*
Factors with a physical activity dimension	*Heavy lifting *Physical hazards *Spatial ability *Unpleasant working conditions	*Technical expertise *Responsibility for equipment *Physical skills *Physical effort *Responsibility for standards *Operational knowledge *Knowledge of machinery, tools and materials	*Safety of others *Stamina *Responsibility for materials *Versatility *Procedural know-how *Fatigue	*Monotony *Visual concentration *Scanning and location of details	*Dexterity *Typing keyboard skills
Factors with a mental activity dimension		*Numerical calculation *Knowledge *Numerical ability *Mathematical reasoning *Problem solving	*Initiative *Originality *Ingenuity *Judgment *Mental effort *Complexity of job *Planning *Verbal comprehension *Verbal expression	*Concentration *Memory *Information ordering	
Factors with a sensory activity dimension		*Differentiating sounds	*Differentiating tastes *Differentiating smells *Visual concentration *Aesthetic appreciation *Tactic sensitivity *Artistic/Musical creativity		

Part 2

2

The objective of Part 2 is to discuss how employers position their pay relative to what competitors are paying. Exhibit II.1 shows how the policy regarding external competitiveness fits into the total pay model. It represents the second of the four major policy decisions in the model. The policy on external competitiveness is important because it expresses the organization's intentions regarding its pay relative to the pay of other employers competing in the same labor and product markets.

External competitiveness involves the determination of a pay level. Three conventional alternatives exist—to lead competition, to match it, or to follow what competitors are paying. Two additional policies emerge from recent practices. One policy is to offer "variable" pay, which varies with the firm's financial success as a result of bonuses paid. During periods of high profits, the pay employees receive may lead the pay offered by other firms. But under weak profits no bonuses are paid and the pay may lag below that offered by others. The other policy is to become the "employer of choice" by emphasizing the total returns in addition to pay such as employment security, added training, opportunity to be part of a highly respected employer, and to work on challenging projects. In practice, some employers use different policies for different units and/or job groups, and there are many different ways to put these policies into practice.

The determination of the policy on external competitiveness depends on three major factors: (1) labor conditions, stemming from competition in the labor market or labor union demands, (2) affordability, stemming from product market conditions and the organization's financial vitality, and (3) the strategic and operating objectives that the organization has established.

External competitiveness is critical to the organization's success. Establishing a pay level translates external competitiveness into practice. The pay level has a twofold effect on pay objectives: (1) it directly affects the employer's operating costs (i.e., labor costs), and (2) it directly affects the employer's ability to attract and maintain a stable and qualified work force. Consequently, the policies and practices related to external competitiveness are among the most critical in compensation management.

In Chapter 6, the major factors affecting external competitiveness policies, consequences of these policies, and theories and research related to them are discussed. Chapter 7 discusses the decisions and techniques that translate an employer's external competitiveness policy into pay level.

External Competitiveness: Determining the Pay Level

EXHIBIT II.1
The Pay Model

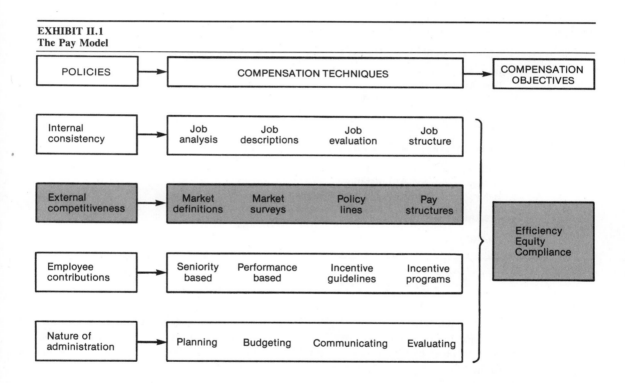

POLICIES	COMPENSATION TECHNIQUES	COMPENSATION OBJECTIVES
Internal consistency	Job analysis Job descriptions Job evaluation Job structure	
External competitiveness	Market definitions Market surveys Policy lines Pay structures	Efficiency Equity Compliance
Employee contributions	Seniority based Performance based Incentive guidelines Incentive programs	
Nature of administration	Planning Budgeting Communicating Evaluating	

167

Chapter

6

External Competitiveness and the Pay Level

Every semester employers make job offers to graduating students. In 1990 students exchanged the data and discovered that the offers ranged from $25,000 to $48,000 per year. The most common was around $37,000. Early in the recruiting season students attributed this range to differences among themselves: grade point average, courses taken, interviewing skills, and analytical and interpersonal abilities. But after some students rejected initial offers, they made an interesting discovery. Employers simply extended the same offer to other students. Why were the offers not changed when extended to different students? If an individual's qualifications do not explain differences in offers, what does? To be sure, some of the pay differences may be related to differences in students, but the better students seemed to get more offers rather than all the higher offers. Location had an effect: higher offers were made by firms located in San Francisco and New York City. The nature of the work also had some effect, with jobs in employment associated with somewhat lower offers than those in compensation and labor relations.

A major difference in job offers was related to the industry to which the different firms belong. Offers from pharmaceuticals, brokerage houses, and petroleum firms tended to exceed those made by consumer products, insurance, banking, and heavy manufacturing firms. Several studies support this significant industry effect on wages. In fact, they report stable industry effects over time; the relatively high paying industries 70 years ago such as autos and pharmaceuticals continue to be relatively high paying today and low wage industries such as education (ouch!) and insurance continue to be lower paying.[1]

What determines these differences in pay levels, and what effects do these differences have on organization performance and employee work behavior? This chapter examines these questions.

EXTERNAL COMPETITIVENESS AND THE PAY MODEL

In practice, policies regarding external competitiveness translate into the employer's pay levels. It is important to understand the two concepts.

> **External competitiveness refers to the pay relationships *among* organizations and the *competitive positions* reflected in these relationships.**

> **Pay level refers to an *average* of the array of rates paid by an employer. It focuses attention on two aspects of pay: (1) the costs of human resources to the employer and (2) the use of pay to encourage workers to seek a job and remain with an employer.**

The link between pay level decisions and operating expenses is easy to understand. Labor costs constitute a significant portion of most organizations' total expenses. Other things being equal, the higher the pay level, the higher the labor costs. Furthermore, the higher the pay level relative to what competition pays, the greater the relative costs to produce similar products. So it would seem that the obvious conclusion is to set the minimum pay level possible.

However, other things are rarely equal. For example, a decision to establish a rel-

---

[1]William T. Dickens and Lawrence F. Katz, "Inter-Industry Wage Differences and Industry Characteristics," in K. Lang and J. Leonard, *Unemployment and the Structure of Labor Markets* (Oxford: Basil Blackwell, 1987); William T. Dickens and Lawrence F. Katz, "Inter-Industry Wage Differences and Theories of Wage Determination" (Cambridge, Mass.: National Bureau of Economic Research Working Paper #2271, 1987); Alan B. Krueger and Lawrence H. Summers, "Reflections on the Inter-Industry Wage Structure," in K. Lang and J. Leonard, *Unemployment and the Structure of Labor Markets* (Oxford: Basil Blackwell, 1987); Alan B. Krueger and Lawrence H. Summers, "Efficiency Wages and the Inter-Industry Wage Structure," *Econometrica,* March 1988, pp. 259–93; and Sumner Slichter, "Notes on the Structure of Wages," *Review of Economics and Statistics,* 32, 1950, pp. 80–91.

atively high pay level may make it easier for the employer to attract and retain a highly qualified work force. One study concluded that high wages and high recruiting costs are substitutes for each other. High-wage employers are able to attract and retain a work force better than low-wage competitors and thus do not have to recruit as extensively. However, other evidence suggests that high-wage employers also expend greater efforts on recruiting—that employers which offer relatively higher wages also exhibit greater recruiting expenses.[2] The logic behind this relationship between high pay level and recruiting behavior is that employers who search more for highly qualified people also pay more to hire them. So the result is that high-paying employers are more likely to attract larger applicant pools and higher quality applicants, which permits such employers to be more selective than would otherwise be the case.

So decisions regarding external competitiveness and pay level are important because they affect the quality of the work force as well as operating expenses and revenues.

No single "going rate." Considering its importance, it is surprising that so little is known about employers' pay policies regarding competitors and their pay level practices. We do know, as graduating students discover each year, that the rates paid for similar jobs and skills vary widely among employers.[3] There is no single "going rate" for a job; rather, an array of rates exists. Notice in Exhibit 6.1 that the salary paid by firms participating in this survey for word processors varies from $6.14 per hour to $12.40 per hour. While some of this difference may be attributable to such factors as experience and seniority within the firm, much of it also reflects different pay levels among employers. The average rate paid by employers ranged from $8.24 per hour to $10.53 per hour.

A survey of aerospace firms reveals wide variation in competitive policies and pay levels.[4] As shown in Exhibit 6.2, the top-paying firm paid more than 21 percent above the average pay in its market, and the bottom one paid more than 13 percent below market (i.e., below the overall average pay of all 21 firms). Despite this apparently wide variation in pay levels, about 70 percent of the firms were within about 10 percent (plus or minus) of the market average.

Even more interesting is the fact that these firms exhibited different competitive positions for different job families. Exhibit 6.3 compares the relationship of the pay levels of two firms (J and S) relative to the market for 13 job families. Note that in company J, average pay for 9 out of 13 job families is above the market. In firm S average pay is above the market in only five job families.

---

[2]John M. Barron, John Bishop, and William C. Dunkelberg, "Employer Search: The Interviewing and Hiring of New Employees," *The Review of Economics and Statistics,* February 1985, pp. 43–52; Harry J. Holzer, "Wages, Employer Costs, and Employee Performance in the Firm," Paper presented at ILR-Cornell Conference on "Do Compensation Policies Matter?" Ithaca, New York, May 24, 1989.

[3]*College Placement Council Salary Survey* is published quarterly by the College Placement Council, Bethlehem, Pa. It reports starting salary offers to college graduates as collected by college placement offices. Data are reported by curriculum, by functional area, and by degree. It is one of several sources employers may use to establish the offers they extend to new graduates.

[4]Ken Foster, "An Anatomy of Company Pay Practices," *Personnel,* September 1985, pp. 67–71.

EXHIBIT 6.1
Salary Survey Results

Word Processing Operator, Lead

Duties

Assumes responsibility for directing work flow through the word processing center or cluster and provides administrative support to principals to improve overall productivity. Uses word processor to type high priority and confidential work.

High school graduate or equivalent, plus three years of work processing (mag card/tape/diskette) experience required.

Job title: Word Process Operator III	*Company Code*	*Minimum Rate*	*Mid Rate*	*Maximum Rate*	*Average Rate*	*Employee Population*
	D	$9.34	$10.88	$12.40	$10.53	1
	Y	$8.23	$9.69	$11.14	$10.53	1
	E	$8.53	$10.07	$11.60	$10.17	3
	YY	$8.71	$10.14	$11.56	$10.01	1
	B	$7.66	$9.59	$11.49	$9.37	2
	N	$7.69	$9.62	$11.55	$9.37	14
	W	$6.68	$10.07	$11.51	$9.05	1
	XX	$7.72	$9.07	$10.89	$9.02	12
	OO	$6.19	$8.05	$9.90	$8.57	2
	Q	$7.22	$9.63	$11.46	$8.49	3
	MM	$6.38	$7.99	$9.59	$8.29	2
	G	$6.14	$7.59	$9.05	$8.24	1
	R	$6.94	$8.55	$10.14	$8.24	3
Straight Average		$7.49	$9.31	$10.94	$9.25	46
Weighted Average		$7.56	$9.31	$11.08	$9.15	

Source: Dallas Area Electronics Survey. Survey sponsors: Recognition Equipment, Rockwell International, Collins Radio Group, and Texas Instruments Inc.

EXHIBIT 6.2
The Relationship of Company Pay Scales to Market Average

	All Jobs (n = 21)		
Company	*Percent*	*Company*	*Percent*
A	+ 21.2	L	− .2
B	+ 17.5	M	− 1.4
C	+ 12.4	N	− 2.0
D	+ 8.7	O	− 4.5
E	+ 7.7	P	− 6.9
F	+ 7.4	Q	− 7.5
G	+ 5.1	R	− 8.1
H	+ 4.2	S	− 10.5
I	+ 2.8	T	− 11.5
J	+ 2.6	U	− 13.6
K	+ 2.5		

The highest 10 percent pay 16.5 percent above market: the highest 25 percent pay 7.5 percent above. The lowest 10 percent pay 11.3 percent below market: the lowest 25 percent pay 7.2 percent below.

Source: Reprinted by permission of the publisher from Kenneth E. Foster, "An Anatomy of Company Pay Practices," *Personnel*, September 1985, p. 68. © 1985 by the American Management Association.

EXHIBIT 6.3
The Relationship of Company Pay Scales to Market Average

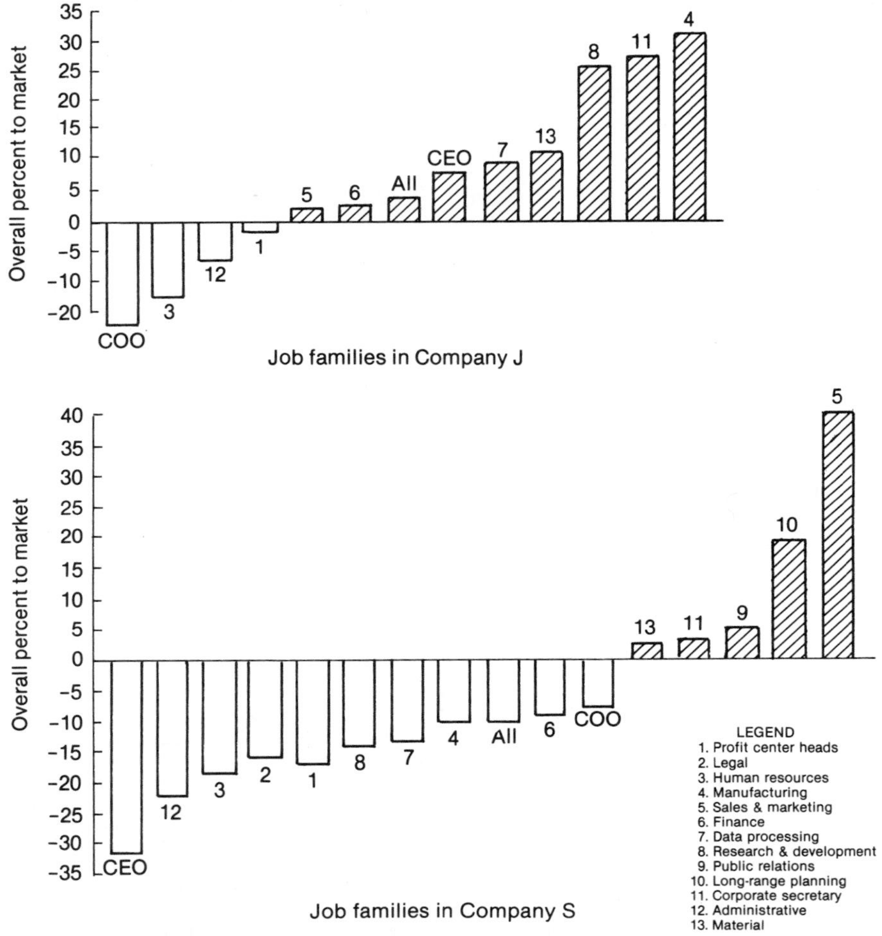

Job families in Company J

Job families in Company S

LEGEND
1. Profit center heads
2. Legal
3. Human resources
4. Manufacturing
5. Sales & marketing
6. Finance
7. Data processing
8. Research & development
9. Public relations
10. Long-range planning
11. Corporate secretary
12. Administrative
13. Material

Source: Reprinted by permission of the publisher from Kenneth E. Foster, "An Anatomy of Company Pay Practices," *Personnel*, September 1985, pp. 69–70. © 1985 by the American Management Association.

While it is risky to infer different competitive policies from these data, it is clear that different employers in the same industry exhibit different pay levels regarding their competitors.[5] Other evidence also suggests that different employers within the same industry adopt different policies and practices regarding external competition and pay

---

[5]Erica Groshen, "Why Do Wages Vary Among Employers?" *Economic Review* Quarter 1, 1988, pp. 19–38; John Dunlop, "The Task of Contemporary Wage Theory," in *New Concepts in Wage Determination*, eds. George W. Taylor and Frank C. Pierson (New York: McGraw-Hill, 1975).

levels.[6] The next section discusses the theories and research related to understanding the factors that determine these differences.

FACTORS INFLUENCING EXTERNAL COMPETITIVENESS AND PAY LEVEL

The factors that affect the determination of external competitiveness and pay level are grouped in Exhibit 6.4. They include the pressures exerted by (1) competition in labor markets for workers with sought-after skills and abilities; (2) competition in product and service markets, which affects the financial condition of the firm; and (3) characteristics unique to each organization and its work force, such as its ability to pay, business strategies, and the productivity and experience of its work force. These factors act in concert to influence pay levels set during the design and administration of pay systems.

EXHIBIT 6.4
Factors Influencing Pay Level

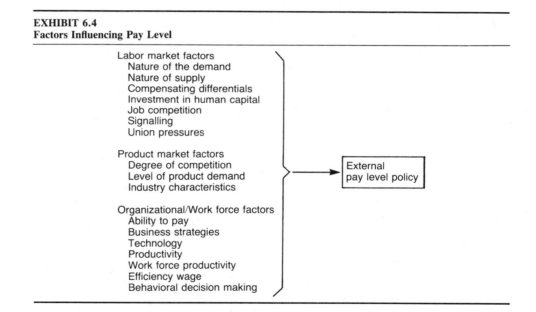

Labor market factors
Nature of the demand
Nature of supply
Compensating differentials
Investment in human capital
Job competition
Signalling
Union pressures

Product market factors
Degree of competition
Level of product demand
Industry characteristics

Organizational/Work force factors
Ability to pay
Business strategies
Technology
Productivity
Work force productivity
Efficiency wage
Behavioral decision making

External pay level policy

[6]Foster, "Anatomy"; George Milkovich, "Compensation Systems in High Technology Companies," in A. Kleingartner and C. S. Anderson, eds., *Human Resource Management in High Technology Firms* (Lexington, Mass.: Lexington Books, 1987), pp. 103–14; Barry Gerhart and George T. Milkovich, "Organizational Differences in Managerial Compensation and Financial Performance," Working Paper 89-09, Center for Advanced Human Resource Studies, Cornell University, Ithaca, New York, 1989; Frederic L. Pryor, "Incentives in Manufacturing: The Carrot and the Stick," *Monthly Labor Review,* July 1984, pp. 40–43; and David Balkin and Luis Gomez-Mejia, "The Relationship between Short-Term and Long-Term Pay Incentives in the High Technology Industry," Working paper, College of Business, Northeastern University, 1985.

LABOR MARKETS

The notion of a market is deceptively simple. Compensation managers often refer to it: "Our pay levels are based upon the market," "We pay competitively with the market," or "We are market leaders." For pay purposes, what precisely are markets?

Economists conceive of them as two basic types: the quoted price and the bourse.[7] Stores that label each item's price or ads that list a job opening's starting wage are examples of quoted price markets. Bourses involve haggling over the terms and conditions; buying a house or signing professional athlete's contracts are examples. Graduating students usually find themselves in a quoted market, though some haggling over the offer may occur. Both types involve an exchange between buyers and sellers; the "buyers" are employers and the "sellers" are workers. In labor markets the mechanisms developed to facilitate the exchange range from college recruiting to want ads and employment agencies.

Regardless of the mechanism, an exchange among employers and workers is necessary and does occur. The exchange involves sharing and evaluating information about the job and inducements offered by the employer and the skills and contributions offered by the worker. If the inducements and contributions offered are acceptable to both parties, some kind of a contract is executed. At times the contract is formal, such as those made with unions, professional athletes, and executive officers. At other times the agreement is informal, with an implied understanding or a brief letter. The result of the workings of the labor market is the allocation of employees to job opportunities at certain pay rates.

How Markets Work

Understanding markets requires analysis of the demand and supply of labor.[8] On the demand side, emphasis is on employers' hiring behavior and how much employers are able and willing to pay for labor. On the supply side, the focus is on the qualifications of workers and the pay that they are willing to accept in exchange for their services. Exhibit 6.5 shows a simple illustration of demand (line D) and supply (line S) for M.B.A.s. The vertical axis represents pay rates from $20,000 a year to $70,000 a year. The horizontal axis scale is the number of M.B.A.s demanded, ranging from 100 to 1,000. At the market level, demand is the sum of all employers' requirements for M.B.A.s at various pay levels. In a downward-sloping demand schedule, the higher the M.B.A. salaries, the fewer M.B.A.s employers will demand. Similarly, the entire market supply of M.B.A.s is the sum of all M.B.A.s who would be interested and available for jobs at different pay levels. In the illustration, the market-determined rate for M.B.A.s is $40,000. That is the rate at which the demand and supply of M.B.A.s are equal. We can think of the pay level as always affected by interaction of supply and demand in the market.

---

[7]For more extended discussion of labor markets, see Arne L. Kalleberg and Aage B. Sorensen, "The Sociology of Labor Markets," *Annual Review of Sociology*, 1979, pp. 351–79; and Michael J. Piore, "Fragments of a 'Sociological' Theory of Wages," *American Economics Association*, May 1973, pp. 377–84.

[8]Ronald G. Ehrenberg and Robert S. Smith, *Modern Labor Economics*, 3rd ed. (Glenview, Ill.: Scott, Foresman, 1988).

EXHIBIT 6.5
Supply and Demand for M.B.A.s in the Short Run

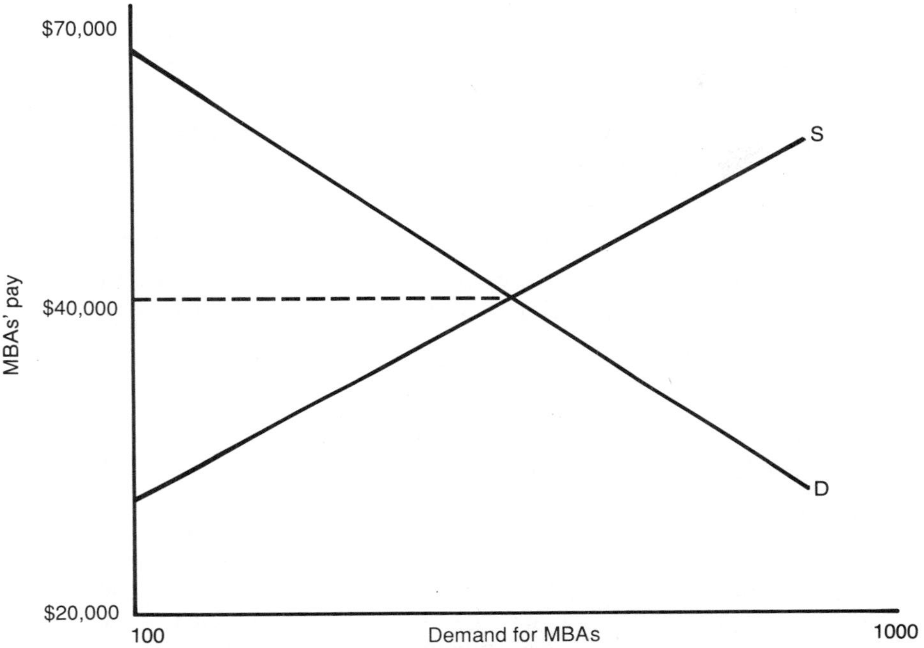

Labor Demand and the Marginal Revenue Product Model

Let us now switch our level of analysis from all employers to the single employer operating in the market. In analyzing a single employer's wage setting and employment behavior, economists simplify the environment with four basic assumptions.[9]

1. Employers seek to maximize profits (the difference between total revenues and total expenses).
2. Human resources are homogeneous and therefore interchangeable; an M.B.A. is an M.B.A. is an M.B.A.
3. The pay rates include *all* costs associated with employing human resources (holidays, benefits, and training, in addition to wages).
4. The markets faced by employers are competitive. This is an important assumption. It implies that there are so many buyers and sellers at any given time that the decisions made by any single employer or worker has negligible impact on the market.

---

[9]For a more generalized discussion of marginal productivity, turn to a basic labor economics text such as Ehrenberg and Smith, *Modern Labor Economics,* or F. Ray Marshall, Vernon M. Briggs, Jr., and Allan G. King, *Labor Economics* (Homewood, Ill.: Richard D. Irwin, 1984).

In the near term, when an employer cannot change technology or capital and natural resources, its level of production can change only if the level of human resources employed is changed. Under such conditions:

> **The additional revenue generated when the firm employs one additional unit of human resources, with other factors held constant, is called the marginal revenue of labor.**

> **The additional output associated with the employment of one additional human resources unit, with other factors held constant, is the marginal product of labor.**

For example, if a compensation consulting firm can service 10 clients per month with two M.B.A.s and 16 with three, the marginal product (the change in output associated with adding additional units of labor) of employing the third M.B.A. is six. But the marginal product of a fourth M.B.A. may not be the same as the marginal product of the third M.B.A. In fact, when we add a fourth M.B.A. to the consulting firm, the marginal productivity falls to four. (Four additional clients can be serviced.) This diminishing marginal productivity results from the fact that as human resources expand, each additional worker has a progressively smaller share of the other factors of production with which to work. Recall that in the short term other factors of production (e.g., office space, computer services) were fixed. As more M.B.A.s are brought into the firm, the marginal productivity must eventually decline.

In the short term, a single employer's demand for labor curve coincides with its marginal product of labor curve. The marginal product curve is downward sloping, indicating that each added unit of labor yields a progressively smaller increment in output.

In order to maximize profits (the first assumption), the employer will continue to employ additional labor until the marginal revenue generated by hiring the last employee is equal to the marginal expenses associated with employing that worker. Marginal revenue is simply the marginal product times the price consumers pay for that product. Since profits equal total revenues minus total expenses, if the labor's marginal revenue exceeds its marginal costs, profits are increased by hiring that additional unit of labor. Conversely, if marginal revenue is less than labor's marginal costs, the employer would lose money on the last hire and could increase profits by reducing labor. Hence, the level of employment that is consistent with profit maximization is that level at which the marginal revenue of the last hire is equal to its marginal costs.

Exhibit 6.6 shows the marginal revenue product model at both the level of the market and of a single employer. The pay level ($40,000) is determined at the market level stated earlier (left side of Exhibit 6.6). The interaction of the sum of *all* employers' demand for human resources and supply of human resources determines the level em-

EXHIBIT 6.6
Demand and Supply at the Market and Firm Level

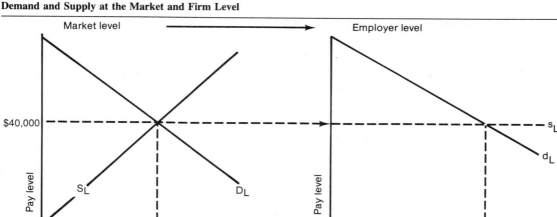

ployers must pay. The employer is a pay level "taker," rather than pay level "maker." On the right side of Exhibit 6.6, supply and demand are analyzed at the level of the individual employer. The market has determined the pay rate ($40,000), and at that rate the individual employer can hire as many M.B.A.s as desired. The supply and demand lines intersect at 20; that is, this employer's marginal revenue will equal marginal cost upon hiring the twentieth M.B.A. So the task for a compensation manager is theoretically simple under the marginal product model: Determine the pay level set by market forces.

Objections to the marginal productivity model. A common objection is that employers have no idea what the marginal productivity of employees is. Compensation managers just do not ask, "What is the marginal revenue product of the last M.B.A. we want to hire?" Perhaps they do consider it, but simply express it differently. At Upjohn, before a new M.B.A. (or any degreed professional) is hired, the manager must justify it by comparing the expected compensation expenses to specific returns expected over a five-year period.[10]

Other objections to the model question its ability to handle the complexities of determining pay in the real world. The model's assumptions oversimplify the real world. For example, the assumed degree of competition among buyers and sellers does not exist,

[10]Henry L. Dahl, "Measuring the Human ROI," *Management Review*, January 1979, pp. 44–50.

nor are factors of production homogeneous, nor are all firms profit maximizers (some maximize market share, long-term profits, and so on). Despite these objections, the model still provides a valuable analytical framework for compensation managers.

Ideally, under the marginal productivity model we would pay individuals according to some function of their productivity times the market price of their product (marginal revenue product = marginal product × price). This is the perfect outcome measure in a conceptual sense. Unfortunately, there are some operational problems in measuring the outcome, specifically:

1. Placing a value on the goods or services an individual produces.
2. Determining individual values on products and services that are produced through joint efforts of different workers with a variety of talents. Labor is heterogeneous, not homogeneous.
3. Factoring the contributions of other resources (capital and raw materials) in the production process.

As a consequence of the difficulty of measuring marginal productivity and marginal revenue, compensation managers propose hypotheses about what types of things produce value in their organizations rather than measuring marginal revenue product directly. In the last two chapters we discussed job evaluation and compensable factors (skills required, financial accountability, external and internal contacts, etc.). In cases where the compensable factors are defined in terms of what management values in work, job evaluation can be thought of as assessing the job's contribution to organization goals (i.e., its marginal revenue product). Partial support for this notion is found in the policy-capturing (regression) approaches to establish the weights for compensable factors. This notion that compensable factors reflect marginal values of work must be treated with caution. Compensable factors are usually defined as input (skills, contacts, responsibilities), not output or the value of the output for each job. Marginal productivity concepts may be applied in establishing the maximum and minimum rates jobs should be paid as well as linking the size of pay increases to performance or productivity improvements. So compensation decisions can be consistent with marginal productivity concepts, and these concepts can help us understand compensation decisions.

Labor Supply

In economic models, the supply of labor is a line or curve (lines S and s in Exhibit 6.6) representing the average pay required to attract different numbers of employees. Like demand curves, the exact shape of the supply of labor varies depending on the assumptions. In perfectly competitive markets, an employer faces a horizontal (elastic) supply curve: The market determines the price, and the individual employer can hire all the employees it wants, at that price. (See Exhibit 6.6, right side.) This model assumes that many workers are seeking jobs, they possess perfect data about job openings, and no barriers to mobility among jobs (no discrimination, licensing provisions, or union membership requirements) exist.

As in the analysis of labor demand, these assumptions greatly simplify the real world.

Perhaps some small employers, such as those in the service industry (e.g., fast foods and convenience stores), operate in such an environment, but most major employers do not.

As the assumptions of the model change to more accurately reflect reality, so do the supply curves. With an upward-sloping curve, from left to right, as shown in Exhibit 6.6, market level means that increased levels of human resources become available at higher pay levels. As pay increases, more people are willing to take a job. This relationship is not meant to imply that pay is the sole determinant of human resource supply. It does imply that the pay level is an important factor influencing the supply of labor.

An upward-sloping supply of labor results from several factors. These include the "net advantage" offered to an individual, the training and investment in human capital required, the degree of competition for job openings, and union pressures.

Compensating differentials and net advantage. More than 200 years ago Adam Smith argued that individuals consider the "whole of the advantages and disadvantages of different employments" and make decisions based on the alternative with the greatest "net advantage."[11] By this he meant that employers must offer higher pay rates to attract workers when

1. Greater time and expense is necessary to acquire the skill and experience required to perform the work.
2. Job security is tenuous.
3. Working conditions are disagreeable.
4. Chances of succeeding on the job are lower.

The theory of compensating wage differentials is the recent rendition of Adams Smith's "net advantage" idea. It suggests that differences in employers' pay levels result from actual (though perhaps unobserved) differences in both jobs and employees. For example, differences in chances for promotion, opportunities to gain experience and training, flexible work schedules, and coworker and supervising relationships as well as location and ease of commuting to and from work all enter into differences among employers. The level of pay necessary to attract and retain employees becomes part of this broader array of differences among employers. Keeping in mind that it is very difficult to measure and control all these factors that may go into "net advantage" calculation, research suggests that aside from high risk of physical injury, the support for the theory of compensating wage differentials is weak.[12] It does, however, have intuitive appeal— if employers wish to increase the number and/or quality of human resources willing to accept employment, they may raise the pay level to offset advantages found in other alternatives.

---

[11]Thomas A. Mahoney, *Compensation and Reward Perspectives* (Homewood, Ill.: Richard D. Irwin, 1979), p. 123.

[12]C. Brown, "Equalizing Differences in the Labor Market," *Quarterly Journal of Economics* 94, 1980, pp. 113–34; and Krueger and Summers, "Efficiency Wages and the Inter-Industry Wage Structure."

Training and investment in human capital. The theory of human capital, perhaps the most influential economic theory for explaining pay differences, is based on the premise that greater earnings flow to those who improve their productive abilities by investing in themselves.[13] Productive abilities are improved by investing in training and even in one's physical health. The expense of acquiring this training and health may create an upward-sloping supply curve. According to the human capital model, the value of an individual's skills and abilities is a function of the time, expense, and other resources expended to acquire them. Consequently, jobs that require long and expensive training (engineering, M.B.A.s, physicians) should receive higher pay levels than other jobs, such as clerical work and even elementary school teaching, which require less investment. According to this logic the time and expenses associated with acquiring the skills act as a barrier and restrict the ease of entry into occupations. Increasing the pay level for these occupations will induce people to develop their human capital and overcome the restrictions. So as pay level increases, the number of people willing to overcome barriers through training increases, creating an upward-sloping supply curve. Research does support the relationship between years of education and experience and earnings, although there is some evidence that suggests that carrying this to a ridiculous extreme—i.e., getting a Ph.D—is not as sound an investment as getting bachelors and masters degrees.[14]

Job competition. The job competition model asserts that workers do not compete for pay in labor markets.[15] Rather, pay for jobs is "quoted" or established, and workers compete through their qualifications for the job opportunities. A pool of applicants develops for every opportunity and individuals in the pool are ranked by prospective employers according to the skills, abilities, and experience required for the job. As the employer dips further and further into the applicant pool, individuals will require more training and will be less productive even though in a quoted market they will receive the same wage. Accordingly, the expenses (pay plus training) associated with each additional unit of labor in the pool increases, leading to an upward-sloping supply of labor curve.

Signalling. The notion of signalling is related to both human capital and job competition models.[16] Managers' decisions about pay "signal" to prospective employees and those currently holding jobs. Thus, pay levels that lead or that offer greater bonus opportunities send different signals from those that meet competitors' pay or offer no bonuses. Signalling works the other way too. Individuals who are better trained (e.g., more schooling, better schools), have higher gpa's in relevant courses, and have related

---

[13]Gary S. Becker, *Human Capital* (Chicago: University of Chicago Press, 1975).

[14]T. N. Daymont and P. J. Andrisiani, "Job Preferences, College Major, and the Gender Gap in Earnings," *Journal of Human Resources,* 19, 1984, pp. 408–28; and Barry Gerhart, "Gender Differences in Current and Starting Salaries: The Role of Performance, College Major, and Job Title," Center for Advanced Human Resource Studies, Cornell University, Working Paper, 88-06, 1988.

[15]Lester C. Thurow, *Generating Inequality: Mechanisms for Distribution in the U.S. Economy* (New York: Basic Books, 1975).

[16]M. Spence, "Job Market Signalling," *Quarterly Journal of Economics,* August 1973, pp. 355–79.

experiences signal prospective employers that they are likely to be better performers. So both investments in human capital (degrees, grades, experience) and pay decisions about level (lead, match, lag) and mix (higher bonuses, benefit choices) act as signals and presumably help better match employees and organizations.

Employer size and other factors. The size of an employer also influences the shape of the supply curve. There is some evidence that larger organizations tend to pay more than smaller ones.[17] Under full-employment conditions, an employer who dominates the labor market has relatively few alternatives from which to attract new applicants. Any increase in employment requires that additional applicants must be induced to enter the labor supply, perhaps from schools, retirement, or more distant areas. Similarly, local applicants have very few alternatives and may have to commute to distant areas if they are rejected by the dominant employer. Corning Glass's influence in Corning, New York, might be an example. Such a dominant employer has relatively wide latitude in determining pay levels, since few alternative jobs exist. However, once the local labor supply is employed, small increases in the pay levels may not be effective in attracting more applicants. Then the supply curve, while upward sloping, may take on the shape of a "step" function, and require large pay increases to attract additional people. Rather than increasing the pay, the firm may opt to lower the job requirements (hire less skilled workers) but this pay savings would tend to be offset by increased training expenses. Small employers competing with a single dominant employer will experience considerable pressure to match the dominant employer's pay level or offer other advantages in order to obtain sufficient labor.

Finally, several other factors, such as geographic barriers, union requirements, lack of information about job openings, the degree of risk involved, and the degree of unemployment present in the market may all influence the supply of labor. For example, during high unemployment the supply curve would become relatively horizontal until the excess labor is absorbed.

In summary, the labor supply curve faced by firms in the short term depends on an individual's perceptions of net advantage, the extent of investment in human capital required, the degree of competition for job openings, the firm's size relative to the market, and other factors. The shape of the supply curve may vary from horizontal, with abundant supply at a given pay level, to upward sloping, requiring higher pay to increase the supply.

Union pressures. Employees organize unions to bargain collectively with management for outcomes they believe are unavailable to them as individuals. Wages and fringe

---

[17]Richard Lester, "Pay Differentials by Size of Establishment," *Industrial Relations*, October 1967, pp. 57–67; Wesley Mellow, "Employer Size and Wages," *Review of Economics and Statistics*, 1982, pp. 495–501; Stanley H. Masters, "Wages and Plant Size: An Interindustry Analysis," *Review of Economics and Statistics*, August 1969, pp. 341–45; David S. Evans and Linda S. Leighton, "Why do Smaller Firms Pay Less?" *Journal of Human Resources*, 24, 2, pp. 299–318; Andrew Weiss and Henry Landau, "Wages, Hiring Standards, and Firm Size," *Journal of Labor Economics*, 2, 4, pp. 477–99; and John E. Garen, "Worker Heterogeneity, Job Screening, and Firm Size," *Journal of Political Economy* 93, 4, pp. 715–39.

benefits, along with job security and grievance handling, are among the most important outcomes. When evaluating their unions, members ranked wage gains first, grievance handling second, fringes third, and job security fourth.[18] Unions' objectives are affected by economic conditions, political considerations within the union, and members' personal needs, among other factors.

Economic models suggest that unions' two basic goals are higher pay and increased membership. Increases in both are preferred, but usually trade-offs occur. If pay (marginal costs) increases more rapidly than productivity (marginal product) and the employer is unable to pass the increased costs on to the consumer, then employment (union membership) may be reduced. On occasion unions may succeed in negotiating both increased wages and membership.[19]

Labor economists have studied the effects of unions on wage levels for years. The relative wage level of union versus nonunion employees seems to depend on the degree of concentration in the industry, the ability to pass wage increases on to consumers in the form of price increases, and the degree that the industry is unionized. Research suggests that unionized employees earn higher wages as compared to nonunion workers. Typical differences range from 5 to 15 percent.[20] The union impact on wages depends on the time period.[21] The union/nonunion wage differential tends to be greatest during depressions or recessions and least during periods of expansion. For example, during 1932–33 (depression years), union presence may have meant more than 25 percent higher wages for unionized compared to nonunion workers.[22] The differential reached a low of about 2 percent in the late 1940s and was below 10 percent in the mid-1980s. In a study of the effects of unions on pay levels of public sector employers, the average wage effect of public sector unions is estimated at +5 percent.[23] The greatest effects are reported for fire fighters (up to 18 percent differential attributed to presence of a union). At the

---

[18]Casey Ichniowski and John Delaney, "Causes and Consequences of How Unionized Employees Get Paid," ILR-Cornell Research Conference on "Do Compensation Policies Matter?" Ithaca, New York: May 23–25, 1989; Thomas A. Kochan, Harry C. Katz, and Robert B. McKersie, *The Transformation of American Industrial Relations* (New York: Basic Books, 1986); Peter Cappelli and Robert B. McKersie, "Labor and the Crisis in Collective Bargaining," in T.A. Kochan, ed., *Challenges and Choices Facing American Labor* (Cambridge, Mass.: MIT Press), 1985, pp. 227–45; Peter Cappelli, "Competitive Pressures and Labor Relations in the Airline Industry," *Industrial Relations,* Fall 1985, pp. 316–38; and Peter Cappelli, "Plant-Level Concession Bargaining," *Industrial and Labor Relations Review,* October 1985, pp. 90–104.

[19]Cappelli, "Plant-Level Concession Bargaining."

[20]H. Gregg Lewis, "Union Relative Wage Effects: A Survey of Macro Estimates," *Journal of Labor Economics,* January 1983, pp. 1–27. Also, Kochan, Katz, and McKersie, *Transformation of American Industrial Relations.*

[21]D.J.B. Mitchell, "Union versus Nonunion Wage Norm Shifts," Working Paper, UCLA, September 1985; Brian Becker, "Concession Bargaining: The Meaning of Union Gains," *Academy of Management Journal,* June 1988, pp. 377–87.

[22]Richard B. Freeman and James Medoff, *What Do Unions Do?* (New York: Basic Books, 1984).

[23]David Lewin, "Public Sector Labor Relations: A Review Essay," in *Public Sector Labor Relations: Analysis and Readings,* eds. D. Lewin, P. Feuille, and T. Kochan (Glen Ridge, N.Y.: Thomas Horton and Daughters, 1977).

other extreme, teachers' unions have not had as great an effect, with only 1 to 4 percent pay level differentials attributed to unions. In sum, it appears that the presence of unions does have a positive effect on pay levels, and this effect is greatest in the private sector during economic downturns and diminishes as the economy expands.

Of practical concern to the compensation manager is defining the specific objectives of each union that represents the organization's employees. Unfortunately, little research has been done that permits translating those objectives into practice. One study measured union member preferences for bargaining outcomes.[24] Using pay increases as a base, it found the proportion of members preferring pension improvements, 42 percent; health insurance, 40 percent; job security, 21 percent; and grievance handling improvement, 15 percent.

Settlements with unions may also influence the compensation of nonunion employees.[25] For example, compensation managers frequently adjust management fringe benefits and services to at least match those negotiated with the union. Pay levels for nonunion supervisors and clerical workers often are set to maintain a differential with union-negotiated wage levels. Finally, some employers adopt higher pay levels to help maintain a union-free status.

Relevant Markets and Multiple Pay Levels

As a practical matter, it has long been recognized that there is no such thing as a single, homogeneous labor market.[26] Rather, employers operate in many labor markets, each with unique demand and supply configurations. A major task for compensation managers is to define the labor markets that are relevant for pay purposes and to establish the appropriate pay levels. The three factors usually used to determine the relevant labor markets are the occupation (qualifications required), the geography (willingness to relocate and/or commute), and the other employers involved (particularly those who market similar goods or services).

Economists conceive of labor markets in terms of all three factors. They consider the skills and qualifications required in an occupation as important because they tend to limit mobility among occupations. This includes licensing and certification requirements as well as training and education. Accountants, for example, would have some difficulty in becoming dentists. Labor markets are organized around occupations.[27]

Qualifications interact with geography to further define the scope of the relevant labor markets. Some skills, such as those possessed by degreed professionals (accountants,

---

[24]Craig A. Olson, "Scaling Union Member Preferences for Bargaining Outcomes," Unpublished paper, Krannert Graduate School of Management, Purdue University, 1979.

[25]Freeman and Medoff, *What Do Unions Do?*

[26]F. Ray Marshall, Allan G. King, and Vernon M. Briggs, Jr., *Labor Economics: Wages, Employment and Trade Unionism* (Homewood, Ill.: Richard D. Irwin, 1984).

[27]Walter Fogel, "Occupational Earnings: Market and Institutional Influences," *Industrial and Labor Relations Review,* October 1979, pp. 24–35; and Krueger and Summers, "Reflections on the Inter-Industry Wage Structure."

engineers, physicians), are recruited nationally. Others (technicians, crafts, and operatives) are recruited regionally and still others (office workers), locally. However, the geographic scope of a market is not fixed. It changes in response to workers' willingness to relocate or commute certain distances. This "propensity to be mobile" in turn may be affected by personal and economic circumstances as well as the pay level established by an employer. Configurations of local markets are even shaped by the availability of convenient public transportation. Furthermore, the geographic limits may not be the same for all in a broad skill group. All M.B.A.s (not a homogeneous group) do not operate in a national market; some firms recruit them regionally, others nationally.

In addition to the occupation and its geography, the industry in which the employer competes also affects the relevant labor markets.[28] Industry effects occur by relating the qualifications to particular technologies and experience as well as by placing a limit on the employer's ability to pay, discussed in the next section. The importance of qualifications and experiences tailored to particular technologies is often overlooked in theoretical analysis of labor markets. But the plant manager of General Motors' diesel locomotive facilities in LaGrange knows that machinists and millwrights who help manufacture parts for locomotives have very different qualifications than those Seattle machinists and millwrights who help Boeing manufacture airplanes.

Surprisingly little research has been done on determining the relevant labor markets for pay determination. Some work has been done with respect to the availability of various skills by minority groups and gender for employment and goal setting in affirmative action.[29] But compensation managers regularly define the relevant markets for various types of labor as part of the process of collecting external pay data. If the markets are incorrectly defined, the estimates of other employers' pay rates may be incorrect and the pay level inappropriately established. Most of the work on defining relevant markets has evolved through wage and salary survey practices. On this issue, academic research seems to offer little guidance to the compensation professional. For example, we have not analyzed the applications for job vacancies to determine the nature of markets. Nor have we ever systematically collected data on the time it takes to fill a job vacancy. Beyond exit interviews, little is known about where valued employees go when organizations fail to retain them and what role pay plays in these decisions.[30]

PRODUCT MARKETS AND ABILITY TO PAY

Affordability and competitive pressures, both national and global, are major factors affecting pay levels. Any organization must, over time, receive enough revenues to cover compensation and other expenses. In the private sector, revenues are generated through

---

[28]Richard H. Thaler, "Interindustry Wage Differentials," *Journal of Economic Perspectives,* forthcoming.

[29]For example, see Frank Krzystofiak and Jerry Newman, "Evaluating Employment Outcomes: Availability Models and Measures," *Industrial Relations,* Fall 1982, pp. 277–92; and Caroline L. Weber and Sara L. Rynes, "Determinants of Job Pay: A Policy-Capturing Investigation," Working paper, Center for Advanced Human Resource Studies, Cornell University, 1988.

[30]Leonard A. Wolff, "Where Do the Workers Go?" *Personnel Administrator,* April 1989, pp. 76–81.

sales of products and services. It follows that an employer's ability to pay is constrained by its ability to compete. So the nature of the product market affects external competitiveness and the pay level the firm sets.[31]

The degree of competition among producers and the level of the demand for products are the two key product market factors. Both affect the ability of the organization to change the prices of its products and services. If prices cannot be changed without suffering loss of revenues due to decreased sales, then the ability of the employer to pay higher rates is constrained.

In effect, the product market factors put a lid on the maximum pay level that an employer can set. If the employer pays more, then it has two options. It can try to pass on the higher pay level through price increases or hold prices fixed and allocate a greater share of total revenues to cover labor costs.

Consider the U.S. auto firms' recent experiences. For many years automakers were able to pass on increased pay levels to the consumer in the form of increased car prices. While competition among the the "Big Three" existed, they all passed on the pay increases. But then the product market revolutionized. The degree of competition from Japan and Korea increased, and due to a slowed economy, the total demand for cars actually declined. Both of these factors constrained the firms' ability to pay and their ability to change the pay level. In response, some autoworkers took pay cuts, accepted smaller wage increases, and agreed to the use of self-managed work teams intended to improve productivity. Publicly available data suggest that General Motors' direct labor costs (blue collar) still account for about 25 percent of total costs, compared to the 15 to 20 percent experienced by Toyota and Honda in their U.S. plants. The wage rates are equal; the Japanese transplants are simply more efficient, and so require less direct labor hours per car.[32]

So the nature of the product demand and the degree of competition in the industry influence the pay level and the ability to change it over time. An employer's ability to finance higher pay levels through price increases depends on the product market conditions. Employers in highly competitive markets will be less able to raise prices without loss of revenues. At the other extreme, monopolists of a product (single sellers) with a very strong demand for the product will be able to raise prices.

Other factors besides the product market conditions affect the ability to pay. Some of these have already been discussed. The productivity of labor, the technology employed, the level of production relative to plant capacity available, and the extent of nonhuman resource expenses all affect ability to pay. These factors vary more across than within industries. The technologies employed and other conditions (e.g., consumer tastes) may differ among auto manufacturers but the differences are relatively small when compared to the technologies and product demand in other industries such as oil or banking. These across-industry differences permit firms to adopt different pay levels.

---

[31]Brian Becker, "Concession Bargaining: The Impact on Shareholders' Equity," *Industrial and Labor Relations Review,* January 1987, pp. 268–79.

[32]Peter F. Drucker, "Low Wages No Longer Give Competitive Edge," *Wall Street Journal,* March 16, 1988, p. 32.

Pay contours. Variations in pay levels from industry to industry are well documented. Dunlop credited differences in wages paid to Boston truck drivers to the existence of wage contours, which he defined as

> a stable group of wage-determining units (bargaining units, plants, or firms) which are so linked together by (1) similarity of product markets, (2) resort to similar sources for a labor force, or (3) common market organization (custom) that they have common wage-making characteristics. The wage rates for a particular occupation in a particular firm are not ordinarily independent of all other wage rates; they are more closely related to the wage rates of some firms than to others.[33]

He noted that truck drivers in the coal industry for example were paid wage rates of about 75 percent of those paid to drivers in the oil industry. These observations, which apply to compensation managers, truck drivers, and most jobs, indicate that employers recruiting from the same labor supply may nonetheless pay significantly different wages. To these data we can add those from Foster's study shown in Exhibits 6.2 and 6.3. Not only do pay levels for the same job differ by industry, they also differ among employers within the same industry and the same geographic location.

ORGANIZATION AND WORK FORCE FACTORS

Conditions in the labor market and product market can be thought of as setting the limits within which the pay level can be established. Since the pay level directly affects operating costs, it must be set with an eye toward competitors' costs and ability to pay. Hence the conditions in the product market set the maximum beyond which the organization will be unable to competitively price its good and services. The labor market pressures establish the minimum pay level that serves to attract and retain a pool of qualified workers. The floor to the minimum is set by minimum-wage legislation. If the compensation manager sets the pay level too low, managers will have trouble attracting and holding the types of employees required. Set the pay level too high and the employer's ability to sell products will be affected.

So the pressures in the product and labor markets create a range of possibilities within which the compensation manager can recommend the pay level be set. "Management in different organizations vary in their motivation patterns (willingness to pay) and in their compensation policies, and they can often set a pay level at various points within the range of possibilities. It is naive . . . to talk of the 'competitive wage,' 'the equilibrium wage' or the 'wage that clears the market.' "[34]

Until now much of the discussion assumed employers operated in product markets and sought profits. Public sector employers do not face product market pressures as

---

[33]Dunlop, "The Task of Contemporary Wage Theory." Also see David A. Pierson and Thomas A. Mahoney, "Labor Market and Employer Ability to Pay as Wage Contour Influences," *Southern Business Review,* Fall 1982, pp. 87–95.

[34]Richard A. Lester, "A Range Theory of Wage Differentials," *Industrial and Labor Relations Review,* July 1952, pp. 483–500.

private sector employers do. Their revenues are generated through legislative budget allocations. These budgets are, in turn, a function of the taxes levied in various jurisdictions. While perhaps not as finely tuned as some product markets, the voters' willingness to pay increased taxes for the services rendered acts as an upper boundary on the pay level analogous to product market forces.

Ability to Pay and Affordability

As noted, the organization's ability to pay directly affects its pay levels. Hence, differences in pay levels observed among employers are related to differences in their ability to afford them. Considerable evidence supports this relationship. Most of the research to date has focused on executive pay. However, a few studies do examine managerial, professional, and blue collar pay levels. We know, for example, that firms with higher profits pay their executives more. An organization with 10 percent larger sales growth pays its executives an average of 3 percent more.[35] And top executive pay has also been linked to stockholder returns (stock prices and dividends). The relation is positive, but small, with a $1,000 change in shareholder wealth (appreciation + dividends) corresponding to a $0.025 change in executive salary plus bonus.[36] A recent study suggested that while an organization's financial performance does affect the pay level, it has a greater effect on the ratio of bonus to base pay and the percent of the workforce eligible for long-term incentives. Specifically, an increase of 10 percent in the ratio of bonus to base pay was related to a .95 percent greater return on assets.[37]

Willingness to pay and pay strategies. Faced with a range of possibilities for setting the pay level, managers survey competitors in labor and product markets to estimate the salaries paid by others. Management motivations and strategies for setting the organization pay level relative to others may differ.[38] Some may opt to set the pay level relatively high in the range to "lead" competition. To the extent possible, they strive to buffer the organization from pressures in the labor and product markets. A lead position is designed to ensure few difficulties in recruiting and hiring as well as to induce the best qualified to apply and hold turnover to a desired level. However, a lead policy without offsetting productivity gains results in higher unit labor costs.

---

[35]George P. Baker, Michael C. Jensen, and Kevin J. Murphy, "Compensation and Incentives: Practice vs. Theory," *Journal of Finance*, July 1988, pp. 593–616.

[36]Ibid.

[37]Gerhart and Milkovich, "Organizational Differences in Managerial Compensation and Financial Performance"; also see Baker, Jensen, and Murphy, "Compensation and Incentives," and George Milkovich and Bonnie Rabin, "Firm Performance: Does Executive Compensation Really Matter?" in F. Foulkes, ed., *Executive Compensation in the 1990s* (Boston: Harvard Business School Press, 1990) for reviews of this literature.

[38]Sara L. Rynes, Donald P. Schwab, and Herbert G. Heneman III, "The Role of Pay and Market Pay Variability in Job Application Decisions," *Organizational Behavior and Human Performance* 31 (1983), pp. 353–64; and Kenneth G. Wheeler, "Perceptions of Labor Market Variables by College Students in Business, Education, and Psychology," *Journal of Vocational Behavior* 22 (1983), pp. 1–11.

Others may decide to "pay with competition" (set the pay level at the average or median of going rates); others may choose to "follow" competition with pay but offer other advantages (job security or short commuting distances) that offset the higher pay offered by competitors. These policies and their consequences are discussed again in the next chapter. At this point it is important to know that employers have options regarding their pay policies toward competitors. Further, as we have already noted, that policy must be coordinated with the overall strategies for managing human resources.

Work force characteristics. The characteristics of the work force, such as its productivity, experience and union affiliation, may affect the employer's pay level decision and consequently its competitive position. Employees with high productivity and more experience may be able to command higher salaries than less productive or less experienced workers. Union affiliation, as we have already noted, affects the pay level, and some evidence suggests that firms with higher proportions of male employees also seem to have pay levels that are higher than the average paid by competing firms. While more research is required, it seems clear that unique characteristics of each organization and its work force affect the variations in pay levels and competitive policies that we observed earlier in this chapter.

Efficiency wage theory. Efficiency wage theory is based on the premise that employees' on-the-job behaviors are very sensitive to decisions about pay levels. Accordingly, employers who set pay levels to lead competitors have more productive workers who, in turn, generate higher profits. The improved productivity comes from three sources: reduced supervision costs, decreased turnover, and improved satisfaction and loyalty to the organization. Economists who seem to value their own jargon say that "monitoring" costs (supervision) decline and decrease workers incentives to "shirk" (screw around) because shirking increases the chances of losing the high paying jobs. Thus, higher wage employers experience higher productivity due to lower monitoring costs and less shirking.[39]

The turnover explanation emphasizes employer's cost of hiring and training. A lead pay level reduces turnover because few better alternatives exist. The loyalty and commitment explanation is closely related. It argues that higher pay levels lead to employee satisfaction with pay and hence to greater loyalty and commitment. We have already seen that the relationship between pay level and satisfaction is reported in behavioral research.[40] But the relationship between satisfaction and productivity is complex. Some suggest that higher performing employees tend to be more satisfied, rather than satisfied employees being more productive.[41]

---

[39]Thaler, "Interindustry Wage Differentials."

[40]H.G. Heneman III, "Pay Satisfaction," in *Research in Personnel and Human Resources Management,* Vol. 3, ed. K.M. Rowland & G.R. Ferris (Greenwich, Conn.: JAI Press, 1985), pp. 115–39.

[41]Larry L. Cummings and Donald P. Schwab, *Performance in Organizations* (Glenview, Ill.: Scott, Foresman, 1973).

Behavioral Decision Models: The Process

Most economic models make heroic assumptions about how individuals react to different pay levels. Rational behavior, or optimizing expected value, is the basic assumption of individual behavior. As we have discussed, higher levels of pay are presumed to elicit less "shirking," greater investment in education and experience, higher average quality, and so on. The image springs to mind of a calculator generating present values of stream of expected payoffs among an array of options. Common sense, not always a reliable source, suggests that those around us seem to behave differently. Nonrational is a more apt descriptor—some suggest irrational.

Given the limited research on how pay level decisions are made or their consequences, the behavioral decision models offer added insights. They focus on how decisions are made and on the devices or crutches individuals use to make decisions. Two such crutches are *representativeness* and *anchoring*. They often lead to nonrational decisions.

Representativeness refers to how a particular event is presumed to represent the entire population. Consider the following example: A manager facing a decision to lead, match, or follow competitors' pay is likely to base that decision on nonrepresentative events. Perhaps a valued employee recently left for a higher paying job. The reason may have had little to do with relative pay but more to other factors such as spouse changing jobs, etc. The point is that individuals faced with decisions tend to overlook how representative are the data on which they base their decision. Rather, they tend to rely on recent and salient events, regardless of their uniqueness.

Anchoring refers to the fact that decision makers tend to focus on the first objective data provided and make only small adjustments from this position. One example is that once the results of a survey reveal what competitors are paying for a job, it is unlikely that managers will deviate from that rate. It serves as an anchor regardless of how representative the data are or how valuable the job is to the particular firm.

Behavioral decision models attempt to capture how managers actually make decisions rather than presuming a rational model.[42]

CONSEQUENCES OF PAY LEVEL DECISIONS

Earlier we noted the degree of competitiveness of the pay level has two major consequences: (1) its effect on operating expenses and (2) its effect on employee attitudes and work behaviors. These consequences, shown in Exhibit 6.7, have been discussed throughout this chapter. All we will do here is to note again that the competitive policy and the pay level are key decisions that affect the performance of the organization.

The pay level directly affects operating expenses and indirectly affects revenues. Wages paid represent an expense, so any decision that affects their level is important. Revenues are indirectly affected by the quality of the work force induced to join and the

[42]D. Kuhneman, & A. Tversky, "Prospect Theory, An Analysis of Decisions Under Risk," *Econometrica*, 47, (2), pp. 263–291, 1979; A. Tversky & D. Kuhneman, "Framing of Decisions and the Psychology of Choice," *Science*, 211 (30), pp. 453–458, January 1981.

productivity and experience levels of those who stay. Reduction in turnover of high performers, increased experience levels, increased probability of remaining union free, and reduction of pay-related grievances and work stoppages are examples of the work behaviors presumed to be affected by pay level decisions. The behavioral effect of pay levels was illustrated in 1988 in Alaska when the national media covered the saga of the three whales entrapped by the advancing ice. A "free-the-whales" effort was launched by the U.S. Government, and a Soviet ice breaker pitched in. Inuits were paid $16 an hour to chainsaw breathing holes for the entrapped whales. When the lucrative government jobs aren't available, the Inuits hunt whales. Clearly, pay level affects Inuit behavior.

From a practical perspective, the manager of the pay system must consider all these factors. The next chapter is devoted to how to set the external competitiveness policy and examines the alternative practices for putting that policy into practice.

From a research perspective, disentangling the relationship among pay level decisions and employee behaviors and organization performance is difficult. We do know that pay level decisions are related to firm performance in the case of the top executives and managerial and professional employers. We also know that the pay mix (bonuses to base pay and long term incentives) appears to be more important than the overall pay level. However, the link between pay levels and the behaviors listed in Exhibit 6.7 remain to be studied.

Before we proceed, let us reemphasize that the major reason we are interested in the external competitiveness policy and the pay level is that they have profound consequences on the organization objectives. As we have already noted, very little research exists to guide us in making pay level decisions. We have clearly established that differences among organizations' competitive policies and pay levels exist. What remains to be better demonstrated are the potential effects different policies will have.

EXHIBIT 6.7
Some Consequences of Pay Levels

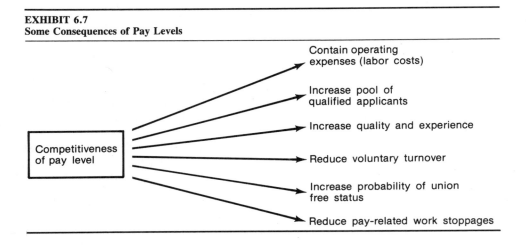

SUMMARY

The pay model used throughout this book emphasizes four basic policy issues—consistency, competitiveness, contributions, and administration. It also emphasizes that policies regarding these four issues need to be designed to achieve specific pay objectives. This section is concerned with external competitiveness, or pay comparisons among organizations. Does Apple Computer pay its bookkeepers the same wage that Virginia Electric and Power pays bookkeepers? Probably not. Different companies pay at different rates; the average of the overall array of rates in an organization constitutes the pay level. Each job family or functional specialty within the organization may have its own pay level. To achieve the objectives stipulated for the pay system, the pay level must be properly positioned relative to competitors. The next chapter discusses how the compensation professional determines this policy and considers the decisions involved and the variety of techniques available to implement decisions.

REVIEW QUESTIONS

1. Distinguish policies on external competitiveness from policies on internal consistency. Why is external competitiveness so important?
2. What factors influence an organization's external competitiveness?
3. What does marginal revenue product have to do with pay?
4. What pay level does the efficiency wage theory predict? Does the theory accurately predict organization behavior? Why or why not?
5. How does the behavioral decision model modify the conventional economic perspective on pay levels?
6. What are the consequences of a lead and/or lag policy?

Compensation Application
Unimerge Corporation

Unimerge Corporation has recently developed a job evaluation plan using the Hay Guide Chart-Profile Method (see Appendix A on page 574). The plan applies to all managerial and professional jobs at Unimerge. Hay consultants have worked with a committee from Unimerge to evaluate all jobs and to develop a job structure based on point assignments. Use of the plan has the solid backing of top management, which has been concerned with the haphazard and inconsistent methods previously used for evaluating and pricing jobs at Unimerge.

The compensation committee has now turned to the task of pricing jobs based on the point evaluations and the resulting structure. While the exact pricing methods are still under discussion, it has been agreed that Hay point ranges will be pegged to compensation ranges.

As methods for pricing the structure are being discussed in more detail, Unimerge's Vice President for Data Processing raises an issue that has just occurred to him. While he feels that the data processing jobs have been evaluated correctly, he notes that the market for these jobs has been very volatile. He has been forced over and over again to match outside pay offers in order to retain critical personnel. If the salaries are determined by Hay points, how will he be able to do this in the future? One of the other committee members suggests that when this occurs, the job in question could be assigned a higher point value.

1. You are the compensation manager responsible for maintaining the compensation program. How do you respond to the concerns of the data processing vice president?
2. How do you respond to the other committee member who proposes assigning a higher point value to jobs with volatile markets?
3. What policy and rationale do you propose for Unimerge for handling such situations in the future?

Designing the Pay Level and Structure

"The desired position in compensation is to be above the market—equal to or better than."

"Our pay philosophy is to be, on the average, better than average."

"The policy for pay and benefits is to be in the top 10 percent."

"The company pays a slight premium in its nonunion plants over the wages paid in the general geographic area for similar work at union plants."

"The pay policy, an unwritten one, is to be competitive with the area. We use our own surveys. We check midpoints, and while the policy is to pay slightly above, in practice we pay at the midpoint. The salaried employees are below midpoint and the hourly people are at the midpoint."

"Our goal is to be in the 65th percentile nationally."[1]

All the above statements are different organizations' policies regarding the competitive position of their pay. Competitive position refers to the comparison of the compensation offered by one employer relative to that paid by its competitors. In the last chapter we discussed the factors that influenced these policies. The amount and types of the compensation competitors offer—base salary, incentive potential, types of benefits—are critical. Other factors that influence an employer's competitive position include the nature of competitors in its product/service markets and labor markets. Labor market factors include the supply of qualified workers and the demand for these workers from other firms. Organizational factors such as the employer's financial condition, technology, work force demographics, productivity, and the influence of unions may also influence a firm's competitive pay policies. In this chapter we examine how organizations use these factors to determine their competitive position and design externally competitive pay levels and structures.

MAJOR DECISIONS

The major techniques and decisions involved in setting an externally competitive pay and designing the corresponding pay structures are shown in Exhibit 7.1. They include (1) clarify the employer's external pay policy; (2) determine the issues to be addressed in a survey; (3) design and conduct surveys; (4) interpret and apply survey results; and (5) design ranges, flat rates, and/or incentives. The approaches associated with each decision are discussed in the rest of the chapter. As you read through the chapter, you will become aware that each new decision may cause an employer to revise previous decisions. So the process may be better described as circular than linear. For example, the use of incentives (decision 5) may cause the employer to revise its external policy or decide that a specialized survey is needed to determine what types of incentives other employers are using. Or, a firm may discover that its competitors are offering day care for children of their employees. The point is that as data change, policy decisions may change.

---

[1]Fred K. Foulkes, *Personnel Policies in Large Nonunion Companies* (Englewood Cliffs, N.J.: Prentice-Hall, 1980).

EXHIBIT 7.1
Determining Externally Competitive Pay Levels and Structures

| External competitiveness: Pay relationships among organizations | → | Policy determination | → | Market definition | → | Conduct pay surveys | → | Draw policy lines | → | Competitive pay levels and structures |

Some Major Decisions in Pay Level Determination
- Determine pay level policy
- Define purpose of survey
- Design and conduct survey
- Interpret and apply results
- Design ranges, flat rates, incentives

Determine Competitive Pay Policy: Conventional and New Directions

There are three conventional policies: to lead, to meet, or to follow competition. How does an employer choose a policy? In 1948, Lester had 63 firms rank seven factors they felt were most important in setting pay policies.[2] His results reveal that rates paid by other employers in the area or industry, and union pressures, were most important, and the firm's financial position and company profits were least important. As shown in Exhibit 7.2, the Conference Board survey of 280 firms in 1978 and 1983 reports a shift in the importance of factors.[3] Industry patterns dropped to fourth place in 1983, while a firm's specific financial situation, its productivity or labor costs and expected profits (ability to pay) were listed as the most important. Union-related factors, rated extremely important in the earlier Lester study, were among the least important in the more recent Conference Board studies. Consequently, while the factors considered in setting pay may be stable, their relative importance may vary over time.

Given the choice to match, lead, or lag, evidence suggests that the most common policy is to *match* rates paid by competitors.[4] Thirty years ago, one study found that managers tended to base the "matching" policy on three factors: (1) failure to match competitors' rates would increase employee pay dissatisfaction; (2) over the long term, lower rates would limit the organization's ability to recruit; and (3) management was somehow obligated to pay prevailing rates. However, this study also found that employees were largely unaware of pay levels offered by other organizations. A more recent study of large, nonunionized companies found that most employers say they try to lead or at least match competition. This policy was seen as important for maintaining union-free status.[5] However, a firm's actual pay policy may differ from its stated policy, depending on which surveys and statistics are used, whether or not all forms of compensation are

[2]Richard A. Lester, *Company Wage Policies* (Princeton, N.J.: Princeton University Press, 1948).

[3]*The New Look in Wage Policy and Employee Relations* (New York: The Conference Board, 1983).

[4]Kenneth E. Foster, "An Anatomy of Company Pay Practices," *Personnel*, September 1985, pp. 67–71.

[5]Lloyd G. Reynolds, *The Structure of Labor Markets* (Westport, Conn.: Greenwood Press, 1951); Foulkes, *Personnel Policies*.

EXHIBIT 7.2
The Relative Importance of Factors Used to Set Wage Objectives in Corporations in 1978 and 1983

Rank	1978	1983
1	Industry patterns	Productivity or labor trends in this company
2	Local labor market conditions and wage rates	Expected profits of this company
3	Expected profits of this company	Local labor market conditions and wage rates
4	Productivity or labor cost trends in this company	Industry patterns
5	Consumer price index increases	Consumer price index increases
6	Influence of this settlement on other wage settlements or nonunion wage levels, or both	Internal (company) wage patterns (historical)
7	Potential losses from a strike	Influence of this settlement on other settlements or nonunion wage levels, or both
8	Internal (company) wage patterns (historical)	Internal (company) benefit patterns (historical)
9	Internal (company) benefit patterns (historical)	Potential losses from a strike
10	Major union settlements in other industries	National labor market conditions and wage rates
11	National labor market conditions and wage rates	Major union settlements in other industries

Note: The sample comprised 197 major U.S. corporations which, in both 1978 and 1983, ranked factors used in settling company wage objectives, with 1 being the most important factor and 11, the least important.
    Source: Audrey Freedman, *The New Look in Wage Policy and Employee Relations* (New York, The Conference Board, 1985).

considered (base pay, incentives, benefits, etc.) and how well jobs are matched across competitors.

Policy effects. What difference does the competitive pay policy make? The basic premise is that the competitiveness of pay will affect compensation objectives and ultimately the organization's performance. The probable effects of alternative policies are shown in Exhibit 7.3.

EXHIBIT 7.3
Probable Relationships between External Pay Policies and Objectives

	Compensation Objectives				
Policy	Ability to Attract	Ability to Retain	Contain Labor Costs	Reduce Pay Dissatisfaction	Inrease Productivity
Pay above market (lead)	+	+	?	+	?
Pay with market (match)	=	=	=	=	?
Pay below market (lag)	−	?	+	−	?
Variable pay	?	?	+	?	+
Employer of choice	+	+	+	−	?

Pay with competition (match). A pay with competition policy tries to ensure that an organization's wage costs are approximately equal to those of its product competitors and that its ability to attract people to apply for employment will be approximately equal to its labor market competitors. This policy avoids placing an employer at a disadvantage in pricing products or in maintaining a qualified work force. But it may not provide an employer with a competitive advantage in its labor markets.

Lead policy. A lead policy maximizes the ability to attract and retain quality employees and minimizes employee dissatisfaction with pay. Or a lead policy may offset less attractive features of the work. Military combat pay is a classic example. The relatively high pay offered by brokerage firms that offsets the lack of employment security is another.

Many employers are able to pass higher pay rates on to consumers in the form of higher product prices. Sometimes an entire industry can pass high pay rates on to consumers if pay is a relatively low proportion of total operating expenses or if the industry is highly regulated. Petroleum and financial (brokerage firms) are examples of such industries.

If Chevron or Exxon adopts a pay leadership position in its industry, do any advantages actually accrue to them? If all firms in the industry have similar technologies and operating expenses, then the lead policy must provide some competitive advantage that outweighs the higher costs. Hence, firms in an entire industry (e.g., petroleum) may gain advantage over firms in other industries (e.g., manufacturing), which compete for employees with similar skills (e.g., secretaries, accountants, programmers). But no unique advantage accrues to specific firms *within* the petroleum industry—unless a firm leads within its industry, too.

Does a lead policy really permit the employer to select the best of the applicant pool? Assuming the employer is able to select the most qualified from this pool, does this higher quality talent translate into greater productivity, lower unit labor costs, improved product quality, and increased innovation? We don't know. There is no research to support (or refute) these assumptions that underlie a pay leadership policy.

Lag policy. Setting a lag pay policy to follow competitive rates may hinder a firm's ability to attract potential employees (Exhibit 7.3). A lag policy's effect on turnover is not at all clear. While lower pay levels probably contribute to turnover, pay may be only one of many factors influencing turnover.[6] For example, alternative jobs available and length of service undoubtedly play a role. It is unclear how dissatisfied employees must be with pay before they will leave. Additionally, it is possible to lag competition on pay

---

[6]Raymond A. Noe, Brian D. Steffy, and Alison E. Barber, "An Investigation of the Factors Influencing Employees' Willingness to Accept Mobility Opportunities," *Personnel Psychology,* Autumn 1988, pp. 559–80; Richard Ippolito, "Why Federal Workers Don't Quit," *Journal of Human Resources* 22, No. 2, (1987), pp. 281–99; Alan Krueger, "The Determinants of Queues for Federal Jobs," *Industrial and Labor Relations Review,* July 1988, pp. 567–81; Hyder Lakhani, "The Effect of Pay and Retention Bonuses on Quit Rates in the U.S. Army," *Industrial and Labor Relations Review,* April 1988, pp. 430–38; Timothy W. Lee and Richard Mowday, "Voluntarily Leaving an Organization: An Empirical Investigation of Steers and Mowday's Model of Turnover," *Academy of Management Journal,* December 1987, pp. 721–743.

but lead on other aspects of rewards (e.g., challenging work, desirable location, outstanding colleagues).

NEW POLICY DIRECTIONS: VARIABLE PAY—EMPLOYER OF CHOICE

Lead, meet, lag are the conventional policy options. Some employers adopt unconventional policies; two typical examples are *variable compensation* and becoming the *employer of choice*. Under a variable pay policy, a firm offers the potential of greater earnings if its performance is strong, (e.g., profitsharing or incentive pay). Union Carbide's Chemicals and Plastic Division offers employees the opportunity to earn a bonus of up to 40 days pay if the Division operating profits exceed certain targets ($280 million in 1990). However, Carbide repositioned its base pay to 5 percent below its usual "match" the market position. So Carbide's policy is to follow the market by 5 percent but to pay a bonus, which yields a slight lead position if the company's performance is strong. Other firms such as DuPont and Borg Warner have similar policies.

Note the potential effects of this competitive position. Lagging by 5 percent actually reduces labor costs. According to advocates, the variable pay policy is intended to focus employee attention on the firm's financial performance and motivate productivity improvements. Its effects on turnover and ability to attract probably depend on individual employees. Some employees may want to share the gains and risks inherent in a business. Others may not, preferring greater certainty in their pay increases.

An *employer of choice* policy is more complex than the other options. Basically it embeds the external competitive position in the firm's entire human resource policies. The competitive policy may be to offer challenging work, employment security, and pay that in some sense fits these other policies. Hence, IBM probably leads its competitors with its tradition of employment security, extensive retraining opportunities, employee assistance programs, and the like. But it meets or even follows with its cash compensation. A competitor such as Apple may lead with pay but lag on the extensive nonfinancial aspects of employment. The point is that some employers' policies in the external market reflect pay as part of the total pattern of human resource policies.

In summary, adopting a competitive pay policy is akin to establishing a niche in the market; there are conventional and new directions in external pay policies. Unfortunately, there is little evidence of the consequences of these different options. It is not known whether the effects of pay level on the financial performance of a firm, its productivity, or its ability to attract and retain employees is sufficient to offset the effects on payroll costs. Nor is it known how much of a pay level variation makes a difference—will 5 percent, 10 percent, or 15 percent be a noticeable difference? While lagging competitive pay could have a noticeable reduction in short-term labor costs, it is not known if this gain is accompanied by a reduction in the quality and performance of the work force. Similarly, we simply do not know the effects of the variable or employer of choice options.

So where does this leave the compensation professional? In the absence of convincing evidence, the least-risk approach is to set the pay level to match competition, though some employers set different policies for different skills. They may adopt a lead policy for critical skills, such as computer design engineers in the semiconductor industry, or financial analysts in brokerage houses. A match policy may be set for less critical skills, and a lag policy for jobs that are easily filled in the local labor market. A study of TRW, a large, highly decentralized firm, found that different business units established a variety of pay level policies. Some of these differences reflected different industries in which the units operate (automotive versus defense related). Other differences reflected varying labor market conditions (high unemployment in Michigan and Ohio versus lower unemployment in Los Angeles) and business strategies (cost-plus defense contracts versus the highly competitive microchip market). General Electric, another diversified firm, emphasizes in its communications to employees that the pay level policies are set independently by each of its business divisions. Under such decentralized approaches, an obvious concern is to achieve some degree of control and uniformity of policies, at least at the corporate level.

No matter what external pay policy is selected, it needs to be translated into practice. A first step is to identify the relevant external labor markets and then survey that market to determine existing pay practices.

WHY CONDUCT A SURVEY?

Most firms conduct or participate in several different pay surveys. Some writers claim that larger employers participate in up to 100 surveys in a single year, though data from only a few surveys are used to make compensation decisions.[7]

An employer will conduct or participate in a survey for a number of reasons: (1) to adjust the pay level in response to changing external pay rates, (2) to establish or price the pay structure, (3) to analyze personnel problems that may be pay related, (4) to attempt to estimate the labor costs of competitors in its product markets, or (5) to respond as "good citizens" to requests from other employers or public agencies.

Pay Level

Most organizations make adjustments to employees' pay on a regular basis. Perhaps as a result, employees have come to expect ever-increasing wages. Such adjustments can be based on performance, seniority, or simply the overall upward movement of pay rates in the economy. Market surveys provide information on pay rates among other employers. Periodic changes in overall rates must be known in order to maintain or adjust a firm's wage level in relationship to the market. A movement away from the tradition of regular (annual) adjustments in the pay level may be underway, particularly in industries facing competition from foreign products with lower unit labor costs. Our experience suggests that some employers are delaying the adjustments of pay levels in an attempt to remain competitive with these foreign competitors. Others are adopting variable pay increases that do not roll into an employees' base pay, thereby reducing the rate of increase in labor costs.

---

[7]Robert C. Ochsner, "The Future of Compensation Measurement in the United States," paper presented at a symposium on compensation measurement sponsored by the Bureau of Labor Statistics, U.S. Department of Labor, Washington, D.C., March 19, 1987.

Pay Structure

As noted in Chapter 4 on job evaluation, some firms go directly from job descriptions to market pricing for most of their jobs and deemphasize job evaluation. Under such an approach, the pay structure heavily depends on the data obtained through market surveys. Many employers also use market surveys as a check to validate their own job evaluation results. For example, internal job evaluation may place data processing jobs at the same level in the job structure as some secretarial jobs. But if the market shows vastly different pay rates for the two types of jobs, most employers will recheck their evaluation process to see if the jobs have been properly evaluated. Some will establish a separate structure for the data processing work. Thus, the job structure that results from job evaluation may not match the pay structure found in the external market. Reconciling these two is a major issue confronting compensation professionals. As with so many procedures, it requires informed judgment based on the organization's specific circumstances and objectives.

Pay-Related Personnel Projects

Surveys used for special projects, often in response to problems that may be pay related, also provide important data. Examples include a survey of competitors' compensation practices for positions in which a company is experiencing abnormally high turnover among good performers. Many special studies are used to appraise the starting salary offers or current pay practices for targeted groups, for example, patent attorneys, retail sales managers, or chemical engineers. Using another example, employers tend to rely on market data to justify pay differences among men and women in lawsuits brought under Title VII of the Civil Rights Act. Employers have successfully argued that the difference in pay between nurses and craft workers is due to pay differences found in the external markets for these skills.[8] This argument rests on the defensibility of the market data collected through wage surveys. Consequently, compensation professionals need to ensure that their surveys will withstand legal challenges.[9]

Estimate Competitors' Unit Labor Costs

Some firms, particularly in high competitive businesses such as producers of microcomputers, autos, and specialty steel products, are beginning to use salary survey data in their financial analysis of competitors' product pricing and manufacturing practices. Industrywide labor cost estimates are reported in the Employment Cost Index (ECI), which measures quarterly changes in employer costs for employee compensation.[10] For example, employee compensation in private industry cost employers $13.42 per hour worked in

---

[8]*Briggs* v. *City of Madison* 1982 W.D. Wisc. 436 F Supp. 435.

[9]Sara L. Rynes and G. T. Milkovich, "Wage Surveys: Dispelling Some Myths about the 'Market Wage,' " *Personnel Psychology,* Spring 1986, pp. 71–90.

March 1989. Wages and salaries made up 73.2 percent of the costs and averaged $9.83, while benefits made up the remaining 26.8 percent and averaged $3.60. So it is possible to compare average costs in a specific firm to the all-industry or specific-industry averages. However, this comparison has limited value, since industry averages may not reflect relevant competitors, and the ECI gives undue weight to unionized firms.

Good Corporate Citizen

The final purpose of surveys—to be a "good corporate citizen"—is least important. Some employers participate in many surveys simply as a courtesy to other employers. Due to the personnel expenses involved, other employers have become very selective in agreeing to participate in surveys.

Survey results serve as crucial input for decisions that ultimately affect a firm's compensation objectives of efficiency and equity. An employer's labor costs and the competitiveness of its products can be affected by conclusions drawn from survey data. Thus, surveys must be designed and managed carefully since their results are so significant to the organization. A first step to insure careful management is to identify the key issues the employer seeks to resolve in the survey.

DESIGN AND CONDUCT SURVEYS

Surveys provide the data for setting the pay policy relative to competition and translating that policy into pay levels and structures. A survey is defined as:

> **The systematic process of collecting and making judgments about the compensation paid by other employers.**

The basic decisions in designing and conducting pay surveys are discussed in the following sections.

What Is the Relevant Market?

The answer to this question depends on the purpose of the survey. To make decisions about pay levels and structures or to estimate competitors' labor costs, the relevant labor market includes those employers with whom an organization competes for employees. While a statistician may design a survey to sample a broad population, salary surveys

---

[10]G. Donald Wood, "Employment Cost Index Series to Replace Hourly Earnings Index," *Monthly Labor Review,* July 1988, pp. 32–35.

are typically designed to capture a narrower population, i.e., the competition. And competitors forming the relevant markets are typically defined by:

1. The occupation or skill required.
2. The geographic distance employees are willing to commute (or relocate).
3. Employers who compete for same skills.
4. Employers who compete with same products.

So the definition of relevant labor market will vary, depending on the purpose of the survey and the particular work and skills being examined.

Exhibit 7.4 shows how qualifications interact with geography to define the scope of relevant labor markets. As the importance of the qualifications and complexity of qualifications increase, the geographic limits also increase. Competition tends to be national for managerial and professional skills, but local or regional for clerical and production skills. However, these generalizations do not always hold true. In areas with high concentrations of scientists, engineers, and managers (e.g., Boston, Los Angeles or Palo Alto), the primary market comparison may be regional, with national data used only secondarily.

In major metropolitan areas, the relevant market may be defined by commuting times and patterns. Some studies show that most people are willing to commute up to 45 minutes (one way) to work.[11] But obviously this varies by locale as well as by personal and economic circumstances. Further, managers can influence the willingness of people to commute through actions other than setting higher pay levels.[12] For example, a firm may lobby the local transit authority for convenient bus routes and schedules or may sponsor company-owned vans and car pooling programs. One New York City department store buses 160 workers from Brooklyn to its suburban stores during busy holiday seasons so that the stores will have an adequate supply of sales personnel. Faced with a shortage of school teachers, New York City went to Spain to recruit qualified teachers who were willing to commit themselves to a job in New York for at least two years. These examples show the variety of steps employers will take to increase the supply of labor before they will raise wages. But even raising wages may not work. For example, when Giant Foods raised its hourly pay fifty cents above the minimum wage in the Chicago area, Wendy's and Burger King quickly followed suit. The result was that Giant Food was paying more for the employees it already had, but was still shorthanded. So from the perspective of attracting qualified people, both skills and geography (willingness to relocate or commute) are important factors in defining the relevant labor market.

From the perspective of cost control and ability to pay, the most important factor in defining the relevant market is competition in the product/service market. The pay rates of product/service competitors will affect both their costs of operations and their financial condition (e.g., ability to pay). Deregulation of the airline industry brought about com-

---

[11]David Peterson, "Defining Local Labor Markets," in *Perspectives on Availability,* ed., Kenneth McGuinness (Washington, D.C.: Equal Employment Advisory Council, 1977).

[12]Thomas H. Stone and Sarosh Kuruvilla, "The Wage Comparison Process in a Local Labor Market," (University of Iowa: working paper, 1988).

EXHIBIT 7.4
Relevant Labor Market Focus

Group	National	Regional	Local
1. Executive/managers	94%	2%	4%
2. Professional/scientist	75%	21%	4%
3. Technician	14%	30%	56%
4. Office/clerical	3%	6%	91%

Source: *1989 Wyatt Survey of Large Corporation Practices.*

petition in fare pricing for the first time in the industry's history. It also meant that many airlines sought wage reductions in order to price fares competitively. So inclusion of product/service competitors in the wage survey is vital. However, this becomes a problem when the major competitors are based in countries with far lower pay rates, such as South Korea, Brazil, or China.

Some writers argue that if the skills are tied to a particular industry, as underwriters, actuaries, and claims representatives are to insurance, it makes sense to define the market on an industry basis.[13] If skills such as accounting, sales, or clerical are not limited to one particular industry, industry considerations are less important. But that position ignores financial objectives of the employer. Pricing labor competitively with others who offer similar products and services is necessary to achieve the organization's financial objectives. Within these product/service market constraints, occupational and geographic factors come into play. Additionally, a firm's size (number of employees, total revenues, and assets) reflects its market dominance. If one firm dominates and becomes a "wage maker" rather than a "wage taker," a survey that omitted that firm would not accurately capture the market.

EEO Considerations

A final consideration in determining the relevant market relates to EEO. As noted earlier, market data are increasingly being used in pay discrimination litigation to defend pay differentials.[14] If market data are to serve as criteria to explain and justify pay practices, the definition of the relevant markets and the survey methodology must be defensible. This means that procedures and decisions must be

1. *Documented.* An organization's policies regarding external wage comparisons are specified, and actions taken in conducting surveys are consistent with these policies.
2. *Business related.* Firms competing with similar products/services are included.

---

[13]Felicia Nathan, "Analyzing Employers' Costs for Wages, Salaries, and Benefits," *Monthly Labor Review,* October 1987, pp. 3–11.

[14]*Kouba and EEOC* v. *Allstate Insurance Company,* 1982, 691 F. 2d 873; and *Briggs* v. *City of Madison,* W. D. Wisc. 1982, 436 F. Supp. 435. Also see *In the Matter of Boston Survey Group,* Mass. Superior Court, Docket No. 56341, August 2, 1982; and Rynes and Milkovich, "Dispelling Myths."

3. *Work related.* Employers of similar skills within similar geographic areas are included. Caution should be exercised here since some employers, by virtue of the nature of their product market or pressure from their unions may be able and/or willing to pay more (e.g., Arthur Anderson may be willing to pay its accountants in Chicago more than the Marshall Field department store pays its Chicago accountants, since accountants are more critical to generate revenues in Arthur Anderson than they are in Field's).

How Many Employers?

There are no firm rules on how many employers to include in a survey. Large firms with a lead policy may exchange data with only a few (6 to 10) top-paying competitors. A small organization in an area dominated by two or three employers may decide to survey only smaller competitors. National surveys conducted by consulting firms may include over 100 employers. Clients of these consultants often stipulate special analyses that report pay rates by selected industry groups, geographic region, and/or their pay levels (e.g., top 10 percent).

Who to Involve?

In most organizations the responsibility for managing the survey lies with the compensation professional. But since the pricing of human resources has a powerful effect on the bottom line, selected operating managers and employees are often involved, too. A recurrent theme in this text has been the need to get user acceptance through involvement in procedure design. This point is valid for job analysis, job evaluation, selecting compensable factors, and also for pricing. Including managers and employees on task forces and/or surveying employees to discover what firms they use for pay comparisons make sense. Not only does broader involvement increase understanding and probably acceptance of results, but also employees can be sources of suggestions about which employers to include and about the accuracy of the data other firms provide.

Third parties, outside consulting firms, are often used as protection from possible "price-fixing" lawsuits. The trade-off in hiring a third party versus managing the survey internally usually involves less control over the decisions that determine the quality and usefulness of the data when outsiders conduct the survey.

The specter of charges of price-fixing is real.[15] Suits have been filed alleging that the exchange of survey data violates Section One of the Sherman Act, which outlaws conspiracies in restraint of trade, but thus far the suits have all been settled out of court. Typically, it has been the courts' interpretation of the Sherman Act that survey participants

---

[15]Gary D. Fisher, "Salary Surveys—an Antitrust Perspective," *Personnel Administrator,* April 1985, pp. 87–97, 154.

are guilty of price-fixing if the overall effect of the information exchange is to interfere with competitive prices and artificially hold down wages. One case involved the Boston Survey Group, a 34-member association, which exchanged data on wages for a variety of clerical jobs. The survey reported the salaries of individuals in each job classification surveyed; each participating firm's information was clearly identified, and the results were reported by industry group. 9 to 5, a political action group, asked the Massachusetts State Attorney General's office to investigate. A consent decree agreed to by the Boston Survey Group stipulates:

- The data from each participant will no longer be identified.
- Only aggregated information will be reported for each participant; salaries of individual employees will not be published.
- No data will be published on a per-industry basis.
- Data will not be reported if there are fewer than 10 people in a job.
- Members may choose to allow their employees to see the aggregated survey results for their own jobs.

Prohibiting exchange of industry data eliminated the ability to make product comparisons. This might not be important in clerical jobs, but industry groups are important when making comparisons for wages for other skills and jobs. For example, a Hewlett-Packard marketer's job is probably more similar to that of an AT&T Information Systems marketer than it is to one in Union Carbide. If the skills in question are generalized and thus transferable, then industry data can safely be ignored. However, industry data are crucial from a competitive product market perspective. Further, if the skills are highly specialized (e.g., semiconductor designer) then they may be industry specific and are not available across industries. The point is that if we are going to start regulating the collection of wage data, more caution than was apparently exercised by the Boston Survey Group is necessary.

Make or Buy?

The decision to retain outside expertise or design one's own survey includes a complex set of trade-offs. The availability of staff time and talent and the desire to control the quality of analysis and results are often given as reasons to tailor one's own survey. On the other hand, consulting firms offer a wide choice of ongoing surveys covering almost every job family and industry group imaginable.

Criteria for selecting. Opinions about the value of alternative consultant surveys are rampant; research is not. Do Hay, Executive Compensation Services (ECS), TPF&C, or MCS's 777 surveys of managerial pay yield significantly different results? Many firms select one survey as their primary source and use others to cross-check or "validate" the results. Yet little systematic study of differences in market definition, participating firms, types of data collected, analysis performed, and/or results is available. Of increasing importance, can these various surveys successfully withstand pay discrimination litigation?

EXHIBIT 7.5
An Example of BLS Survey Data

Weekly earnings of office workers in establishments employing 500 workers or more in Chicago, IL, July 1988

Occupation and Industry Division	Number of Workers	Average Weekly Hours (Standard)	Weekly Earnings (in dollars)		
			Mean	Median	Middle Range
Secretarial and Keyboarding Occupations					
Secretaries	8,427	39.0	446.00	435.00	381.00–499.00
Manufacturing	2,479	39.5	451.00	435.00	390.00–499.00
Nonmanufacturing	5,948	39.0	443.50	435.50	374.50–499.50
Transportation and utilities	734	39.5	506.00	481.50	461.50–593.00
Secretaries I	970	38.5	414.50	405.00	343.00–477.00
Manufacturing	238	38.5	402.50	387.50	356.00–431.50
Nonmanufacturing	732	38.5	418.00	421.00	336.00–477.00
Transportation and utilities	246	38.5	506.50	477.00	477.00–602.00
Secretaries II	1,296	39.5	381.00	380.00	332.00–432.50
Manufacturing	267	39.5	394.00	386.50	357.00–413.00
Nonmanufacturing	1,029	39.5	377.50	376.00	318.00–438.50
Transportation and utilities	62	40.0	412.00	444.50	342.50–481.50
Secretaries III	3,003	39.0	432.50	422.50	375.50–482.00
Manufacturing	1,000	39.5	431.00	420.50	385.50–468.00
Nonmanufacturing	2,003	39.0	433.50	422.50	369.00–490.00
Transportation and utilities	180	40.0	508.50	512.00	431.00–593.00
Secretaries IV	1,989	39.0	481.50	468.50	417.50–526.00
Manufacturing	633	39.5	473.00	473.00	431.00–517.50
Nonmanufacturing	1,356	38.5	485.50	468.00	414.00–533.50
Transportation and utilities	194	40.0	492.50	475.50	419.00–519.50

Professional consultants who design employment tests for applicant selection report the test's performance against a set of measurements (reliability, validity, etc.). Analogous standards for pay surveys have not yet evolved. For example, issues of sample design and statistical inference are seldom considered.

Publicly available data. The Bureau of Labor Statistics (BLS) is a major source of publicly available pay data.[16] It publishes area wage studies, industry wage studies, a National Survey of Professional, Administrative, Technical, and Clerical Pay (PATC), an Employee Benefits Survey, which reports the incidence of various benefits in the private sector, local area wage surveys (AWS), and the Employment Cost Index (ECI),

---

[16]U.S. Department of Labor, Bureau of Labor Statistics, *BLS Measures of Compensation* (Washington, D.C.: U.S. Government Printing Office, 1977). Bulletin 1941.

the measure of changes in employee compensation costs discussed earlier. In addition, most states and even some counties provide pay data to the public.

Exhibit 7.5 illustrates the nature of the BLS data. The data are inexpensive and readily available. Public sector employers seem to use BLS data more often than do private sector employers. Some private sector firms track the rate of change in BLS data as a cross-check on other surveys and for examining geographic differentials for various nonexempt jobs (e.g., file clerks in Chicago versus file clerks in Durham, North Carolina).

Which Jobs to Include?

A general guideline for all survey issues is to keep things simple. Select as few employers and jobs as necessary to accomplish the purpose. The more complex the survey, the less likely employers are inclined to participate unless the survey results are important to them also.

Benchmark jobs approach. Typically, only key or benchmark jobs are included in surveys. Descriptions of the benchmark jobs are included in the survey so that participants can match the survey job with the correct job in their organization. Benchmark jobs are defined as reference points having the following characteristics:

- The contents are well known, relatively stable, and agreed upon by the employees involved.
- The supply and demand for these jobs are relatively stable and not subject to recent shifts.
- They represent the entire job structure under study.

EXHIBIT 7.6
Representative Benchmark Jobs

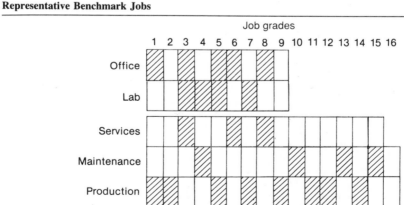

- A sizable proportion of the work force is employed in these jobs.
- Some employers use the percentage of incumbents who are women and men to try to ensure that the benchmarks are free of possible employment discrimination.

Exhibit 7.6 shows a profile of an organization's functional areas (e.g., production, maintenance, services, laboratory, and office) and job grades. Benchmark jobs anchor the comparisons of competitive pay rates with descriptions of similar types of work. Selecting a benchmark job from each shaded grade ensures coverage of the entire work domain for these functional areas. Including the entire domain of work and jobs held by large numbers of employees helps ensure the accuracy of the work relatedness of decisions based on survey results.[17] Hence the benchmarks chosen should represent all levels in the organization and, if possible, all functions.

Skill-based/global approach. Rarely do several organizations have identical jobs. This is particularly true in organizations that emphasize production work teams and task forces, or continuously adapt jobs to meet changing conditions. Recall the description of knowledge-based pay systems in Chapter 3. The skill-based approach may be better suited to survey pay levels in these situations.

With a skill-based approach, the rates paid to every individual employee in an entire skill group or function (e.g., all chemical engineers, or all computer scientists) become the reference point. Exhibits 7.7 and 7.8 show external market data for engineers with bachelor's degrees. These data permit determination of rates paid to engineers as well as that rate's relationship to years-since-degree (YSD). A skill-based approach simply substitutes a particular skill (represented by a B.S. in engineering in the example) and experience (YSD) for detailed descriptions of work performed.[18]

Job value approach. This approach to matching survey job requires an employer to use its job evaluation plan to evaluate the benchmark jobs provided in the survey and to compare those results to internal job evaluations.[19] The magnitude of difference in job evaluation results provides a guideline for making similar adjustments in the market data collected for the survey job.

So the real issue is to ensure that the jobs or skill groups included in the survey

---

[17]Bruce Ellig, *Executive Compensation—A Total Pay Perspective* (New York: McGraw-Hill, 1982); Robert J. Greene, "How to Improve Job Pricing Techniques," *Compensation and Benefits Management,* Spring 1985, pp. 223–28.

[18]Harold B. Guerci, "Compensation Programs for Scientists and Professionals in Business," in *Handbook of Wage and Salary Administration,* ed. M. Rock (New York: McGraw-Hill, 1984), pp. 53/1–53/10.

[19]Kenneth E. Foster, "Acquiring Competitive Information from Surveys: An Empirical Approach," in *Handbook of Wage and Salary Administration,* 2nd ed., ed. Milton L. Rock (New York: McGraw-Hill, 1984), pp. 42/1–42/13; Edward Perlin, Irvin Bobby Kaplan, and John M. Curcia, "Clearing Up Fuzziness in Salary Survey Analysis," *Compensation Review,* Second Quarter 1979, pp. 12–25.

EXHIBIT 7.7
Frequency Distribution
—All Engineers, All Companies

YEARS SINCE BS

MONTHLY SALARY	0	1	2	3	4	5	6	7	8	9	10	11	12	13	14	15	16	17	18	19	20	21	22	23	24	25	26	27	28	29	30	31	32	33	34	35	36	37	TOTAL
6950 - OVER																					2	3	3		2	2	2		2	2	6	1	3	1	1	1		10	40
6825 - 6949																							1	1						2		1	3				1		9
6700 - 6824																	1							1			2	1	1		2			1			1	2	12
6575 - 6699																		1		1	2	2	3	1				1	1	1			1			2	1	2	14
6450 - 6574																2	4		3	1		3	1	1		2			4	1	1	2	1	3	2	2	4	9	31
6325 - 6449													1			1	2	3	4	4	4			1	3		2	3	1	1	2	3	2	2	2	1	1	5	24
6200 - 6324																	1	2	3	3		6		5	2	2	4	3	4	3	2	4	3	2	3	3	4	5	42
6075 - 6199											1			2			1	2	4	4	4	2	5	5	3	3	6	3	2	2	3	3	2	5	2	4	1	6	43
5950 - 6074																2	4	3	3	4	4		5	5	4	4	6	6	3	4	4	4	3	2	5	3	4	8	44
5825 - 5949										1			1	5	1	5	6	6	4	3	6	2	5	6	2	2	6	6	5	4	6	5	4	5	3	4	2	6	63
5700 - 5824														7	5	5	2	2	4	4	2	6	5	6	4	4	2	7	6	4	3	2	2	2	5	3	6	8	70
5575 - 5699										3		1		7	11	11	4	9	3	3	6	3	6	5	9	6	4	3	5	4	5	5	7	5	4	4	8	11	95
5450 - 5574									1	4	1			4	10	10	7	5	9	4	7	3	6	6	4	2	6	8	6	2	3	2	3	3	5	3	3	10	97
5325 - 5449									2	4				8	11	11	8	11	5	7	8	10	5	7	9	4	2	7	11	4	5	7	7	4	3	5	3	15	102
5200 - 5324									4	3	2			7	9	11	7	9	13	4	7	7	9	6	6	9	7	3	9	8	3	7	3	5	4	4	7	16	116
5075 - 5199									2	4		1	1	5	7		12	5	12	3	11	10	12	13	7	7	6	5	7	12	5	2	6	3	5	5	2		151
4950 - 5074							1	1	11	5	3	4	5	8	21	11	7	11	9	13	6	4	8	8	9	2	9	7	7	8	3	7	11	7	5	4	2	19	173
4825 - 4949								1	14	7	2	8	4	2	14	10	6	9	12	12	9	10	6	13	7	4	10	8	9	4	5	8	3	3	2	4	2	20	178
4700 - 4824					4		3	10	12		8	13	5	19	15	21	13	12	7	8	7	7	18	11	6	9	8	6	8	12	3	2	6	2	4	2	1	21	180
4575 - 4699					5	4	6	12	16	7	14	8	4	9	14	14	8	11	9	9	11	10	8	15	9	5	5	6	3	4	5	6	11	3	5	2	2	17	210
4450 - 4574				4	8	8	13	16	13	12	8	13	17	11	7	11	14	11	12	12	7	3	6	8	6	6	8	8	6	9	3	5	6	3	3	3	1	18	192
4325 - 4449				9	8	7	11	13	20	15	14	12	13	19	21	21	15	14	10	13	10	11	13	8	9	9	10	6	8	4	10	2	7	3	5	3	1	27	232
4200 - 4324				8	4	8	14	18	18	18	8	15	15	13	16	19	9	6	9	13	7	6	14	8	6	6	7	8	8	12	7	5	3	2	5	4	1	10	216
4075 - 4199				12	11	8	11	12	15	15	14	12	13	9	11	14	19	12	12	6	11	10	12	13	9	9	10	5	6	4	5	8	6	7	3	4	2	19	290
3950 - 4074	4		14	19	15	4	14	7	18	8	8	15	15	19	16	15	14	14	9	9	7	7	18	3	6	6	9	8	3	9	3	2	11	5	2	5	2	20	281
3825 - 3949		14	24	15	8	11	22	20	10	7	14	16	13	13	13	11	13	15	11	12	10	9	5	13	11	4	8	3	6	4	5	4	3	1		4	1	24	262
3700 - 3824	8	17	19	18	4	18	19	19	8	8	8	12	10	9	7	9	12	10	7	8	8	6	6	15	5	4	6	4	3	9	7	10		3			1	18	255
3575 - 3699	11	27	20	15	11	17	17	13	10	7	4	15	17	13	8	7	9	6	11	9	10	8	9	3	5	5	8	5	6	4	5	6	10	4	5			27	234
3450 - 3574		8	15	20	15	18	8	10	14	12	8	15	15	16	16	21	8	5	6	6	4	9	8	9	4	4	6	3	3	9	7	2	3	1	2	3	1	7	205
3325 - 3449		42	19	15	12	5	18	12	10	9	12	12	8	9	14	14	4	6	5	7	10	5	6	2	7	7	3	2	6	2	4	3		4		2	1	7	193
3200 - 3324	29	35	22	10	7	8	9	12	9	9	16	12	9	11	5	5	6	5	4	7	9	3	3	5	5	2	2	6	3	4	4	3		3	1			5	176
3075 - 3199	16	37	10	4		10	8	20	15	13	13	8	11	8	14	4	4	9	5	4	10		6	1	2	1	1		3	3								3	174
2950 - 3074	13	11	4	15	10		4	7	8	14	4	5	2	5	5	6	6	5		5	3	4	5	7	1	1		1	2		3				1				155
2825 - 2949	10		6	12	8	11	14	18	10	8	14	9	11	3	8	7	2	9	9	2	6		4	5	3		3	2	6	2	4		4			2		1	174
2700 - 2824	4	8	24	19	15	18	11	10	7	10	8	5	7	3	6	2	2	5	9		6	8	6	1		4	2		3	1	7	4		3				1	189
2575 - 2699		11	17	20	18	13	17	8	18	4	4	3	5	1	4	3	5	6	5	2	3	5	2	2				2		2	6	1	1	4					158
2450 - 2574	29	27	22	15	7	4	4	2		7	3	2	4	1	1	3	3	4	4	5			4	3	1	1	2	1		4	4	4				2		1	172
2325 - 2449	16	35	10	14	8	10	5	3	2		1	3			2	2	2	2		2	3	1	5	5	2		2		1		1		3		1			1	116
2200 - 2324	13	11	6	1	10		2		1		1	1	5	1		2	3	1	1	3			1	1		1	1		1	2			1						48
UNDER 2200	10	6	6		4		2	3									1	2			3											3	4	1				1	29
TOTAL	62	120	142	117	105	87	116	167	165	131	139	166	145	154	193	221	187	174	170	164	179	148	183	170	168	137	128	119	131	124	111	109	103	89	74	91	82	354	5425
MEDIAN	2458	2455	2553	2728	2804	2976	3195	3295	3429	3455	3858	3908	3924	4005	4089	4186	4188	4304	4422	4429	4432	4512	4503	4524	4595	4630	4551	4762	4439	4655	4585	4682	4782	4950	4828	4772	4899	4950	4035
MEAN	2433	2447	2564	2711	2752	2854	3008	3199	3332	3434	3501	3665	3598	3924	4189	4209	4239	4421	4466	4475	4438	4637	4583	4638	4665	4629	4629	4741	4669	4657	4821	4738	4851	4828	4741	4899	4860	4887	4090
STD. DEV.	110	170	243	275	289	344	388	428	479	491	513	583	527	673	678	699	729	791	798	856	932	861	951	807	839	859	819	826	897	979	897	929	965	1010	1011	943	963	887	1051

Source: Organization Resources Counselors, Inc.

209

EXHIBIT 7.8
Percentile Curves
Years Since First Degree versus Monthly Salary • All Engineers, All Companies

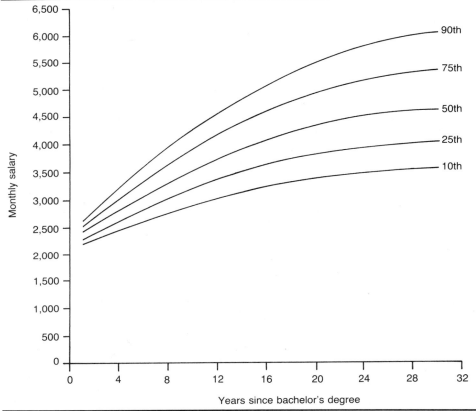

Source: Organization Resources Counselors, Inc.

provide data that will be useful. Depending on the purpose of the survey, either the key jobs approach, the skill-based approach, or the job value approach can help.

What Information to Collect?

There are three basic types of data typically requested: (1) information about the nature of the organization, (2) information about the total compensation system, and (3) specific pay data on each incumbent in the jobs under study. Exhibit 7.9 lists the basic data elements and the logic for including them.

No survey includes all the data that will be discussed. Rather, the data collected

EXHIBIT 7.9
Data Elements to Consider for Surveys and Their Rationale

Basic Elements	*Examples*	*Rationale*
Nature of organization		
Identification	Company, name, address, contact person.	Further contacts
Financial condition	Assets, sales, profits (after taxes).	Indicates nature of the product/service markets, the ability to pay, size, and financial viability.
Size	Profit centers, product lines.	Importance of specific job groups to business success.
	Total number of employees.	Impact on labor market.
Structure	Organizational charts.	Indicates how business is organized.
Nature of total compensation system		
Cash forms used	Basic pay, pay increase schedules, long- and short-term incentives, bonuses, cost of living adjustments, overtime and shift differentials.	Indicates the mix of compensation offered. Used to establish a comparable base.
Noncash forms used	Composition of benefits and services, particularly the degree of coverage and contributions to medical and health insurance and pensions.	
Incumbent and job		
Date	Date effective.	Need to update rates to current date.
Job	Match generic job descriptions. Number of employees supervised and reporting levels describe scope of responsibilities.	Indicates degree of similarity with survey's key jobs.
Individual	Years since degree, education, date of hire.	Indicates training and tenure of incumbents.
Pay	Actual rates paid to each individual, total earnings, last increase, bonuses, incentives.	

depends on the purpose of the survey and the jobs and skills included. Since no standards or guidelines on what to collect have been developed, managers must rely on their expertise and experience to make that decision.

Nature of the organization. Information about the nature of the organization should permit assessment of the similarities and differences among organizations in the survey. Financial information, size, and organization structure are usually included. Surveys of executives and upper level positions include more detailed financial and reporting relationships data. The logic for including this additional data is that compensation for these jobs is more directly related to the organization's financial performance. More often than not, the financial data are simply used to group firms by size expressed in terms of sales or revenues.

Nature of the total pay system. All the basic forms of pay need to be covered in a survey in order to assess the similarities and differences in the entire pay packages offered and to accurately assess competitors' practices. For example, employers are increasingly offering various forms of team awards and incentives along with the base pay. Further, some employers roll these awards into the base pay, while others do not, and still others roll only a percentage of them into employees' base pay. Inconsistent reporting (or not reporting) these awards will distort the data.

Yet it is particularly difficult to include *all* the pay forms in detail. For example, including details on benefits such as medical coverage deductibles, flexible benefit options, and even vacation policies quickly makes a survey too cumbersome to be useful. Methods to handle this problem range from a brief description of a benchmark benefit package to including only the most expensive and variable benefits or asking for an estimate of total benefit expenses as a percent of total labor costs. Including some estimate of total compensation is needed to assess the entire compensation package offered by competitors.

Incumbent data. The most important data in the survey are the *actual* rates paid to each incumbent. Total earnings, hours worked, date and amount of last increase, and bonus and incentive payments are included. However, the usefulness of each element needs to be balanced against the cost of trying to collect it.

Enough data must be available to appraise the match between the benchmark jobs in the survey and jobs within each company. Some personal data on each incumbent (e.g., tenure on job, educational degrees) are also included to facilitate matching. The degree of match between the survey's key jobs and each company's jobs is assessed by various means. Hay Associates, for example, has installed the same job evaluation plan in many companies that participate in their surveys. Consequently, jobs in different organizations can be compared on their total job evaluation points and the distribution of points among the compensable factors. Other surveys simply ask participants to judge the degree of match, using a scale similar to the following one.

> Please check ( ) degree to which your job matches the benchmark job described in the survey:
>
> My company's job is . . .
>   Of moderately less value   ( )
>   Of slightly less value   ( )
>   Of equal value   ( )
>   Of slightly more value   ( )
>   Of moderately more value   ( )

Still other survey designers periodically send teams of employees familiar with the key jobs to visit each participating organization to discuss the matches. Many public agency and trade association surveys simply rely on each participant to match the key jobs as closely as possible. The BLS has perhaps the most rigorous job matching process. It includes site visits and detailed job analysis.

International data. International competition requires international pay comparisons. Most large consulting firms conduct international surveys. Exhibit 7.10 is an example of TPF&C's report on cash remuneration practices in 20 countries. International surveys raise additional issues of comparability because legal regulations and tax policies, as well as customs, vary among countries. For example, because of tax reasons, Korean executives rarely receive incentive pay, and some South American countries mandate cost of living adjustments, which makes the timing of the survey data collection crucial. Companies with worldwide locations use local surveys for jobs filled locally, and international surveys only for top executive and managerial jobs.

EXHIBIT 7.10
Example of International Survey Data Reported by Compensation Consulting Firm

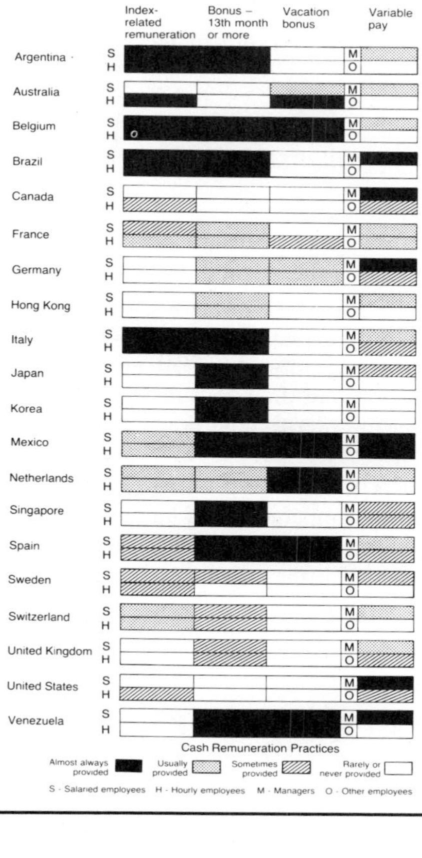

EEO-related data. To date, no surveys collect data specifically for EEO purposes. Since market data are frequently important in explaining pay differences between men and women, data such as length of time required to fill vacancies may be collected to more fully assess labor market conditions. For example, the fact that the city of Madison had difficulty attracting public health sanitarians to fill job vacancies was an important factor for the court that examined the pay differences between sanitarians (predominantly men) and nurses (predominantly women).[20]

Accuracy of data. A compensation manager cautions that "most surveys are not of sufficient quality to justify their use for anything more than indicators of general salary levels and trends."[21] Despite the acceptance by courts of market data as legal justification for salary differentials, the whole area of collection, analysis, and interpretation has not been subject to the same scrutiny as hiring practices and testing. Whether it should is another question. Certainly, a sound, business-related rationale for every step in the process is important. But fine distinctions using data that are extremely general may be faulty. Some survey data provide a general guide to assess the adequacy of the whole pay structure, but not necessarily the pay of specific jobs. Other surveys are designed to price specific jobs, and still others to assess only the rate of change in the rates paid. The purpose of the survey needs to be kept in mind when judging the data.

How to Collect the Data?

Two basic methods are used to collect pay data—interviews (in person or by phone) and mailed questionnaires. The purpose of the survey and the extensiveness of the data required usually determine the method. Special studies or double checking results is often done through phone interviews. Mailed questionnaires similar to the one used by Wyatt in Exhibit 7.11 are probably most common. The Bureau of Labor Statistics (BLS), the most experienced wage surveyor of all, uses extensive field interviews. Obviously, this approach is costly and time consuming. Some organizations use field visits every second or third year in order to hold down costs.

Many aspects of pay surveys have been ignored by researchers. Little can be said about the effects of different formats in the accuracy of the data obtained. Little is known about ensuring comparability of key job matches or matching benefit packages. We don't even know how representative the survey participants are of some markets. The same lack of research plagues the analysis of survey results.

---

[20]*Briggs* v. *City of Madison.*

[21]T. Michael Fain, "Conducting Surveys," in *Handbook of Wage and Salary Administration,* 2nd ed., pp. 32/3–32/11.

EXHIBIT 7.11
Survey Questionnaire used by Compensation Consulting Firm

Instructions and Position Descriptions

1. Reporting Multiple Locations: If your company operates more than one location, we urge you to submit data on as many of those locations as possible. ECS is committed to expanding the number of cities and states we publish. The inclusion of responses on multiple locations will enhance our geographic coverage and help ensure that data for the states and metropolitan areas in which you operate contain sufficient sample to yield meaningful results.

A separate questionnaire should be completed for each location (each operation with a different zip code).

2. Positions to be Reported: Report positions of a supervisory nature that fall below the level of middle management and above those filled by hourly-rated and nonexempt employees. Supervisory jobs constitute the first line of management. Because much of LEVEL 1 supervisor's working time may be spent performing work of the type supervised (i.e. group leader; working supervisor), some positions may be classified as nonexempt. See level guides and position descriptions for further clarification.

3. Effective Date: Report all data in effect as of January 1, 1989.

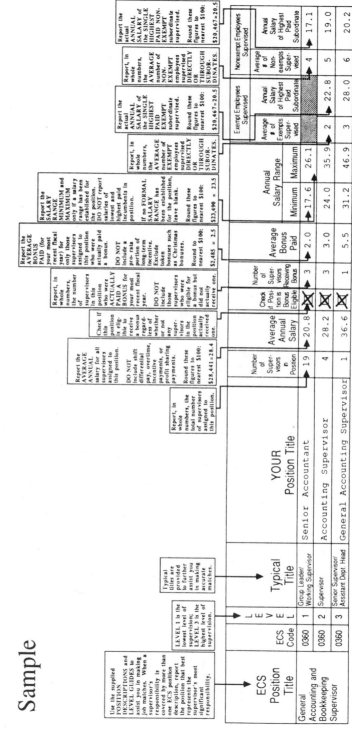

Sample

Source: Executive Compensation Service.

INTERPRET AND APPLY SURVEY RESULTS

To discover how survey data is actually analyzed, Belcher interviewed 34 compensation professionals. He reports:

> Every organization uses its own methods of distilling information from the survey; uses different surveys for different purposes; and uses different methods for company surveys. I could find no commonality in these methods of analysis by industry, by firm size or by union presence. For example, some did nothing except read the entire survey, some emphasized industry data, others geographic competitors (commuting distances), some made comparisons with less than five competitors, some emphasized only large firms, others throw out the data from large firms.[22]

Diversity rules in analyzing survey data. This probably reflects the pragmatism of compensation managers who adjust their analysis to deal with a variety of circumstances. It may also reflect that many current approaches to analysis are not well grounded in business and work-related logic and therefore will not be able to withstand a legal challenge.

Check the Accuracy and Usefulness of the Data

If no standard approach exists, how should analysis proceed? A common first step is to check the accuracy of the job matches. Job descriptions will be included with the survey data. However, even descriptions that match perfectly do not indicate how various companies value the same job, or their pay policies in reference to that job.

Leveling. If the job description is similar, but not identical, the survey data may be weighted according to its closeness of the match. This technique is called survey leveling.[23] Based on a scale such as shown on p. 212, if the job in the survey has slightly less responsibility, some analysts adjust the survey data (e.g., multiplied by 8) to bring it closer in comparability. Conversely, the survey data could be adjusted upward if the survey job has greater responsibility.

Typical analysis. Becoming familiar with the actual numbers in a survey is a necessary first step to assess its accuracy and usefulness. Exhibit 7.12 shows a survey provided by Organization Resources Counselors, Inc., for participants in their Salary Information Retrieval System. This particular exhibit was prepared for company P844, a pharmaceutical firm, and reports wages on a business applications programmer/analyst position.

---

[22]Letter from D. W. Belcher to G. T. Milkovich, in reference to D. W. Belcher, N. Bruce Ferris, and John O'Neill, "How Wage Surveys Are Being Used," *Compensation and Benefits Review,* September–October 1985, pp. 34–51.

[23]Bruce Ellig, ed., *Compensation and Benefits: Design and Analysis* (Scottsdale, Ariz.: American Compensation Association, 1985).

EXHIBIT 7.12
Survey Report Prepared by Compensation Consulting Firm

REPORT PREPARED FOR COMPANY   P844   LOMELI PHARMACEUTICALS

Annotations:
- Modifier (A = stronger match; B = exact match; C = weaker match)
- SIRS job family   SIRS subfamily   Level of job (3 = senior)
- Company number
- Benchmark job code and title
- Company's salary grade or job evaluation points
- Salary range: minimum, midpoint or control point (*), maximum
- Status under Fair Labor Standards Act
- Salary range percentage spread minimum to maximum
- Base salary plus bonus or incentive compensation
- Your company's data, including internal job code, in boldface for easy reference
- Number of incumbents reported to job

CO NO: 09·04   MOD: TO14   LEVEL 3   4821

CO NO	MOD	JOB TITLE / INTERNAL JOB CODE	NO OF INC	ACTUAL SALARIES AVG	LOW	HIGH	RANGE MIN	MIDPT/CNTRL	RANGE MAX	%SP	GR/PTS	FL SA	TOTAL COMP
		TO14 PROGRAMMING/ANALY-BUSINESS APPLICATIONS											
E067	B	PROG/ANALYST BUSINESS-SR	2	32396	32240	32500	25520	31564	37908	50	53	E	33692
E008	C	SR DATA PROC ANALYST	5	32656	28288	35464	25584	35464	45344	77	A4		34145
P023	B	PROGRAMMER ANALYST SR	13	34892	31980	39156	25584	37310	49036	92	11	E	34892
D032	B	MGMT SYSTEMS ANALYST SR	8	34892	33852	35880	31460	39520	47580	51	11	E	34892
E009	B	PROGRAMMER/ANALYST SR	8	35388	31500	38400	29160	37860	46560	60	11	E	35388
E017	B	MCS 2 - BUSINESS	297	35620	28756	45604	29980	39468	49556	69	12	E	35620
G002	B	PRINCIPAL BUSINESS PROG	1	36240	36240	36240	31740	39360	46980	48	A4		36240
P019	B	PRGRMMR/ANALYST SENIOR	12	36868	33000	43836	31460	41678	51896	65	73	E	36868
E231	B	PROGRAMMER ANALYST SR	3	37260	34560	39540	28896	37596*	45096	56	08	E	38750
E111	C	PROGRAMMER ANALYST SR	3	37536	34560	41520	28896	37002	45108	56	08	E	37536
P221	B	PROG/ANALY III	3	37980	37980	37980	30936	39600	48264	56	08	E	37980
E008	B	ADP ANALYST	4	38948	34840	43160	27144	39364	51584	90	45	E	38948
E035	B	SR SYS ANALYST GEN	22	39204	27000	48195	33600	42000	50400	50	28	E	38904
P844	**B**	**SYSTEMS DEV SPEC III**	**3**	**39252**	**37392**	**42300**	**27744**	**39836**	**51528**	**88**	**28**	**E**	**39252**
A012	B	ADMIN INFO SYS PROG/ANL	9	40040	35776	43628	33436	39676	45360	75	05	E	42242
K215	B	COMPUTING ANL SR	7	40196	31200	44096	33096	39676	48204	60	14	E	40196
E020	B	PROGRAMMER/ANALYST SR	4	40352	36600	44096	35880	42340	48860	55	08	E	40352
E015	C	PROGRAMMER ANALYST II	4	40417	39000	44200	31252	39052	56628	58	14	E	40417
C026	B	SR SYSTEMS ANALYST	13	40760	36912	44704	31120	40400	49700	47	47	E	40760
E003	B	PROGRAMMER/ANALYST SR	6	40812	37560	44100	31920	39900	47880	50	09	E	40760
E017	A	MCS 3 - BUSINESS	125	41392	32556	50960	31920	42510	52884	60	46	E	40812
E111	B	PROG/SYS ANALYST (SR)	1	41772	40800	42600	32136	41646	50796	65	13	E	41392
B110	B	PROGRAMMER ANALYST III	103	41772	34560	51240	32296	43200	54096	50	09	E	41520
F007	B	SR PROGRAMMER/ANALYST	24	41988	29784	52740	34560	44748	55068	50	05	E	41772
P122	B	SR PROGRAMMER/ANALYST	1	42840	42840	42840	32400	41500	50600	56	13	E	41988
E003	A	PROGRAMMER ANALYST BUS	10	43080	39852	43992	32400	43360	53400	61	08	E	42840
S037	B	MGMT SYS ANALYST SR	2	43160	42276	44720	30680	40820	50960	66	47	E	43160
E034	B	ANALYS BUS SYSTEMS SR	1	44720	44720	44720	31564	44258	53352	69	17	E	44720
Q154	B	PROGRAMMER ANALYST STAFF	4	45032	45032	45032	35828	45136	54444	52	18	E	45032
E231	A	PROGRAMMER ANALYST STAFF	4	47436	44580	53040	36600	47604*	57096	69	10	E	47436
Q018	A	INFO SYS ANALYST SR	4	47700	44644	49008	32700	44790	56880	74	23	E	47700
E015	B	PROGRAMMER ANALYST I	1	48308	48308	48308	33540	41912	50284	60	49	E	48308
P005	B	SR MIS SPEC	1	50492	50492	50492	34216	45604*	54704	60	10	E	50492
		26 COMPANIES TOTAL INCUMBENTS	696										
		COMPANY P844 AVERAGE	3	39252	37392	42300	27744	39836	51528	86	28	E	39252
		MARKET WEIGHTED AVERAGE	693	38570	36314	44659	31179	40999	50801	63	A4		38647
		MARKET SIMPLE AVERAGE		40360			31667	41143	50475	59			40596
		MARKET ARITHMETIC AVERAGE MIDPOINT LOW		32396	27000	32500	25220	31564	37908	48			33692
		HIGH		50492	50492	53040	36600	47604	57096	92			50492
		3 COMPANIES MATCHING MODIFIER C	12	36463	33949	40394	28577	37172	45768	60			37083
		23 COMPANIES MATCHING MODIFIER B	513	37531	36731	42817	31194	40530	49712	59			37587
		6 COMPANIES MATCHING MODIFIER A	168	41893	39801	49982	34133	44675	54962	61			41996

Source: Organization Resources Counselors, Inc.

217

EXHIBIT 7.13
Scatterplot/Frequency Distribution of Salaries for Business Applications Programmers/Analysts (in thousands)

$ (in thousands)

Frequency	32	33	34		36	37	38	39	40	41	42	43	44	45	46	47	48	49	50
	2		13	297	1	3		22	9	125	1	1	10	1	1	4	1		1
		8	2		12	1			7	3			2			4			
									1	103									
									4	24									
									13										
									6										
Total	7	0	15	305	13	4	4	22	40	255	1	1	12	1	1	8	1	0	1

Scatter plots/frequency distribution. Let us use these data to illustrate some typical analyses. A scatter plot/frequency distribution of wages for each job, similar to the one in Exhibit 7.13 is a useful first step. A scatter plot provides a visual picture, or a "snapshot," of the relationships found in the data. For example, Exhibit 7.13 shows that almost all the salaries are between $35,000 and $42,000. In this case, the one salary above $50,000 may be considered an outlyer—an extreme value that falls beyond the majority of the data points. Distributions can vary in their shape. Unusual distributions require further analysis to assess the usefulness of the data. They may reflect problems with job matches, widely dispersed pay rates, or employers with widely divergent pay policies. One wag has suggested that if the data look reasonable, it is probably the result of two large, offsetting errors.

If the purpose of the survey is relatively simple, for example, to simply check on the going rate of entry level messengers, a frequency distribution may provide an adequate analysis. More typically, additional analysis is required. Measures to summarize the data in the frequency distribution are used.

Central Tendency

Mean, weighted mean, median, and mode are all measures of central tendency that are used in analyzing survey data. They summarize the data into one number. For example, take a closer look at the salaries that company E008 in Exhibit 7.12 pays its five senior data processing analysts. These five individual salaries are listed in Exhibit 7.14. The average, or mean wage, is $32,656 (sum of wages paid divided by the number of people), and this is the number reported in the survey. But there are alternative measures of central tendency, which may sometimes paint a different picture of the actual data than does the mean. Median, for example, is the middle measure in an array of data from highest to lowest. And mode is the most frequently occurring measure. Mean is a common measure used, but if outlyers, or extreme values, are a problem, median is often substituted, on the grounds that the mean is distorted by the outlyers.

When combining data from many companies, as in the summary statistics found near the bottom of Exhibit 7.12, using the mean wage from *each company* gives equal weight

---

EXHIBIT 7.14
Measures of Central Tendency: Mean, Median, and Mode

5 senior data processing analysts salaries—Company E008

$28,288
$30,460
$33,604
$35,464
$35,464

Mean = $32,656; sum of wages divided by number of people
Median = $33,604; in a continuum, the middle wage
Mode = $35,464; the most frequently occurring wage

Weighted mean: Each company's mean wage is weighted by the number of people reported in that company

to every company in the survey (simple average). The programmer wage paid by company G002, which has only one individual in that position, counts as much as the wage paid by E017, where there are 297 programmers. An alternative is a **weighted mean,** which is more representative of the market rate on a supply-demand basis. It weights *each individual employee* wage equally. A weighted mean combines all the data in the frequency distribution. Each company's mean wage is weighted by the number of people in that company who occupy that job. There are separate summary lines in Exhibit 7.12 for the mean (simple average) and the weighted mean.[24]

Dispersion

Dispersion refers to the distribution of rates around a measure of central tendency. Dispersion can be examined among the distribution of rates for each job, or for the entire sample of companies in the survey.

   Standard deviation is probably the most common statistical measure of dispersion. It refers to how far from the mean each of the items in a frequency distribution is located. In the frequency distribution based on data in Exhibit 7.12 the standard deviation is $4423.92, which means that 68 percent of the salaries lie within ± 1 standard deviation or between $35,914 and $44,762.

   Percentiles and quartiles are commonly used descriptions of salary distributions. Exhibit 7.8 shows the 10th, 25th, 50th, 75th, and 90th percentile curves for engineers' salaries. Ten percent of all engineers in the survey receive salaries below the 10th percentile, while 90 percent receives salaries above that line. Quartiles correspond to the 25th (Q1), 50th (Q2), 75th (Q3), and 100th (Q4) percentile. Recall from the introduction to this chapter that one organization's policy was to "be in the top 10 percent," another's was "to be in the 65th percentile nationally." A 65th percentile would mean that 65 percent of all companies' pay rates are at or below that point, and 35 percent are above.

   Ranges exist if two or more rates are paid for the same job. As we have seen, not all programmers within the same organization receive the same salary. Most companies as a matter of policy establish a minimum and maximum salary for each position, which sets the limits within which individual programmers' salaries fall, depending on performance or experience. Exhibit 7.12 gives the ranges established by each survey participant for this particular job.

   From these data, *range spreads* can be calculated using the formula:

$$\text{Range spread} = \frac{\text{Maximum} - \text{minimum}}{\text{Minimum}}$$

---

[24]This particular survey report includes more than one job per company. For example, company E008 senior data processing analyst position and its ADP analyst position are both included. The first job is labeled C, a weaker match. The second is labeled B, an exact match with the survey job. The last three lines of Exhibit 7-12 separate data based on the strength of the job match. More commonly, a survey would report only one match per company, with little information provided that would allow the user to assess the strength of that match.

The higher the percent, the greater the dollar distance between minimum and maximum salaries. A later section of this chapter will discuss how to design salary ranges within a pay system.

COMBINE JOB EVALUATION AND MARKET SURVEYS

Before further reviewing more mechanics, it is useful to step back a moment and reconsider what we are trying to accomplish with surveys. One objective is to design pay levels and structures that employees feel are fair and equitable and that will help accomplish management's objectives. Two components of the pay model are emerging, and their relationship to each other is depicted in Exhibit 7.15.[25]

- An *internally equitable job structure* based on *job analysis* and *job evaluation* has been developed and is shown on the horizontal axis in Exhibit 7.15.
- Rates paid by *competitors in the external market* for benchmark jobs in that structure are based on the survey. The purpose of the survey is to help position pay competitively in the external market (the vertical axis in Exhibit 7.15).

EXHIBIT 7.15
Relationship between Internal Consistency and External Competitiveness

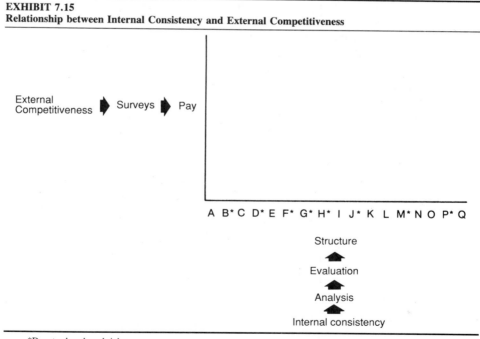

*Denotes benchmark jobs.

[25]Nancy Brown Johnson and Ronald A. Ash, "Incorporating the Labor Market into Job Evaluation: Clearing the Cobwebs," working paper, University of Kansas School of Business, Lawrence, Kans., 1985.

The next steps are to construct the market pay lines, to update the market data, and to set the employer's pay policy line and design the pay structure.

Construct Market Pay Lines

We have discussed the distribution of market rates reported for each job (e.g., scatter plot/frequency distribution Exhibit 7.13) and typical approaches to analyze these rates. But a survey rarely focuses on a single job. Rather, data are gathered for any number of different jobs. These jobs may be related (e.g., computer programmers and computer operators), or they may cover a broader range of work. If the purpose of the survey is to set pay rates for a number of jobs with respect to the market, a way is needed to combine data from all the surveyed jobs. A market pay line does this by summarizing rates of the various jobs found in the market.

There are a number of approaches used to construct market pay lines. A fruitful beginning is to construct a frequency distribution of rates for each of the surveyed jobs, as shown in Exhibit 7.16. Note that job structure (job evaluation points) is the X axis and $ is the Y axis value. Each survey participant's mean rates for the benchmark jobs (B, D, F, H, M, P) are on the Y axis. The frequency of the rates provides a third dimension to the exhibit, similar to a topographic map. In our example, rates for some of the jobs form a normal bell-shaped distribution (jobs D, H, and M), for other jobs the distribution is less normal (B, F, and P). But these plots provide too much data. One way to summarize the data is to fit a line to the midpoints (central tendency) of these

EXHIBIT 7.16
Relationship Between Job Structure and Market Survey Data

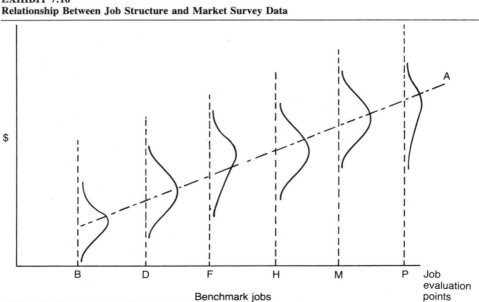

distributions. (Line A, Exhibit 7.16). A straight line or a curve is most useful, even though midpoints for some jobs (F, H, and P) may not fall on this line. Additional lines may be drawn to represent various percentiles in the distributions of job rates (e.g., a 60 percent line would indicate that 60 percent of market rates fall below this line).

A market line may be drawn freehand on the basis of simple inspection of the data as was Line A. For statistically more accurate results, the regression technique is commonly used. Regression fits a line which minimizes the variance of observations around it. An appendix to this chapter provides additional information on regression and interpreting its results. The result is a market pay line which summarizes the distribution of going rates in the market.

So at this point, the survey data have been analyzed for accuracy, and summarized via a market line to make the information more manageable. Another step is to update or "age" the data.

Update the Survey Data

Three to six months (or more) may pass before all participating firms return their survey, data are coded and analyzed, and the report is available for use in decision making. By this time the survey data may be outdated if market rates have already changed. Consequently, the data are usually updated to forecast the competitive rates for the future date when the pay decisions will be implemented.

There are two issues involved in updating (often called "aging") the survey data. The first is *how much* (the amount) to update the data and the second is the *time horizon*. The amount chosen is based on several factors, including historical trends in the market data based on current and previous surveys, economic forecasts (prospects for the economy and the markets in which the employer operates, consumer price index, etc.), and the manager's judgment.

The time horizon includes the current period and the plan period—the period (usually 12 months) in which the compensation plan will be implemented and operate.

Exhibit 7.17 illustrates one of several approaches for updating. In the example, the pay rates collected in the survey were in effect as of January 1 of the *current year*. The compensation manager will use these data for pay decisions that will go into effect January 1 of the next year, labeled *plan year* in the exhibit. According to historical trends reported in this and past surveys, the pay rates have been increasing by approximately 5 percent annually. If we assume the future will be like the past, then the market pay line is multiplied by 1.05 to account for the rise in pay that is expected to occur during the *current year*. To estimate what the market rates will be by the *end* of the plan year, a judgment is made about the rate of increase expected during the plan year and survey results are updated again on the basis of this judgment. In Exhibit 7.17, the assumed 6 percent increase during the plan year may be based on an expected increase in demand for the particular skills included in this survey. By the end of the plan year, the assumption is that the market will have increased by a factor of 1.13 (1.05 × 1.06 = 1.13), or 13 percent, over January 1 of the current year.

Now that the survey data are updated, the employer's pay level can be set.

EXHIBIT 7.17
Updating Survey Data: An Illustration

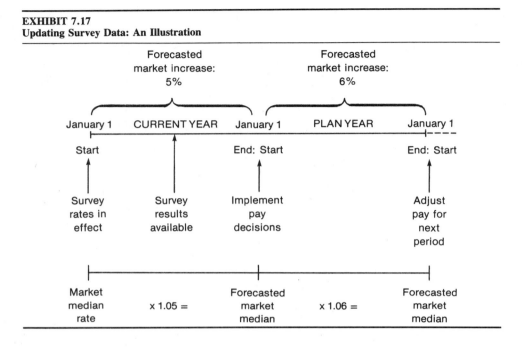

Set the Employer's Pay Level

Markets are dynamic, reflecting decisions of employers, employees, unions, and government agencies. As a result, wages paid by competitors change over time. And competitors adjust their wages at different times. Universities typically adjust to match the academic year. Unionized employers adjust to correspond to dates negotiated in labor agreements. Many employers adjust each employee's pay on the anniversary of the employee's date of hire. Even though all these changes do not occur smoothly and uniformly throughout the year, as a practical matter it is common practice to assume that adjustments do occur uniformly over the time period.

Exhibit 7.18 shows market movement through time. Note that the market pay line, set through regression analysis and updated to the start of the plan year, is expressed as a single point, A: the midpoint of this updated market line. At the start of the plan year, the midpoint is at A. Let's assume that the wages will increase by 6 percent during the year—to A^1. The solid line, AA^1, depicts the market's movement during the year.

Because an individual company typically sets its pay level only once per period, its pay level will be at the same point at both the beginning and the end of the plan year, represented by horizontal line, BB^1. Exhibit 7.18 also shows the three conventional competitive policy options: lead, match, lag. The point is to set the firm's line consistent with the organization's desired external competitiveness policy. In the case of lead policy, the illustration shows an organization setting its pay level (e.g., the median or mean rate) so it will be at least *equal* to the market's midpoints at the *end* of the plan year. A lead

EXHIBIT 7.18
Putting Pay Level Policy into Practice

Policy	Mechanics	Illustration
I. Lead competition	Set our midpoint pay line (50th percentile or average) at the start of plan year to match competition by the *end* of the plan year or Set our midpoint pay (50th percentile) to match competition's 60 or 75th percentile or Set our midpoint pay to match only a few selected top paying competitors	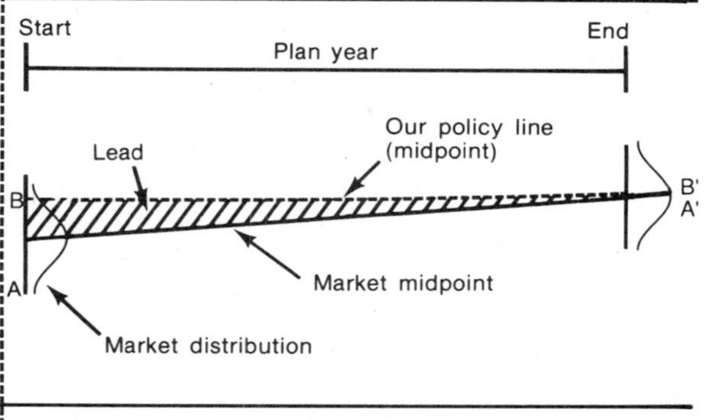
II. Pay with competition (lead/lag)	Set our midpoint pay line to match competition's at mid-year	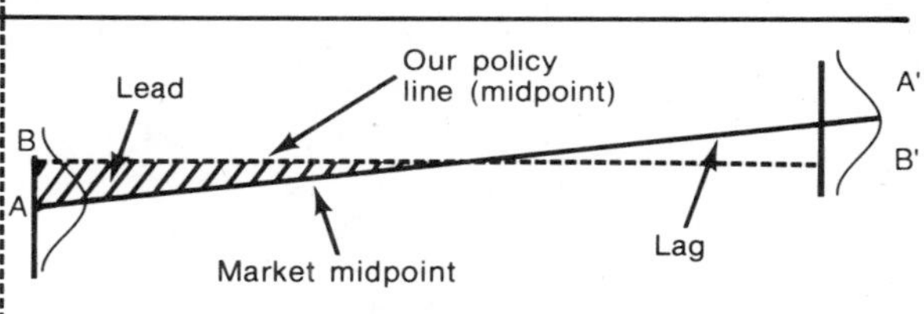
III. Follow competition	Set our midpoint pay line to be less than or match competition's at the *start* of the plan year	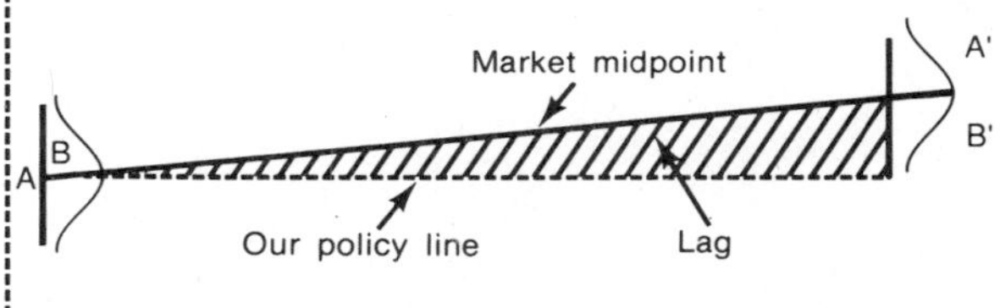

policy requires that they set it *above* the market rates at the start of the plan year. As the year progresses, the market rates are expected to increase so that the degree by which the organization increases its pay level again for the following plan year.

Employers may use other techniques to apply a lead policy. Midpoint pay may be pegged at the market's 60th or 75th percentile, or midpoint pay may match only a few top-paying competitors.

To establish a match policy, the organization may use a lead/lag mechanism. The pay level is set so that it leads competition for half the year and lags for the other half. A "follow competition" policy involves setting the organization pay level so that it lags the market level during the year.

Recognize that practice does not always match policy. For example, the employer in Figure A of Exhibit 7.19 espouses a "match competition" policy but because of the method used, it only "matches" competition on the first day of each year. The rest of the time its pay level is lagging its competitors. To achieve the "matches competition" policy

EXHIBIT 7.19
Lead-Lag: Matching Practice to Policy

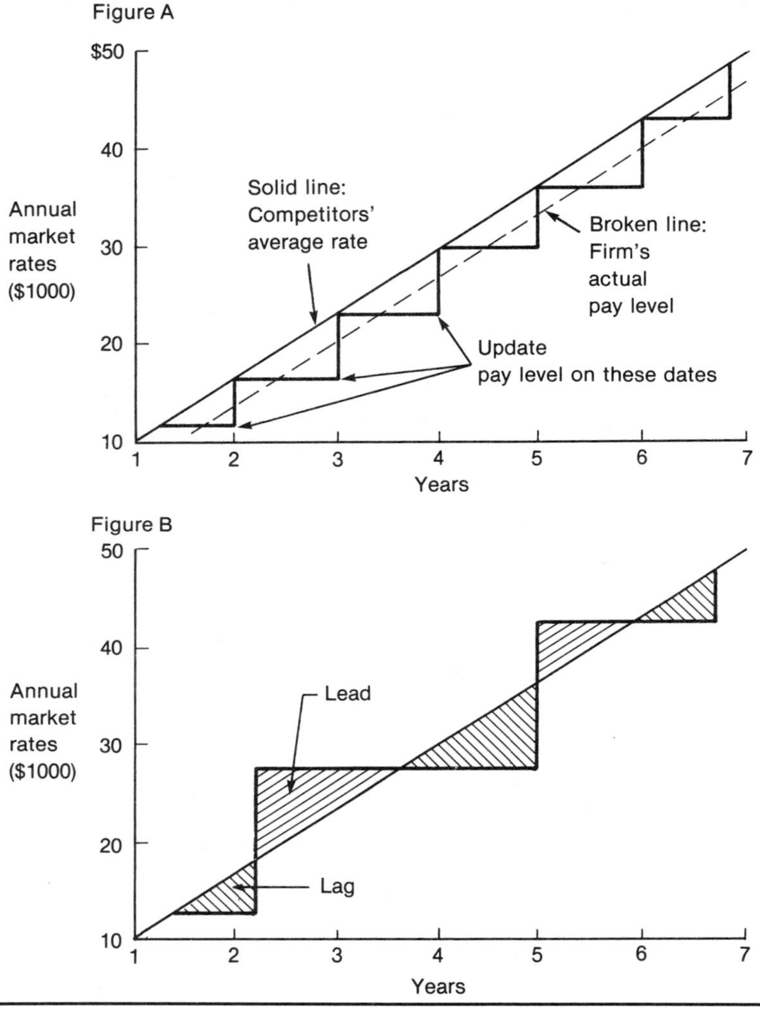

Figure A

Figure B

the employer must "saw tooth" the market rate (Figure B), that is, set its pay level so it leads half the time and lags the other half.

Compare with Competition

Survey data are also used to analyze how an organization's current rates compare to the rates paid by competition. These analyses are relatively straightforward and there may be as many different approaches to them as there are compensation professionals. The total cash compensation of auto component assemblers in a major U.S. firm versus its

EXHIBIT 7.20
Comparing Pay at Major Motors with Competitors' Pay

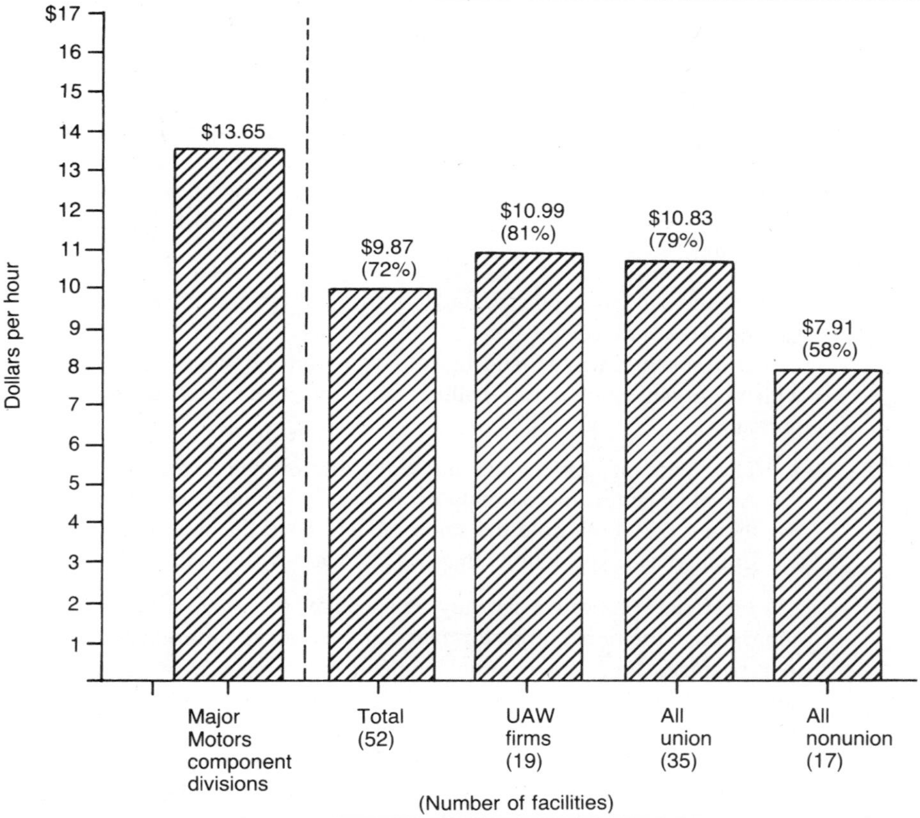

competition is shown in Exhibit 7.20. Note the $13.65 paid by Major Motors exceeds the $9.87 (72% of $13.65) all company average, and the $10.99 (81% of $13.65) paid by other firms organized by the United Auto Workers. The point of this analysis is to assess the competitiveness of Major Motors' current wages. We would expect that, based on its lead position, Major Motors experiences low turnover, has a queue of applicants for every job vacancy, but risks higher labor costs (assuming similar employment levels among its competitors).

DESIGN PAY RANGES

The pay policy line has now been established based on the organization's competitive policy regarding the external market and the survey that provided data on competitors' pay. The next step is to design pay ranges for jobs inside the organization. A pay range exists whenever two or more rates are paid to incumbents in a given job.

Why Bother with Ranges?

Ranges provide a mechanism to deal with pressure from the external labor market and within the organization.[26] The wide variation of rates paid for similar jobs and skills reflects two *external* pressures:

1. The existence of quality variations (skills, abilities, experience) among individuals in the external market (e.g., company A has stricter hiring requirements for its buyer position than does company B, even though job descriptions are identical).
2. The recognition of differences in the productivity-related value to employers to these quality variations (e.g., buyers are more important to Neiman-Marcus than they are to Wal-Mart).

Both of these factors translate into a variety of rates in the external market rather than a single market rate for buyers.

Differences in rates paid to employees on the same job also should be consistent with an organization's pay policies and objectives. Hence ranges reflect the *internal* pressures:

1. The intention to recognize individual performance variations with pay (e.g., Buyer A makes better, more timely decisions for Neiman-Marcus than does Buyer B, even though they both hold the same job and have the same responsibilities).
2. Employees' expectations that pay increases will occur over time.

From an internal consistency perspective, the range established for any job should approximate the range of performance or experience differences that an employer wishes to recognize. From an external competitive perspective, the range acts as a control device.[27] A range maximum sets the lid on what the employer is willing to pay for that work; the range minimum sets the floor.

But not all employers use ranges. For example, in cases where collective bargaining contracts establish wages, single *flat rates* rather than ranges are paid for each job. For example, all Senior Machinists II receive $14.50 per hour regardless of performance or seniority. This flat rate is often set to correspond to some midpoint on a survey of that job.

Constructing Ranges

Designing ranges is relatively simple. There is no "best" approach, but four basic steps are typically involved.

1. *Develop classes or grades.* In Exhibit 7.21 the horizontal axis is the job structure generated through job evaluation. Recall that a grade or class is a grouping of different

---

[26]Jeff S. Emans and William W. Seithel, "Remedying Salary Inequities: Cleaning Up Your Act Systematically," *Compensation and Benefits Review,* July-August 1985, pp. 14–23.

[27]James D. Finch, "Computerized Retrieval of Pay Survey Data, Linking Compensation Practices to Business Strategies," *Personnel Administrator,* July 1985, pp. 31–38.

EXHIBIT 7.21
Construct Grades or Classes

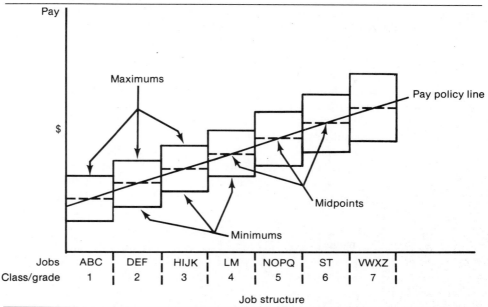

jobs; thus, each grade is made up of a number of jobs. The jobs in each grade are considered substantially equal for pay purposes. They may have approximately the same job evaluation points (e.g., within 20 or 30 points in a 500-point job evaluation plan). Each grade will have its own pay range, and all the jobs within the grade have that same range. Jobs in different grades (e.g., jobs D, E, and F in grade 2) should be dissimilar to those in other grades (grade 1, jobs A, B, and C) and will have a different range.

The use of job grades enhances an organization's ability to move people among jobs within a pay grade with no change in pay.[28]

But there are disadvantages to using salary grades, too. While grading recognizes the imprecision in job evaluation, it may be difficult to construct grades so that all jobs of identifiably similar content lie within the same grade. If jobs with relatively close job evaluation point totals fall on either side of grade boundaries (e.g., jobs E, F, and G have point totals within 30 points of each other, but E and F are in one grade, and G is in another), the magnitude of difference in salary treatment may be out of proportion to the magnitude of difference in job content. Resolving such dilemmas requires an understanding of the specific jobs, the needs of the organization, and the pressures it faces.

---

[28]Martin Wolf, "Solving Technical Problems in Establishing the Pay Structure," in *Handbook of Wage & Salary Administration*.

In Chapter 4 we stated that the number of grades or classes depended on the variety and diversity of the jobs involved, traditions in the workplace, and the career paths in the organization. To this list we now add the results of the survey data, particularly the slope of the pay curve and the pay differentials that are established between the grades. What is the correct number of job grades? Once more, our answer is, "it depends." Designing the grade structure that "fits" each organization involves trial and error until one seems to fit the best without too many problems.

2. ***Select Desired Range (midpoint, minimum and maximums).*** Determining the midpoints for each range is important. They are usually set to correspond to the competitive policy established earlier. Hence, the policy line represents the organization's competitive pay policy relative to the competitor's pay for similar work. And each range's midpoint is based on the pay policy line as shown in Exhibit 7.21. The midpoint becomes the *competitive objective* or control point. In the example below the midpoint is 100 percent of the competitive objective, the maximum is 115 percent, and the minimum is 85 percent of the competitive objective.

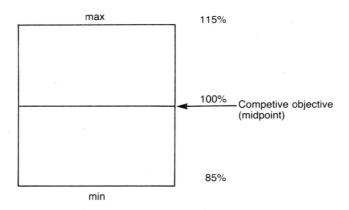

The desired range spread is based on some judgment about how the ranges support career paths, promotions, and other organization systems. In the above example, the range spread is approximately 35 percent.[29] Range spreads seem to vary between 10 to 120 percent. Top level management positions commonly have range spreads of 60 to 120 percent; entry to mid-level professional and managerial positions, between 35 to 60 percent; for office and production work, 10 to 25 percent is common. The underlying logic is that wider range spreads in the managerial jobs are designed to reflect the greater opportunity for individual discretion in the work.

Another, perhaps better basis on which to determine the desired range spreads is what makes good sense for the particular employer. Surveys usually provide data on both the actual maximum and minimum rates paid, as well as the ranges established

---

[29]The formula for range spread is on page 220. A range spread of 35% corresponds to ± 15% of the midpoint. A 50% range spread equals the midpoint ± 35%.

by policy (turn back to Exhibit 7.13 for an example). Some compensation professionals use the actual rates paid, particularly the 75th and 25th percentiles (if available) to establish the maximums and minimums. Others examine alternatives to insure that the range spread selected includes at least 75 percent of the rates paid for the work based on the survey data. In the end, range spread is based on judgment that weighs all these factors.

Once the midpoint (based on the pay policy line) and the range spread (based on judgment) are specified, minimums and maximums are calculated:

Minimum = Midpoint ÷ [100% + (1/2 range spread)]
Maximum = Minimum + (range spread × minimum)

For example, if the recommended range spread is 30 percent, and the midpoint is $10,000,

Minimum = $10,000 ÷ (1 + .15) = $8,695
Maximum = $8,695 × (.30 × $8695) = 8695 + 2609 = $11,304

3. **Degree of Overlap.** If A and B are two adjacent pay grades, the degree of overlap is defined as

$$\frac{\text{Maximum}_A - \text{Minimum}_B}{\text{Minimum}_B}$$

What difference does overlap make? Consider the two extremes shown in Exhibit 7.22. A high degree of overlap and low midpoint differentials in Figure A indicate small

EXHIBIT 7.22
Range Overlap

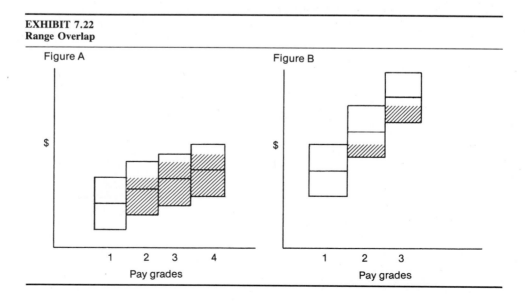

differences in the value of jobs in the adjoining grades. Such a structure results in promotions (title changes) without much change in pay. On the other hand, in Figure B, few grades and ranges result in wider range midpoint differentials and less overlap between adjacent ranges, and permit the manager to reinforce a promotion—a movement into a new range—with a larger pay increase. At some point the differential must be great enough to induce employees to seek and/or accept the promotion or to undertake the necessary training required. However, there is little research to indicate how much of a differential is necessary to influence employees to take on additional responsibilities or invest in training.[30]

A related issue is the size of pay differentials between supervisors and the employees they supervise. A supervisory job would typically be at least one pay range removed from the jobs it supervises. While a 15 percent pay differential has been offered as a rule of thumb, large range overlap, combined with possible overtime or incentive pay available in some jobs but not in supervisory jobs, could make it difficult to maintain such a differential.

Geographic Differentials—Locality Pay

Many employers have historically maintained one national pay structure for their managerial-professional work force and separate schedules tied to local pay rates for their blue collar and clerical employees. But increasing differences in costs of living in different locations make recruiting and transferring professional employees difficult. The FBI has documented the problems that arise with a single structure.[31] In New York City, starting salaries for FBI agents in 1986 was less than $25,000, compared to over $35,000 for New York City detectives. Not only is the FBI experiencing difficulty in retaining agents in New York City, it is having difficulty in transferring them from more rural regions to high cost (and high crime) areas such as New York City and Los Angeles. For example, an agent transferred from Omaha will face living costs 56 percent higher in Boston. Many large employers are considering the use of geographic differentials based in part on local and regional differences in living costs. However, pay differences based on local and regional data may become so disconnected as to cause dissatisfaction and lack of cooperation among coworkers across locations. Omaha FBI agents may feel underpaid if Boston-area salaries for agents are raised. Several consulting firms offer geographic differential surveys and some employers base their differentials on a few key items such as cost of housing.

---

[30]P. Varadarajan and C. Futrell, "Factors Affecting Perceptions of Smallest Meaningful Pay Increases," *Industrial Relations,* Spring 1984, pp. 278–86; and Linda Krefting, Jerry Newman, and Frank Krzystofiak, "What is a Meaningful Pay Increase?" in *Perspectives on Compensation,* eds. L. Gomez-Mejia and D. Balkin (Englewood Cliffs, N.J.: Prentice-Hall, 1987).

[31]*1989 Survey of Locality Pay Practices in Large U.S. Corporations,* conducted for the U.S. Office of Personnel Management by the Wyatt Company, Philadelphia, Pa.; L. D. Tanner, "Developing a Locality Pay System," *Classification and Compensation Society Newsletter,* June 1988, pp. 1–5; G. L. Stelluto, "Federal Pay Comparability," *Monthly Labor Review,* June 1979, pp. 18–29; and Office of Personnel Management, *Update of Federal Pay Comparability,* (Washington, D.C.: Government Printing Office, 1988).

BALANCING INTERNAL AND EXTERNAL PRESSURES: ADJUSTING THE PAY STRUCTURE

Establishing the pay ranges for work reflects a balance between competitive pressures and pressures for internal consistency and fairness. Up until now we have made a distinction between the job structure and the pay structure. A job structure is generated through the process of job analysis and job evaluation. In it jobs are ordered on the basis of total points (point plan), classes and grades (classification plan), or ranks (ranking plan). The pay structure, on the other hand, is anchored by the organization's pay policy line, which is set using the market rates paid for key jobs.

Reconciling Differences

The problem with using two methods to create a structure is that you are likely to get two different structures. The order in which jobs are ranked on internal (job evaluation) and external (market surveys) factors may not completely agree. Certainly differences between the market rate and the job evaluation rank warrant a review of the basic decisions in evaluating and pricing that particular job. This may entail reviewing the job analysis, the job description sheets, and the evaluation of the job. It also means reexamining the market data as it pertains to the job in question. Often this reanalysis solves the problem. In cases where discrepancies persist, experienced judgment is required. Sometimes survey data are discarded; sometimes benchmark job matches are changed. Studies that examined the relative importance managers place on external versus internal factors reported that external market data weigh more heavily than internal job evaluation data. One possible explanation is that market data are considered to be more objective in disputes.[32] Too frequently, decisions are made on the basis of expediency, and these decisions can undermine the integrity of the pay system. Reclassifying a market-sensitive job (supply and demand imbalance) into a higher salary grade, where it will tend to remain long after the imbalance has been corrected, will only create additional problems in the long run. Creating a special range that is clearly designated as market responsive may be a better approach.

Compression

Compression problems are classic examples of an imbalance between external competitive pressures and internal equity.[33] Compression results when wages for those jobs filled from outside the organization are increasing faster than the wages for jobs filled from within the organization. The result is that as pay differentials among jobs become very small, the traditional pay structure becomes compressed. A classic example is an employer with a large number of jobs at or near the minimum wage. Whenever Congress legislates

---

[32]Sara Rynes, Caroline Weber, and George Milkovich, "Effects of Market Survey Rates, Job Evaluation and Job Gender on Job Pay," *Journal of Applied Psychology* 74, 1, 1989, pp. 114–23.

[33]Thomas J. Bergmann, Frederick S. Hills, and Laurel Priefert, "Pay Compression: Causes, Results, and Possible Solutions," *Compensation Review* 15, no. 2 (1983), pp. 17–26.

an increase in the minimum wage, or labor market conditions necessitate raising entry level wages, the employer must decide whether to shift the entire wage structure upward in order to maintain differentials, or to narrow it. Either decision can be costly, in dollars and/or employee dissatisfaction.

Compression is also an issue in professional work (engineers, lawyers, professors) where new graduates command salaries almost equal to those of professionals with three to five years experience. A study of business school professors found that a decision to boost faculty quality by paying premium salaries for the best new assistant professors available backfired, because rates for the rest of the faculty were not increased, too.[34] Dissatisfaction among older faculty led to the rapid loss of the best professors, who were able to find other jobs. With only the less marketable professors remaining, the overall faculty quality declined. (The older the authors of this text get, the greater the importance we attach to studies that recommend raising salaries for older professors.)

In sum, the process of balancing internal and external pressures is a matter of judgment, made with an eye to the objectives established for the pay system. De-emphasizing internal pay relationships may lead to feelings of inequitable treatment among employees. These in turn may reduce employees' willingness to share new ideas on how to improve the work or improve the product's quality. Inequitable internal pay relationships may also lead employees to seek other jobs, file grievances, form unions, go out on strike, or refuse to take on greater job responsibilities. Neglecting external pay relationships, however, will affect both the ability to attract job applicants and the ability to hire those applicants who match the organization's needs. External pay relationships also influence the organization's labor costs and hence its ability to compete in the product/services market.

SUMMARY

This chapter has detailed the basic decisions and techniques involved in setting pay levels and designing pay ranges. Most organizations survey other employers' pay rates to determine competitive rates paid in the market. An employer using the survey results considers how it wishes to position its pay in the market: to lead, to match, or to follow competition. This policy decision may be different for different business units and even for different job groups within a single organization. The pay policy is then translated into practice by setting pay policy lines. These lines reflect the employer's position in the market and serve as reference points around which pay ranges are established.

The use of ranges is a recognition of both external and internal pressures. No single going rate for a job exists in the market; an array of rates exists. This array results from variations in the quality of employees for that job and differences in employer policies and practices. It also reflects the fact that employers differ in the value they attach to the jobs and qualifications. Internally, the use of ranges is consistent with variations in the

---

[34]Luis R. Gomez-Mejia and David B. Balkin, "Causes and Consequences of Pay Compression: The Case of Business Schools," working paper, Management Department, University of Florida, Gainesville, Fla., November 1984.

discretion present in jobs. Some employees will perform better than others; some employees are more experienced than others. Pay ranges permit employers to value and recognize these differences with pay.

Let us step back for a moment to review what has been discussed and preview what is coming. We have examined two components of the pay model. Internal consistency issues and techniques include job analysis, job descriptions, and job evaluation. These techniques determine a job structure. External competitiveness issues and techniques include policy determination, survey design and analysis, setting the pay policy line, and designing pay ranges. The next part of the book will examine issues involved in employee contributions—paying the individuals who perform the work. This is perhaps the most important part of the book. All that has gone before is a prelude, setting up the pay levels and pay structures within which individual employees are to be paid.

REVIEW QUESTIONS

1. Which competitive pay level policy would you recommend to an employer? Why? Does it depend on circumstances faced by the employer? Which ones?

2. How would you go about designing a survey for setting pay for welders? How would you go about designing a survey for setting pay for financial managers? Do the issues differ? Will the techniques used and the data collected differ? Why or why not?

3. What factors determine the relevant market for a survey? Why is the definition of the relevant market so important?

4. In what situations would you recommend your employer use benchmark jobs in survey? When would you recommend a skill-based or job valuation approach?

5. What do surveys have to do with pay discrimination?

6. Why are pay ranges used? Does their use assist or hinder the achievement of internal consistency? External competitiveness?

Appendix
Regression Analysis

Using the mathematical formula for a straight line,

y = a + bx,
y = dollars,
x = job evaluation points,
a is the y value (in dollars) at which x = 0, i.e., the straight line crosses the y axis,
b is the slope of the line.

If b = 0, the line is parallel to the x axis and all jobs are paid the same, regardless of job evaluation points. Using the dollars from the market survey data and the job evaluation points from the internal job structure, solving this equation enables the analyst to construct a line based on the relationship between the internal job structure and market rates. An upward sloping line means that greater job evaluation points are associated with higher dollars. The market line can be written as

pay for job A = a + (b × job evaluation points for job A),
pay for job B = a + (b × job evaluation points for job B), etc.

The issue is to estimate the values of a and b in an efficient manner, so that errors of prediction are minimized. This is what "least squares" regression analysis does.

For many jobs, particularly high level managerial and executive jobs, job evaluation is not used. Instead, salaries are related to some measure of company size (sales volume, operating revenues) as a measure of responsibility through the use of logarithms. In such situations, x and y are converted to logarithms (in base 10), and the equation for a straight line becomes

log y = a + b(log x)

where x is sales or revenues (in millions of dollars), and

y = current compensation (in thousands of dollars).

Example: Given sales and compensation levels for a sample of jobs, assume that

a = 1.7390
b = 0.3000

Using the equation log y = 1.7390 + 0.3000 (log x), one can calculate the current market rate for the chief executive in a company with sales of $500 million.

1. First set x = 500, that is, 500,000,000 with six zeros dropped.
2. Log x = 2.6990
3. Multiply log x by 0.3000, which is the coefficient of the variable log x in the given equation. This results in a value of 0.8997.
4. Add to 0.8097 the constant in the equation, 1.7390. The result, 2.5487, is the value of log y.

5. The chief executive's total current compensation is the antilog of log y, which is 354. Read in thousands of dollars it is $354,000.

Equation: log y = 1.7390 + 0.3000 (log x)

    x = $500,000,000 = 500

    log x = 2.6990

    log y = 1.7390 + 0.3000 (2.6990)

    log y = 1.7390 + 0.8097

    log y = 2.5487

    antilog y = 354

    y = $354,000

Note: Logarithm tables are found in most algebra textbooks.

Compensation Application
Comparing Faculty Salaries

Cornell University is frequently ranked as one of the top universities in the country. It is by far the largest employer in Ithaca, New York. Cornell is organized into two colleges, statutory and endowed. The statutory college includes the Agricultural, Human Ecology, and Industrial and Labor Relations Schools. The statutory colleges are considered a public university. About one-third of their budget is provided by New York State, and their tuition is comparable to other state-supported universities. The endowed schools—the arts and sciences, engineering, and architecture—are private. Tuition is on a level with Harvard, Princeton, and Yale. The following article by David Folkenflik recently appeared in the Cornell Daily Sun.

CORNELL FACULTY SALARIES REMAIN UNCOMPETITIVE WITH TOP COLLEGES[34]

Cornell professors received pay raises commensurate with the national university average for the 1988–89 school year and slightly above the rate of inflation, but salary levels continue to lag behind comparable institutions, according to faculty and top administrators.

Many University officials, including President Frank H. T. Rhodes, believe the salary levels may prove to be a source of difficulty for the University in its quest to recruit and retain top faculty.

"We see that, on average, we pay about 10 percent below the marketplace," said Geoffrey V. Chester, dean of the College of Arts and Sciences.

Figures released by the Financial Policy Committee indicate that the University has become less competitive for faculty salaries in relationship with Ivy League schools and other "peer institutions"—for both endowed and statutory colleges.

Faculty Salaries 1988–89								
	All Public Universities		Cornell (Statutory)		All Private Universities		Cornell (Endowed)	
	Salary	1-yr. Increase	Salary	1-yr.* Increase	Salary	1-yr. Increase	Salary	1-yr.* Increase
Full Professor	$54,240	5.9%	$57,100	8.3%	$64,800	6.3%	$62,800	6.2%
Assoc. Professor	39,570	5.7	43,600	8.4	43,680	6.1	44,000	7.1
Assistant Professor	33,400	6.1	35,100	8.2	36,650	7.1	37,700	7.7

*1-yr. increase based on continuing faculty members eligible for Cornell's Institutional Planning and Analysis (IPA) Survey.

Information Courtesy of IPA and the American Association of University Professors.

---

[34]Adapted from an article by David Folkenflik that appeared in the *Cornell Daily Sun* on May 1, 1989, p. 1.

"In the early '80s, the endowed colleges of Cornell was ranked tenth" in faculty salaries among top four-year private universities, said Ronald D. Ehrenberg, a member of the financial policy committee. "Now, in the private part of the University, we're just not competitive," he said.

The tables released by another committee member peg Cornell's endowed schools as the 16th highest paying private institution, behind not only top-ranked Harvard and Stanford Universities, but Columbia University, the University of California at Berkeley and the Massachusetts Institute of Technology.

Cornell's State University of New York (SUNY) units, however, are in an even worse position than their endowed counterparts, Ehrenberg said.

Professors at the state colleges—the College of Agriculture and Life Sciences, the School of Industrial and Labor Relations, the College of Veterinary Medicine and the College of Human Ecology—receive yearly percentage increases commensurate with faculty at other SUNY schools, but start with lower base salaries.

Average raises from 1987–88 to 1988–89 for full faculty in the endowed colleges worked out to 6.2 percent; for associate professors, 7.1 percent; and for assistant professors, 7.7 percent, according to the figures released by the IPA. The figures for the pay hikes cover only continuing faculty members eligible for the IPA survey, and include raises caused by promotions.

"If you go on the figures, we're competing with second-echelon institutions" rather than Ivy League schools and other top universities, said one financial policy committee member.

DISCUSSION QUESTIONS (Use Spreadsheet Software, If Available)

1. Using graph paper, chart the salaries reported in the table. Put the three jobs—assistant professor, associate professor, and full professor—on the X axis. Put salary levels on the Y axis. Connect the points to make a pay line for each comparison. You should then have four lines on your chart, one connecting the salary levels at All Public Universities, another connecting the salary levels at Cornell (statutory), etc. Differentiate your lines by either using color, or different combinations of dots and dashes. Label the lines.

2. How is Cornell defining its relevant market? Do you agree with their distinction? Add a fifth line, the average salary at Cornell line, by combining data from Cornell (statutory) and Cornell (endowed), and calculating an average. Should the other jobs at Cornell be compared against similar markets? For example, should office, clerical, and technicians in the endowed schools be compared to rates paid in other endowed schools? Or should different markets be used for different groups of jobs?

3. What is Cornell's pay level when compared to the market? Does it matter who they compare to?

4. The cost of living in Ithaca, New York, is relatively low in comparison to the Boston area (Harvard, MIT), New York City (Columbia), and California (Stanford, Berkeley). Does this matter? Should it matter to managers designing and administering the Cornell pay system?

5. The table in the newspaper article also gives percent salary increases granted in 1988–89.

   a. Why do you think Cornell (endowed) gives different percentages to fulls, associates, and assistants? What effect will such a policy have on the slope of their pay line? What effect will it have on average pay? What effects do you think it may have on professors' attitudes and behaviors and subsequently on the university's effectiveness?

b. Assume that Cornell (endowed) will give these same percent increases next year. Calculate the new salaries after the raises are granted. On a new graph, draw in 1988–89 Cornell (endowed) salaries (from your previous graph) and the new 1989–90 salaries. Based on this, what future problems may Cornell anticipate?

c. If you are familiar with spreadsheet software, project the salary increases for all comparisons five years into the future using a computer. Graph the resulting salaries, and compare the slope and relative positions of the lines in five years with the present. Did anything change? If so, what are the implications of this result?

Part 3

Thus far we have concentrated on two components of the pay model (Exhibit III.1). Internal consistency and the practices to ensure it-job analysis and job evaluation—provide guidance relating jobs to each other in terms of the content of the work and the relative contributions of the jobs to the organization's objectives. External competitiveness, or comparisons with the external labor market, raises issues of proper survey definitions, setting policy lines, and arriving at competitive pay levels and equitable pay structures. This part of the book deals with a third critical dimension of the pay system design and administration—paying individual employees performing the job.

How much should one employee be paid relative to another when they both hold the same jobs in the same organization? If this question is not answered satisfactorily, all prior efforts to evaluate and price jobs may have been in vain. For example, the compensation manager determines that all systems analysts should be paid between $18,000 and $26,000. But where in that range is each individual paid? Should a good performer be paid more than a poor performer? If the answer is yes, how should performance be measured and what should be the differential reward? Similarly, should the systems analyst with more years' experience (i.e., higher seniority) be paid more than a co-worker with less time on the job? Again, if the answer is yes, what is the trade off between seniority and performance in assigning pay raises? As Exhibit III.1 suggests, all of these questions involve the concept of employee contribution. For the next three chapters we will be discussing different facets of employee contribution.

Chapter 8 considers how pay affects performance. In particular, two questions are addressed: First, *should* pay systems be designed to affect performance? Second, *can* pay systems be designed to affect performance? Many of the answers to these questions come from theories of motivation and empirical research evaluating strategies to motivate employees in the workplace.

Chapter 9 focuses on more subjective performance measurement systems and their relationship to compensation in general and pay increases in particular.

Chapter 10 looks at pay systems that assume performance can be objectively measured. In these times of productivity stagnation, such incentive systems are becoming increasingly attractive to organizations.

Employee Contributions: Determining Individual Pay

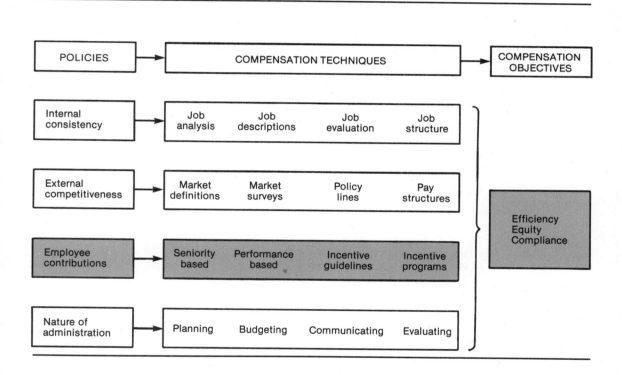

POLICIES	→	COMPENSATION TECHNIQUES	→	COMPENSATION OBJECTIVES
Internal consistency	→	Job analysis Job descriptions Job evaluation Job structure		
External competitiveness	→	Market definitions Market surveys Policy lines Pay structures		Efficiency Equity Compliance
Employee contributions	→	Seniority based Performance based Incentive guidelines Incentive programs		
Nature of administration	→	Planning Budgeting Communicating Evaluating		

The Little Red Hen: A Productivity Fable

Once upon a time there was a little red hen who scratched about the barnyard until she uncovered some grains of wheat. She turned to other workers on the farm and said: "If we plant this wheat, we'll have bread to eat. Who will help me plant it?"

"We never did that before," said the horse, who was the supervisor.

"I'm too busy," said the duck.

"I'd need complete training," said the pig.

"It's not in my job description," said the goose.

"Well, I'll do it myself," said the little red hen. And she did. The wheat grew tall and ripened into grain. "Who will help me reap the wheat?" asked the little red hen.

"Let's check the regulations first," said the horse.

"I'd lose my seniority," said the duck.

"I'm on my lunch break," said the goose.

"Out of my classification," said the pig.

"Then I will," said the little red hen, and she did.

At last it came time to bake the bread.

"Who will help me bake the bread?" asked the little red hen.

"That would be overtime for me," said the horse.

"I've got to run some errands," said the duck.

"I've never learned how," said the pig.

"If I'm to be the only helper, that's unfair," said the goose.

"Then I will," said the little red hen.

She baked five loaves and was ready to turn them in to the farmer when the other workers stepped up. They wanted to be sure the farmer knew it was a group project.

"It needs to be cleared by someone else," said the horse.

"I'm calling the shop steward," said the duck.

"I demand equal rights," yelled the goose.

"We'd better file a copy," said the pig.

But the little red hen turned in the loaves by herself. When it came time for the farmer to reward the effort, he gave one loaf to each worker.

"But I earned all the bread myself!" said the little red hen.

"I know," said the farmer, "but it takes too much paperwork to justify giving you all the bread. It's much easier to distribute it equally, and that way the others won't complain."

So the little red hen shared the bread, but her co-workers and the farmer wondered why she never baked any more. [From *Federal News Clip Sheet,* June 1979.]

W hat contributions do compensation policies and practices make to the success of an organization? To answer this question we have to understand the factors that influence the success of an organization. Strategy researchers suggest that organizations succeed or fail depending on how well they adapt to changes in the environment.[1] The auto industry provides a classic example. Over the past 15 years foreign competition has severely affected the success of automobile companies. For companies like General Motors to meet this threat several factors influencing the long-run success of organizations need to be considered. First, **costs** must be controlled. To combat foreign firms, the cost of making cars must be more competitive. Second, these auto makers have become too bureaucratic, that is, beset by so many rules and layers of reporting relationships that

---

[1]Charles W. Hofer and D. Schendel, *Strategy Formulation: Analytical Concepts* (St. Paul, Minn.: West Publishing, 1978).

rapid response to a changing environment is all but impossible. The internal **structure** of organizations, particularly large ones, should allow for greater flexibility in adapting to changes in the environment (e.g., changes in technology, changes in the labor or product market). Third, the very **culture and value system** of a firm may need to be reshaped to meet the new challenges that accompany a changing environment. For example, the auto industry is no longer insulated. Executives in the Big Three cannot simply be content with doing things the way they have always been done. More willingness to take risks needs to be encouraged. Employees at all levels of the organization should be encouraged to make suggestions for change. To do this, though, a firm needs to **attract and retain** high quality employees and **motivate** them to perform in ways that will help the organization compete effectively. This chapter briefly discusses the role of compensation in the first four of these objectives. The majority of the chapter, though, focuses on the role of compensation in motivating performance by employees.

THE ROLE OF COMPENSATION IN CONTROLLING COSTS

The relationship between compensation and product/service costs seems obvious. Labor is a factor of production. Control compensation costs and product costs are also affected. Even though this linkage is obvious, cost control has not always been a central concern of compensation professionals. When a firm faces little competition in its product or service market there is a tendency to worry less about labor costs.[2] Consider a simple example. It used to be common for companies to negotiate or unilaterally agree to provide a quality health care package, without any particular regard for the cost of that package. When health care costs began to soar in the 1970s, firms were caught in the difficult position of either absorbing the rapid increases or cutting back on the quality of the health care package provided. A better cost control strategy would have made costs the central issue of negotiations from the beginning. The firm negotiates a fixed dollar obligation which may or may not pay for the desired health care package. When the cost of this package rises, the company is only obligated to continue paying the fixed dollar cost negotiated earlier. Increasing the company contribution to cover cost escalation could be a topic of negotiation. No preset agreement to provide the total health package exists. Seemingly little shifts like this in focus toward cost issues have been a major trend in compensation in general and benefits determination in particular during the 1980s. (This issue is discussed in greater detail in Chapters 11 and 12.)

The emphasis on cost control in compensation packages is also evident in wage concession bargaining (Chapter 17) and in the design of alternative compensation systems (Chapter 10). A primary focus in all these efforts is identifying ways to pay people fairly and still improve the cost-competitive stance of the organization.

---

[2]Allan M. Cartter, *Theory of Wage and Employment* (Homewood, Ill.: Richard D. Irwin, 1959).

COMPENSATION AND THE STRUCTURE OF ORGANIZATIONS

A number of authors have stressed that long term organizational success depends on attention to the environment and the way it changes.[3] To the extent employees in an organization can rapidly identify changes in the environment and make sound decisions based on those changes, market share and profitability may rise. Part of the success in monitoring the environment depends on the way organizations structure themselves.[4] The amount of formalization and centralization in the structure of an organization may govern its ability to cope with a changing environment. Formalization refers to the number of rules an organization imposes on its workers and the extent to which these rules govern decision making of individuals.[5] In effect, formalization of rules forces explicit guidelines on employees, defining what they should or should not do and reducing willingness to explore alternative courses of action.[6] In contrast, low formalization allows employees more latitude in exploring new ways of coping with changes in the environment.[7] .

There is also fairly consistent agreement that decentralization permits an organization to respond more rapidly to its environment.[8] Rather than requiring separate business units to direct all decisions to a central headquarters, individual units are given greater latitude to respond to their unique environmental demands as they see fit. A classic example arose in the food industry during the early 1980s. Consumer preferences for cookies were shifting to the "soft batch" variety. Nabisco was slow to notice and respond to this trend. As a result, competitors cut into Nabisco's market share. Shortly thereafter, Nabisco began to decentralize their operations so each business unit could respond more rapidly to changes in both consumer tastes and competitor tactics. To encourage this greater autonomy at the local business unit level, Nabisco also restructured its compensation system to reward appropriate behaviors.

In theory, compensation specialists should be able to design reward systems that reinforce employees to work effectively in organizations varying in the level of formal-

---

[3]F. E. Lawler and E. L. Trist, "The Causal Texture of Organizational Environments," *Human Relations* 18 (1965), pp. 21–32; and B. Hedberg, "How Organizations Learn and Unlearn," in *Handbook of Organizational Design,* vol. 1, eds. P. C. Nystrom and W. H. Starbuck (New York: Oxford University Press, 1981), pp. 3–28.

[4]J. Pfeffer and G. Salancik, *The External Control of Organizations: A Resource Dependence Perspective* (New York: Harper & Row, 1978).

[5]D. C. Carroll, "Implications of On-Line, Real-Time Systems for Managerial Decision Making," in *The Management of Aerospace Programs,* ed. W. L. Johnson (Tarzana, Calif.: American Astronautical Society, 1967), pp. 345–70; R. H. Hall, "Technological Policies and Their Consequences," in *Handbook of Organizational Design,* vol. 2, eds. P. C. Nystrom and W. H. Starbuck (New York: Oxford University Press, 1981), pp. 320–35; and J. D. Thompson, *Organizations in Action* (New York: McGraw-Hill, 1967).

[6]Carroll, "Implications of On-Line, Real-Time Systems for Managerial Decision Making" and Thompson, *Organizations in Action.*

[7]Hall, "Technological Policies and Their Consequences."

[8]Hedberg, "How Organizations Learn and Unlearn"; and R. B. Duncan, "The Ambidextrous Organization: Designing Dual Structures for Innovation," *The Management of Organization Design,* vol. 1, eds. R. H. Kilmann, L. R. Pondy, and D. P. Slevin (New York: Elsevier North-Holland, 1976), pp. 167–88.

ization and centralization. Unfortunately, we know relatively little about how compensation systems should be designed to reinforce the existing structure. Reward systems have long been acknowledged as motivators of employee behavior, but we do not know what compensation features would reinforce employees to behave optimally in organizations with different levels of formalization and centralization.[9]

What literature does exist linking traditional organization theory variables to compensation focuses exclusively on the design of managerial reward systems in different structural environments.[10] The most promising of these studies found that steady state firms (those whose growth has leveled off) tended to have less compensation at risk and base incentive distribution on corporate performance.[11] Evolutionary firms depended more heavily on incentives and linked their distribution to division performance.

COMPENSATION AND AN ORGANIZATION'S VALUE SYSTEM

One of the more popular theories today with long run implications for compensation practices is called agency theory.[12] The central tenets of this theory are: 1) An organization and its employees may conflict in the goals they want to achieve, and 2) the organization and its employees differ in the amount of risk they are willing to take in achieving any particular goal. Another way of expressing these differences is to focus on the conflict in value systems between an organization and individual employees. Coca Cola, in the late 1970s, faced this problem. Employees were comfortable with an internal environment where risk taking was avoided. "Coke is number one and always will be" seemed to be the prevailing attitude. Little product innovation occurred. Tab was one of the few new products introduced over the previous 50 years. The organization realized, though, that this conservative value system would hinder new product development, and changing tastes in a diet-conscious America demanded new diet products. Over the next few years Coke changed the internal value system by making risk taking acceptable. Diet Coke, Caffeine-Free Coke, and Cherry Coke were the result. How can a compensation system contribute to this restructuring of employee value systems to better align them with organizational needs? Such questions have prompted compensation experts to experiment more with gain sharing plans, profit sharing plans, and stock option plans (all discussed in greater detail in Chapter 10). Each of these incentive packages share a common feature:

[9]P. Stonich, "The Performance Measurement and Reward System: Critical to Strategic Management", in *Organizations by Design: Theory and Practice,* eds. M. Jelinek, J. Litterer, and R. Miles (Homewood, Ill., Richard D. Irwin, 1986).

[10]N. A. Berg, "What's Different about Conglomerate Management," *Harvard Business Review* 47 (6), 1969, pp. 112–20; J. Kerr, "Diversification Strategies and Managerial Rewards: An Empirical Study," *Academy of Management Journal* 28 (1), 1985, pp. 155–79; R. A. Pitts, "Incentive Compensation and Organizational Design," *Personnel Journal* 53, 1974, pp. 338–48; and M. Salter, "Tailor Incentive Compensation to Strategy," *Harvard Business Review* 51, 1973, pp. 94–102.

[11]J. Kerr, "Diversification Strategies and Managerial Rewards: An Empirical Study," *Academy of Management Journal* 28 (1), 1985, pp. 155–79.

[12]K. Eisenhardt, "Agency Theory: An Assessment and Review," *Academy of Management Review* 14, no. 1 (1989), pp. 57–74.

employees are encouraged (i.e., compensated more) to adopt the goals and values of the organization. For example, consider a manager with a value system that favors decisions that maximize short-run profits. If an organization wants to encourage a more long-range outlook, it can introduce a stock option package. Managers receive payoffs tied to stock prices. Managers now have an incentive to avoid decisions that may have good immediate profit potential but hurt long-run success of the company. A concern over stock prices and the compensation tied to this index shapes a more long-range orientation.

COMPENSATION AND ATTRACTING/RETAINING GOOD EMPLOYEES

Organizations have long realized the role of pay in the selection process. If an applicant pool is too small to insure selection of sufficient numbers of qualified employees, one standard strategy is to raise the relative wage to attract more applicants.[13] In fact, the most recent economic thought, termed "efficiency wage theory," suggests that organizations may be perfectly rational in offering wages greater than required by the market to attract workers. When firm A offers higher wages than its competitors, so the theory goes, employees face greater risks when they perform at substandard levels. If caught, it is relatively more difficult, that is, longer unemployment, to find a comparable alternative job. Presumably, then, workers are less likely to shirk their task demands.[14]

Traditional selection theory also supports the basic logic of paying wages above the market clearing level. As noted in Chapter 7, paying above the market rate triggers several phenomena. First, the higher relative wage makes the opening more attractive. Recruitment is easier and more individuals apply for the job. Second, the larger pool of applicants means more opportunity to select individuals whose abilities better match job requirements. The better a match between individual abilities and job requirements, the higher the expected job performance, other things being equal.[15]

An essential ingredient in this scenario is the role of pay. This does not suggest that pay is the sole factor that attracts individuals to a firm. However, there is relatively strong evidence that job seekers do set a minimum pay level, and any wage offered lower than that minimum standard leads to refusal of an otherwise acceptable job offer.[16]

THE ROLE OF COMPENSATION IN MOTIVATING EMPLOYEES TO PERFORM

What leads one employee to do a better job than another? In general there appear to be three factors that influence performance. First is the quality of the match between job

[13]Lloyd Reynolds, *Labor Economics and Labor Relations* (Englewood Cliffs, N.J.: Prentice-Hall, 1982).

[14]Robert E. Hall and David M. Lilien, "Efficient Wage Bargains under Uncertain Supply and Demand," *The American Economic Review* 69, no. 5 (1979), pp. 868–79; "Why Unemployment Sometimes Lingers On Stirs Renewed Interest," *The Wall Street Journal*, December 26, 1985, pp. 1, 26; and Ian M. McDonald and Robert M. Solow, "Wage Bargaining and Employment," *The American Economic Review* 71, no. 5 (1981), pp. 896–908.

[15]L. H. Lofquist and R. V. Dawis, *Adjustment to Work* (New York: Appleton-Century-Crofts, 1969).

[16]H. R. Sheppard and A. H. Belitsky, *The Job Hunt* (Baltimore, Md.: Johns Hopkins University Press, 1966).

requirements and individual ability. Everyone has heard stories of the supersalesperson who, when promoted to sales management, turned out to be worse than average. Skills that are exceptional for one line of work might be useless in another. Beyond the requirements/ability match though, there is the complex dimension of motivation. Why are some employees motivated to use their skills to best advantage while other employees "loaf" at every available opportunity? Finally, even highly skilled employees who are motivated to perform sometimes encounter conditions beyond their control (e.g., the bank loan officer with a goal to increase loans is hampered by an unexpected sharp increase in interest rates).

All of these factors have been discussed in greater detail elsewhere.[17] Exhibit 8.1 illustrates these factors and suggests the potential role compensation may play to influence them. As the exhibit suggests, compensation policies and practices may affect performance levels indirectly through the level of employee aptitude and skills (factors 1 and 2), and directly through employee motivation (choice to expend effort, degree of effort, and persistence of effort). The focus in the remainder of this chapter is on the role of compensation as a motivator of employee performance.

EXHIBIT 8.1
Determinants of Employee Performance and the Role of Compensation

Determinant	Primary Source of Organizational Influence	Secondary Source of Organizational Influence
1. Aptitude level	Level of employee aptitude influenced by quality of selection policies and practices.	Quality of selection is affected by number of applicants, which is influenced by compensation and reward practices.
2. Skill level	Level of employee aptitude influenced by quality of selection policies and practices.	Quality of selection is affected by number of applicants, which is influenced by compensation and rewards, quality of training.
3. Choice to expend effort.	Degree to which compensation practices are tied to employee performance.	
4. Choice of degree of effort to expend	Degree to which compensation practices are tied to employee performance.	
5. Choice to persist	Degree to which compensation practices are tied to employee performance.	
6. Understanding of work	Quality of job descriptions and supervisory explanations of performance requirements.	Quality of performance appraisal process.
7. Facilitating and inhibiting condition not under control of the individual	Unknown.	Unknown.

[17]John P. Campbell and Robert Pritchard, "Motivation Theory in Industrial and Organizational Psychology," in *Handbook of Industrial and Organizational Psychology,* ed. Marvin Dunnette (Chicago: Rand McNally, 1976).

Motivation → Pay → Performance Relationships

Many psychologists interested in the area of motivation agree that the key issue is the goal-directed nature of behavior.[18] If compensation managers could discover why behavior occurs and why it is directed toward one of countless possible goals, considerable progress could be made in improving employee job performance. Consider, for example, two operatives who work side by side on an assembly line in an automotive plant. One of the workers makes the appropriate welds in a timely fashion as cars pass on the assembly line. The other expends considerable energy in finding ways to "beat the system": welds are missed, or coat hangers are welded to parts of the body that are virtually undiscoverable until an owner takes the car in with complaints about an "irritating rattle." Each of these two employees works on the same line, with similar environments; each receives the same pay and works the same hours. Yet obviously their behavior is directed to entirely different goals.

Each of the following theories sheds some light on this and countless other motivation problems experienced in the real world. The orientation taken will be to discuss these theories as they may bear on job performance. Again, particular emphasis will be placed on the role pay assumes in the motivation-performance link.

Content theories. Content theories can be distinguished by their emphasis on what motivates people, rather than how people are motivated. The key variable in most of these theories is different types of needs. It has been speculated that psychologists have enumerated several hundred needs that are thought to motivate people.[19]

The two most well known content theories include the work by Maslow[20] and by Herzberg, Mausner, and Snyderman.[21] Maslow's theory is based on a hierarchy of five needs (Exhibit 8.2), each assumed to motivate behavior in varying degrees. Maslow argues that lower level needs in the hierarchy are prepotent: Behavior is directed toward satisfying physiological needs of themselves and their families. After obtaining a job that ensures consistent satisfaction of that need, the security need becomes dominant. Behavior is then directed toward obtaining physical and emotional security. Higher-order needs become progressively more important as lower-order needs are satisfied. One of the major problems with this approach is that it is extremely difficult to identify which needs are prepotent at any given time. Without this information it is virtually impossible to determine how a work environment should be structured to improve performance. For example,

---

[18]Edwin Locke and J. Bryan, "Cognitive Aspects of Psychomotor Performance: The Effect of Performance Goals on Level of Performance," *Journal of Applied Psychology* 50 (1966), pp. 286–91; and Edwin Locke, "The Motivational Effect of Knowledge of Results: Knowledge or Goal Setting?" *Journal of Applied Psychology* 51 (1967), pp. 324–29.

[19]Edward Lawler III, *Pay and Organizational Effectiveness: A Psychological View* (New York: McGraw-Hill, 1971).

[20]Abraham Maslow, *Motivation and Personality* (New York: Harper & Row, 1954).

[21]F. Herzberg, B. Mausner, and B. Snyderman, *The Motivation to Work* (New York: John Wiley & Sons, 1959).

EXHIBIT 8.2
Maslow's Hierarchy of Needs

1.	Physiological needs	The need for food, water, and air.
2.	Safety needs	The need for security, stability, and the absence from pain, threat, or illness.
3.	Social needs	Need for affection, belongingness, love.
4.	Esteem needs	Need for personal feelings of achievement or self-esteem and also a need for recognition or respect from others.
5.	Self-actualization needs	Need to become all one is capable of becoming, to realize one's own potential or achieve self-fulfillment.

research indicates that needs vary by age, geographic location (urban/rural), socioeconomic status, and gender to name a few. There is even speculation that the needs of the general population have been shifting over time toward a greater concern for such higher level needs as autonomy and self-actualization.[22]

In comparison, Herzberg's theory is very similar to Maslow's.[23] He argues that two types of factors are present across organizations: hygienes and motivators. Hygiene factors include such things as company policy and administration, supervision, salary, interpersonal relations, and working conditions. Motivators are represented by opportunities for advancement, achievement, responsibility, and recognition. In essence, it might be argued that Maslow's theory has gravitated in the same direction as Herzberg's. If in fact most lower-order needs are generally satisfied in our affluent society, then individual needs that are prepotent in Maslow's framework include esteem and self-actualization.[24] As conceived by Maslow, these needs are very similar to Herzberg's conception of advancement, achievement, and recognition. Since these factors are prepotent, they assume responsibility for a great deal of the goal direction of individuals. In Herzberg's terms they become the motivators, the factors that can lead to job satisfaction if met by the organization. The one major difference that can be inferred from these two theories is the function assumed by pay. As already indicated, numerous studies have shown that pay can serve to satisfy, to some extent, Maslow's needs. In contrast, Herzberg's work is often interpreted as if he argued that pay is solely a hygiene factor. Pay is necessary at sufficient levels to thwart job dissatisfaction, but it is not appropriate for motivating behavior. In fact, this assessment is not correct. While Herzberg's theory can be attacked on a number of grounds, it is inappropriate to assume Herzberg relegated pay only to the status of a hygiene factor.[25] The original work by Herzberg also demonstrated that pay takes on significance as a source of satisfaction when it is perceived as a form of recognition or reward. In this context pay provides feedback to an employee in the form of recognition for achievement.

---

[22]Theodore Roszak, *The Making of a Counter Culture: Reflections on the Techno-Cratic Society and Its Youthful Opposition* (Garden City, N.Y.: Doubleday, 1969).

[23]Herzberg, Mausner, and Snyderman, *The Motivation to Work.*

[24]Roszak, *The Making of a Counter Culture.*

[25]R. J. House and L. A. Wigdor, "Herzberg's Dual-Factor Theory of Job Satisfaction and Motivation: A Review of the Evidence and a Criticism," *Personnel Psychology* 20 (1967), pp. 369–90.

It is apparent from this summary of content theories that pay can serve to satisfy needs and impact on motivation. This discussion, however, has been silent on the mechanism by which this occurs. In fact, this is a general criticism of content theories. While it is apparent that pay can motivate behavior, one category of which is job performance, it is not at all clear how organizations can use pay to achieve this goal. In the following discussion of process theories of motivation more emphasis is placed on explaining the mechanisms that lead to motivation.

Process theories. Process theories of motivation focus on how people are motivated. They certainly recognize the role of content theories in examining the types of needs and reinforcers that are part of the motivational process, but they also attempt to explain how this process operates.

In explaining how motivation operates, some theories prominently mention the importance of rewards, including compensation. Others, while presumably acknowledging some role for compensation, focus on other factors that affect individual motivation.

Operant conditioning theory and Expectancy theory both grant a prominent role to rewards (e.g., compensation). Pay motivates job performance to the extent merit increases and other work-related rewards are allocated on the basis of performance.

Much of the operant conditioning literature focuses on the types of reinforcement schedules that best motivate high performance. Do workers respond better when rewards are based on their individual performance, or when their work units' success is the major determinant of rewards? Is a continuous reinforcement schedule (after each performance unit) motivationally superior to a variable reinforcement schedule? A summary of these findings is included in Chapter 9.

Of even greater interest to researchers over the past two decades has been the utility of expectancy, or VIE theory. VIE is an acronym for Valence (V), Instrumentality (I), Expectancy (E). Borrowing from earlier works,[26] Campbell and Pritchard present an excellent composite picture of the variables important in a VIE model.[27] Exhibit 8.3 summarizes this model.

The key variable to be explained in this model is effort level. According to Exhibit 8.3, effort level depends on three factors: (1) expectancy, (2) valence, and (3) instrumentality. Expectancy is viewed as a subjective probability estimate made by an individual as to whether a specific level of effort will result in task accomplishment. For example, if you were to have a test on the subject matter of this chapter tomorrow, what do you think the probability would be of getting an "A" if you studied hard for five hours tonight? In an organizational context employees would assess whether or not they could accomplish specific assignments made by their supervisor. These probabilities are assessed in numbers

---

[26]V. H. Vroom, *Work in Motivation* (New York: John Wiley & Sons, 1964); G. Graen, "Instrumentality Theory of Work Motivation: Some Experimental Results and Suggested Modifications," *Journal of Applied Psychology* 53, no. 2 (1969), pp. 1–25; L. W. Porter and E. E. Lawler, *Managerial Attitudes and Performance* (Chicago, Ill.: Dorsey Press, 1968); and Campbell and Pritchard, "Motivation Theory."

[27]Campbell and Pritchard, "Motivation Theory."

EXHIBIT 8.3
A Composite Expectancy-Valence Model

| Force to expend specific level of effort | Expectancy that specific level of effort will/will not accomplish task | Valence of task goal accomplishment/failure | Instrumentality of task accomplishment/failure for job outcomes | Valence of job outcomes | Instrumentality of job outcomes for need satisfaction | Valence of "basic" needs |

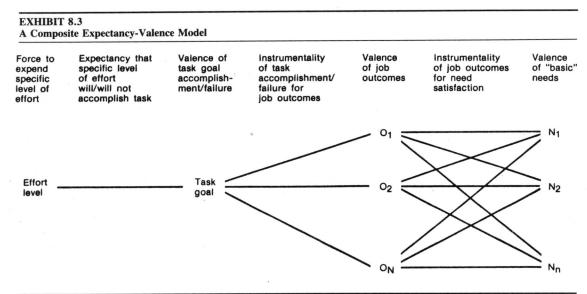

Note: For purposes of simplicity, this schematic portrays only one level of effort and one level of success on one task goal. A similar set of relationships exists for alternative levels of effort and alternative tasks or alternative levels of success.

Source: John P. Campbell and Robert Pritchard, "Motivation Theory in Industrial and Organizational Psychology," in *Handbook of Industrial and Organizational Psychology,* ed. Marvin Dunnette (Chicago: Rand McNally, 1976). Copyright © 1976, Marvin D. Dunnette. Reprinted by permission of John Wiley & Sons, Inc.

between .00 and 1.00. As the probability of a goal accomplishment rises (approaches 1.00), the probability of expending a specific amount of effort rises.

The second factor in this model is goal valence. How much does an individual value (i.e., what is the anticipated satisfaction from) task accomplishment? To link Maslow's hierarchy of needs with this model, a task that satisfies a prepotent need, would have a relatively high valence. Carrying the earlier illustration further, if you did not place a high value on earning an "A" in tomorrow's exam, even though it was within your capability (i.e., high expectancy), you would be less likely to expend the necessary effort. From an individual's perspective in an organization, consider a reward of a promotion offered for successful accomplishment of a lengthy and difficult task. Most supervisors offering this promotion would assume subordinates would value highly this type of reward. Consider, however, the employees who are content with their existing job responsibilities and do not want to assume greater job responsibility. The low valence attached to this reward may lead to lower effort expenditure, a disappointment to supervisors who assume their employees hold consistent values.

Normally, completion of a task is not considered to have value in and of itself. In one sense this is correct. Most people associate work in organizations with the rewards that can be obtained from successful completion of that task. Actually, though, there is a reasonably large body of literature to indicate tasks can offer intrinsic rewards that occur simply because of performance and completion of a task.[28] So a task goal can have a valence attached to it. More traditionally, though, people think about the rewards that result from task accomplishment, the so-called extrinsic rewards (e.g., pay, promotion) because they are outcomes resulting from performance of the task. It is in this linkage where the third component, instrumentality, becomes important. Assuming an employee accomplishes a task, what is the probability that a desired outcome or reward will result? If it is estimated that the subjective probability of obtaining a reward given task accomplishment is 1.00, then an employee is more likely to expend the necessary effort to start this sequence in motion. Instrumentality, as was true for expectancy, is expressed as a subjective probability varying between .00 and 1.00. Carrying the example with the test grade one step further, students might attempt to estimate the probability that obtaining an "A" on an exam tomorrow will result in an "A" for the entire course. Or, going even further, they might estimate the probability that obtaining an "A" in this course will lead to a good job offer. It is not a coincidence, for example, that finance majors probably expend more effort on obtaining "A's" in their finance courses. They view these courses as more relevant to their chosen career goals. When students talk about course relevance in this context, they are expressing judgments that are considered instrumentalities in this model.

You will notice that the model in Exhibit 8.3 carries the idea of valences and instrumentalities beyond the first level outcomes and their attached valences. In fact, this is a reasonable expression of reality that also portrays the role of pay in this model as it affects motivation. As Opsahl and Dunnette have noted, pay can serve as an *instrument* (this term is derived from the word *instrumentality* taken from the model).[29] Consider the manager who obtains a pay raise for an employee who performs well. By itself the pay raise may have no value. However, it can have a high instrumentality. Pay can be used to purchase goods that have a high valence. Given sufficient money the subjective probability that money can be used to buy a wide variety of desired goods is quite high (i.e., high instrumentality).

Note: This chain of events was triggered by a manager who established the pay-for-performance link. At least from an employee's perspective, *pay for performance* is partially an issue of instrumentality: "If I perform at the *desired* level considered excellent by my company, what is the probability I will be rewarded in turn with a corresponding pay increase?" Involved in this question is whether or not the company is viewed as paying for performance (i.e., allocating pay raises differentially to employees based on level of performance). This is just one of several questions that will be addressed after discussing the last theory relevant to the issues of pay for performance.

---

[28]See, for example, McNaly Csikszentmihalyi, "Play and Intrinsic Rewards," *Journal of Humanistic Psychology* 4 (1979), pp. 16-22; A. Bandura, *Social Learning Theory* (Englewood Cliffs, N.J.: Prentice-Hall, 1977); and E. Deci, "Notes on the Theory and Metatheory of Intrinsic Motivation," *Organizational Behavior and Human Performance* 15 (1975), pp. 130–45.

[29]R. L. Opsahl and M. D. Dunnette, "The Role of Financial Compensation in Industrial Motivation," *Psychological Bulletin* 66 (1966), pp. 94–118.

Equity theory. There has been some question about whether this theory is really a distinct theory or whether it can be subsumed under VIE theory.[30] Since equity theory plays such an important role in compensation, though, separate discussion is included here.

While there are a number of models[31] dealing with the equity concept, two have generated sufficient research or intriguing potential to warrant discussion. Adams argues that individuals compare their inputs and outcomes to those of some relevant other person in determining whether they are equitably (fairly) treated.[32] Stated another way, the comparison process can be expressed as a comparison of ratios:

$$\frac{Op}{Ip} \text{ compared to } \frac{Oo}{Io}$$

where:

$$Op, Oo = \text{Outcomes of person (p) or other (o)}$$

$$Ip, Io = \text{Inputs of person (p) or other (o)}$$

This model suggests that people compare the reward they receive, relative to the inputs they have to make to receive those rewards, to the same ratio for some relevant other. If the two ratios are not equal, the consequence is motivation to reduce the "perceived" inequity. A key in this explanation is the word *perceived*. The inequity could result because some individuals evaluate and classify as inputs and outcomes factors that other individuals might consider irrelevant. For example, a physically attractive salesperson might consider that a relevant input and expect to be compensated higher than a less attractive individual, other things being equal. Yet the organization may consider this an irrelevant input, pay the two individuals equally, and never realize that the person views it as an inequitable exchange. Correspondingly, a person might evaluate an outcome as relevant that the organization is not even aware exists. As an example, consider a supervisor who keeps a particular employee abreast of information about company activities affecting the employee's job. Potentially, the supervisor could view this as a reward, treating the subordinate as a member of the "in" group, privy to information not disseminated to other subordinates.[33] If this is not perceived as a reward by the subordinate, yet the supervisor views it as a reward for above-average performance, feelings of inequity may result.

---

[30]Lawler, *Pay and Organizational Effectiveness;* Campbell and Pritchard, "Motivation Theory."

[31]G. C. Homans, *Social Behavior: Its Elementary Forms* (New York: Harcourt Brace Jovanovich, 1961); E. Jaques, *Equitable Payment* (New York: John Wiley & Sons, 1961); M. Patche, *The Choice of Wage Comparisons* (Englewood Cliffs, N.J.: Prentice-Hall, 1961); J. S. Adams, "Wage Inequities, Productivity, and Work Quality," *Industrial Relations* 3, no. 1 (1963), pp. 9–16; and J. S. Adams, "Injustices in Social Exchange," in *Advances in Experimental Social Psychology,* vol 2, ed. L. Berkowitz (New York: Academic Press, 1965), pp. 267–99.

[32]Ibid.

[33]Fred Dansereau, G. Graen, and W. Haga, "A Vertical Dyad Linkage Approach to Leadership within Formal Organizations: A Longitudinal Investigation of the Role Making Process," *Organizational Behavior and Human Performance* 13 (1975), pp. 46–70.

The impacts this perceived inequity may have on motivation and subsequent performance are pointed out by Adams.[34] Granted, inequity is viewed in this theory as a source of motivation. However, the consequences do not necessarily bode well for improved performance. As Adams notes, people can (1) cognitively distort their or other's inputs and/or outcomes, (2) attempt to change their or other's inputs and/or outcomes, (3) change the comparison person, or (4) reduce their involvement in the exchange relationship. Several of these consequences have negative implications for performance. For example, accusing employees of being rate busters and using social sanctions to get them to reduce outcomes could be viewed as an effort to get others to reduce inputs. An even better example would include certain unionization efforts. Consider a company that has a union representing all blue-collar workers. If nonunionized clerical workers do not receive raises commensurate with those obtained by unionized workers, one possible outcome could be efforts by clerical workers to form their own union. This is particularly true if clerical workers use the unionized blue-collar workers as relevant others and perceive that rewards for the two groups are out of balance, given inputs. In this case, disgruntled clerical workers could view unionization as a way to improve outcomes and reestablish equity.[35]

The role money plays in equity theory is quite evident. Money is only one of many outcomes that are evaluated in the exchange relationship. But since money is one of the most visible components, and frequently one of the easiest to modify, it becomes extremely important. As will be pointed out later, much of the research in equity theory involves varying pay levels or work level required and noting the inequity and subsequent behavior that occurs.

The second equity model of interest here was formulated by Elliot Jaques.[36] The major part of this model relevant to this discussion deals with Jaques's conception of how inequity arises. From Jaques's perspective, feelings of inequity are not dependent on the existence of a relevant other whose ratio of inputs to outcomes differs from the target person's ratio. Rather, Jaques suggests that the relevant comparison in determination of equity is an internal standard. Presumably individuals have some internal standard of fairness based on accumulated past experiences against which current conditions are compared to determine fairness of, for example, current pay. From a compensation administrator's perspective, this can cause problems. A well-constructed and administered job evaluation system may reduce feelings of inequity in comparison with what other persons in the company may be receiving. If an internal standard is employed, however, any experiences in other organizations become relevant. This requires a compensation administrator to be equitable with respect to practices of other organizations. (Note: Adam's equity theory does not preclude a relevant other who is external to the organization. Consequently the same implications could be inferred for this theory. However,

---

[34]Adams, "Injustices in Social Exchange."

[35]Chris Berger, Craig Olson, and John Boudreau, "The Effects of Unions on Work Values, Perceived Rewards, and Job Satisfaction," presented at the National Academy of Management meetings, August 1980.

[36]Jaques, *Equitable Payment*.

it has been speculated that relevant other is more likely to be a co-worker than someone outside the firm.)

Most of the research relating equity theory to performance has stimulated inequity by either underpaying or overpaying individuals for tasks and then recording the impact on performance. At best the research has had mixed support.[37] Efforts during the 1980s have focused more on refining equity models to improve prediction and attempting to identify the behavioral and attitudinal consequences of inequity.[38]

Social Information Processing Theory. Recall that need theories focused on internally generated needs that induced behaviors designed to reduce these needs. Social information processing (SIP) theory counters need theory by focusing on external factors that motivate performance.[39] According to SIP theory, workers pay attention to environmental cues (e.g., performance levels of coworkers, goals imposed by supervisors, etc.) by cognitively processing this information in a way that may alter personal work goals, expectancies, and perceptions of equity.[40] In turn this influences job attitudes, behavior, and performance. By far the strongest evidence that external factors influence motivation comes from the goal-setting research of Locke and associates.[41] A review of this literature indicates that the vast majority of studies on goal setting find a positive impact of goal setting on performance. Workers assigned "hard" goals consistently do better than workers told to "do your best."[42]

Notice, nothing in this discussion of SIP theory has suggested a role for compensation in the motivational process. Part of the reason may be that researchers are divided on whether compensation has an additive, interactive, or independent influence on goal setting. Locke and associates suggest that pay affects performance only by affecting the level of goals or individual commitment to achieving goals already established.[43] A second perspective views goal setting and compensation as independent.[44] Any positive, or negative, influences of goal setting or compensation on performance are not enhanced or diminished by their joint presence. Countering this argument of independence, a third line of research argues the joint presence of incentives and goal setting conditions has a

---

[37]Dyer and Schwab, "Personnel/Human Resource Management Research."

[38]D. M. Messick and K. S. Cook, eds., *Theory of Equity: Psychological and Sociological Perspectives* (New York: Praeger Publishers, 1983).

[39]Terence R. Mitchell, Miriam Rothman, and Robert C. Liden, "Effects of Normative Information on Task Performance," *Journal of Applied Psychology* 70, no. 1 (1985), pp. 48–55.

[40]Ibid.

[41]Edwin A. Locke, Karyll N. Shaw, Lise M. Saari, and Gary P. Latham, "Goal Setting and Task Performance: 1969-1980," *Psychological Bulletin* 90 (1981), pp. 125–52.

[42]Ibid.

[43]Locke, Shaw, Saari, and Latham, "Goal Setting and Task Performance."

[44]R. D. Pritchard and M. I. Curtis, "The Influence of Goal Setting and Financial Incentives on Task Performance," *Organizational Behavior and Human Performance* 10 (1973), pp. 175–83; and J. R. Terborg and H. E. Miller, "Motivation, Behavior, and Performance: A Closer Examination of Goal Setting and Monetary Incentives," *Journal of Applied Psychology* 63 (1978), pp. 29–39.

negative effect on performance.[45] Perhaps the best summary, though, is to admit we still do not know enough about the motivational and cognitive processes that lead goal setting and compensation to trigger higher performance.[46] The next section explores this relationship between pay and performance.

PAY FOR PERFORMANCE: THE POSITIVE EVIDENCE

Early in this chapter discussion centered on the factors presumed to affect performance. Ideally, this would lead to identification of strategies that can be used by organizations to improve employee performance. This discussion has been leading up to the question: "Is pay the answer?" Can employee motivation and performance be affected by devising different pay strategies? The answer to this question depends on the answer to three subquestions: 1) Is money important to individuals? 2) Should pay increases be based on performance? 3) Is pay based on performance?

Is Money Important to Individuals?

From the motivational theories discussed earlier it is apparent there is no instinctive or basic need for money. Money becomes important insofar as it can satisfy recognized needs. For example, Lawler and Porter found that highly paid managers are more satisfied in the security need and the esteem need than low paid managers.[47] Lawler infers from this and other research that money is capable of satisfying physiological, security, and esteem needs.[48] If these needs are satisfied by other means, or if they are not currently prepotent (in Maslow's terminology), then money is seen as having lower instrumental value and is not particularly useful in motivating desired behavior.

If different needs are, in fact, prepotent across individuals, this information could be used to design a pay-for-performance system. Lawler argues for a two-step sequential process: 1) identify groups for which differential need strength is evident and 2) devise selection strategies that will identify those individuals who have needs that can be satisfied through a pay system tied to performance.[49] Such a strategy, if successful, would permit organizations that subscribe to a pay-for-performance philosophy to implement a wage and salary system designed to use pay for improved performance.

Until this occurs, however, there is evidence that organizations may be experiencing problems by assuming that applicants and employees place a high value on monetary rewards. One study indicates that applicants rate salary only ninth out of eighteen different

[45]J. Mowen, R. Middlemist, and D. Luther, "Joint Effects of Assigned Goal Level and Incentive Structure on Task Performance: A Laboratory Study," *Journal of Applied Psychology* 61 (1981), pp. 598–603.

[46]Donald J. Campbell, "The Effects of Goal-Contingent Payment on the Performance of a Complex Task," *Personnel Psychology* 37 (1984), pp. 23–40.

[47]E. Lawler and L. Porter, "Perceptions Regarding Management Compensation," *Industrial Relations* 3 (1969), pp. 41–49.

[48]Lawler, *Pay and Organizational Effectiveness*.

[49]Ibid.

types of rewards when evaluating the attractiveness of a particular job opportunity.[50] Compounding this problem, when applicants become employees, there is evidence that managers overestimate the importance of pay to subordinates.[51] Given a belief that pay can motivate performance, supervisors become disillusioned when improved performance does not result from pay increases. This failure results in a general condemnation of pay as a motivator. In reality, however, it may be more advantageous not to view money as the supreme motivator, but rather as one of the numerous factors in the work environment that affects employee motivation.

For example, it appears that one of the other factors affecting employee motivation is **the way that rewards are distributed.** There is strong evidence that employees are concerned not only about fairness in the amount of rewards they receive (distributive justice), but also in the means used to distribute those rewards (procedural justice).[52] Employees who perceive that they are being treated fairly in the way rewards are distributed (as opposed to the actual amount they receive), exhibit more trust in their supervisors and greater commitment to their organization.[53] Making efforts to allocate rewards in ways that are perceived as being fair seems to have positive payoffs! When we discuss design of compensation systems at the end of this chapter we will discuss ways to be fair in greater detail.

Should Pay Increases Be Based on Performance?

Given that money can satisfy at least a subset of basic needs, the question now becomes, "Should salary increases be based on level of performance?" Substantial evidence exists that management and workers alike believe pay should be tied to performance.

Dyer et al. asked 180 managers from 72 different companies to rate 9 possible factors in terms of the importance they should receive in determining size of salary increases.[54] As Exhibit 8.4 indicates, workers believe the most important factor for salary increases should be job performance. Following close behind is a factor that presumably would be picked up in job evaluation (nature of job) and a motivational variable (amount of effort expended). Two other studies support these findings.[55] Both college students and a second

---

[50]Barry Posner, "Comparing Recruiter, Student, and Faculty Perceptions of Important Applicant Job Characteristics," *Personnel Psychology* 34 (1981), pp. 329–37.

[51]F. A. Heller and L. W. Porter, "Perceptions of Managerial Needs and Skills in Two National Samples," *Occupational Psychology* 40 (1966), pp. 1–13.

[52]Robert Folger and Mary Konovsky, "Effects of Procedural and Distributive Justice on Reactions to Pay Raise Decisions," *Academy of Management Journal* (in press); and Jerald Greenberg, "A Taxonomy of Organizational Justice Theories," *Academy of Management Review* 12, no. 1 (1987), pp. 9–22.

[53]Folger and Konovsky, "Effects of Procedural and Distributive Justice on Reactions to Pay Raise Decisions."

[54]L. Dyer, D. P. Schwab, and R. D. Theriault, "Managerial Perceptions Regarding Salary Increase Criteria," *Personnel Psychology* 29 (1976), pp. 233–42.

[55]John Fossum and Mary Fitch, "The Effects of Individual and Contextual Attributes on the Sizes of Recommended Salary Increases," *Personnel Psychology* 38 (1985), pp. 587–603; and F. Hills, K. Scott, S. Markham, and M. Vest, "Merit Pay: Just or Unjust Desserts," *Personnel Psychology* 32, no. 9 (1987), pp. 53–59.

EXHIBIT 8.4
Mean Ratings of Criteria That *Should Be* Used to Determine Size of Salary Increases

	Criteria	Mean Rating
1.	Level of job performance	6.23
2.	Nature of job	5.91
3.	Amount of effort expenditure	5.56
4.	Cost of living	5.21
5.	Training and experience	5.15
6.	Increases outside organization	4.64
7.	Budgetary considerations	4.53
8.	Increases inside organization	3.69
9.	Length of service	3.31

Source: L. Dyer, D. P. Schwab, and R. D. Theriault, "Managerial Perceptions Regarding Salary Increase Criteria," *Personnel Psychology* 29 (1976), pp. 233–42. © 1976, Personnel Psychology, Inc.

group of managers ranked job performance as the most important variable in allocating pay raises.

The role that performance levels should assume in determining pay increases is less clear-cut for blue collar workers.[56] As an illustration, consider the frequent opposition to compensation plans that are based on performance (i.e., incentive piece-rate systems). Actually, much of the discontent with performance-based plans is a reaction to the specific type of plan and the way it is administered. Lawler notes that "in many situations opposition to incentive pay comes about because the employees feel they cannot trust the company to administer incentive schemes properly."[57] From this data it appears there is some belief among **employees** that pay should be based on performance, particularly if the company can be trusted to administer the performance-based plan effectively.

From an organization's perspective we can ask the same question: **should** pay be based on performance? Assume a company does tie pay to performance. What are the payoffs? One school of thought argues that designing reward systems to meet employee expectations can increase job satisfaction.[58] In turn, this increase in job satisfaction may lower both absenteeism and turnover, and increase job performance. Estimates place the savings to a company from an increase of just one-half a standard deviation in job satisfaction at more than $25,000 in today's dollars.[59]

Do workers, in fact, perform better when they receive pay contingent upon level of performance? Consider, for example, the Episcopal Diocese of Newark, N.J. Starting in 1986, priests were paid according to performance. Priests qualify for salary raises based on achievement of goals such as parish growth and quality of sermons. Apparently the

---

[56]Opinion Research Corporation, *Wage Incentives* (Princeton, N.J.: Opinion Research Corporation, 1946); Opinion Research Corporation, *Productivity from the Worker's Standpoint* (Princeton, N.J.: Opinion Research Corporation, 1949); L. V. Jones and T. E. Jeffrey, "A Quantitative Analysis of Expressed Preferences for Compensation Plans," *Journal of Applied Psychology* 48 (1963), pp. 201–10.

[57]Lawler, *Pay and Organizational Effectiveness*, p. 61.

[58]Edward Lawler, "Pay for Performance: A Strategic Analysis," in Gomez-Mejia and Balkin, eds. (1987).

[59]Philip Miruis and Edward Lawler, "Measuring the Financial Impact of Employee Attitudes," *Journal of Applied Psychology* 62, no. 1 (1977), pp. 1–8.

Church believes that tying pay to performance will enhance Church goals. Is there any hard data to support this belief?

Numerous studies indicate that tying pay to performance has a positive impact on employee performance.[60] A common type of study is to introduce an incentive system and observe whether workers, whose pay is now directly dependent upon level of output, increase their levels of performance. Several studies indicate that introduction of an incentive system (e.g., piece rate) results in higher performance than occurs for workers receiving hourly pay.[61] One particularly well-designed study found that incentive plans lead employees to work smart, finding work behaviors that increase productivity.[62] Even more encouraging, the long-term productivity gains reported in this study appear to be even greater than gains reported from analyses of more short term results.

Another approach is to look at the top performing organizations and see if they are also the top payers. Most commonly, these studies look at the compensation of Chief Executive Officers (CEO) in relation to organizational profits. While several studies have found negative relationships, one survey found that the best performing companies pay 21 percent more in base salary to their CEOs, 67 percent more in the combined base salary and short term incentives, and 140% more when the package also includes long-term incentives. The authors contend that previous studies were flawed because they failed to control for organizational size when studying the pay-performance relationship.[63]

One recent article summarizes the reasons why a company should pay for performance as follows.[64] First, money can serve as an effective motivator of performance for employees. Following from this motivation increase, a good merit program tying pay to performance will then improve productivity, reduce costs, and increase competiveness.[65] Second, superior employees resent automatic increases. As the little red hen found in the beginning of this chapter, working harder than other workers for the same level of rewards is not very satisfying and may result in reduced performance. Third, if the company develops a good pay-for-performance program, it must spell out exactly what is expected

---

[60]George Green, "Instrumentality Theory of Work Motivation," *Journal of Applied Psychology* 53, no. 2 (1965), pp. 1–25; Lawler, "Manager's Attitudes"; D. P. Schwab and L. Dyer, "The Motivational Impact of a Compensation System on Employee Performance," *Organizational Behavior and Human Performance* 9 (1973), pp. 215–25; R. D. Pritchard, D. W. Leonard, C. W. Von Bergen, Jr., and R. J. Kirk, "The Effects of Varying Schedules of Reinforcement on Human Task Performance," *Organizational Behavior and Human Performance* 16 (1976), pp. 205–30; and Donald Schwab, "Impact of Alternative Compensation Systems on Pay Valence and Instrumentality Perceptions," *Journal of Applied Psychology* 58 (1973), pp. 308–12.

[61]G. F. Latham and D. L. Dossett, "Designing Incentive Plans for Unionized Employees: A Comparison of Continuous and Variable Ratio Reinforcement Schedules," *Personnel Psychology* 31 (1978), pp. 47–61.

[62]John Wagner, Paul Rubin, and Thomas Callahan, "Incentive Payment and Non-Managerial Productivity: An Interrupted Time Series Analysis of Magnitude and Trend," *Organizational Behavior and Human Decision Processes* 42 (1988), pp. 47–74.

[63]E. T. Redling, "Myth v. Reality: The Relationship between Top Executive Pay and Corporate Performance," *Compensation Review* 4 (1981), pp. 16–24.

[64]Thomas Rollins, "Pay for Performance: Is it Worth the Trouble?" *Personnel Administrator* 33, no. 5 (1988), pp. 42–47.

[65]Frederick W. Cook & Co., Inc., "Improving Merit Pay Effectiveness," Compensation Conference, The Conference Board (1988).

of employees. Knowing what is expected and how it relates to the success of the organization gives employees a better sense of ownership and involvement in the mission of the company.

Is Pay Based on Performance?

Whether due to blind faith, belief in expert testimony, or positive review of existing research, there are many companies that claim to base pay on performance.[66] Two recent polls consistently found about 90 percent of large public and private sector organizations claiming to have at least a portion of their compensation designed to tie pay to performance.[67] Even nonprofit organizations are interested in such programs, with 34 percent claiming to have pay-for-performance components in their compensation package.[68] This is up from just 10 percent of the nonprofit firms professing to have pay-for-performance components only 5 years earlier!

Even though companies report, in increasing numbers, that they tie pay to performance, there is considerable evidence that an effective linkage is hard to achieve. Claiming to have a pay-for-performance plan does not necessarily mean it is implemented well or that it will necessarily work effectively.

PAY FOR PERFORMANCE: THE NEGATIVE EVIDENCE

Perhaps the biggest movement toward a pay-for-performance system was mandated by the Civil Service Reform Act of 1978. This act required that 50 percent of any pay increase was to be automatic, but the other 50 must be performance-based. Here was an excellent opportunity to determine whether basing pay on performance (in part) would lead to improvements in productivity. One study of managers in the Social Security Administration, an agency covered by the act, found merit pay had no impact on organizational performance.[69] Using a combination of objective (e.g., average number of days to pay certain claims) and subjective performance measures, there were no significant effects on performance from going to a merit pay system.

Two other recent studies also portray a gloomy outlook for firms trying to implement pay-for-performance components. One survey of 16 organizations found 76 percent of employees receiving raises within 2 percent (above or below) the budget.[70] Little differ-

---

[66]Bruce R. Ellig, *Executive Compensation: A Total Pay Perspective* (New York: McGraw-Hill, 1982); Edward E. Lawler, *Pay and Organizational Development* (Reading, Mass.: Addison-Wesley Publishing, 1981).

[67]Laurie Hays, "All Eyes on DuPont's Incentive Pay Plan," *Wall Street Journal*, December 5, 1988, p. B1; and "Dramatic Growth in Use of Incentives Attributed to Global Competition," *Compflash 88,* no. 11 (1988), p. 1.

[68]Ibid.

[69]Jane L. Pearce, William B. Stevenson, and James L. Perry, "Managerial Compensation Based on Organizational Performance: A Time Series Analysis of the Effects of Merit Pay," *Academy of Management Journal* 28, no. 2 (1985), pp. 261–78.

[70]Kenneth Teel, "Are Merit Raises Really Based on Merit?" *Personnel Journal,* March 1986, p. 88–92.

entiation in actual raises occurred, even though these firms reported a policy of paying for performance. A closer look at the distribution of performance ratings in one company illustrates one major reason why pay for performance may not always be successful. Over the period 1983-1985, a team of researchers tracked the performance ratings of 800 employees in a large West Coast Transit organization.[71] Ninety-eight percent of the time— over three different rating periods—employees were rated as **average or better** (3510 ratings out of 3561). Despite the best of intentions, pay-for-performance systems may not work. In this example either the vast majority of employees were average or better (which is statistically unlikely) or supervisors were not making the tough decisions to give poor performers the ratings they deserved. This highlights what some experts contend is a major problem with research on pay for performance: Most of the evidence arguing against a pay-for-performance system is based on problems in implementing the system.[72] Some of the road blocks pose serious problems. As examples consider the following:[73] First, it appears, as we have already noted, that supervisors find it difficult to make the tough rating choices and give poor evaluations when they are deserved. Second, even if managers were willing to make the tough decisions, many appraisal forms require fine distinctions in performance levels that may be difficult for managers to understand and use. Third, even in companies that embrace the pay-for-performance concept, cost controls and modest budget increases make it difficult to reward outstanding employees. Fourth, the way appraisals are timed almost guarantees that the merit increases that typically follow will be much later than the actual performance to be rewarded. Any basic psychology book tells us that effective reinforcement of behavior should occur as soon after the behavior occurs as possible. Otherwise the reinforcement value diminishes. Fifth, most employees consider themselves above average in performance. Exhibit 8.5 illustrates just how strong this upward rating bias is when employees evaluate themselves.

Any willingness by a manager to make the tough decisions we talked about earlier (i.e., to rate poor performers at the low end of the rating scale) is likely to be at odds with inflated self-ratings. The performance review is perceived as biased and results in dissatisfaction. Finally, some people argue that the idea of rewarding individual performance may run contrary to organizational needs for group cohesiveness. Emphasis on individuals, the key to merit pay plans, may foster independence and lessen the motivation to help and work with others.

The next section of this chapter looks at ways to improve the changes that a pay-for-performance system will work. This involves both general issues in designing a performance measurement system and in designing the corresponding compensation system.

---

[71]Hills, Scott, Markham, and Vest, "Merit Pay: Just or Unjust Desserts."

[72]Clay W. Hamner, "How to Ruin Motivation with Pay," *Compensation Review* (Third Quarter 1975), pp. 88–98; Herbert H. Meyer, "The Pay-for-Performance Dilemma," *Organizational Dynamics,* Winter 1975, pp. 71–78; and *CompFlash,* "Companies Praise Pay-for-Performance Programs."

[73]Cook & Co., Inc., "Improving Merit Pay Effectiveness"; and Rollins, "Pay for Performance: Is it Worth the Trouble?"

EXHIBIT 8.5
Self Ratings for Selected Employee Groups

Self Ratings	Employee Group			
	Blue-Collar Group Plant A	Blue-Collar Group Plant B	Engineers in Research Laboratory	Accountants in Several Companies
Top 10%	46%	40%	29%	37%
Top 25%	26	28	57	40
Top 50%	26	28	14	20
Bottom 50%	1	2	0	3
Bottom 25%	0	0	0	0
Bottom 10%	0	0	0	0
No response	1	2	0	0
	100%	100%	100%	100%

Reprinted by permission of the publisher, from "The Pay-for-Performance Dilemma," by Herbert H. Meyer, *Organizational Dynamics*, Winter 1975, p. 44. © 1975, American Management Association, New York. All rights reserved.

MEASURING AND PAYING FOR PERFORMANCE: DESIGN ISSUES

According to the pay model developed in Chapter 1, we should have three objectives in designing compensation systems to measure employee contributions. First, the system must be efficient. The design should contribute to improved productivity and savings in labor costs. In large part this objective is the focus of Chapter 10, where we discuss the different types of alternative reward systems and their impacts on productivity/labor costs. The second objective in designing the system concerns compliance with legal requirements. Chapters 13 and 14 deal specifically with this objective. Here we deal with the third objective of the compensation system: making sure it is equitable or fair.

Two types of fairness are concerns for employees. The first type is fairness in the amount that is distributed to employees. Not surprisingly, this type of fairness is labeled **distributive justice.**[74] Does an employee view the amount of compensation received as fair? As we discussed earlier in the section on equity theory, perceptions of fairness here depend on the amount of compensation actually received relative to inputs (e.g., productivity) compared against some relevant standard. Notice several of the components of this equity equation are frustratingly removed from the control of the typical supervisor or manager working with employees. A manager has little influence over the size of an employee's pay check. This is influenced more by external market conditions, pay policy decisions of the organization, and the occupational choice made by the employee. Even decisions about how much of a pay increase to give are typically constrained by budget limitations. Managers also don't have much influence on whom an employee chooses as a relevant other (i.e., someone to compare against when evaluating rewards received in relation to work performance provided).

[74]John Thibaut and Laurens Walker, *"Procedural Justice: A Psychological View* (Hillsdale, N.J.: John Wiley & Sons, 1975).

Managers do have somewhat more control, though, over the second type of equity. Employees are also concerned about the fairness of **procedures** used to determine the amount of rewards they receive. As also noted in Chapter 2, employees expect **procedural justice.** Evidence suggests that organizations that use fair procedures and supervisors who are viewed as fair in the means they use to allocate rewards are perceived as more trustworthy and command higher levels of commitment.[75] Some research even suggests that pay satisfaction of employees may depend more on the procedures used to determine pay than on the actual level distributed![76] This concern for fairness in procedures is something that organizations and supervisors can directly influence in a cost-effective way. For the remainder of this chapter we outline the stages in measuring performance and subsequently determining compensation. Issues of procedural fairness or justice for each of the stages are considered.

These stages correspond to the sequence of events most people might expect to occur in the appraisal and reward process. The first stage includes development of performance standards or expectations. What will be expected of workers for satisfactory or higher performance? And will rewards be allocated on the basis of that performance or on some other basis (e.g., allocate the same amount to each employee regardless of performance). Once the standards and allocation norms are determined, decisions are made about how much performance data will be collected and how it will be collected. This performance data is then used in the actual appraisal and both are input to a final appraisal rating for each employee. Following this, the organization must decide when compensation increases will be given and how much they will be. Any disagreements from employees about the level of rewards or process used should go to some form of appeals board. And finally, policies and procedures are established to communicate how this entire process operates. Each of these stages can add to or subtract from perceptions of procedural fairness. To the extent the organization and its supervisors can create fair processes, a relatively low cost means to enhance employee satisfaction and the general attractiveness of the organization are established.

EXHIBIT 8.6
Stages in Measuring and Paying for Performance

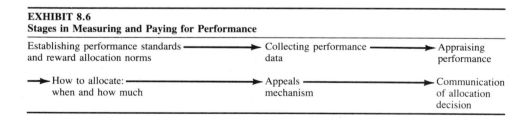

---

[75]Robert Folger and Mary Konovsky, "Effects of Procedural and Distributive Justice on Reactions to Pay Raise Decisions."

[76]S. Alexander and M. Ruderman, "The Role of Procedural and Distributive Justice in Organizational Behavior," *Social Justice Research* 1 (1987), pp. 177–198.

Establishing Performance Standards and Reward Allocation Norms

Performance standards. Based on research from a number of different areas, there appear to be at least four rules for making sure performance standards are perceived as fair. First, the standards should represent all the concerns of the employees to be evaluated later.[77] One major task to ensure employee concerns are covered is to make sure an updated job description is used as the foundation for deciding what performance dimensions should be measured. Second, the level of performance on each dimension should not be so hard as to be viewed as impossible. Apparently, though, employees will accept as fair standards that are challenging.[78] Third, employees should be informed what these performance standards are.[79] Finally, employees perceive the whole process as fairer when they are informed about the standard early during the rating time period rather than at some later point.

Allocation norms. A company should also ensure that the rules that will govern how much of an increase employees will receive are spelled out clearly. The natural inclination is to assume the size of an increase will depend upon how well an employee performs. Better performers receive larger increases. We know, though, that companies do not always pay for performance. Exhibit 8.7 identifies the five allocation rules and gives examples of what they entail.

Apparently each of these five rules are used under different circumstances. The equity rule, not surprisingly, is used most frequently when the organization is committed to paying for performance and achieving increased productivity.[80] The equality rule is more appropriate when social harmony is an important outcome, that is, when a company needs employees to work together cooperatively.[81] No research studies have identified occasions when the reciprocity rule might be used, but we might speculate that supervisors with high moral and ethical standards might "do unto others as they would have done unto themselves." Basing increases on need (need rule), interestingly, used to be a fairly common argument for justifying higher wages for men than women. After all, the argument went, men have a family to support while women are only working for "pin money." Compensation administrators today are more sensitive to the fallacies apparent in this argument. Apparently, though, a need-based allocation mechanism is still used

---

[77]G. S. Leventhal, "Fairness in Social Relationships," in *Contemporary Topics in Social Psychology*, eds. J. W. Thibaut, J. G. Spence, and R. C. Carson (1976), pp. 211–39.

[78]Locke, Shaw, Saari, and Latham, "Goal Setting and Task Performance."

[79]Hamner, "How to Ruin Motivation with Pay"; Nathan B. Winstanley, "Are Merit Increases Really Effective?" *Personnel Administrator* 4 (1982), pp. 23–31; and Robert H. Rock, "Pay-for-Performance: Accent on Standards and Measures," *Compensation Review* 16, no. 3 (1984), pp. 15–23.

[80]Jerald Greenberg, "Looking Fair vs. Being Fair: Managing Impressions of Organizational Justice," in *Research in Organizational Behavior*, Vol. 12, eds. B. Staw and L. Cummings (JAI Press, 1990).

[81]G. S. Leventhal, "Fairness in Social Relationships," in *Contemporary Topics in Social Psychology*, eds. J. W. Thibaut, J. T. Spence, and R. C. Carson (Morristown, N.J.: General Learning Press, 1976a), pp. 211–39.

EXHIBIT 8.7
Rules for Allocation Rewards

Rule	Example
1. Equity rule	Salary increases based on inputs (performance)
2. Equality rule	All receive the same increase regardless of performance (across-the-board increases)
3. Reciprocity rule	Golden rule (treat others as you would like to be treated)
4. Need rule	More to those with greater need
5. Contract rule	Allocate according to prior agreements

Source: Adapted from Gerald Leventhal, "The Distribution of Rewards and Resources in Groups and Organizations," in *Equity Theory: Toward a General Theory of Social Interaction,* eds. Leonard Berkowitz and Elaine Walster, Advances in Experimental Social Psychology, volume 9 (New York: Academic Press, 1976), pp. 92–131.

when the recipient is a close personal friend of the person allocating the increase.[82] Finally, a contract rule indicates rewards are allocated based on preestablished agreements. Formal examples of this criterion are evident in any union setting. Less formal examples, though, might appear in different types of incentive systems. Employees are told up front that the compensation they receive will be strictly tied to the number of units produced or the cost savings achieved. The schedule of payouts for different levels of performance is agreed to in advance.

Collecting Performance Data

Procedural justice also means that supervisors should collect information about employee behavior in a fair manner. Best efforts should be made to ensure accurate data.[83] This includes specifying in advance the rules that will be used for collecting performance data.[84] For example, one study found that employees consider the appraisal process as more fair when the supervisor uses a diary to collect performance data.[85] Combining these suggestions, it appears that the employee and supervisor should discuss how the supervisor will keep track of performance, and that recorded observations (such as in a diary) are viewed favorably.

The Performance Appraisal Interview

Given that the majority of performance evaluations are based on subjective judgments of supervisors, and not on objective criteria (e.g., units produced), many employees feel that ratings are biased. Substantial evidence exists to support this position. For example, several studies have shown that raters can agree reasonably well in their relative ratings

---

[82]M.J. Lerner, "The Justice Motive in Human Relations and the Economic Model of Man: A Radical Analysis of Facts and Fictions," in *Cooperation and Helping Behavior: Theories and Research,* V. Derlega and J. Grezlak, eds. (New York: Academic Press, 1982), pp. 121–145.

[83]Winstanley, "Are Merit Increases Really Effective?"; and J. Greenberg, "Using Diaries to Promote Procedural Justice in Performance Approach," *Social Justice Review,* in press.

[84]Leventhal, "Fairness in Social Relationships."

[85]Greenberg, "Using Diaries to Promote Procedural Justice in Performance Approach."

of employees, but they do not discriminate particularly well across rating dimensions.[86] Dunnette and Borman have noted that "this means that different raters and/or methods tend to rank ratees similarly but that different facets or dimensions of job performance are poorly differentiated."[87]

Chapter 9 covers in great detail the appraisal interview and forms to best ensure bias-free results. We should note here, though, that efforts to appear fair in the actual interview seem to depend on whether subordinates are allowed to participate (provide their view of performance) and feel they have some input into the final decision.[88] Also, the behavior of the supervisor conducting the appraisal is important. Subordinates who perform well view the process as more fair when they are told by supervisors that the appraisal results are based on performance. Subordinates who do badly want to know the supervisor is concerned about their welfare (e.g., "I am sorry to give you such a low rating").[89] A bit of compassion goes a long way!

How to Allocate: When and How Much

When to Appraise. When should appraisals be conducted? One survey indicates that employees prefer appraisals once per year.[90] The number probably should be more often for new (probationary) employees and employees who are having a difficult time meeting performance expectations. A more controversial issue concerning timing of appraisals centers on the gap that should exist between the appraisal interview and the actual granting of compensation increases. One classic study indicated that appraisals should be used to help develop the employee.[91] Unfortunately, when the developmental aspect of the appraisal was combined with decisions about salary increases, employees focused only on the increase they were to get and any hope for development was lost. This concern generated bountiful prescriptions about how to solve the problem. The most common suggestion was to have the developmental interview separated by several months from an interview to discuss salary changes. None of the suggestions seemed to resolve the problem. Fortunately, one recent well-designed study indicates that it may be possible

---

[86]R. F. Burnaska and T. D. Hollman, "An Empirical Comparison of the Relative Effects of Rater Response Biases on Three Rating Scale Formats," *Journal of Applied Psychology* 59 (1974), pp. 307–12; and B. A. Freedman and E. F. Cornelius, "Effect of Rater Participation in Scale Construction on the Psychometric Characteristics of Two Rating Scale Formats," *Journal of Applied Psychology* 61 (1976), pp. 210–16.

[87]Marvin Dunnette and Martin Borman, "Personnel Selection and Classification Systems," *Annual Review of Psychology* 30 (1979), p. 488.

[88]F. Landy, J. Barnes, and K. Murphy, "Correlates of Perceived Fairness and Accuracy of Performance Evaluation," *Journal of Applied Psychology* 63 (1978), pp. 751–54.

[89]J. Greenberg, "Using Explanations to Manage Impressions of Performance Appraisal Fairness," Paper presented at the 1988 Academy of Management Meetings, Anaheim, Calif. (1988).

[90]J. Laumeyer and T. Beebe, "Employees and Their Appraisal," *Personnel Administrator,* December 1988, pp. 76–80.

[91]H. Meyer, E. Kay, and J. French, Jr., "Split Roles in Performance Appraisal," *Harvard Business Review* 43 (1965), pp. 123–29.

to combine developmental and salary discussions in the same appraisal interview.[92] Salary discussion actually helped foster positive appraisal outcomes, particularly for employees with clear performance problems. When supervisors discussed salary and combined it with a clear communication of performance problems, poor performers found the appraisal more helpful, were more satisfied with the whole process, and perceived the greatest amount of subsequent performance improvement.[93] This is further evidence that supervisors can make a difference! Paying attention to the way the appraisal is conducted has positive impacts.

How much of an increase should be given. How large should pay increases be? There are three obvious actors with vested interests in the answer to this question, and each must be considered in arriving at an effective level of merit increase. First, the organization seeks to minimize payroll costs while maintaining some level of performance output. An individual occupying a job then should receive a raise (from the organization's perspective) whose magnitude is a function of individual performance, occupational marketability, centrality of both job and individual for achievement of organizational goals, and, of course, budget constraints.[94] Research indicates salary magnitude decreases when budgets are smaller and increases when performance is higher or when the job is central to the organization mission, other things equal.[95] A second participant in the salary increase process is an employee's supervisor. Recent research on salary increment decision making indicates that supervisors in general tend to follow an adjustment approach to allocating salary raises. This type of system allocates larger raises to employees who are underpaid relative to peers at the same performance level.[96] Future research will need to determine what factors affect the type of allocation scheme supervisors select and identify ways to insure procedures used by supervisors are consistent with organizational goals.

The final actor in the salary increase process is, of course, the employee receiving the pay increase. Considerable recent research indicates there are differences across individuals in the size of a meaningful pay increase.[97] Presumably, if an organization offers a pay raise that is too small from an employee's perspective, the raise will not have the impact desired by the organization. Most current research focuses on factors that differentiate people in terms of how they attach value to money, and in particular, pay increases. Pay increases seem to be valued either because of their positive impact

---

[92]J. Bruce Prince and Edward Lawler III, "Does Salary Discussion Hurt the Developmental Performance Appraisal," *Organizational Behavior and Human Decision Processes* 37 (1986), pp. 357–75.

[93]Ibid.

[94]John Fossum and Mary Fitch, "Effects of Individual and Contextual Attributes on the Size of Recommended Salary Increases," *Personnel Psychology* 38 (1985), pp. 587–602.

[95]Ibid.

[96]M. H. Birnbaum, "Perceived Equity of Salary Policies," *Journal of Applied Psychology* 68 (1983), pp. 49–59.

[97]Linda A. Krefting, Jerry M. Newman, and Frank Krzystofiak, "What is a Meaningful Pay Increase?" prepared for *Compensation: An Applied Approach,* Luis R. Gomez-Mejia and David B. Balkin, eds. (Reston, Va.: Reston Publishing, forthcoming).

on the purchasing power of the individual or because of their significance as a form of organizational recognition.[98] In the former case salary increase magnitude would probably be compared against the size of the cost of living index. After all, a 6 percent increase during periods of 9 percent inflation is hardly grounds for celebration in the struggle to increase personal purchasing power. In contrast, if money is a form of organizational recognition, employees become concerned about the level of their raises in comparison to raises of others in the company. High relative raises act as feedback that performance is considered good by the powers that be.[99]

The total of this research indicates that appropriate pay size is not a fixed value. While we have made some progress in identifying the factors organizations consider important in establishing pay increase guidelines (Chapter 14), there are still huge gaps in our understanding of supervisory and subordinate reactions to these pay guidelines. To the extent either party is unhappy with the allocation scheme or pay raise level devised by the organization, unintended and potentially counterproductive consequences may be the result.

Appeals Mechanisms

One of the important roles that unions serve in organizations is to protect members against decisions that are viewed as unfair. The grievance process lets employees challenge decisions they see as unjust. Apparently such an appeals mechanism, whether mandated by a union contract or implemented by management unilaterally (Chapter 15 discusses this further), represents an important element of justice.[100] Opportunities should exist for appraisal decisions to be modified.

Communications

Many organizations adopt a policy of **pay secrecy.** According to studies by Lawler, this pay secrecy leads managers to regularly misperceive the levels of compensation of subordinates, peers, and superiors.[101] The nature of these errors tends to restrict the range of perceived salaries: Superiors are thought to receive less than their actual salaries and subordinates/peers appear to receive more than is actually the case. This tends to compress

---

[98]Linda A. Krefting and T. A. Mahoney, "Determining the Size of a Meaningful Pay Increase," *Industrial Relations* 11 (1977), pp. 83–93.

[99]Krefting and Mahoney, "Determining the Size of a Meaningful Pay Increase"; Frank Krzystofiak, Jerry M. Newman, and Linda A. Krefting, "Determining the Size of a Meaningful Pay Increase," *Proceedings of the Midwest Academy of Management* (1982a), pp. 191–99; and Frank Krzystofiak, Jerry Newman, and Linda Krefting, "Pay Meaning, Satisfaction, and Size of a Meaningful Pay Increase," *Psychological Reports* 51 (1982b), pp. 660–62.

[100]G. S. Leventhal, J. Karuza, and W. R. Fry, "Beyond Fairness: A Theory of Allocation Preferences," in *Justice and Social Interaction,* ed. G. Mikula (New York: Springer Verlag, 1980), pp. 167–218.

[101]E. E. Lawler, "Managers' Perception of their Subordinates' Pay and of their Superiors' Pay," *Personnel Psychology* 18 (1965), pp. 413–22; Edward Lawler III, "Secrecy and the Need to Know," in *Managerial Motivation and Compensation,* eds. Henry Tosi, Robert House, and Marvin Dunnette (East Lansing, Mich.: Michigan State University Press, 1972), pp. 455–76.

the perceived wage scale and lowers motivation to perform: Subordinates with fewer job responsibilities are earning almost as much and any effort to obtain a promotion would result in a lower (perceived) increase than was felt justified. Hamner argues that the secrecy surrounding pay increases may lead managers to believe that there is no direct relationship between pay and performance.[102] The alternative is to explain how pay raises are determined and announce all raises/promotions resulting from this stated policy.[103] Chapter 15 covers the development of these communication procedures in greater detail.

SUMMARY

On a superficial level the idea of pay for performance sounds like a viable policy to improve employee performance in organizations. After all, numerous studies have been summarized that show that employees who believe pay is dependent on performance actually perform at a higher relative level. Three key problems exist in translating this philosophy into a working practice. First, employees must value pay. While there is reasonable evidence to suggest that pay, at least indirectly, can satisfy individual needs, it should not be assumed that pay is the preeminent motivator capable of solving all organizational motivation problems. In essence, pay alone will not lead to achievement of high performance expectations. This leads to the second point. If pay is to assume a role as a motivator of performance, other detractors from this goal must be eliminated. This means an organization must develop sound human resources systems (e.g., selection, planning, performance evaluation, training) to complement the wage and salary system. Supervisors also must be trained to interact with subordinates about job expectations and provide feedback about job performance. Compensation does not, and never will be able to, exist in a vacuum. Even the best designed compensation system will falter when other human resources systems are inadequately designed to meet organizational needs.

The third problem in developing a pay-for-performance system centers on the fact that employees must believe that pay is tied to performance. This implies more than a policy statement to this effect. Organization practices must convey that pay is actually tied to performance. This precipitates a number of thorny issues: 1) a reasonable amount of salary increases must be allocated to merit so that performance differences translate into meaningful differences in pay raises, 2) supervisors must be trained to discriminate among subordinates in performance, 3) supervisors must be willing and able (i.e., trained) to provide feedback to employees about performance, 4) this feedback must be accompanied by a supportive environment in which supervisors view their roles partially as facilitators of employee performance (i.e., that performance is essentially a team effort), and 5) these practices must be adhered to consistently over time.

It is not surprising that organizations fail to tie pay to performance effectively. When confronted with the choice between a commitment to all that pay for performance implies

---

[102]Hamner, "How to Ruin Motivation with Pay."

[103]J. Greenberg, "Cultivating an Image of Justice: Looking Fair on the Job," *Academy of Management Executive* 2, no. 2 (1988), pp. 155–57.

and adopting a far more tranquil strategy with fewer payoffs, the choice is frequently made to avoid the more costly long term strategy. If this is the choice, then we should stop deluding ourselves that pay motivates performance and search for other strategies to motivate performance.

REVIEW QUESTIONS

1. Name the five factors affecting the long run success of organizations that can be influenced by compensation. Give examples of each.
2. How would VIE theory be used to argue that tying pay to performance will increase performance? Would this also be true for someone who does not consider money important?
3. How does equity theory help to explain why companies go out to the external labor market and conduct salary surveys?
4. Cite four reasons why pay for performance may not work in an organization.
5. How does procedural justice differ from distributive justice. Why might a supervisor have more control over the level of procedural justice in his department than the level of distributive justice?
6. Give five examples of the way an organization might increase the perceived fairness of its performance appraisal process.

Compensation Application
Quayle Pharmaceutical

Quayle Pharmaceutical is a medium-sized pharmaceutical company located in Sherwood, New Jersey. Most of Quayle's profits over the past 20 years have been generated by high volume production of drugs used by veterinarians in the care of domesticated animals. Since there is only a small markup in this market, Quayle must make its profit from high volume. With somewhat loose quality control laws for drugs distributed to veterinarians, Quayle historically has been able to achieve unit production levels that are high for the pharmaceutical industry.

Unfortunately, in the past two years productivity has significantly deteriorated at Quayle. Records for the past five years are provided in Exhibit 1. In addition, turnover and absenteeism are up (Exhibits 2 and 3).

John Lancer, president of Quayle Pharmaceutical, is deeply concerned. The key to Quayle's success has always been its high productivity and resulting low unit production costs. For some reason profits have been down 18 percent during the past two years (1988 = -13 percent; 1989 = -23 percent). Mr. Lancer has an annual stockholders' meeting in two weeks and he is determined he will go in with some answers. Maybe they can't correct the drop-off in time for the meeting, but heads will roll if he doesn't get some answers. All department heads subsequently are sent detailed letters outlining the profit picture and requesting explanations.

EXHIBIT 1
Quayle Pharmaceutical Productivity Trends, 1985–1989*

1985	1986	1987	1988	1989
127,000	123,000	122,786	104,281	100,222

*Dollars gross revenue generated per employee in 1967 dollars.

EXHIBIT 2
Turnover Percentages, All Occupations, 1985–1989

1985	1986	1987	1988	1989
14%	12.5%	19.0%	20.2%	21.1%

EXHIBIT 3
Absenteeism, Average Days per Employee, 1985–1989

1985	1986	1987	1988	1989
*	*	9.6	9.7	10.2

*Records not available.

EXHIBIT 4
Attitude Survey toward Compensation: Level and Administration

N = 1,427 (87 percent response rate)
Questions 1–15

Column A Scaling	*Column B Scaling*	*Column C Scaling*
1 = Very important to me	1 = Very satisfied	1 = Very dependent
2 = Important to me	2 = Satisfied	2 = Dependent
3 = Neither important nor unimportant	3 = Neutral	3 = Unsure
4 = Unimportant to me	4 = Dissatisfied	4 = Rarely dependent
5 = Very unimportant to me	5 = Very dissatisfied	5 = Never dependent

Indicate how important the following rewards available to Quayle employees are to you in column A. Indicate how satisfied you are with the level Quayle delivers in column B. How dependent are these rewards on your performance? (Column C)

		A	B	C
1.	A good salary	2	2	4
2.	An annual raise equal to or greater than the cost of living	1	2	5
3.	A profit sharing plan	5	3	3
4.	Paid sick days	5	3	5
5.	Vacation	3	1	5
6.	Life insurance	4	1	5
7.	Pension	4	1	5
8.	Medical plan	3	1	5
9.	Opportunity for advancement	2	5	5
10.	Job security	1	2	2
11.	Good supervisors	2	2	5
12.	Opportunity to develop new skills	2	5	5
13.	Good co-workers	3	3	5
14.	Steady hours	3	2	2
15.	Feedback about performance	1	5	3

Ralph Simpson is the top human resources person at Quayle Pharmaceutical. As Director of Human Resources Management he was informed by John Lancer three weeks ago that a marked drop in profits had occurred over the past year. Mr. Simpson offers the data in Exhibit 4 as a possible explanation for the profit decline.

1. Do Exhibits 1, 2, and 3 suggest any problems that might explain or be related to the profit declines?

2. Given the discussion of motivation theory in your text, do the data in Exhibit 4 suggest that productivity declines may be due to motivation problems? What other human resource management explanations are plausible?

Compensation Application
Tinker Food Markets

Tinker Food Markets were founded by Jonathan Tinker in Philadelphia shortly after the Depression. Since 1938 the chain has grown from 1 store to 86 supermarkets in Pennsylvania and southern New York. Until 1948 the stores were operated by one of Mr. Tinker's descendants. In 1948 the firm went public and the Tinker family gradually moved out of leadership roles. By all accounts, Tinker's problems stem from this period of Tinker family withdrawal. The company is now heavily unionized, with virtually all nonexempt employees and approximately 15 percent of the exempt employees unionized. Pay raises for union employees are across-the-board and negotiated between the union and management. Nonunion employees generally receive an across-the-board increase also, generally pegged to the union's negotiated rate. Performance appraisals are conducted by supervising employees. The appraisal form consists of one performance-related question: "Overall, how well do you think this employee performed during the past year?" Employees are not told the results of this appraisal and it is generally believed that the question is only used to determine promotability.

Employees have no opportunity to respond to poor ratings and, in fact, don't even know when ratings are poor. The end result is suspicion and mistrust. There have been numerous complaints that the system must be unfair. In general the complaints tend to come from the poorer performers. Supervisors respond very rapidly to these complaints, though, and usually ensure that the person receives a larger than average raise to lessen the dissatisfaction.

1. The new Tinker management would like to establish a pay-for-performance system. What does this mean for them?
2. What changes will have to be made in the way the system operates now?
3. How might these changes be implemented?
4. Which of the nonmonetary changes do you think will help motivate better performance? Defend your position.

Subjective Performance Evaluation and Merit Pay

The Harper

According to one version of Aesop's fables, a man who used to play upon the harp, and sing to it, in little alehouses, and made a shift in those narrow confined walls to please the dull sots who heard him, from hence entertained an ambition of shewing his parts on the public theatre, where he fancied he could not fail of raising a great reputation and fortune in a very short time. He was accordingly admitted upon trial; but the spaciousness of the palace, and the throng of the people, so deadened and weakened both his voice and instrument, that scarcely either of them could be heard, and where they could, his performance sounded so poor, so low, and wretched, in the ears of his refined audience, that he was universally hissed off the stage.

Moral: As beauty is in the eyes of the beholder, so too is a performance evaluation in the eyes of the rater.

Chapter 8 covered the global issues involved in designing compensation systems to reflect individual and organizational performance. Now we narrow the focus by discussing the actual process of appraising performance to determine how much of a pay increase, if any, employees should receive. This chapter describes performance appraisal systems that depend on subjective measures of individual performance to determine the size of pay increases employees should receive. As such, this chapter explores traditional methods of linking pay and performance. The next chapter concentrates on less traditional ways to pay employees. A large part of this discussion centers on compensation techniques when performance can be measured fairly objectively. Objective performance data lends itself readily to objective counting and verification procedures. A punch press operator who works all day to produce 3,000 widgets can readily verify this number if desired. This objective evaluation system, in turn, is the foundation for pay systems heavily dependent on output. The sophisticated linkages between pay and output (e.g., variable levels, timing, and even forms of pay) are possible only because output measurement is so free from distortion.

This chapter deals with an entirely different set of circumstances. In the majority of jobs, objective performance standards are not feasible. Either job output is not readily quantifiable or the components that are quantifiable do not reflect important job dimensions. A secretarial job could be reduced to words per minute and errors per page of typing. But many secretaries, and their supervisors, would argue this captures only a small portion of the job. Courtesy in greeting clients and in answering phones, initiative in solving problems without running to the boss, dependability under deadlines—all of these intangible qualities can make the difference between a good and a poor secretary.

How, then, should performance be measured when the data are so elusive? What does a unit of courtesy or initiative look like? Such subjective concepts require subjective judgments for performance evaluation. This chapter deals with the continuing efforts to find evaluation formats and strategies to reduce this subjectivity. The ultimate goal, as yet not achieved, is to find ways to evaluate performance that are perceived as fair and that accurately reflect work output. Until this is accomplished, though, employees quite naturally will be reluctant to have pay systems finely tuned to "measured" variations in performance. At the very least, charges that the evaluation process is political will abound.[1] As a consequence, employees and unions sometimes argue, pay systems related to subjective performance evaluation ought to reflect only gross changes in output.

Unfortunately, organizations operate as if their appraisal systems are more accurate than they actually are.[2] Quite naturally, then, employees feel inequitably treated. One poll, in fact, found 30 percent of employees believed their performance appraisals were ineffective. This credibility gap and the growing general concern about errors in appraisal have spurred research to improve accuracy in appraisal. Early research along these lines centered on identifying appraisal formats that would improve the accuracy of rater efforts. More recent attention has focused on the raters themselves, attempting to identify how raters process information used to derive appraisal ratings. Knowing how raters process information, including how irrelevant information plays a role in the evaluation of employees, may permit more effective training programs designed to show raters appropriate procedures. The first two sections of this chapter deal with these two research directions and the useful information they have uncovered.

PERFORMANCE EVALUATION FORMATS

Exhibit 9.1 illustrates six types of evaluation formats falling into two general categories.[3] By themselves in one category are all evaluation methods involving some ranking procedure to compare employees with each other. All other procedures compare performance data against one of three absolute standards: adjectives, behaviors, and outcomes. Finally,

EXHIBIT 9.1
Standards of Comparison Used in Different Rating Formats

	Relative Comparison against:	*Absolute Comparison against:*		
	Performance of Other Employees	*Adjective Descriptors*	*Expected Job Behaviors*	*Expected Job Outcomes*
Type of Format	1. Ranking 6. Essay	2. Adjective checklist 3. Standard rating scale	4. Behaviorally anchored rating scale (BARS)	5. Management by objectives (MBO)

[1]Clinton Longnecker, Henry Sims, and Dennis Gioia, "Behind the Mark: The Politics of Employee Appraisal," *Academy of Management Executive* 1(3) (1987), pp. 183–93.

[2]Daniel Ilgen and Jack Feldman, "Performance Appraisal: A Process Focus," *Research in Organizational Behavior*, vol. 5 (1983), pp. 141–97.

[3]Larry L. Cummings and Donald P. Schwab, *Performance in Organizations* (Glenview, Ill.: Scott Foresman, 1973).

EXHIBIT 9.2
Usage of Performance Evaluation Formats

	Type of System	Usage (%) By Type of Employee	
		Nonexempt	*Exempt*
1.	Standard rating scale	52	32
2.	Essay	30	
3.	Management by objectives or other objective-based system	19	73
4.	Behaviorally anchored scale	28	24
5.	Other	33	32

(Percentages total more than 100 percent because of multiple systems in different companies.)

Source: Based on a survey of 256 firms from a population of 1300 large organizations completed by Drake, Beam and Morin. Drake, Beam and Morin: New York, 1983.

an essay format, because of the wide discretion allowed a rater in completing an evaluation, could involve any of the above formats. Exhibit 9.2 illustrates the relative popularity for some of these formats in industry.

Ranking Procedures

Employees are compared against each other in terms of the overall value of their performance to the organization. There are several ways these rankings can be obtained. First is a straight ranking procedure. The highest performer is identified and successive individuals are ordered by level of overall performance. A second strategy involves alternate ranking. The top and bottom performers in the unit are identified and removed from the list. From the remaining list, then, the next best and worst performers are selected. This process continues until all employees have been ranked. Third, on a paired comparison procedure, each employee is compared (paired) with every other employee. One's ranking depends on the number of total times an employee is ranked higher in performance than the other employee in each pair.

Finally, forced distribution ranking literally forces evaluators to distribute rankings according to some predetermined distribution. A typical procedure would be to approximate a normal distribution:

Number of Employees	*Lowest 10%*	*Next 20%*	*Middle 40%*	*Next 20%*	*Highest 10%*
40	4	8	16	8	4

Adjective Checklists

For an adjective checklist, raters must check the descriptors that most reflect an employee's performance. Each descriptor previously has been evaluated to determine how favorable or unfavorable it is for successful job performance (e.g., aloof, demanding, temperamental).[4] A variant on this format also attempts to equate checklist items for social desirability (perceived positive or negative connotations generally attached to a word). For whichever format is used, though, the overall performance score is the sum of scores on each of the items checked.

Standard Rating Scales

All of the variants on rating scales share two underlying commonalities. First, one or more performance standards are developed and each is defined for the appraiser. Second, each performance standard has a measurement scale attached to it, indicating varying levels of performance on that dimension. Appraisers rate appraisees by checking the point on the scale that best represents the appraisee's performance level. Variations on the rating scale format occur in the extent to which points or anchors along the scale are defined. For example, Exhibit 9.3 compares two different anchoring methods.

Employees are assigned a scale level reflecting their performance on each dimension. Overall performance is some weighted performance average (weighted by the importance the organization attaches to each dimension) of the ratings on all dimensions. Appendix A at the end of this chapter gives examples of standard rating scales and the total appraisal form for some well-known organizations. As a brief illustration, though, consider Exhibit 9.4.

This employee is rated slightly above average. An alternative method for obtaining

---

EXHIBIT 9.3
Methods of Anchoring Rating Scales

			Single Word Anchor Scale		
Performance dimension					
	(1)	*(2)*	*(3)*	*(4)*	*(5)*
Leadership ability	Well above average.	Above average.	Average.	Below average.	Well below average.
			Short Phrase Anchor Scale		
Performance dimension					
	(1)	*(2)*	*(3)*	*(4)*	*(5)*
Job knowledge	Is extremely well informed about all facets of job.	Is well informed on important dimensions of job.	Has sufficient knowledge of job dimensions to perform job adequately.	Lacks necessary information about job dimensions.	Is misinformed or lacks knowledge on important job dimensions.

---

[4]Frank Barron, "Complexity-Simplicity as a Personality Variable," in *Problems in Human Assessment,* eds. Douglas Jackson and Samuel Messick (New York: McGraw-Hill, 1967).

EXHIBIT 9.4
An Example of Employee Appraisal

Employee: George T. Mahoney
Job title: supervisor, shipping and receiving

Performance Dimension	Dimension Rating					Dimension Weight
	Well Below Average 1	*Below Average* 2	*Average* 3	*Above Average* 4	*Well Above Average* 5	
Leadership ability				x		.2 (× 4) = .8
Job knowledge					x	.1 (× 5) = .5
Work output				x		.3 (× 4) = 1.2
Attendance			x			.2 (× 3) = .6
Initiative			x			.2 (× 3) = .6
			Sum of rating × weight			= 3.7
			Overall rating			= 3.7

an overall rating is to allow the rater discretion in rating both performance on the individual dimensions and in assigning an overall evaluation. In this case the weights from the far right column of Exhibit 9.4 would not be used, and the overall evaluation would be based on a subjective and internal assessment by the rater.

Behaviorally Anchored Rating Scales

Behaviorally anchored rating scales (BARS) are a variant on standard rating scales in which the various scale levels are anchored with behavioral descriptions directly applicable to jobs being evaluated (Exhibit 9.5). By anchoring scales with concrete behaviors, firms adopting a BARS format hope to make evaluations less subjective. Now when raters decide on a rating they have a common definition (in the form of a behavioral example)

EXHIBIT 9.5
Behaviorally Anchored Rating Scale: Resident Adviser, University Housing

Performance Dimension
   Concern for individual dorm residents: Attempts to get to know individual dorm residents and responds to their individual needs with genuine interest. This resident adviser could be expected to:

Rating Scale

(1)	*(2)*	*(3)*	*(4)*	*(5)*
Recognize when a floor member appears depressed and ask if person has problem he/she wants to discuss.	Offer floor members "tips" on how to study for a course he/she has already taken.	See person and recognize him/her as a floor member and say "hi."	Be friendly with a floor member; get into discussion on problems, but fail to follow up on the problem later on with student.	Criticize a floor member for not being able to solve his/her own problems.

EXHIBIT 9.6
Procedures in Developing a Behaviorally Anchored Rating Scale

---

1. Supervisors of a group of employees, performing similar jobs, are asked to identify those broad sets of job activities that comprise the job. For programmer analysts, examples of such "performance dimensions" might be coding and documentation.

2. The same supervisors generate a set of critical incidents (behaviors they have seen performed by subordinates) that represent actual examples of very good and very poor subordinate performance on each of the dimensions.

3. Each member of a second, independent group of supervisors then is instructed to categorize each incident into the performance dimension most appropriate. If there is not high agreement among the supervisors (e.g., 70 percent) about which category an incident belongs in, the incident is deleted as being too ambiguous.

4. For each remaining incident the same group of supervisors rates the incident on a "good-bad" continuum, typically using a 1 to 5 scale. Items with high disagreement between supervisors (e.g., standard deviations greater than 1.0) are also discarded as being too ambiguous.

5. The remaining incidents may be used to anchor the various scale points on a numerical scale for each performance dimension. For example, an incident with a mean rating (from the second supervisory group) of 2.5 would be used as an anchor one half of the way between the scale values of 2 and 3. Presumably these anchors allow supervisors to compare their employees against a common set of standards, thereby reducing error.

6. The resultant set of performance dimensions, each with a set of ordered and scaled incidents, is referred to as BARS.

---

of, for example, average performance. This directly addressed a major criticism of standard rating scales: different raters carry with them into the rating situation different definitions of the scale levels (e.g., different raters have different ideas about what "average work" is). The six steps in developing a behaviorally anchored rating scale are listed in Exhibit 9.6.

Management by Objectives (MBO)

There is a major obstacle to defining MBO. As has been noted elsewhere: "MBO, like ice cream, comes in 29 flavors."[5] Since this comment was written, both the number of ice cream flavors and the number of different approaches to MBO have increased. Despite this confusion, a working definition can be developed. (Components of successful MBO programs are illustrated in Exhibit 9.7). MBO is both a planning and appraisal process. Organization goals or plans are identified from the strategic plan of the company and each successively lower level in the organizational hierarchy is charged with identifying work objectives that will support attainment of organizational goals. This identification of work objectives is a participatory process requiring discussion between both supervisor and subordinate in identifying appropriate goals.[6] Once goals have been mutually deter-

---

[5]J. S. Hodgson, "Management by Objectives: The Experiences of a Federal Government Department," *Canadian Public Administration* 16, no. 4 (1973), pp. 422–31.

[6]Mark L. McConkie, "A Clarification of the Goal Setting and Appraisal Processes in MBO," *Academy of Management Review* 4, no. 1 (1979), pp. 29–40.

EXHIBIT 9.7
Components of a Successful MBO Program

	*Total Number of Responses**	*Percentage of Authorities in Agreement*
1. Goals and objectives should be specific.	37	97
2. Goals and objectives should be defined in terms of measurable results.	37	97
3. Individual goals should be linked to overall organization goals.	37	97
4. Objectives should be reviewed "periodically."	31	82
5. The time period for goal accomplishment should be specified.	27	71
6. Wherever possible, the indicator of the results should be quantifiable; otherwise, it should be at least verifiable.	26	68
7. Objectives should be flexible; changed as conditions warrant.	26	68
8. Objectives should include a plan of action for accomplishing the results.	21	55
9. Objectives should be assigned priorities of weights.	19	50

*In this table the total number of responses actually represents the total number of authorities responding; thus, the percentages also represent the percent of authorities in agreement with the statements made.

Source: Mark L. McConkie, "A Clarification of the Goal Setting and Appraisal Process in MBO," *Academy of Management Review* 4, no. 1 (1979), pp. 29–40. © 1979, Academy of Management Review.

mined, they become the standards against which employee performance is evaluated. Level of performance evaluation is directly equated with degree of goal accomplishment. The final evaluation (overall rating) is expressed numerically and represents a subjective estimate of both goal difficulty and degree of attainment, e.g., hard goals that are completely achieved should result in an overall rating of five on a scale with five as the maximum.

A review of firms using MBO indicates generally positive improvements in performance for both individuals and the organization.[7] This is accompanied by managerial attitudes toward MBO as a method of evaluation that become more positive over time, particularly when the system is revised periodically to reflect feedback of participants. Managers are especially pleased with the way MBO provides direction to work units, improves the planning process, and increases superior/subordinate communication. On the negative side, MBO appears to require more paperwork and increase both performance pressure and stress.[8]

---

[7]Stephen Carroll, "Management by Objectives: Three Decades of Research and Experience," in *Current Issues in Human Resource Management: Commentary and Readings,* eds. Sara Rynes and George Milkovich (Plano, Tx.: Business Publications, Inc., 1986).

[8]Ibid.

Essays

Using an open-ended format, the appraiser is asked to write an essay description of employee performance. Since the descriptors used could range from comparisons with other employees through adjectives, behaviors, and goal accomplishments, the essay format can take on characteristics of all the formats discussed previously.

EVALUATING PERFORMANCE APPRAISAL FORMATS

A review of the literature indicates five dimensions against which different appraisal formats can be compared: (1) employee development potential (amount of feedback about performance the form offers), (2) administrative ease, (3) personnel research potential, (4) cost, (5) validity. Admittedly, different organizations will attach different weights to these dimensions. For example, a small organization in its formative years is likely to be very cost conscious. A larger organization with more pressing affirmative action commitments might place relatively high weight on validity and nondiscrimination criteria and show less concern about cost issues. A progressive firm concerned with employee development will demand a format allowing rich employee feedback. Less enlightened organizations may be concerned solely with costs. These dimensions are explained below.[9]

Employee Development Criteria

Does the method communicate the goals and objectives of the organization? Is feedback to employees a natural outgrowth of the evaluation format, such that employee development needs are identified and can be attended to readily?

Administrative Criteria

How easily can evaluation results be used for administrative decisions concerning wage increases, promotions, demotions, terminations, and transfers? Comparisons among individuals for personnel action require some common denominator for comparison. Typically this is a numerical rating of performance. Evaluation forms that do not produce numerical ratings cause administrative headaches.

Personnel Research

Does the instrument lend itself well for validating employment tests? Applicants predicted to perform well can be monitored through performance evaluation. Similarly, the success of various employees and organizational development programs can be traced to impacts on employee performance. As with the administrative criteria, though, evaluations typically need to be quantitative to permit the statistical tests so common in personnel research.

---

[9]Bruce McAfee and Blake Green, "Selecting a Performance Appraisal Method," *Personnel Administrator* 22, no. 5 (1977), pp. 61–65.9.2.

Economic Criteria

Does the evaluation form require a long time to develop initially? Is it time-consuming for supervisors to use in rating their employees? Is it expensive to use? All of these factors increase the format cost.

Validity

By far the most research on formats in recent years has focused on reducing error and improving accuracy. Success in this pursuit would mean decisions based upon performance ratings (e.g., promotions, merit increases, could be made with greater confidence). In general, the search for the "perfect format" to eliminate rating errors (see Exhibit 9.8 for definitions and examples of true rating errors) and improve accuracy has been unsuccessful. The high acclaim, for example, accompanying introduction of BARS has not been supported by research.[10] Exhibit 9.9 provides a relative comparison among the six

---

EXHIBIT 9.8
True Rating Errors: An Illustration and Definition

	(1)	*(2)*	*(3)*	*(4)*
High	Al	Al / Sue / Bill (top)		
True Performance	Sue	Rated Performance	Rated Performance	Rated Performance — Al / Sue / Bill (middle)
Low	Bill		Al / Sue / Bill (bottom)	
	No error	Leniency error	Severity error	Central tendency error

Error

Leniency—Rated performance consistently exceeds true score performance of ratees.

Severity—Rated performance consistently lower than true score performance of ratees.

Central tendency—Rated performance falls in middle of rating scale, irrespective of true score performance of ratees.

Halo—Rating on one performance dimension strongly influences (i.e., highly correlated with) rating on other performance dimensions, irrespective of true score relationship across dimensions.

---

[10]H. John Bernardin, "Behavioral Expectation Scales v. Summated Ratings: A Fairer Comparison," *Journal of Applied Psychology* 62 (1977), pp. 422–27; H. John Bernardin, Kim Alvares, and C. J. Cranny, "A Recomparison of Behavioral Expectation Scales to Summated Scales," *Journal of Applied Psychology* 61 (1976), pp. 284–91; C. A. Schriesheim and U. E. Gattiker, "A Study of the Abstract Desirability of Behavior-Based v. Trait-Oriented Performance Rating," *Proceedings of the Academy of Management* 43 (1982), pp. 307–11; and F. S. Landy and J. L. Farr, "Performance Rating," *Psychological Bulletin* 87 (1980), pp. 72–107.

EXHIBIT 9.9
An Evaluation of Performance Appraisal Formats

	Employee Development Criteria	Administrative Criteria	Personnel Research	Economic Criteria	Validity
Ranking	Poor—ranks typically based on overall performance, with little thought given to feedback on specific performance dimensions.	Poor—comparisons of ranks across work units to determine merit raises are meaningless. Other administrative actions similarly hindered.	Average—validation studies can be completed with rankings of performance.	Good—inexpensive source of performance data. Easy to develop and use in small organizations and in small units.	Average—good reliability but poor on rating errors, especially halo.
Adjective checklist	Average—general problem areas identified for employee, but little information on extent of problem or behaviors/outcomes necessary to change evaluation.	Average—adjective rankings can be tallied for merit decisions.	Good—checklists equated for social desirability may yield relatively uncontaminated performance data.	Average—expensive to develop.	Good—usually good content validity and equating items for social desirability will reduce rating errors.
Standard rating scales	Average—general problem areas identified. Some information on extent of developmental need is available, but no feedback on necessary behaviors/outcomes.	Average—ratings valuable for merit increase decisions and others. Not easily defended if contested.	Average—validation studies can be completed, but level of measurement contamination unknown.	Good—inexpensive to develop and easy to use.	Average—content validity is suspect. Rating errors and reliability are average.
Behaviorally anchored rating scales	Good—extent of problem and behavioral needs are identified.	Good—BARS good for making administrative decisions. Useful for defense if contested because job-relevant.	Good—validation studies can be completed and measurement problems on BARS less than many other criterion measures.	Average—expensive to develop but easy to use.	Good—high content validity. Some evidence of inter-rater reliability and reduced rating errors.
Management by objectives	Excellent—extent of problem and outcome deficiencies are identified.	Poor—MBO not suited to merit income decisions. Level of completion and difficulty of objectives hard to compare across employees.	Poor—nonstandard objectives across employees and no overall measures of performance make validity studies difficult.	Poor—expensive to develop and time consuming to use.	Excellent—high content validity. Low rating errors.
Essay	Unknown—depends on guidelines for inclusions in essay as developed by organization or supervisors.	Poor—essays not comparable across different employees considered for merit or other administrative actions.	Poor—no quantitative indices to compare performance against employment test scores in validation studies.	Average—easy to develop but time consuming to use.	Unknown—unstructured format makes studies of essay method difficult.

rating formats in terms of their performance on the five dimensions for evaluating appraisal formats.

HOW RATERS PROCESS INFORMATION

The 1980s ushered in an explosion of research on how people process information to arrive at, among other things, final performance ratings. Many experts believe this is a potentially more fruitful research direction to help improve performance rating than previous efforts directed at rating formats.[11] Already this research has yielded models of how people review information and make judgments.[12] Combine this with systematic research testing parts of these models and quickly there is a developing body of information on how to improve the rating process.

Models of the Appraisal Process

Cognitive models tend to outline the performance appraisal process in similar ways. Raters go through stages, some of them quite unconscious when they attempt to rate the performance of other employees. First, the rater observes behavior of a ratee. Second, this behavior is encoded as part of a total picture of the ratee (e.g., one way of saying this is that we form stereotypes about people). Third, we store this information in memory, which is subject to both short and long term decay. Simply put, we forget things! Fourth, when it comes time to evaluate a ratee, the rater reviews the performance dimensions and retrieves stored observations/impressions to determine their relevance to the performance dimensions. Finally, the information is reconsidered and integrated with other available information as the rater makes the final ratings.[13]

Quite unintentionally, when people process this information, errors occur. And they can occur at any of the stages. For example, when people process this information, behavior is sometimes observed incorrectly. Impressions are formed that are incorrect stereotypes of employees. When information is stored some of it may be forgotten. Recall is also influenced by extraneous factors. At virtually every stage raters can make errors that result in evaluations that are not an accurate reflection of employee performance. Fortunately, some high quality research has allowed us to identify, and thus try to correct, some of the errors made in rating other employees.

Errors in the Rating Process

Ideally raters should attend exclusively to performance-related factors when they observe employee behavior. In fact all of the processing stages should be guided by **performance**

---

[11]Landy and Farr, "Performance Rating."

[12]Ilgen and Feldman, "Performance Appraisal: A Process Focus."

[13]Landy and Farr, "Performance Rating"; A. S. Denisi, T. P. Cafferty, and B. M. Meglino, "A Cognitive View of the Performance Appraisal Process: A Model and Research Propositions," *Organizational Behavior and Human Performance* 33 (1984), pp. 360–96; Jack M. Feldman, "Beyond Attribution Theory: Cognitive Processes in Performance Appraisal," *Journal of Applied Psychology* 66, no. 2 (1981), pp. 127–48; and W. H. Cooper, "Ubiquitous Halo," *Psychological Bulletin* 90 (1981), pp. 218–44.

relevancy. Unless a behavior (or personality trait) affects performance it should not influence performance ratings! Fortunately, studies show that performance actually does play an important role, perhaps the major role, in determining what rating a supervisor gives a subordinate.[14] On the negative side, though, there are many other factors that appear to influence ratings (i.e., they cause errors in the evaluation process).[15]

Errors in observation (attention). Generally, researchers have varied three types of input information to see how raters observe and what they attend to. The first set of data manipulated are characteristics of the ratees themselves. There is reasonably consistent information that males are rated higher than females (other things equal) and that the rating of Blacks and Whites depends on the race of the rater (same race, higher ratings).[16]

Researchers also vary characteristics of the input data to see if this influences performance ratings. Both the pattern of performance (performance gets better or worse over time) and the variability of performance (consistent vs. erratic) influence performance ratings, even when the level of performance is controlled.[17] Not surprisingly, workers with an ascending pattern of performance are seen as more motivated, while those who are more variable in their performance are tagged as lower in motivation. All of us have seen examples of workers (and students) who intuitively recognize this type of error and try to use it to their advantage. The big surge of work at the end of an appraisal period is often designed to "color" a rater's perceptions.

---

[14]Leo Leventhal, Raymon Perry, and Philip Abrami, "Effects of Lecturer Quality and Student Perception of Lecturer Experience on Teacher Ratings and Student Achievement," *Journal of Educational Psychology* 69, no. 4 (1977), pp. 360–74; Angelo Denisi and George Stevens, "Profiles of Performance, Performance Evaluations, and Personnel Decisions," *Academy of Management* 24, no. 3 (1981), pp. 592–602; Wayne Cascio and Enzo Valenzi, "Relations among Criteria of Police Performance," *Journal of Applied Psychology* 63, no. 1 (1978), pp. 22–28; William Bigoness, "Effects of Applicant's Sex, Race, and Performance on Employer Performance Ratings: Some Additional Findings," *Journal of Applied Psychology* 61, no. 1 (1976), pp. 80–84; and Dorothy P. Moore, "Evaluating In-Role and Out-of-Role Performers," *Academy of Management Journal* 27, no. 3 (1984), pp. 603–18.

[15]H. J. Bernardin and Richard Beatty, *Performance Appraisal: Assessing Human Behavior at Work* (Boston: Kent Publishing, 1984).

[16]Edward Shaw, "Differential Impact of Negative Stereotyping in Employee Selection," *Personnel Psychology* 25 (1972), pp. 333–38; Benson Rosen and Thomas Jurdee, "Effects of Applicant's Sex and Difficulty of Job on Evaluations of Candidates for Managerial Positions," *Journal of Applied Psychology* 59 (1975), pp. 511–12; Gail Pheterson, Sara Kiesler, and Philip Goldberg, "Evaluation of the Performance of Women as a Function of their Sex, Achievement, and Personal History," *Journal of Personality and Social Psychology* 19 (1971), pp. 114–18; W. Clay Hamner, Jay Kim, Lloyd Baird, and William Bigoness, "Race and Sex as Determinants of Ratings by Potential Employers in a Simulated Work Sampling Task," *Journal of Applied Psychology* 59, no. 6 (1974), pp. 705–11; and Neal Schmitt and Martha Lappin, "Race and Sex as Determinants of the Mean and Variance of Performance Ratings," *Journal of Applied Psychology* 65, no. 4 (1980), pp. 428–35.

[17]Denisi and Stevens, "Profiles of Performance, Performance Evaluations, and Personnel Decisions"; William Scott and Clay Hamner, "The Influence of Variations in Performance Profiles on the Performance Evaluation Process: An Examination of the Validity of the Criterion," *Organizational Behavior and Human Performance* 14 (1975), pp. 360–70; and Edward Jones, Leslie Rock, Kelly Shaver, George Goethals, and Laurence Ward, "Pattern of Performance and Ability Attributions: An Unexpected Primacy Effect," *Journal of Personality and Social Psychology* 10, no. 4 (1968), pp. 317–40.

Errors in storage and recall. Research suggests that raters store information in the form of trait-based schemata.[18] More importantly perhaps, people tend to recall information in the form of schemata or trait categories also. For example, a rater observes a specific behavior (i.e., an employee resting during what are obviously work hours). The rater stores this information not as the specific behavior, but rather in the form of a trait, such as "that worker is lazy." Specific instructions to recall information about the ratee, as for a performance review, elicits the trait—lazy. Evidence indicates that in the process of forming impressions or making predictions about others, people organize behavioral information into trait categories.[19] Further, in the process of recalling information, rater recall may be colored by, or consistent with, the schema (trait categorization or implicit personality theory) but inconsistent with actual events.[20] The entire rating process then may be heavily influenced by these cognitive schema that we adopt; and the schema may or may not be accurate! One of the most obvious examples of this processing error is evident in sex stereotyping. A female ratee is observed, not as a ratee, but as a female ratee. A rater may form impressions based on stereotypic beliefs about women rather than the reality of the work situation. Performance ratings are then influenced by the gender of the ratee, quite apart from any performance information. Errors in storage and recall also appear to arise from memory decay. At least one study indicates that rating accuracy is a function of the delay between performance and subsequent rating. The longer the delay, the less accurate the ratings.[21]

Errors in evaluation. The context of the actual evaluation process also can influence evaluations.[22] Several researchers indicate how the purpose of evaluation affects the rating process. Supervisors who know ratings will be used to determine merit increases are less likely to discriminate among subordinates than when the ratings will be used for other purposes.[23] Being required to provide feedback to subordinates about their ratings also

---

[18]Landy and Farr, "Performance Rating"; Bernardin and Beatty, *Performance Appraisal: Assessing Human Behavior at Work.*

[19]K. M. Jeffrey and W. Mischel, "Effects of Purpose on the Organization and Recall of Information in Person Perception," *Journal of Personality* 47 (1979), pp. 297–419; and C. Hoffman, W. Mischel, and K. Masse, "The Role of Purpose in the Organization of Information about Behavior: Trait-Based v. Goal-Based Categories in Person Cognition," *Journal of Personality and Social Psychology* 4 (1981), pp. 211–25.

[20]N. Cantor and W. Mischel, "Traits v. Prototypes: The Effects on Recognition and Memory," *Journal of Personality and Social Psychology* 35 (1977), pp. 38–48; R. J. Spiro, "Remembering Information from Text: The 'State of Schema' Approach," in *Schooling and the Acquisition of Knowledge,* eds. R. C. Anderson, R. J. Spiro, and W. E. Montague (Hillsdale, Calif.: Erlbaum Assoc., 1977); and T. K. Srull and R. S. Wyer, "Category Accessibility and Social Perception: Some Implications for the Study of Person Memory and Interpersonal Judgments," *Journal of Personality and Social Psychology* 38 (1980), pp. 841–56.

[21]Robert Heneman and Kenneth Wexley, "The Effects of Time Delay in Rating and Amount of Information Observed on Performance Rating Accuracy," *Academy of Management Journal* 26, no. 4 (1983), pp. 677–86.

[22]Robert Liden and Terence Mitchell, "The Effects of Group Interdependence on Supervisor Performance Evaluations," *Personnel Psychology* 36, no. 2 (1983), pp. 289–99.

[23]Winstanley, "How Accurate Are Performance Appraisals?"; Landy and Farr, "Performance Rating"; and Heneman and Wexley, "The Effects of Time Delay in Rating and Amount of Information Observed on Performance Rating Accuracy."

yields less accuracy than a secrecy policy.[24] Presumably anticipation of an unpleasant confrontation with the angry ratee "persuades" the rater to avoid confrontation. How? By giving ratings that are higher than justified.

IMPROVING EVALUATIONS

Raters are capable of making errors in all the stages of information processing that characterize the rating process. Thus far this chapter has been quite pessimistic about the potential to correct this situation. This section identifies what is known about improving evaluation—the so-called "tips to a better appraisal."

Format Selection

Historically, the selection of a performance appraisal has been guided primarily by fads and fashions. Organizations have been disposed to jump on the proverbial "band wagon" by adopting the latest "in" format. Little consideration is given to the organization's needs, employee needs, or the types of jobs being evaluated. These factors are vital in the strategic selection of a performance appraisal format. And, because these factors vary across organizations and within organizations, across jobs and individuals, a contingency approach to format selection may be the most appropriate strategy. The argument is made that no single evaluation format may be entirely appropriate across all jobs and individuals in an organization. It may be appropriate to adopt different appraisal formats for different situations. Advocates of this contingency approach argue that the nature of the task and/or past performance of the individual may warrant an array of formats rather than a single format.

Keeley suggests that the choice of an appraisal format is dependent on the type of tasks being performed.[25] He argues that tasks can be ordered along a continuum from those that are very routine in nature to those for which the appropriate behavior for goal accomplishment is very uncertain. In Keeley's view, different appraisal formats require assumptions about the extent to which correct behavior for task accomplishment can be specified. The choice of an appraisal format requires a matching of formats with tasks that meet the assumptions for that format. At one extreme of the continuum are behavior-based evaluation procedures that define specific performance expectations against which employee performance is evaluated. Keeley argues that behaviorally anchored rating scales fall into this category. The behavioral anchors define specific performance expectations representing different levels of performance possible by an employee. Only for highly routine, mechanistic tasks is it appropriate to specify behavioral expectations. For these routine tasks it is possible to identify the single sequence of appropriate behaviors to accomplish a goal. Consequently it is possible to identify behavioral anchors for a per-

---

[24]Cummings and Schwab, *Performance in Organizations*.

[25]Michael Keeley, "A Contingency Framework for Performance Evaluation," *Academy of Management Review* 3 (July 1978), pp. 428–38.

formance scale that illustrate varying levels of attainment of the proper sequence of activities.

However, when tasks become less routine, it becomes more difficult to specify a single sequence of procedures that must be followed to accomplish a goal. Rather, multiple strategies are both feasible and appropriate to reach a final goal. Under these circumstances, Keeley argues the appraisal format should focus on evaluating the extent to which the final goal is accomplished.[26] Thus, for less certain tasks a management by objective (MBO) strategy would be appropriate. As long as the final goal can be specified, performance can be evaluated in relation to that goal without specifying or evaluating the

---

EXHIBIT 9.10
A Contingency Evaluation Approach Based on Past Employee Performance

Program	Past Employee Performance	Type of Tasks Assigned to Employee	Appropriate Evaluation Format
Developmental Action Program (DAP)	Consistently high performance in past with demonstrated potential for growth.	Tasks for which there is considerable discretion in way goals are accomplished.	1. MBO. 2. BARS.
Maintenance Action Program (MAP)	1. Average acceptable performance with low potential for growth, or 2. Above average performance working on job with low discretion.	Tasks for which: 1. Clearly defined and communicated goals are established, and 2. The method for carrying out tasks is frequently improved by the technology or the supervisor, and 3. Close direction and frequent evaluation is possible.	1. Conventional trait rating. 2. BARS. 3. Weighted checklist. 4. Forced choice.
Remedial Action Program (RAP)	Employees who are clearly below acceptable performance standards.	Highly structured tasks for which it is possible to: 1. Provide feedback about why performance is inadequate, 2. Provide behavioral critical incidents to point out examples of poor and acceptable performance, 3. Develop a structured program for correction with performance measures and time perspectives clearly explained and frequently reviewed.	1. BARS.

Source: L. L. Cummings and D. P. Schwab, *Performance in Organization* (Glenview, Ill.: Scott, Foresman, 1973). Reprinted with permission.

---

[26]Ibid.

behavior used to reach that goal. The focus is exclusively on the degree of goal accomplishment.

At the other extremes of the continuum are tasks that are highly uncertain in nature. A relatively low consensus exists about the characteristics of successful performance. Moreover, the nature of the task is so uncertain it may be difficult to specify expected goals. For this type of task, Keeley argues that judgment-based evaluation procedures are most appropriate. Subjective estimates are made by raters about the levels of employee performance on tasks for which neither the appropriate behavior nor the final goal are well specified. The extent of this uncertainty makes this type of appraisal very subjective, and may well explain why trait-rating scales are openly criticized for the number of errors that result in performance evaluation.

A second contingency approach advocated by Cummings and Schwab combines both a task dimension and an evaluation of past employee performance in determining the appropriate appraisal format.[27] Unlike Keeley's approach, however, the appropriate format is determined by past employee performance and not task specificity. Cummings and Schwab argue that the type of tasks assigned to an individual should be a function of past performance. High performers are given tasks that have relatively uncertain behavioral requirements and perhaps even uncertain goal specifications. Presumably this is both a reward to the employee and an affirmation by the supervisor that performance need not be monitored as closely. In contrast, average and below average performers are assigned to tasks that are increasingly more specified in terms of behavioral requirements. In turn, the level of task specificity defines the appropriate evaluation format. Exhibit 9.10 outlines the various approaches recommended by Cummings and Schwab and the evaluation formats they feel are appropriate for each.

Training Raters

Although there is some evidence that training is not effective,[28] or is less important in reducing errors than other factors,[29] the majority of findings are quite supportive of training raters as an effective method to reduce appraisal errors.[30] Rater training programs can

---

[27]Cummings and Schwab, *Performance in Organizations.*

[28]H. J. Bernardin and E. C. Pence, "Effects of Rater Training: Creating New Response Sets and Decreasing Accuracy," *Journal of Applied Psychology* 6 (1980), pp. 60–66.

[29]Sheldon Zedeck and Wayne Cascio, "Performance Appraisal Decision as a Function of Rater Training and Purpose of the Appraisal," *Journal of Applied Psychology* 67, no. 6 (1982), pp. 752–58.

[30]H. J. Bernardin and M. R. Buckley, "Strategies in Rater Training," *Academy of Management Review* 6, no. 2 (1981), pp. 205–12; D. Smith, "Training Programs for Performance Appraisal: A Review," *Academy of Management Review* 11, no. 1 (1986), pp. 22–40; B. Davis and M. Mount, "Effectiveness of Performance Appraisal Training Using Computer Assisted Instruction and Behavioral Modeling," *Personnel Psychology* 3 (1984), pp. 439–52; H. J. Bernardin, "Effects of Rater Training on Leniency and Halo Errors in Student Ratings of Instructors," *Journal of Applied Psychology* 63, no. 3 (1978), pp. 301–8; and J. M. Ivancevich, "Longitudinal Study of the Effects of Rater Training on Psychometric Error in Ratings," *Journal of Applied Psychology* 64, no. 5 (1979), pp. 502–08.

be divided into three distinct categories[31]: (1) Rater error training, in which the goal is to reduce psychometric errors (i.e., leniency, severity, central tendency, halo) by familiarizing raters with their existence; (2) Performance dimension training, with supervisors exposed extensively to the performance dimensions to be used in rating; and (3) performance standard training—designed to provide raters with a standard of comparison or frame of reference for making ratee appraisals. Several generalizations about ways to improve rater training can be summarized from this research. First, lecturing to ratees about ways to improve ratings is generally ineffective. Second, individualized or small group discussion sections are more effective in conveying proper rating procedures. Third, when these sessions are combined with extensive practice and feedback sessions, the rating accuracy is significantly improved. Fourth, longer training programs (more than two hours) are generally more successful than shorter programs. Fifth, performance dimension training and performance standard training (as explained) generally work better than rater error training, particularly when the two superior methods are combined together. Finally, the greatest success has come from efforts to reduce halo errors and improve accuracy. Leniency errors have proved the most difficult form of error to eliminate. This shouldn't be surprising. Think about the consequences to a supervisor of giving inflated ratings versus accurate or even deflated ratings. The latter two courses are certain to result in more complaints, and possibly reduced morale. The easy way out is to artificially inflate ratings.[32] Unfortunately, this positive outcome for supervisors may come back to haunt them. With everyone receiving relatively high ratings there is less distinction between truly good and poor performers, and less emphasis on pay for performance.

Eliminating Errors in the Actual Appraisal

Several researchers have indicated that errors can also be prevented in the planning and actual conduct of appraisal interviews.[33] While Exhibit 9.11 provides a detailed discussion of the elements of a good appraisal, the essence can be distilled down to seven require-

---

[31]Bernardin and Buckley, "Strategies in Rater Training."

[32]Longnecker, Sims, and Gioia, "Behind the Mask: The Politics of Employee Appraisal."

[33]Bernardin and Buckley, "Strategies in Rater Training"; Winstanley, "How Accurate Are Performance Appraisals?"; Bernardin and Pence, "Effects of Rater Training: Creating New Response Sets and Decreasing Accuracy"; J. M. Ivancevich, "Subordinates' Reactions to Performance Appraisal Interviews: A Test of Feedback and Goal Setting Techniques," *Journal of Applied Psychology* 67 (1982), pp. 581–87; D. Cederblom, "The Performance Appraisal Review: A Review, Implications and Suggestions," *Academy of Management Review* 7 (1982), pp. 219–27; S. Snell and K. Wexley, "Performance Diagnosis: Identifying the Causes of Poor Performance," *Personnel Administrator*, April 1985, pp. 117–27; J. M. Ivancevich and J. T. McMahon, "The Effects of Goal Setting, External Feedback, and Self-Generated Feedback on Outcome Variables: A Field Experiment," *Academy of Management Journal* 25 (1982), pp. 359–72; and A. S. Denisi and W. A. Blencoe, "Level and Source of Feedback and Determinates of Feedback Effectiveness," *Proceedings of Academy of Management* 42 (1982), pp. 175–79.

EXHIBIT 9.11
Tips on Appraising Employee Performance

Preparation for the Performance Interview

1. Keep a weekly log of individual's performance. Why?
   A. It makes the task of writing up the evaluation simpler. The rater does not have to strain to remember six months or a year ago.
   B. It reduces the chances of some rating errors (e.g., recency, halo).
   C. It gives support/backup to the rating.
2. Preparation for the interview should *not* begin a week or two before it takes place. There should be continual feedback to the employee on his/her performance so that (*a*) problems can be corrected before they get out of hand, (*b*) improvements can be made sooner, and (*c*) encouragement and support are ongoing.
3. Allow sufficient time to write up the evaluation. A well-thought-out evaluation will be more objective and equitable. Sufficient time includes (*a*) the actual time necessary to think out and write up the evaluation, (*b*) time away from the evaluation, and (*c*) time to review and possibly revise.
4. Have employees fill out an appraisal form prior to the interview. This prepares employees for what will take place in the interview and allows them to come prepared with future goal suggestions, areas they wish to pursue, and suggestions concerning their jobs or the company.
5. Set up an agreed-upon, convenient time to hold the interview (at least one week in advance). Be sure to pick a nonthreatening day.
6. Be prepared!
   A. Know what you are going to say. Prepare an outline (which includes the evaluation and future goal suggestions).
   B. Decide on developmental opportunities *before* the interview. Be sure you know of possible resources and contacts.
   C. Review performance interview steps.
7. Arrange the room in such a way as to encourage discussion.
   A. Do not have barriers between yourself and the employee (such as a large desk).
   B. Arrange with secretary that there be no phone calls or interruptions.

Performance Appraisal Interview (Steps)

1. Set the subordinate at ease. Begin by stating the purpose of the discussion. Let the individual know that it will be a two-way process. Neither superior nor subordinate should dominate the discussion.
2. Give a general, overall impression of the evaluation.
3. Discuss each dimension separately. Ask the employee to give his/her impression on own performance first. Then explain your position. If there is a problem on some, try *together* to determine the cause. When exploring causes, urge the subordinate to identify three or four causes. Then, jointly determine the most important ones. Identifying causes is important because it points out action plans which might be taken.
4. Together, develop action plans to correct problem areas. These plans will flow naturally from the consideration of the causes. Be specific about the who, what, and when. Be sure to provide for some kind of follow-up or report back.
5. Close the interview on an optimistic note.

Communication Technique Suggestions

1. Do not control the interview—make it two-way. Do this by asking open-ended questions rather than submitting your own solutions. For example, rather than saying, "Jim, I'd like you to do these reports over again," it would be better to say, "Jim, what sort of things might we do here?" Avoid questions that lead to one-word responses.
2. Stress behaviors and results rather than personal traits. Say, "I've noticed that your weekly report has been one to two days late in the last six weeks," rather than, "You tend to be a tardy, lazy person."
3. Show interest and concern. Instead of saying, "Too bad, but we all go through that," say, "I think I know what you're feeling. I remember a similar experience."
4. Allow the subordinate to finish a sentence or thought. This includes being receptive to the subordinate's own ideas and suggestions. For example, rather than saying, "You may have something there, but let's go back to the real problem," say, "I'm not certain I understand how that relates to this problem. Why don't you fill me in on it a bit more?"

These last four suggestions emphasize problem analysis rather than appraisal. Of course, appraisal of past performance is a part of problem analysis, but these suggestions should lead to a more participative and less defensive subordinate role. These suggestions will also help improve creativity in problem solving. The subordinate will have a clearer understanding of why and how he/she needs to change work behavior. There should be a growth of climate of cooperation, which increases motivation to achieve performance goals.

ments:[34] (1) maintain records of employee performance, both as documentation and to jog the memory, (2) conduct a performance diagnosis to determine in advance if the problem arises because of motivation, skill deficiency, or external environmental constraints[35]—in turn this tells the supervisor whether the problem requires "motivation-building," training, or efforts to remove external constraints, (3) participation in appraisal between superior and subordinate—not unilateral "discussion," (4) promote goal achievement through team effort between supervisor and subordinate, (5) goal setting to focus work efforts and provide a basis for comparison of results versus goals, (6) focused discussions, with performance and ways to improve it as the target, (7) minimal criticism with focus on the future and strategies to achieve future goals.

EQUAL EMPLOYMENT OPPORTUNITY (EEO) AND PERFORMANCE EVALUATION

Equal employment opportunity and affirmative action have influenced human resource decision making for more than 20 years now. While there are certainly critics of these programs, there has been at least one important trend traceable to the civil rights vigil in the workplace. Specifically, EEO has forced organizations to document decisions and to insure they are firmly tied to performance or expected performance. Nowhere is this more apparent than in the performance appraisal area. Performance appraisals are subject to the same scrutiny as employment tests. Consider the use of performance ratings in making decisions about promotions. In this context, a performance appraisal takes on all the characteristics of a test used to make an initial employment decision. If employees pass the test (i.e., are rated highly in the performance evaluation process), they are predicted to do well (i.e., have promotion potential) at higher level jobs. This interpretation of performance evaluation as a test, subject to validation requirements, was made in *Brito* v. *Zia Company*.[36] In this case, Zia Company used performance ratings based on a rating format to lay off employees. The layoffs resulted in a disproportionate number of minorities being discharged. The court held that:

> Zia, a government contractor, had failed to comply with the testing guidelines issued by the Secretary of Labor, and that Zia had not developed job-related criteria for evaluating employees' work performance to be used in determining employment promotion and discharges which is required to protect minority group applicants and employees from the discriminatory effects of such failure.[37]

---

[34]Winstanley, "How Accurate Are Performance Appraisals?"; Bernardin and Buckley, "Strategies in Rater Training"; Ivancevich, "Subordinates' Reactions to Performance Appraisal Interviews: A Test of Feedback and Goal Setting Techniques"; Cederblom, "The Performance Appraisal Interview: A Review, Implications and Suggestions."

[35]Snell and Wexley, "Performance Diagnosis: Identifying the Causes of Poor Performance."

[36]*Brito* v. *Zia Company,* 478 F. 2d. 1200 (1973).

[37]Ibid.

Since the Brito case there has been growing evidence that the courts have very specific standards and requirements for performance appraisal.[38] Two studies, summarizing the factors influencing court evaluations of performance appraisal systems, identified a total of six factors that appear to make a difference.[39] First, courts are favorably disposed to appraisal systems that give specific written instructions on how to complete the appraisal. Presumably, more extensive training in other facets of evaluation would also be viewed favorably by the courts. Second, organizations tend to be able to support their cases better when the appraisal system is behaviorally based rather than trait oriented. In part this probably arises because behaviorally oriented appraisals have more potential to provide workers feedback about developmental needs. Third, as pointed out by every basic personnel book ever printed, and reinforced by this text, the presence of adequately developed job descriptions provides a rational foundation for personnel decision making of every form. The courts reinforce this by ruling more consistently for defendant (company) when their appraisal systems are based on sound job descriptions. Fourth, courts also approve of appraisal systems that require that supervisors feed back to employees results of the appraisal. Absence of secrecy permits employees to identify weaknesses and to challenge undeserved appraisals. Fifth, the courts seem to like evaluation systems that incorporate a review of any performance rating by a higher level supervisor(s). Finally, and perhaps most importantly, the courts have consistently suggested that the key to fair appraisals depends on consistent treatment across ratees, regardless of race, color, religion, sex, or national origin. The focal question then becomes "are similarly situated individuals treated similarly?"

What will the probable thrust be of future EEO cases dealing with performance appraisal? If performance evaluations continue to be treated as tests, a number of trends can be predicted. First, the courts will continue to require that performance standards are content valid (i.e., they must be related to the job being evaluated). This means that dimensions on which performance is to be rated must be derived from job analysis, reflecting content of the job in question. Second, it is also likely the courts will insist that performance evaluations be as free as possible from errors based on subjective judgments (e.g., halo, leniency, severity, central tendency). Partial support for these predictions comes from a Supreme Court case, *Albermarle Paper Co. v. Moody.*[40] In

---

[38]G. L. Lubben, D. E. Thompson, and C. R. Klasson, "Performance Appraisal: The Legal Implications of Title VII," *Personnel* 57, no. 3 (1980), pp. 11–21; H. Feild and W. Halley, "The Relationship of Performance Appraisal System Characteristics to Verdicts in Selected Employment Discrimination Cases," *Academy of Management Journal* 25, no. 2 (1982), pp. 392–406; *Albermarle Paper Company* v. *Moody*, U.S. Supreme Court, no. 74–389 and 74–428, 10 FEP Cases 1181 (1975); also *Moody* v. *Albermarle Paper Company*, 474 F. 3d. 134.

[39]Feild and Hally, "The Relationship of Performance Appraisal System Characteristics to Verdicts in Selected Employment Discrimination Cases"; and Gerald Barrett and Mary Kernan, "Performance Appraisal and Terminations: A Review of Court Decisions Since Brito v. Zia with Implications for Personnel Practices," *Personnel Psychology* 40 (1987), pp. 489–503.

[40]*Albermarle Paper Company* v. *Moody;* also *Moody* v. *Albermarle Paper Company.*

this case, Albermarle used a rating system based on overall job performance to evaluate employee performance. The Court found this inappropriate:

> Albermarle's supervisors were asked to rank employees by a "standard" that was extremely vague and fatally open to divergent interpretations. Each job grouping contained a number of different jobs, and the supervisors were asked, in each grouping to "determine which ones (employees) they felt, irrespective of the job that they were actually doing, but in their respective jobs, did a better job than the person they were rating against. . . ." There is no way of knowing precisely what criteria of job performance the supervisor was considering, the same criteria or whether, indeed, any of the supervisors actually applied a focused and stable body of criteria of any kind.[41]

A third possible requirement for performance evaluation could be that the process be empirically validated (i.e., some demonstration that the performance ratings for employees predict, in the case of promotions, performance on the job after promotion). If this requirement is mandated, current organizational practices will have to be dramatically altered. In a survey of company performance appraisal practices, not 1 of 217 companies using performance appraisal results to make promotion decisions had completed an empirical study to determine if the ratings were a good predictor of later job performance after promotion.[42]

If EEO infiltrates the performance evaluation area to any serious extent, two formats appear most likely to survive the encounter: behaviorally anchored rating scales and management by objectives. Each requires close attention to job content in establishing performance dimensions or objectives. Each focuses on assessment of concrete observable performance dimensions. And each has the latitude to provide employees with specific feedback about performance, lessening the chances of charges based on subjective biases.

In effect, EEO may force a renaissance in performance evaluation. An incentive will exist for organizations to consider carefully the issues discussed in this chapter and elsewhere in constructing a nonbiased performance evaluation system.

TYING PAY TO SUBJECTIVELY APPRAISED PERFORMANCE

Most people have come to expect at least annual pay increases. The difficulty arises in trying to shape these expectations so that employees view raises as a reward for performance. Chapter 8 illustrated this difficulty in theoretical terms. Now it is addressed from a pragmatic perspective. Very simply, organizations frequently grant increases that are not designed or communicated to be related to performance. The three pay increase guidelines that fit this mold will be discussed briefly before outlining a standard based on merit.[43]

---

[41]Schlei and Grossman, *Employee Discrimination Law,* p. 173.

[42] Robert I. Lazer, "The Discrimination Danger in Performance Appraisal," in *Contemporary Problems in Personnel,* eds. W. Hammer and F. Schmidt (Chicago: St. Clair Press, 1977), pp. 239–45.

[43]*Compensating Salaried Employees during Inflation: General vs. Merit Increases* (New York: Conference Board, Report no. 796, 1981).

Two types of pay increase guidelines provide equal increases to all employees. The first, a general increase, typically is found in unionized firms. A contract is negotiated that specifies an across-the-board (equal) increase for each year of the contract. Similar increases would occur because of cost-of-living adjustments (COLA), but these would be triggered by changes in the consumer price index (CPI) (Chapter 17).

The third form of guideline comes somewhat closer to tying pay to performance. Longevity (seniority) increases tie pay increases to a progression pattern based on seniority. For example, a pay grade might be divided into 10 equal steps, and employees move to higher steps based on seniority. To the extent performance improves with time on the job, this method has the rudiments of paying for performance.

By far the most popular form of pay guideline for exempt employees is one based on merit or performance.[44] Invariably these guidelines take one of two forms. The simpler version specifies pay increases permissible for different levels of performance.

Performance level	*(1)* Outstanding	*(2)* *Very* Satisfactory	*(3)* Satisfactory	*(4)* *Marginally* Satisfactory	*(5)* Unsatisfactory
Merit Increase	10–12%	7–10%	5–7%	3–5%	0%

Increase ranges may be included in each performance category to give supervisors some discretion in the amount of increases. A variant on this guideline would also include a third dimension representing time between increases. Better performers might receive increases every 8 months while the poorest performers might have to wait 15 months to 2 years for their next increase.

More complex guidelines tie pay not only to performance but also to position in the pay range. Exhibit 9.12 illustrates such a system for a food market firm. The percentages in the cells of Exhibit 9.12 are changed yearly to reflect changing economic conditions, but they usually maintain two relationships across all organizations. First, as would be expected in a pay-for-performance system, lower performances are tied to lower pay

EXHIBIT 9.12
Performance Rating Salary Increase Matrix

Position in Range / Performance Rating	Unsatisfactory	*Improvement Needed*	Competent	Commendable	Superior
Fourth quartile	0%	0%	4%	5%	6%
Third quartile	0%	0%	5%	6%	7%
Second quartile	0%	0%	6%	7%	8%
First quartile	0%	2%	7%	8%	9%
Below minimum of range	0%	3%	8%	9%	10%

---

[44]Ibid.

increases. In fact, in many organizations the poorest performers receive no merit increases. The second relationship is that pay increases decrease (percentage) as employees move through a pay range. For the same level of performance, employees low in the range receive higher percentage increases than employees who have progressed farther through the range. In part this is designed to forestall the time when employees reach the salary maximum and have salaries frozen. In part, though, it is also a cost-control mechanism tied to budgeting procedures, as discussed in Chapter 15.

Given a salary increase matrix, merit increases are relatively easy to determine. From Exhibit 9.12 an employee at the top of his pay grade who receives a "competent" rating would receive a 4 percent increase in base salary. A new trainee starting out below the minimum of a pay grade would receive a 10 percent increase for her "commendable" performance rating.

Designing Merit Guidelines

Designing merit guidelines involves answering four questions. First, what should the poorest performer be paid as an increase? Notice, this figure is seldom negative! Wage increases are, unfortunately, considered an entitlement. Wage cuts tied to poor performance are very rare. Most organizations, though, are willing to give no increases to very poor performers.

The second question involves average performers. How much should they be paid as an increase? Most organizations try to ensure that average performers are kept whole relative to cost of living. This dictates that the midpoint of the merit guidelines equal the percentage change in the local or national cost-of-living index (usually the CPI). So following this guideline, the 6 percent increase for an average performer in the second quartile of Exhibit 9.12 would reflect the change in CPI for that area. In a year with lower inflation, all the percentages in the matrix probably would be lower.

Third, how much should the top performers be paid? In part, budgetary considerations (Chapter 15) answer this question. But there is also growing evidence that employees vary in the size of increases that they consider meaningful (Chapter 8). Continuation of this research may help determine the approximate size of increases not only for top performers but for all employees.

Finally, matrices can differ in the size of the differential between different levels of performance. Exhibit 9.12 basically rewards successive levels of performance with 1 percent increases (at least in the portion of the matrix where any increase is granted). A larger jump between levels would signal a stronger commitment to recognizing performance with higher pay increases. Most companies balance this, though, against cost considerations. Larger differentials cost more. When money is tight this option is less attractive.

SUMMARY

The process of appraising employee performance can be both time-consuming and stressful. These costs are compounded if the appraisal system is poorly developed or if a supervisor lacks appropriate training to collect and evaluate performance data. Development of a sound appraisal system(s) requires an understanding of organizational objectives balanced against the relative merits of each type of appraisal system. For example, despite its inherent weaknesses an appraisal system based on global ranking of employee performance may be appropriate in smaller organizations that, for a variety of reasons, choose not to tie pay to performance. In contrast, a sophisticated management-by-objective appraisal system may not be appropriate for such a company.

Similarly, training supervisors effectively to appraise performance requires an understanding of organizational objectives. We know relatively little about the ways in which raters process information and evaluate employee performance. However, a thorough understanding of organizational objectives combined with a knowledge of common errors in evaluation can make a significant difference in the quality of appraisals.

REVIEW QUESTIONS

1. Feldspar Corporation manufactures speciality iron products (e.g., fancy gates and fences). One job involves operation of machines that form molten metal into different parts of gates and fences. The job is fairly low level and classified as a nonexempt position. Without any further information, which of the six types of appraisal formats do you think would be most appropriate? Justify your answer.
2. From question 1, what further information would you like to have in order to decide on an appropriate format. Explain why the different pieces of information are important in your decision-making process.
3. What do you think should be included in the design of a performance appraisal process to lessen the probability that your company would be accused of discrimination in performance appraisal?
4. If you wanted to ensure that employees had good feedback about performance problems and strengths, which format would you recommend using? Why?
5. Assume that you had one employee fall into each of these cells in Exhibit 9.12 (25 employees in the company). How much would base salary increase in dollars if the current average salary in the company is $15,000. (Assume ratings are randomly distributed by salary level, so that you can use $15,000 as your base salary for calculation in each of the cells.)

APPENDIX

Examples of Appraisal Forms: 3M, Xerox (next 10 pages)

> Note: The form for Xerox Corporation allows managers to identify different performance factors for each job. Once factors are listed, though, a standard rating format is used.

3M'S POSITION-TAILORED
PERFORMANCE REVIEW

MAIL TO:	Manager's Name J. J. Mc Habe	Manager's Address	Date Prepared

Employee Name John T. Doe		Personnel Action Code	Employee Number 1234567
Position Title Sales		Country Canada	Date PDQ Completed 01/04/83
Functional Area Engineering		Date Entered Present Position / /	Appraisal Period From / / To / /

Section I–Overall Performance

Check the box below that best summarizes this employee's overall job performance in terms of the job requirements. Your rating should take into account

1. The degree to which the job requirements have been satisfied.
2. The difficulty of the job requirements.
3. The employee's methods for satisfying job requirements.

☐	Excellent	Achievements consistently far exceed the position's key objectives.
☐	Better than satisfactory	Achievements consistently meet and frequently exceed the position's key objectives or requirements.
☐	Satisfactory	Achievements consistently meet the position's key objectives or requirements. Accomplishments may exceed work requirements in some areas.
☐	Needs further improvement	Achievements partially meet the position's key objectives or requirements. With improvement, performance should become satisfactory.
☐	Unsatisfactory	Achievements do not meet the position's key objectives or requirements.

Major job responsibilities during appraisal period: List, in order of importance, what this employee was supposed to do during this appraisal period.

Time spent in major functions	
80%	Representing
70%	Coordinating
60%	Administration
50%	Consulting
40%	Monitoring business indicators
30%	Controlling
20%	Supervising
12%	Other
10%	Planning and organizing

Accomplishments for this appraisal period: List significant accomplishments or results achieved during this appraisal period related to the major job responsibilities listed above. Explain any lack of results.

3M'S POSITION-TAILORED PERFORMANCE REVIEW	John T. Doe PDQ Completed 01/04/83

Section II–Performance Factors

This section contains nine job performance factors, definitions of these factors, and examples of each factor. Rate this employee's job performance by:

1. Reading the definitions and examples of each factor.
2. Rating the employee on each factor by placing an X in the appropriate box of the shaded column. If a factor is not applicable, write "NA" in the Comments section for that factor.

The Comments section for each factor can be used to expand upon the ratings made.

1. **Economics management:** Uses information, finances, equipment, and supplies to maximize long-term profit; achieves forecasts and objectives.

   - Determining plans and performance objectives of an organization the size of 3M, worldwide.
   - Determining plans and performance objectives of an organization the size of a sector.
   - Determining plans and performance objectives of an organization the size of a group or international geographic area.
   - Forecasts manpower requirements.
   - Reviews and, if necessary, revises budget allocations.

Far exceeds requirements	
Exceeds requirements	
Meets all requirements	
Partially meets requirements	
Does not meet requirements	
Comments:	

2. **Emphasizing goals and productivity:** Setting and attainment of high performance standards for self and group in line with company goals.

   - Developing implementation strategy for long-range plans.
   - Planning and coordinating the introduction of new products or services.
   - Determining plans to phase out unprofitable products/services.
   - Setting selling prices.
   - Making additions to headcount that are within the approved budget.

Far exceeds requirements	
Exceeds requirements	
Meets all requirements	
Partially meets requirements	
Does not meet requirements	
Comments:	

3. **Organizing and facilitating work:** Plans, organizes, and ensures effective job performance through oral and written communication and delegation of tasks to subordinates.

   - Hiring an individual for an approved position.
   - Determining reductions in employee headcount, should this become necessary.
   - Revising the structure of an organization having 400 or more employees.
   - Evaluating an organization of 200–400 employees to determine the best allocation and utilization of resources.
   - Scheduling work of subordinates so that it flows evenly and steadily.

Far exceeds requirements	
Exceeds requirements	
Meets all requirements	
Partially meets requirements	
Does not meet requirements	
Comments:	

4. **Managing subordinates:** Emphasizes cooperation and teamwork among subordinates; motivates subordinates.

   - Allocating and scheduling resources to ensure that they will be available when needed.
   - Developing operational policies and procedures under which managers are expected to perform.
   - Establishing parameters to guide the planning of organizations in excess of 800 employees.
   - Giving guidance to other organizations for planning beyond one year.
   - Recommending changes in policy and procedures.

Far exceeds requirements	
Exceeds requirements	
Meets all requirements	
Partially meets requirements	
Does not meet requirements	
Comments:	

3M'S POSITION-TAILORED PERFORMANCE REVIEW	John T. Doe PDQ Completed 01/04/83

5. Knowledge of job: Has and regularly updates knowledge of job-related concepts and/or skills.

- Determining implementation methods for meeting operational objectives established by others.
- Makes use of assigned administrative or technical staff.
- Defines areas of responsibility for managerial personnel.
- Interacts face-to-face with subordinates on an almost daily basis.
- Assigns priorities for others on no less than a quarterly basis.

	Far exceeds requirements
	Exceeds requirements
	Meets all requirements
	Partially meets requirements
	Does not meet requirements

Comments:

6. Problem solving and decision making: Monitors and analyzes situations, identifies problems, and makes appropriate decisions to resolve problems.

- Develops executive level management talent.
- Reviews subordinates' work almost continually.
- Reviews subordinates' work methods for possible increases in productivity.
- Motivates subordinates to change or improve performance.
- Analyzes subordinates' weaknesses and training needs.

	Far exceeds requirements
	Exceeds requirements
	Meets all requirements
	Partially meets requirements
	Does not meet requirements

Comments:

7. Appraisal and development of subordinates: Evaluates subordinates objectively on a regular basis and is active in the setting and attainment of objectives for subordinates.

- Guides subordinates on technical aspects of the job.
- Monitors subordinates' progress toward objec. of unit and adjusts activ. as necessary to reach them.
- Provides complete instructions to subordinates when giving assignments.
- Delegates work, assigns responsibility to subordinates, and establishes appropriate controls.
- Maintains a smooth working relationship among various individuals who need to work cooperatively.

	Far exceeds requirements
	Exceeds requirements
	Meets all requirements
	Partially meets requirements
	Does not meet requirements

Comments:

8. Equal opportunities: Utilizes skills and talents of subordinates and ensures equal opportunities for all subordinates.

	Far exceeds requirements
	Exceeds requirements
	Meets all requirements
	Partially meets requirements
	Does not meet requirements

Comments:

9. Other:

	Far exceeds requirements
	Exceeds requirements
	Meets all requirements
	Partially meets requirements
	Does not meet requirements

Comments:

3M'S POSITION-TAILORED PERFORMANCE REVIEW	John T. Doe PDQ Completed 01/04/83

Section III–Development Plan

This section helps develop the jobholder's skills as they pertain to this position.

Relative strengths	Specific recommendations for better utilizing strengths	Target date
	Manager:	
	Employee:	
	Human resources:	

Relative weaknesses	Specific recommendations for improving current job performance	Target date
	Manager:	
	Employee:	
	Human resources:	

3M'S POSITION-TAILORED PERFORMANCE REVIEW	John T. Doe PDQ Completed 01/04/83

Section IV–Overall Comments

Comments of J. J. Mc Habe

Comments of reviewer

Comments of John T. Doe

Section V–Signatures

This performance review has been reviewed and discussed with the employee:

Employee Signature: John T. Doe	Manager Signature: J. J. Mc Habe	Reviewer Signature
Date	Date	Date

XEROX EXEMPT SALARY
PROGRAM PERFORMANCE APPRAISAL

Name	
Title	
Division/Department	
Period reviewed from	To
Reviewed by	
Title	

Descriptions of Ratings
Used in this Performance Appraisal
(all ratings should be made in whole numbers)

Rating	Description
5	Exceptional performance
4	Consistently exceeds expected level of performance
3	Expected level of performance
2	Less than expected level of performance
1	Unsatisfactory performance

Part I

Employee lists activities in order of importance.

Manager appraises performance against standards of performance considered attainable most of the time by a majority of employees qualified to perform the assignment.

Activity (to be completed by the employee):

Appraisal (to be completed by the manager):

Activity:

Appraisal:

Activity:
Appraisal:
Activity:
Appraisal:

Part IV

Summary appraisal and/or additional comments:

Overall summary appraisal:
(check the overall rating)

In reaching the summary rating the manager is expected to consider each of the activities. Since the weightings assigned to various activities are intended merely to show their relative importance, no precise formula should be applied. Managers are to exercise sound judgment and discretion in reaching the summary rating.

Unsatisfactory performance	Less than expected level of performance	Expected level of performance	Consistently exceeds expected level of performance	Exceptional performance

Written by	Title	Date

Additional approvals

Employee review of the performance appraisal:
I have reviewed this appraisal and discussed the contents with my manager. My signature means that I have been advised of my performance and does not necessarily imply that I agree with the appraisal or the ratings.

Employee signature:	Date

Employee's comments (optional): If the employee wishes to do so, any comments concerning the appraisal, for example, agreement or disagreement, may be indicated here.

Salary range:	Minimum $	Midpoint $	Maximum $	Date as of

Compensation Application
Great Lakes Ornamental Supplies

Great Lakes Ornamental Supplies (GLOS) designs and manufactures metal stair railings for commercial and residential customers. The company was founded in 1946 by Jake Weatherbee, a man fiercely dedicated to building the highest quality railings possible. This emphasis on high quality quickly established a reputation for Jake and ensured him continuing business from customers interested in top quality products. Between 1946 and 1975 Jake's share of the market gradually rose to 9 percent. Since then the market has stabilized and Jake has been quite content to maintain his market share and reputation for quality.

Jake's senior vice president in this enterprise is Amos Taylor. Amos began his career with GLOS in 1952 as Jake's first full-time salesperson. Repeated success as the top salesperson led to Amos's promotion to vice president of sales in 1964 and senior vice president in 1972. Amos, too, is proud of the quality railings GLOS designs and manufactures. He has frequently been heard to tell customers: "I don't have to be a salesman with these railings, they sell themselves."

Amos's nephew, Larry Hart, is vice president for manufacturing. He has a reputation as a demanding but fair boss. Workers are expected to come to work on time and complete assignments as directed. If they perform up to expectations, Larry will back them up 100 percent in fighting for wage increases and other forms of reward.

Larry has a meeting today with Jake. He's certain Jake wants to talk about the annual wage increases. He hopes Jake has recommended a large increase for the welding department. Despite high turnover rates those guys have really pulled together and done a good job. Despite a 25 percent reduction in departmental employment over the past year, the gang has turned out as many units as they did last year.

Role for Jake Weatherbee

You have a meeting today with Larry Hart, your vice president for manufacturing. Larry is a good man but you're a bit concerned he doesn't share your love of GLOS. Certainly he doesn't seem to care as much as you about quality. Over the past four months there have been four complaints about structural weaknesses in newly installed railings. This is more complaints than the company normally gets in a year! To convey your displeasure you have decided to increase the budget of the welding department only 3 percent. You hope when word gets around that all the other departments received a 10 percent increase, the welding department will improve its performance. If this doesn't work, maybe it's time to reprimand Larry Hart.

Role for Larry Hart

You are very concerned about the way wage increases are allocated at GLOS. When you first started with the company in 1968 there were only 75 employees. Since Jake knew everyone and could keep track of their performance, it seemed appropriate that he determine both departmental budgets and individual wage increases. Since 1965, though, the company has grown to 217 employees. It is apparent that Jake simply can't know all the employees well enough to recommend individual raises. Moreover, there is also some evidence that Jake isn't aware of departmental records either. You have had three people leave the welding department in the past year. These were the first turnovers in that department in four years. Rumor has it among the welders that the company doesn't appreciate them. They turn out more units than anyone else in the industry, yet no one seems to care. You care; and you have tried to show it. But you'd better back up your words with cold, hard cash. You have prepared records showing improved productivity in the group. You are particularly proud of this since the unit switched over to a new welding process. It took some getting used to, but the group worked extra hard and got the job done, even short three welders. You think they deserve large raises and replacements for the lost workers.

It's time to meet with Jake Weatherbee.

1. What is the strategic plan of the company? How well does it fit in with compensation practices?
2. What compensation problems exist in GLOS? How does the issue of equity play a role?
3. What other elements of the reward system (i.e., other elements of the system that reinforce behavior) aren't operating well? What changes in behavior will be necessary for Jake and Larry to correct those problems?

Compensation Application
Keysoft Enterprises Appraisal Interview

Keysoft writes and markets software packages for microcomputers. Founded in 1973 by two former employees of IBM, Keysoft gradually has moved to a place of prominence and respect in this highly competitive and volatile industry. Last year the company employed 150 people. At that time James Burton III, president of Keysoft, decided to introduce a formal Human Resources program. Part of this program is a new appraisal system for exempt employees illustrated in Exhibit 1. Mr. Burton borrowed this appraisal format from a friend who owns a string of convenience food stores. This will be the first time the appraisal forms have been tried out on Keysoft employees.

Students will play each of the two roles, Sarah Brown and Jeff Morrow. Each participant should read the company history and the assigned role. Sarah Brown also should read about conducting an appraisal interview (see Exhibit 9.11). Both employees should fill out the appraisal form in Exhibit 1, rating Jeff on the dimensions indicated. This will provide a starting point for discussions during the interview.

Role for Sarah Brown, Supervisor

Today you will be conducting your first appraisal interview with the new format Jim Burton has been pushing. Frankly you wish you could try it out on someone besides Jeff Morrow. While he's been a very good employee in the past, you notice that in the last six months his performance has dropped. He doesn't seem to get along very well anymore with the other creative programmers. One incident, in particular, sticks out. Jeff was working on a new spreadsheet program when Sam Daniels asked for help on one of the games he was creating. Not only did Jeff refuse, but he starting screaming at Daniels to do his own work. You can't tolerate this kind of behavior. Employees are expected to cooperate with each other.

You're also concerned that Jeff hasn't been creating as many software programs lately. Normally he can write about two programs a year. But he has been working on this program for almost a year with no tangible output. Jeff just doesn't seem to be as productive as he used to be.

Role for Jeff Morrow, Programmer

Keysoft just isn't the company it used to be. All your problems started about two years ago. About that time they hired a bunch of new programmers who just don't have that creative flair. You helped them for the first year. But they keep coming back for more and more. It got to the point about six months ago where you had to tell them to do their own work. Sam Daniels is the worst of the lot. He's in over his head and expects you to bail him out. You're tired of covering for him. In fact, you lost your temper with him about five months ago. You regret screaming at him but he just won't let you do your job.

You are excited about the upcoming appraisal interview with Sarah Brown, your

EXHIBIT 1
Appraisal Form—Exempt Employees

☐ Annual   ☐ Interim   ☐ Probationary   Original to local file, duplicate to employee.

Employee's Name (Last, First, Middle initial)	File Number	Job Title	Company Seniority Date	Organization Code No.

Evaluation Period	Instructions: Rate the employee on the major performance areas listed below by placing an "X" on the scale. Be sure to consider the entire year's performance, not just a major or recent occurrence. You should be able to substantiate your rating with measurable and/or observable information. Include appropriate written comments of a summary nature for each performance category shown below.
From To	
/ / / /	

PRODUCTIVITY/VOLUME OF WORK: Examples—Contribution to unit objectives, revenue generation, calls, data input, passengers processed, does his/her share.

Comments:

Far below what   About the same   Far above what
others in the   as others   others
group contribute   contribute   contribute

QUALITY OF WORK: Examples—Errors, customer contact skills, complaint letters, completeness of assignment, files in order, appearance (if related to job).

Comments:

Far below   About the same   Far above
others in the   as others in the   others in the
group   group   group

TEAMWORK: Examples—Works well with other employees, helps others when time is available, supportive of decisions, works well in group situations.

Comments:

Not concerned   Usually puts the   Outstanding
about the needs   needs of the   team player,
of the team   team ahead of   always puts
                         own needs   team needs first

INTERPERSONAL RELATIONS: Examples—Communication skills, ability to get along with customers, peers, and management.

Comments:

Lacks   Demonstrates   Has
interpersonal   good interpersonal   outstanding
skills, very   relations and is   interpersonal
often has   effective in   relations with
conflicts with   dealing with   customers and/
customers and/   customers and/   or members of
or members of   or members of   the group
the group   the group

DEPENDABILITY/ATTENDANCE:	Days Absent	No. of Occurrences	Days Late
Comments:			

Summary Comments:

Evaluator's signature	Date	Reviewed by: Evaluator's Supervisor's signature	Date
	/ /		/ /
Signature of employee (Optional)	Date	Conference with employee held on:	Date
	/ /		/ /

supervisor. She didn't give you as big a raise last year as you deserved, but you're sure she'll make up for it this year. After all, didn't you carry three programmers for almost a year with some of your more creative ideas? Besides that, you are almost done with that spreadsheet program that has taken a year to write. It's by far the most sophisticated program you've ever written. If it doesn't outperform the market leaders and make the company $2 million in the first year, you'll be very surprised. You can smell success, and you're sure Sarah will be just as enthusiastic.

Following Jeff and Sarah's interview, students should discuss the following questions.

1. Were any of the difficulties in the appraisal interview magnified because of the poor quality of the appraisal format? Explain your answer.

2. Was Sarah Brown able to recognize where differences of opinion existed with Jeff Morrow? Was she able to resolve these differences? What is (are) the key(s) to successfully resolving these differences?

3. Do you think Jeff Morrow's performance will improve as a result of this interview? Why or why not?

Compensation Application
Evaluating Keysoft's Performance Appraisal System

Keysoft Enterprises (see History of Keysoft in the previous Compensation Application, the Keysoft Appraisal Interview case) uses a performance evaluation form (Exhibit 1) to appraise incumbents of the seven nonexempt jobs described below. Identify the strengths and weaknesses of this evaluation form relative to the criteria outlined in Chapter 9 of your text (i.e., employee development criteria, administrative criteria, personnel research, economic criteria, and validity). Be specific in your discussion.

JOB DESCRIPTIONS FOR KEYSOFT NONEXEMPT JOBS

Messenger

1. *Duties:* Performs under direct supervision, collection, sorting, and distribution of mail and incoming and outgoing interoffice correspondence as required. Performs errands and other related duties. Distributes or collects miscellaneous materials. Posts bulletin board notices. Operates simple mechanical reproduction machines, such as ditto duplicator and addressograph, and collates reports.
2. *Requirements for entering:* High school graduate or equivalent. Must be physically fit, must give evidence of intelligence, ability, and responsibility to indicate possible eventual ability to advance to higher rated work.

Typist

1. *Duties:* Performs under general supervision typing of technical and business correspondence, reports, and statements, including long carriage statement work and setting up of tables taken from copy or from machine. Performs other types of miscellaneous clerical work and acts as receptionist when required.
2. *Requirements for entering:* High school graduate or equivalent. Must demonstrate ability to satisfactorily pass company typist test by performing accurately at the rate of at least 50 words per minute.

Secretary

1. *Duties:* Schedules appointments, gives information to callers, takes dictation, and otherwise relieves officials of clerical work and minor administrative and business details.
   a. Reads and routes incoming mail.
   b. Locates and attaches appropriate file to correspondence to be answered by employer.
   c. Takes dictation by hand or by machine and transcribes notes on typewriter.
   d. Composes and types routine correspondence.

EXHIBIT 1
Keysoft Nonexempt Performance Appraisal

Name _____ Date of Hire _____

Position _____ Department _____

Absentee Record: _____ Miscellaneous illness   _____ Total
                  _____ Single illness   _____ Days late
                  _____ Other

PLEASE COMPLETE AND RETURN TO THE HUMAN RESOURCES DEPARTMENT NO LATER
THAN: _____

Rating Scale:

| 1 = Unacceptable performance | 2 = Minimally acceptable performance | 3 = Average performance | 4 = Good performance | 5 = Outstanding performance |

Number		Rating	Comments
1	Theoretical knowledge		
2	Business maturity and productivity		
3	Willingess to act and make decisions		
4	Analytical capacity		
5	Quality of work and judgment		
6a	Personality in internal relations		
6b	Tact and persuasiveness in customer and public relations		
7a	Leadership		
7b	Organizational ability and control		
8	Physical capacity		
	Overall evaluation =		

    e. Files correspondence and other records.
    f. Answers telephone and gives information to callers or routes calls to appropriate official.
    g. Schedules appointments for employer.
    h. May oversee clerical workers.

2. *Requirements for entering:* High school graduate or equivalent. Must be neat in appearance and have a pleasing personality. Must have broad experience in stenographic work and have demonstrated the capacity to handle secretarial duties as well as the qualities of integrity and intelligence.

Intermediate Clerk I (General)

1. *Duties:* Under general supervision or under the direction of a higher rated clerk performs a wide range of specialized clerical and/or payroll duties of an analytical nature, some of which may be in the scope of or be a part of the duties of other clerical jobs. May also direct the work of one or more lower rated clerks; and in so doing, may plan and lay out tasks for such individuals. May use usual office machines and equipment, calculating machines, etc. May have numerous contacts with vendors, common carriers, or government agencies.
2. *Requirements for entering:* High school graduate or equivalent. Must have four years of experience in clerical duties. Must have demonstrated ability to analyze the problems arising in previous assignments, to handle a variety of detail pertaining to established procedures, as well as the ability to exercise discretion concerning operating routine and detail. Must have experience necessary to originate investigations of various phases of work assignments or to assemble data for the purpose of such investigations.

Programming Clerk I

1. *Duties:* Under general supervision, carries out a variety of duties to assist technical personnel by relieving them of the routine tasks involved in project work, computer programming, and preparation of work for the computer. May be called upon to write computer programs of a moderate complexity, or parts of such programs. May act as contact with remote users of the computer to receive data, prepare it for submission to the computer, and return answers to the remote user. May direct the work of lower rated programming clerks and staff assistants.
2. *Requirements for entering:* Education requirements are the same as for Programming Clerk II. Must have received for at least one year the top progression rate of Programming Clerk II and have demonstrated a higher caliber of aptitude, skill, and job performance.

Programming Clerk II

1. *Duties:* Under general supervision, carries out a variety of duties to assist technical personnel by relieving them of the routing tasks involved in project work, computer programming, and preparation of work for the computer. May be called upon to write simple computer programs or parts of programs. May act as contact with remote users of the computer to receive data, prepare it for submission to the computer, and return answers to the remote users. May assist higher and lower rated clerical personnel in the performance of their work as required.

2. *Requirements for entering:* High school graduate from college preparatory course or equivalent, with two years of algebra, plane geometry, and at least one physical science. Two years of experience as math clerk, or the equivalent in outside training or experience. Demonstration of ability by successful passing of the appropriate written test of achievement, or by successful completion of a two-year course in computer programming in a recognized technical school. Must exhibit a higher caliber of aptitude, skills, and job performance.

Senior Programming Clerk

1. *Duties:* Under limited supervision, performs a variety of advanced clerical duties to assist technical personnel by relieving them of selected tasks involved in project work, computer programming, and preparation of work for the computer. May be called upon to code or write programs of greater complexity than are undertaken by Programming Clerk I, or parts of such programs. May act as contact with remote users of the computer to receive data, prepare it for submission to the computer, and return answers to remote users. May direct the work of lower rated programming clerks and staff assistants.

2. *Requirements for entering:* Educational requirements are the same as for Programming Clerk II. Must have received for at least one year the top progression rate of Programming Clerk I and have demonstrated a higher caliber of aptitude, skill, and job performance. Must have complete knowledge of functional and operating procedures of clerical programming group (if applicable; or must be able to work along in the conduct of the required duties if the work assignments are so constituted) and must have demonstrated capacity to assume responsibility and to exercise soundly independent judgment and initiative.

Compensation Application
Developing a Merit Pay Guide for Keysoft Enterprises

As noted in the history of Keysoft Enterprises in the second Compensation Application, James Burton III (president of Keysoft) wants to upgrade the existing human resources system. One part of the system that will follow the same format, though, is the merit pay guide. Please read about merit pay guides in Chapter 9 of your text. Exhibit 1 shows the merit pay guide used by Keysoft last year. Next year's guide should follow the same general format. Specifically: (1) higher performers should receive larger increases, (2) employees with salaries in lower quartiles of a pay grade should receive larger increases than employees in higher quartiles, and (3) average performers with salaries in the middle of a pay grade should receive increases equal to the cost of living. In addition, Mr. Burton would like the new merit guide to reflect the following policy decisions:

1. Performance differences between employees should be rewarded with even larger salary-increase differences between employees than in past years.
2. No red circle employee should receive a pay increase.
3. Total increases should not exceed 8 percent on average for all employees.

Develop a merit pay guide to reflect these policies. Remember, there is no one right answer, but you should document how your merit pay guide conforms to Keysoft policies.

EXHIBIT 1
Merit Pay Guide for Last Year

Position in Salary Range / Performance	Well below Average		Below Average		Average		Above Average		Well above Average	
Above grade maximum (red circle)	0		2		3		4		5	
		0		0		5		5		15
Q4	0		3		4		5		6	
		0		0		10		10		15
Q3	0		4		5		6		7	
		0		0		5		25		10
Q2	2		5		6		7		8	
		0		2		9		9		10
Q1	2		6		7		8		9	
		0		3		6		5		6

Notes: 1. Cost of living rose 6 percent last year.
2. Numbers at lower right corner of each cell represent the number of employees falling into that cell during the previous year. These figures should be used to calculate budgetary implications of any proposed merit guide.

Alternatives to Traditional Reward Systems

One way of looking at the relationship between an organization and its employees is in the form of a contract. The organization offers inducements (or rewards) that should be designed to satisfy employee **needs.** In return, employees provide contributions of their own in the form of work output.[1] For an organization to achieve its business objectives, it must identify ways to ensure that this work output of employees will support business objectives. This requires the design of **effective reward administration and performance measurement systems.** An effective reward system is designed to satisfy

---

[1]C. I. Barnard, *The Function of the Executive* (Cambridge, Mass.: Harvard University Press, 1938); and J. March and H. Simon, *Organizations* (New York: John Wiley & Sons, Inc., 1958).

employee needs and reinforce job behaviors consistent with organizational objectives. An effective performance measurement system is designed to translate business objectives into some set of performance expectations and then measure employee performance against those expectations.

Reward administration system: A system to identify pay levels, components, and timing that best match individual needs and organizational requirements.

Performance measurement system: A system to determine the correspondence between worker behavior/task outcomes and job expectations (performance standards).

Thus far this book has presented a traditional view of reward administration systems in organizations. Jobs are evaluated according to some criteria of internal worth to the organization (Chapter 4). The external worth of jobs is assessed through salary surveys indicating what other firms pay for their jobs (Chapter 7). Based on some combination of internal and external measures of worth, jobs are assigned pay grades. Movement within those grades is based on individual performance (Chapter 9) or some other measure of personal characteristics (e.g., job tenure).

Although this characterization of compensation still dominates organizational practices, alternative reward systems do exist, and these alternatives are becoming more and more prevalent. Exhibit 10.1 summarizes a number of interesting statistics, all of which show a rising trend toward use of alternative reward systems.

Columns 1–5 in Exhibit 10.1 show how long companies who are currently using one or more of the alternative reward systems have had them in existence. Profit-sharing plans (16.9 percent of the companies with current plans have had them for 25 years or longer) and individual incentive plans (13.3 percent of companies report histories of more than 25 years) have the longest histories in companies. Column 6 indicates the percentage of companies currently using the different types of plans, and column 7 reports the expected increase in adoption. Profit sharing and individual incentives currently are most popular, with about 30 percent of the firms using such plans. The greatest future interest, though, (in percentage terms) is in pay-for-knowledge systems, small group incentives, and gain-sharing plans.

Along with this growth in alternative reward systems has been a relative decline in some of the more traditional compensation practices. For example, in a sample of 1598 respondents from 857 companies, significant numbers indicated they will either eliminate or significantly reduce participation in across-the-board increases (36 percent), cost-of-living increases (28 percent), and merit increases (25 percent).[2] Although this survey

---

[2]Carla O'Dell, *Major Findings from People Performance and Pay,* American Productivity Center, 1986.

EXHIBIT 10.1
Alternative Reward Systems and Their Longevity in Organizations

	Years experience with different plans (% of companies)						
	1	*2*	*3*	*4*	*5*	*6*	*7*
Type of Plan	*25+ yrs*	*16–25 yrs*	*11–15 yrs*	*6–10 yrs*	*1–5 yrs*	*Current Use*	*(%) Projected Increase*
Individual incentive plan	13.3	12.2	10.2	22.1	42.3	28	31
Small group incentive plan	6.2	8.4	6.2	17.4	61.8	14	70
Gain-sharing plan	2.8	.7	4.9	18.7	72.9	13	68
Profit-sharing plan	16.9	17.4	14.5	21.5	29.5	32	20
Pay-for-knowledge plan	6.7	0.0	1.7	23.4	68.4	5	75
All salaried work force	13.7	20.9	15.8	25.9	23.7	11	29

Adapted from: Carla O'Dell, *Major Findings from People Performance and Pay*, American Productivity Center, Houston, TX, 1986.

anticipates a decline in the use of traditional merit increases, there is still widespread use of individual performance appraisal, and efforts to link these appraisals to individual merit increases (see Chapter 9 for this discussion).

In the next section we talk about why alternative reward systems are becoming popular. Subsequent sections describe the different types of plans along with their relative strengths and weaknesses for satisfying employee needs and motivating performance consistent with organizational objectives.

WHAT ARE ALTERNATIVE REWARD SYSTEMS AND WHY ARE THEY INCREASINGLY POPULAR?

Exhibit 10.1 illustrates the types of innovations that we group under alternative reward systems. In one way or another, all of these alternatives represent experiments by organizations to better tie individuals to organizations and to better link rewards given to employees to performance of the organization. Such programs are becoming increasingly popular for several reasons. First, both increasing domestic and international competition force companies to be even more cost conscious than in prior eras. Most of these reward systems attempt to control costs by better linking rewards to performance increases. One study of 4500 organizations found that the single factor that best explained why organizations adopted alternative reward systems was increased domestic and foreign competition.[3] Second, the rate of technological change seems to be increasing, with new products and new methods of production introduced at what sometimes appears to be a bewildering pace. This creates at least two types of instability. First, organizations that fail to capitalize on new technologies and to recognize new product opportunities face an unstable future. Their competitors threaten to steal market share and/or erode profits. If this happens a second kind of instability arises: the instability workers feel when their jobs are threatened by layoffs. Currently, compensation experts are focusing on ways to design reward systems so that workers will be able and willing to move quickly into new jobs and new ways of performing old jobs. The ability and incentive to do this comes from reward systems that more closely link worker interests with the objectives of the company.

ALTERNATIVE REWARD SYSTEMS

All Salaried Work Force

Exhibit 10.1 indicated that 11 percent of organizations have moved to an all salaried work force. The mechanics of this are self evident. Both exempt employees, who traditionally are paid a salary rather than an hourly rate, and nonexempt employees receive a prescribed amount of money each pay period that is not primarily dependent on the number of hours worked. Companies adopt this type of plan to lessen the "we versus them" attitude that sometimes separates management and workers. By paying all workers under the same system, with no "second class" citizens, the hope is that an all salaried work force will more readily share the aspirations of management and work toward the objectives of the firm.

Firms that adopt an all salaried plan are still subject to provisions of the Fair Labor Standards Act (Chapter 13). Employers still pay nonexempt employees time and one-half for any hours worked over forty during the week. Hence the advantages of a salaried work force are not in cost savings but rather in perceptions of greater loyalty and commitment to the organization.

Pay-For-Knowledge Systems

As noted in Chapter 3, pay-for-knowledge plans (skill-based pay plans) exist in approximately 5–8 percent of companies in the United States.[4] These plans vary compensation as a function of the number of different jobs or skills that employees are able to perform competently. General Foods offers an illustrative example from their Maxwell House Coffee Plant in Houston. Since 1985, 135 maintenance workers have been classified into four skill groups: 1) Maintenance Workers, 2) Machine Adjusters, 3) Refrigeration Mechanics, and 4) Instrument and Electrical Maintenance Personnel. Each of the four groups

---

[3]Ibid.

[4]"Pay For Knowledge," *Wall Street Journal,* December 16, 1986, p. 1.

has multiple proficiency levels, and compensation increases are tied to learning multiple jobs at ever higher levels of proficiency. For example, the maintenance worker position is divided into five levels. Each of the first four levels is worth 15 cents extra (paid as a separate check on a quarterly basis), and the last level is worth 40 cents more.[5]

The General Foods example is fairly typical. Most plans have about 10 skill units, but maximums are reported as high as 100 different skill units.[6] Most companies limit the number of skills a person is allowed to learn (mean = 4) for fear that an employee will become "a Jack of all trades, master of none." In turn for learning these new skills, employees receive increases in compensation.

Perhaps the most interesting feature of pay-for-knowledge plans is the way they reverse the trend towards increased specialization that has been the hallmark of American industry since the turn of the century. Pay-for-knowledge systems encourage diversification in workers. The major impetus for paying workers to broaden their skill base appears to be the flexibility it offers for firms to quickly change business and product/service emphasis in response to changing technologies and changing consumer demand.[7] Two by-products of this greater flexibility are increased work force stability and greater job security for employees.[8] Workers with multiple job skills can be moved quickly into jobs where there is high demand. If sales of pocket calculators drop for Hewlett-Packard while personal computer sales boom, workers with skills in both areas can be reassigned easily. Supporters of pay-for-knowledge systems also claim that workers will be more satisfied with their jobs and company, be more motivated, be more productive, and have less absenteeism/turnover.[9] In reality, the positive impact of pay-for-knowledge systems may be less impressive, but early feedback is still very encouraging.[10] One study of 20 plants with pay-for-knowledge systems did find increased commitment, satisfaction, and worker productivity. Management also reported labor cost reductions.[11] Interestingly, these companies also reported broad scale improvements in labor-management relationships. Presumably the work force stability and job security resulting from a pay-for-knowledge system contributed to a perception that management was concerned about the welfare of labor, even during periods of fluctuating product demand.

On the negative side of the ledger, pay-for-knowledge systems are more costly, both in terms of compensation costs and training costs. In fact, the program with General Foods that we reported earlier costs about $50,000 per year in increased training costs,

---

[5]Bureau of National Affairs, *Changing Pay Practices: New Developments in Employee Compensation,* (Washington, D.C.: BNA, 1988).

[6]Nina Gupta, Timothy Schweizer, and G. Douglas Jenkins, "Pay for Knowledge Compensation Plans: Hypotheses and Survey Results," *Monthly Labor Review,* October 1987, pp. 40–43.

[7]Bureau of National Affairs, *Changing Pay Practices.*

[8]Ibid.

[9]Ibid.

[10]Gupta, Schweizer, and Jenkins, "Pay for Knowledge Compensation Plans: Hypotheses and Survey Results."

[11]Ibid.

and this is for a group of just 135 workers. Critics of pay-for-knowledge systems are also skeptical about claims for increased productivity and reduced labor costs.[12] How, they ask, can workers trained in several different jobs perform all of them better than a group of workers trained in only one job area. This flaunts a major tenet of industrial engineering, i.e., that specialization improves efficiency. Perhaps more experience with pay-for-knowledge systems and more reports on their effectiveness will resolve this question.

Pay Plans Based on Objective Measures of Performance

Alternative plans. Exhibit 10.2 outlines the characteristics of pay plans based on objective performance measures.

Two of these plans are sufficiently similar to cause confusion. Gain-sharing plans and profit-sharing plans both measure performance of a large group (division or total company) to determine the size of the payout. The major distinction, though, is in the measure of performance. Gain-sharing plans focus on fairly straightforward measures of unit productivity or cost savings (e.g., labor cost savings, material cost savings). Profit-sharing plans, in contrast, may have complex measures of profit. Profit is dependent on the type of depreciation procedures used, the level of bad debt expenses, and changes in economic conditions. Notice, all of these factors are beyond the control of workers and may contribute to feelings that personal performance is not the main determinant of the size of incentives.

So far the alternative reward systems we have discussed (all salary plans and pay-for-knowledge plans) have not been, fundamentally, pay-for-performance plans. Both of the previous plans focused more on characteristics of the individuals (exempt vs. nonexempt distinction, number of skill competencies) than on their performance. Why would an organization choose to do this, to consciously pay for something other

EXHIBIT 10.2
Incentive Based Pay Plans

Performance Measure	*Plan Type*
Individual units of output	Individual incentive plan
Units of output for a small group	Small group incentive
Units of output or cost savings for a division or entire organization	Gain-sharing plan
Profitability of division or organization	Profit-sharing plan
Value of stock	Employee stock ownership plan

---

[12]Ian Ziskin, "Knowledge-Based Pay! A Strategic Analysis," *ILR Report,* 24(1), (August 1974), pp. 16–22.

than performance? After all, Chapter 8 illustrated the potential motivation and performance advantages of tying compensation as closely as possible to performance. The answer is simple. Organizations are limited in their ability to tie pay to performance by their ability to measure performance. Some jobs do not have easily definable performance outcomes. How do we measure the performance of an engineer whose job involves making cars more aerodynamic? What is the increased dollar value of a car with a better drag coefficient (wind resistance)? Other jobs have a defined output but no single individual is responsible for the entire product or service. Working on an assembly line in Detroit yields cars at the rate of one every minute or less, but the added value of any single worker is difficult to separate from the contributions of other employees.

To the extent performance of individuals is difficult to measure objectively, organizations must resort to more subjective measures of individual worth. And as performance becomes more difficult to measure, organizations are, not surprisingly, less willing to tie pay directly to performance. Exhibit 10.3 illustrates this point.

When output is concrete and measurable, evaluation of performance is straightforward. A supervisor simply determines if quantity standards are being met. The major debate in this type of setting, as noted later, is over the difficulty of the performance standards. What level of output should an employee be expected to achieve to receive a specific reward level? When performance can be measured this objectively, pay systems may be quite sophisticated, including some of the incentive and gain-sharing plans to be discussed shortly.

In contrast, when evaluation standards and performance data are more subjective, organizations must channel more effort to the development of evaluation systems that are perceived as accurate and fair (Chapter 9). The evaluation process is considerably more elaborate and complex. Perhaps because these systems are more subjective, and employee acceptance more tenuous, pay systems tied to them are less complex and less rigidly dependent on evaluation of performance.

EXHIBIT 10.3
The Link Between Performance Measurement Problems and Pay

	Smallest work unit for which output can be measured		
	Individual	*Small Group*	*Division or Company*
Base pay	may be based directly on performance (individual incentive system)	determined by traditional job evaluation and market pricing	determined by traditional job evaluation and market pricing
Extra compensation	None. All is function of individual performance. May have group or company plan if desire to tie pay to overall performance of organization	Small group incentive plan possible. Extra compensation then tied to group performance. May use subjective performance evaluation and give merit increases	Gain-sharing, profit-sharing, or employee stock ownership plan possible

ISSUES IN ADOPTION AND DEVELOPMENT OF PERFORMANCE-BASED PAY PLANS

Adoption Issues

About 20 years ago, a series of factors was discovered that related to incentive system adoption. Interestingly, incentive plans tend to be more prevalent in industries sharing four characteristics:[13]

1. High labor costs
2. High cost competition in product markets
3. Slow or nonexistent advancements in technology
4. High potential for production bottlenecks

In large part, these observations still tend to be borne out. Consider the clothing industry. Labor is a large proportion of total costs for production of clothing. The market is extremely cost competitive, particularly when international production of clothing along the Pacific Rim is considered. The technology for making clothing has not advanced very quickly, and there is a reasonably high potential for bottlenecks in the production of the final good. Similar kinds of problems face the steel industry, which in recent years has been accused of being negligent in its adoption of new technologies. This, combined with severe competition from overseas steel markets, makes the advantages of incentive systems appear more attractive.

In contrast, the automobile industry has traditionally been relatively restrained in its use of incentive systems. While it faces problems similar to the steel industry in terms of foreign competition, technological advances tended, in the past, to keep labor costs down to a level where price competition with foreign producers was at least feasible. This, combined with the United Auto Workers' stand against incentive systems, had resulted in relatively infrequent adoption of them. As we will see in Chapter 17, though, the Big Three all adopted profit-sharing plans in the 1980s. A large part of this change can be explained by the need to control costs and to assume a more competitive stance in the international automobile market.

Since this early study was done, a number of other factors have been identified that affect incentive system adoption: 1) organizational strategy, 2) managerial value system, 3) organizational design and work relationships, 4) unit and individual performance standards, and 5) unit and individual performance.

Organizational strategy. As organizations grow and change to meet environmental demands, the design of compensations systems to support both change and stabilization is vital. Research on this change process and the accommodation of compensation systems to change has focused thus far on linking compensation design to diversification strategy.[14]

---

[13]Robert B. McKersie, Carroll F. Miller, and William E. Quarterman, "Some Indicators of Incentive Plan Prevalence," *Monthly Labor Review,* May 1964, pp. 271–76.

[14]Jeffrey Kerr, "Diversification Strategies and Managerial Rewards: An Empirical Study," *Academy of Management Journal* 28, no. 1 (1985), pp. 155–79; and R. A. Pitts, "Incentive Compensation and Organization Design," *Personnel Journal* 53 (1974), pp. 338–44.

As organizations prosper and grow they must decide, as part of their overall organizational strategy, what the nature of the growth (if any) will be. For example, organizations can choose to diversify into new product or service lines. Should this diversification be through acquisition of existing firms or through internal expansion? Further, if the decision is to expand, will it be along similar or different product lines? Research indicates that the decision to diversify and the mode (acquisition or expansion) have impacts on compensation system design.[15]

Some organizations pride themselves on stability and growth through "tried and true" methods, that is, growth through internally generated diversification or through further penetration of existing markets.[16] It is just these organizations that are also likely to have compensation systems that promote stable employment relationships. Rewards are based on seniority. Any incentive systems used in this type of organization are likely to take a long run perspective on profits and are apt to foster interdependence between divisions through goals emphasizing *both* divisional and organizational performance.[17]

In contrast, some firms adopt a more risk-taking approach to growth, actively prospecting for acquisitions and generally pursuing external diversification programs.[18] These organizations promote more entrepreneurial behavior for employees.[19] Entrepreneurial behavior is reinforced by designing bonus and incentive systems that encourage autonomy and competitive drive. Bonuses may assume a much larger role in these organizations than in those characterized by more conservative values.[20] Incentives are likely to stress short term performance on relatively objective measures of divisional performance. Concern for shaping cooperative behavior between units is conspicuously absent. Autonomy and competition are valued, and the compensation system reflects these concerns.[21]

Management values. A related factor influencing compensation design is the existing management value system. Incentive systems are more readily accepted when management values promote stable work relationships. Trust between workers and management is strong.[22] This trust evolves, in part, as workers experience a work environment

---

[15]R. A. Pitts, "Incentive Compensation and Organization Design"; Kerr, "Diversification Strategies and Managerial Rewards: An Empirical Study"; R. P. Reumelt, "Diversity and Profitability," paper presented at the Academy of Management meetings, Western Region, Sun Valley, Idaho, 1977.

[16]M. Leonitiades, *Strategies for Diversification and Change* (Boston: Little, Brown, 1980).

[17]Arch Patton, "Why Incentive Plans Fail," *Harvard Business Review,* May-June 1972, pp. 58–66; Kerr, "Diversification Strategies and Managerial Rewards: An Empirical Study"; and Jerry M. Newman, "Selecting Incentive Plans to Complement Organizational Strategy," in *Current Trends in Compensation Research and Practice,* eds. L. Gomez-Mejia and D. Balkin (Englewood Cliffs, N.J.: Prentice Hall, 1987), pp. 14–24.

[18]Leonitiades, *Strategies for Diversification and Change.*

[19]Pitts, "Incentive Compensation and Organization Design"; and M. S. Salter, "Tailor Incentive Compensation to Strategy," *Harvard Business Review* 51, no. 3 (1973), pp. 94–102.

[20]Kerr, "Diversification Strategies and Managerial Rewards."

[21]Newman, "Selecting Incentive Plans to Complement Organizational Strategy."

[22]Patton, "Why Incentive Plans Fail"; Kerr, "Diversification Strategies and Managerial Reward: An Empirical Study"; Pitts, "Incentive Compensation and Organization Design"; and Robert McKersie, "The Promise of Gainsharing," *ILR Report* 24(1) (1986), pp. 7–11.

where cyclical employment patterns are avoided and fears of job loss diminish. In turn, this stability lessens fears that introduction of an incentive system is a "management plot" to increase production and lay off workers. Trust also evolves when management is willing to listen to the suggestions of workers by involving them in the design and implementation of the system.[23]

Continued viability of an incentive system, though, depends on management's ability to face the more difficult behavioral consequences of incentive compensation. Remember, incentives create a spread between the pay levels of individuals and groups. As the spread increases so may the dissatisfaction of lower paid individuals. Organizations and managers unable to bear the heat of this disapproval should avoid incentive systems.

Organizational design and work relationships. A compensation system also complements the way organizational units are designed to interact. Autonomous units with sole responsibility for particular goods or services are ideal for objective, results-oriented performance measures. Independent units can be held accountable for successfully meeting targets; and incentive systems can tie rewards to these performance targets.[24]

As autonomy decreases, though, divisional performance measures become less viable. Rather, the interdependence among groups, divisions, and the organization in decision making is reflected in performance measures and incentive standards that reflect combined performance of all three entities.

Unit and individual performance standards. The last section may leave the impression that performance standards are easily manipulated and can trigger all sorts of desired performance. Be careful! Research indicates that inappropriate choice of performance standards is the single biggest cause of certain incentive system failures. If performance cannot be measured validly and objectively, the potential advantage of incentive systems is greatly reduced.[25]

Unit and individual performance. Compensation, as noted earlier, is intended to attract, retain, and motivate workers. Incentive systems are useful on the last of these objectives: when performance is below par, incentives may motivate higher performance. However, it is not clear that incentives are nearly so effective in helping to attract or retain employees. One survey indicates 72 percent of blue collar workers, and 56 percent of white collar workers, would prefer straight wages over any type of incentive plan.[26]

Adoption of an incentive system probably has implications for the types of workers

[23]McKersie, "The Promise of Gainsharing."

[24]Pitts, "Incentive Compensation and Organization Design"; Newman, "Selecting Incentive Plans to Complement Organizational Strategy"; and Organizational Analysis and Practice, *Strategic Issues in Reward Systems: An Analysis of Incentive Systems* (Ithaca, N.Y.: Organizational Analysis and Practice, 1982).

[25]Organizational Analysis and Practice, *Strategic Issues in Reward Systems;* Jude T. Rich and John A. Larson, "Why Some Long-Term Incentives Fail," *Compensation Review* 16, no. 1 (1984), pp. 26–37.

[26]Bureau of National Affairs, *Changing Pay Practices: New Developments in Employee Compensation,* Bureau of National Affairs, 1988.

such a system might attract. What does an economically motivated person look like? Is there any such animal? Can selection strategies be developed to fill jobs with these people? Or can current employees be trained in this need? While little empirical work addresses the issue, motivation theories from Chapter 8 suggest the process that might apply in determining whether an incentive system is favorably viewed. Specifically, equity theory suggests that the reward value relative to effort must be greater than 1.00 (reward exceeds effort) and that the ratio should favorably compare to other relevant employees. Furthermore, expectancy theory indicates the monetary reward must be valued, the performance-pay link must be visible, and employees must believe that effort leads to high performance.[27]

For a different perspective on factors to consider in selecting an incentive/gain-sharing plan, Exhibit 10.4 notes a more general set of issues in incentive system adoption. In general, incentive systems lead employees to work smarter and more independently, be cost conscious, and produce at a higher rate. On the negative side, incentive systems may lead to deteriorating product quality (particularly if quantity is rewarded and quality is neglected). Another negative side effect is greater mistrust of any management activities that give even the slightest sign that either performance standards or payout rates will be adversely changed.

EXHIBIT 10.4
Pros and Cons, Incentive (payment by results) Plans

Advantages

1. Payment-by-results systems can make a substantial contribution to a rise in productivity, to lower production costs, and to increased earnings or workers.
2. In general, less direct supervision is required to maintain reasonable levels of output than under payment by time.
3. Workers are encouraged to pay more attention to reducing lost time and to make more effective use of their equipment.
4. In most cases, systems of payment by results, if accompanied by improved organizational and work measurement, enable labor costs to be estimated more accurately than under payment by time and so facilitate the application of modern systems of standard costing and budgetary control.

Disadvantages

1. Generally, introduction of a payment-by-results system leads to a deterioration in the quality of the product. Additional expense is involved in the application of an adequate system of quality control.
2. If the task is set too high or there is a low guaranteed minimum wage, the health, efficiency, and morale of the workers may be adversely affected.
3. The risk of accidents may be increased.
4. Inaccurate rate setting under an incentive scheme or wide differences in the ability or capacity of workers working in close proximity may lead to large differences in earnings and ill-feelings between the workers.
5. Additional expense involved in employing the personnel required to install and administer a system of payment of results; in some cases this expense may be out of proportion to the potential savings in costs.
6. Workers may tend to oppose the introduction of new machinery or methods, or other changes in conditions of production, which would necessitate a restudy of the job.

Source: Pinhas Schwinger, *Wage Incentive Systems* (New York: Halsted, 1975). © 1975, Keter Publishing Company.

---

[27]Organizational Analysis and Practice, *Strategic Issues in Reward Systems*.

Development Issues

Should rewards be paid to individual employees for individual performance? Or should larger groups be the unit of focus? What should be the standard that triggers incentives? And what should be the form (frequency of incentives)? All of these issues are discussed in this section.

Group or individual plans? level of aggregation? Level of aggregation refers to the size of the work unit for which performance is measured (e.g., individual, work group, department, plant, organization) and to which rewards are distributed. The issue is important for three reasons. First, **contrasting motivational forces** are unleashed by an organization's decision to aggregate. What type of employee behavior best fits organizational needs? Individual incentive systems are generally associated with more competition, increased pressure on individuals to perform and to accept responsibility for their own actions, increased risk-taking behavior, and lower acceptance of management values/job demands that do not directly affect incentive output.[28] Alternatively, group incentive plans reinforce behaviors that promote collective rather than individual success. The perceived connection between pay and performance may be lessened, but this may be offset by an increase in cooperation and joint effort among employees working for a shared reward based on aggregate performance. In deciding on an appropriate plan, organizations ought to consider the four factors noted in Exhibit 10.5.[29] Also note, though, the trend in recent years has been away from individual incentive plans and towards group plans.[30] The concern seems to be that individual incentive plans are extremely costly and difficult to administer. Further, unions fear that individualized pay will be based on "biased" management standards. Couple these constraints with a growing interest in increased teamwork/cooperation and the movement to group plans becomes more understandable.

Of course, combinations of these plans are also possible. One of the most popular is to measure performance at the plant or total organization level but to distribute rewards at the individual level, based on some supervisory evaluation of individual performance. One variation currently used by a prominent organization is illustrated in the Appendix at the end of this chapter.

A second reason why the issue of aggregation is important centers on **technical constraints.** The nature of an organizations technology, both in production and in information processing, constrains choice. In general, individual incentive systems are less appropriate where:[31]

---

[28]Organizational Analysis and Practice, *Strategic Issues in Reward Systems;* Pinhas Schwinger, *Wage Incentive Systems* (New York: Halsted, 1975); Kerr, "Diversification Strategies and Managerial Rewards: An Empirical Study"; and Salter, "Tailor Incentive Compensation to Strategy."

[29]Edward Lawler III, *Pay and Organization Development* (Reading, Mass.: Addison-Wesley Publishing, 1981).

[30]Hewitt Associates, *An Overview of Productivity-Based Incentive Systems,* May 1985, Document P3022/2625.

[31]Organizational Analysis and Practice, *Strategic Issues in Reward Systems;* Schwinger, *Wage Incentive Systems.*

EXHIBIT 10.5
Factors Influencing Aggregation Level

Characteristic	*Individual Level of Incentives Appropriate*	*Group Level of Incentives—Unit, Department, Organization— Appropriate*
Performance measurement	Good measures of individual performance exist. Task accomplishment not dependent on performance of others.	Output is group collaborative effort. Individual contributions to output cannot be assessed.
Organizational adaptability	Individual performance standards are stable. Production methods and labor mix relatively constant.	Performance standards for individuals change to meet environmental pressures on relatively constant organizational objectives. Production methods and labor mix must adapt to meet changing pressures.
Organizational commitment	Commitment strongest to individual's profession or superior. Supervisor viewed as unbiased and performance standards readily apparent.	High commitment to organization built upon sound communication of organizational objectives and performance standards.
Union status	Nonunion. Unions promote equal treatment. Competition between individuals inhibits "fraternal" spirit.	Union or nonunion. Unions less opposed to plans that foster cohesiveness of bargaining unit and which distribute rewards evenly across group.

1. individual contributions of workers are difficult to measure, either because of interdependent work flows or because of machine controlled work pace;
2. work stoppages are regular and uncontrollable;
3. the management information and cost accounting systems are relatively primitive.

The key to these constraints is that performance must be measurable and the agent (who completed the work) must be identifiable. Usually these constraints become more severe the lower the level of analysis (e.g., individuals).[32] After all, any organization can provide performance data (e.g., profits) for the entire organization. When the unit of analysis is smaller though, it becomes more and more difficult to decide on objective measures of performance and to attribute that performance to specific individuals or groups.

Finally, level of aggregation is also important because the choice **frequently influences the objectivity of the performance standards** and, consequently, the type of pay system that evolves. If the existing information system can provide only very subjective supervisory ratings at the individual level of performance, it may be appropriate to focus on a higher level measure. Moving to higher levels of aggregation yields performance measures with a more objective base (profit, cost effectiveness). And, as noted earlier, these objective performance measures allow implementation of compensation systems directly tied to (group) output.

---

[32]Newman, "Selecting Incentive Plans to Complement Organizational Strategy."

EXHIBIT 10.6
Illustration of a Bonus Payment System In a Large Retail Store

Time Frame for Goal Attainment	Performance Standard	Bonus
June 1989–June 1990	Increase sales volume by 6% and reduce customer complaints by 10%	20% of base pay as of June 1990

Form of incentive. Incentive and gain-sharing plans can involve three forms of payment: base pay, incentive payment, and bonus. Base pay, if used at all in an incentive scheme, is a guaranteed level of payment irrespective of output. Typically, this base pay compensates for such activities as handling customer returns, fielding complaints, and waiting for machines to be repaired. All these examples restrict employee production, which is typically tied to incentive payments. Consequently, this alternative compensation may be considered appropriate.

An incentive payment is any form of pay tied directly to achievement of performance standards. Wage payment, then, directly or indirectly is tied to performance of the organization. Employee costs rise and fall in line with the health of the firm.

A bonus is a lump sum payment to an employee in recognition of goal achievement. Typically the goal is not expressed in standard output but represents a major step toward achievement of organizational goals. Herein lies a distinct advantage. Performance goals can be changed yearly to reflect the changing nature of organizational objectives.[33] Upon completion, a previously agreed-upon bonus is owed the employee (frequently a percentage of base pay; see Exhibit 10.6).

One industry where bonuses are particularly popular is the highly competitive, high technology industry. A Hay survey of 33 large high tech companies showed that the top 7 percent of managerial, professional, and technical employees were eligible for bonuses. In smaller high tech organizations (less than 100 million sales versus 1 billion sales for the larger companies) 47 percent of all managerial, professional, and technical employees get bonuses. These percentages are generally higher than are found in other manufacturing industries (e.g., large manufacturing firms average approximately 3 percent participation rates).[34]

Another form of payment attaining some popularity over the past several years is lump sum payments. Lump sum payments are generally granted in lieu of wage increases and are preferred because base pay and pay-related benefits do not change. In the first nine months of 1988, 26 percent of all contracts provided for lump sum payouts.[35] Chapter 17 covers lump sum awards in greater detail.

Frequency of incentives. Instrumental conditioning experiments indicate that rewards work best when administered immediately after task completion. This conjures up

[33]J. Moynahan, *Designing an Effective Sales Compensation Program* (New York: Amacom, 1980).

[34]CompFlash, "Survey Shows Bonuses Are the Way to Go," *AMA CompFlash 85-07* (1985), p. 4.

[35]U.S. Department of Labor, *Current Wage Developments* (Washington, D.C., 1988), p. 26.

images of monkeys pressing bars and immediately receiving bananas from a chute. Obviously, this kind of compensation system would not be very popular or practical with humans. The most frequent concession is to pay incentives on standard time schedules: weekly, monthly, quarterly, and yearly. Unfortunately, though, task cycles are not conveniently equal to calendar cycles.[36] Employees end up receiving incentives at times far removed from the accomplishments triggering the rewards. A more viable strategy would adopt a performance contract mechanism. Upon completion of agreed-upon work at an agreed-upon date, an incentive will be paid. If the time frame is too short to make payment practical, regular feedback about incentive accumulations should be provided until payment can be made.

Another subset of the frequency question is the issue of long-term and short-term incentive plans. Much of the popular press has criticized American business for taking too short a perspective on organizational goals. Emphasizing short-run profits to the detriment of longer-run objectives, so this argument runs, frequently hurts us in international competition with firms such as Japan, which take a more long-range perspective on business prospects. It is true that short-term incentive plans are more prevalent in American companies than long-term plans. For example, one study found 75 percent of firms (n = 110) had short-term plans while only 55 percent had long-term incentive plans.[37] However, there is increasing emphasis on designing incentive plans that both meet organizational objectives *and* are consistent with incentive plans of differing durations.[38] This focus shifts discussions away from the less productive question, "should we use short-term or long-term incentive plans," toward the more relevant question, "what should be the nature of the mix and objectives of each type of plan." Organizational success then becomes a function of identifying consistent short- and long-run goals and insuring both are met. Several authors suggest a key element in forging this interdependence is selecting appropriate measures of organizational performance.[39] Both the financial research literature and the human resources management literature currently are debating the relative merits of such organizational effectiveness measures as earnings per share, return on equity, return on investments, and growth.[40] Exhibit 10.7 illustrates measures used by different organizations.

Finally, the frequency question also can be looked at from an entirely different perspective. How does an organization with stringent cost constraints still employ an incentive system? Consider a bank hard hit by deregulation during the early 1980s. Bank officers want to offer tellers an incentive payment based on their ability to sell new bank

---

[36]P. Clark, *Organizational Design* (London: Travistock, 1972).

[37]CompFlash, "Short-Term Plans Outnumber Long-Term Plans," *AMA CompFlash 85-06* (1985), p. 1.

[38]Bruce R. Ellig, "Incentive Plans: Short-Term Design Issues," *Compensation Review* 16, no. 3 (1984), pp. 26–36; and Peat Marwick, "Capital Accumulation and Long-Term Incentive Practices in the 500 Top Industrial Companies," Compensation Briefs Research Report, February 1986.

[39]Ellig, "Incentive Plans: Short Term Design Issues"; Rich and Larson, "Why Some Long Term Incentives Fail."

[40]Bruce R. Ellig, "Incentive Plans: Over the Long Term," *Compensation Review* 16, no. 2 (1984), pp. 39–54; and Ellig, "Short Term Design Issues."

EXHIBIT 10.7
Common Performance Measures Used in Incentive Plans

Measure	Definition	Organization
1. Operating margin (percent)	*Total sales and revenues less total costs and expenses* divided by total sales and revenues.	American Motors, American Airlines.
2. Operating return on assets	*Operating income* divided by average total assets.	General Motors, Borg-Warner, Federated Department Stores, Texas Instruments.
3. Earnings per share	*Income available to common stockholder* divided by average number of common shares outstanding.	Jewel Company, Winn Dixie Stores.

products, but they face constraints on their ability to pay incentives if the employees are too successful in their promotional efforts. Organizations are adopting incentive lottery programs to cover just these circumstances. Employees who exceed standard output (e.g., opening 30 new savings accounts per month) do not receive a minuscule incentive payment with little or no motivational impact (e.g., $.20 per new account). Rather, their performance earns them "lottery tickets" that apply toward a much larger payoff. The cost of both the traditional program and the lottery program are identical. A lottery, though, capitalizes on the reward value of taking a risk.[41]

INCENTIVE (PERFORMANCE-BASED) PAY PLANS

Individual Incentive Plans

All incentive plans have one common feature: an established standard against which worker performance is compared to determine wages. For individual incentive systems this standard is compared against individual worker performance. From this basic foundation, a number of seemingly complex and divergent plans have evolved. Before discussing the more prevalent of these plans, however, it is important to note that each varies along two dimensions and can be classified into one of four cells illustrated in Exhibit 10.8.

The first dimension on which incentive systems vary is in the method of rate determination. Plans either set up a rate standard based on units of production per time period or in time period per unit of production. On the surface, this distinction may appear trivial but, in fact, the deviations arise because tasks have different cycles of operation.[42] Short-cycle tasks, those that are completed in a relatively short period of time, typically have as a standard a designated number of units to be produced in a given time period. For long-cycle tasks, this would not be appropriate. It is entirely possible that only one

---

[41]Karen Evans, "On the Job Lotteries: A Low Cost Incentive That Sparks Higher Productivity," *Personnel*, April 1988.

[42]Thomas Patten, *Pay: Employee Compensation and Incentive Plans* (New York: Macmillan, 1977); and Schwinger, *Wage Incentive Systems*.

EXHIBIT 10.8
Individual Incentive Plans

		Method of Rate Determination	
		Units of production per time period	*Time period per unit of production*
	Pay constant function of production level	*(1)* Straight piecework plan.	*(2)* Standard hour plan.
Relationship between production level and pay	*Pay varies as function of production level*	*(3)* Taylor differential piece-rate system. Merrick multiple piece-rate system.	*(4)* Halsey 50–50 method. Rowan plan. Gantt plan.

task or some portion may be completed in a day. Consequently, for longer-cycle tasks, the standard is typically set in terms of time required to complete one unit of production. Individual incentives are based on whether or not workers complete the task in the designated time period.

The second dimension on which individual incentive systems vary is the specified relationship between production level and wages. The first alternative is to tie wages directly to output, so that wages are some constant function of production. In contrast, some plans vary wages as a function of production level. For example, one common variation is to provide higher dollar rates for production above the standard than for production below the standard.

Specific plans. Each of the plans discussed in this section has as a foundation a standard level of performance determined by some form of time study, or job analysis completed by an industrial engineer or trained personnel administrator. (Exhibit 10.9 provides an illustration of a time study.) The variations in these plans occur in either the way the standard is set or the way wages are tied to output. Following Exhibit 10.8 there are four general categories of plans.

1. Cell 1. The most frequently implemented incentive system is a straight piecework system. Rate determination is based on units of production per time period, and wages vary directly as a function of production level. A standard is developed reflecting the units of output a worker is expected to complete in, say, an hour. Workers are paid for each unit of output. Consequently workers who consistently exceed the established standard receive higher than average wages.

   The major advantages of this type of system is that it is easily understood by workers and, perhaps consequently, more readily accepted than some of the other

EXHIBIT 10.9
Example of a Time Study

Task: Drilling operation.

Elements:
1. Move part from box to jig.
2. Position part in jig.
3. Drill hole in part.
4. Remove jig and drop part in chute.

Notes and remarks	Observation number	Elements			
		(1)	*(2)*	*(3)*	*(4)*
	1	.17	.22	.26	.29
	2	.17	.22	.27	.34
	3	.16	.21	.28	.39
	4	.18	.21	.29	.29
	5	.19	.20	.30	.36
	6	.25	.21	.31	.31
	7	.17	.23	.29	.33
Observed time		.17 (mode)	.21 (mode)	.29 (median)	.33 (mean)
Effort rating	(130%)	1.30	1.30	1.30	1.30
Corrected time		.2210	.2730	.3370	.4290
Total corrected time					1.2600

Allowances:
fatigue	5%		
personal needs	5%		
contingencies	10%		
Total	20% (of total corrected time of 1.2600)		.2520
Total allotted time for task			1.5120

Source: From *Performance Appraisal and Review Systems* by Stephen J. Carroll and Craig E. Schneier. Copyright © 1982 by Scott, Foresman and Company. Reprinted by permission.

incentive systems. The major disadvantages center on the difficulty in setting a standard. For example, the industrial engineer charged with establishing a standard for the drilling operation in Exhibit 10.9 may be expected to observe numerous drillers performing the task. The time study expert would then derive a standard indicating the number of holes it should be possible to drill in a given time period by workers performing at a normal rate. The accuracy of the industrial engineer's measurements, the workers chosen to observe, and the definition of a normal rate of speed all influence the final standard.[43] An inappropriate standard can result in labor dissension (too high a standard) or excessive labor costs (too low a standard). Either outcome is likely to result in deteriorating labor-management relations. Consequently great care must be taken to ensure that both management and the workers have a role in establishing standards. Very frequently in unionized firms this is formally ensured through inclusion of standards as a negotiable issue in the contract language.

---

[43]Stephen Carroll and Craig Schneier, *Performance Appraisal and Review Systems* (Glenview, Ill.: Scott Foresman, 1982).

EXHIBIT 10.10
Illustration of a Straight Piece-rate Plan

Piece-rate standard (e.g., determined from time study)	10 units/hour
Guaranteed minimum wage (if standard is not met)	$ 5.00/hour
Incentive rate (for each unit over 10 units)	$ .50/unit

Examples of worker output   *WAGE*
10 UNITS or less $5.00/hour (as guaranteed)
20 UNITS   20 × $ .50 = $10.00/hour
30 UNITS   30 × $ .50 = $15.00/hour

---

2. Cell 2. There are two relatively common plans that set standards based on time per unit and tie incentives directly to level of output: 1) standard-hour plans and 2) Bedeaux plans. A standard-hour plan is a generic term for plans setting incentive rate based on completion of a task in some expected time period. A common example can be found in any neighborhood gasoline station or automobile repair shop. Let us assume you need a new transmission. The estimate you receive for labor costs is based on the mechanic's hourly rate of pay, multiplied by a time estimate for job completion derived from a book listing average time estimates for a wide variety of jobs. If the mechanic receives $30 per hour and a transmission is listed as requiring four hours to remove and replace, the labor costs would be $120. All this is determined in advance of any actual work. Of course, if the mechanic is highly experienced and fast, the job may be completed in considerably less time than indicated in the book. However, the job is still charged as if it took the quoted time to complete. This is the basic mechanism of a standard hour incentive plan. If a task can be completed in less than the designated time, a worker is still paid at a rate based on the standard time allotted for that job times an hourly rate. Standard hour plans are more practical than a straight piecework plan for long-cycle operations and jobs that are nonrepetitive and require numerous skills for completion.[44]

   A Bedeaux plan provides a variation on straight piecework and standard hour plans. Instead of timing an entire task, a Bedeaux plan requires division of a task into simple actions and determination of the time required by an average skilled worker to complete each action. After the more fine time analysis of tasks, the Bedeaux system functions similarly to a standard hour plan. Workers receive a wage incentive for completing a task in less than standard time. This incentive is a direct function of the time saved in completing the task.

3. Cell 3. The two plans included in cell 3 provide for variable incentives as a function of units of production per time period. Both the Taylor plan and the Merrick plan provide different piece rates, depending on the level of production relative to the standard. To illustrate this, consider the contrasts of these plans with a straight piece-rate plan. A straight piece-rate plan varies wages directly with output. If workers reach standard production, they receive the standard wage. Eighty percent of standard

---

[44]Patten, *Pay: Employee Compensation and Incentive Plans;* Schwinger, *Wage Incentive Systems.*

EXHIBIT 10.11
Illustrations of the Taylor and Merrick Plans

Piece-rate standard				10 units per hour
Standard wage				$ 5.00/hour
Piecework rate				

Output	Taylor rate per unit	Taylor wage	Merrick rate per unit	Merrick wage
7 units/hour	$.50/unit	$3.50	$.50/unit	$3.50
8 units/hour	$.50/unit	$4.00	$.50/unit	$4.00
9 units/hour	$.50/unit	$4.50	$.60/unit	$5.40
10 units/hour	$.50/unit	$5.00	$.60/unit	$6.00
11 units/hour	$.70/unit	$7.70	$.70/unit	$7.70
12 + units	calculations at same rate as for 11 units			

production results in 80 percent of standard wage. Plotting a graph with percentage of standard production on one axis and percentage gain in base hourly rate on the other, the slope for a straight piece-rate system would be 1.00. Both the Taylor and Merrick plans would have variable slopes depending on production levels of workers. For example, the Taylor plan establishes two piecework rates. One rate goes into effect when a worker exceeds the published standard for a given time period. This rate is set higher than the regular wage incentive level. A second rate is established for production below standard, and this rate is lower than the regular wage.

The Merrick system operates in the same way, except three piecework rates are set: 1) high—for production exceeding 100 percent of standard; 2) medium—for production between 83 percent and 100 percent of standard; and 3) low—for production less than 83 percent of standard.[45]

Both these systems are designed to reward highly the efficient worker and penalize the inefficient worker. Quite obviously there are infinite variations on the number and type of piecework rates that could be established. While these two plans are designed to encourage the highly efficient, they are not as penalty-laden for less efficient workers as their now defunct predecessors.

4. Cell 4. The three plans included in cell 4 provide for variable incentives as a function of a standard expressed as time period per unit of production. The three plans include the Halsey 50-50 method, the Rowan plan, and the Gantt plan.

The Halsey 50-50 method derives its name from the shared split between worker and employer of any savings in direct cost. An allowed time for a task is determined via time study. The savings resulting from completion of a task in less than the standard time are allocated 50-50 (most frequent division) between the worker and the company.

The Rowan plan is similar to the Halsey plan in that an employer and employee both share in savings resulting from work completed in less than standard time. The major distinction in this plan, however, is that a worker's bonus increases as time required to complete the task decreases. For example, if the standard time to complete

---

[45]Schwinger, *Wage Incentive Systems*.

a task is 10 hours and it is completed in 7 hours, the worker receives a 30 percent bonus. Completion of the same task in six hours would result in a 40 percent bonus above the hourly wage for each of the six hours.

The Gantt plan differs from both the Halsey and Rowan plans in that standard time for a task is purposely set at a level requiring high effort to complete. Any worker who fails to complete the task in standard time is guaranteed a preestablished wage. However, for any task completed in standard time or less, earnings are pegged at 120 percent of the time saved. Consequently worker's earnings increase faster than production whenever standard time is met or exceeded.

Group Incentive Plans (Gain-Sharing Plans)

In one sense, group incentive plans are similar to individual incentive plans. An attempt is made to tie pay to performance by giving workers an additional payment when there has been an increase in profits or a decrease in costs to the firm. All plans begin by comparing inputs to outcomes. In this case labor inputs are compared to some measure of production outputs. In a basic sense incentives are awarded when some base period calculation of labor inputs and production outputs are exceeded, either by reducing labor inputs, increasing production outcomes, or both. It should be stressed, though, that these improvements do not necessarily result because employees individually or collectively decide to work harder. Indeed, it is probably more common that improvements arise because employees work smarter, identifying means to perform tasks more efficiently without working harder.

Deviation from individual incentive plans obviously arises because incentives are based on some measure of group performance rather than individual performance. Incentives are based on a comparison of present profits or costs against historical cost accounting data on the same figures. When the organization achieves greater profits or lower costs relative to a base year, groups participating in the incentive plan receive a portion of the accrued funds.

Complexity is introduced into these formulas, though, because different organizations have different goals. Different strategies and management value systems yield different solutions to some of the common questions organizations must answer in selecting one of the several different types of gain-sharing plans:[46]

1. *Strength of reinforcement.* What role should base pay assume relative to incentive pay? Incentive pay tends to encourage only those behaviors that are rewarded. For example, try returning an unwanted birthday present to a store that pays its sales force solely for new sales! Tasks that carry no rewards are only reluctantly performed (if at all!).

2. *Productivity standards.* What standard will be used to calculate whether employees will receive an incentive payout? Almost all gain-sharing plans use a historical stan-

---

[46]Max Bazerman and Brian Graham-Moore, "PG Formulas: Developing a Reward Structure to Achieve Organizational Goals," in *Productivity Gainsharing,* eds. Brian Graham-Moore and Timothy Ross (Englewood Cliffs, N.J.: Prentice-Hall, 1983).

dard. A historical standard involves choice of a prior year's performance to use for comparison with current performance. Which baseline year should be used, though? If too good (or too bad) a comparison year is used, the standard will be too hard (easy) to achieve, with obvious motivational and cost effects. One possible compromise is to use a moving average of several years (e.g., the average for the past five years, with the five-year block changing by one year on an annual basis).

One of the major problems with historical standards is the problems that changing environmental conditions can cause.[47] For example, consider the company that sets a target of 6 percent return on investment based on historical standards. When this level is reached, it triggers an incentive for eligible employees. Yet, in a product market where the average for that year is 15 percent return on investment, it is apparent that no incentive is appropriate for our underachiever.[48] Such problems are particularly insidious during economic swings and for organizations that face volatile economic climates. Care must be taken to ensure that the link between performance and rewards is sustained. This means that environmental influences on performance, not controllable by plan participants, should be factored out when identifying incentive levels.

3. *Sharing the gains: split between management and workers.* Part of the plan must address the relative cuts between management and workers of any profit or savings generated. This also includes discussion of whether an emergency reserve (gains withheld from distribution in case of future emergencies) will be established in advance of any sharing of profits.

4. *Scope of the formula.* Formulas can vary in the scope of inclusions for both the labor inputs in the numerator and productivity outcomes in the denominator.[49] For example, the standard could be as narrowly defined as reducing labor costs or it could incorporate a wide range of alternative organizational goals. Efforts to improve quality could be reinforced by focusing on reductions in customer complaints, increases in market share, or some other measure selected to reflect management concerns. Great care must be exercised, though, to ensure that the behaviors reinforced actually affect the desired bottom line goal. Getting workers to expend more effort, for example, might not always be the desired behavior. Increased effort may bring unacceptable levels of accidents. Or it may even be preferable to encourage cooperative planning behaviors that result in smarter, rather than harder, work.

5. *Perceived fairness of the formula.* Not all incentive systems cover all employees in a firm.[50] In fact it is common to limit eligibility to individuals in key positions whose income exceeds certain minimum standards.[51] When multiple plans are implemented

[47]Rich and Larson, "Why Some Long Term Incentives Fail."

[48]Patton, "Why Incentive Plans Fail."

[49]Newman, "Selecting Incentive Plans to Complement Organizational Strategy."

[50]John Belcher, "Design Options for Gain Sharing," American Productivity Center, unpublished paper, 1987.

[51]Ellig, "Incentive Plans: Short Term Design Issues."

EXHIBIT 10.12
Determinants of a Successful Gain-Sharing Plan

Factor	What the Best Companies Do	What the Rest Do
Eligibility	To be eligible a person must impact on some measurable factor of importance to the company	Based on job level
Compensation Mix	At risk is larger percentage of total pay with 200–300% of base pay typical	At risk pay is no more than 100% of base pay
Basis of reward formula	Performance	More attuned to what competitors give than any measure of performance
Time period	Plan length geared to time necessary to achieve objectives	Calendar or fiscal year yardstick
Distribution of rewards	20% receive no award 20% receive minimum 20% receive more than minimum but less than maximum 40% receive fully competitive cash incentive	Many more receive maximum award

Source: Adapted from J. Schuster and P. Zingheim, "Designing Incentives for Top Financial Performance," *Compensation and Benefits Review*, 1986, 18(3), 39–48.

that cover different groups of employees and have different goals, coordination to ensure equity becomes increasingly important.

6. *Ease of administration.* Sophisticated plans with involved calculations of profits or costs can become too complex for existing company information systems. Increased complexities also require more effective communications and higher levels of trust among participants.

One survey of 50 executives in different companies expresses the "formula" for a successful gain sharing plan in slightly different terms.[52] Exhibit 10.12 illustrates these "ingredients."

Exhibit 10.13 illustrates three different formulas that can be used as the basis for gain-sharing plans. The numerator, or input factor, is always some labor cost variable, expressed in either dollars or actual hours worked. Similarly, the denominator is some output measure such as net sales or value added. Each of the plans determines employees' incentive based on the difference between the current value of the ratio and the ratio in some agreed-upon base year. The more favorable the current ratio relative to historical standard, the larger the incentive award.[53] The three primary types of gain-sharing plans,

---

[52]Jay Schuster and Patricia Zingheim, "Designing Incentives for Top Financial Performance," *Compensation and Benefits Review* 18(3) (1986), pp. 39–48.

[53]Newman, "Selecting Incentive Plans to Complement Organizational Strategy."

EXHIBIT 10.13
Three Gain-Sharing Formulas

	Scanlon plan (single ratio variant)	Rucker plan	Improshare
Numerator of ratio (input factor)	Payroll costs	Labor cost	Actual hours worked
Denominator of ratio (outcome factor)	Net sales (plus or minus inventories)	Value added	Total standard value hours

Adapted from M. Bazerman and B. Graham-Moore, "P.G. Formulas: Developing a Reward Structure to Achieve Organizational Goals," in *Productivity Gainsharing*, ed. B. Graham-Moore and T. Ross (Englewood Cliffs, N.J.: Prentice-Hall, 1983).

differentiated by their focus on either cost savings (the numerator of the equation) or some measure of profits (the denominator of the equation), are noted below.

Cost Savings Plans

Scanlon plan. Scanlon plans are designed to lower labor costs without lowering the level of a firm's activity. Incentives are derived as a function of the ratio between labor costs and sales value of production (SVOP).[54] The SVOP includes sales revenue and the value of goods in inventory. To illustrate how these two figures are used to derive incentives under a Scanlon plan, consider Exhibit 10.14.

Rucker plan. The Rucker plan involves a somewhat more complex formula than a Scanlon plan for determining worker incentive bonuses. Essentially, a ratio is calculated that expresses the value of production required for each dollar of total wage bill. Consider the following illustration.[55]

1. Assume accounting records show the company put $.60 worth of electricity, materials, supplies, and so on into production, to produce $1.00 worth of product. The value added is $.40 for each $1.00 of sales value. Assume also that records show that 45 percent of the value added was attributable to labor; a productivity ratio (PR) can be allocated from the formula:
2. PR $\times$ 45% = 1.00. Solving yields PR = 2.22.
3. If the wage bill equals $100,000, the *expected* production value is the wage bill ($100,000) $\times$ PR (2.22) = $222,222.22.
4. If *actual* production value equals $280,000.00, then the savings (actual production value minus expected production value) equals $57,777.78.
5. Since the labor contribution to value added is 45 percent, the bonus to the work force should be .45 $\times$ $57,777.78 = $26,000.00 (rounded).
6. The savings are distributed as an incentive bonus according to a formula: 75 percent of the bonus is distributed to workers immediately and 25 percent is kept as an

---

[54] A. J. Geare, "Productivity from Scanlon Type Plans," *Academy of Management Review* 1, no. 3 (1976), pp. 99–108.

[55] Ibid.

EXHIBIT 10.14
Examples of a Scanlon Plan

1989 Data (base year) for Alcon, Ltd.	
SVOP	= $10,000,000
Total wage bill	= 4,000,000
$\dfrac{\text{Total wage bill}}{\text{SVOP}}$	= 4,000,000 ÷ 10,000,000 = .40 = 40%
Operating month, August 1987	
SVOP	= $950,000
Allowable wage bill	= .40 ($950,000) = $380,000
Actual wage bill (August)	= 330,000
Savings	= 50,000
$50,000 available for distribution as a bonus.	

emergency fund to cover poor months. Any excess in the emergency fund at the end of the year is then distributed to workers.

Implementation of the Scanlon/Rucker Plans

There are two major components vital to the implementation and success of a Rucker- or Scanlon-type plan: 1) a productivity norm and 2) development of effective worker committees. Development of a productivity norm requires both effective measurement of base year data and acceptance by workers and management of this standard for calculating bonus incentives. Effective measurement requires that an organization keep extensive records of historical cost relationships and make them available to workers or union representatives to verify cost accounting figures. Acceptance of these figures, assuming they are accurate, requires that the organization choose a base year that is neither a "boom" nor a "bust" year. The logic is apparent. A boom year would reduce opportunities for workers to collect bonus incentives, and a bust year would lead to excessive bonus costs for the firm. The base year chosen also should be fairly recent, allaying worker fears that changes in technology or other factors would make the base year unrepresentative of a given operational year.

The second ingredient of Scanlon/Rucker plans is a series of worker committees (also known as productivity committees or bonus committees). The primary function of these committees is to evaluate employee and management suggestions for ways to improve productivity and/or cut costs. Operating on a plantwide basis in smaller firms, or a departmental basis in larger firms, these committees have been highly successful in eliciting suggestions from employees. It is not uncommon for the suggestion rate to be above that found in companies with standard suggestion incentive plans.[56]

It is this climate the Scanlon/Rucker plans foster that is perhaps the most vital element of success. Numerous authors have pointed out that these plans have the best chance for

---

[56]Ibid.

success in companies with competent supervision, cooperative union-management attitudes, strong top management interest and participation in the development of the program,
and management open to criticism and willing to discuss different operating strategies.
It is beyond the scope of this discussion to outline specific strategies adopted by companies
to achieve this climate, but the key element is a belief that workers should play a vital
role in the decision-making process.

Similarities and Contrasts between Scanlon and Rucker Plans

Scanlon and Rucker plans differ from individual incentive plans in their primary focus.
Individual incentive plans focus primarily on using wage incentives to motivate higher
performance through increased effort. While this is certainly a goal of the Scanlon/Rucker
plans, it is not the major focus of attention. Rather, given that increased output is a
function of group effort, more attention is focused on organizational behavior variables.
The key is to promote faster, more intelligent, and acceptable decisions through participation. This participation is won by developing a group unity in achieving cost savings,
a goal that is not stressed, and often stymied, in individual incentive plans.

Even though Scanlon and Rucker plans share this common attention to groups and
committees through participation as a linking pin, there are two important differences
between the two plans. First, Rucker plans tie incentives to a wide variety of savings,
not just the labor savings focused on in Scanlon plans.[57] Second, this greater flexibility
may help explain why Rucker plans are more amenable to linkages with individual
incentive plans.

Improshare

Improshare (IMproved PROductivity through SHARing) is a relatively new gain-sharing
plan that has proven easy to administer and to communicate.[58]

First, a standard is developed that identifies the expected hours required to produce
an acceptable level of output. This standard comes either from time and motion studies
conducted by industrial engineers or from a base period measurement of the performance
factor. Any savings arising from production of agreed-upon output in fewer than expected
hours are shared by the firm and by the worker.[59]

Exhibit 10.15 compares these three types of gain-sharing programs on the five dimensions discussed earlier.[60]

Profit-Sharing Plans

The second general category of group incentive plans includes all profit-sharing plans,
whether the profit shared is distributed currently or deferred until later (typically at

[57]Patten, "Pay: Employee Compensation and Incentive Plans"; Schwinger, *Wage Incentive Plans.*

[58]Graham-Moore et al., *Productivity Gainsharing.*

[59]Newman, "Selecting Incentive Plans to Complement Organizational Strategy."

[60]Ibid.

EXHIBIT 10.15
A Comparison among Gain-Sharing Plans

		Behavioral and Organizational Issues in Choosing a Plan			
	Strength of reinforcement	Scope of formula	Perceived fairness of formulation	Ease of administration	Production variablity
Scanlon	Reinforcement hindered because incentives tied to group performance.	Narrowly concerned with labor costs and sales.	Simplicity of formula and broad base of cooperation yield perception of fairness.	Simplicity makes administration easy.	Rapid peaking of production cycles not easy to deal with.
Rucker	Reinforcement only hindered because incentives tied to group performance.	Even more narrow than Scanlon in that sales value of production is corrected for inflation.	Complexity slightly reduces perceived fairness. Requires somewhat less cooperative effort than Scanlon.	Value added concept and formula exclusions difficult to administer.	Formula for calculating value added specifically deals with changing economic conditions.
Improshare	Reinforcement only hindered because incentives tied to group performance.	Narrow measures of labor hours saved.	Lack of employee involvement in development of plan may reduce perceived fairness.	Simplicity makes administration easy.	Management must closely monitor inventory to ensure variability in economic conditions is reflected in production changes.

retirement, disability, severance, or death).[61] While provisions of the Employee Retirement Income Security Act (ERISA) have taken some of the incentive out of implementing incentive plans, recent estimates still suggest that about 20 percent of the private nonfarm work force receives some kind of profit sharing.[62] In the past three or four years, though, there has been a shift to thrift savings plans (Chapter 12) and away from profit-sharing plans, largely because of the instability of corporate profits. This comes despite some evidence that profit sharing may result in significant performance improvements.[63]

Profit-sharing plans, as is evident from the name, focus on profitability as the standard for group incentives. These plans typically can be found in one of three combinations. First, cash or current distribution plans provide full payment to participants soon after profits have been determined, usually quarterly or annually. As might be expected, the incentive value of profit distribution declines as the time between performance and payoff increases and as the size of the payoff declines relative to previous years. Second, deferred plans have a portion of current profits credited to employee accounts, with cash payment made at time of retirement, disability, severance, or death.[64] Because of certain tax advantages, this is the fastest-growing type of profit-sharing system, with approximately 80 percent of the companies with some form of profit-sharing plans using the deferred option.[65] The median range of profits distributed runs from 14 percent to about 33 percent.[66] Third, combination plans incorporate aspects of both current and deferred options. A portion of profits is immediately distributed to employees with the remaining amount set aside in designated accounts. About 20 percent of all companies with profit-sharing plans have this option.

There are certain similarities between profit-sharing plans and the other group incentive plans discussed. Both types of plans foster a climate where cost-cutting suggestions are more acceptable to employees. Furthermore, both types of plans are designed to pay out incentives when the organization is most able to afford them. However, the similarities end here. While a cash or current distribution plan carries some motivational incentive, thus resembling Scanlon/Rucker plans, deferred-payment plans more closely resemble a pension fund. The incentive value of working to increase current profits when rewards are distributed much later is, at best, minimal. To balance this disadvantage, profit-sharing plans have two distinct advantages. First, they do not require elaborate cost accounting systems to calculate incentives to be allocated to employees. Second, and perhaps more important, profit-sharing plans have been implemented in organizations that cover the entire spectrum in size. Admittedly there are definite tendencies for smaller organizations to opt for a current distribution plan and for larger organizations to choose

[61]Robert McCaffery, *Managing the Employee Benefits Process* (New York: AMACOM, 1983).

[62]Bureau of National Affairs, "Incentive Pay Schemes Seen as a Result of Economic Employee Relation Change," *BNA Daily Report,* October 9 1984, pp. cc-1.

[63]General Accounting Office, "Productivity Sharing Programs: Can They Contribute to Productivity Improvement?" March 31, 1981 (Washington, D.C.: government document).

[64]Schwinger, *Wage Incentive Systems.*

[65]McCaffery, *Managing the Employee Benefits Process.*

[66]Patten, "Pay: Employee Compensation and Incentive Plans"; Schwinger, *Wage Incentive Systems.*

the deferred option, but until there is more evidence that Scanlon/Rucker plans can be adapted successfully to larger organizations, profit-sharing plans seem to represent the major alternative for organizations of any size.

Effectiveness of Gain-Sharing Plans

Although there are many case studies of gain-sharing programs in the literature, very few of them report hard data collected in a well-controlled study. Many of the better studies, however, do report positive results from such plans. The General Accounting Office, for example, interviewed 36 companies with gain-sharing programs. Estimates indicated an average of 17 percent savings from these programs.[67] Perhaps the best study, though, reports an extensive literature search on gain-sharing studies.[68] Of the 33 programs with sufficient detail for comparison, virtually all reported only post hoc analyses; hence it is virtually impossible to make any but the most preliminary conclusions. The data are encouraging, though: (1) some level of productivity increase, rise in quality, or cost reduction was reported by 75 percent of the companies; (2) 75 percent of the companies indicated an increase in ideas, suggestions, and innovations by employees; (3) among participants the programs were generally popular, with 64 percent reporting improved morale or quality of work life; and (4) about 50 percent of the participants reported improved communications, either between superiors and subordinates, labor and management, or both.

Why do gain-sharing programs work? Unfortunately there is almost no information available to answer this question.[69] The most plausible speculation, though, suggests that gain-sharing programs succeed because they change the culture of the firm. Employees at all levels develop a broader perspective about the organization's objectives and greater commitment to achieving them.[70]

REVIEW QUESTIONS

1. What does level of aggregation mean in compensation? How does it relate to development of incentive plans?
2. Given the following information calculate the incentive payout to an employee under a straight piece-rate system and under a Taylor plan for each level of output. At what output level does a worker earn more under the Taylor plan?

    Assume guaranteed minimum wage of $3.75 under **straight piece rate,** none under Taylor.

---

[67]General Accounting Office, "Productivity Sharing Programs: Can They Contribute to Productivity Improvement?"

[68]R. J. Bullock and E. E. Lawler, "Gainsharing: A Few Questions and Fewer Answers," *Human Resource Management* 23, no. 1 (1984), pp. 23–40.

[69]Ibid.

[70]Ibid.

Straight piece rate = 75 cents per unit

Taylor piece rate = 50 cents per unit up to standard, $1.00 per unit if standard is exceeded.

Standard production = 5 units per hour

Don't forget the minimum wage provision!

Worker Output	Earning under straight piece rate	Earnings under Taylor
4 per hour		
5 per hour		
6 per hour		
7 per hour		
8 per hour		

3. How do profit-sharing plans differ from Scanlon/Rucker type plans?
4. What might be the problems in implementing an individual incentive plan in a company with a long history of labor strikes and grievances?

Appendix

Example of an Integrated Incentive Plan (Selected Sections)

J. C. Penney Company
Management Incentive Plan Guide
General Office, Zone, and District Personnel

This material sets forth the principles, policies, and procedure that will guide the administration of the Penney incentive plan for general office, zone, and district management personnel. It is presented in the following sections:

1. Purpose and Philosophy of the Plan.
2. Eligibility for Participation.
3. The Incentive Fund.
4. Distribution of the Incentive Fund.
   a. Allocating Department and Zone Funds.
   b. Determining Individual Awards.
5. Timing and Method of Payment.
6. Summary of Responsibilities for Plan Administration.

PURPOSE AND PHILOSOPHY OF THE PLAN

The purpose of the management incentive plan is to motivate Penney management personnel to increase company profits. In order to achieve this objective, incentive payments will be related directly to company profit performance, department performance, zone performance (where applicable), and individual performance.

The philosophy underlying the plan recognizes that both salary and incentive payments play a part in providing recognition and rewards that help motivate individual performance. However, incentive payments differ from salaries in two respects. One is that incentive payments are one-time, rather than continuing, payments. A second is that incentive payments are related directly to profits, whereas salaries are related to the long-term value of the job as performed by the incumbent. Because of these differences in the characteristics of these two forms of compensation, there will be differences in the way they are administered.

Some of the more important differences resulting from the one-time character of incentive payments are the following:

1. Incentive payments will tend to reflect company and individual performance in the year just ended; while salary payments, since they are the cumulative result of successive salary reviews, will reflect performance over a longer period of time.
2. Incentive payments can be used with more flexibility than salary adjustments to reward outstanding performance. This is primarily because the company can grant an unusually large incentive award in one year without committing itself to higher compensation costs in future years.
3. Incentive payments can be used to penalize as well as to reward. While salaries customarily move upward only, incentive awards may be reduced from one year to the next either because of lower company profits or because of poorer individual performance.

The second major distinction between incentive payments and salary adjustments lies in the relationship to company profits. Salaries are related to company profits only remotely. With incentive payments there is a direct, immediate relationship. This relationship has been established to motivate all Penney associates who influence company profits significantly to make a maximum contribution toward this key objective.

The greater an individual's opportunity to influence company profits, the more logical it is that he should have an important stake in those profits. Hence the proportion of total compensation paid in the form of incentive award, rather than salary, will be greatest for those associates with greatest degree of responsibility for company profits. Consequently, changes in company profits will have a more pronounced effect on the total compensation of higher level executives than on the compensation of those at lower levels.

It has been traditional in the Penney Company to place heavy emphasis on relating individual compensation to profits—store profits in the case of store management, and company profits in the case of general management. The salary portion of total compensation traditionally has been relatively modest. Despite the rise in salary levels under the new salary plan, the spirit of this tradition will be continued in order to maintain management incentive to build profits. Consequently, salaries, particularly for higher level positions, will be lower than salaries paid by other companies for comparable positions, and incentive awards (at least in reasonably good profit years) will be larger than those paid by other companies.

ELIGIBILITY FOR PARTICIPATION

Eligibility for the management incentive plan is limited to those associates whose responsibilities are such that they make a significant impact on company profits, either long term, short term, or both. Eligibility shall be determined by analysis of each Penney associate's opportunity to contribute to profits. Since position grades in the salary structure reflect the relative worth of positions, they serve as a useful point of departure for determining eligibility. However, they shall not be applied automatically but shall be used as a general guide.

Eligibility shall begin at a lower level in the salary structure for zone and district positions than for general office positions. The reason is that transfers between zone and district positions and store positions can be made more easily if the compensation patterns for these two groups are compatible. Incentive payments for store personnel begin at a relatively low total compensation level (and rightly so, because these incentive payments are based on profits or sales at the store level); whereas incentive payments for general office personnel are applied only to those at higher compensation levels with an opportunity to influence company profits (because these incentive payments are related to company profits). Thus, if zone and district eligibility did not begin well below the compensation level required among the general office group, transfers between store positions and zone and district positions would require unusually large salary adjustments.

To determine eligibility, the following ground rules shall be applied in each area of operations.

For the general office, the plan shall include all associates who are classified in grade 10 and above, plus selected associates whose positions are in grade 9. Corporate department heads shall review the performance of associates in grade 9 annually and nominate for eligibility in the coming year those whose performance is considered superior. These nominations shall be subject to review and approval by the Pay Administration Committee.

For zone and district positions, the plan shall include all associates who are classified in grade 7 and above, plus selected associates from grade 6. Zone managers shall review performance of associates in grade 6 annually and nominate for eligibility in the coming year those whose performance is considered superior. These nominations shall be subject to review and approval by the director of store operations and the Pay Administration Committee.

From time to time, the board of directors may wish to grant special awards for outstanding accomplishments to associates who are not eligible for regular incentive payments. Such special awards shall not be taken from the management incentive fund.

THE INCENTIVE FUND

In order to relate incentive awards to company profits, all awards shall be paid from a fund generated by company profits. The amount of this incentive fund for any year shall be determined by the following formula: 5 percent of net profits before deducting federal taxes and before deducting the incentive fund itself, but after deducting 10 percent of invested capital (total shareholders' equity plus any long-term debt).

For example, using the appropriate figures for 1960, the incentive fund calculation would be:

Net profits before deducting federal taxes and incentive fund.	$97,425,000
10 percent of invested capital (shareholders' equity only, since there was no long-term debt).	− 30,825,000
	$66,600,000
	× 5%
Incentive fund.	$ 3,330,000

If we assume that net profits before deducting federal taxes and the incentive fund increase to $110,000,000 and that invested capital increases to $400,000,000, the calculations would be:

Net profits before deducting federal taxes and incentive fund.	$110,000,000
10 percent of invested capital.	$-40,000,000$
	$\overline{\$\ 70,000,000}$
	$\times\ 5\%$
Incentive fund.	$\overline{\$\ \ \ 3,500,000}$

Thus, when company profits increase by more than 10 percent of any additional invested capital, the fund will increase; when company profits do not increase as much as 10 percent of added invested capital, the fund will decrease.

The provision for a deduction or "set-aside" of 10 percent of invested capital accomplishes two purposes:

1. It ensures that the fund will increase only if the company earns at least a reasonably good return on any increased capital investment. (A 10 percent before-tax return can be considered "reasonably good" in today's investment market.) It thus helps focus attention on protection of the shareholders' interests.

2. It maximizes the impact of profit on the fund, hence emphasizes the need for building profits.

In order to ensure that individual incentive payments are directly related to company profit performance, substantially all of the fund generated in one year shall be distributed at the close of that year. No reserve shall be established to even out the effect of good and poor profit years, nor shall any ceiling be established on the size of the fund. (However, company directors have the authority to reduce an unreasonably large fund.)

Although care has been taken to develop an incentive fund formula that minimizes the need for future change, it is possible that unforeseen changes in conditions will necessitate such a change. It shall be the responsibility of the Board Management Compensation Committee to review the fund formula annually, with the assistance of the comptroller and manager of pay administration, and to decide on any changes that are needed.

DISTRIBUTION OF THE INCENTIVE FUND

The intent in distributing the incentive fund is to provide appropriate recognition for both individual and group performance. Group performance at the overall company level is recognized by the fact that the size of the fund itself depends on company profit performance. Group performance at the general office and zone levels is recognized by allocating the fund among general office departments and the zones (including districts) on a basis that takes the performance of each group into account. Individual performance is recognized by determining the portion of the department or zone allocation to be awarded to plan participants on the basis of their individual performance.

Compensation Application
Assessing the Environment for Developing an Incentive Plan

Tasks

1. Identify an organization for which you can get reasonably thorough information about products, methods of production, nature and extent of competition, morale of workers, and attitude of company toward workers. Your information source might be: (a) yourself in past or current jobs, (b) a friend or relative, (c) classmates.
2. Develop a structured interview questionnaire outlining the questions that you think need to be asked to assess whether your company could benefit from an incentive system. Be sure that your questions cover all the areas of concern noted in Chapter 10 of your text.
3. Which type of incentive or gain-sharing plan do you think would be most effective in your organization? Extensively document your position. If no incentive system would be appropriate, also defend your position.

Compensation Application
"The Ratebusters"

Carlisle Controls manufactures small servocontrol valves used in aircraft of all kinds, including space shuttles regularly sent into orbit. About 75 percent of Carlisle's business comes from government contracts. To win these contracts Carlisle must bid lower (among other requirements) than other competitors. Up until five years ago this wasn't difficult. Carlisle had no competitors! At that time, though, a patent on the valve ran out and a number of other organizations began machining these parts. To reduce labor costs, Carlisle implemented an incentive system based on the following rate schedule:

Number Valves Machined per Hour*	Payment Schedule
10	$ .60 per valve
11–20	.80 per valve
21 +	1.00 per valve

*Counted only if 0 defects.

Of the 10 machinists operating on this schedule, 9 produce an average of 12 valves per hour. Rarely does this group turn out less than 10 valves or more than 15 in an hour. The 10th machinist is an exception. He regularly machines between 23 and 25 valves per hour.

According to an industrial engineering consultant that Carlisle hired last year, the separate motions involved in machining a valve require 2.5 minutes. With allowances for fatigue and personal needs each valve could be machined in three minutes by a trained machinist working under normal conditions.

Role for Alan Young

You are 29 years old, married, and have two children. Six months ago your mother-in-law moved in with your family. Since you believe very strongly in the family unit, you are happy to have her; but the extra financial burden has been difficult to bear. To meet the extra costs you have been working especially hard to turn out more valves and earn a higher incentive. In the past you have always tried to produce around 18–20 valves an hour. The guys have kidded you about being a ratebuster, but it just seemed like good-natured jibes. Now you are turning out 25 valves during a good hour. You've always been good with machines, plus you know a few tricks to cut down the number of movements needed to machine a valve. Sure you have to press to turn out the last three in an hour, but it's worth it to know your family has a comfortable income.

Lately you have noticed the other machinists don't seem to be as friendly. There have even been occasional flashes of anger when one or two guys have noticed how many valves you were finishing. It's now to the point where George King wants to talk to you. George is one of the machinists you like; but if he tries to pressure you to reduce your output . . . well he can go stuff it.

Role for George King

You have been with Carlisle for 15 years now, second highest seniority in the department. You think Carlisle is a good place to work. They try to look after their people. The only time Carlisle hasn't done right by you was during the last big slump in the aerospace industry. All but three machinists in your department were laid off that time. You're determined you won't go through another stretch of unemployment like that again. Eighteen months without a job almost made you an alcoholic and destroyed your marriage. You've got everything back together again and nothing is going to mess things up.

The guys you work with are all pretty straight; all except Al Young, that is. He's always been a bit of a maverick. Most of the guys have agreed to hold production to 15 or less pieces. Who cares what that industrial engineer said was possible. It is too tough to turn out 20 pieces every hour. Besides, if everyone increases their output, what's to stop Carlisle from getting rid of some of the guys. It just isn't worth it. Now all of a sudden Al Young is turning out as many as 25 pieces an hour. The guys tolerated it when he did 20 pieces an hour, but now he's rubbing your nose in it. It's time to set that guy straight. In fact, maybe you'll just go see him now.

Students will play the roles of George King and Alan Young. Each will rationalize his position. Their meeting should address the following issues.

1. Given your understanding of corporate America, are George King's concerns legitimate?
2. What might Carlisle do to reduce the existing tension between Alan and the rest of the group?
3. How do you think an industrial engineer establishes productivity standards? How might these standards be flawed?

Compensation Application
Minnesota Electric

Minnesota Electric makes lamps for residential customers and high intensity bulbs for commercial use. The industry is quite competitive, with foreign manufacturers claiming 40 percent of the market. Profits and sales have risen in all but six of the years since the company was founded in 1958. All six years shared one common attribute: new housing sales were at record lows. Eighty percent of Minnesota Electric's market is in furnishing fixtures for new homes.

Minnesota Electric is viewed as a good company to work for. They believe strongly in employee participation and in the basic dignity of workers. This attitude is reflected in the successful operation of quality circles, the continuing presence of highly effective suggestion plans, and the general high morale of employees. Further evidence of this commitment to its employees is Minnesota Electric's reluctance to reduce its work force when demand drops. In fact, there have been no general work force reductions in 22 years. Reductions in overtime have generally been sufficient reaction to decreased demand.

You have the following information about Minnesota Electric:

	1984	1985	1986	1987	1988
Sales value of production (SVOP)	$15,000,000	$17,500,000	$19,000,000	$16,000,000	*
Total wage bill	5,000,000	6,000,000	9,000,000	8,000,000	*

	Current Operating Month, January 1990
Sales value of production	$1,500,000
Wage bill	666,666

*Data available in four weeks. Changeover to new computer system delayed output.

Minnesota Electric has decided to implement a Scanlon Plan for the 610 workers in its New Brighton, Minnesota, plant. Given the above information and your knowledge of Scanlon Plans (and incentive systems in general) from the text, design a Scanlon Plan and determine the bonus to be distributed as of the coming January. At a minimum your plan should include:

1. An implementation strategy, including specific communication tools.
2. Development of a target standard against which current wages and SVOP can be compared. This should include justification for which historical data is used and why.

Part

The area of employee benefits represents more of a mystery than any other covered thus far in this book. The reason is simple. Benefit practices today frequently are based on faith rather than facts. Consider, for example, the compensation objectives noted in the pay model, Exhibit IV.1.

Does effective employee benefits administration facilitate organization performance? Or do employee benefits impact upon an organization's ability to attract, retain, and motivate employees? Conventional wisdom says employee benefits can affect retention, but there is little research to support this conclusion. A similar lack of research surrounds each of the other potential payoffs to a sound benefits program.

Is it any wonder, then, why firms are becoming increasingly concerned about the steadily rising cost of benefits? They represent a labor cost with no apparent returns.

Balanced against this is the perception of employee benefits as an entitlement. Employees believe they are entitled to continued benefits as a term of employment. Efforts to reduce benefit levels or eliminate parts of the package altogether would meet with employee resistance and dissatisfaction.

Somewhere between these two perspectives is the probable truth about employee benefits. Operating on this assumption, this part of the book takes the perspective that organizations must control costs of benefits wherever possible and increasingly seek ways to maximize the returns from benefit expenditures. As a first step in this direction, Chapter 11 identifies issues that organizations should face in developing and maintaining a benefits program. A model of the benefits determination process also is presented to provide a structure for thinking about employee benefits.

Chapter 12 provides a summary of the state of employee benefits today. Hopefully this will provide the groundwork for the innovative and effective benefit packages of tomorrow.

Employee Benefits

EXHIBIT IV.1
The Pay Model

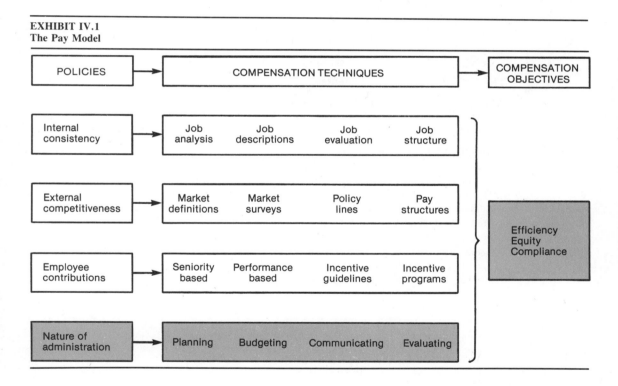

| POLICIES | → | COMPENSATION TECHNIQUES | → | COMPENSATION OBJECTIVES |

Internal consistency → Job analysis · Job descriptions · Job evaluation · Job structure

External competitiveness → Market definitions · Market surveys · Policy lines · Pay structures

Employee contributions → Seniority based · Performance based · Incentive guidelines · Incentive programs

Nature of administration → Planning · Budgeting · Communicating · Evaluating

Efficiency
Equity
Compliance

363

The Benefits Determination Process

Item 1: Oneida silversmith employees can rent, at reduced rates, cottages and campsites on company-owned property on New York's Lake Oneida.[1]

Item 2: Ingersoll Rand Company, Woodcliffe Lake, N.J., lets staffers plant gardens on its grounds and even plows, fertilizes, and waters the plots.[2]

---

[1]Andrea Stone, "Innovative Benefit Programs Perk Up," *USA Today*, January 31, 1986, p. 30.

[2]*The Wall Street Journal*, June 10, 1980, p. 1.

Item 3: Other benefits from assorted companies: Hypnosis cure for smoking; tear gas classes; weekly barbecue; high school graduation gift; on-site barber shop; on-site department store; company pro shop.[3]

Item 4: Half of payroll costs may go for employee benefits by decade's end, up from 37 percent currently, some consultants predict.[4]

Are items 1–3 isolated cases of liberal employee benefits, or do they foreshadow a reality predicted by the doomsayers in item 4. How can employee benefits expand this rapidly, especially when we compare with the following brief chronicle of "benefits" of the past.[5]

- A carriage shop published a set of rules for employees in 1880 that stated, in part: "Working hours shall be from 7 A.M. to 9 P.M. every day except the Sabbath. . . . After an employee has been with this firm for five years he shall receive an added payment of five cents per day, provided the firm has prospered in a manner to make it possible. . . . It is the bounden duty of each employee to put away at least 10 percent of his monthly wages for his declining years so he will not become a burden upon his betters."
- In 1915, employees in the iron and steel industry worked a standard 60 to 64 hours per week. By 1930 that schedule had been reduced to 54 hours.
- It was not until 1929 that the Blue Cross concept of prepaid medical costs was introduced.
- Prior to 1935 only one state (Wisconsin) had a program of unemployment compensation benefits for workers who lost their jobs through no fault of their own.
- Before World War II very few companies paid hourly employees for holidays. In most companies employees were told not to report for work on holidays and to enjoy the time off, but their paychecks were smaller the following week.

In comparison to these benefits from the past, today's reality seems staggering. Although esoteric benefits are the rarity, private sector organizations still expend on average $10,708 per employee on benefits costs (1987), up from $7,000 in 1983.[6]

---

[3]Hewitt Associates. "Innovative Benefits" (Lincolnshire. Ill.: Hewitt Associates. 1982).

[4]*The Wall Street Journal.* June 10, 1980, p. 1.

[5]Robert W. McCaffery. *Managing the Employee Benefits Program* (New York: American Management Association. 1972).

[6]U.S. Chamber of Commerce. *Employee Benefits, 1983* (Washington, D.C.: U.S. Chamber of Commerce. 1984); and U.S. Chamber of Commerce. *Employee Benefits, 1988.* (Washington, D.C.: U.S. Chamber of Commerce. 1988).

> **Employee benefits—that part of the total compensation package, other than pay for time worked, provided to employees in whole or in part by employer payments (e.g., life insurance, pension, workers' compensation, vacation).**

Employee benefits can no longer realistically be called "fringe benefits." Benefits represent an ever escalating percentage of total payroll, as illustrated in Exhibit 11.1.[7]

Around these average figures there is considerable variation by industry. The clothing industry is on the low end, paying benefits averaging only 28.5 percent of payroll; and the primary metals industry is on the high end, with benefits averaging 54.2 percent of payroll (1987).[8] By any standard, though, benefits represent a huge cost for the private sector. Costs were in excess of 813 billion dollars in 1987 alone![9] As a more tangible example of the cost to industry, General Motors estimates that it pays more for employee medical benefits alone than it does for all the steel necessary to produce its yearly output of automobiles![10]

Probably the most important statistic in Exhibit 11.1 is the trend shown in cost of benefits. Benefits rose from 25 percent of payroll in 1959 to 39 percent of payroll in 1987. Over one 20-year period (1955–1975) employee benefit costs rose at a rate almost four times greater than employee wages or the consumer price index.[11] A similar comparison for the period 1963-1987 shows the rate of growth has slowed (benefit costs rose twice as fast as wage costs), but organizations still express extreme concern for controlling the cost of benefits.[12] Experts agree that this concern is legitimate, and the problem is only expected to get worse. The aging of the workforce alone is expected to dramatically increase both pension and health care costs for companies.[13] Before exploring ways to rationally plan and administer benefits programs in a cost effective manner, the next section outlines reasons for this growth in employee benefits.

---

[7]U.S. Chamber of Commerce, *Employee Benefits, 1980* (Washington, D.C.: U.S. Chamber of Commerce, 1981); and U.S. Chamber of Commerce, *Employee Benefits, 1988,* (Washington, D.C.: U.S. Chamber of Commerce, 1988).

[8]U.S. Chamber of Commerce, *Employee Benefits, 1988* (Washington, D.C.: U.S. Chamber of Commerce, 1988).

[9]Ibid.

[10]Hallie Kintner and Ernest B. Smith, "General Motors Provides Health Care Benefits to Millions," *American Demographics,* May 1987, pp. 44–45.

[11]John Hanna, "Can the Challenge of Escalating Benefits Costs Be Met?" *Personnel Administration* 27, no. 9 (1977), pp. 50–57.

[12]U.S. Chamber of Commerce, *Employee Benefits, 1988* (Washington, D.C.: U.S. Chamber of Commerce, 1988).

[13]Kintner and Smith, "General Motors Provide Health Care Benefits to Millions"; Health Research Institute, "1985 Health Care Cost Containment Survey," (Walnut Creek, Calif.: Health Research Institute).

EXHIBIT 11.1
Changes in Benefit Costs: 1959, 1969, 1987

	1959	*1969*	*1987**
Percentage of payroll (total)	24.7	31.1	39.0
Legally required benefits	3.5	5.3	9.0
Pension, insurance, and other agreed-upon payments	8.5	10.4	15.2
Rest periods and lunch breaks	2.2	3.1	2.7
Payment for time not worked (holidays, vacations, etc.)	8.4	10.1	11.0
Miscellaneous	2.1	2.2	1.1

*Percentage of payroll
Source: Adapted from U.S. Chamber of Commerce Annual Benefits Surveys.

WHY THE GROWTH IN EMPLOYEE BENEFITS?

Wage and Price Controls

During both World War II and the Korean War the federal government instituted strict wage and price controls. The compliance agency charged with enforcing these controls was relatively lenient in permitting reasonable increases in benefits. With strict limitations on the size of wage increases, both unions and employers sought new and improved benefits to satisfy worker demands.

Unions

The climate fostered by wage and price controls created a perfect opportunity for unions to flex the muscles they had recently acquired under the Wagner Act of 1935. Several National Labor Relations Board rulings during the 1940s conferred legitimacy upon negotiations over employee benefits. Absent the leverage to raise wages very much, unions fought for the introduction of new benefits and the improvement of existing benefits. Success on this front during the war years led to further postwar demands. Largely through the efforts of unions, most notably the auto and steelworkers, several benefits common today were given their initial impetus: pattern pension plans, supplementary unemployment compensation, extended vacation plans, and guaranteed annual wage plans.[14]

Employer Impetus

It would be a mistake to assume that the war years provided the only incentive fostering a receptive benefits climate. In fact, many of the benefits in existence today were provided at employer initiative. Much of this employer receptivity can be traced to pragmatic

---

[14]McCaffery, *Managing the Employee Benefits Program.*

concerns about employee satisfaction and productivity. Rest breaks were often implemented in the belief that fatigue increased accidents and lowered productivity. Savings and profit-sharing plans (e.g., Procter & Gamble's profit-sharing plan was initiated in 1885) were implemented to improve performance and provide increased security for worker retirement years. Indeed, many employer-initiated benefits were designed to create a climate in which employees perceived that management was genuinely concerned for their welfare.

Cost Effectiveness of Benefits

Another important impetus for the growth of employee benefits is their cost effectiveness in three situations. The first cost advantage is that most employee benefits are not taxable. Provision of a benefit rather than an equivalent increase in wages avoids payment of federal and state personal income tax. Remember, though, recurrent tax reform proposals continue to threaten the favorable tax status granted to many benefits. In the last several years, several standard benefits have had their tax exempt status threatened, including:

1. Portions of employer health contributions.
2. Group life insurance premiums.
3. Dependent life insurance.
4. Educational assistance.
5. Legal services.
6. Cafeteria pay plans.[15]

Already there has been one minor casualty, with the Deficit Reduction Act (Defra) of 1984 limiting the types of benefits that can be included in cafeteria plans (e.g., no parking fees paid, limits on vacation homes). Obviously, taxation of any or all of these benefits would reduce or eliminate their advantage over allocating the corresponding amount to direct wages.

A second cost effectiveness component of benefits arises because many group-based benefits (e.g., life, health, and legal insurance) can be obtained at a lower rate than could be obtained by employees acting on their own. Group insurance also has relatively easy qualification standards, giving security to a set of employees who might not otherwise qualify (e.g., an employee with a heart condition who becomes eligible for group life insurance at a nonprohibitive rate after being denied individual insurance).

Third, a well-developed benefits plan that meets employee needs may yield advantages far beyond the dollar cost. In an economic sense, if the utility of the cash value of a benefit is less than the utility of the benefit itself, the organization is better off providing the benefit.

---

[15]Carson E. Beadle, "Taxing Employee Benefits: The Impact on Employers and Employees," *Compensation Review* 17, no. 2 (1985), pp. 12–19.

Government Impetus

Obviously the government has played an important role in the growth of employee benefits. Three employee benefits are mandated by either the state or federal government: Worker's Compensation (State), Unemployment Insurance (Federal) and Social Security (Federal). In addition, most other employee benefits are affected by such laws as the Employee Retirement Income Security Act (ERISA affects pension administration) and various sections of the Internal Revenue Code. Chapter 12 covers the impact of the government in greater detail.

THE VALUE OF EMPLOYEE BENEFITS

Exhibit 11.2 shows the relative importance attached to different types of benefits across three different studies.[16]

In general the three studies reported in Exhibit 11.2 show fairly consistent results. For example, medical payments are regularly listed as one of the most important benefits employees receive. These rankings have added significance when we note that health care costs are the most rapidly growing and the most difficult to control of all the benefit options offered by employers.[17] In 1988, health care costs alone were estimated at $2,135 per employee.[18]

Given the rapid growth in benefits and the staggering cost implications, it seems only logical that employers would expect to derive commensurate return on this investment. In fact, there is at best only anecdotal evidence that employee benefits are cost justified. This evidence falls into three categories.[19] First, employee benefits are widely claimed to help in the retention of workers. Benefit schedules are specifically designed to favor longer term employees. For example, retirement benefits increase with years of service, and most plans do not provide for full employee eligibility until a specified number of years of service has been reached. Equally, amount of vacation time increases with years

---

[16]This table was compiled from three different sources. Some of the reward components rated in some of the studies were not traditional employee benefits and have been deleted from the rankings here. The three studies were: *Wall Street Journal,* "The Future Look of Employee Benefits," September 8, 1988, p. 23 (Source: Hewitt Associates); Kermit Davis, William Giles, and Hubert Feild, *How Young Professionals Rank Employee Benefits: Two Studies* (Brookfield, Wisc.: International Foundation of Employee Benefit Plans, 1988); and Kenneth Shapiro and Jesse Sherman, "Employee Attitude Benefit Plan Designs," *Personnel Journal,* July 1987, pp. 49–58.

[17]Mary Fruen and Henry DiPrete, "Health Care in the Future" (Boston, Mass.: John Hancock, 1986); HRM Update, "Health Plan Increases" (New York: The Conference Board, May 1988); Kintner and Smith, "General Motors Provides Health Care Benefits to Millions"; Health Research Institute, "1985 Health Care Cost Containment Survey" (Walnut Creek, Calif.: Health Research Institute); and North West National Life Insurance Co., "Ten Ways to Cut Employee Benefit Costs" (1988).

[18]North West National Life Insurance Co., "Ten Ways to Cut Employee Benefit Costs" (1988).

[19]Donald P. Crane, *The Management of Human Resources,* 2nd ed. (Belmont, Calif.: Wadsworth, 1979); Foegen, "Are Escalating Employee Benefits Self-Defeating?" *Pension World* 14, no. 9 (September 1978), pp. 83–84, 86.

EXHIBIT 11.2
Ranking of Different Employee Benefits

	Study		
	1	*2*	*3*
Medical	1	1	3
Pension	2	3	8
Paid vacation and holidays	3	2	X (Not Rated)
Sickness	4	X	5
Dental	5	X	6
Profit sharing	6	X	2
Long-term disability	7	X	7
Life insurance	8	X	4

of service; and finally, employees' savings plans, profit-sharing plans, and stock purchase plans frequently provide for increased participation or benefits as company seniority increases. By tying these benefits to seniority, it is assumed that workers are more reluctant to change jobs.

There is also some research to support this common assumption that benefits increase retention. Two studies uncovered a negative relationship between fringe benefit coverage and job change patterns.[20] Higher benefits reduced mobility. A more detailed follow-up study, though, found only two specific benefits curtailed employee turnover: pensions and medical coverage.[21] Virtually no other employee benefit had a significant impact on turnover.

Employee benefits also are lauded for their presumed impact on employee satisfaction. One survey by the Opinion Research Corporation casts doubt on this claim, though. Between 1970–1984 satisfaction with employee benefits dropped 17 percent.[22] The lowest satisfaction marks go to disability, life, and health insurance.[23] Current estimates indicate only 62 percent of workers have a favorable attitude about their overall benefits package.[24] Why have satisfaction ratings fallen? One view holds that benefits satisfaction falls as cost cutting companies attempt to reduce coverage and also shift more of the costs to employees.[25] A second view is more pessimistic, arguing that benefits plans fail to meet

---

[20]Olivia Mitchell, "Fringe Benefits and Labor Mobility," *Journal of Human Resources* 17, no. 2 (1982), pp. 286–98; and Bradley Schiller and Randal Weiss, "The Impact of Private Pensions on Firm Attachment," *Review of Economics and Statistics* 61, no. 3. (1979), pp. 369–80.

[21]Olivia Mitchell, "Fringe Benefits and the Cost of Changing Jobs," *Industrial and Labor Relations Review* 37, no. 1 (1983), pp. 70–78.

[22]Employee Benefit Research Institute, ed., *America in Transition: Benefits for the Future* (Washington, D.C.: EBRI, 1987).

[23]*The Wall Street Journal,* April 30 1985, p. 1.

[24]Kenneth P. Shapiro and Jesse A. Sherman, "Employee Attitudes Benefit Plan Designs," *Personnel Journal,* July 1987, pp. 49–53.

[25]George Dreher, Ronald Ash, and Robert Bretz, "Benefit Coverage and Employee Cost: Critical Factors in Explaining Compensation Satisfaction," *Personnel Psychology* 41, no. 2 (1988), pp. 237–254.

either employer or employee needs. In this view simply pumping more money into benefits is inappropriate. Rather, employers must make fundamental changes in the way they approach the benefits planning process. Companies must realize that declining satisfaction with benefits is a result of long term changes in the work force. Ever-increasing numbers of women in the labor force, coupled with increasing numbers of dual career families and higher educational attainments, suggest changing values of employees.[26] Changing values, in turn, necessitate a reevaluation of benefits packages.

Finally, employee benefits are also valued because improved retention and increased satisfaction will, some organizations hope, have bottom line effects on profitability. This is consistent with the old adage: "A happy worker is a productive worker."

Unfortunately the research supporting these declarations is relatively scant, particularly in relation to the huge costs incurred in the name of employee benefits. Further cause for pessimism comes from several studies indicating employees are not aware of, or undervalue, the benefits provided by their organization. For example, in one study employees were asked to recall the benefits they received. The typical employee could recall less than 15 percent of them. In another study with a somewhat different approach, MBA students were asked to rank-order the importance attached to various factors influencing job selection.[27] Presumably the large percentage of labor costs allocated to payment of employee benefits would be justified if benefits turned out to be an important factor in attracting good MBA candidates. Of the six factors ranked, employee benefits received the lowest ranking. Opportunity for advancement (1), salary (2), and geographic location (3) all ranked considerably higher than benefits as factors influencing job selection. Compounding this problem, these students also underestimated the percentage of payroll spent on employee benefits. Slightly less than one half (46 percent) of the students thought that benefits comprised 15 percent or less of payroll. Nine out of 10 students (89 percent) thought benefits accounted for less than 30 percent of payroll. Only 1 in 10 students had a reasonably accurate (39 percent of payroll) or inflated perception of the magnitude of employee benefits.[28]

The ignorance about the value of employee benefits inferred from these studies can be traced to both attitudinal and design problems. Looming largest is the attitude problem. Benefits are taken for granted. Employees view them as a right with little comprehension of, or concern for, employer costs.[29]

One possible salvation from this money pit comes from recent reports that employees are not necessarily looking for more benefits but rather greater choice in the benefits they receive.[30] In fact, up to 70 percent of employees in one study indicated they would be

---

[26]Ibid.

[27]Richard Huseman, John Hatfield, and Richard Robinson, "The MBA and Fringe Benefits," *Personnel Administration* 23, no. 7 (1978), pp. 57–60.

[28]Ibid.

[29]Foegen, "Are Escalating Employee Benefits Self-Defeating?"

[30]Employee Benefit Research Institute, ed., *America in Transition: Benefits for the Future* (Washington, D.C.: EBRI, 1987).

willing to pay more out of pocket for benefits if they were granted greater choice in designing their own benefits package. Maybe better benefits planning, design, and administration offer an opportunity to improve benefits effectiveness.

KEY ISSUES IN BENEFITS PLANNING, DESIGNING AND ADMINISTRATION

Benefits Planning and Design Issues

First, and foremost, the components of a benefits plan should complement the remainder of the compensation program.[31] For example, if a major compensation objective is to attract good employees, the benefits program would be designed with this in mind. Benefits would be designed with rapid, or instant, eligibility provisions and attractive vesting requirements. Conversely, an organization with a turnover problem might choose to design a benefits package that improves progressively with seniority, thus providing a reward for continuing service.

Second, the benefits plan should be competitive, adequate, and cost effective. To be competitive, an employer might establish an objective that the overall value of a benefits package would be comparable to that of designated firms in a benefits survey. To be adequate, however, more subjective evaluations come into play. Most organizations evaluating adequacy consider the financial liability of employees with and without a particular benefit (e.g., employee medical expenses with and without medical expenses benefits). There is no magic formula for defining benefits adequacy.[32] In part, the answer may lie in the relationship between benefits adequacy and the third plan objective: cost effectiveness. More organizations need to consider whether employee benefits are cost justified. Consider, for example, the health care area. There was a 93 percent increase in health care prices between 1973 and 1980. Health care increases continue to exceed other cost increases. The end result is higher deductibles and greater sharing of premium payments with employees. At the extreme, some experts have even suggested limiting health coverage solely to catastrophic illness. Any cost savings would then be shared with employees. Such cost-benefit analyses must become a stronger feature in both planning and administration of benefits.

Benefits Administration Issues

Three major administration issues arise in setting up a benefits package: (1) Who should be protected or benefitted? (2) How much choice should employees have among an array of benefits? (3) How should benefits be financed?[33]

Every organization has a variety of employees with different employment statuses.

---

[31]Jerry Rosenbloom and G. Victor Hallman, *Employee Benefit Planning* (Englewood Cliffs, N.J.: Prentice-Hall, 1981).

[32]M. Meyer, *Profile of Employee Benefits* (New York: The Conference Board, Report no. 813, 1981), p.2.

[33]Rosenbloom and Hallman, *Employee Benefit Planning*, pp. 427–31.

EXHIBIT 11.3
Benefits Comparison: Part-timers versus Full-timers

	Percent of Firms Giving Benefits to	
Benefit	Part-timers	Full-timers
All benefits	14.6	100
Health	21.2	99
Retirement	29.8	86
Vacation	33.6	95

Source: U.S. Chamber of Commerce, Employee Benefits 1988. Reprinted by permission.

Should these individuals be treated equally with respect to benefits coverage? Exhibit 11.3 illustrates that companies do indeed differentiate treatment based on employment status. Part-timers receive, proportionately, far fewer benefits than full-time employees.

As a second example, should retired automobile executives be permitted to continue purchasing cars at a discount price, a benefit that could be reserved solely for current employees? In fact, a whole series of questions need to be answered:

1. What probationary periods (for eligibility of benefits) should be used for various types of benefits? Does the employer want to cover employees and their dependents more or less immediately upon employment or provide such coverage for employees who have established more or less "permanent" employment with the employer? Is there a rationale for different probationary periods with different benefits?
2. Which dependents of active employees should be covered?
3. Should retirees (as well as their spouses and perhaps other dependents) be covered, and for which benefits?
4. Should survivors of deceased active employees (and/or retirees) be covered? And if so, for which benefits? Are benefits for surviving spouses appropriate?
5. What coverage, if any, should be extended to employees who are suffering from disabilities?
6. What coverage, if any, should be extended to employees during layoff, leaves of absence, strikes, and so forth?
7. Should coverage be limited to full-time employees?[34]

The answers to these questions depend on the policy decisions regarding adequacy, competition, and cost effectiveness discussed in the last section.

The second administrative issue concerns choice (flexibility) in plan coverage. In the standard benefits package employees typically have not been offered a choice among employee benefits. Rather, a package is designed with the "average" employee in mind and any deviations in needs simply go unsatisfied. The other extreme (discussed in greater detail later) is represented by "cafeteria-style" plans. Under this concept employees are permitted great flexibility in choosing benefits options of greatest value to them. Picture

---

[34]Ibid.

EXHIBIT 11.4
Example of Possible Options in a Flexible Benefits Package

	Package			
	A	*B*	*C*	*D*
Health	No	No	No	Yes
Dental	No	No	No	Yes
Vision	No	Yes	Yes	Yes
Life insurance	1 × AE*	2 × AE	2 × AE	3 × AE
Dependent care	Yes	No	No	No
401 K savings	No	No	No	No
Cash back	Yes	No	No	No

*AE = Average earnings

an individual allotted x dollars walking down a cafeteria line and choosing menu items (benefits) according to their attractiveness and cost. The flexibility in this type of plan permits the structuring of packages with maximum impact on employee needs.[35] Exhibit 11.4 illustrates a typical choice among packages offered to employees under a Flexible Benefits System.

It seems that employers consider the advantages noted in Exhibit 11.5 to far outweigh the disadvantages. A recent survey of 292 organizations reports usage of Flexible Benefits packages by 40 percent of the companies, with another 47 percent voicing plans to introduce such a plan within two years.[36]

Even companies who are not considering a Flexible Benefits Program are offering

EXHIBIT 11.5
Advantages and Disadvantages of Flexible Benefit Programs

Advantages

1. Employees choose packages that best satisfy their unique needs.
2. Flexible benefits help firms meet the *changing* needs of *changing* work force.
3. Increased involvement of employees and families improves understanding of benefits.
4. Flexible plans make introduction of new benefits less costly. The new option is added merely as one among a wide variety of elements from which to choose.
5. Cost containment: Organization sets dollar maximum. Employee chooses within that constraint.

Disadvantages

1. Employees make bad choices and find themselves not covered for predictable emergencies.
2. Administrative burdens and expenses increase.
3. Adverse selection. Employees pick only benefits they will use. The subsequent high benefit utilization increases its cost.
4. Subject to nondiscrimination requirements in Section 125 of the Internal Revenue code.

[35]TPF & C Survey Report, *Flexible Benefit Programs: A Comprehensive Look at Flexible Spending Accounts and Broad-Based Plans* (New York: Towers, Perrin, Forster & Crosby, 1985).

[36]*The Wall Street Journal*, March 19, 1985, p. 1.

EXHIBIT 11.6
Advantages of Different Types of Benefit Financing Plans

Arguments for noncontributory financing:

1. All eligible employees are covered: Under a noncontributory plan, all eligible employees who have completed the probationary period, if any, are covered by the plan. This feature can avoid employee and public relations problems that might arise under a contributory plan. For example, otherwise eligible employees may not elect coverage under a contributory plan and hence, they and/or their dependents may not be covered when a loss or retirement occurs.
2. Tax efficiency: In most cases, employer contributions to an employee benefit plan do not result in current gross income to the covered employees for federal income tax purposes, even though these contributions are normally deductible by the employer as a reasonable and necessary business expense.
3. Group purchasing advantages: To the extent that all eligible employees are covered, as opposed to less than all under a contributory plan, the employer may be able to secure more favorable group rates or other conditions of coverage than would otherwise be the case.
4. Union or collective bargaining pressures: Labor unions generally favor noncontributory plans.
5. Ease and economy of administration: Since payroll deduction is not necessary under a noncontributory plan, benefit and accounting records are easier to maintain.

Arguments for contributory financing:

1. More coverage and/or higher benefits possible: Given a certain level of employer contribution toward the cost of an employee benefit plan, employee contributions may make possible a more adequate plan, or they may enable a plan to be installed in the first place.
2. Possible greater employee appreciation of the plan: When employees contribute to a plan, they will have greater appreciation for the benefits that they are helping to finance. They will not take such benefits for granted.
3. Possible lessening of abuses of benefits: In a vein similar to the previous argument, employees will be less likely to abuse an employee benefit plan if they know that such abuses may increase their own contribution rates.

Arguments for employee-pay-all financing:

1. Separate optional plans may be offered: Some employers offer employees the opportunity of purchasing additional, supplementary coverages at group rates, without individual underwriting, which are separate from the benefits of the regular employee benefit plan. These coverages might include, for example, additional accident insurance, life insurance, hospital-indemnity coverage to supplement Medicare. These additional coverages are normally on an employee-pay-all basis.
2. Benefits not otherwise available: Employee-pay-all financing may be the only basis on which an employer feels it can offer the coverage. In the future, such a plan might be shifted to a contributory or even to a noncontributory basis.

Source: Jerry S. Rosenbloom and G. Victor Hallman, *Employee Benefit Planning*, 1981, pp. 427, 429–34. Reprinted by permission of Prentice-Hall, Englewood Cliffs, N.J.

---

greater flexibility and choice. Such plans might provide, for example, (1) optional levels of group term life insurance; (2) the availability of death or disability benefits under pension or profit-sharing plans; (3) choices of covering dependents under group medical expense coverages; (4) a variety of participation, cash distribution, and investment options under profit-sharing, thrift, and capital accumulation plans.[37]

The level at which an organization finally chooses to operate on this choice/flexibility dimension really depends on its evaluation of the relative advantages/disadvantages of

---

[37]Kenneth Shapiro, "Flexibility in Benefit Plans," in *1983 Hay Compensation Conference Proceedings* (Philadelphia: Hay Management Consultants, 1983).

flexible plans noted in Exhibit 11.5.[38] A key consideration is the increased scrutiny of the Internal Revenue Service. Section 125 of the Internal Revenue Code outlines a series of requirements that a company must meet in setting up a Flexible Benefits package.[39] The most important of these restrictions is a nondiscrimination clause (i.e., a plan may not give significantly higher benefits to highly compensated executives relative to average employees). In fact, the average benefits for non-highly compensated employees must equal or exceed 75 percent of the average benefits for highly compensated executives.

The final administrative issue involves the question of financing benefits plans. Alternatives include:

1. Noncontributory (employer pays total costs).
2. Contributory (costs shared between employer and employee).
3. Employee financed (employee pays total costs for some benefits—by law the organization must bear the cost for some benefits).

Exhibit 11.6 shows the arguments for each of these three methods of financing. In general, organizations prefer to make benefits options contributory, reasoning that a "free good," no matter how valuable, is of less value to an employee. Furthermore, employees have no personal interest in controlling the cost of a free good.

COMPONENTS OF A BENEFITS PLAN

Exhibit 11.7 outlines a model of the benefits determination process over time. The remainder of this chapter briefly explains the model and then reviews each of its important components.

The central dynamic of a benefits program involves a negotiating process. While the term *negotiating* typically is associated with a union environment, the process is viewed much more broadly here. Negotiation in this context involves a maximum bilateral effort to satisfy the preferences of both the employer and employee. The crucial element of this process is that it involves a *joint* determination of a benefits package. Joint determination implies that maximal effectiveness of a benefits program requires a reorientation in benefits planning, design, and implementation. Given the costs of benefits, it is no longer appropriate for top executives or benefits managers to make assumptions about employee needs and design programs based on these all-too-frequently faulty assumptions. Nor is it realistic for employees to expect employers readily to provide every benefit that may "catch their fancy." Rather, employers must develop mechanisms to identify employee needs and to determine the potential costs of these benefits. Correspondingly, employees

---

[38]Commerce Clearing House, *Flexible Benefits* (Chicago: Commerce Clearing House, 1983); American Can Company, *Do It Your Way* (Greenwich, Conn.: American Can Co., 1978); and L. M. Baytos, "The Employee Benefit Smorgasbord: Its Potential and Limitations," *Compensation Review,* First Quarter 1970, pp. 86–90; *Wall Street Journal,* "Flexible Benefit Plans Become More Popular," December 16, 1986, p. 1; and Richard Johnson, *Flexible Benefits: A How To Guide,* (Brookfield, Wisc.: International Foundation of Employee Benefit Plans, 1986).

[39]Johnson, *Flexible Benefits: A How To Guide.*

EXHIBIT 11.7
A Model of the Benefits Determination Process

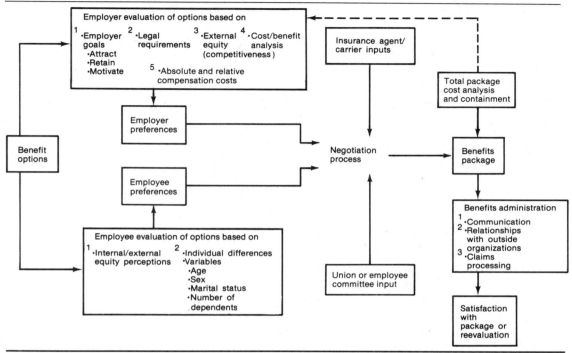

must expect that the negotiation process involving benefits will be placed in a much broader cost framework that mandates employer consideration of total package costs—a consideration which, in all likelihood, will yield more employer opposition to new benefits options in the decades ahead.

Participating in this negotiation process are a number of interested parties with varying levels of input into the final benefits package. Two of the minor participants are insurance agents and union negotiators. Insurance agents may become involved by providing cost information on different alternatives. Unions, if present, play a somewhat larger role by negotiating for benefits that best represent the collective needs of employees.

Far larger roles in the choice of a final benefits package are played by both employee and employer and their preferences. The next sections review the factors that affect these sets of preferences.

Employer Preferences

As Exhibit 11.7 indicates, a number of factors affect employer preference in determining desirable components of a benefits package. One of the most important, but least effectively considered, is the structure of the package existing from prior years. Many benefits managers fail to recognize the difficulty of eliminating an options once it has been established and accepted by employees. Historically, benefits managers negotiated or provided benefits on a "package" basis rather than a cost basis. The current cost of a benefit would be identified and, if the cost seemed reasonable, the benefit would be provided for (or negotiated with) employees. The crucial error in this process was a failure to recognize that rising costs of this benefit were expected to be borne by the employer. The classic example of this phenomenon is health care coverage. An employer considering a community based medical plan like Blue Cross during the early 1960s no doubt agreed to pay all or most of the costs of one of the Blue Cross options. As costs of this plan skyrocketed during the 60s and 70s, the employer was expected to continue coverage at the historical level. In effect, the employer became locked into a level of coverage rather than negotiating a level of cost. In subsequent years, then, the spiraling costs were essentially out of the control of the benefits manager.

Admittedly, in subsequent years coverage may be reduced or employee contributions on an option may be required, but the blow to employee perceptions of equity may be severe. A more prudent strategy to determine employer preferences would be a complete cost-benefit analysis and forecasts of future costs *prior to* adopting a particular option.

Cost-benefit analysis. A major reason for the proliferating costs of benefits programs is the narrow focus of benefits administrators. Too frequently the costs/benefits of a particular benefit inclusion are viewed in isolation, without reference to total package costs or forecasts of rising costs in future years. To control spiraling benefits costs, administrators should adopt a broader, cost-centered approach. As a first step, this approach would require policy decisions on the level of benefits expenditures acceptable both in the short and long run. The ability of benefits administrators to control costs within these parameters would be an important dimension in their performance evaluations. As a second step, this approach would require benefits administrators, in cooperation with insurance carriers and armed with published forecasts of anticipated costs for particular benefits, to determine the cost commitments for the existing benefits package. Budget dollars not already earmarked may then be allocated to new benefits that best satisfy organizational goals. Factors affecting this decision include an evaluation of benefits offered by other firms and the competitiveness of the existing package. Also important is compliance with various legal requirements as they change over time (Chapter 12). Finally, the actual benefit of a new option must be explored in relation to employee preferences. Those benefits that top the list of employee preferences should be evaluated in relation to current and future costs. Because future cost estimates may be difficult to project, it is imperative that benefits administrators reduce uncertainty. If a benefit forecast suggests future cost containment may be difficult, the benefit should be offered to employees only on a cost-sharing basis. Management determines what percentage of cost it can afford to bear within budget projections, and the option is offered to employees on a cost-sharing basis, with projected increases in both employer and employee costs communicated openly. In the negotiation process, then, employees or union representatives can evaluate their preference for the option against the forecasted cost burden. In effect, this approach defines the contribution an employer is willing to make, in advance. And it avoids the constraints of a defined benefit strategy that burdens the employer with continued provision of that defined benefit level despite rapidly spiralling costs.

External equity. Two important considerations establish external equity in a benefits program. One of the issues that must be confronted is the absolute level of benefits payments relative to important product and labor market competitors. A policy decision must be made about the position (market lead, market lag, or competitive) the organization wants to maintain in its absolute level of benefits relative to the competition. Many employers adopt a benefit a competitor has initiated only to find some time later that it is inappropriate given the makeup of the organization. A classic example is the employer who installs an education reimbursement plan in an organization with an aging work force. Data suggest this composition of employees is less likely to use this benefit, and consequently place relatively low value on it.

One of the best strategies to determine *external equity* is to conduct a benefits survey. Alternatively, many consulting organizations, professional associations, and interest groups collect benefits data that can be purchased. Perhaps the most widely used of these surveys is the annual benefits survey conducted by the U.S. Chamber of Commerce. To illustrate typical inclusions in a survey, the survey used by the U.S. Chamber of Commerce is reproduced in Exhibit 11.8.[40]

Legal requirements. Since the turn of the century both the state and federal governments have shown considerable interest in the benefits area. In particular, governmental policy consistently has been to legally require employers to provide a cushion of economic and social security. Employers are legally required to finance all or part of the costs of workers' compensation, unemployment insurance, social security, and pension plans.[41]

Absolute and relative compensation costs. Any evaluation of employee benefits must be placed in the context of total compensation costs. Cost competitiveness means the total package must be competitive—not just specific segments. Consequently, decisions on whether to adopt certain options must be considered in light of the impact on total costs and in relationship to expenditures of competitors (as determined in benefits surveys such as the Chamber of Commerce survey discussed later in this chapter).

Employee Preferences

Employee preferences for various benefit options are determined by individual needs. Those benefits perceived to best satisfy individual needs are most highly desired. In part these needs arise out of feelings of perceived equity or inequity. For example, consider government employees living in the same neighborhood as autoworkers. Imagine the dissatisfaction with government holidays created when they discover the autoworkers are home the whole week between Christmas and New Year's Day. The perceived unfairness of this difference need not be rational. But it is, nevertheless, a factor that must be considered in determining employee needs. Occasionally this comparison process leads to a "bandwagon" effect where new benefits offered by a competitor are adopted without

---

[40]U.S. Chamber of Commerce, *Employee Benefits,* 1988.

[41]James Ledvinka, *Federal Regulation of Personnel and Human Resource Management* (Belmont, Calif.: Kent Publishing, 1982).

EXHIBIT 11.8
U.S. Chamber of Commerce: Benefits Survey

Please return the completed questionnaire to:
ECONOMIC POLICY DIVISION/EMPLOYEE BENEFITS SURVEY
U.S. CHAMBER OF COMMERCE/WASHINGTON, D.C. 20062

CONFIDENTIAL

EMPLOYEE BENEFITS SURVEY—1988

For Office Coding— Leave Blank
———————— A 1
———————— 6
————————
————————
———— 27
——— 30
— 32
— 33

INSTRUCTIONS

1. **It is confidential**—Data from individual firms will not be disclosed. Data will be published only in the form of totals for groups of companies. Only the researchers will see your questionnaire(s).

2. **Company coverage**—If you have several divisions or plants, data covering any *typical* group of employees will be satisfactory.

3. **Employees covered in survey**—We are surveying *both* hourly-paid and salaried employees, if this break-out is available. If a separate breakout is not available for hourly and salaried employees please use the survey on the following page for reporting the combined totals for all employees.

   If the break-out is available, please fill out separate surveys for hourly-paid and salaried employees. The hourly-paid employee survey begins on this page and the salaried employee survey begins on page 5.

   ### HOURLY-PAID EMPLOYEE SURVEY AND/OR COMBINED TOTAL OF SALARIED AND HOURLY PAID EMPLOYEES IF NOT AVAILABLE SEPARATELY

   We will continue to survey hourly-paid employees under the guidelines used in the past for purposes of historical comparison. Therefore, when filling out the questionnaire surveying hourly-paid workers, *include data for workers whose pay varies with the number of hours worked.* In addition, include data for *salaried* employees if their pay varies if they work overtime or less than full-time; but do not include them if they receive their regular pay regardless of hours worked.

   Organizations having difficulty making this employee separation between hourly-paid and salaried workers (e.g., banks, hospitals, financial institutions) should include all nonsupervisory employees and all working supervisors in this hourly-paid employee survey, *regardless of method of payment.* However, please *exclude* all officers of company.

4. **Approximate or incomplete data**—If you are unable to give exact data for the various items, please give estimates—*your best estimate is much better than a zero.* If you cannot break down the data on payments exactly as they are outlined, please give the data that is available. Also, please indicate the items or benefits for which payments were made, but for which you cannot give separate figures.

1

EXHIBIT 11.8
(Continued)

Show actual data or best estimate for employees covered in survey.

A. GROSS PAYROLL FOR EMPLOYEES IN SURVEY:

- For this item, report *actual* wages. Report pay prior to employee deductions for all income and payroll taxes, pay deferral programs, such as 401k plans, and other insurance and deductions. Report on line A-1 the straight-time wages for all hours, including pay for time *not* worked, plus payments in lieu of vacations and holidays.

- Report premium and bonus payments on lines other than line A-1. Thus, if your firm paid $15,000 in overtime pay and the overtime rate is time and one-half, put $10,000 on line A-1, and $5,000 in premium pay on line A-2.

Total amount for 1988

1. Straight-time for employees in survey	$_____	34
2. Overtime premium pay	$_____	46
3. Holiday premium pay	$_____	58
4. Shift differential	$_____	70
5. Earned incentive or production bonus	$_____	82
6. Other (Specify: _____)	$_____	94
7. TOTAL GROSS PAYROLL	$_____	106

Box (lines 2-6): Include BONUS AND PREMIUM PAY ONLY on lines 2-6. Report straight-time pay on line 1.

B. LEGALLY-REQUIRED PAYMENTS (*employer's* share only):

1. Old-Age, Survivors, Disability, and Health Insurance (employer FICA taxes) and Railroad Retirement Tax	$_____	118
2. Unemployment Compensation (federal and state taxes)	$_____	130
3. Workers' Compensation (estimate cost if self-insured)	$_____	142
4. State sickness benefits insurance	$_____	154
5. Other (Specify: _____)	$_____	166
6. TOTAL	$_____	178

C. RETIREMENT AND SAVINGS PLAN PAYMENTS (*employer's* share only):

- ITEM C-4 (PENSION AND INSURANCE PREMIUMS)—For pension and insurance premiums, report *net* payments after deducting any dividends or credits returned to employer by insurer.

1. Defined benefit pension plan contributions (a defined benefit plan is one that is insured by the Pension Benefit Guaranty Corporation involving a promise to pay a fixed level of benefits on retirement)	$_____	190
2. Defined contribution plan payments (a defined contribution plan is one that provides for an individual account for each participant and for benefits based on the amount contributed to the participant's account)		
a. 401K or similar payments (employers share only)	$_____	202
b. Profit-sharing payments (employer contributions are based on current profits of the business, fluctuating with current profit levels)	$_____	214
c. Stock bonus and employee stock ownership plans (ESOP)	$_____	226
3. Money purchase plans	$_____	238
4. Pension plan premiums (net) under insurance and annuity contracts (insured and trusteed)	$_____	250
5. Costs of plan administration (please estimate the administrative costs paid separately or as part of contributions to the plan)	$_____	262
6. Other (Specify: _____)	$_____	274
7. TOTAL	$_____	286
8. Please report the number of employees participating in your company's retirement and savings plan programs	_____	298

D. LIFE INSURANCE AND DEATH BENEFITS (*employer's* share only):

- Exclude premiums for life insurance purchased under a pension plan. Such premiums should be reported under item C-4.

1. Life insurance premiums (net)	$_____	304
2. Death benefits not covered by insurance	$_____	316
3. TOTAL	$_____	328

EXHIBIT 11.8
(Continued)

E. MEDICAL AND MEDICALLY-RELATED BENEFIT PAYMENTS (*employer's* share only):
1. Hospital, surgical, medical, and major medical insurance premiums (net) .... $_____ 340
2. Self-insured hospital, surgical, medical, and major medical payments............................. $_____ 352
3. Short-term disability, sickness or accident insurance (company plan or insured plan) .... $_____ 364
4. Long-term disability or wage continuation (insured, self-administered, or trust) .... $_____ 376
5. *Retiree* (payments for retired employees) hospital, surgical, medical, and major medical
insurance premiums (net) .... $_____ 388
6. Self-insured *retiree* (payments for retired employees) hospital, surgical, medical, and major
medical payments .... $_____ 400
7. Dental insurance premiums .... $_____ 412
8. Vision care and prescription drugs .... $_____ 424
9. Physical and mental fitness programs .... $_____ 436
10. Medically-related benefits for *former* workers and family members, such as the continuation
of health benefit payments after termination of employment (do not include payments to
retirees and/or for maternity leave) .... $_____ 448
11. Other (Specify: _____) .... $_____ 460
12. TOTAL .... $_____ 472

F. PAID REST PERIODS, COFFEE BREAKS, LUNCH PERIODS, WASH-UP TIME,
TRAVEL TIME, CLOTHES-CHANGE TIME, GET-READY TIME, ETC.
- This should be reported if time is paid for, whether or not there is a formal work rule
providing for such time off. A simple rule of thumb is that if employees typically take two
10-minute rest periods per day, this would amount to approximately 4% of gross payroll; if
two 15-minute breaks are taken, the figure would come to 6% of gross payroll (Item A-7). $_____ 484

G. PAYMENTS FOR TIME NOT WORKED:
1. Payments for or in lieu of vacations (for estimating purposes, each day of paid vacation =
.00385 x straight-time pay) .... $_____ 496
   If unable to estimate a dollar figure, please indicate the average number of days of vacation an
   employee receives a year. _____
2. Payments for or in lieu of holidays (for estimating purposes, each paid holiday = .00385 x
straight-time pay)... $_____ 508
   If unable to estimate a dollar figure, please indicate the average number of paid holidays an
   employee receives a year. _____
3. Sick leave pay.. $_____ 520
4. Parental leave (maternity and paternity leave payments) .... $_____ 532
5. Payments required under guaranteed workweek or work year—only that part that represents
payment for time not worked .... $_____ 544
6. Payments for State or National guard duty; jury, witness, and voting pay allowances;
payments for time lost due to death in family; or other personal reasons .... $_____ 556
7. Other (Specify: _____) .... $_____ 568
8. TOTAL .... $_____ 580

H. MISCELLANEOUS BENEFIT PAYMENTS (*employer's* share only):
1. Discounts on goods and services purchased from company by employees .... $_____ 592
2. Employee meals furnished by company... $_____ 604
3. Child care: a. On-site child care.. $_____ 616
               b. Third-party provided care... $_____ 628
4. Parking... $_____ 640
5. Employee education expenditures (tuition refunds, seminar attendance, etc.) .... $_____ 652
6. Payments for legal counselling .... $_____ 664
7. Payments to union stewards or officials for time spent in settling grievances or in negotiating
agreements .... $_____ 676
8. Christmas or other special bonuses (not tied to profits), service awards, suggestion awards, etc..... $_____ 700
9. Other (Specify: _____) .... $_____ 712
10. TOTAL .... $_____ 724

CONFIDENTIAL

3

EXHIBIT 11.8
(Concluded)

I. EMPLOYEE PAYROLL DEDUCTIONS (*employee's* share only):
- For this question, report deductions from *employee* pay. Employer contributions are reported in questions B-E.
1. Old-Age, Survivors, Disability, and Health Insurance (employee FICA taxes) and Railroad Retirement Taxes .... $_____ 736
2. Retirement and Savings Plan payments (including 401K and similar programs) .... $_____ 748
3. Life insurance premiums .... $_____ 760
4. Medical and Medically-Related Benefits Payments .... $_____ 772
5. Other (Specify: _____). Do not include deductions for
   income tax. .... $_____ 784
6. TOTAL .... $_____ 796

J. EMPLOYEE HOURS
- These figures include hours worked or paid for (including time actually worked, *plus* holidays, vacation, sick leave, and other time paid for but not worked).
1. Total hours of a **typical full-time employee**
   during 1988: _____ $\times$ 52 = _____ 808

   average number of hours   total hours
   per week per employee   during 1988
                                  per employee

2. Total hours of **all** employees in survey during 1988:
   - The total number of hours worked or paid for of all employees covered in the survey, corresponds to earnings given on line A-1.

   _____ $\times$ _____ = _____ 812

   total hrs. during 1988   full-time equivalent   total hours of
   per employee   employees included   all employees
                             in your survey data   in 1988
                             for 1988

PRIMARY STANDARD INDUSTRIAL CLASSIFICATION CODE (SIC Code) = _____
- If you do not know your SIC Code, please give a description of the major type of business and/or the principal lines or products manufactured or handled.

_____
_____

SUPPLEMENTAL QUESTIONS

For Office Coding— Leave Blank

__ __ __ **B1**

Please answer the following questions:
1. Does your firm have a fixed benefit plan or a cafeteria plan (a cafeteria plan is one that allows employees to choose between benefits and/or benefit plans)?
   (Check appropriate box)
   Fixed Benefit Plan .... F ☐
   Cafeteria Plan .... C ☐   6
2. What is the estimated percentage of part-time workers as the percentage of your total work-force (part-time workers are those who work less hours than the normal work week)? .... _____ 7
3. If you provide benefits to part-time employees, which benefits do you provide?
   All .... Yes ☐   No ☐   12
   Health .... Yes ☐   No ☐   13
   Retirement .... Yes ☐   No ☐   14
   Vacations .... Yes ☐   No ☐   15
   Bonuses .... Yes ☐   No ☐   16
   Others (please specify: _____)
4. Please estimate the total annual cost for administering your benefit costs that are not included in the above cost data on employee benefits.
   a. Estimated annual internal costs of administering benefits programs not included in the above data on benefit costs .... $_____ 17
   b. Estimated annual cost of outside consultants, attorneys and other persons consulted regarding the administration of benefits programs .... $_____ 29
   c. Other (please specify) .... $_____ 41
5. Does your organization provide for the following:
   a. Does your firm sponsor wellness programs, such as health fairs, blood pressure tests etc? .... Yes ☐   No ☐   53
   b. Do you believe these programs are an effective way of reducing health care costs? .... Yes ☐   No ☐   54
   c. Do you believe health promotion programs are an effective way of enhancing productivity and reducing absenteeism? .... Yes ☐   No ☐   55

Please list the name, title and phone number of the person who is responsible for filling out this questionnaire in case our researchers have any questions.

(___) _____

_____
Name   Title   Phone Number

careful consideration simply because the employer wants to avoid hard feelings. This phenomenon is particularly apparent for employers with strong commitments to maintaining a totally or partially nonunion work force. Benefits obtained by a unionized competitor or a unionized segment of the firm's work force are frequently passed along to nonunion employees. While the effectiveness of this strategy in thwarting unionization efforts has not been demonstrated, many nonunion firms would prefer to provide the benefit as a safety measure.

A major assumption in empirical efforts to determine employee preferences is that preferences are somehow systematically related to what are termed demographic differences. The demographic approach assumes that demographic groups (e.g., young versus old, married versus unmarried) can be identified for which benefits preferences are fairly consistent across members of the group. Furthermore, it assumes that meaningful differences exist between groups in terms of benefit preferences.

There is some evidence that these assumptions are only partially correct. In an extensive review of employee preference literature, Glueck traced patterns of group preferences for particular benefits.[42] As one might expect, older workers showed stronger preferences than younger workers for pension plans.[43] Also, families with dependents had stronger preferences for health/medical coverage than families with no dependents.[44] The big surprise in all these studies, though, is that many of the other demographic group

---

EXHIBIT 11.9
Questionnaire Formats for Benefits Surveys

A. Ranking method
Rank order the following benefits from 1 (high) to 4 (low) in terms of their value to you.
_____Health/medical coverage.
_____Extended holiday schedule.
_____Pension plan.
_____Life insurance.

B. Likert-type scale
How important are each of the following benefits to you (check one for each benefit).

	(1) Very Important	(2) Important	(3) Neutral	(4) Unimportant	(5) Very Unimportant
Health/medical coverage	_____	_____	_____	_____	_____
Extended holiday schedule	_____	_____	_____	_____	_____
Pension plan	_____	_____	_____	_____	_____
Life insurance	_____	_____	_____	_____	_____

---

[42]William F. Glueck, *Personnel: A Diagnostic Approach* (Plano, Tex.: Business Publications, 1978).

[43]Ludwig Wagner and Theodore Bakerman, "Wage Earners' Opinions of Insurance Fringe Benefits," *Journal of Insurance,* June 1960, pp. 17–28; and Brad Chapman and Robert Otterman, "Employee Preference for Various Compensation and Benefits Options," *Personnel Administrator* 25 (November 1975), pp. 31–36.

[44]Stanley Nealy, "Pay and Benefit Preferences," *Industrial Relations,* October 1963, pp. 17–28.

breakdowns fail to result in differential benefit preferences. Traditionally, it has been assumed that benefit preferences ought to differ among males versus females, blue collar versus white collar, married versus single, young versus old, and families with dependents versus those with none. Few of these expectations have been borne out by these studies. Rather, the studies have tended to be more valuable in showing preference trends that are characteristic of all employees. Among the benefits available, health/medical and stock plans are highly preferred benefits, while such options as early retirement, profit sharing, shorter hours, and counseling services rank among the least-preferred options. Beyond these conclusions, most preference studies have shown wide variation in individuals with respect to benefit preferences.

The weakness of this demographic approach has led some organizations to undertake a second and more expensive empirical method of determining employee preference: surveying individuals about needs. One way of accomplishing this requires development of a questionnaire on which employees evaluate various benefits. For example, Exhibit 11.9 illustrates two types of questionnaire formats.

While other strategies for scaling are available (e.g., paired comparison), the most important factor to remember is that a consistent method must be used in assessing preferences on a questionnaire. Switching between a ranking method and a Likert-type scale may, by itself, affect the results.[45]

A third empirical method of identifying individual employee preferences is commonly known as a flexible benefit plan (also called, at various times, a cafeteria style plan or a supermarket plan). As previously noted, employees are allotted a fixed amount of money and permitted to spend that amount in the purchase of benefit options. From a theoretical perspective, this approach to benefits packaging is ideal. Employees directly identify the benefits of greatest value to them, and by constraining the dollars employees have to spend, benefits managers are able to control benefits costs.

The Negotiation Process

It would be nice to believe that determination of benefits is a bilateral process. Unfortunately, there are numerous cases where this appears not to be true. In some cases organizations provide benefits without consulting employees about their preferences. In other cases a union representing employees will push hard for a benefit that is granted by management's negotiator without conferring with the benefits managers about long-term cost implications. Neither strategy is optimal. Rather, multiple groups should be involved in a negotiating process, and this holds true whether the firm is unionized or not. On management's side, the labor relations expert (if any) must be in constant touch with the benefits manager to identify options and their cost implications. In turn, the benefits manager must decide whether the organization should directly finance the benefit or obtain indirect coverage through an agent or carrier. If this latter option is chosen, the agent can provide valuable costing information and suggestions on plan design.

---

[45]George T. Milkovich and Michael J. Delaney, "A Note on Cafeteria Pay Plans," *Industrial Relations,* February 1975, pp. 112–16.

EXHIBIT 11.10
Job Description for Employee-Benefits Executive

Position

The primary responsibility of this position is the administration of established company benefits programs. Develops and recommends new and improved policies and plans with regard to employee benefits. Assures compliance with ERISA requirements and regulations.

Specific Functions

1. Administers group life insurance, health and accident insurance, retirement programs, and savings plans.
2. Processes documents necessary for the implementation of various benefits programs and maintains such records as are necessary.
3. Recommends and approves procedures for maintenance of benefits programs and issues operating instructions.
4. Participates in the establishment of long-range objectives of company benefits programs.
5. Conducts surveys and analyzes and maintains an organized body of information on benefits programs of other companies.
6. Informs management of trends and developments in the field of company benefits.
7. Gives advice and counsel regarding current developments in benefits programs.
8. Acts as liaison between company and banks, insurance companies, and other agencies.
9. Conducts special studies as requested by management.

In addition, the employee-benefits executive may be responsible for various employee services, such as recreation programs, advisory services, credit unions, and savings bond purchase programs.

Source: Robert McCaffery, *Managing the Employee Benefits Program* (New York: American Management Association, 1983), p. 25.

From the employee's side, unions must be sensitive to which benefit options are most important to union members. Formal or informal polling provides the input for initial demands. As cost implications are determined and as the relative priority of specific benefits becomes clearer for both parties, the negotiations can proceed more rationally.

Administering the Benefits Program

The job description for an employee-benefits executive found in Exhibit 11.10 indicates that administrative time is spent on two functions that require further discussion: (1) communicating about the benefits program, and (2) claims processing.[46]

Employee Benefits Communication

The most frequent method for communicating employee benefits today is probably still the employee benefits handbook.[47] A typical handbook contains a description of all benefits, including levels of coverage and eligibility requirements. To be most effective, this benefits manual should be accompanied by group meetings and videotapes.[48] While some organizations may supplement this initial benefits discussion with periodic refreshers

---

[46]McCaffery, *Managing the Employee Benefits Program*.

[47]Towers, Perrin, Forster, and Crosby, "Corporate Benefit Communication . . . Today and Tomorrow," (1988).

[48]Ibid.

EXHIBIT 11.11
Typical Benefits Objectives

Objective	Respondents Indicating This Is a Primary Objective (%)
1. Increase employee understanding of plan objectives	82*
2. Increase employee appreciation of the benefits program	81
3. Increase employee knowledge of the cost of providing benefits	41
4. Obtain employee cooperation in controlling benefit costs	36
5. Encourage employees to take responsibility for their own financial security	16
6. Maintain the company's commitment to open employee communications	16

*Multiple responses permitted
Source: Towers, Perrin, Forster, and Crosby (1988), "Corporate Benefit Communication . . . Today and Tomorrow."

(e.g., once per year), a more typical approach involves one-on-one discussions between the benefits administrator and an employee seeking information on a particular benefit.

In recent years the dominance of the benefits handbook is being challenged by personalized benefits statements generated by computer software programs specially designed for that purpose. These tailor-made reports provide a breakdown of package components and list selected cost information about the options. Many experts predict that the future of benefits communications includes interactive computer programs where employees can enter questions into the computer and have the computer provide basic benefits counseling.[49]

Despite this and other innovative plans to communicate employee benefit packages, failure to understand benefits components and their value is still one of the root causes of employee dissatisfaction with a benefits package.[50] We believe an effective communications package must have three elements. First, an organization must spell out its benefit objectives and ensure that any communications achieve these objectives. Exhibit 11.11 outlines typical benefits objectives.

Second, the program should make use of the most effective presentation mediums. Exhibit 11.12 indicates the effectiveness ratings for a variety of communications tools.

And finally, the content of the communications package must be complete, clear, and free of the complex jargon that so readily invades benefits discussions. The amount of time/space devoted to each issue should vary closely with both perceived importance of the benefit to employees and with expected difficulty in communicating option alternatives.[51]

[49]Ibid.

[50]Reported in "Yoder-Heneman Creativity Award Supplement," *Personnel Administration* 26, no. 11 (1981), pp. 49–67.

[51]Benefits, "How Do You Communicate? It May No Be Nearly As Well As You Think," *Benefits,* December 1988, pp. 13–15; and Kevin Greene, "Effective Employee Benefits Communication," in David Balkin and Luis Gomez-Mejia, *New Perspectives on Compensation* (Englewood Cliffs, N.J.: Prentice-Hall, 1987).

EXHIBIT 11.12
Effectiveness of Different Communications Tools

Communications Tool	Rating	5 = highly effective 1 = highly ineffective
Memos	3.4	
Special brochures	3.8	
Employee handbooks	3.3	
Small group meetings	4.2	
Personalized benefit statements	4.3	
Letters to employee's home	3.5	
Companywide publications	3.3	
"Live" slide shows	3.8	
Large group meetings	3.6	
Bulletin boards	3.1	
Videotapes	4.0	
Employee annual reports	2.4	
Slides/audiotapes	3.7	
Individual discussions with supervisors	3.4	
Benefit newsletters	3.6	
Telephone hotlines	3.6	
Electronic communications	3.3	
Films	3.5	

Source: Towers, Perrin, Forster, and Crosby (1988), "Corporate Benefit Communication . . . Today and Tomorrow."

Relationship with Outside Organizations

Virtually all employee benefits come under the scrutiny of some government agency. Some employee benefits, such as the legally required unemployment compensation, worker's compensation and social security, require extensive liaison with government agencies. For example, worker's compensation and unemployment compensation claims by employees require employer contacts with the appropriate agencies. Companies that establish a reputation of being communicative and cooperative can expect objective reviews of all claims and challenges to claims.

Claims Processing

As noted by one expert, claims processing arises when an employee asserts that a specific event (e.g., disablement, hospitalization, unemployment) has occurred and demands that the employer fulfill a promise of payment.[52] As such, a claims processor must first determine whether the act has, in fact, occurred. If the answer is yes, the second step involves determining if the employee is eligible for the benefit. If payment is not denied at this stage, the claims processor calculates payment level. It is particularly important at this stage to ensure coordination of benefits. If multiple insurance companies are liable for payment (e.g., working spouses covered by different insurers) a good claims processor

---

[52]Bennet Shaver, "The Claims Process," in H. Wayne Snider, ed., *Employee Benefit Management*, pp. 141–52.

can save from 10 to 15 percent of claims cost by ensuring that the liability is jointly paid.[53]

While these steps are time-consuming, most of the work is quite routine in nature. The major job challenges come in those approximately 10 percent of all claims where payment is denied. A benefits administrator must then become an adroit counselor explaining the situation to the employee in a manner that conveys the equitable and consistent procedures used.

Cost Analysis and Containment

Cost containment is easily the biggest issue in benefits planning and administration today. Escalating costs of the 1960s and 1970s, combined with disappointing evidence that benefits have little impact on shaping positive employee behaviors, have molded the cost-cutting drives of the 1980s. Increasingly, employers are auditing their benefits options for cost containment opportunities. The terminology of cost containment is becoming a part of every employee's vocabulary; Exhibit 11.13 provides definitions of some common cost containment terms. Additional discussion of cost containment strategies for specific benefits is included in Chapter 12.

Monitoring the Benefits Environment

The model of the benefits process (Exhibit 11.7) presented earlier has a final variable—satisfaction with pay package. In effect, this variable is included because a benefits

---

EXHIBIT 11.13
A Basic Primer of Cost Containment Terminology

Deductibles—an employee claim for insurance coverage is preceded by the requirement that the first $x dollars be paid by the claimant.

Coinsurance—a proportion of insurance premiums are paid by the employee.

Benefit Cutbacks—corresponding to wage concessions some employers are negotiating with employees to eliminate or reduce employer contributions to selected options.

Defined Contribution Plans—employers establish the limits of their responsibility for employee benefits in terms of dollar contribution maximum.

Defined Benefits Plans—employers establish the limits of their responsibility for employee benefits in terms of a specific benefit and the options included. As the cost of these options rises in future years the employer is obligated to provide the benefit as negotiated, despite its increased cost.

Dual Coverage—in families where both spouses work there is frequently coverage of specific claims from each employer's benefit package. Employers cut costs by specifying payment limitations under such conditions.

Benefit Ceiling—establishing a maximum payout for specific claims (e.g., limiting liability for extended hospital stays to $150,000).

---

[53]Thomas Fannin and Theresa Fannin, "Coordination of Benefits: Uncovering Buried Treasure," *Personnel Journal,* May 1983, pp. 386–91.

package must have a monitoring process. The key to this monitoring function is that both employers and employees must periodically (at *least* once yearly) assess whether specific components and the total benefits package are meeting desired goals. From the employer's perspective, it is important to ensure: compliance with changing legal requirements, competitiveness with relevant organizations, and cost effectiveness of existing options. In turn, employees must evaluate how well benefits satisfy their changing needs. To the extent either party is dissatisfied with the outcomes of this monitoring process, it may signal a need for change in some of the benefits components discussed in the next chapter.

SUMMARY

Given the rapid escalation in the cost of employee benefits over the past 15 years, organizations would do well to evaluate the effectiveness of their benefits adoptions, retention, and termination procedures. Specifically, how does an organization go about selecting appropriate employee benefits? Are the decisions based on sound evaluation of employee preferences balanced against organizational goals of legal compliance and competitiveness? Do the benefits chosen serve to attract, retain and/or motivate employees? Or are organizations paying billions of dollars of indirect compensation without any tangible benefit? This chapter has outlined a benefits determination process that identifies major issues in selecting and evaluating particular benefit choices. The next chapter catalogues the various benefits available and discusses some of the decisions confronting a benefits administrator.

REVIEW QUESTIONS

1. Why is it more difficult to control costs under a defined benefits program versus a defined contributions program?

2. Assume an organization (Company A) develops a benefits program in the following way. First it identifies the major demographic groups in the organization. Then the company offers benefits known to be highly desired by people in those demographic groups in general (i.e., more senior employees prefer larger allocations to pensions). What kinds of problems could arise using this type of strategy to design a benefits program?

3. Assume a second organization (Company B) decides to adopt a flexible benefits program. If it has an identical demographic makeup to the organization in question 2, what kinds of new problems do you think would arise and what types of problems would be eliminated in comparison to Company A in question 2.

4. How is the concept of external equity similar or different in discussing pay versus benefits?

5. Design a program to communicate effectively an employee benefits program. What are the key elements of this communication?

Benefits Options

uman resources professionals share three widely held views about benefits admin-istration. First, the number of employee benefits and the laws affecting them have been escalating rapidly. Second, a good benefits administrator can save an organization sub-stantial sums of money through proper benefits plan design and effective administration of benefits. Third, proficiency in benefits plan administration requires years of experience. The first two of these statements were endorsed in Chapter 11. The third statement, however, requires qualification. Admittedly, the number of benefits options and choices

---

EXHIBIT 12.1
Categorization of Employee Benefits

Type of Benefit

---

1. Legally required payments
   (employers' share only)
   a. Old-Age, Survivors, Disability, and Health Insurance (employer FICA taxes) and Railroad Retirement Tax.
   b. Unemployment compensation.
   c. Workers' compensation (including estimated cost of self-insured).
   d. State sickness benefits insurance.

2. Retirement and saving plan payments
   (employers' share only)
   a. Defined benefit pension plan contributions (401 K type).
   b. Defined contribution plan payments.
   c. Profit sharing.
   d. Stock bonus and employee stock ownership plans (ESOP).
   e. Pension plan premiums (net) under insurance and annuity contracts (insured and trusted).
   f. Administrative and other cost.

3. Life insurance and death benefits
   (employers' share only)

4. Medical and medically-related benefit payments (employers' share only)
   a. Hospital, surgical, medical, and major medical insurance premiums (net).
   b. Retiree (payments for retired employees) hospital, surgical medical, and major medical insurance premiums (net).
   c. Short-term disability, sickness or accident insurance (company plan or insured plan).
   d. Long-term disability or wage continuation (insured, self-administered, or trust).
   e. Dental insurance premiums.
   f. Other (vision care, physical and mental fitness benefits for former employees).

5. Paid rest periods, coffee breaks, lunch periods, wash-up time, travel time, clothes-change time, get-ready time, etc.

6. Payments for time not worked
   a. Payments for or in lieu of vacations.
   b. Payment for or in lieu of holidays.
   c. Sick leave pay.
   d. Parental leave (maternity and paternity leave payments).
   e. Other.

7. Miscellaneous benefit payments
   a. Discounts on goods and services purchased from company by employees.
   b. Employee meals furnished by company.
   c. Employee education expenditures.
   d. Child care.
   e. Other.

EXHIBIT 12.2
Summary: Percent of Full-Time Employees by Participation[1] in Employee Benefit Programs, Medium and Large Firms,[2] 1986

Employee benefit program	All employees	Professional and administrative employees	Technical and clerical employees	Production employees
Paid:				
Holidays	99	99	100	98
Vacations	100	99	100	100
Personal leave	25	33	35	15
Lunch period	10	3	4	17
Rest time	72	58	69	82
Funeral leave	88	87	87	88
Jury-duty leave	83	96	96	90
Military leave	66	74	72	58
Sick leave	70	93	93	45
Sickness and accident insurance	49	28	35	69
Wholly employer financed	41	22	28	59
Partly employer financed	8	6	7	9
Long-term disability insurance	48	68	60	30
Wholly employer financed	38	52	47	24
Partly employer financed	10	16	13	6
Health insurance[3]	95	96	94	96
Employee coverage:				
Wholly employer financed	54	52	45	61
Partly employer financed	41	45	49	35
Family coverage:				
Wholly employer financed	35	33	28	41
Partly employer financed	60	64	66	55
Life insurance	96	97	96	95
Wholly employer financed[4]	87	87	87	86
Partly employer financed	10	10	9	9
Retirement[5]	89	92	92	87
Defined benefit pension	76	78	78	74
Wholly employer financed[4]	71	73	74	69
Partly employer financed	5	5	3	5
Defined contribution plan	47	53	55	40
Wholly employer financed[6]	33	33	36	31
Partly employer financed	15	20	19	9
Capital accumulation[7]	23	31	29	16
Wholly employer financed[6]	6	6	6	5
Partly employer financed	18	25	23	11

[1]Participants are workers covered by a paid time off, insurance, retirement, or capital accumulation plan. Employees subject to a minimum service requirement before they are eligible for a benefit are counted as participants even if they have not met the requirement at the time of the survey. If employees are required to pay part of the cost of a benefit, only those who elect the coverage and pay their share are counted as participants. Benefits for which the employee must pay the full premium are outside the scope of the survey. Only current employees are counted as participants; retirees are excluded.

[2]See appendix A for scope of study and definitions of occupational groups.

[3]Includes less than 0.5 percent of employees in plans that did not offer family coverage.

[4]Includes participants in noncontributory basic plans who may contribute to the cost of supplemental plans in these benefit areas. Supplemental plans are not tabulated in this bulletin.

[5]The total is less than the sum of the individual items because many employees participate in both defined contribution plans. Defined contribution plans include money purchase pension plans, and profit sharing, savings and thrift, stock bonus, and employee stock ownership plans in which employer contributions must remain in the participant's account until retirement age, death, disability, separation from service, age 59 1/2, or hardship.

[6]Employees participating in two or more plans are counted as participants in wholly employer financed plans only if all plans are noncontributory.

[7]Includes plans in which employer contributions may be withdrawn from participant's account prior to retirement age, death, disability, separation from service, age 59 1/2, or hardship. Excludes pure cash profit sharing, stock option, and stock purchase plans.

Note: Because of rounding, sums of individual items may not equal totals.

Source: U.S. Department of Labor, Employee Benefits in Medium and Large Firms, 1986, Bulletin 2281, 1987.

can, at times, be quite overwhelming. Even trained human resource professionals can err in their evaluation of the package. For example, one study asked both college graduates and human resource professionals to rank order 11 different benefits equated for costs to a company.[1] The HR professionals' role was to estimate the graduates' responses. Surprisingly, at least to the recruiters, the college graduates placed high value on medical/life insurance, company stocks, and pensions. Lesser importance was placed on holidays and scheduling conveniences (e.g., flextime, four-day work week). The recruiters systematically underestimated the value of most of the top benefits and overestimated the value of the time and schedule benefits. Despite the surprises, though, and despite the obvious magnitude of benefits information, there are still some basic issues that can be identified as equally relevant across different organizations. These commonalities serve as a foundation for aspiring benefits plan administrators. After categorizing benefits, these issues will be discussed as they relate to each benefit category. Exhibit 12.1 provides the most widely accepted categorization of employee benefits. In their annual report based on a nationwide survey of employee benefits, the U.S. Chamber of Commerce identifies seven categories of benefits.[2] Since this breakdown is familiar to benefits plan administrators, it will be used to organize this chapter and illustrate important principles affecting administation of each benefit type. Exhibit 12.2 provides Department of Labor data on employee participation in selected benefits programs.[3] Notice the high rate of participation for such common benefits as life/health insurance and pension plans. These participation rates are only exceeded by those of legally required benefits. Exhibit 12.3 compares participation rates between private sector firms and state/local governments. In general, a greater percentage of employees are covered in the private sector.

EXHIBIT 12.3
A Comparison of Private v. Public Sector Participation in Employee Benefits Programs

| | *All Employees* | |
| | *Private Sector Medium and Large Firms (%)* | *Public Sector State/Local Government (%)* |
Benefit Program		
Paid days off	99	81
Sickness and accident insurance	49	14
Long term disability insurance	48	31
Health care	95	93
Life insurance	96	85
Retirement plans	89	98

[1]Kermit Davis, William Giles, and Hubert Feild, "Compensation and Fringe Benefits: How Recruiters View New College Graduates' Preferences," *Personnel Administrator*, January 1985, pp. 43–50.

[2]U.S. Chamber of Commerce, *Employee Benefits, 1987* (Washington, DC: Chamber of Commerce, 1988).

[3]U.S. Department of Labor, *Employee Benefits in Medium and Large Firms, 1986*, Bulletin 2281, 1987.

LEGALLY REQUIRED BENEFITS

Virtually every employee benefit is *affected* by statutory or common law (many of the limitations are imposed by tax laws). In this section the primary focus will be on benefits that are *required* by statutory law: workers' compensation, social security, and unemployment compensation. In addition, we will look at equal employement opportunity laws as they affect employee benefits—a legal minefield for benefits managers, lawyers, and executives.

Workers' Compensation

Workers' compensation is an insurance program that is paid for by the employer and designed to protect employees from expenses incurred for a work-related injury or disease. An injury or disease qualifies for workers' compensation if it results from an accident that occurred during the course of employment. An employee may receive workers' compensation benefits for:

1. Permanent total disability and temporary total disability.
2. Scheduled injuries—loss of use of a body member.
3. Survivor benefits for fatal injuries.
4. Medical expenses.
5. Rehabilitation.
6. Disfigurement.

Workers' compensation can consist of either monetary reimbursement or payment of medical expenses. The amount of compensation is based on fixed schedules of minimum and maximum payments. Disability payments are often tied to the employee's earnings, modified by such economic factors as the number of dependents.

The employee receives workers' compensation, regardless of fault in an accident. Detailed record keeping of work accidents, illnesses, and deaths are required by state statute.

States require that employers obtain workers' compensation insurance through a private carrier or, in some states, through participation in a state fund. The employer is liable for premium payments; the employee does not pay for this insurance.

Some states provide "second injury funds" to relieve an employer's liability when a preemployment injury combines with a work-related injury to produce a disability greater than that caused by the latter alone. For example, if a person with a known heart condition breaks an arm in a fall triggered by a heart attack, medical treatments for the heart condition would not be paid from workers' compensation insurance; treatment for the broken arm would be compensated.

Exhibit 12.4 summarizes the most common features of the various state laws.[4]

The cost of workers' compensation, as well as level of protection, varies widely

---

[4]U.S. Chamber of Commerce, *Analysis of Workers' Compensation Laws, 1985* (Washington, DC: Chamber of Commerce, 1985), Publication no. 6803.

EXHIBIT 12.4
Commonalities in State Workers' Compensation Laws

Issue	*Most Common State Provision*
Type of law	• Compulsory (N = 47 states)
	• Elective (N = 3 states)
Self insurance	• Self-insurance permitted (N = 47 states)
Coverage	• All industrial employment
	• Farm labor, domestic servants and casual employees usually exempted.
	• Compulsory for all or most public sector employees (N = 47 states)
Occupational diseases	• Coverage for all diseases arising out of and in the course of employment. No compensation for "ordinary diseases of life."

from state to state. In some states employers pay more for workers' compensation than they do for state income tax. In fact the overall cost of workers' compensation was 29.3 billion in 1985, a rise of 16 percent over the previous year.[5] Many employers claim that rising costs are overloading the system.[6] Some employers argue the high costs of workers' compensation are forcing them to uproot established businesses in states with high costs to relocate in lower cost states.[7] Why these rapid cost increases? At least three factors seem to play a role.[8] First, medical costs continue to skyrocket. Over 30 percent of workers' compensation costs can be traced to medical expenses. Second, some employers use workers' compensation as a surrogate for more stringent unemployment insurance programs. Rising numbers of employees, fearing recession and possible layoffs, fake new illnesses or stall reporting back after existing illnesses. Finally, workers' compensation also faces a serious threat from inclusion of new illnesses for coverage under the law. The most common new inclusion is stress related ailments. The number of claims for stress induced illness doubled between 1979 and 1984.[9]

Unfortunately, these cost problems appear to be spiralling. One study indicates the number of workers' compensation claims depend directly on the size of benefits specified in the state law.[10] So when benefits rise, the number of claims rise. Equally disturbing, though, when the number of claims rise, state legislators have a tendency to vote for more generous benefits.[11]

If this cost spiral is to be broken, legislators and benefits administrators need to better understand how the system works. First we provide a brief history of workers' compen-

---

[5]Philip Polakoff and Paul O'Rourke, "Workers' Compensation: A New Look at an Old Problem," *Benefits Quarterly*, 5(1), 1989, pp. 27–41.

[6]Business Week, "The Worsening Ills of Workers' Comp," *Business Week*, October 12, 1987, p. 46.

[7]Ibid.

[8]Ibid.

[9]Ibid.

[10]J. Paul Leigh, "Analysis of Workers' Compensation Using Data on Individuals," *Industrial Relations* 24(2), 1985, pp. 247, 256.

[11]Ibid.

sation. This is followed by a discussion of program objectives and an evaluation of success against these objectives.

The first workers' compensation state laws to survive the constitutionality question were passed in 1911. By 1920, all but six states had passed some form of workers' compensation law. All 50 states currently have one. The passage of these first laws is attributable to two related factors. First, prior to passage of the first state laws (1907–1908), the accident rate in industry attained an unacceptable level: "approximately 30,000 workers died from occupational-related accidents."[12]

In addition to this high accident rate, workers had no protection for work-related accidents. The only source of remedy for workers injured on the job required legal resolution.

Under common law prevailing at that time, injured employees rarely received favorable treatment in the court. An employer could use any one of three defenses with reasonable assurance of success: (1) "contributory negligence"—recovery denied to the worker if it could be shown the worker contributed in any way to the injury, (2) "fellow servant" doctrine—recovery denied if a coworker contributed in some way to the accident, (3) "assumption of risk"—as a last resort an employer could claim that the employees knew of the job hazards and willingly assumed them upon acceptance of employment.

Needless to say, many accident cases were successfully defended by employers using one of these three lines of defense. As accident rates mounted, however, public support grew for some form of worker compensation.

The result of this rising sentiment, tempered by more than 60 years of experience and modification, is the modern workers' compensation system. According to the National Commission on State Workmen's Compensation Laws, the existing workers' compensation system should achieve five major objectives.[13] The following paragraphs outline these objectives and assess the degree to which they have been achieved.

First, workers' compensation is designed to pay certain, prompt, and reasonable compensation to victims of work accidents. Little can be said about the promptness of payments, since few jurisdictions collect or report such data. The reasonableness of compensation, however, is more easily assessed. Most states attempt to provide an injured worker with 50 to 67 percent of lost income. According to one authority, though, this compensation level frequently is not achieved in practice.[14] Numerous states set maximum weekly benefits that fall below the target policy. Of even more concern, many jurisdictions provide for benefits that are below the poverty threshold. While some progress has been made in the years since these data were collected (1971–1972), considerable room for improvement still exists.

Second, workers' compensation attempts to eliminate delays, costs, and wastes of personal injury litigation. The existing system is based on the no-fault concept, presumably eliminating the need to undertake costly battles to establish guilt or innocence. This goal

---

[12]Robert J. Paul, " Workers' Compensation: An Adequate Employee Benefit?" *Academy of Management Review*, October 1976, p. 113.

[13]Ibid.

[14]Ibid.

has been largely achieved, despite some administrative problems in minimizing delays and costs.

Third, the law seeks to study and attempts to reduce the number of accident cases rather than to conceal them. While data on accident reduction records are not widely available, workers' compensation has two components that could provide incentive for development of a safe work environment. First, since most employers are experience rated (insurance premiums vary directly with the number of accidents experienced), they have a monetary incentive to reduce accidents.[15] Second, most laws require accurate records on accident data which, if assembled, could provide added insight into safety modification procedures appropriate for various industries. Unfortunately, many employers do not respond to this component of the law. Consequently, the resulting accident data are often sketchy and of little value in accident prevention.

Perhaps the most convincing evidence that workers' compensation laws have not met public expectations about accident prevention can be inferred from passage of the Occupational Safety and Health Act (OSHA) of 1970.[16] The provisions of OSHA are designed to improve working conditions in industry, thereby reducing worker accidents and job-related illnesses. Passage of the act suggests that the reactive approach (i.e., react to injuries after the fact through compensation) is insufficient incentive to stem job-related accidents.

Fourth, workers' compensation requires firms to provide prompt and adequate medical treatment. This provision has been a major contribution of workers' compensation laws. Most jurisdictions provide full medical treatment for injured workers without legal limitation on the time or cost of treatment.

Fifth, the law provides for rehabilitation of workers unable to return to their former jobs. Prior to the early 1970s this provision was the least effective aspect of existing workers' compensation programs. However, massive reforms of the law during the 1970s have resulted in additional rehabilitative benefits while a disabled employee enrolls in a retraining program.

Social Security

Today most working Americans and their families are protected by social security. Whether a worker retires, becomes disabled, or dies, social security benefits are paid to replace part of the lost family earnings. Indeed, ever since its passage in 1935, the Social Security Act has been designed and amended to provide a foundation of basic security for U.S. workers and their families. Exhibit 12.5 identifies initial coverage of the law and subsequent broadening of this coverage over the years.[17]

---

[15]Ibid.

[16]James Ledvinka, *Federal Regulation of Personnel and Human Resource Management* (Belmont, Calif.: Wadsworth Publishing, 1982).

[17]William J. Cohen, "The Evolution and Growth of Social Security," in *Federal Policies and Worker Status Since the Thirties*, ed. J.P. Goldberg, E. Ahern, W. Haber, and R.A. Oswald (Madison, Wis.: Industrial Relations Research Association, 1976), p. 62.

EXHIBIT 12.5
Social Security through the Years

1935:   **Original provisions of the law**
        Federal old-age benefits program.
        Public assistance for the aged, blind, and dependent children who would not otherwise qualify for
            social security.
        Unemployment compensation.
        Federal state program for maternity care, crippled children's services, child-welfare services.
        Public health services.
        Vocational rehabilitation services.

        Changes in the law since 1935
1939:   Survivor's insurance added to provide monthly life insurance payments to the widow and
            dependent children of a deceased worker.
1950–
1954:   Old-age and survivor's insurance was broadened.
1956:   Disability insurance benefits provided to workers and dependents of such employees.
1965:   Medical insurance protection to the aged and later (1973) the disabled under age 65 (medicare). ✓
1972:   Cost-of-living escalator tied to the consumer price index—guaranteed higher future benefits for all
            beneficiaries.
1974:   Existing state programs of financial assistance to the aged, blind, and disabled were replaced by
            SSI (supplemental security income) administered by the Social Security Administration.

The money to pay these benefits comes from the social security contributions made by employees, their employers, and self-employed people during working years. As contributions are paid in each year, they are immediately used to pay for the benefits to current beneficiaries. Herein lies a major problem with social security. While the number of retired workers continues to rise (because of earlier retirement and longer life spans), no corresponding increase in the number of contributors to social security has offset these costs. Combine these increases with other cost stimulants (e.g., liberal cost-of-living adjustments) and the outcome is not surprising. To maintain solvency, there has been a dramatic increase in both the maximum earnings base and the rate at which that base is taxed. Exhibit 12.6 illustrates the trends in tax rate, maximum earnings base, and maximum tax for social security.

The combined impact of these schedules for employers is twofold. Consider, for example, employees who earned $45,000 in 1990. They will have deducted from their wages $3,442 (7.65 percent of $45,000). The first obvious impact on an employer is that he must also pay $3,442. Less obviously, though, an employer should consider this social security contribution when determining appropriate pension benefits. A targeted level of pension benefits that neglects social security contributions results in retirement income subsidized by the employer in excess of forecasted objectives.

It is generally agreed that current funding levels will produce a massive surplus in the 1990s. Current baby boomers will reach their peak earnings potential and subsidize a much smaller generation born during the 1930s. Forecasts project a 70 billion dollar surplus in 1996 alone. As Exhibit 12.7 starkly projects, this surplus is expected to turn into a substantial shortfall sometime after the year 2015. By that time baby boomers will be at retirement age and too few workers will be contributing to the fund to balance the outflow. One proposed solution is to hold current surpluses in anticipation of future

EXHIBIT 12.6
Tax Rates, Maximum Earnings Base, and Maximum Social Security Tax

	Taxation Rate on Covered Earnings				Maximum Social Security Tax (dollars)
Year	For Retirement Survivors and Disability Insurance (percent)	For Hospital Insurance (percent)	Total (percent)	× Maximum Earnings Base (dollars)	
1978	5.05%	1.00%	6.05%	× $17,700	$1,070.85
1979	5.08	1.05	6.13	× 22,900	1,403.77
1980	5.08	1.05	6.13	× 25,900	1,587.67
1981	5.35	1.30	6.65	× 29,700	1,975.05
1982	5.40	1.30	6.70	× 32,400	2,170.80
1983	5.40	1.30	6.70	× 35,700	2,391.90
1984	5.40	1.30	7.0	× 37,800	2,646.00
1985	5.70	1.35	7.05	× 39,600	2,791.80
1986	5.70	1.45	7.15	× 42,000	3,003.00
1987	5.70	1.45	7.15	× *	—
1990	6.2	1.45	7.65	× *	—
2000	6.2	1.45	7.65	× *	—

*Automatic adjustments based on average earnings level.
Source: Social Security Administration (SSA) Bulletin No. 79-10044, 1979, and Annual Statistical Supplement.

EXHIBIT 12.7
Social Security: Projected Surpluses and Shortfalls

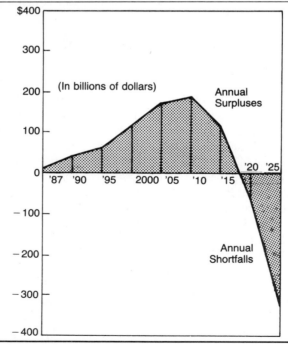

Source: Social Security Administration.

deficits. Unfortunately, it is unclear whether legislators will be able to resist using current and projected Social Security excesses to fund other program deficits.

Benefits under social security. The majority of benefits under Social Security fall into one of four categories: (1) old age or disability benefits paid to the covered worker, (2) benefits for dependents of retired or disabled workers, (3) benefits for surviving family members of a deceased worker, and (4) lump sum death payments. To qualify for these benefits, a worker must meet certain insured status requirements. Essentially the requirements can be distilled down to working in a covered employment and earning a specified amount of money ($470.00 in 1988) for each quarter year of coverage. Forty quarters of coverage will insure any worker for life. The amount received under the four benefits categories noted above varies, but in general is tied to the amount contributed during eligibility quarters. The maximum benefit for a family in 1988 was just under $1,500.00 per month.

Unemployment Insurance

The earliest union efforts to cushion the effects of unemployment for their members (c. 1830s) were part of benevolent programs of self-help. These efforts took the form of crises contributions by working members for their unemployed brethren.[18] With passage of the unemployment insurance law (as part of the Social Security Act of 1935), this floor of security for unemployed workers became less dependent upon the philanthropy of fellow workers. Since unemployment insurance laws vary state by state, this review will cover some of the major characteristics of different state programs.

Financing. Unemployment compensation paid out to eligible workers is financed exclusively by employers who pay federal and state unemployment insurance tax. The tax amounts to 6.2 percent of the first $7,000 earned by each worker. The state unemployment commission (or its equivalent) receives 5.4 percent of this 6.2 percent, and the remainder goes to the federal government for administrative costs and to repay federal government loans to the extended unemployment compensation account. All states allow for experience rating, charging lower percentages to employers who have terminated fewer employees. The tax rate may fall to 0 percent in some states for employers who have had no recent experience with former employees collecting chargeable unemployment insurance, and rise to 10 percent for organizations with large numbers of layoffs. These percentages translate into state unemployment taxes ranging from a high of $680.00 per worker in Alaska to a low of $175.00 in Nebraska.[19]

---

[18]Raymond Munts, "Policy Development in Unemployment Insurance," in *Federal Policies and Worker Status Since the Thirties*, ed. Goldberg, Ahern, Haber, and Oswald, pp. 89–106.

[19]Eugene Carlson, "Firm Unemployment Taxes Fell in Most States This Year," *Wall Street Journal*, December 29, 1987, p. 15.

Eligibility. To be eligible for benefits, an unemployed worker must: (1) be able, available, and actively seeking work; (2) not have refused suitable employment; (3) not be unemployed because of a labor dispute (except Rhode Island and New York); (4) not have left a job voluntarily; (5) not have been terminated for gross misconduct; and (6) have been previously employed in a covered industry or occupation, earning a designated minimum amount for a designated period of time.

These eligibility criteria eliminate many individuals who might otherwise qualify for UI.[20] As an example, of the 5,076,000 people unemployed in 1974, "672,000 had never been in the labor force and therefore failed to meet the minimum employment earnings criterion. Another 431,000 were teenagers who had left the labor force and subsequently reentered; they also were unlikely to have met the minimum employment earnings criterion. Additionally, 585,000 people were prime-age adults who voluntarily left their jobs and so were ineligible. These 1,688,000 persons, one third of the unemployed, were very likely ineligible for UI benefits."[21]

Coverage. All workers except a few agricultural and domestic workers are currently covered by unemployment insurance (UI) laws. These covered workers (97 percent of the work force) must still meet eligibility requirements to receive benefits.

Duration. Until 1958 the maximum number of weeks any claimant could collect UI was 26 weeks. However, the 1958 and 1960–61 recessions yielded large numbers of claimants who exhausted their benefits, leading many states temporarily to revise upward the maximum benefits duration. The most recent modification of this benefits duration (1982) involves a complex formula that ensures extended benefits in times of high unemployment. Extended benefits will be paid when either of two conditions prevails: (1) when the number of insured unemployed in a state reaches 6 percent, or (2) when the rate experienced is greater than 5 percent and at least 20 percent higher than in the same period of the two preceding calendar years over a 13-week time frame.[22]

Weekly benefits amount. Those unemployed workers who do meet eligibility requirements are entitled to a weekly benefit amount designed to equal 50 percent of the claimants' lost wages. A recent study indicates, though, that most states do not reach this 50 percent target level.[23] Nor do benefits appear to cover even the minimum nondeferable expenditures (e.g., minimum outlay for food and housing) faced by the average recipient.[24] Recognizing this problem, some states recently raised their benefits levels.

---

[20]Gary S. Fields, "Direct Labor Market Effects of Unemployment Insurance," *Industrial Relations 16*, no. 1 (February 1977), pp. 33–44.

[21]Ibid.

[22]C. Arthur Williams, John S. Turnbull, and Earl F. Cheit, *Economic and Social Security*, 5th ed. (New York: John Wiley & Sons, 1982).

[23]Elchanan Cohn and Margaret Capen, "A Note on the Adequacy of UI Benefits," *Industrial Relations*, 26(1), 1987, pp. 106–111.

[24]Ibid.

EXHIBIT 12.8
Cost Elements in Replacing a Terminated Worker

	Direct	Indirect	Total
Added overhead costs			
Employment agency fee	$___	$___	$___
Advertising	___	___	___
Recruitment	___	___	___
Public relations activities	___	___	___
Processing applications	___	___	___
Interviewing, reference check	___	___	___
Psychological testing	___	___	___
Orientation materials (films, brochures)	___	___	___
Medical exam	___	___	___
Accounting and payroll entries	___	___	___
Pension plan, health insurance	___	___	___
Workers' compensation premiums	___	___	___
Increased social security payments	___	___	___
Increased unemployment insurance premiums	___	___	___
Added operating costs			
On-the-job training	___	___	___
Supervisor's time with new employee	___	___	___
Formal training program participation	___	___	___
Material spoilage	___	___	___
Increased inspection	___	___	___
Temporary employees hired to make up for low output of new hires	___	___	___
Overtime paid to maintain productivity	___	___	___
Loss of productivity between separation of former employee and hire of new employee	___	___	___
Loss of productivity between time of decision to quit (discharge) and actual quit (discharge)	___	___	___
Severance pay	___	___	___
Estimated cost per replacement	$___	$___	$___

Source: Allan Janoff, "You Can Reduce Your Unemployment Taxes." Reprinted from the January 1976 issue of *Personnel Administrator*, copyright 1976, The American Society for Personnel Administration, 606 North Washington Street, Alexandria, VA 22314, $40 per year.

Controlling unemployment taxes. Every unemployed worker's unemployment benefits are "charged" against one or more companies. The more money paid out on behalf of a firm, the higher is the unemployment insurance rate for that firm. Couple the increased insurance premiums with the costs of replacing a terminated worker (Exhibit 12.8), and it is apparent that the costs of terminations are high. Efforts to control these costs quite logically should begin with a well-designed human resources planning system. Realistic estimates of human resources needs will reduce the need for hasty hiring and morale-breaking terminations. Additionally, a benefits administrator should attempt to audit prelayoff behavior (e.g., lateness, gross misconduct, absenteeism, illness, leaves of absence) and compliance with UI requirements after termination (e.g., job refusals, insufficient duration of covered work).

EQUAL EMPLOYMENT OPPORTUNITY AND BENEFITS

Two Equal Employment Opportunity laws have substantial impacts on benefits policy and procedures: Title VII of the Civil Rights Act of 1964 and the Age Discrimination in

Employment Act (1967). Both laws have provisions outlawing differential contributions to or coverage from benefit plans when such differential treatment is based on protected group status (in these cases, sex and age).

Civil Rights Act

Title VII of the Civil Rights Act prohibits discrimination in terms and conditions of employment (including benefits) that is based on race, color, religion, sex, or national origin. One interpretive issue related to benefits that has arisen since passage of the act involves sex discrimination. In particular, should pregnant women be permitted health, disability, and/or sick leave benefits because of pregnancy? In the 1976 case of *Gilbert v. General Electric Corporation* the Supreme Court held that the disability insurance program was not sex discriminatory under Title VII.[25] Reasoning that men and women were covered under the GE plan equally except for one condition, pregnancy, the Court ruled no insurance plan must be all inclusive. This decision met with sufficient opposition from women's organizations, unions, civil rights groups, and sympathetic legislators to be overturned by law in 1978. The pregnancy disability amendment, as it is called, "prohibits the denial of health, disability, or sick leave benefits to pregnant women temporarily disabled by childbirth itself or by a medical condition incurred before or after childbirth." Such coverage applies only if a valid benefits plan is already in effect and if the pregnant employee is medically able to work.

A second area where sex discrimination may exist is in pension plans. Two types of plans have been alleged to be discriminatory:

1. A plan requiring women to contribute a higher premium than men in order to receive the same benefits as a man, other things equal.
2. A plan requiring women to contribute the same amount but receive less benefits than a man, other things equal.

The Supreme Court in the *Manhart* case (reaffirmed and extended in the *Norris* case) rejected the defense that the higher payment rate was justified on actuarial grounds because women as a class live about five years longer than men; therefore, the cost of a pension plan for the average retired woman was greater than the cost for the average retired man. In rejecting this claim, the Supreme Court agreed that actuarial tables show the average woman living longer than the average man. However, for many individual cases, women live shorter lives than men. Title VII clearly applies to the individual and, thus, the Court ruled against decisions based on class characteristics. This decision means not only that women receive the same pension but also contribute the same amount, other things equal. The added costs of this coverage, therefore, are borne by the company.

Age Discrimination in Employment Act

The Age Discrimination in Employment Act prohibits job-related discrimination against individuals over 40 years of age. In addition, the Omnibus Budget Reconciliation Act of

---

[25]429 US 125.

1986 prohibits employers from discriminating on the basis of age for pension accrual.[26] All employees working beyond "the normal retirement age" will continue to receive credit for time worked and have contributions made into their retirement plans.

The remainder of this chapter examines employee benefits that are not legally required. However, if the employer chooses to provide these benefits, many of them are subject to certain regulatory and taxation laws (e.g., pensions, profit sharing, life insurance, educational benefits). The review follows the categorization listed earlier in this chapter.

RETIREMENT AND SAVINGS PLAN PAYMENTS

The last chapter noted that a high relationship exists between employee age and preference for a pension plan. While this need for old age security may become more pronounced as workers age, it is also evident among younger workers.

This security motive and certain tax advantages have fostered the rise of pension programs. As Exhibit 12.3 indicated, the vast majority of employers (private sector = 89 percent; public sector = 95 percent) choose to provide this benefit as part of their overall package. Pension programs provide income to an employee at some future time as compensation for work performed now. Two types of pension plans will be discussed in varying degrees here: (1) defined benefit and (2) defined contribution plans.

Defined Benefit Plans

In a defined benefit plan an employer agrees to provide a specific level of retirement pension, which is expressed as either a fixed dollar or percentage-of-earnings amount that may vary (increase) with years of seniority in the company. The firm finances this obligation by following an actuarially determined benefits formula and making current payments that will yield the future pension benefit for a retiring employee. Only about 29 percent of all pension plans are this variety, but they exist primarily in large organizations. This translates into 80 percent of all pension participants being covered by these plans.

Defined benefit plans generally follow one of three different formulas. The most common approach (54 percent) is to calculate average earnings over the last 3–5 years of service for a prospective retiree and offer a pension that is a function of this earnings average and years of seniority. Plans that are considered generous typically target for pensions equal to 50 to 80 percent of final-average earnings. At the low end of the "generosity" scale are plans that target for 30 to 50 percent of final-average pay. The second formula (14 percent of companies) for a defined benefits plan uses average career earnings rather than earnings from the last few years: other things equal this would reduce the level of benefit for pensioners. The final formula (28 percent of companies) commits an employer to a fixed dollar amount that is not dependent on any earnings data. This figure generally rises with seniority level.

---

[26]Public Law No. 99-507, 100 Stat. 1975 (1986).

EXHIBIT 12.9
The High Cost of Job-Hopping
(Pensions based on one percentage point for each year of service multiplied by final salary)

		Years of Service	Percentage Point Credit	Final Salary	Annual Pensions
Employee A	1st job	10	10%	× $ 35,817 =	$ 3,582
	2nd job	10	10	× 64,143 =	6,414
	3rd job	10	10	× 114,870 =	11,487
	4th job	10	10	× 205,714 =	20,571
				Total Pension:	$42,054
Employee B	1st job	40	40	× 205,714 =	82,286
				Total Pension:	$82,286

Note: Figures assume starting salary of $20,000 and 6% annual inflation rate.
Pay increases match inflation rate.
Source: Federal Reserve Bank of Boston

The level of pension a company chooses to offer depends on the answer to several questions. First, what level of retirement compensation would a company like to set as a target, expressed in relation to preretirement earnings. Second, should Social Security payments be factored in when considering the level of income an employee should have during retirement. About one third of the plans monitored by the Department of Labor have a provision for integration with social security benefits.[27] One integration approach reduces normal benefits by a percentage (usually 50 percent) of social security benefits.[28] Another feature employs a more liberal benefits formula on earnings that exceed the maximum income taxed by social security. Regardless of the formula used, about two thirds of U.S. companies do not employ the cost-cutting strategy. Once a company has targeted the level of income it wants to provide employees in retirement, it makes sense to design a system that integrates private pension and social security to achieve that goal. Any other strategy is not cost effective.

Third, should other postretirement income sources (e.g., savings plans that are partially funded by employer contributions) be integrated with the pension payment? Fourth, a company must decide how to factor seniority into the payout formula. The larger the role played by seniority, the more important pensions will be in retaining employees. Most companies believe that the maximum pension payout for a particular level of earnings should only be achieved by employees who have spent an entire career with the company (e.g., 30 to 35 years). As Exhibit 12.9 vividly illustrates, job hoppers are hurt financially by this type of strategy.

[27]Frumkin and Schmitt, "Pension Improvements Since 1974 Reflect Inflation, New U.S. Law," pp. 66–78.

[28]Jerry S. Rosenbloom and G. Victor Hallman, *Employee Benefit Planning* (Englewood Cliffs, NJ: Prentice-Hall, 1981).

Defined Contribution Plans

Defined contribution plans require specific contributions by an employer, but the final benefit received by employees is unknown, depending on the investment success of those charged with administering the pension fund.

There are two popular forms of defined contribution plans. A 401 (K) plan, so named for the section of the Internal Revenue Code describing the requirements, is a savings-type plan in which employees are allowed to defer income up to a $7,000.00 maximum. Employers match employee savings, typically at the level of fifty cents for each dollar deferred. The maximum deferral level rises from $7,000.00 depending on changes in the Consumer Price Index (e.g., 1988 = $7,313).

The second type of plan, described in greater detail in Chapter 10, is an Employee Stock Ownership Plan (ESOP). In a basic ESOP a company makes a tax deductible contribution of stock shares or cash to a trust. The trust then allocates company stock (or stock bought with cash contribution) to participating employee accounts. The amount allocated is based on employee earnings. When an ESOP is used as a pension vehicle (as opposed to an incentive program) the employees receive cash at retirement based upon the stock value at that time. ESOPs have one major disadvantage that limits their utility for pension accumulations. Many employees are reluctant to "bet" most of their future retirement income on just one investment source. If the company's stock takes a downturn, the result can be catastrophic for employees approaching retirement age.

The advantages and disadvantages of each type of plan are outlined in Exhibit 12.10. Possibly the most important of the factors noted in Exhibit 12.10 is the differential risk borne by employers on the cost dimension. Defined contribution plans have known costs from year one. The employer agrees to a specific level of payment that only changes through negotiation or through some voluntary action. In contrast, defined contribution plans commit the employer to a specific level of benefit. Errors in actuarial projections can add considerably to costs over the years. Perhaps for this reason, defined contribution plans have been more popular for new adoptions over the past 15 years.

Not surprisingly, both of these deferred compensation plans are subject to stringent tax laws. For deferred compensation to be exempt from current taxation, specific requirements must be met. To qualify (hence labeled a "qualified" deferred compensation plan), an employer cannot freely choose who will participate in the plan. This requirement eliminated the common practice of discriminating in favor of executives and other highly

EXHIBIT 12.10
Relative Advantages of Different Pension Alternatives

	Defined Benefit Plan	*Defined Contribution Plan*
1.	Provides an explicit benefit which is easily communicated	Unknown benefit level is difficult to communicate
2.	Company absorbs risk associated with changes in inflation and interest rates which affect cost	Employees assume these risks
3.	More favorable to long service employees	More favorable to short-term employees
4.	Employer costs unknown	Employer costs known up front

compensated employees. The major advantage of a qualified plan is that the employer receives an income tax deduction for contributions made to the plan even though employees may not yet have received any benefits. The disadvantage arises in recruitment of high-talent executives. A plan will not qualify for tax exemptions if an employer pays high levels of deferred compensation to entice executives to the firm, unless proportionate contributions also are made to lower level employees.

The Appendix illustrates one example of the language used in describing pension benefits.

ERISA

Private pension plans ran into serious criticism in the recession of the early 1970s for a number of reasons. Many people who thought they were covered were not because of complicated rules, insufficient funding, irresponsible financial management, and employer bankruptcies. Some pension funds, including both employer-managed and union-managed funds, were accused of mismanagement; other pension plans required long vesting periods. The Employee Retirement Income Security Act was passed in 1974 in response to these criticisms.

ERISA does not require that employers offer a pension plan, but pension plans in existence are rigidly controlled by ERISA provisions. These provisions were designed to achieve two goals: (1) "to protect the interest of 35 million workers who are covered today by private retirement plans and (2) to stimulate the growth of such plans."

The actual success of ERISA in achieving these goals has been mixed at best. In the first two full years of operation (1975–1976) more than 13,000 pension plans were terminated. A major factor in these terminations, along with the recession, was ERISA. Employers complained about the excessive costs and paperwork of living under ERISA. Some disgruntled employers even claimed ERISA was an acronym for "Every Ridiculous Idea Since Adam." To examine the merits of these claims, let us take a closer look at the major requirements of ERISA.

General requirements. ERISA requires that employees be eligible for pension plans beginning at age 21. Employers may require one year of service as a precondition for participation. The service requirement may be extended to 3 years if the pension plan offers full and immediate vesting.

Vesting and portability. These two concepts are sometimes confused but have very different meanings in practice. Vesting refers to the length of time an employee must work for an employer before he or she is entitled to benefits accruing in the pension plan. The vesting concept has two components. First, any contributions made by the employee to a pension fund are immediately and irrevocably vested. The vesting right becomes questionable only with respect to the employer's contributions. As mandated by ERISA, and amended by the tax reform act of 1986, the employer's contribution must vest at least as quickly as one of the following two formulas: (1) full vesting after five years, or (2) 20 percent after three years and 20 percent each year thereafter (full in seven years).

The vesting schedule an employer uses is often a function of the demographic makeup of the work force. An employer who experiences high turnover may wish to use the five-year service schedule. By so doing, any employee with fewer than five years' service at time of termination receives no vested benefits. Or the employer may use the second schedule in the hopes that earlier benefits accrual will reduce undesired turnover. The strategy adopted is, therefore, dependent on organizational goals and work force characteristics.

Portability of pension benefits becomes an issue for employees moving to new organizations. Should pension assets accompany the transferring employee in some fashion?[29] ERISA does not require mandatory portability of private pensions. On a voluntary basis, though, the employer may agree to let an employee's pension benefits transfer to the new employer. For an employer to permit portability, of course, the pension rights must be vested.

Fiduciary responsibility. Today over $400 billion exist in private pension accounts in the United States. Unrestrained investment of these funds by a company representative could lead to substantial abuse.[30] Consequently ERISA stipulates that the fiduciary entrusted with investment decisions is legally obligated to follow a "prudent man" rule. Included in the operational definition of a prudent man are certain prohibitions against investments made in self-interest.

Pension benefit guaranty corporation. Despite the wealth of constraints imposed by ERISA, the potential still exists for an organization to go bankrupt, or in some way fail to meet its vested pension obligations. To protect individuals confronted by this problem, employers are required to pay insurance premiums to the Pension Benefit Guaranty Corporation (PBGC) established by ERISA. In turn, the PBGC guarantees payment of vested benefits to employees formerly covered by terminated pension plans.

LIFE INSURANCE

One of the most common employee benefits offered by organizations is some form of life insurance. Typical coverage would be a group term insurance policy with a face value of one to two times the employee's salary. Most plan premiums are paid completely by the employer, and slightly over 80 percent include retiree coverage. The policy provides protection against loss of life for a specified period, but provides no cash surrender value or investment value. About two-thirds of all policies include accidental death and dismemberment clauses. To discourage turnover, almost all companies make this benefit forfeitable at termination.

Life insurance is one of the benefits heavily affected by movement to a flexible benefits program. A typical program provides a core of basic life coverage (e.g., $25,000)

---

[29]Susan M. Philips and Linda P. Fletcher, "The Future of the Portable Pension Concept," *Industrial and Labor Relations Review 30* (1977), p. 197.

[30]Mark Gertner, "ERISA and the Investment Decision Making Process: The Past, the Present, and the Future," *Employee Benefits Journal,* June 1985, pp. 28–35.

and then permits employees to choose greater coverage (e.g., in increments of $10,000–25,000) as part of their optional package.

MEDICAL AND MEDICALLY RELATED PAYMENTS

General Health Care

The American health system today costs in excess of $500 billion annually. Health care costs represented 5.9 percent of gross national product in 1965 and 10.5 percent in 1983. There was a 400 percent increase in health care costs between 1970 and 1981.[31] More costly technology, increased numbers of elderly, and a system that does not encourage cost savings have all contributed to the rapidly rising costs of medical insurance. In the past 10 years, though, employers have begun to take steps designed to curb these costs. After a discussion of the types of health care systems, these cost-cutting strategies will be discussed.

An employer's share of health care costs is contributed into one of five health care systems: (1) a community-based system, such as Blue Cross; (2) a commercial insurance plan; (3) self-insurance; (4) a health maintenance organization (HMO); or (5) a preferred provider organization (PPO).

Of these five, plans 1 through 3 operate in a similar fashion. Two major distinctions exist, however. The first distinction is in the manner payments are made. With Blue Cross, the employer-paid premiums guarantee employees a direct service, including room, board, and any necessary health services covered by the plan. Coverage under a commercial insurance plan guarantees fixed payment for hospital service to the insured, who in turn reimburses the hospital. And finally, a self-insurance plan implies that the company provides coverage out of its own assets, assuming the risks itself within state legal guidelines. A Johnson and Higgins Survey claims self-funding is on the rise, with 46 percent of the companies surveyed claiming some level of self-funding. The most common strategy is to couple self-funding with stop loss coverage, essentially an insurance policy covering costs in excess of some predetermined level (e.g., $50,000.00).[32]

The second distinction is in the way costs of medical benefits are determined. Blue Cross operates via the concept of community rating. In effect, insurance rates are based on the medical experience of the entire community. Higher use of medical facilities results in higher premiums. In contrast, insurance companies operate off a narrower experience rating base, preferring to charge each company separately according to its medical facility usage. Finally, of course, the cost of medical coverage under a self-insurance program is directly related to usage level, with employer payments going directly to medical care providers rather than to secondary sources in the form of premiums.

As a fourth delivery system, health maintenance organizations offer comprehensive benefits for a fixed fee. Health maintenance organizations offer routine medical services

---

[31]Daniel Stone and E. G. Sue Reitz, "Health Care Cost Containment and Its Impact on Employee Relations," *Personnel Administrator 29* (1984), pp. 27 –33.

[32]*Wall Street Journal*, "Self Funding: Many Companies Try it for Health Benefits," June 2, 1987, p. 1.

at a specific site. Employees make prepayments in exchange for guaranteed health care services on demand. By emphasizing preventive treatment and early diagnosis, HMOs reduce the need for hospitalization to about one half the national average.[33] By law, employers of more than 25 employees are required to provide employees the option of joining a federally qualified HMO. If the employee opts for HMO coverage the employer is required to pay the HMO premium or an amount equal to the premium for previous health coverage, whichever is less.

Finally, preferred provider organizations represent a new form of health care delivery in which there is a direct contractual relationship between and among employers, health care providers, and third-party payers.[34] An employer is able to select providers (e.g., selected doctors) who agree to price discounts and strict utilization controls. In turn, the employer influences employees to use the preferred providers through financial incentives. Doctors benefit by increasing patient flow. Employers benefit through increased cost savings. And employees benefit through wider choice of doctors than might be available under an HMO. Whether other benefits or disadvantages of PPOs surface depends on broader exposure and experimentation with this newest cost-cutting alternative.

Health Care: Cost Control Strategies

There are basically three general strategies available to benefit managers for controlling the rapidly escalating costs of health care.[35] First, organizations can motivate employees to change their demand for health care, through changes in either the design or the administration of health insurance policies.[36] Included in this category of control strategies are: (1) deductibles (the first x dollars of health care cost are paid by the employee); (2) coinsurance rates (premium payments are shared by company and employee); (3) maximum benefits (defining a maximum payout schedule for specific health problems); (4) coordination of benefits (ensure no double payment when coverage exists under the employee's plan and a spouse's plan); (5) auditing of hospital charges for accuracy; (6) requiring preauthorization for selected visits to health care facilities; (7) mandatory second opinion whenever surgery is recommended.[37]

The second general cost control strategy involves changing the structure of health care delivery systems and participating in business coalitions (for data collection and dissemination). The trend toward HMOs and PPOs falls under this category. Even under

---

[33]Janice Ross, "Attacking Soaring Health Benefit Costs," *Pension World 14*, no. 1 (1978), p. 51.

[34]Thomas Billet, "An Employer's Guide to Preferred Provider Organizations," *Compensation Review 16*, no. 4 (1984), pp. 58–62.

[35]Regina Herzlinger and Jeffrey Schwartz, "How Companies Tackle Health Care Costs: Part I," *Harvard Business Review 63* (July–August 1985), pp. 69–81.

[36]David Rosenbloom, "Oh Brother, Our Medical Costs Went Up Again," Paper presented for the Health Data Institute, March 16, 1988.

[37]Herzlinger and Schwartz, "How Companies Tackle Health Care Costs: Part I"; Regina Herzlinger, "How Companies Tackle Health Care Costs: Part II," *Harvard Business Review 63* (September–October 1985), pp. 105–121.

EXHIBIT 12.11
Selected Cost Control Strategies and Their Effectiveness

Cost Control Strategy	Number of Companies Using Strategy	Percentage Considering Strategy	
		Most Effective	*Least Effective*
Claims and use review	137	46	7
Auditing insurers	189	42	18
Business coalitions	182	30	18
Offer alternative delivery systems	138	28	15
Identify high-cost providers	109	11	7
Cost control task forces	114	10	3
Company negotiated provider contracts	38	7	1
Company negotiated hospital contracts	17	6	1

Source: Regina Herzlinger, "How Companies Tackle Health Care Costs: Part II," *Harvard Business Review* 63, September–October 1985, p. 109.

more traditional delivery systems, though, there is more negotiation of rates with hospitals and other health care-delivery agents.

The final cost strategy involves promotion of preventive health programs. No-smoking policies and incentives for quitting smoking are popular inclusions here. But there is also increased interest in healthier food in cafeterias/vending machines, on-site physical fitness facilities, and early detection screening to identify possible health problems before they become more serious.[38] One review of physical fitness programs found fitness led to better mental health and improved resistance to stress. There also was some evidence of increased productivity, increased commitment, decreased absenteeism, and decreased turnover.[39] Exhibit 12.11 shows typical cost control strategies and an assessment of how effective each has been.

Dental Insurance

A rarity 20 years ago, dental insurance is now quite prevalent. Dental insurance is a standard inclusion for 91 percent of the major U.S. employers.[40] This translates into over 100 million workers with some form of dental insurance.

In many respects dental care coverage follows the model originated in health care plans. The dental equivalent of HMOs and PPOs are standard delivery systems. For example a dental HMO enlists a group of dentists who agree to treat company employees in return for a fixed monthly fee per employee.[41]

---

[38]W. Robert Nay, "Worksite Health-Promotion Programs," *Compensation and Benefits Review*, 17(5), 1985, pp. 57–64.

[39]Loren Falkenberg, "Employee Fitness Programs: Their Impact on the Employee and the Organization," *Academy of Management Review*, 1987, 12(3), pp. 511–522.

[40]Carroll Roarty, "Biting Dental Insurance Costs," *Personnel Administrator*, 33(11), 1988, pp. 68–71.

[41]"Dental Insurance Program Gains Favor Among Firms," *The Wall Street Journal*, September 21, 1984, p. 31.

EXHIBIT 12.12
An Example of a Multitiered Salary Continuation Plan

Duration of Illness	Percentage of Salary to Individual
Less than 26 weeks	100
26–52 weeks	75
More than 52 weeks	See long-term disability plan

Organizations may only pay that portion not covered by social security and up to a maximum dollar amount, e.g., $100,000.

Fortunately for employers, dental insurance costs have not spiraled like health care costs. In part this is due to stringent cost control strategies (e.g., plan maximum payouts are typically $1,000 or less per year), but the excess supply of dentists in the United States also has helped keep costs competitive.[42] Dental costs remain relatively stable at around .8–1.0 percent of payroll.[43]

Vision Care

Vision care dates back only to the 1976 contract between the United States Auto Workers and the Big 3 auto makers. Since then, this benefit has spread to other auto-related industries and parts of the public sector. Most plans are noncontributory and usually cover partial costs of eye examination, lens, and frames.

Short and Long-Term Disability

A number of benefit options provide some form of protection for disability. For example, workers' compensation covers disabilities that are work related. Even social security has provisions for disability income to those who qualify. Beyond these two legally required sources, there are two similar sources of disability income: employee salary continuation plans and long-term disability plans.

Many companies have some form of salary continuation plan that pays out varying levels of income depending on duration of illness. At one extreme is short-term illness covered by sick leave policy and typically reimbursed at a level equal to 100 percent of salary.[44] After such leave benefits run out, disability benefits become operative. The benefit level is typically less than 100 percent of salary, and may be multitiered. An example of a multitiered plan follows the quite liberal formula noted in Exhibit 12.12.

Most private disability income benefits are provided through plans underwritten by

---

[42]Harry Sutton, "Prescription Drug and Dental Programs," *Compensation and Benefits Review*, 18(4), 1986, pp. 67–71.

[43]Ibid.

[44]Employee Benefit Plan Review, "Disability Plan Survey Identifies Common Elements," *Employee Benefit Plan Review 10* (April 1981), p. 9.

insurance companies. Typically these plans become effective when an employee salary continuation plan expires. So, for example, an injured worker covered by the payment schedule in Exhibit 12.12 would start collecting long-term disability (LTD) after 52 weeks.[45] Most company LTD plans then provide between 50 and 66 percent of an employee's wages for a period varying between two years and life.

PAID TIME OFF DURING WORK HOURS

Paid rest periods, lunch periods, wash-up time, travel time, clothes-change time, and get-ready time benefits are self-explanatory. Most work-time-off arrangements evolved historically on an informal basis or were negotiated in labor contracts.

PAYMENT FOR TIME NOT WORKED

Included within this category are several self-explanatory benefits:

1. Paid vacations and payments in lieu of vacation.
2. Payments for holidays not worked.
3. Paid sick leave.
4. Payments for National Guard or army or other reserve duty; jury duty and voting pay allowances; payments for time lost due to death in family or other personal reasons.

Judging from employee preferences discussed in the last chapter and from observation of negotiated union contracts, pay for time not worked continues to be a high-demand benefit. Twenty years ago it was relatively rare, for example, to grant time for anything but vacations, holidays, and sick leave. Now many organizations have a policy of ensuring payments for civic responsibilities and obligations. Any pay for such duties (e.g., National

EXHIBIT 12.13
Payment for Time Not Worked

Paid Leave Type	Average Private Sector 1986	Average State and Local Government 1987
Rest period	24 minutes/day	29 minutes/day
Holidays	10/year	11/year
Vacation	8.8 days for 1 yr. service	12 days for 1 year service
	20.6 days for 20 yr. service	21 days for 20 yr. service
Funeral leave	3.2 days/occurrence	4 days/occurrence
Military leave	11.5 days/year	17 days/year
Jury Duty	as needed	as needed
Sick Leave	15.2 days/year with full pay after 1 year service	13 days/year with full pay after 1 year service

Source: U.S. Department of Labor Bulletins 2281 (1986) and 2309 (1987).

[45]William Wiatrowski, "Employee Income Protection against Short Term Disability," *Monthly Labor Review*, February 1985, pp. 33–38.

Guard, jury duty) are usually nominal, so companies often supplement this pay, frequently to the level of 100 percent of wages lost. There is also increasing coverage for parental leaves. Maternity and, to a lesser extent, paternity leaves are much more common than 25 years ago.

Exhibit 12.13 outlines the average paid leave time for covered employees.

MISCELLANEOUS BENEFITS

Child Care

As of 1988 approximately 3,500 companies offered day care as a benefit.[46] Over the next 15 years more and more companies are projected to open day care centers for the preschool children of employees. In part these centers are intended as a tool to attract and retain employees. Impending labor shortages in the 1990s, combined with greater labor force participation by both parents, make day care an attractive option for the decade ahead.

Legal Insurance

Prior to the 1970s, prepaid legal insurance was practically nonexistent. In recent years, however, prepaid legal insurance has become an increasingly popular benefit, with recent estimates placed at 30 million enrollees.[47] Tremendous variety exists in the structure, options, delivery systems, and attorney compensation mechanisms. Across these plans, there are still some commonalities. A majority of plans provide routine legal services (e.g., divorce, real estate matters, wills, traffic violations) but exclude provisions covering felony crimes, largely because of the expense and potential for bad publicity. Employees with legal problems either select legal counsel from a panel of lawyers selected by the firm (closed-panel mechanism) or freely choose their own lawyers with claims reimbursed by an insurance carrier.

SUMMARY

Since the 1940s employees benefits have been the most volatile area in the compensation field. From 1940 to 1980 these dramatic changes came in the form of more and better forms of employee benefits. The result should not have been unexpected. Employee benefits are now a major, and many believe prohibitive, component of doing business. Look for the decade of the 1990s to be dominated by cost-saving efforts to improve the competitive position of American industry. A part of these cost savings will come from tighter administrative controls on existing benefit packages. But another part, as already seen in the auto industry, may come from a reduction in existing benefits packages. If

---

[46]Jaclyn Fierman, "Child Care: What Works—and Doesn't." *Fortune*, November 21, 1988, pp. 165–176.

[47]William Giese, "Cover Story," *USA Today*, July 9, 1987, p. 1.

this does evolve as a trend, benefits administrators will need to develop a mechanism for identifying employee preferences (in this case "least preferences") and use those as a guideline to meet agreed-upon savings targets.

REVIEW QUESTIONS

1. Are Workers' Compensation Laws effective? Defend your answer.
2. Why are people concerned about funding social security payments if there is currently a surplus (tax exceeds payouts)?
3. Why are Defined Contribution Pension Plans gaining in popularity in the United States?
4. Explain the role of experience rating in employee benefits. Use Unemployment Insurance to illustrate your case.
5. Which of the benefits in this chapter seem best suited to linking benefit level with seniority?

Appendix: Pfizer Benefits Program

YOUR BENEFITS AT PFIZER

At first glance, the Pfizer Employee Benefit Program—like all such programs—may appear to be an assortment of unrelated Plans. Actually, each Pfizer benefit has been developed and improved to take care of you—*and* in many cases your dependents—in certain types of situations when extra financial assistance is needed.

There are four major types of coverage in the Pfizer Employee Benefit Program: survivors' assistance, disability protection, health care and retirement income—all of which are outlined in this brochure. In addition, you and your family may enjoy many other benefits throughout your active Pfizer career. These include: holidays, vacations, educational assistance, matching gifts, scholarships, military leave and active duty training allowances, and adoption benefits—highlights of which are also shown in this brochure.

All in all, the Pfizer Employee Benefit Program gives you and your family a full range of financial protection and security—above and beyond your regular earnings as an employee. Actually, these benefits represent a substantial *addition* to your earnings and many allow certain tax advantages.

In addition to your Pfizer benefits, Social Security provides income and medical benefits to you and/or your qualified dependents upon disability, death or retirement. Workers' Compensation also provides cash, income, medical and death benefits to you and certain family members if you qualify as the result of a job-related accident.

As you can see, the various benefits in the Pfizer Program and those provided by law work together to give you and your family well-rounded protection when it's needed most.

Each Plan in the Benefit Program has been carefully designed with the welfare of our employees in mind. The Plans are continually reviewed to make certain they remain up to date and to ensure that they are accomplishing the job they were intended to do. In fact, we feel that the Program is one of the best to be found anywhere today.

417

Survivor Benefits	Coverage
Life Insurance . . . pays benefits to your beneficiary whatever the cause of your death.	**Basic**—Approximately *two times* your annual compensation—maximum benefit of *$500,000*—until your normal retirement date—reduced amounts thereafter. Part of your Life Insurance continues into retirement—at no cost to you. **Supplemental**—Choice of approximately one, two or three times your annual compensation, up to a maximum benefit of *$500,000*.
Accidental Death and Dismemberment Coverage . . . pays *additional* benefits to your beneficiary if you die—or to you if you suffer dismemberment as a result of an accident.	Amounts equal to your Basic and Supplemental Life Insurance for: • loss of life • loss of any two limbs or entire sight of both eyes (one-half of the coverage for loss of one limb or entire sight of one eye).
Business Travel Accident Insurance . . . pays *additional* benefits to your beneficiary if you are killed on a covered Company business trip—or to you, if you lose sight or limb.	*Six* times your annual compensation— *Minimum $50,000/maximum $500,000*—for loss of life, any two limbs or entire sight of both eyes. *One-Half* of insurance amount— *Minimum $50,000/maximum $250,000*—for loss of one limb or entire sight of one eye.

Disability Benefits	Coverage		
Short Term Disability . . . helps continue part of our pay for temporary absences from work because of illness or injury.	Service	Full Salary	Half Salary
	Less than 10 years	6 months	0
	10 but less than 15 years	6 months	3 months
	15 or more years	6 months	6 months
Long Term Disability Plan . . . helps continue part of your pay if you become ill or are injured and cannot work.	60% of your insured monthly compensation *up* to a maximum monthly benefit of *$3,600* including Workers' Compensation, Social Security disability benefits and any other Pfizer Group Plan Benefits.		

Health Care Benefits	Coverage
For you and each of your covered dependents: **Comprehensive Medical Plan** . . . provides coverage for a broad range of medical services. Three types of expenses are covered by the Plan—Type A, Type B and Type C.	*TYPE A EXPENSES*—100% of reasonable and customary charges, with no deductible required, for certain cost-effective services such as second surgical opinions, outpatient surgery and outpatient diagnostic x-rays and lab tests. *TYPE B EXPENSES*—100% of reasonable and customary charges for semi-private hospital room and board and special services or intensive care charges *after* the deductibles are met. Most hospital benefits are payable for as long as each hospital confinement lasts—except for confinements for treatment of alcoholism and drug abuse. For those conditions, hospital benefits are payable for up to a lifetime maximum of 365 days. *TYPE C EXPENSES*—80% of reasonable and customary charges for all other covered services and supplies not included as Type A or Type B expenses *after* the deductibles are met.

Health Care Benefits	*Coverage*
	DEDUCTIBLES

- Calendar year Plan deductible of $200 per individual/$500 per family for most Type B and Type C expenses.
- Hospital deductible of $100 per confinement—in addition to the calendar year Plan deductible, if not previously satisfied—up to a maximum of three hospital deductibles per person per calendar year.
- Services received in a hospital emergency room
    - —$25 deductible per visit for treatment or outpatient surgery within 72 hours of an accident;
    - —$25 per visit deductible *and* calendar year Plan deductible (if not previously satisfied) for all other services performed in a hospital emergency room.

EMPLOYEE OUT-OF-POCKET MAXIMUM

- An out-of-pocket calendar year maximum of $2,000 per family applies to all covered expenses not reimbursed by the Plan, including the deductibles. Thereafter, the Plan will pay 100% of additional covered charges incurred during the remainder of that calendar year. (Expenses for the treatment of alcohol and drug abuse may not be applied toward the out-of-pocket maximum.)

PLAN MAXIMUMS

- Unlimited lifetime dollar maximum for most covered charges.
- $50,000 per person combined lifetime maximum for outpatient psychiatric visits and outpatient treatment of alcoholism and drug abuse.
- $50,000 per person maximum for hospice care.

Dental Plan
. . . pays benefits for a wide variety of dental procedures—*including orthodontia*—with no deductible at all.

100% of reasonable and customary charges for most forms of preventive and diagnostic care—*and*
50% of reasonable and customary charges for repair or replacement of natural teeth—*up to*

$1,000 per person each calendar year—*with*
$10,000 in lifetime benefits per peron—*plus*
$1,000 in lifetime benefits per person for orthodontia alone.

Retirement Benefits	*Coverage*

Retirement Annuity Plan
. . . is designed to pay an income for life to you and—in the case of your death—to your surviving spouse.

The pension plan has two formulas and the one which produces the *higher* benefit for you is used. One formula provides a benefit based on 1.4% of your Pfizer Career Earnings for service up to 35 years. The other formula provides a benefit based on 1.75% of your Pfizer Career Earnings for service up to 35 years less a portion of your projected Primary Social Security benefit. Career Earnings are determined by multiplying the *average* of your earnings for your highest consecutive five calendar years prior to January 1, 1987 times years of service prior to January 1, 1987 and then adding your actual earnings from 1987 to the date you retire. If you are *not* married when your retirement benefit commences, you will receive a straight life annuity payable only to you, unless you choose an optional payment method. If you are *married* when payments begin, your benefits will be in the form of a 50% joint and survivor annuity *unless* your spouse signs a waiver and consent form permitting you to choose a payment option other than a joint and survivor annuity.

Retirement Benefits	Coverage
	Normal retirement is age 65.
	Early retirement is any time after age 50 with at least 10 years of service if your age and service equals 65 or more. If you retire early, your pension will be reduced *unless* your age plus service equals 90 or more, and you are at least age 60 when you retire.
	Late retirement is anytime after age 65.
	Vesting—i.e., your right to a pension—occurs after 5 years of service.
Savings and Investment Plan . . . affords you the opportunity to accumulate finds towards retirement through your contributions and Company contributions made on your behalf. Contributions may be made on a before-tax basis, after-tax basis or a combination of both. Company contributions vest at a rate of 20% per year.	Contributions from 2%–15% of your regular earnings, up to the maximum permitted by current laws and regulations, may be made to the Plan. The Company matches these contributions dollar for dollar on the first 2% of your pay that is contributed to the Plan and 50¢ for every dollar on the next 4% of your pay that is contributed to the Plan. You can invest in one, two or all three investment funds. All Company matching contributions are invested in Pfizer common stock. *Vesting* is full and immediate for the value of your own contributions and at 20% for each year in which you participate in the Plan on the value of Company contributions; *up to 100%* after 5 years. If you are married, your spouse will *automatically* be your primary beneficiary *unless* your spouse signs a waiver and consent form permitting you to name someone else as a primary beneficiary.

Compensation Application
Mondaille Hydraulics

Mondaille Hydraulics manufactures pumps for construction equipment and residential homes. In six months contract negotiations are scheduled with the bargaining representative for all blue collar workers, Local 1099 of the United Auto Workers. The president of your company, Forrest Sutton, is convinced that he must get concessions from the workers if Mondaille is to compete effectively with increasing foreign competition. In particular, Mr. Sutton is displeased with the cost of employee benefits. He doesn't mind conceding a small wage increase (maximum 3 percent), but he wants the total compensation package to cost 3 percent less for union employees during the first year of the new contract. Your current costs are shown in Exhibit 1.

Your labor relations assistant has surveyed other companies obtaining concessions from UAW locals. You also have data from a consulting firm which indicates employee preferences for different forms of benefits (Exhibit 2). Based on all this information you have two possible concession packages, which the union just might accept, labeled Option 1 and Option 2 (Exhibit 3).

EXHIBIT 1
Current Compensation Costs

Average yearly wage	$16,224.00
Average hourly wage	$ 9.86
Dollar value of yearly benefits, per employee	$ 6,084.00
Total compensation (wages plus benefits)	$21,638.76
Daily average number of hours paid	7.5

Benefits (by category)	Dollar Cost/ Employee/Year
1. Legally required payments (employer's share only)	$1,459
a. Old-age, survivors, disability, and health insurance (FICA taxes)	951
b. Unemployment compensation	229
c. Workers' compensation (including estimated cost of self-insured)	262
d. Railroad Retirement Tax, Railroad unemployment and cash sickness insurance, state sickness benefits insurance, etc.	16
2. Pension, insurance, and other agreed-upon payments (employer's share only)	2,069
a. Pension plan premiums and pension payments not covered by insurance-type plan (net)	885
b. Life insurance premiums; death benefits; hospital, surgical, medical, and major medical insurance premiums, etc. (net)	954
c. Short-term disability	65
d. Salary continuation or long-term disability	49
e. Dental insurance premiums	49
f. Discounts on goods and services purchased from company by employees	16
g. Employee meals furnished by company	32
h. Miscellaneous payments (compensation payments in excess of legal requirements, separation or termination pay allowances, moving expenses, etc.).	16
3. Paid rest periods, lunch periods, wash-up time, travel time, clothes-change time, get-ready time, etc. (90 minutes)	573

(continued)

EXHIBIT 1
(Concluded)

4.	Payments for time not worked	1,623
	a. Paid vacations and payments in lieu of vacation (16 days average)	803
	b. Payments for holidays not worked (9 days)	557
	c. Paid sick leave (10 days maximum)	213
	d. Payments for State or National Guard duty; jury, witness, and voting pay allowances; payments for time lost due to death in family or other personal reasons, etc.	49
5.	Other items	360
	a. Profit-sharing payments	196
	b. Contributions to employee thrift plans	49
	c. Christmas or other special bonuses, service awards, suggestion awards, etc.	65
	d. Employee education expenditures (tuition refunds, etc.)	32
	e. Special wage payments ordered by courts, payments to union stewards, etc.	16
Total		$6,084.00

1. Cost out these packages given the data in Exhibits 1 and 2 and the information contained from various insurance carriers and other information sources (Exhibit 4).
2. Which package should you recommend to the president? Why?
3. Which of the strategies do you think need not be negotiated with the union before implementation?

EXHIBIT 2
Benefit Preferences

Benefit Type or Method of Administering	Importance to Workers
Pensions	87
Hospitalization	86
Life insurance	79
Paid vacation	82
Holidays	82
Long-term disability	72
Short-term disability	69
Paid sick leave	70
Paid rest periods, lunch periods, etc.	55
Dental insurance	51
Christmas bonus	31
Profit sharing	21
Education expenditures	15
Contributions to thrift plans	15
Discount on goods	5
Fair treatment in administration	100

Note: 0 = Unimportant; 100 = Extremely important.

EXHIBIT 3
Two Possible Concession Packages

Option 1

Implement COPAY for Benefit	*Amount of COPAY*
Pension	$200.00
Hospital, surgical, medical and major medical premiums	250.00
Dental insurance premiums	15.00

Reduction of Benefit

Eliminate 10-minute paid break (workers leave work 10 minutes earlier)

Eliminate one paid holiday per year

Coordination with legally required benefit; Social Security coordinated with
   Mondaille pension

Option 2

Improved claims processing
   Unemployment compensation
   Workers' compensation
   Long-term disability

Require probationary period (one year) before eligible for:
   Discounts on goods
   Employee meal paid by company
   Contributions to employee thrift plans

Deductible ($100 per incident)
   Life insurance; death benefits; hospital, etc.
   Dental insurance

COPAY	*Amount of COPAY*
Hospital, surgical, medical and major medical premiums	$200.00

EXHIBIT 4
Analysis of Cost Implications for Different Cost-Cutting Strategies: Mondaille Hydraulics

Cost-Saving Strategy	*Savings as Percent of Benefit-Type Cost*
COPAY	Dollar for dollar savings equal to amount of COPAY
Deductible ($100 per incident)	
Life insurance premiums, death benefits, hospital, etc.	6%
Dental insurance	30
Require probationary period before eligible (one year)	
Discount on goods and services	10
Employee meals furnished by company	15
Contributions to employee thrift plans	10
Improved claims processing	
Unemployment compensation	8
Workers' compensation	3
Long-term disability	1
Coordination with legally required benefits	
Coordinate Social Security with Mondaille Pension Plan	15

Part **5**

We have now completed the discussion of three basic policies in the pay model used in this book. The first, which focused on determining the structure of pay, dealt with internal consistency. Determining the pay level based on external competitiveness was the second, and the third dealt with determining the pay for individual employees according to their contributions. Policy decisions regarding consistency, competitiveness, and contributions are directed at achieving the objectives of the pay system.

Before taking up the fourth basic policy decision, the nature of administration, we need to consider the significant role government and legislation play in the management of compensation. Laws and regulations are the most obvious intervention by government into compensation management. Laws serve to regulate pay decisions, much as employer policies do. Minimum wage legislation is the most obvious example. Others include the Equal Pay Act and Title VII of the Civil Rights Act, which prohibit pay discrimination.

But government is more than a source of laws and regulations. It is a major player in the marketplace, and consequently affects both the supply and demand for labor. Government affects the demand for labor in several ways: as a major employer, as a consumer of goods and services, and through its fiscal and monetary policies. Similarly, it affects the supply of labor—as a competitor looking to employ labor but also by setting licensing standards (e.g., teachers, physicians, barbers) and through appropriating funds for education and training programs that affect the nature of skills possessed by potential employees.

This part of the book has two chapters devoted to examining government as a major force to be considered in the design and management of pay systems (see Exhibit V.1). Chapter 13 examines government's role in general and also several laws. Pay discrimination, a critical concern in contemporary compensation management, is considered in Chapter 14.

Government's Role and Compliance

EXHIBIT V.1
The Pay Model

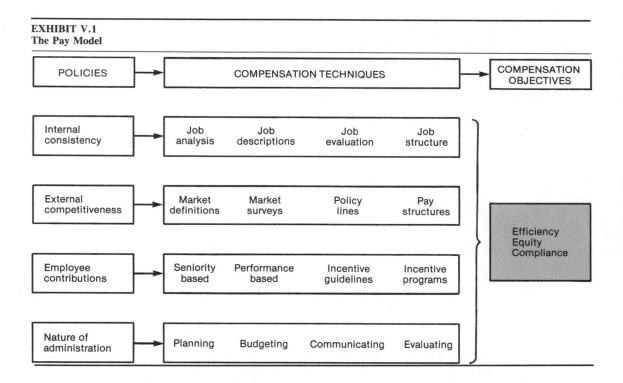

POLICIES	COMPENSATION TECHNIQUES	COMPENSATION OBJECTIVES
Internal consistency	Job analysis — Job descriptions — Job evaluation — Job structure	
External competitiveness	Market definitions — Market surveys — Policy lines — Pay structures	Efficiency Equity Compliance
Employee contributions	Seniority based — Performance based — Incentive guidelines — Incentive programs	
Nature of administration	Planning — Budgeting — Communicating — Evaluating	

13 The Government's Role in Compensation

A majority of the workers in the cotton mills are under 16, and the ages of them run down to 6 and 7. . . . The hours that these children work is well nigh incredible. Either they toil from six in the morning until six at night, or from six at night until six in the morning. The average daily wage of the men is 57 cents, of the women 39 cents, of the children 22 cents.[1] Said one . . . superintendent of a . . . glass plant: "I shall oppose every attempt at improved child-labor laws. Some people are born to work with their brains and some with their hands. Look at these," pointing to a line of "glass" boys, "they are not fitted to do anything else."[2]

---

[1]Edwin Markham, Benjamin B. Lindsey, and George Creel, *Children in Bondage* (New York: Hearst's International Library Company, 1914), pp. 25, 46.

[2]Ibid., p. 67.

T he above excerpt describes conditions during a period when employment relations were without government regulation. Today we hear of the economic effect of regulations, but less often about the price paid for unregulated conditions. Like so many aspects of human resource management, balance is required between massive governmental intervention on the one hand and a lack of regulation on the other.

While the degree of enforcement may fluctuate with the political climate, the overall tendency has been toward ever-increasing regulation. Consequently the regulatory climate—the laws and the regulations issued by governmental agencies created to enforce the laws—represents a significant influence on compensation decisions.

GOVERNMENT INFLUENCES ON PAY

The government influences compensation practices and wages both directly and indirectly. Its direct effect on wages is through legislation such as the minimum wage law, which sets a floor on what an employer must pay, or the Equal Pay Act, which requires that pay differences among employees doing the same job cannot be based on the sex of the employee. Through such laws, the government involves itself directly in the wage-setting process. But it also has indirect effects, as shown in Exhibit 13.1. Governmental actions often affect both the demand and supply of labor; consequently, wages are also affected. Protective legislation often restricts the supply of labor in an occupation. For example, requiring plumbers to be licensed restricts the number of people who can legally offer plumbing services. While these licensing requirements are initiated in the name of consumer protection, they also constrain the labor supply and put upward pressure on wages.

Legislation aimed at protecting specific groups also tends to restrict that group's full participation in the labor supply. Compulsory schooling laws, for example, restrict the supply of 15-year-olds available to sell hamburgers. Laws intended to protect women

EXHIBIT 13.1
Indirect Government Influences on Pay

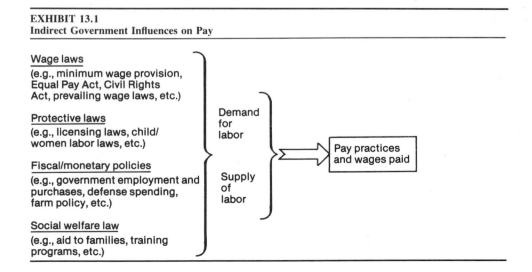

from harsh working conditions also limited the hours women could work and the amount of physical labor they performed. While the intent may have been well-meaning, such laws also may have restricted access to many well-paying occupations. Other indirect effects of government on labor supply and hence wages include government-sponsored training and social welfare programs (e.g., aid to families with dependent children).

Government actions also affect the demand for labor. First, employment at all levels of government has grown from around 6 million employees in 1946 to 17 million in 1988.[3] While the federal government grew rapidly in the 1930s and 1940s, current growth is more rapid at state and local levels. Yearly growth rates at the state and local level of 5 percent were common in the 1960s and the 1970s.[4] In many regions (e.g., state capitals, county seats, etc.) the government is the dominant employer; consequently, it is a major force in determining the wages paid. In addition to being a major employer, government is a major consumer. Federal expenditures as a percent of the GNP have risen from 7.3 percent in 1902 to 22 percent in 1988.[5] A decision by the government to purchase 10 B-757 aircraft from Boeing has a dramatic effect on the demand for labor in Seattle, where Boeing is located.

Government fiscal and monetary policies that affect the economy indirectly affect market forces which, in turn, influence wages. Examples abound. Foreign trade policies, money supply decisions, farm policy—all these governmental actions have indirect effects on wages paid. Restricted farm exports mean farmers will have less money, which means manufacturers of farm equipment and fertilizer will hire fewer people. Lowered interest rates mean more people can afford to purchase houses, which means jobs not only for builders but also for employees of appliance, furniture, and carpet manufacturers. Lower tax rates mean more cash for all taxpayers, which, at least according to some economic theorists, translates into a boost for all employers and an increased demand for labor. Tax subsidies for hiring certain disadvantaged youth have the intent of stimulating a weak demand for such employees. So government's effect on wages is wide-ranging and pervasive.

GOVERNMENT AND THE PAY MODEL

Regulatory compliance is one of the objectives of the pay model used in this book. The compensation techniques (job analysis and evaluation, surveys, ranges, performance appraisal, increase guidelines, and so on) and the results of those techniques (pay levels, pay structures, individual pay, and pay forms) must all be designed to be in compliance with the laws.

Some might argue that laws and regulations serve as constraints rather than objectives in the pay model. Whether or not they constrain depends on the philosophy of compen-

---

[3]U.S. Department of Commerce, Bureau of Census, *Statistical Abstract of the United States,* 1989, 108th ed. (Washington, D.C.: U.S. Government Printing Office, December 1988).

[4]Ibid.

[5]*Economic Report of the President,* transmitted to Congress February 1989 (Washington, D.C.: U.S. Government Printing Office, 1989).

sation management in a particular organization. Laws and regulations can serve as both constraints and objectives.

Regulations as Constraints

Once legislation is passed and interpretive regulations are published, the compensation manager must design systems to comply with them. Whether or not this leads to the results that are intended by legislation, managers must ensure that their practices are in compliance or be willing to go to court to seek clearer interpretation of the laws.

By understanding the regulatory process, managers can better comply with the intent.[6] Organized pressure for legislative action stems from perceived problems in society. If enough support develops, often as a result of compromises and trade-offs, laws are passed. Once passed, agencies enforce the laws through rulings, regulations, inspections, and investigations. Management responds to enforcement by auditing and/or altering personnel practices, defending lawsuits, and lobbying for policy change.

Regulations as Objectives

But if the regulatory process constrains employers' behavior, it also provides opportunities to influence what legislation is passed and how legislation is interpreted. The nature of legislation can also be influenced. Employers lobby through their governmental relations units or through a consortium of employers, such as Business Roundtable or American Compensation Association. Testimony is often given before committees drafting legislation. In order to influence legislation, the compensation professional must establish links with the firm's law department as well as with professional societies.

Employers also influence court interpretation of legislation through defending their practices during litigation, although this is a costly procedure and not one many employers seek. An example of employer influence on legislation is the Equal Pay Act, in which Congress chose skill, effort, responsibility, and working conditions as factors to define equal work.[7] These factors were chosen largely because Congress became aware of them through lobbying efforts and testimony as the criteria commonly used by employers and unions to evaluate jobs. So laws and regulations serve as both objectives and constraints within which to operate. Compensation professionals need to put greater emphasis on proactive activities intended to shape the legislation and regulations or to defend sound pay practices in the courts.

Let us now look at some specific compensation legislation.

---

[6]James Ledvinka, *Federal Regulation of Personnel and Human Resource Management* (Boston: Kent Publishing Company, 1982).

[7]Equal Employment Opportunity Commission, *Legislative History of Titles VII and XI of Civil Rights Act of 1964* (Washington, D.C.: U.S. Government Printing Office, 1968).

MINIMUM WAGES AND COMPENSABLE TIME

The main legislation in this category is the Fair Labor Standards Act and the Portal-to-Portal Act. The Fair Labor Standards Act is the oldest and has the broadest coverage.

Fair Labor Standards Act of 1938 (FLSA)

FLSA covers all employees (with some exceptions discussed later) of companies engaged in interstate commerce or in production of goods for interstate commerce. FLSA has four major provisions:

1. Minimum wage.
2. Hours of work.
3. Child labor.
4. Equal pay.

Minimum wage. When first enacted in 1938, the minimum wage was $.25 per hour. As of January 1981 it was changed to $3.35 per hour. In 1989, President Bush proposed a new minimum of $4.25, to be phased in at the rate of 30 cents an hour over three years. It would be coupled with a training wage of $3.35 that employers would be allowed to pay newly hired workers for the first six months on the job. The Senate has proposed

EXHIBIT 13.2
Basic Hourly Minimum Wage Rates Under State Laws

1.	Alabama	None	27.	Montana	$3.35
2.	Alaska	$3.85	28.	Nebraska	$3.35
3.	Arizona	None	29.	Nevada	$3.35
4.	Arkansas	$3.30	30.	New Hampshire	$3.65
5.	California	$4.25	31.	New Jersey	$3.35
6.	Colorado	$3.00	32.	New Mexico	$3.35
7.	Connecticut	$4.25	33.	New York	$3.35
8.	Delaware	$3.35	34.	North Carolina	$3.35
9.	D.C.	$3.35–$4.85	35.	North Dakota	$2.80–$3.10
10.	Florida	None	36.	Ohio	$2.30
11.	Georgia	$3.25	37.	Oklahoma	$3.35
12.	Hawaii	$3.85	38.	Oregon	$3.35
13.	Idaho	$2.30	39.	Pennsylvania	$3.70
14.	Illinois	$3.35	40.	Puerto Rico	$0.24–$4.00
15.	Indiana	$2.00	41.	Rhode Island	$4.00
16.	Iowa	None	42.	South Carolina	None
17.	Kansas	$2.65	43.	South Dakota	$3.35
18.	Kentucky	$3.35	44.	Tennessee	None
19.	Louisiana	None	45.	Texas	$3.35
20.	Maine	$3.75	46.	Utah	$2.50–$2.75
21.	Maryland	$3.35	47.	Vermont	$3.65
22.	Massachusetts	$3.75	48.	Virginia	$2.65
23.	Michigan	$3.35	49.	Washington	$3.85
24.	Minnesota	$3.65–$3.85	50.	West Virginia	$3.35
25.	Mississippi	None	51.	Wisconsin	$3.35
26.	Missouri	None	52.	Wyoming	$1.60

instead an increase to $4.65. Both the Senate and the White House propose exempting from coverage small businesses with gross annual sales under $500,000.[8] Forty-seven states also have minimum wage laws (shown in Exhibit 13.2), which cover employees exempt from FLSA. Coverage of the minimum wage provision does not extend to all employees. For example, current regulations allow the Department of Labor to authorize pay for full-time students at 83 percent of the federal minimum wage, but the certification period cannot exceed one year. Exemptions may also be granted for handicapped workers, apprentices, and learners. The bulk of such exemptions are utilized in the restaurant industry.[9]

Effects of minimum wage provisions. Minimum wage legislation was intended to provide an income floor for workers in society's lowest paid and least productive jobs. Who benefits by changes in the minimum wage rates? Some evidence suggests that adult women have been the primary beneficiaries, because higher rates have attracted them into full-time from part-time employment. Other evidence suggests that all workers have benefited; as the pay rate at the lowest end of the scale has moved up, so have pay rates above it, in order to maintain pay differentials among jobs.

The shift in the pay structure resulting from an increased minimum wage is greater in some industries than others. For example, the lowest rates paid in the steel, chemical, oil, and pharmaceutical industries are well above minimum wage; any legislative change would have little direct impact on the labor bill of employers in these industries. Changes in the minimum wage will greatly affect labor costs of retailing and service firms, however. These businesses employ many clerks and sales personnel at or near the minimum wage. As the minimum increases, the increase ripples upward through the entire pay structure. Hence, pay of all personnel is increased to maintain pay differentials. The resulting higher labor bill increases the possibility of substituting capital for jobs (e.g., introducing automated inventory control systems, or prepacked frozen french fries) or holding down employment levels (e.g., fewer sales personnel) to control labor costs.

Employment effects. Some economists believe that employment opportunities for inexperienced and unskilled youth are hurt by the minimum wage. Employers may reason that the skills this group possesses are not commensurate with their costs. If a higher wage is to be paid the employer will try to find more experienced or skilled workers. The high rate of unemployment among teenagers is consistent with this argument.

So people working at or near the minimum wage who continue to work definitely do benefit from mandated minimum wage increases, and other workers in higher level jobs in those same companies may also benefit. Yet as labor costs increase, fewer workers will be hired if the increased costs cannot be passed on to consumers or offset by increased productivity.

---

[8]"Senate Panel Approves Minimum Wage Increase," *New York Times,* March 9, 1989, p. A20.

[9]July 16, 1982, Federal Register (47 FR 31010).

Hours of work. The overtime provisions of the FLSA require payment at one and a half times the standard for work over 40 hours per week.[10] There is a "union contract exemption" covering employees working under guaranteed annual employment agreements. Many union contracts provide for overtime after a shorter work week, some as short as 25 hours.[11]

The overtime provision is aimed at sharing available work. It seeks to make hiring more workers a less costly option than scheduling overtime for current employees. But overtime pay for current employees is often the least costly option. This is due to (1) an increasingly skilled work force, with higher training costs per employee and (2) higher fringe benefits, the bulk of which are fixed per employee. These factors have lowered the point at which it pays employers to schedule longer hours and pay the overtime premium, rather than hire, train, and pay fringes for more employees. Models to examine the break-even points between working overtime and hiring additional workers have been designed. These models compare added expense of time and a half wages to the added fringe benefits and training costs required for new hires.

Several amendments to increase the overtime penalty have been proposed over the years. These typically seek to increase the penalty, reduce the standard workweek to less than 40 hours, or repeal some of the exemptions. Only about 58 percent of all employees are covered by the overtime provision at present.

Effects of the overtime provision. Unions typically support efforts to raise the overtime wage because they believe such a change will result in higher employment levels and more union members. Employers typically oppose efforts because changes will result in greater costs for them.

Some researchers have investigated overtime's effect on worker satisfaction. Generally, as hours of work increase, both pay satisfaction and job satisfaction decrease. But any negative effects of overtime vary with the reasons for using overtime. For example, is overtime scheduled because of growing workload, or because of inefficient work scheduling? If overtime is required because of what employees consider to be inadequate management, they are probably going to resent the requirement. Nonetheless, most union contracts specify that overtime hours be offered to members on the basis of seniority.

So what difference does overtime make to the compensation professional? The hours-of-work provision of FLSA requires that records be kept of actual time worked by employees in covered jobs. This brings up two issues of interest: (1) What is and is not included in "actual time worked"? and (2) Which jobs are covered?

Exempt and nonexempt. Whether jobs are classified as exempt or nonexempt from the FLSA is of major importance. Nonexempt jobs must comply with the FLSA, which means they must be paid time and a half for hours worked overtime and extensive records

---

[10]29 Code of Federal Regulations, Chap. V, Secs. A.3–A.5

[11]T. A. Kochan, H. C. Katz, and N. R. Mower, "Worker Participation and American Unions," in *Challenges and Choices Facing American Labor,* ed. T. Kochan (Cambridge, Mass.: MIT Press, 1985), pp. 271–306.

EXHIBIT 13.3
Some Exemptions to the Minimum Wage and Overtime Provisions of the Fair Labor Standards Act

Section 13 (a)(1)	Outside salesmen, professional executive, and administrative personnel ("including any employee employed in the capacity of academic administrative personnel or teacher in elementary or secondary schools")
Section 13(a)(3)	Employees of certain seasonal amusements or recreational establishments.
Section 13(a)(5)	Fishing and first processing at sea employees.
Section 13(a)(6)	Agricultural employees employed by farms utilizing fewer than 500 man-days of agricultural labor, employed by a member of their immediate family, certain local seasonal harvest laborers and seasonal hand harvest laborers 16 years of age or under, and employees principally engaged in the range production of livestock.
Section 13(a)(7)	Employees exempt under Section 14 of the Act (certain learners, apprentices, students and handicapped workers).
Section 13(a)(12)	Seamen on foreign vessels.
Section 13(a)(15)	Babysitters employed on a casual basis and persons employed to provide companion services.
Section 7(b)	Certain employees under collectively bargained guaranteed annual wage plans and wholesale or bulk petroleum distribution employees.
Section 7(i)	Certain commission salesmen in retail or service establishments.
Section 13(b)(1)	Motor carrier employees.
Section 13(b)(2)	Railroad employees.
Section 13(b)(3)	Airline employees.
Section 13(b)(6)	Seamen.
Section 13(b)(12)	Agricultural employees.
Section 13(b)(15)	Maple sap employees.
Section 13(b)(29)	Employees of amusement or recreational establishments located in a national park or national forest or on land in the National Wildlife Refuge System.

must be kept and filed with the Department of Labor. Overtime pay is not required for exempt jobs, nor is recordkeeping of hours worked. Today the FLSA, amended several times since it was first passed in 1938, covers many jobs. However, there are exemptions, and they are the most complex part of the act. Some of the exemptions are shown in Exhibit 13.3. For example, professional, executive, and administrative jobs are exempt. So are many jobs in the transportation industry.

Some exemptions suspend only certain provisions of the act, while others suspend all provisions. Some apply to all employees of certain businesses, others to only certain employees. To compound the confusion, exemptions may overlap. Repeated amendments to the act have made the distinction between exempt and nonexempt difficult to determine. One writer observed, "As soon as the distinction between exempt and nonexempt begins to emerge clearly from court cases, the act is amended, setting off a new round of court cases."[12]

The Wage-Hour Division of the Department of Labor, which is charged with enforcement of the FLSA, provides strict criteria that must be met in order for jobs to be considered professional and exempt from minimum wage and overtime provisions. Professionals must:

---

[12]Ledvinka, *Federal Regulation.*

Do work requiring knowledge generally acquired by prolonged, specialized study, or engage in original and creative activity in a recognized artistic field.

Consistently exercise discretion or judgment.

Do work that is primarily intellectual and nonroutine.

Devote at least eighty percent of their work hours to such activities.[13]

There are also criteria for exempt status for executives. Executives must:

Primarily undertake management duties.

Supervise two or more employees.

Have control (or at least great influence) over hiring, firing, and promotion.

Exercise discretionary powers.

Devote at least 80 percent of their work hours to such activities.[14]

There are similar criteria for administrative and sales workers and employees in transportation and other industries as well.[15]

Child labor. The child labor provision of FLSA states that minors must be over 18 to work in hazardous occupations and above 16 or 14 in other occupations. The age varies, depending on the type of work and whether or not the employer is the child's parents. Workers under 16 may not work more than three hours on any school day or eight hours on nonschool days. They cannot work more than 18 hours a week when school is in session or 40 hours when it is not. Workers age 16 and 17 have no hourly restrictions.

During the 1950s through 1970s, the child labor provision generated little controversy. But violations in child labor laws have doubled in the 1980s. Exhibit 13.4 shows this trend. In the early 1980s, the rate was approximately 9,000 violations a year. In 1988, it was over 20,000 violations, and most child-labor experts say the inspectors are catching only a fraction of the violations. Restaurants, retailers, and supermarkets are the biggest employers of teenagers. As the supply of older teenagers dwindles, these employers say they are forced to hire younger workers. Many of the violations concern children working too late in the evening or too many hours. While working too late at the supermarket is a far cry from the dangers in sweatshops that spurred initial passage of child labor laws, the number of violations has become a cause for concern. States vary in their responses to the situation. Some states have liberalized their laws, particularly in allowing young teenagers to work later into the evening (until 7 p.m. for 14- and 15-year-olds). Other states have called for greater restrictions, on the grounds that educational achievement suffers if young students work part-time. The rise in teen-age employment, including workers as young as 14, is particularly noticeable in areas where the overall employment rate is low—3 to 5 percent.

The fourth major provision of FLSA, equal employment, will be discussed in the

---

[13]29 Code of Federal Regulations, Chap. V, Sec. 541.3.

[14]Ibid., Sec. 541.1

[15]Ibid., Secs. 541.2 and 541.500.

EXHIBIT 13.4
Violations of the Child Labor Law Are Increasing

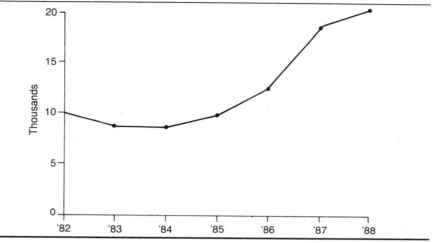

next chapter. Equal employment was not covered in the original 1938 FLSA. It was added as an amendment in 1963, called the Equal Pay Act, and is today of major importance. The whole topic of wage discrimination merits a separate chapter. (See Chapter 14.)

Portal-to-Portal Act of 1947

Recall that FLSA requires records of time actually worked by covered employees. But when does the workday begin? Is it when the employee arrives at the actual job site? Or on the employer's premises? Think of working in an underground coal mine. Underground travel time to get to the actual site where coal is being extracted is under the control of the employer and may be substantial. According to current interpretation of FLSA and the courts, this travel time should be part of the hours worked and included in calculating pay and overtime rates. But in *Anderson* v. *Mt. Clemens Pottery* the courts extended this "travel time" concept to manufacturing, ruling that time spent walking between the plant gate and the work bench as well as time spent on certain "make-ready" activities was all "compensable working time."[16] A flood of lawsuits for wages owed followed, prompting Congress to pass the Portal-to-Portal Act. The act provides that time spent on activities before beginning or after completion of the "principal activity" is compensable only if payment is required under a contract or has customarily been counted as work time prior to the *Mt. Clemens* case. In other words, if time spent on make-ready activities was not counted as work hours before, the employer need not begin counting that time now. This addition of "custom" is the most important feature of the act.

---

[16]*Anderson v. Mt. Clemens Pottery Co.*, 6 WH Cases 595, USDC E. Michigan.

The next group of laws set pay for work done to produce goods and services contracted by the federal government. These are called "prevailing wage" laws.

PREVAILING WAGE LAWS

A government-defined prevailing wage is the minimum wage that must be paid for work done on covered government projects or purchases. The original purpose was to prevent the government from undercutting local workers. For example, if a government project of the magnitude of Hoover Dam were to pay low wages to construction workers, its sheer force of size could drive down the entire wage structure in the area. So the government has required that surveys identify the prevailing wage in an area, and that wage becomes the mandated minimum wage on the government-financed project. Thus, the prevailing wage becomes a new minimum wage.

Contractors object to this requirement because it frequently means they have to match a wage rate that only a minority of area workers, 30 percent, are receiving. Business and taxpayer groups argue that prevailing rates results in higher costs than necessary on government projects. Unions, on the other hand, argue that fringe benefits are not included in the calculation of prevailing wages, and therefore it understates actual rates.

In 1982 new regulations went into effect that define prevailing wage in any area as (1) the wage paid to a majority of area employees in the job classification (that provision remained unchanged from the previous regulations) *or* (2) a wage calculated under a new weighted average formula, if a majority of area employees do not happen to work at a single rate.[17]

The main prevailing wage laws are (1) Davis-Bacon (1931), which covers mechanics and laborers on public construction projects with expenditures over $2,000; (2) Walsh-Healey Public Contracts Act (1936), which extends the provisions of Davis-Bacon to manufacturers or suppliers of goods for government contracts over $10,000; (3) Service Contract Act (1965), which extends coverage to suppliers of services in excess of $2,500 (e.g., cleaning, catering) to the federal government; and (4) National Foundation Arts and Humanities Act (1965), which covers professionals, laborers, and mechanics working on projects that receive funding from the Foundation. Only those employees directly engaged in producing or furnishing for the federal contract are covered; other employees of the manufacturer/supplier are not.

In addition to a prevailing wage, Walsh-Healey also requires:

1. One and a half times the regular pay rate for hours over 8 per day or 40 per week must be paid.
2. Sanitary and nonhazardous working conditions must be maintained.
3. Payroll records must be kept.
4. Employees must be above 16 years.

Walsh-Healey predates the FLSA. The FLSA duplicates some Walsh-Healey requirements and extends them to additional employees.

---

[17]May 28, 1982, Federal Register (47 FR 23644).

EXHIBIT 13.5
Federal Laws: Equal Employment Opportunity

Regulation	Major Provisions
Equal Pay Act	A 1963 amendment to FLSA; equal pay required for male and female workers doing "substantially similar work" in terms of skill, effort, responsibility, and working conditions. Exemptions allowed for seniority, merit pay, and piece work systems.
Title VII of Civil Rights Act	(1) Prohibits discrimination in all employment practices on basis of race, sex, color, religion, national origin, or pregnancy.
	(2) Bennett Amendment links Title VII and the Equal Pay Act by providing that it is not unlawful to differentiate on the basis of sex in determining pay if such differentiation is authorized by the Equal Pay Act.
Age Discrimination Act	Protects employees aged 40 and over against age discrimination.
Pregnancy Discrimination Act	Disability and medical benefits plans cannot single out pregnancy for differential treatment. Pregnancy must be covered to same extent that other medical conditions are covered.

Up to this point we have discussed the FLSA, the Portal-to-Portal Act, and prevailing wage legislation, much of which was originally passed in the 1930s and 1940s in response to social issues of that time. In the 1960s, the equal rights movement pushed different social problems to the forefront. The Equal Pay Act and the Civil Rights Act were passed. Because of their substantial impact on human resource management and compensation, they are discussed at length in the next chapter. Additional rights legislation includes the Pregnancy Discrimination Act and the Age Discrimination in Employment Act (Exhibit 13.5).

EQUAL RIGHTS LEGISLATION

Age Discrimination in Employment Act of 1967

The Age Discrimination in Employment Act, passed in 1967 and amended in 1978 and 1986, protects workers age 40 and over from employment discrimination due to age.[18] To date this act has been applied principally to retirement, promotion, and layoff policies, but it applies to all personnel decisions. The 1986 amendment forbids mandatory retirement (formerly legal at age 70) for all except fire fighters, police officers, and tenured professors(!), an exception of acute personal interest.[19] The 1986 amendment also appointed a committee including professors to analyze the consequences of lifting the exception for professors. The committee has five years to make a recommendation, a time frame that further perpetuates the stereotype of absent-minded professors. The purpose of the act is to "promote employment of older persons on their ability rather than

---

[18]29 U.S.C. Sec. 621–634 (1970 and Supp. V. 1975) as amended by Public Law 95-256 (1978).

[19]And also to Professor Glenn Thiel. We thank him for calling the amendment to our attention.

age; to prohibit arbitrary age discrimination in employment; to help employers and workers find ways of meeting problems arising from the impact of age on employment." The law forbids limiting or classifying employees in any way that would adversely affect their status because of age; reducing any employee's wage rate to comply with the act; or discriminating in compensation or terms of employment because of age. Individual states frequently have laws protecting employees not covered by federal law.

Age discrimination focuses attention on the compensation issue of paying for performance and the relationship between performance and age. For example, the career stage literature often assumes a "decline" stage in later years, though the age of decline varies. However, the literature on aging does not support such an assumption. Variations in performance exist at all ages, including among older workers. A pay system that purports to pay for performance must be sure that performance appraisal systems are not biased by age, or that appraisers do not assume a lower performance level simply because a worker is older.[20]

In most cases it is difficult to document age discrimination because age is so closely correlated to seniority, and it is not illegal to vary treatment of employees on the basis of seniority. Another difficulty in pinpointing age discrimination is the frequently higher base position of an older worker. For example, older workers have lower promotion rates than younger workers, but this difference reflects the lower number of possible positions available into which older workers could be promoted. Additionally, lower salary increases for older workers may reflect their higher position in the pay ranges for particular jobs. To lessen the impact of any performance declines on costs, some experts recommend a base price for adequate performance in a job, and a bonus for quantifiable results above satisfactory. The chapters on employee contributions discuss various ways of linking pay and performance. But the best advice in regard to the regulatory compliance objective is to avoid assuming performance differences on the basis of age, sex, race, or other illegal criteria. The focus should be on accurate performance appraisal.

Pregnancy Discrimination Act of 1978

This act is actually an amendment to Title VII of the Civil Rights Act. It requires employers to extend to pregnant women the same disability and medical benefits provided other employees. The Pregnancy Discrimination Act forbids exclusion of pregnancy from the list of disabilities for which the employer compensates absent employees. It does not require an employer to offer a disability plan, nor does it prevent a dollar limit being placed on reimbursement of medical costs. The law merely places disability benefits for pregnant employees on an equal footing with those of nonpregnant employees.

In *McNulty* v. *Newport News Shipbuilding* (1983), the Supreme Court applied the Pregnancy Discrimination Act to pregnancy benefits received by spouses of male employees. The employer had set a limit on maternity benefits for employee spouses, but did not limit payments for any other medical conditions for either employees or spouses of employees. The Court ruled that a limitation on pregnancy coverage for spouses is

---

[20]*Mistressa* v. *Sandia Corp*. U.S. District Court 21, FEP Cases 1671, 1978.

legal only if the same limitation also applied to other medical coverage for spouses. No limitation can be put on pregnancy expenses that is not applied to other medical conditions. The decision does not bar employers from limiting all medical costs for dependents, say to 50 percent of expenses, if they impose the same limit on all dependents, regardless of sex. All employee spouses must be treated the same and while this treatment need not be identical to treatment for employees, maternity benefits cannot be treated differently from other medical conditions.

Equal Benefits Payouts versus Equal Benefit Costs

The issue of equal benefit treatment for all employees is complicated by the insurance industry practice of charging differential rates based on sex (Exhibit 13.6). For example, because women as a group live longer than men, they theoretically collect pensions for a greater number of years and therefore are more costly for the pension provider unless the monthly pension payment is made smaller. If a pension is taken as a lump-sum payment, or paid out over a limited number of years, then the sex of the pensioner makes no difference. But if the pensioner wishes to purchase an annuity that will continue payments until death, a woman will receive a lower monthly annuity payment than a man will, assuming both retire at the same age and both pay the same lump sum for their annuity. For years many employers required greater pension contributions from women employees than from men, or alternatively, paid lower annuities to women than to men when they retired. But in 1978 the Supreme Court ruled that an employer violates Title

EXHIBIT 13.6
How Much More Women Pay for Insurance than Men

Coverage	Lifetime Cost Differential for Women
Medical	
Typical hospital-surgical policy from State Farm Mutual for years 25 to 64. $100 daily room and board; $2,000 surgical. Includes pregnancy complications. Excludes normal pregnancy, childbirth	+ $ 6,862
Disability	
Typical disability policy for years 25 to 64 from Allstate Life. $700/ month base benefit. Excludes pregnancy, childbirth, miscarriage, abortion. Includes complications and nonelective caesarean section	+ 4,854
Life insurance and pension	
Typical policy for age 65 retirement from Minnesota Mutual. Life insurance before age 65, $100,000. Monthly pension starting at age 65, $1,000. Pay premiums for years 35 to 54. Dividends estimated by company deducted	+ 5,856
Automobile	
Typical liability and physical damage policy, using factors rated by Insurance Services Office. Primary classifications: youthful operator; good student; unmarried; owner or principal operator; drive to work or business use, medium-size town. For years 17 to 24	− 1,840
Total difference	$15,732

Source: National Organization for Women.

VII of the Civil Rights Act if it requires unequal pension plan *contributions* based on sex.[21] The fact that women as a group live longer than men does not justify unequal treatment of a specific woman employee, who may or may not live longer than any specific male employee. Lower courts have applied this reasoning to pension *benefits* or payouts in addition to pension contributions.

WAGE AND PRICE CONTROLS

Wage control programs typically aim at maintaining low inflation at low levels of unemployment. They frequently focus on limiting the size of the pay raises as well as the rate of increases in the prices charged for goods and services.

Control programs can vary in their stringency. In 1942, for example, wages were frozen at a level that prevailed on September 15 of that year. The government established "going rates" for key occupations and then permitted pay increases up to the minimum of a going rate bracket. Benefits could be instituted only if employers could show that they were customary in an area. Despite these restrictions, because of the demand and supply imbalances created by World War II, the basic wage increased 24 percent between January 1941 and July 1945.

Another freeze was ordered in 1951, but by now many union members had labor contracts that provided automatic wage increases tied to the cost of living as well as annual "productivity" raises.[22] Once stabilization officials decided to permit the continued operation of these contracts, they were forced to sanction similar raises for other groups of employees.

Rather than an across-the-board wage freeze, the Council of Economic Advisers (CEA) in the early 1960s tried a more moderate approach. It tied wage rate and benefit increases to overall productivity increases, reasoning that acceptance of this guide would maintain stability of labor cost per unit of output for the overall economy. But productivity is only one of many factors related to pay, and any national productivity rate is meaningless when applied to a specific employer's productivity.

In 1971 the Nixon administration, facing a 6 percent inflation rate and an unemployment level just over 5 percent, imposed freeze and control measures that rivaled those of World War II. These policies were able to slow inflation to just over 3 percent through most of 1971 and 1972. But once the controls were relaxed, prices rose rapidly: over 6 percent in 1973 and 11 percent in 1974. Some economists interpret the rapid growth of postcontrol inflation as proof that the controls were effective and should have remained in place. Others interpret the same data to indicate that wage-price controls merely redistributed inflation over time but did not eliminate it.

The Council on Wage and Price Stability during the Carter administration tried to minimize problems by opting for less encompassing voluntary wage guidelines. Employers were provided formulas to determine their own compliance with pay standards. Those

---

[21]*Los Angeles Dept. of Water and Power* v. *Manhart et al.*, 435 U.S. 702, 1978.

[22]Solomon Fabricant, "Which Productivity? Perspectives on a Current Question," *Monthly Labor Review*, June 1962, pp. 18–24.

that did not comply were subject to government scrutiny and possible government manipulation of import restrictions and government purchases to favor employers who complied and penalize noncompliance. However, even though flexibility had been a goal of the program, an absolute standard soon developed, along with a bureaucracy to consider exceptions to the standard.

So wage controls or guidelines can vary in the broadness of application and in the stringency of the standard. The standard for allowable pay increases can range from absolute denial during a freeze to increases equal to some productivity or price change measure.

Eventually any freeze or outside control exerted at an arbitrary point in time cannot help but be inequitable to some employers and employees, since the wage-setting process is ongoing. Both unions and managers are united in their concern for employee equity under wage controls. They are also united in their interest in the administration of a government control program. Programs usually start out simple, but as requests for exceptions mount, so does the bureaucracy. The administrators of the 1978–80 Carter pay guidelines prided themselves on an average response time to requests for exceptions of 40 days. But in periods in which responses are required to meet rapidly changing conditions, affected employees are not willing to wait 40 days, and compensation professionals are forced to figure ways around the regulations.

In the face of possible bureaucratic and employee equity problems, how can compensation managers best protect their employees and managers facing government intervention in the wage-setting process? Those companies that seem to suffer the least disruptions are the ones that have sound and flexible compensation systems in place, with well-thought-out policies that demonstrably have been followed in the past. Such companies can document what they have done and why they did it, and are far more able to handle government intervention than employers that have no formal pay systems and cannot justify their behavior. The same is true with any other area of government interest, be it meeting FLSA pay and recordkeeping requirements, or complying with equal rights legislation. A system based on work- and business-related logic is an employee's and employer's best protection.

REGULATION OF BENEFITS

We have already mentioned the requirements that benefits packages must be nondiscriminatory on the basis of sex, race, religion, and national origin. Additional governmental effects on benefit options are discussed in Chapter 12. Government has its impact in two ways. The first is by legally requiring that some specific benefits be provided, either at employer expense or as an expense shared between employer and employee. Workers' compensation, social security, and unemployment insurance are all legally required. Workers' compensation and unemployment insurance are completely employer-financed, whereas employees and employers jointly contribute to social security.

The second way the government influences benefits is through its tax policy. Benefits are, in general, tax-free to employees and a tax-deductible expense to employers, providing certain conditions are met. These conditions change frequently, almost with every legislative session, but their general aim is to ensure that a benefit package is structured to be available to all employees rather than to a select few, and to be sure that tax-free cash is not funneled to employees under the guise of benefits, thus escaping the long arm of the Internal Revenue Service. These issues are discussed in the benefits chapters.

SUMMARY

Compliance with laws and regulations is treated as an objective in the pay model. It can be a constraint and/or an opportunity.

The regulatory environment faced by a compensation professional certainly constrains the decisions that can be made. Once laws are passed and regulations published, employers must comply. But a proactive compensation manager can influence the nature of regulations and their interpretation. Astute professionals must be aware of legislative and judicial currents, to protect both employers' and employees' interests, and to ensure that compensation practices conform to judicial interpretation.

How can a compensation professional best undertake these efforts? First, join professional associations to stay informed on emerging issues and to act in concert to inform and influence public and legislative opinion. Second, constantly review compensation practices and the results of their application. The equitable treatment of all employees is the goal of a good pay system, and that is the same goal of the legislation. Where interpretations of equitable treatment differ, informed public discussion is required. Such discussion cannot occur without the input of informed compensation professionals.

REVIEW QUESTIONS

1. What is the nature of government's role in compensation?
2. Explain why changes in the minimum wage can have differential effects on employees.
3. How could a compensation professional examine the effect of minimum wage on a specific employer's labor bill?
4. Your employer's production manager has recommended adding a third shift of workers. What advice can you give?
5. What kinds of proactive activities can an employer undertake to enhance the regulatory environment?
6. Could the pay objective or regulatory compliance ever conflict with other objectives? Could it conflict with the employer's notion of consistency or competitiveness? An employee's notion of equity? If so, how would you deal with such situations?

Compensation Application
Amendments to Minimum Wage Legislation

Over the years, a number of changes have been proposed to the minimum wage provision of the Fair Labor Standards Act. Prepare a brief report outlining the effects of ONE of the proposed changes listed below. Find out if there is currently any legislative activity regarding this change. You may have to use your library's information service to track current activity.

In your report, answer these questions:

WHAT PROBLEM will this change address? Who will it help? Who will it hurt? Do you think such a change is a good idea? If you were a legislator, would you vote for such an amendment?

A different student should research each proposed change. Reports should then be presented to the class. Presenters should be prepared to answer questions and defend their vote. After discussion, the entire class will vote on the proposals.

PROPOSED CHANGES

a. A youth differential allowing a lower rate for jobs held by unskilled, inexperienced workers.
b. Elimination of the bulk of exemptions.
c. Elimination of the entire minimum wage provision.
d. Index the minimum wage to reflect changes in the Consumer Price Index. (Chapter 15 contains a discussion of the Consumer Price Index.)
e. Index the minimum wage to reflect changes in average hourly earnings in private business.
f. Reduce noncompliance by permitting class action lawsuits, increasing penalties, and targeting enforcement efforts.
g. Limit student certification exemptions to high school students.

Chapter

14 Pay Discrimination

The . . . wage curve . . . is not the same for women as for men because of the more transient character of the service of the former, the relative shortness of their activity in industry, the differences in environment required, the extra services that must be provided, overtime limitations, extra help needed for the occasional heavy work, and the general sociological factors not requiring discussion herein. Basically then we have another wage curve . . . for women and not parallel with the men's curve.[1]

It has been suggested that the concept of discrimination is vague. In fact it is clear and simple and has no hidden meanings. To discriminate is to make a distinction, . . . and these differences in treatment which are prohibited . . . are those based on the five forbidden criteria: race, color, religion, sex, and national origin. [Floor debate preceding passage of Title VII, Interpretive Memorandum, Senators Clark and Case, floor managers, Title VII, 110 Congressional Record 7218 (1964)][2]

The pay practice described above, taken from a 1939 job evaluation manual, is now prohibited by law. Discriminatory practices, such as paying women and minorities less than white men for equal work, contributed to the need for legislation. Legislation, in turn, requires interpretation by regulatory agencies and courts. And despite the assurances offered during the heat of congressional debates, definitions of pay discrimination and the interpretation of the laws enacted to prohibit it have been neither clear nor simple. The laws pertaining to pay discrimination, their interpretation, and implications for pay systems are the subject of this chapter.

PAY DISCRIMINATION: WHAT IS IT?

Over 20 years have passed since the laws intended to prohibit pay discrimination were enacted; while a number of issues have been settled, some remained unresolved. To better understand pay discrimination, it is useful to begin by distinguishing between *access* and *valuation* discrimination.[3]

Access Discrimination

Access discrimination focuses on the staffing and allocation decisions made by employers (e.g., recruiting, hiring, promoting, training, and layoffs). Access discrimination denies particular jobs, promotions, or training opportunities to qualified women or minorities.

---

[1]The job evaluation manual was introduced as evidence in *Electrical Workers (IUE) v. Westinghouse Electric Corp.*, 632 F.2d 1094, 23 FEP Cases 588 (3rd Cir. 1980), cert. defined, 452 U.S. 967, 25 FEP Cases 1835 (1981).

[2]Interptetive memorandum, Title VII, 110 Cong. Rec. 7213 (1964).

[3]Kenni Judd and Luis Gomez-Mejia, "Comparable Worth: A Sensible Way to End Pay Discrimination, or the Looniest Idea Since Looney Tunes?" in *Perspectives on Compensation*, eds. L. Gomez-Mejia and David Balkin (Englewood Cliffs, N.J.: Prentice-Hall, 1987); and Thomas A. Patten, Jr., *Fair Pay.* (San Francisco, Calif.: Jossey-Bass Publishers, 1988).

Signs of such discrimination still persist. For example, more than half of all women workers are employed in only 20 out of a total of 427 occupations.[4] Analyzing how employers share employment and training opportunities with minority and women is beyond the intent of this book, but the interested reader will find the references useful for further study.

Valuation Discrimination

Valuation discrimination focuses on the pay women and minorities receive for the jobs they perform. The Equal Pay Act makes it clear that it is discriminatory to pay minorities or women less than males when performing equal work (i.e., working side by side, in the same plant, doing the same work, producing the same results). This definition of pay discrimination hinges on the standard of equal pay for equal work.

But many believe this definition does not go far enough.[5] They believe that valuation discrimination can also occur when men and women hold entirely different jobs (i.e., when job segregation or access discrimination has forced women or minorities into a limited range of jobs). For example, office and clerical jobs are typically staffed by women, and craft jobs (electricians, welders) are typically staffed by men. Is it illegal to pay employees in one job group less than employees in the other, if the two job groups contain work that is not equal in content or results, but is "in some sense of comparable worth" to the employer?

Here, the proposed definition of pay discrimination hinges on the standard of equal pay for work of comparable worth. Existing federal laws do not support this standard. However, several states have enacted laws that require a comparable worth standard for state and local government employees. There are moves afoot to extend such legislation to other states and eventually to the private sector, as the province of Ontario, Canada, has done. In the United States, state and local governments have been more receptive than the federal government.[6]

---

[4]Toby Parcel, "Comparable Worth, Occupational Labor Markets and Occupational Earnings: Results from the 1980 Census," *Pay Equity: Empirical Inquiries* (Washington, D. C.: National Academy of Science, 1989); Elaine Sorensen, "Measuring the Effect of Occupational Sex and Race Composition on Earnings," *Pay Equity: Empirical Inquiries* (Washington, D. C.: National Academy of Science, 1989); Jack Fiorito, Charles Greer, and Robert C. Dauffenbach, "Uniformity and Variation in Occupational Earnings Determination: Potential Sources of Incomparable Worth," *Journal of Management,* 12, 1(1986), pp. 61–74; and Reuben Gronau, "Sex-related Wage Differentials and Women's Interrupted Labor Careers—the Chicken or the Egg," *Journal of Labor Economics* 6, 31 (1988), pp. 277–301.

[5]B. F. Reskin and H. I. Hartmann, eds., *Women's Work, Men's Work: Segregation on the Job* (Washington, D.C.: National Academy Press, 1986).

[6]"General Accounting Office to Conduct Pay Equity Study of the Federal Workforce," (Washington, D.C.: National Committee on Pay Equity, March 16, 1989); Alice Cook, *Comparable Worth: A Case Book of Experiences in States and Localities, 1986 Supplement,* Industrial Relations Center, University of Hawaii at Manoa, Honolulu, HI.; and *Survey of State-Government Level Pay Equity Activity 1988,* National Committee on Pay Equity, Washington, D.C. (no date); and *Pay Equity Implementation Series* (Toronto, Ontario, Canada: The Pay Equity Commission). This is a series of guidelines addressing questions regarding implementation of the province's pay equity legislation. The Introduction was published in March 1988. By January 1989 Series # 15 was available.

So two standards for defining pay discrimination need to be considered—equal pay for equal work, and equal pay for work of comparable worth. For an understanding of the legal foundations of each, let us turn to the legislation and key court cases.

THE EQUAL PAY ACT

The two major laws prohibiting pay discrimination are the Equal Pay Act (EPA) of 1963 and Title VII of the Civil Rights Act of 1964.[7] The EPA was the first modern statute directed at eliminating discrimination in the job market. It forbids wage discrimination between employees on the basis of sex when employees perform equal work on jobs in the same establishment requiring equal skill, effort, and responsibility and performed under similar working conditions. . . . Pay differences between equal jobs can be justified when that differential is based on (1) a seniority system; (2) a merit system; (3) a system measuring earnings by quality or quantity of production; or (4) any factor other than sex.[8]

Reducing wages of the higher-paid employee in order to achieve compliance is also prohibited. The Act embraces the "equal work" definition of pay discrimination. It permits comparisons among equal jobs only, and defines equal work by four factors: (1) skill, (2) effort, (3) responsibility, and (4) working conditions. As noted during our discussion of job evaluation (Chapters 4 and 5), these factors, or some variation of them, are commonly used in most job evaluation plans.

Pay differences are permitted under the EPA's four *affirmative defenses*. Differences in pay among men and women doing equal work are legal if these differences are based on (1) seniority, (2) quality of performance, (3) quality or quantity or production, or (4) some factor other than sex.

The Act is deceptively simple, yet numerous court cases have been required to clarify its provisions, particularly its definition of equal. Three major issues involve defining:

Equal work: How equal is equal?;

Equal skill: effort, responsibility, and working conditions;

Factors other than sex.

Some noteworthy cases are summarized in Exhibit 14.1.

Definition of Equal

After years of judicial indecision, the court in 1970 established guidelines to define equal work in the *Schultz v. Wheaton Glass Company* case. Wheaton Glass Company maintained

---

[7]The 14th Amendment also provides equal treatment under the law and some cases involving pay discrimination have been heard under it, especially since *Mescall v. Burrus,* 603 F.2d 1266, 1271 (7th Cir. 1979); most, however, have been brought jointly with a Title VII claim.

[8]29 U.S.C. § 206(d) (1979). Since the EPA is an amendment to the Fair Labor Standards Act, it originally exempted the same occupational groups as did the FLSA. However, with the passage of the Education Amendments of 1972, EPA exemptions for bona fide executives, administrators, professionals, and outside salesmen were eliminated [29 U.S.C. § 213(a) (1970)].

EXHIBIT 14.1
Selected Wage Discrimination Cases

Major cases	Issues	Findings	Implications for compensation practices
Schultz v. *Wheaton Glass,* 1970 421 F. 2d 259	Two jobs had been historically segregated by sex with the men's jobs carrying the higher pay rate. This pay differential was based on the fact that men sometimes performed tasks the women did not. Performance of these extra tasks was considered of economic benefit to the company.	Pay differential was based on sex since the jobs performed by men and women were nearly identical with respect to skill, effort, responsibility and working conditions; additional tasks performed by men did not justify wage difference since the tasks were not performed by all men in the job.	Under EPA, equal pay for equal work means equal pay for "substantially similar" work. Evaluation of jobs must reflect real differences in skill, effort, responsibility and working conditions if wage differentials are to be justified. "Economic benefit" of the additional tasks is not a legitimate "other than sex" factor.
Corning Glass Works v. *Brennan,* 1974 417 U.S. 188	Some night shift jobs had originally been open only to men and carried a higher rate than the same day shift jobs open to women. Although the employer later opened the night shift jobs to all and established a uniform shift differential, the original wage difference for men was preserved.	A shift difference could be a factor other than sex, but in this case the shift differential was explained by a desire of the employer to compensate men, who worked at night, more than women, who worked during the day.	Traditional considerations involved in development of universal job factors will be considered by the court, but are not necessarily legal.
Lemons v. *City and County of Denver,* 1980 620 F. 2d 228	Plaintiffs argued that nurses were underpaid by the city, which paid the prevailing wage for their occupation in the community, because the community had historically discriminated against women's jobs.	There is no authorization under Title VII to adjust market disparities. As long as there is equal access to all jobs, there is no need to disregard community wage rates in assessing job worth.	The market factor is legitimate in job pricing so long as all jobs involved are equally open to both sexes.
Gunther v. *County of Washington,* 1981 U.S. Supreme Court 451 U.S. 161	Plaintiffs used employer's deviation from job evaluation plan as evidence of intentional discrimination.	The court found that this case did not involve the notion of comparable worth but that "to hold sex-based wage discrimination violates Title VII only if it also violates the EPA would be denying relief to victims of discrimination who did not hold the same job as a high paid man."	Illegal wage discrimination can also exist outside of "substantially equal" jobs. Proof of such discrimination is found in pattern of personnel practices.
Spaulding v. *University of Washington,* 35 FEP Cases 217 (9th Cir. 1984)	Faculty of a predominantly female department claimed that they were underpaid on the basis of sex in comparison with faculty of other comparable departments. Defendant claimed reliance on external market rates in setting wages, an employment practice that plaintiffs stated was discriminatory in impact although facially neutral.	Existence of wage differences between similar jobs is not sufficient to establish intent to discriminate. Employer's nonpay behavior did not show discriminatory intent. A compensation system based on market forces is not the type of specific employment practice necessary to support a disparate impact claim.	Use of wage survey data that incorporates past sex discrimination in the relevant market does not subject the employer to disparate impact claims. "(E)mployers deal with the market as a given and do not meaningfully have a 'policy' about it."

EXHIBIT 14.1
(Concluded)

Major cases	Issues	Findings	Implications for compensation practices
American Federation of State, County, and Municipal Employees (AFSCME) v. State of Washington, 578 F. Supp. 846, (W.D. Wash. 1983)	Employee union claimed that the state discriminated when it failed to implement a comparable-worth study which it had commissioned. Study had been commissioned in response to widespread allegations of discrimination. The study showed that employees in female-dominated jobs were compensated less than employees in male-dominated jobs, although *the dissimilar jobs were of comparable worth*.	Commissioning the study does not require the state to implement its recommendations. Although the state may choose to enact a comparable worth plan, it is not obligated to eliminate economic inequalities that it did not create in the market. "Economic reality is that the value of a particular job to an employer is but one factor influencing the rate of compensation for that job."	Setting wages according to prevailing market rates is not evidence of intent to discriminate. Employer is not bound by a study it commissions, but may use it as a diagnostic tool. Labor market conditions, bargaining demands and the possibility that another study could give different results may also be considered.

two job classifications for selector packers in its production department, male and female. The female job class carried a pay rate 10 percent below that of the male job class. The company claimed that the male job class included additional tasks that justified the pay differential, such as shoveling broken glass, opening warehouse doors, doing heavy lifting, and the like. The plaintiff claimed that the extra tasks were infrequently performed, and not all men did them.[9] Further, these extra tasks performed by some of the men were regularly performed by employees in another classification ("snap-up boys"), and these employees were paid only 2 cents an hour more than the women. Did the additional tasks performed by some members of one job class render the jobs unequal? The court decided not. It ruled that the equal work standard required only that jobs be *substantially* equal, not identical. The extra duties performed by the men did not justify paying the men 10 percent more than the women were paid. "Substantially equal work" based on the *Wheaton Glass Company* case has become the standard for assessing whether or not jobs are equal.

Additionally, the courts have generally held that the *actual work performed* is the appropriate data to use when deciding if jobs are substantially equal. This was established in several cases where it was found that the duties employees actually performed were different from those in the written descriptions of the job. These cases reinforce the point made in the chapter on job analysis: Compensation decisions must be based on the actual work employees perform, and any summary of that work, such as written job descriptions, must accurately capture that work.

---

[9]Plaintiffs are those who bring suit to obtain a remedy for injury to their rights. Defendants are those (usually the employer) who explain practices to answer the suit.

Definitions of the Four Factors

The Department of Labor provides these definitions of the four factors.[10]

- Skill: Experience, training, education, and ability as measured by the performance requirements of a particular job.
- Effort: Mental or physical. The amount or degree of effort (not type of effort) actually expended in the performance of a job.
- Responsibility: The degree of accountability required in the performance of a job.
- Working conditions: The physical surroundings and hazards of a job including dimensions such as inside versus outside work, heat, cold, and poor ventilation.

Guidelines to clarify these definitions have evolved through court decisions.

Differences in effort and skill requirements for hospital aides (females) and orderlies (males) were examined in *Brennan* vs. *Prince William Hospital.*[11] The primary tasks of both jobs involved general patient care. However, the hospital claimed that additional tasks assigned male orderlies required greater effort (e.g., restraining violent patients, dealing with disoriented patients) or greater skill (e.g., catheterization) than did any of the additional tasks assigned female aides, despite the fact that the hiring and organizational training requirements for the two jobs were identical.

The hospital had formerly grouped orderlies and aides into one job classification and paid one wage rate. The hospital preferred to have orderlies assigned to assist with male patients, and aides assigned to women's wards. But when the hospital ran into difficulty in attracting a sufficient number of orderlies (males), it divided the two jobs into two classifications, assigned a few additional job duties to the orderlies, and raised the wage attached to that job. The court found that additional duties (catheterization) were performed infrequently, and that newly hired orderlies were paid the higher wage even before they had been taught the additional task. Therefore the wage discrepancy was not justified.

For an employer to support a claim of *unequal* work, the following conditions must be met:

1. The effort/skill/responsibility must be substantially greater in one of the jobs compared.
2. The tasks involving the extra effort/skill/responsibility must consume a *significant amount* of time for *all* employees whose additional wages are in question.
3. The extra effort/skill/responsibility must have *a value commensurate* with the questioned pay differential (as determined by the employer's own evaluation).

---

[10]U.S. Department of Labor, *Women Workers Today* (Washington, D.C.: 1976); U.S. Department of Labor, *The Earnings Gap between Women and Men* (Washington, D.C.: 1976); U.S. Department of Labor, *Equal Pay for Equal Work under the Fair Labor Standards Act* (Washington, D.C.: Interpretative Bulletin, August 31, 1971); and U.S. Department of Labor, *Brief Highlights of Major Federal Laws and Order on Sex Discrimination on Employment* (Washington, D.C.: February 1977).

[11]*Brennan* v. *Prince William Hospital Corporation,* 503 F.2d 282 (4th Cir. 1974) *cert. denied,* 420 U.S. 972 (1975).

Cooper and Barrett compared a number of cases that provide information on what constitutes equal.[12] While they agree with the general pattern identified above, they point out that questions remain. For example, according to various court rulings, where 36 percent or more of time is spent in additional duties, jobs are dissimilar. Where 10 percent or less of the time is spent in additional duties, jobs are similar. (However, in one orderlies versus aides case, the 2 percent of the time that orderlies drove ambulances convinced the First Circuit Court that the jobs were unequal.) But that still leaves the range between 10 and 36 percent.

The courts have also dealt with equal working conditions. In *Brennan* v. *Corning Glass Works,* Corning claimed that night and day shift inspector jobs were unequal because the time of day work constituted "dissimilar working conditions." Prior to 1925, Corning operated two day shifts at its glassware plants, and all inspection work was performed by women. But the introduction of automatic production equipment made a night shift desirable. Because state protective legislation prohibited women from working at night, the company had to recruit male employees from the two day shifts to work as night inspectors. The male employees who transferred to night inspector demanded substantially higher wages than those paid to the women inspectors on the two day shifts. In 1944, the plants were organized, and the union negotiated a plant-wide shift differential, but this change did not eliminate the higher base wage paid to male night inspectors.

In 1969, a new collective bargaining agreement abolished future separate base wages for day and night shift inspectors, but allowed the differential to persist for those inspectors hired before January 20, 1969.

The 1974 court ruled that the jobs were not dissimilar; time of day did not constitute dissimilar working conditions because the definition of working conditions in Corning's job evaluation plan did not include shift differentials. Corning had to pay women back wages equal to what they would have received had they earned the night inspector rate. Shift differentials are not illegal, but if they are paid, the employer must clearly state that its purpose is to compensate workers for unusual conditions, and it must be separate from the base wage for the job.

Factors Other than Sex

Under the Equal Pay Act *unequal* pay for equal work may be justified through the four affirmative defenses: seniority, merit, performance-based incentive system, or a factor other than sex. Factors other than sex include shift differentials, temporary assignments, bona fide training programs, differences based on ability, training, or experience, and others.[13]

---

[12]Elizabeth A. Cooper and Gerald V. Barrett, "Equal Pay and Gender: Implications of Court Cases for Personnel Practices," *Academy of Management Review 9,* no. 1 (1984), pp. 84–94.

[13]Bona fide is interpreted here as (1) established, either formally or informally; (2) systematically applied in a nondiscriminatory fashion; and (3) communicated to all covered employees. H.R. Rep. No. 309, 88th Cong. 1st Sess. 3 (1963).

Recently factors other than sex were interpreted as a broad general exception that may include business reasons advanced by the employer. In *Kouba* v. *Allstate*,[14] Allstate Insurance Company paid its new sales representatives a minimum salary during their training period. After completing the training, the sales reps received a minimum salary or their earned sales commissions, whichever was greater. The minimum salary paid during training needed to be high enough to attract prospective agents to enter the training program, yet not so high as to lessen the incentive to earn sales commissions after training. Allstate argued that the minimum salary needed to be calculated individually for each trainee, and the trainee's past salary was a necessary factor used in the calculation. But Allstate's approach resulted in women trainees generally being paid less than male trainees, since women had held lower paying jobs before entering the program. Allstate maintained the pay difference resulted from acceptable business reasons: a factor other than sex.

Lola Kouba didn't buy Allstate's arguments. She argued that acceptable business reasons were limited to "those that measure the value of an employee's job performance to his or her employer." But the court rejected Kouba's argument. It said that Allstate's business reasons for a practice must be evaluated for reasonableness. A practice will not automatically be prohibited simply because wage differences between men and women result.

The court did not say that Allstate's "business" reasons were justified. It did say that Allstate's argument could not be rejected *solely because the practice perpetuated historical differences in pay*. Rather, Allstate needed to justify the business relatedness of the practice.

The case was settled out of court, so no legal clarification of Allstate's rationale was ever provided. Thus, the definition of "factor other than sex" remains somewhat murky. It does seem that pay differences for equal work can be justified for demonstrably business-related reasons. But what is and is not demonstrably business related has not yet been catalogued.

Reverse Discrimination

Several cases deal with the important issue of reverse discrimination against men, when pay for women is adjusted. In these cases, men have claimed that they were paid less than women doing similar work, simply because they were men. In one case, the University of Nebraska created a model to calculate salaries based on values estimated for a faculty member's education, field of specialization, years of direct experience, years of related experience, and merit.[15] Based on these qualifications, the university granted raises to 33 women whose salaries were less than the amount computed by the model. However, the university made no such increases to 92 males whose salaries were also

---

[14]*Kouba and EEOC* v. *Allstate Insurance Company,* 691 F.2d 873 (1982).

[15]*Board of Regents of University of Nebraska* v. *Dawes,* 522 F.2d 380, 11 FEP Cases 283 (8th Cir. 1976); 424 U.S. 914, 12 FEP Cases 343 (1976). The *Dawes* and *Ende* cases are contrasted in K. M. Weeks, "Equal Pay: The Emerging Terrain," *College and University Law,* Summer 1985, pp. 41–60.

below the amount the model set for them based on their qualifications. The court found this system a violation of the Equal Pay Act. It held that, in effect, the university was using a new system to determine a salary schedule, based on specific criteria. To refuse to pay employees of one sex the minimum required by these criteria was illegal.

In another case, the male faculty at Northern Illinois University sued to have a model the university developed to adjust women faculty salaries applied to them, also.[16] But there was an important difference. The regional Office of Civil Rights had found reasonable cause to believe that Northern Illinois University was discriminating against women faculty. The university did not dispute this finding. Instead, it sought to correct salary differences based on a model similar to the one used at Nebraska.

The NIU model was used to allocate *a one-time salary adjustment* to overcome the results of past discrimination against women, and was not a permanent change in the compensation system. Therefore the court ruled that it did not need to be applied to men. Nebraska, on the other hand, used a salary model that was *not* tailored to correct past discrimination. Rather, Nebraska developed a new way to calculate salaries and therefore must apply it to all faculty members equally.

So what does this have to do with compensation management? Viewed collectively, the courts have provided reasonably clear directions. The design of pay systems must incorporate a policy of equal pay for substantially equal work. The determination of substantially equal work must be based on the actual work performed (the job content) and must reflect the skill, effort, and responsibility required, and the working conditions. It is legal to pay men and women who perform substantially equal work differently if the pay system is designed to recognize differences in performance, seniority, quality and quantity of results, or certain factors other than sex, in a nondiscriminatory manner. Further, to minimize vulnerability to reverse discrimination suits, if a new pay system is designed, it must be equally applied to all employees. If, on the other hand, a one-time adjustment is made to correct past problems, it need only apply to the affected group.

But what does this tell us about discrimination on jobs that are *not substantially equal*—dissimilar jobs? For example, suppose that almost all women employees work in one job classification: office/clerical. Further suppose that the employer granted cost of living increases semiannually to all job classes *except* the office/clericals. The office/clerical jobs are not "substantially equal" to the other jobs, so the Equal Pay Act does not apply. Can the office/clerical employees still charge their employer with pay discrimination? Yes, under Title VII of the Civil Rights Act.

TITLE VII OF THE CIVIL RIGHTS ACT

Title VII prohibits discrimination on the basis of sex, race, color, religion, or national origin in any employment condition, including hiring, firing, promotion, transfer, com-

---

[16]*Ende v. Board of Regents of Northern Illinois University,* 37 FEP Cases 575 (7th Cir. 1985). Peter Saucier wonders whether affirmative action plans are "a factor other than sex" in "Affirmative Action and the Equal Pay Act," *Employee Relations Law Journal* 11, no. 2 (Winter 1985/86), pp. 453–66.

pensation, and admission to training programs.[17] Title VII was amended in 1972 and 1978. The 1972 amendments strengthened enforcement and expanded coverage to include employees of government and educational institutions, as well as private employers of more than 15 persons. The pregnancy amendment of 1978 made it illegal to discriminate based on pregnancy, childbirth, or related conditions.

Defining Discrimination

Since 1964 the courts have evolved two theories of discrimination behavior under Title VII: (1) disparate treatment and (2) disparate impact. Exhibit 14.2 contrasts the two theories.

Disparate treatment. Disparate or unequal treatment includes those practices in which an organization treats minorities or women less favorably than others are treated, either openly or covertly. Under this definition, a practice is unlawful if it applies different standards to different employees, for example, based on seniority for women but performance for men (different standards). The mere fact of unequal treatment may be taken as evidence of the employer's intention to discriminate.

Disparate impact. Personnel practices that have a differential *effect* on members of protected groups are illegal under the disparate or unequal impact theory of Title VII, unless the differences can be justified as necessary to the safe and efficient operation of the business or are work related. The major case that established this interpretation of Title VII is *Griggs* v. *Duke Power Co.,*[18] in which the Court struck down employment tests and educational requirements that screened out a greater proportion of blacks than

---

EXHIBIT 14.2
Discriminatory Behavior

Disparate treatment	*Disparate impact*
1. Different standards for different individuals or groups.	1. Same standards have differing consequences.
2. Intent to discriminate may be inferred by behaviors.	2. Discrimination shown by general statistical impact; discriminatory intent need not be present.
3. Employer can justify actions by absence of discriminatory intent and exercise of reasonable business judgment.	3. Employer can justify pay differences through business necessity.

---

[17]29 U.S.C. § 206 (d) (1) (1970). Its coverage is broader, also. Employers, employment agencies, labor organizations, and training programs involving 15 or more employees and some 120,000 educational institutions fall under its jurisdictions.

[18]*Griggs v. Duke Power Co.,* 401 U.S. 414 (1971).

whites. Even though the practices were applied equally—both blacks and whites had to pass the tests—they were prohibited because (1) they had the consequence of excluding a protected group (blacks) disproportionately and (2) they were not related to the jobs in question.

Under the disparate impact theory of discrimination, whether or not the employer intended to discriminate is irrelevant. Thus a personnel decision can, on its face, seem neutral, but if the results of it are unequal, the employer must demonstrate that the decision is either work related or a business necessity.

These two theories of discrimination have been well established in employment or access discrimination issues.[19] They have been more difficult to apply to pay issues. The difficulty stems from the fact that different pay may be legal for dissimilar work. To understand the evolving status of pay discrimination under Title VII, we examine two basic questions.

1. Can pay discrimination exist in different pay rates for dissimilar jobs?
2. What constitutes pay discrimination in dissimilar jobs?

Pay Discrimination and Dissimilar Jobs

The Supreme Court, in *Gunther* v. *County of Washington* (Exhibit 14.1), determined that pay discrimination may occur in establishing pay differences for dissimilar jobs. In this case, four jail matrons in Washington County, Oregon, claimed that their work was comparable to that performed by male guards. The women matrons guarded one-tenth the number of prisoners for which the male guards were responsible. The rest of their job responsibilities were of a clerical nature.

Both the county's own wage survey and its assessment of job worth had indicated that the matrons should be paid about 95 percent as much as the guards. Instead, their pay was only about 70 percent that of the guards. Lower courts refused to consider the matrons' case on the grounds that their evidence did not *meet the equal work requirement of the Equal Pay Act*. The Supreme Court overturned the lower courts and stated that a Title VII pay case was not bound by the definitions of equal work or the affirmative defenses of the Equal Pay Act.

Prior to *Gunther,* the relationship between EPA and Title VII was unclear. Many felt that the existence of the Equal Pay Act meant that all pay discrimination charges had to be brought under that law and meet the law's definitions of equal work and the four defenses.[20] But in *Gunther*, the Supreme Court ruled that "to hold that sex-based wage discrimination violates Title VII only if it also violates the EPA would be denying relief to victims of discrimination who did not hold the same jobs as a higher paid man." The Court also went out of its way to state what it was *not* ruling on:

---

[19]Walter Fogel, "Intentional Sex-Based Pay Discrimination: Can It Be Proven?" *Labor Law Journal,* May 1986, pp. 291–299.

[20]Garth Mangum and Stephen Mangum, "Comparable Worth Confusion in the Ninth Circuit," *Labor Law Journal,* June 1986, pp. 357–65.

We emphasize at the outset the narrowness of the question before us in this case. Respondents' claim is not based on the controversial concept of "comparable worth," under which the plaintiff might claim increased compensation on the basis of a comparison of the intrinsic worth or difficulty of their job with that of other jobs in the same organization or community. Rather, respondents seek to prove, by direct evidence, that their wages were depressed because of intentional sex discrimination, consisting of setting the wage scale level lower than its own survey of outside markets and the worth of the jobs warranted.

(The case was returned to a lower court for additional evidence of discrimination, and was eventually settled out of court.)

So the *Gunther* case established that charges of pay discrimination on dissimilar (not equal) jobs could be brought under Title VII. But it did not consider what might constitute pay discrimination in dissimilar jobs under Title VII. To examine this question we discuss three possible approaches: (1) where the employer exhibited a pattern of discrimination in many of its personnel practices beyond wage setting, (2) where the employer used market data to justify pay differences, and (3) where the employer conducted a pay equity study using job evaluation to determine jobs of "comparable worth."

Proof of Discrimination: Pattern of Personnel Practices

Under this approach, employees seek to prove that discrimination pervades the entire employment relationship, including the pay system. In *Taylor* v. *Charley Brothers Company*,[21] a wholesale distributor maintained two separate departments based on what products were handled, not on what work was done. For example, warehouse workers who handled frozen food were in department 1; those who handled health and beauty aids were in department 2. Charley Brothers hired only men for the first department; women applicants were not even considered for positions in that department. If female applicants specifically requested department 1, they were told that the work there required greater physical strength, but they were not told that jobs in department 1 also paid more. Additional evidence indicated that no males were considered for jobs in department 2, and that both company officials and union officials discouraged female employees from bidding for jobs in department 1. Clearly, the company's hiring and job assignment policies violated Title VII in that women were denied equal access to jobs, but did its pay policies discriminate, too? The Court held that both the EPA and Title VII were violated. In those jobs that were substantially equal in both departments 1 and 2—receivers, order selectors, and pack-up persons—the differential pay meant that the EPA was violated. But the Court went beyond this and said that Charley Brothers intentionally discriminated in its entire pay system. Women were paid substantially less than men in the all-male department simply because they worked in a department populated only by women and not because the jobs they performed were inherently worth less than jobs performed by men. The Court took as evidence of the company's intent to discriminate the fact that it never had undertaken any type of evaluation of any of the jobs, its practice of segregating women within the one department, and various discriminatory remarks

---

[21]*Taylor* v. *Charley Brothers Company*, 25 FEP Cases 602 (W. D. Pa. 1981).

made by officials of the company.[22] Sufficient proof of Charley Brothers' intention to discriminate was shown through the pattern of its personnel practices, including pay, regardless of the dissimilarity of the jobs involved.

Cases of such blatant discrimination are probably rarer today. It is relatively easy to obtain agreement as to the existence of discrimination in situations where evidence exists in almost every personnel decision. Most situations are less clear.

Consider, for example, the case in which the pay rates for two obviously dissimilar jobs are determined. Examples include the pay rates for nurses versus tree trimmers or nurses versus sanitarians or even professors of nursing versus professors of business administration. If these jobs are dissimilar and if no pattern of discrimination in hiring, promotion, or other personnel decisions exists, then what constitutes pay discrimination?

Proof of Discrimination: Use of Market Data

In the case of *Lemons* v. *The City and County of Denver* (Exhibit 14.1), nurse Mary Lemons claimed that her job, held predominantly by women, was illegally paid less than the jobs held predominantly by men (tree trimmers, sign painters, tire servicemen, etc.). Lemons claimed that the nurse's job required greater education and skill. Therefore, to pay the male jobs more than the nurses' jobs simply because the male jobs commanded higher rates in the local labor market was discriminatory. She argued that the market reflected historical underpayment of "women's work." Lemons claimed the existence of pay differences for women's versus men's work was a sign of job discrimination. The court disagreed, adding that "market disparities are not among those Title VII seeks to adjust." Thus, the situation identified by *Lemons*—pay differences in dissimilar jobs— did not by itself constitute proof of intent to discriminate.

In another case, *Briggs* v. *City of Madison,* pay differences between *substantially similar* jobs were considered. Here the court determined that, if jobs are substantially similar, then the existence and size of any pay differences are relevant in establishing discrimination. The court ruled that though the jobs of nurse and public health sanitarian were not equal, they were "substantially similar." But the pay differences between the two jobs were great. The court felt that if the jobs were similar, the pay should be, too. The fact that it wasn't constituted initial evidence of discrimination because

> it rests upon the logical premise that jobs which are *similar* in their requirements of skill, effort, and responsibility and in their working conditions are of comparable value to an employer. . . . Jobs of comparable value would be compensated comparably but for the employer's discriminatory treatment of the lower paid employees.[23]

---

[22]The union was also accused of discrimination against female employees. The courts accepted as evidence discriminatory statements made by union leaders, but did not hold them liable for their behaviors, since they had not made the hiring and allocation decisions.

[23]George T. Milkovich, "Wage Discrimination and Comparable Worth," *ILR Report* 19, no. 2 (Spring 1982), pp. 7–12; Ronald L. Oaxaca, "Sex Discrimination in Wages," *Discrimination in Labor Markets*, eds. O. Ashenfelter and A. Rees (Princeton, N.J.: Princeton Press, 1973); and E. Robert Livernash, ed., *Comparable Worth: Issues and Alternatives* (Washington, D.C.: Equal Employment Advisory Council, 1980).

However, the city of Madison successfully rebutted the initial case of discrimination with evidence from the external labor market. According to labor market data, sanitarians throughout the state were paid salaries comparable with those in Madison. The salary the city was offering for sanitarians was raised because the city had experienced difficulty (long periods to fill job vacancies) in attracting qualified sanitarians. So the city was able to justify the pay differences using market data.[24]

The courts have continually upheld employers' use of market data to justify pay differences for different jobs. *Spaulding* v. *University of Washington* (Exhibit 14.1) developed the argument in greatest detail. In this case, the predominantly female faculty of the Department of Nursing claimed that it was illegally paid less than faculty in other departments.

Spaulding alleged disparate treatment in setting nursing professors' pay in comparison to pay in "comparable" departments. The statisticians for Spaulding presented a model that controlled for the effects of level of education, job tenure, and other factors. They asserted that any pay difference not accounted for in their model was discrimination. But the courts have been dubious of statistics. Such an approach to defining discrimination has been likened to the owner of a missing piece of jewelry concluding that it must be in the kitchen, "because I've looked through every other room in the house." Far better to define discrimination directly, rather than concluding that it is "whatever is left."[25] The *Spaulding* judge observed that the model "unrealistically assumed the equality of all master's degrees, ignored job experience prior to university employment and ignored detailed analysis of day-to-day responsibilities." Without such data, "we have no meaningful way of determining just how much of the proposed wage differential was due to sex and how much was due to academic discipline."

But the court went beyond criticizing the model. It ruled on the use of competitive market data as a policy. The court held that every employer who is constrained by market forces must consider market values in setting labor costs. "Naturally, market prices are inherently job-related." Employers who rely on the market deal with it as a given and do not meaningfully have a "policy" about it in the relevant Title VII sense, according to the court. Allowing reliance on the market to constitute a facially neutral policy for disparate impact purposes "would subject employers to liability for pay disparities with respect to which they have not, in any meaningful sense, made an independent business judgment."

---

[24]In 1983, Madison, Wisconsin's city government enacted guidelines requiring that the wage structures of private businesses that contract with the city be reviewed "to determine whether comparable pay exists for comparable positions." To comply, vendors must set percentage goals for hiring women and minorities and maintain the same percentage goals for distribution of salaries. For example, if a contractor's work force is 30 percent female, 30 percent of its wages must be paid to females. [Information from Lawrence Lorber, J. Robert Kirk, Stephen Samuels, and David J. Spellman III, *Sex and Salary* (Alexandria, VA.: The ASPA Foundation, 1985).]

[25]Orley Ashenfelter and Ronald Oaxaca, "The Economics of Discrimination: Economists Enter the Courtroom," *American Economic Review,* May 1987, pp. 321–25; and Victor Fuchs, *Women's Quest for Economic Equality* (Cambridge, Mass.: Harvard University Press, 1988).

Is there a "market policy"? Recall from the market survey discussion (Chapter 7) all the decisions that go into designing and conducting a survey. What employers constitute the "relevant market"? Does the relevant market vary by occupation? Do different market definitions yield different wage patterns? Clearly, judgment is involved in answering these questions. Yet the courts have thus far neglected to examine those judgments for possible bias. Perhaps the pattern of judgment does indeed constitute a "policy" in a Title VII sense.

Spaulding and other court cases have tended to view the market as a "given" that allows little room for discretion. If that is so, then according to Rynes and Milkovich, the employer's role is to "find out precisely what that rate is. If, on the other hand, a *range* of possible wages exists for any given job, then . . . the observed, or measured, market wage will depend on where the wage data is collected, . . . (and) *sampling* becomes critical."[26]

Should market survey procedures be subject to the same issues that surround other statistical procedures (e.g., availability analysis for fairness in hiring and promotion, or validity and job-relatedness of tests)? While Rynes and Milkovich do not take a position on this question, they point out that "judgment enters into virtually every step of the wage survey process, and each successive judgment may modify the eventual results." Clearly not all employers are the "price takers" that the courts have assumed.[27]

Proof of Discrimination: Jobs of "Comparable Worth"

A third approach to attempting to determine pay discrimination on jobs of dissimilar content hinges on finding a standard by which to compare the value of jobs. The standard must be two things. First, it must permit jobs with dissimilar content to be declared equal or "in some sense comparable."[28] Second, it must permit pay differences for dissimilar jobs that are not comparable. Job evaluation has been proposed as that standard.[29] If an employer's own job evaluation study shows jobs of dissimilar content to be of equal value to the employer, then isn't failure to pay them equally proof of intent to discriminate? The issue has been considered in *AFSCME* v. *State of Washington* (Exhibit 14.1).

In 1973, the state of Washington commissioned a study of the concept of comparable worth (discussed later in this chapter) and its projected effect on the state's pay system. The study concluded that by basing wages on the external market, the state was paying

[26]Sara L. Rynes and George T. Milkovich, "Wage Surveys: Dispelling Some Myths about the 'Market Wage'," *Personnel Psychology*, Spring 1986, pp. 71–90.

[27]Sara L. Rynes, Caroline L. Weber, and George T. Milkovich, "The Effects of Market Survey Rates, Job Evaluation and Job Gender on Job Pay," *Journal of Applied Psychology* 74, 1, 1989, pp. 114–23.

[28]Reskin and Hartmann, *Women's Work, Men's Work;* and Judith Olans Brown, Phyllis Tropper Baumann, and Elain Millar Melnick, "Equal Pay for Jobs of Comparable Worth: An Analysis of the Rhetoric," *Harvard Civil Rights–Civil Liberties Law Review,* Winter 1986, pp. 127–70.

[29]*Job Evaluation: A Tool for Pay Equity* (Washington, D. C.: National Committee on Pay Equity, November 1987); and Rynes, Weber, and Milkovich, "Effects of Market Survey Rates, Job Evaluation, and Job Gender on Job Pay."

women approximately 20 percent less than it was paying men in jobs deemed of comparable value to the state. The state took no action on this finding, so AFSCME, the employees' union, sued to force implementation of a compensation system based on comparable worth as outlined in the study. The union alleged that since the state was aware of the adverse effect of its present policy, failure to change it constituted discrimination.

The state of Washington has failed to rectify an acknowledged "discriminatory disparity in compensation" on the grounds that it could not afford it. The district court declared this a straightforward "failure to pay case" and ordered the state to change its practices. But the appeals court overruled this order. It found that the district court's interpretation of disparate impact was not "confined to cases which challenge a specific, clearly delineated employment practice applied at a single point." The state was not obligated to correct the disparity, according to the appeals court. An employer merely being aware of adverse consequences for a protected group did not constitute discrimination. "The plaintiff must show the employer chose the particular policy because of its effect on members of a protected class."[30]

AFSCME v. *State of Washington* differs from previous cases that used market data in that this is the first case where the evidence that the jobs were in any sense "equal" was developed by the employer. But even though the state had commissioned the study, it had not agreed to implement the study's results. Therefore the employer had not, in the court's view, admitted the jobs were equal or established a pay system which purported to pay on the basis of "comparable worth" rather than markets.

Rather than appeal, the parties settled out of court. The state revamped its pay system and agreed to make over $100 million in "pay equity" adjustments by 1992.

So where does this leave us? Clearly Title VII prohibits intentional discrimination in compensation if it is based on sex or other proscribed factors, whether or not the employees in question hold the same or different jobs. Discrimination may be proved by direct evidence of an employer's intent (e.g., an overall pattern of behavior that demonstrates disparate treatment). However, "Job evaluation studies and comparable worth statistics alone are insufficient to establish the requisite inference of discriminatory motive."[31] The disparate impact standard, where no proof of discriminatory intent is required, appears to be inappropriate for broad challenges to general compensation policies.

Title VII rulings make it clear that pay discrimination is not limited only to equal jobs; it may also occur in setting different rates for different jobs. It is also clear that the courts are not about to rule use of external market rates illegal. Competitive market pricing, by itself, does not appear to constitute a policy that has disparate impact. Further, to prevail in a disparate treatment allegation, plaintiffs need to demonstrate a pattern of discrimination practices that is specific and deliberate—"regularly and purposefully treat(ing)

---

[30]The AFSCME case is discussed in length in Mangum and Mangum, "Comparable Worth Confusion in the Ninth Circuit."

[31]David A. Cathcart and Pamela L. Hemminger, *Developments in the Law of Salary Discrimination* (Los Angeles: Gibson, Dunn and Crutcher, 1985).

[32]*Taylor* v. *Charles Brothers Company*.

women differently and generally less favorably than men."[32] Simply demonstrating pay differences on jobs that are not equal is insufficient to prove discrimination.

What additional implications for the design and administration of pay systems can be drawn? These court decisions imply that pay differentials between dissimilar jobs will not be prohibited under Title VII if the differences can be shown to be based on the content of the work, its value to the organization's objectives, and the employer's ability to attract and retain employees in competitive external labor markets. The courts appear to recognize that "the value of a particular job to an employer is but one factor influencing the rate of compensation for a job."[33]

ECONOMIC EQUALITY AS A SOCIAL ISSUE

Clearly, present interpretation of federal law in the United States does not mandate a comparable worth theory of discrimination. Why then does the issue persist? It is part of a continuing evolution of the role of women in society. The image of the typical family, father (at work), mother (at home), and two kids, persisted long after statistical evidence showed that women were increasingly switching from work at home to work in the labor force. Exhibit 14.3 documents the upward trend in the labor force participation rate of women. In 1975, 46 percent of all women in the United States were in the labor force. Ten years later, the rate was 54 percent, and by 1995 it is projected to be 60 percent. But even though this trend predates passage of the Equal Pay Act, women have still not achieved economic parity with men.[34] Some people believe that elimination of gender-related pay differentials on equal jobs and opening access to all jobs is sufficient.[35] But many others do not.[36] They believe that despite the equal pay standard, women continue to face severe handicaps in the labor market. To paraphrase Mark Twain, they are "surrounded by insurmountable opportunities." These opportunities present themselves as differences in occupational attainment, and a persistent gap in the wages received by women compared to men.

The Earnings Gap

According to the Bureau of Labor Statistics, women working full time in 1988 had a median weekly wage equal to 70 percent of the weekly wage earned by men. While this difference has fluctuated over time, it has been extremely persistent.[37]

---

[33]*AFSCME* v. *Washington.*

[34]Fuchs, *Women's Quest for Economic Equality.*

[35]Myron Lieberman, "The Conversion of Interests to Principles: The Case of Comparable Worth," *Journal of Collective Negotiations* 15, 2 (1986), pp. 145–52.

[36]Jerald Greenberg and Claire L. McCarty, "Comparable Worth: A Matter of Justice," in *Research in Personnel and Human Resources Management,* vol. 8, K. M. Rowland and G. R. Ferris, eds. (Greenwich, Conn.: JAI Press, 1990).

[37]Heidi Hartmann, "Briefing Paper on the Wage Gap: Women Have Made Slow Steady Progress in the Labor Market Since 1979 But the Wage Gap Has Not Suddenly Narrowed Significantly" (Washington, D.C.: National Committee on Pay Equity, September 22, 1987).

EXHIBIT 14.3
Labor Force Participation Rates of Men and Women 1975–1995

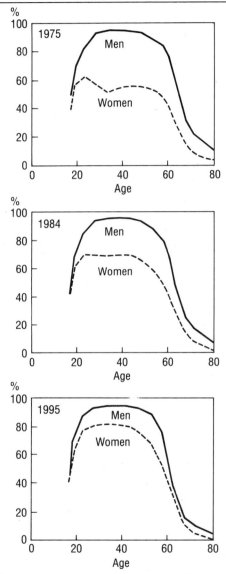

EXHIBIT 14.4
Changes in Women's Earnings as a Percentage of Men's Among Full-Time Workers

Year	Median Annual Earnings (Year-Round)	Median Weekly Earnings (Usual)
1955	63.9	
1960	60.7	
1965	59.9	
1970	59.4	62.3
1975	58.8	62.0
1976	60.2	62.2
1977	58.9	61.9
1978	59.4	61.3
1979	59.7	62.5
1980	60.2	64.4
1981	59.2	64.6
1982	61.7	65.4
1983	63.6	66.7
1984	63.7	67.8
1985	64.9	68.2
1986	64.3	69.2
1987	65.0	70.0
1988	—	70.2

Source: Data through 1983 are from Francine D. Blau and Marianne A. Ferber, *The Economics of Women, Men and Work* (Prentice-Hall, 1986). Annual data for 1984, 1985, 1986.

The size of the gap depends on how it is defined. Comparing weekly earnings gives a higher ratio than comparing annual earnings. If the data are adjusted for differences in hours worked (women on full time schedules work about 6 percent fewer hours than men on full time schedules) the ratio would be about 72 percent.

Historically, the ratio was relatively constant for about 30 years. Exhibit 14.4 shows wage data over time. In 1955, women's median annual earnings were 64 percent of men's, in 1965 they declined to 60 percent, in 1975 they fell to 59 percent, by 1987 they were back to 65 percent—about where they were 30 years earlier. That relatively constant pattern occurred despite the passages of the Equal Pay Act in 1963, the Civil Rights Act of 1965, and the Executive Orders that mandated affirmative action in firms doing business with the federal government—all implemented during the intervening years.

Since 1971, the ratio has risen steadily, reaching 69 percent in 1986. So there is some evidence that in the most recent years the gap is slowly narrowing. The fact remains that an earnings gap exists. Almost any way you measure it, women earn less than men, and the difference is slowly narrowing.

What do we know about why that gap exists? Respected economists agree that many complex and subtly interrelated factors are involved, which is why we never sit next to economists at parties.[38]

Some of the more important factors, shown in Exhibit 14.5, include:

[38]See Dave Barry, *Dave Barry Slept Here* (New York: Random House, 1989), p. 125.

EXHIBIT 14.5
Possible Determinants of Pay Differences

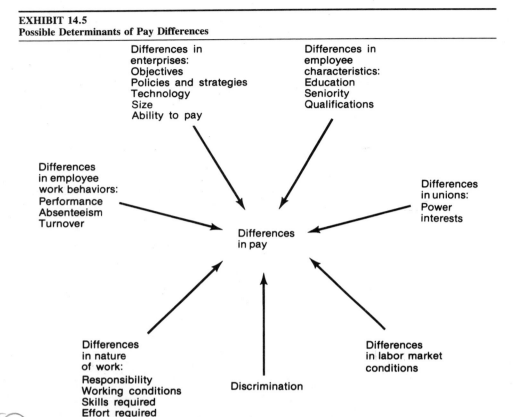

Differences in
enterprises:
Objectives
Policies and strategies
Technology
Size
Ability to pay

Differences in
employee
characteristics:
Education
Seniority
Qualifications

Differences
in employee
work behaviors:
Performance
Absenteeism
Turnover

Differences
in unions:
Power
interests

Differences
in pay

Differences
in nature
of work:
Responsibility
Working conditions
Skills required
Effort required

Discrimination

Differences
in labor market
conditions

Source: George T. Milkovich, "The Emerging Debate," in *Comparable Worth: Issues and Alternatives*, ed. E. Robert Livernash (Washington, D.C.: Equal Employment Advisory Council, 1980).

1. Differences in the occupational attainment and the jobs held by men and women.
2. Differences in personal work-related characteristics and work behaviors.
3. Differences among industries and firms.
4. Differences in union membership.
5. The presence of discrimination.

First let us examine some data, then some conflicting beliefs.

Differences in Occupational Attainment

One of the most important factors, that accounts for much of the remaining 30 percent gap, is the difference in the nature of jobs held by men and women. A variety of data illustrate these differences.

As noted earlier, the Bureau of Labor Statistics reports that half of all working women are employed in only 20 percent of the 427 occupations. And among 427 occupational

EXHIBIT 14.6
Gender and Race Differences in Occupational Distribution, 1988

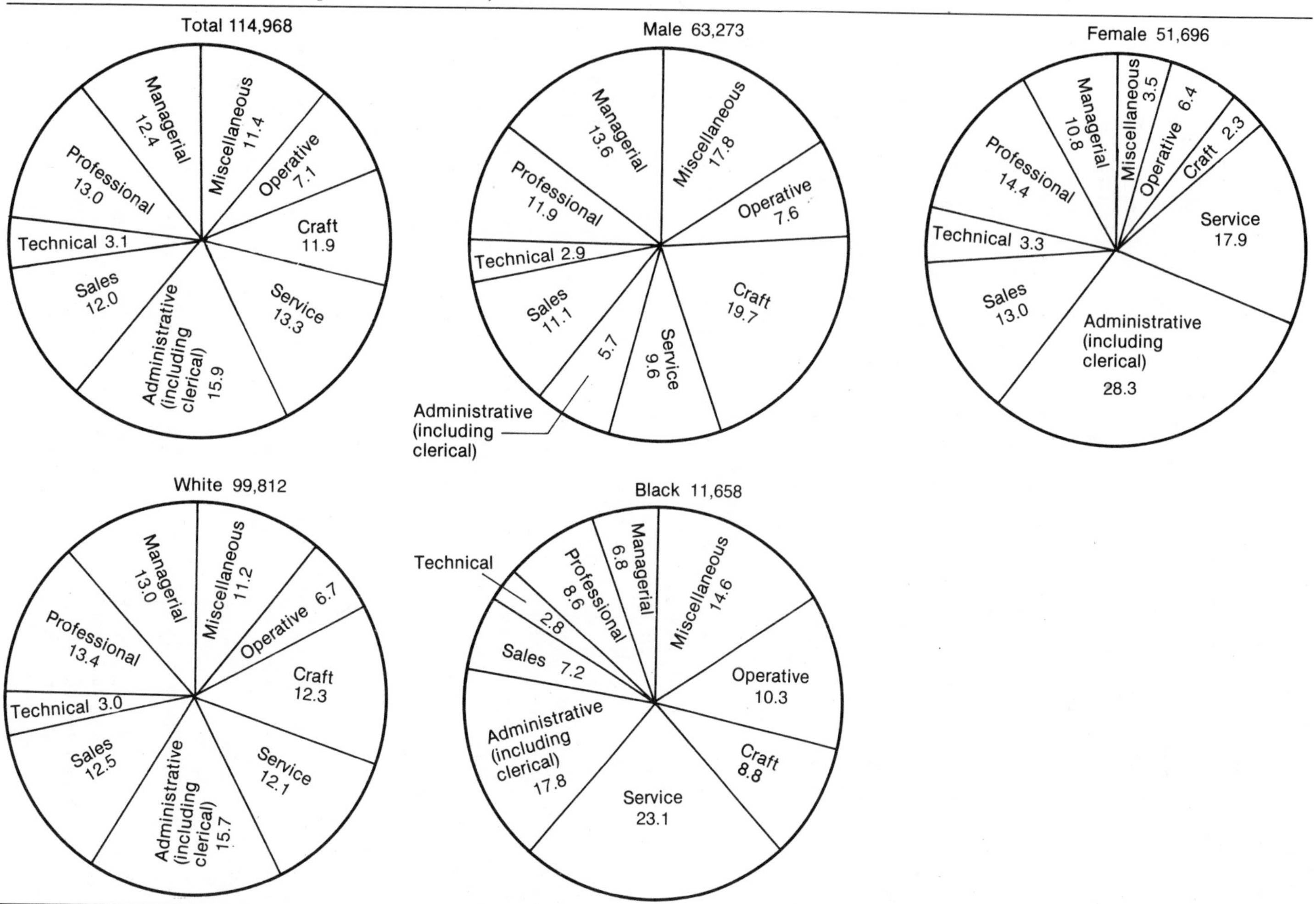

Female 51,696

- Service 17.9
- Administrative (including clerical) 28.3
- Sales 13.0
- Technical 3.3
- Professional 14.4
- Managerial 10.8
- Miscellaneous 3.5
- Operative 6.4
- Craft 2.3

Male 63,273

- Operative 7.6
- Craft 19.7
- Service 9.6
- Administrative (including clerical) 5.7
- Sales 11.1
- Technical 2.9
- Professional 11.9
- Managerial 13.6
- Miscellaneous 17.8

Total 114,968

- Craft 11.9
- Service 13.3
- Administrative (including clerical) 15.9
- Sales 12.0
- Technical 3.1
- Professional 13.0
- Managerial 12.4
- Miscellaneous 11.4
- Operative 7.1

Black 11,658

- Operative 10.3
- Craft 8.8
- Service 23.1
- Administrative (including clerical) 17.8
- Sales 7.2
- Technical 2.8
- Professional 8.6
- Managerial 6.8
- Miscellaneous 14.6

White 99,812

- Operative 6.7
- Craft 12.3
- Service 12.1
- Administrative (including clerical) 15.7
- Sales 12.5
- Technical 3.0
- Professional 13.4
- Managerial 13.0
- Miscellaneous 11.2

Source: U.S. Department of Labor Statistics, *Employment and Earnings*, January, 1989.

classes, 80 percent of women work in which at least 70 percent of employees are women. The distribution of women among occupations differs from that for white men. Exhibit 14.6 shows the different occupational patterns for male, female, white, and black workers.

The 1980 Census lists the highest concentration of black women in the occupations of private household workers, cooks, housekeepers, and welfare aides. Hispanic women tend to be agricultural workers, housekeepers, and electrical assemblers. Black men are concentrated in the occupations of stevedores, garbage collectors, long shore equipment operators, and baggage porters. Hispanic men tend to be farm workers and farm supervisors. The occupations in which women are employed tend to be lowest paying. Thus, the difference in occupational attainment is the major factor accounting for the earnings gap.[39]

Now let's examine the beliefs or theories used to explain the data. Supporters of comparable worth believe the differences in occupational attainment are a reflection of discrimination in society.[40] Discrimination and gender stereotyping in counseling received and courses taken in high school, admission to colleges, and in the hiring and promotion practices of employers have all worked, the argument goes, to allocate or crowd women into a limited number of occupations. Because these occupations are typed as women's work, they are devalued. That is, women's jobs pay less because wage discrimination acts on an entire occupation, not only on individual women workers.

On the other hand, the opponents of comparable worth believe wages are determined primarily by supply and demand; that is, by choices of women and employers. Wages and employment levels are flexible and labor markets adjust, so that the supply available, made up of choices of workers to undertake training required and seek job opportunities, adjusts to equal the demand. If we just get markets competitive and working efficiently, the argument goes, the goal of maximizing profits will eventually lead employers to eliminate discrimination.[41]

According to this view, women make choices about which occupations to train for, when to leave, and enter the work force. From this efficient market perspective, women earn less because the jobs they choose have low productivity and low wages, but those

[39]Linda Subich, Gerald Barrett, Dennis Doverspike, and Ralph Alexander, "The Effects of Sex Role-Related Factors on Occupational Choice and Salary," *Pay Equity: Empirical Inquiries* (Washington, D. C.: National Academy of Science, 1989); and Randall K. Filer, "Occupational Segregation, Compensating Differentials and Comparable Worth," *Pay Equity: Empirical Inquiries* (Washington, D.C.: National Academy of Science, 1989).

[40]Paula England, "Do Men's Jobs Require More Skill than Women's?" *ILR Report* 19, no. 2 (Spring 1983), pp. 20–23.

[41]G. G. Cain, *The Economic Analysis of Labor Market Discrimination: A Survey,* Special Report 37 (Madison: University of Wisconsin, March 1985); Solomon W. Polachek, "Women in the Economy: Perspectives on Gender Inequality," *Comparable Worth: Issue for the 80's,* Vol. 1 (Washington, D.C.: U.S. Commission on Civil Rights, 1985); and Claudia Goldin, *Occupational Segregation by Sex: The Roles of Supervisory Costs and Human Capital, 1890–1940* (Cambridge, Mass.: National Bureau of Economic Research, 1984).

jobs permit women to enter and leave the work force readily; require relatively less training; and are not onerous or dangerous.[42]

But recent data indicate these occupational patterns are changing. Women are gaining access to (are choosing) a wider array of occupations. Exhibit 14.7 shows data from some selected occupations. For example in 1979, 28 percent of computer programmers were women, by 1986 it was 39.7 percent. Similar increases occurred in supervision, lawyers, janitors, and accountants.

EXHIBIT 14.7
Female/Male Hourly Earnings Ratio

| | Full-Time Workers Selected Occupations | | | |
| | 1979 | | 1986 | |
Occupation	Percent Female	Earnings Ratio	Percent Female	Earnings Ratio
Registered nurses	94.6	82	92.7	91
Bookkeepers, accounting and auditing clerks	88.1	66	93.0	74
Nursing aides, orderlies, and attendants	85.1	72	88.3	81
Administrative support occups., misc.	62.9	62	82.4	70
Social workers	60.6	83	60.0	73
Computer operators	56.6	69	63.8	73
Supervisors, food preparation and service occups.	41.6	72	48.2	67
Secondary school teachers	39.7	83	49.1	86
Accountants and auditors	34.0	60	44.7	72
Computer programmers	28.0	80	39.7	81
Janitors and cleaners	15.3	74	21.0	69
Supervisors, production occupations	12.9	62	15.1	67
Lawyers	10.4	55	15.2	63

Source: *Current Population Reports*, Series p-70, No. 10: Table 11, p. 23; Table G, p. 5.

---

[42]G. Johnson and G. Solon, *Pay Differences between Women's and Men's Jobs* (Cambridge, Mass.: National Bureau of Economic Research, Inc., 1984); W. F. Oi, "Neglected Women and Other Implications of Comparable Worth," *Contemporary Policy Issues* (April 1986), pp. 21–32; and J. Roback, *A Matter of Choice: A Critique of Comparable Worth by a Skeptical Feminist* (New York: Priority Press, 1986).

It is a fact that (1) women tend to be employed in female dominated occupations and (2) that wages in these occupations are relatively lower. It is also a fact that (3) women tend to hold the lower paying jobs in each occupation. So while the percentage of women employed is increasing dramatically, new workers are more likely to hold lower paying jobs. Thus, the influx of women into the workforce has also tended to hold down women's earnings.

Based on a recent survey of the research conducted on the earnings gap, no study has been able to explain more than half of the difference between male/female earnings without one or more variables designed to measure differences in occupations and the nature of the work performed. So we know that the nature of the jobs performed is a critical factor.

Differences in Personal Work-Related Characteristics

Differences in employee attributes and behaviors are another important factor explaining the earnings gap. These include differences in experience and seniority within a firm, continuous time in the work force, and education, and the like.

Experience and seniority. To illustrate with some data, consider experience and seniority differences among full time workers. We have already noted that on the average, men work 6 percent more hours per week than women. By the time men and women have been out of school for 6 years, women on average have worked 1.6 years, or 30 percent less than men. After 16 years out of school, women average half as much labor market experience as men.[43]

Research shows that the male/female differential is reduced by about half when women are compared to men with the same years of work experience. While women still lag men in total work force experience (especially in older age groups), the 1987 Report of the Council of Economic Advisors shows that women have increased their job tenure. In 1963, women averaged 2.7 fewer years of tenure with their current employer than men. By 1983, the difference narrowed to 1.4 years. So difference in experience is a critical factor.

Education. So, too, are differences in the level of education and in educational specialty. Currently men and women graduate from college in nearly equal numbers. As you might expect, if the occupations women enter are changing, so too are the college majors chosen by women. And college major is the strongest factor affecting income of college graduates. A major in engineering or business brings the highest income for both men and women; majors in education the lowest.[44] In 1964, 42.5 percent of all bachelors degrees earned by women were in education, and in 1981 it plummeted to 18 percent. Fields attracting women today are those traditionally chosen by men, with the sharpest

---

[43]Fuchs, *Women's Quest for Economic Equality.*

[44]Estelle James, N. Absalam, J. Conaty, and Duc-le To, "College Quality and Future Earnings," working paper, Department of Economics, SUNY Stony Brook, Stony Brook, NY, 1989.

growth in professional degrees. In 1964, women earned only 5 percent of the medical degrees and 4 percent of the law degrees and 3 percent of the MBAs. By 1984, 25 percent of the medical degrees, 32 percent of the law degrees, and 25 percent of the MBAs were earned by women. So we are observing significant shifts in the education/training choices made by women.

Age. We also know the earnings gap varies by age of workers. The gap is larger for older than younger workers. The ratio almost disappears at age 16–19; it is about 96 percent. At age 20–24 it is 89 percent, and at 65 percent for those 55–64 years of age.

Combining factors. While many researchers studied the effects of differences in jobs and occupations and personal characteristics such as experience and education, few studies have looked at their effects on pay difference *over time*. Given that employees' pay at any point in time is a result of many factors that unfold over time, this is a serious omission. One longitudinal study examined starting and current salaries of men and women hired between 1976 and 1986, using data from within a single Fortune 500 firm.[45] Controlling for education degree, college major, and prior experience, males had a 12 percent higher starting salary than females. Among college graduates, college major was a key determinant of gender differences in starting salaries. To compare current salaries, the variables of average performance rating and job title were added to the analysis. This reduced the size of the wage differential to under 6 percent. In a subpopulation of those employees who were college graduates, the differentials were similar, but smaller. When all the variables in the study's model were included, the current salary differential among male college graduates and female college graduates was less than 3 percent. The implication is that women received greater pay *increases* after they were hired than men did, but differences in starting salary remain important and persistent contributors to gender-related pay differences.

These are the facts. But they are also subject to conflicting interpretations and beliefs.

Conflicting interpretations. Some proponents of comparable worth suggest that lower continuous time in the work force and lower tenure with a current employer reflect a woman's childbearing and primary parenting responsibilities, which society has undervalued. Some even go so far as to suggest a "mommy track" exists; some women choose to leave the work force, have children, and reenter, but as part-time workers.[46] Other women choose the "career track" and either forgo child bearing or opt to place children in daycare programs and resume full time employment. If women do voluntarily quit jobs and leave the work force more often than men do (e.g., to move when their husbands change jobs or to have children) naturally they will have less experience and earn less pay. But women may also leave because they are discouraged about being

---

[45]Barry A. Gerhart and George T. Milkovich, "Salaries, Salary Growth, and Promotions of Men and Women in a Large, Private Firm," *Pay Equity: Empirical Inquiries* (Washington, D. C.: National Academy of Science, 1989).

[46]Elizabeth Ehrlich, "The Mommy Track," *Business Week*, March 20, 1989, pp. 126–134.

passed over for promotion, or getting smaller pay increases.[47] What appear to be voluntary choices about child rearing, parenting, or leaving the work force may be simply discouragement at the discrimination faced on the job. In short, discrimination may be operating through these factors. Even granting the differences in experience, tenure, and education, a portion of the earnings gap remains unaccounted for. Advocates attribute that difference to discrimination.

As you might expect, the opponents of comparable worth hold a different set of beliefs. Opponents believe that factors such as these differences (e.g., in education, education specialty, experience, time spent out of the work force) reflect individual choices and preferences. These choices, along with the differences in job held, account for much of the gap.

Differences in Industries and Firms

Another factor affecting earnings differences between men and women is the industry and the firms in which they are employed. Studies report that employees in some jobs can get about a 20 percent pay increase simply by switching industries in the same geographic area while performing basically similar jobs.[48]

There is some evidence that within the same occupations, industries that employ higher percentages of women (e.g. retail, insurance) tend to pay a lower average wage than those firms in industries employing higher percentages of men. In other words, office and clerical workers, most likely women, tend to be paid less in retailing than in manufacturing or chemicals.

Differences in the firm's compensation policies and objectives within a specific industry is another factor that accounts for some of the earnings gap.[49] As noted in chapters 6 and 7, some firms within an industry adopt pay strategies that place them among the leaders in their industry, while other firms adopt policies that may offer more employment security coupled with bonuses and gainsharing schemes. The issue here is whether within an industry some firms are more likely to employ women than other firms and if that likelihood leads to earnings differences.

We also know that the size of a firm is systematically related to differences in wages. Female employment is more heavily concentrated in small firms.[50] Wages of men in large firms are 54 percent higher than wages of men in small firms. That gap was only 37 percent for women in small versus large firms.

---

[47]Gronau, "Sex-related Wage Differentials and Women's Interrupted Labor Careers"; and Barry Gerhart and Nabil El Cheikh, "Earnings and Percentage Female: A Longitudinal Study," Working paper 89–04, Center for Advanced Human Resource Studies, Cornell University.

[48]Erica L. Groshen, "Sources of Wage Dispersion: How Much Do Employers Matter?" Working paper, Harvard University Department of Economics, December 1985.

[49]Kenneth Foster, "An Anatomy of Company Pay Practices," *Personnel* (Sept. 1985), pp. 69–70.

[50]Oi, "Neglected Women and Other Implications of Comparable Worth."

Differences in Union Membership

Finally, we also know that belonging to a union will affect differences in earnings. Belonging to a union in the public sector seems to raise female wages more than it raises male wages.[51] Little research has been devoted to studying the gender effect of union membership in the private sector.

Presence of Discrimination

So we know that a lot of factors affect pay; discrimination may possibly be one of them. But we are not in agreement as to what constitutes evidence of discrimination. While the earnings gap is the most frequently cited example, closer inspection reveals the weaknesses in this statistic.

RESEARCH ON THE EARNINGS GAP: A MIXED BAG

Unfortunately many studies of the earnings gap have little relevance to understanding discrimination in pay-setting practices. Three examples of these limitations are discussed: the use of unexplained residuals as evidence of pay discrimination, inferring employer level behavior from aggregate rather than employer-specific data, and problems with proxies.

Unexplained Residual Approach

A standard statistical approach for determining whether discrimination explains part of the gap is to try to relate pay differences to the factors just discussed above (e.g., occupation, type of work, experience, education, and the like). The procedure typically used is to regress some measure of earnings on those factors thought to legitimately influence earnings. If the average wage of men with a given set of values for these factors is not significantly different from the average wage of women with equal factors, then discrimination is not assumed to occur.

The standard statistical approach is to interpret the residual portion of the gap as discrimination. In fact, Treiman and Hartmann "pose the search for additional explanatory variables as a challenge to those who wish to dispute the interpretation of the residual effects as discrimination."[52]

The residual approach to identifying discrimination brings to mind an observation made by Carl Sagan, Cornell astronomer who hosted a PBS series designed to educate the public about the cosmos. He observed that while space exploration and research has increased our knowledge of the universe, much remains to be learned. He cautioned, "Just because we can't identify a light doesn't make it a space ship." Many people looking

---

[51]Richard B. Freeman and Jonathan S. Leonard, *Union Maids: Unions and the Female Workforce* (Cambridge, Mass.: National Bureau of Economic Research, 1985).

[52]Donald J. Treiman and H. J. Hartmann, eds., *Women, Work and Wages* (Washington, D.C.: National Academy Press, 1981).

at the earnings gap fall into the same trap. Just because we can't explain all the differences in pay between men and women doesn't make it discrimination.

Must this residual earnings disparity be considered a function of discrimination? Consider studies on the earnings of white men. Studies that attempt to explain differences in white men's earnings, using such factors as jobs held and experience, education, time worked and age, are able to account for about 60 to 70 percent of the differences. How can we logically conclude that residual unexplained portion is discrimination among white men?[53]

Theorizing about the nature of the residual is important. But when financial liabilities for pay discrimination are assessed based on unexplained residuals, as they are by the Courts, then more is required than statistical analysis. Statistical studies are just one type of evidence that people need to consider when deciding whether pay differences are attributable to discrimination.

If they do not tell us what portion of the gap is discrimination what do these analyses show? They show that the gap is not fully explained by a number of factors; differences in characteristics of men or women employees, differences in jobs they hold, the occupations they are in, the firms in which they are employed, the industry, and so on. But these studies do not eliminate the possibility that the discrepancy is caused by unmeasured variables other than discrimination. Nor can they rule out that wage and earnings differences are the result of voluntary behaviors.

Inferring from Aggregated Data

Many studies of the earnings gap have little relevance to understanding pay discrimination because actual pay decisions are decentralized: made by individual employers, unions, and employees. Most analysis of the earnings gap is conducted at aggregate levels. Studies using aggregate data often do not adequately include factors actually used in wage determination. This is not always because researchers are not aware of these factors; the omissions are due in large part to two problems. First, there is a lack of adequate publicly available data and second, the proxies used are often too abstract.[54]

Consider a study that treats all employee experiences as equal (measured as age minus years of education minus 5 years) and all fields of education as equal (measured as years of education completed). Common sense and your own experience tell us that there are differences in the types of experience (whether it is continuous with one employer and the type of training received) and that there are differences in the specialties and quality of education (a four-year degree in social work is not equivalent to a four-year degree in electrical engineering). Anyone knowledgeable in pay determination believes that these differences are important in attracting and retaining the work force necessary

[53]Gerhart and Milkovich, "Salary Growth and Promotions in a Large, Private Firm."

[54]Barbara R. Bergmann, "Occupational Segregation, Wages, and Profits When Employers Discriminate by Race or Sex," *Eastern Economic Journal* 1 (1974), pp. 103–16; C. Selden, E. Mutari, M. Rubin, and K. Sacks, *Equal Pay for Work of Comparable Worth* (Chicago: American Library Association, 1982); and Ashenfelter and Oaxaca, "The Economics of Discrimination."

for an effective organization. Hence these differences also affect pay differences. Consider the earnings differential between Mr. and Mrs. Jones. Both have college degrees (his in psychology, hers in computer science), both are in sales (he in shoes and she in computers), and both work for private sector employers (he for J.C. Penney and she for IBM). They probably earn very different salaries, but most aggregate data would report them to have similar skills and education, and similar jobs.

Problems with Proxies

Years of education often serve as a proxy for all the differences in a person's skills and abilities and quality of the education received. Employee performance may be measured as absenteeism, and differences in firms may be measured as differences in industries, treating each firm within an industry as the same. One study even used number of children as a proxy for time spent away from the job.[55] We have reached that point as parents when we better understand a counter point, that the number of teenagers one has will increase the time spent on the job and away from home.

Another problem with the proxies used is that mere possession of a qualification or skill does not mean it is work related. Examples of cab drivers, secretaries, and house painters with college degrees are numerous. In a college town like East Lansing, Michigan it is common for spouses of students to hold down jobs for which they are overqualified, simply to help support themselves and their spouses.

Even if the legitimate factors fully explain pay differences between men and women, discrimination still could have occurred. First, the factors themselves may be tainted by discrimination. For example, past discrimination against women in the admission to engineering schools may have affected their earnings. Another reason is that women may be better qualified on some factors that were omitted or abstracted in the analysis.

In sum, statistical analysis needs to be treated as part of a pattern of evidence and that evidence needs to reflect the wage behaviors of specific firms. Inferring behaviors from unexplained residuals, grossly aggregated data and poor proxies can be misleading. As one reviewer has written, "It is not the quantity of studies that is lacking; it is the quality."[56]

WAGES FOR "WOMEN'S WORK"

Why are jobs held predominantly by women, almost without exception, paid less than jobs held predominantly by men? Are women's jobs fairly valued, by the same standards that are used to value other jobs, or have they been systematically undervalued and/or

---

[55]Barbara Norris, "Comparable Worth, Disparate Impact, and the Market Rate Salary Problem: A Legal Analysis and Statistical Application," *California Law Review* 71, no. 2 (March 1983), pp. 730–40.

[56]Donald P. Schwab, "Using Job Evaluation to Obtain Pay Equity," in *Comparable Worth: Issue for the 80's,* Vol. 1.

underpaid?[57] Do job evaluation systems give adequate recognition to job-related contributions in those jobs held primary by women? An example: the state of Washington conducted a study that concluded that the job of a licensed practical nurse required skill, effort, and responsibility equal to that of a campus police officer. In 1978 the state paid the licensed practice nurse, on average, $739 a month. The campus police officer was paid, on average, $1,070 a month. These salary differences were not related to productivity-related job content characteristics included in the study.[58]

It is this type of wage difference (e.g., nurses' versus police officers' wages) that is controversial. Some argue that pay differences are the result of consistent undervaluing of work done by women, and it ought to be illegal.[59] If jobs require comparable skill, effort, and responsibility, the pay must be comparable, no matter how dissimilar the job content may be. Others respond that pay differences between men and women are the result of many factors, not the least of which are market factors, for which no acceptable substitute is available.[60] And they question who or what, if not market-based factors, will determine wages for such dissimilar jobs as nurses and police officers. But critics respond that current pay differentials based on market forces are discriminatory. The market is faulty, they argue, because it reflects historic *access discrimination,* when employers simply refused to hire women for most jobs.[61] Women were restricted to only a few job categories, resulting in an oversupply of people to fill these jobs and artificially holding down wages for women's jobs relative to the rates paid for other jobs. Pay systems that value jobs today based on their market rates, these critics assert, incorporate and perpetuate this past discrimination against women and minorities. This is so, they argue, because market influences historically tend to undervalue jobs dominated by women (e.g., clerks, nurses, librarians, teachers). Therefore, they argue, jobs held predominantly by women ought to be paid at the market rate for "comparable" jobs held predominantly by men.[62]

But proponents of continuing reliance on market forces in the pay determination process argue that market forces are the best available measure of the value of work and

[57]Sharon Toffey Shepela and Ann T. Viviano, "Some Psychological Factors Affecting Job Segregation and Wages," in *Comparable Worth and Wage Discrimination,* ed. H. Remick (Philadelphia: Temple University Press, 1984).

[58]Helen Remick, "Beyond Equal Pay for Equal Work: Comparable Worth in the State of Washington," in *Equal Employment Policy for Women,* ed. Ronnie Steinberg-Ratner (Philadelphia: Temple University Press, 1980), pp. 405–48; and Ronnie J. Steinberg, " 'A Want of Harmony': Perspectives on Wage Discrimination and Comparable Worth," in *Comparable Worth and Wage Discrimination,* ed. H. Remick.

[59]Paula England, "Socioeconomic Explanations of Job Segregation," in *Comparable Worth and Wage Discrimination,* ed. Remick.

[60]George H. Hildebrand, "The Market System," in *Comparable Worth: Issues and Alternatives,* ed. E. R. Livernash (Washington, D.C.: Equal Employment Advisory Council, 1980).

[61]Bergmann, "Occupational Segregation, Wages, and Profits When Employers Discriminate by Race or Sex."

[62]Helen Remick, "Dilemmas of Implementation: The Case of Nursing," in *Comparable Worth and Wage Discrimination.*

employee qualifications. Whatever its flaws, there exists no adequate substitute. Indeed, market advocates argue that no mechanism that excludes market factors for determining job worth is feasible.[63]

Differing Public Policy Options

All the rhetoric boils down to two basic policy options directed at the reduction of the earnings gap. The first focuses on the access discrimination: ensuring that the distribution of employment and educational opportunities is not discriminatory. The second aims at the realignment of wage structure: valuation discrimination.

During the 1970s, interpretation and enforcement of pay discrimination legislation was consistent with the first strategy: eliminate access discrimination through the fair distribution of employment and education opportunities. Regulatory agencies urged that vacancies in jobs, training, and education programs in which women and minorities were underrepresented (or in some cases excluded) be filled by women and minorities at rates greater than their representation in the available labor supply until the underrepresentation was corrected. Thus, reduction in the earnings differentials was sought through deseg-regating jobs, hiring affirmatively, and offering equal pay for equal work. But many say this is insufficient.

Many women currently in the labor force have invested in years of experience and training for their jobs and simply may not want access to other, higher paying jobs.[64] Proponents of realigning the work structure maintain that focusing solely on job oppor-tunities and equal pay for equal work overlooks the fact that jobs held predominantly by women may be less valued precisely because they are "women's work," rather than for any productivity or work-related attributes of the work performed. The argument is that these wages may have been artificially depressed relative to what those wages would be if the jobs were performed by white males.

Challenging wage alignments will improve women's economic position and will benefit the many children being supported by low-wage-earning women. Thus, they maintain, it becomes a social issue. And if the jobs in which women predominate are being undervalued, then a reevaluation is a matter of social justice.[65]

The first policy option, insuring equal access, relies on the standard of "equal pay for equal work" to eliminate pay discrimination. It insures that women have fair and equal opportunities to all jobs and then insures that they receive equal pay. The second policy option, realignment of the work structure, relies on the comparable worth standard of pay discrimination—equal pay for jobs that are dissimilar in content but of comparable

---

[63]Hildebrand, "The Market System."

[64]Brigette Berger, "Comparable Worth at Odds with American Realities," in *Comparable Worth: Issue for the 80's*, Vol. 1; Michael Evan Gold, *A Dialogue on Comparable Worth* (Ithaca, N.Y.: ILR Press, 1983). Gold provides a thoughtful discussion of the issue of comparable worth and proposed approaches to operationalize the concept.

[65]Greenberg and McCarty, "Comparable Worth: A Matter of Justice."

worth. Let us turn next to examine comparable worth. First, we examine the concept and related legislative developments.

COMPARABLE WORTH

Comparable worth has been debated off and on since World War II.[66] During the debate leading to passage of the Equal Pay Act in the 1960s, a proposed bill read "to prohibit employers from maintaining wage differentials for work of *comparable* character on jobs the performance of which required *comparable* skills."[67] Representative St. George proposed, and the House of Representatives agreed to, the word *equal* for comparable, arguing that

> the term "comparable" lacked meaning and would provide too much latitude to the Department of Labor, who would enforce the bill.[68]

Representative Goodell stated,

> when the House changed the word "comparable" to "equal" the clear intention was to narrow the whole concept. We went from "comparable" to "equal" meaning that the jobs involved should be virtually identical, that they would be very much alike or closely related to each other. We do not expect the Labor Department people to go into an establishment and attempt to rate jobs that are not equal.[69]

The National Academy of Science (NAS) report on the topic recognizes the difficulty of determining comparable worth and suggests that within an employer jobs "in some sense comparable" in their value to the organization ought to be equally compensated whether or not their work content is substantially equal. The NAS authors suggest that rather than being some immutable standard universal to all employers and all jobs across the entire U.S. economy, a comparable worth standard would require only that whatever characteristics of jobs are considered worthy of compensation by a single employer (excluding market considerations) should be equally regarded, irrespective of the sex of the job incumbent.[70]

Legislative Developments

Comparable worth is a political and social issue. People who share a set of beliefs about how pay should be determined in society wish to convince a sufficient number of others

---

[66]Martha May, "The Historical Problem of the Family Wage," *Feminist Studies* 8 (Summer 1982) pp. 399–424; and Ronnie Steinberg-Ratner, "Research: Wage Discrimination and Pay Equity," in *Preliminary Memorandum on Pay Equity,* eds. N. Perlman and B. Ennis (Albany: Center for Women in Government, State University of New York, 1980).

[67]Hearings . . . on H. R. 8898, 10266, Part I, 87th Cong., 2d Sess. (1962).

[68]108 Cong. Rec. 14767-14769.

[69]109 Cong. Rec. 9197.

[70]Treiman and Hartmann, *Women, Work and Wages,* p. 9.

EXHIBIT 14.8
Survey of State-Government Level Pay Equity Activity

State	Research/data collection	Pay equity study	Pay equity adjustments	Year of latest pay equity activity*
Alabama	▨			1985
Alaska				1988*
Arizona	▨			1984
Arkansas				
California	▨		■	1988*
Colorado	▨			1988
Connecticut	▨	☐	■	1988
Delaware				
D.C.	▨	☐		1988
Florida	▨		■	1987
Georgia				
Hawaii	▨	☐	■	1987
Idaho				1988*
Illinois	▨		■	1988*
Indiana	▨			1985
Iowa	▨	☐	■	1988
Kansas	▨			1984
Kentucky	▨			1984
Louisiana	▨			1982
Maine	▨	☐	■	1988
Maryland	▨	☐		1985
Massachusetts	▨	☐	■	1988
Michigan	▨	☐	■	1988*
Minnesota	▨	☐	■	1988
Mississippi	▨			1985
Missouri				
Montana	▨	☐		1985
Nebraska	▨			1978
Nevada	▨			1984
New Hampshire	▨			1986
New Jersey	▨	☐	■	1988
New Mexico	▨	☐	■	1986
New York	▨	☐	■	1988
North Carolina	▨			1985
North Dakota	▨	☐		1988
Ohio	▨	☐		1988
Oklahoma				
Oregon	▨	☐	■	1988
Pennsylvania			■	1987
Rhode Island	▨	☐	■	1988
South Carolina	▨			1988
South Dakota		☐	■	1985
Tennessee	▨			1986
Texas	▨			1981
Utah	▨			1984
Vermont	▨	☐	■	1987
Virginia	▨			1985
Washington	▨	☐	■	1988
West Virginia	▨	☐		1986
Wisconsin	▨	☐	■	1988
Wyoming	▨	☐		1988
Totals:	43	23	20	

*Asterisk indicates that litigation was pending in 1988.

Source: National Committee on Pay Equity, Washington, D.C.

that their approach is "fairer" or more "equitable." The courts do not seem inclined to interpret present laws in a manner that encompasses comparable worth. Consequently, comparable worth proponents continue to lobby for either new legislation or voluntary action on the part of employers which would include the comparable worth standard.

Much of this political activity is occurring in state and local governments.

In New Jersey, for example, the 1985 legislature granted $7 million to raise the lowest four pay ranges up to the salary level of range 5, and to raise ranges 5 through 8 by one range each. Nearly 85 percent of the affected workers were women or minorities. A task force formed to study the state's job evaluation system for possible bias suggested a restructuring to give more possibility of earning job evaluation points in human relation skills (including caregiving and custody), sensory and physical as well as mental effort, and accountability for people and programs as well as for money. The number of points correlates directly to a salary scale of 45 pay ranges with specific dollar amounts. Thus, an increase in points will automatically increase dollars. The task force also called for a $60 million appropriation to cover the adjustments.

In California, the largest sex- and race-based discrimination suit ever filed, affecting nearly 70,000 present and former state workers, went to trial in 1989. The California State Employees Association alleged that the state discriminated by paying job classes dominated by women and minorities less than other job classes. However, a judge dismissed key portions of the suit after finding the evidence ambiguous and the statistical methodology faulty. The union's "expert witnesses" had matched jobs for comparison purposes solely on the basis of job titles, not on job duties. Too bad they hadn't read chapter 7.

By 1989, 20 states had begun or completed "pay equity adjustments" for state civil services, and an additional 23 states had begun "pay equity studies." Exhibit 14.8 shows the present status of comparable worth in all states. Some states specify that wages must be equal for those performing "comparable work," others require pay equity for performing work of a "comparable character."[64] Coverage of these statutes varies from state to state.

Action at the federal level focuses on rhetoric and commissioning studies. A proposal for a "pay equity study" of federal government employees has aroused opposition from business groups, which feel that the study will be structured to conclude that pay adjustments are necessary. Extending this conclusion to the private sector is seen as the next logical step, one that concerns them. The House of Representatives has passed legislation authorizing the study three times, but so far the Senate has refused to take action.

The Mechanics of Comparable Worth

Establishing a comparable worth plan typically involves the following four basic steps:

1. *Adopt a single job evaluation plan for all jobs within a unit.* If employees are unionized, separate plans can be prepared for each bargaining unit and take precedence over previous agreements. The key to a comparable worth system is a single job evaluation plan which serves as the standard for the company jobs with dissimilar content and for establishing pay.

2. *All jobs with equal job evaluation results should be paid the same.* Although each factor in the job evaluation may not be equal, if the total points are equal, the wage rates must also be equal.

3. *Identify general representation (percentage male and female employees) in each job group.* A job group is all positions with similar duties and responsibilities, requires similar qualifications, is filled by similar recruiting procedures, and is paid under the same pay schedule. Typically a female-dóminated job class is defined as 60 percent or more female incumbents; a male-dominated job class has 70 percent or more male incumbents.

4. *The wage to job evaluation point ratio should be based on the wages paid for male dominated jobs* since they are presumed to be free of pay discrimination.

These steps are based on the Province of Ontario and State of Minnesota's laws that mandate comparable worth. Ontario's law applies to all public and private sector employees. Minnesota's only applies to all public sector employees (i.e., the state, cities, school districts, libraries, etc.). The Ontario law states "Pay equity is achieved when the job rate for the female job class is *at least equal* to the job rate for a male job class of equal or comparable value." (Ital. added.)

Consider Exhibit 14.9. The solid dots are jobs held predominantly by women (i.e., female representation greater than or equal to 60 percent). The circles are jobs held predominantly by men (i.e., greater than or equal to 70 percent men). The policy line (solid) for the women's jobs is below and less than the policy line for male jobs (dotted

EXHIBIT 14.9
Job Evaluation Points and Salary

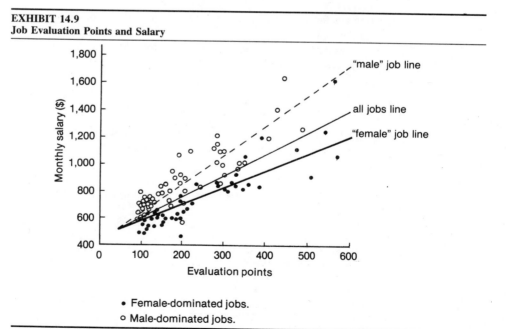

• Female-dominated jobs.
o Male-dominated jobs.

line). A comparable worth policy would use the results of the single job evaluation plan (*x* axis) and price all jobs as if they were male-dominated jobs (dotted line). Thus all jobs with 100 job points would receive $600, all those with 200 points would receive $900, and so on.

Proponents of comparable worth are of two minds when it comes to job evaluation. Some see it as the primary technique for establishing jobs of comparable worth, as illustrated above.[71] Others see it as too subjective to rely on.[72] While there is disagreement, Remick is perhaps the most specific. She defines comparable worth as "the application of a single, biased free point factor job evaluation system within a given establishment, across job families, both to rank order jobs and to set salaries.[73] This definition seeks to minimize the influence of external markets for female-dominated jobs (e.g., markets for clerical or nursing skills). How dollars are actually attached to job evaluation points under such a plan is still being debated. Recent applications (see step 4) use market rates for male-dominated jobs to convert the job evaluation points to salaries. The point-to-salaries ratio of male-dominated jobs are then applied to female-dominated jobs.

Some question the use of male-dominated jobs rather than all job data to establish the relationship between job evaluation points and pay rates. They argue that using only male dominated jobs will artificially inflate other job rates. It presumes, for example, that clerical work is subject to identical union and market forces as police, firefighters, and craft workers. Arbitrators and legislators are struggling with this issue.

Steinberg, in Exhibit 14.10, points out the wide range of point-to-dollar relationships that exist in Minnesota, San Jose, and Washington, all of which work to the detriment of women. For example, in Minnesota both registered nurses (females) and vocational education teacher positions (male) receive 275 job evaluation points, but a $537 difference exists in their monthly pay.

Since past pay legislation has outlawed lowering any wage to make pay equal, a comparable worth policy may require employers to pay all employees at the highest market line or point-to-dollar ratio that exists for any segment of its employees (steps 3 and 4). This translates into the rate paid for jobs held predominantly by men (Exhibit 14.9, the dotted line). Such an arrangement raises a host of issues:

- Would the unions give up their right to negotiate contracts independent of the pay arrangements in the other segments of the organization (i.e., would unions B, C, D,

---

[71]Helen Remick, ed., *Comparable Worth and Wage Discrimination* (Philadelphia: Temple University Press, 1984).

[72]Ruth G. Blumrosen, "Wage Discrimination, Job Segregation and Title VII of the Civil Rights Act of 1964," *University of Michigan Journal of Law Reform* 12, no. 397 (1979), pp. 17–23; Richard W. Beatty and James R. Beatty, "Some Problems with Contemporary Job Evaluation Systems," in *Comparable Worth and Wage Discrimination;* Robert Madigan, "Comparable Worth Judgments," *Journal of Applied Psychology* 70, no. 1 (1985), pp. 137–47; and Robert Grams and Donald Schwab, "An Investigation of Systematic Gender-Related Error in Job Evaluation," *Academy of Management Journal* 28, no. 2 (June 1985), pp. 279–90; Mark Lengnick-Hall, "The Effects of Group Processes on Bias in Job Evaluation," paper presented at 1989 Academy of Management Meetings, Washington, D.C.

[73]Helen Remick, "Major Issues in *a priori* Applications," in *Comparable Worth and Wage Discrimination*, p. 99.

EXHIBIT 14.10
Inequalities in Point-to-Dollar Relationships

A. Inequality of pay in relation to job evaluation points

City or State	Job Title	Monthly Salary	Difference	Number of Points
Minnesota	Registered nurse (F)	$1,723	$537	275
	Vocational education teacher (M)	2,260		275
San Jose, California	Senior legal secretary (F)	665	$375	226
	Senior carpenter (M)	1,040		226
	Senior librarian (F)	898	$221	493
	Senior chemist (M)	1,119		493
Washington State	Administrative services manager A (F)	1,211	$500	506
	Systems analyst III (M)	1,711		426
	Dental assistant I (F)	608	$208	120
	Stockroom attendant II (M)	816		120
	Food service worker (F)	637	$332	93
	Truck driver (M)	969		94

B. Inequality of job evaluation points in relation to pay

City or State	Job Title	Monthly Salary	Point Difference	Number of Points
Minnesota	Health program representative (F)	$1,590	82	238
	Steam boiler attendant (M)	1,611		156
	Data processing coordinator (F)	1,423	65	199
	General repair work (M)	1,564		134
San Jose, California	Librarian I (F)	750	104	228
	Street sweeper operator (M)	758		124

Note: F = Female; M = Male.
Source: Ronnie J. Steinberg, "Identifying Wage Discrimination and Implementing Pay Equity Adjustments," in *Comparable Worth: Issue for the 80's,* Vol. 1 (Washington, D.C.: U.S. Commission on Civil Rights, 1985).

E, etc., have to agree to the same point/dollar relationship as union A, which signed the first agreement)?

- If the individual unions negotiated jointly for the same point/pay relationship, would there be any need for more than one union?
- How would an organization entice people into jobs where there were shortages because of distasteful work, if there were not premium pay for the same points, or more pay for fewer points (as in the sanitarians/nurses case previously discussed)?
- If one unit in a firm pays only base salary, will it have to increase its compensation level if another unit in the same firm introduces an incentive plan suitable for the business sector in which it competes?
- Must a state pay the same dollars for the same points to employees who work and live in a low-cost rural area as they do to employees in the high-cost large cities?
- Must a high-tech company raise the pay of its accountants (male-dominated) to equal the pay of its engineers (also male-dominated) for the same points?[74]

[74]Alvin O. Bellak, "Comparable Worth: A Practitioner's View," in *Comparable Worth: Issue for the 80s,* Vol. 1.

Underlying these points is a more basic one, which is whether legally mandating a job evaluation approach is defensible. Many employers do not use job evaluation at all. A myriad of approaches are used to determine pay ranging from market pricing to knowledge-based pay to gain sharing to maturity curves. A mandated job evaluation approach simply does not fit all circumstances.

Single versus multiple plans. A key issue in designing a comparable worth system is the use of a single job evaluation plan across job families. This issue of single versus multiple plans has not yet been tested in the courts. An employer may be able to justify the use of multiple plans by demonstrating the full range of the work performed and the inadequacy of a single set of factors to adequately describe and evaluate that range of work. In practice, the overwhelming majority of employers that use job evaluation use more than one plan to cover all jobs. A partner of Hay Associates observed,

> We, ourselves, do not know of a single case, in all the years before and after the legislation of 1963 and 1964, where a large and diverse organization in the private sector concluded that a single job evaluation method, with the same compensable factors and weightings, was appropriate for its factory, office, professional, management, technical, and executive personnel in all profit center divisions and all staff departments.[75]

Rosen, Rynes, and Mahoney add,

> The problem of making global assessments of a position's overall contribution to organizational goals and objectives cannot be underestimated. As work increases in complexity and interdependence, it becomes progressively more difficult to define common criteria of worth and to assess the unique contribution of any given position to the organization.[76]

Yet the use of a single plan seems crucial to comparable worth: The NAS study concludes, "Whatever characteristics of jobs are considered worthy of compensation by a single employer should be equally regarded, irrespective of the sex of the job incumbent."[77]

How to conduct such an evaluation in a bias-free manner is difficult to imagine. There is no way to discern with certainty what the absolute point value of any particular job is, despite the ratios found by Steinberg; such a value does not exist. People who advocate such approaches credit job evaluation with more explanatory power than it possesses. By relying solely on job evaluation they are putting all their eggs in a loosely woven basket.

On the other hand, if everyone recognizes that job evaluation provides not an immutable standard, but rather agreed-upon comparisons applicable for one particular setting, then job evaluation does offer an orderly basis for comparing jobs.

---

[75]Ibid.

[76]Benson Rosen, Sara Rynes, and Thomas A. Mahoney, "Compensation, Jobs, and Gender," *Harvard Business Review,* July/August 1983, pp. 170–90.

[77]Treiman and Hartmann, *Women, Work and Wages;* Donald P. Schwab, "Job Evaluation and Pay Setting: Concepts and Practices," in *Comparable Worth: Issues and Alternatives,* ed. E. Robert Livernash (Washington, D.C.: Equal Employment Advisory Council, 1980).

Union Development

Unions support "pay equity" as a concept. Some interpret pay equity to mean comparable worth; others use pay equity as a more all encompassing, less well-defined term. Some unions, such as the American Federation of State, County, and Municipal Employees (AFSCME) and the Communication Workers of America (CWA) actively support comparable worth and have negotiated comparable worth-based pay increases, lobbied for legislation, filed legal suits, and attempted to educate their members and the public about comparable worth.[78]

Collective bargaining has produced more comparable worth pay increases than any other approach. The amount of union support for comparable worth is directly related to its effects on the union's membership. The public sector faces little competition for its services and is frequently better able to absorb a wage increase, since public employees are in a better position to pressure lawmakers than are taxpayers. This probably accounts for the relative success of public employees' unions in bargaining comparable worth pay adjustments.

But trade-offs between higher wages and fewer jobs make some unions reluctant to aggressively support comparable worth. Examples include unions in industries facing stiff foreign competition (e.g., International Ladies' Garment Workers' Union and the United Steel Workers).

Nationally the AFL-CIO adopted a resolution calling for its affiliated unions to:

1. Treat sex-based pay inequities in contract negotiations like all other inequities that must be corrected.
2. Initiate joint union-employer pay equity studies, as AFSCME has already done with a number of public employers.
3. Take all other appropriate action to bring about true equality in pay for work of comparable value and to remove all barriers to equal opportunity for women.

The beauty of "equity adjustments," from a union's perspective, is that because they are a separate budget item, they do not appear to come at the expense of overall pay increases for all union members.[79]

---

[78]Sara Rynes, T. Mahoney, and B. Rosen, "Union Attitudes toward Comparable Worth," in *Pay Equity in Comparable Worth;* Karen Shallcross Koziara, "Comparable Worth: Organizational Dilemmas," *Monthly Labor Review,* December 1985, pp. 13–16; Barbara N. McLennan, "Sex Discrimination in Employment and Possible Liabilities of Labor Unions," *Labor Law Journal,* January 1982, pp. 26–35; *Breaking the Pattern of Injustice* (Washington, D.C.: American Federation of State, County, and Municipal Employees, 1983); *Pay Equity: A Union Issue for the 1980s,* American Federation of State, County, and Municipal Employees, 1625 L Street N.W., Washington, D.C. 20036, 1980; *Ourself: Women and Unions,* Food and Beverage Trades Department, AFL-CIO, Washington, D.C., March 1981; and Lisa Portman, Joy Ann Grune, and Eve Johnson, "The Role of Labor," in *Comparable Worth and Wage Discrimination.*

[79]Marvin J. Levine, "Comparable Worth in the 1980s: Will Collective Bargaining Supplant Legislative Initiatives and Judicial Interpretations?" *Labor Law Journal,* June 1987, pp. 323–34.

International Developments

Canada has gone further than any nation toward requiring a comparable worth pay standard. While the province of Ontario extends its law to the private sector, the Canadian Human Rights Act, in effect since 1978, requires that equal pay for work of equal value be paid to federal employees, approximately 10 percent of the country's work force.

The International Labor Organization (ILO) has had a directive since 1951 promoting "equal pay for work of equal value," but this has been generally interpreted to mean equal pay for equal work. The European Economic Community (EEC) issued an Equal Pay Directive in 1975, specifying elimination of all discrimination on grounds of sex for the "same work or for work to which equal value is attributed." The 12 member states are free to choose the methods most suitable for complying with the directive. As a result of complaints and subsequent court decisions, both Denmark and the United Kingdom were required to change their laws to incorporate the Directive's provisions. In Denmark in 1986, the wage gap in average hourly earnings was 82 percent. In the United Kingdom it was 74 percent.

But while passage of laws may not be sufficient, it also may not be necessary. Sweden's Act on Equality Between Men and Women at Work, in force since 1980, prohibits sex discrimination but does not specify equal pay for work of equal value. Yet the ratio of women's wages in 1985 was 91 percent. The narrowness of the gap has been attributed in part to the Swedish unions' practice of negotiating the largest increases for the lowest-paid workers, which narrows the wage structure and also the wage gap.[80]

Costs

Opposition to comparable worth legislation is almost a reflex action for many employers. Legislation constrains their ability to act, to redesign pay systems, and to meet changing conditions. In addition, legislation usually translates into increased costs. Nevertheless, some employers that oppose a mandated approach to comparable worth are investigating how it could be implemented and its expected costs.

Private sector data on costs of comparable worth adjustments are not available, for competitive reasons. Where adjustments have been made in the public sector, cost data are available.[81] There is a wide variation in the magnitude of costs. Hawaii, for example, appropriated $1 million in 1987 for "equity adjustments," even though a task force found only minimal inequities. In Illinois, AFSCME negotiated one-half percent of payroll, approximately $8 million, to be placed in an "inequity fund" for 1987–88. In Iowa, $32 million worth of comparable worth adjustments affected 60 percent of the state's employees. In contrast, $20 million of adjustments were shared by about 30 percent of Michigan state employees. In New York, the tab was $75 million.

In Minnesota, where coverage extends to all local cities, counties, and school districts,

---

[80]"Closing the Wage Gap: An International Perspective," (Washington, D.C.: National Committee on Pay Equity, October 1988).

[81]"Survey of State-Government Level Pay Equity Activity," *National Committee on Pay Equity.*

costs statewide have averaged 1.7 percent of payroll for school districts, 4.1 percent for cities, and 3.8 percent for counties. At the state level, adjustments totaling $22.2 million, approximately 3.7 percent of payroll, were negotiated for clerical and health care workers. A case at the end of this chapter is adapted from an arbitration hearing in a Minnesota city. The local police felt their pay raises should be comparable to pay raises police officers in other municipalities were receiving, even though the city's "pay equity analysis" dictated a wage freeze. California has already made $36 million worth of adjustments, and is being sued by its employees for more. All of the above figures are direct costs. No one has calculated the indirect costs (higher pensions, sick leave and vacation costs, costs of any benefits that are tied to salary level, administrative costs) of comparable worth adjustments.

How generalizable are these figures? One writer estimated costs at .7 percent to 5 percent of payroll, but did not report the underlying models used to arrive at those estimates.[82] A simple model shown in Exhibit 14.11 allows us to make an initial estimate of the cost of comparable worth adjustments. Perlman and Grune estimate a 5–20 percent pay difference in male-female jobs that have the same job evaluation points in most firms.[83] We can use their 20 percent figure as the size of the wage adjustment required and further assume that 25 percent of the firm's entire payroll is earned by people whose wages need to be increased. Based on the formula in Exhibit 14.11, the adjustment is a 5 percent increase in the employer's total wage bill. In organizations where wage differences are less than 20 percent, or where a smaller percent of the total wage bill is paid to female-dominated jobs, the percentage would be smaller.

A 5 percent increase in total wage costs may not be too high a price for some employers—those that can pass the costs on in the form of higher prices or increased taxes, or those whose overall labor costs are a very small portion of total costs (e.g.,

---

EXHIBIT 14.11
Preliminary Calculations of Comparable Worth's Addition to Wage Bill

$$Percent\ increase\ =\ DF$$

where

D = Percent differential between wage for female-dominated occupations and comparable male-dominated occupations

F = Percent of total wages presently paid to members of female-dominated occupations

If D = 20% F = 30%, comparable worth adds 6 percent to total wage bill.
If D = 15% F = 20%, comparable worth adds 3 percent to total wage bill.

---

[82]Alice Cook, *Comparable Worth: A Case Book of Experiences in States and Localities,* 1986 Supplement, Industrial Relations Center, University of Hawaii at Manoa, Honolulu, HI. See also Richard Arvey and Katherine Holt, "The Cost of Alternative Comparable Worth Strategies," *Compensation and Benefits Review,* September–October 1988, pp. 37–46.

[83]Nancy Perlman and Joy Ann Grune, "Comparable Worth Testimony of the National Committee on Pay Equity," presented before the U.S. House of Representatives, Subcommittees on Civil Service, Human Resources, and Compensation and Employee Benefits, 1982.

petroleum firms). Conversely, those employers facing greater competition and with a higher percentage of employees receiving adjustments will find a 5 percent increase in their wage costs intolerable.

Obviously, the model in Exhibit 14.11 oversimplifies the real costs involved. It calculates the cost for only a single period; it does not include increased cost resulting from benefits tied to pay level (e.g., pensions, overtime pay, social security) and other factors.

Alternatives

While advocates try to gain support for comparable worth by using the term *pay equity—* no one wants to be against equity—many believe the whole notion is wrongheaded for interfering in a system that manages to get people to do unpopular jobs and immoral for holding out false hope. Some call it "changing the rules in the middle of the game, for no good reason."[84] Rather than encouraging women to move into higher paying job categories, the notion in effect penalizes those who have made the effort to do so. For example, if a women takes the training necessary to become a computer programmer only to find the pay differential between clerk and programmer narrowed through comparable worth, her efforts to become a programmer have less monetary worth than she anticipated. Others call comparable worth a "moral imperative," and view it solely as an issue of fairness.[85]

But the pay determination process has always had a political aspect. Minimum wage legislation is an example. Unionized workers have frequently been able to obtain higher wages than comparable unorganized workers. So if women can convince employers to adopt comparable worth, why shouldn't they? The issue then becomes, should it be mandated? Or should it be part of the ongoing collective bargaining process?

The bottom line is that there simply is no intrinsic economic worth to any one job or group of jobs or job structure.[86] Why should a nurse be paid more than a ditch digger? Why should a ditch digger be paid more than a nurse? Within limits, workers are paid what is required—to get people to do work is determined through the confluence of many forces: the markets, unions, individual preferences, and so on. Who is to say another system is "fairer"? Fairer to whom? Put in this manner, comparable worth is clearly a political issue.

Finally, little attention has been paid to how effectively comparable worth will close

---

[84]June O'Neill, "An Argument Against Comparable Worth," in *Comparable Worth: Issue for the 80's*, Vol. 1.

[85]Greenberg and McCarty, "Comparable Worth: An Issue of Fairness."

[86]Frederick S. Hills and Thomas J. Bergmann, "Conducting an Equal Pay for Equal Work Audit," in *Perspectives on Compensation*, eds. L. Gomez-Mejia and D. Balkin (Englewood Cliffs, N.J.: Prentice-Hall, 1987).

the earnings gap.[87] Since differential earnings between men and women are the key rationale given for its adoption, the policy ought to be evaluated in terms of its ability to reduce the gap. As Minnesota and other states proceed, that data will begin to be available. Minnesota is already experiencing a few problems with firefighters who were less enamored with the concept when their job was judged comparable to that of a librarian. The press reports the firefighters suggesting to the public, "next time you have a fire, call a librarian."[88] Perhaps the librarian's response should be, "Next time you want to know what's in a book ask a firefighter." Nevertheless, the results in the states may influence the willingness of the private sector employers as well as Congress to adopt the comparable worth standard as a national policy.

SUMMARY

Pay discrimination laws require special attention for several reasons. First, these laws regulate the design and administration of pay systems. Second, the definition of pay discrimination, and thus the approaches used to defend pay practices, are in a state of flux. Many of the provisions of these laws simply require sound pay practices which should have been employed in the first place. And sound practices are those with three basic features:

1. They are work related.
2. They are related to the mission of the enterprise.
3. They include an appeals process for employees who disagree with the results.

Achieving compliance with these laws rests in large measure on the shoulders of compensation professionals. It is their responsibility to ensure that the pay system is properly designed and managed.

Should comparable worth be legally mandated? Comparable worth is at its core a political issue and, not surprisingly, opinions vary. But how much, if any, comparable worth policy will diminish the earnings differential remains an unanswered question. The earnings differential is attributable to many factors. Discrimination, whether it be access or valuation, is but one factor. Others include market forces, industry and employer differences, union bargaining priorities, and more. Compensation professionals need to critically examine traditional pay practices to ensure they are complying with regulations. Certainly the focus needs to be on pay discrimination.

Is all this detail on interpretation of pay discrimination really necessary? Yes. Without understanding the interpretation of pay discrimination legislation, compensation managers

[87]Heidi Hartmann, ed., *Comparable Worth: New Directions for Research* (Washington, D.C.: National Academy Press, 1985); and Robert Buchele and Mark Aldrich, "How Much Difference Would Comparable Worth Make," *Industrial Relations,* Spring 1985, pp. 222–33.

[88]Cathy Trost, "In Minnesota, 'Pay Equity' Passes Test, but Foes See Trouble Ahead," *The Wall Street Journal,* May 13, 1985, p. 35.

risk violating the law, exposing their employer to considerable liability and expense, and losing the confidence and respect of all employees when a few are forced to turn to the courts to gain nondiscriminatory treatment.

REVIEW QUESTIONS

1. What is the difference between access and valuation discrimination?
2. Differentiate between disparate impact and disparate treatment, using pay practices as your examples. (Your illustrative practices may be legal or illegal.)
3. What is the relationship between the Equal Pay Act and Title VII of the Civil Rights Act?
4. What are the reasons given to indicate a need for a comparable worth standard? Why hasn't a comparable worth standard been embraced by all employers?
5. What are the pros and cons of labor market data in setting wages? Can you defend their use?
6. How would you design a pay system that was based on comparable worth?

Compensation Application
Wayzata Police Officers

BACKGROUND

The following information is based on an actual interest arbitration case that took place in Wayzata, Minnesota, to decide issues contained in the collective bargaining agreement between the City of Wayzata and the Law Enforcement Union. The relevant issue is salary increases for patrol officers.

The union has requested an increase of 5 percent in the first year, and 5 percent in the second year. It bases its proposal on external wage comparisons with other police departments in the Wayzata geographical district and other cities that have been determined demographically comparable. Such market comparisons suggest that the requested salary increases are justified.

The city proposes a wage freeze in the first year, based upon applicable comparisons with other cities and the requirements of Minnesota's Comparable Worth Legislation (CWL). The city argues that CWL considerations manifest a clear legislative intent to downgrade the use of market wage rates and that any raise to be awarded should in no event exceed the 3.25 percent increase already granted to the public works employees.

The debate revolves primarily around the meaning and application of CWL. Applicable statutory provisions read:

1. Every political subdivision of this state shall establish equitable compensation relationships between female-dominated, male-dominated, and balanced classes of employees.
2. The arbitrator shall consider the equitable compensation relationship standards established under this (comparable worth law) together with other standards appropriate to interest arbitration. The arbitrator shall consider both the results of a job evaluation study and any employee objections to the study.
3. Job positions bear reasonable relationships to one another if:
    a. The compensation for positions that require comparable skill, effort, responsibility, working conditions, and other relevant work-related criteria is comparable.
    b. The compensation for positions that require differing skill, effort, responsibility, working conditions, and other relevant work-related criteria is proportional to the skill, effort, responsibility, working conditions, and other relevant work-related criteria required.

ADDITIONAL INFORMATION

The Consumer Price Index (see Chapter 15 for more detail) indicates an overall increase of 4.3 percent during the past year, and a 5.3 percent increase from June of the past year to June of the current year. The increase in CPI during the next year is projected to be between 4.4 percent and 5.2 percent.

Wayzata uses a quantitative job analysis system to support its job evaluation. Exhibit

EXHIBIT 1
Wayzata Pay Equity Analysis
Market Line Generated Using Regression Analysis, with Additional Lines Showing
90% of Market and 110% of Market

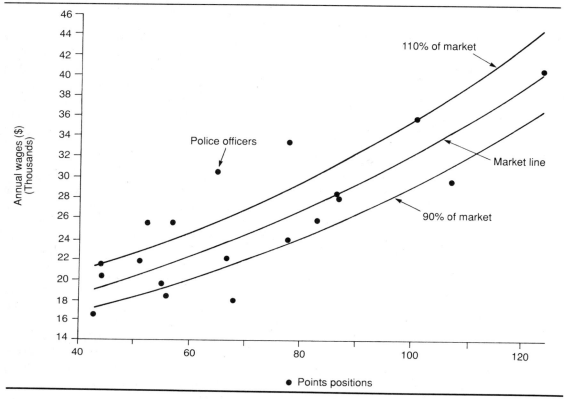

1 shows the police officer's job evaluation points-to-wages ratio, in comparison to ratios for others jobs. It shows an extremely high points-to-wages ratio for this job.

DISCUSSION

Divide the class into thirds. One third is the union team and will present the union arguments. One third will present the city's position. The final one third of the class makes up the arbitration panel, who will issue a decision.

ISSUES FOR THE UNION

As expert witness for the union, you will want to evaluate the current system for job evaluation. Will a quantitative job evaluation process produce results useful in a comparable worth setting? Will it effectively/sufficiently differentiate between a wide range of jobs? Should there be a mechanism through which employees can offer feedback on the final outcome (i.e., job descriptions and job evaluation scores)? What questions and issues are relevant to the determination of salaries in a comparable worth state?

Do not focus on this particular job evaluation method. Rather, focus on job evaluation per se, and whether a quantitative job evaluation method developed to cover a wide range of jobs can adequately evaluate the police officers' jobs. Is job evaluation really "measurement" or merely rules for negotiation? Wayzata is a wealthy community; emphasize your market comparisons with other police departments.

ISSUES FOR THE CITY

How might you respond to the union's criticisms regarding the quantitative job evaluation process as applied to the police officers' jobs? Is it realistic to expect that job evaluation be an objective measure for which we can achieve reliability and validity, or is it better characterized as a subjective process designed and continually modified to value work such that it "works" for the system and its participants? How important is employee participation in the JE process? Why? How does the language of the CW Law treat market wage rates or external relationships as a determinant of compensation relationships? Are the revenues and expenditures incurred by the city relevant to the determination of police officers' pay raises? How should market data be handled, and what are relevant comparisons?

ISSUES FOR THE ARBITRATOR

As the arbitrator, you have the legal duty to decide how to weigh the usefulness of the job evaluation system against the legislative intent of CWL. What conclusions might the legislation lead you to in terms of the relevance of market data for determining compensation relationships? What types of data might constitute "other standards" appropriate to interest arbitration? How will your decision about police officers' wages impact the wages of female-dominated professions valued comparably? Should police officers be treated specially by receiving awards greater than those for comparable jobs outside of law enforcement? Should the financial burden to the city of raising wages for female-dominated classes be a consideration in your decision about police officers' wages? Does the projected rise in price levels as indicated by the CPI make a difference?

Part

6

Let us return to the pay model, shown in Exhibit VI.1. We have covered three basic policy decisions—consistency, competitiveness, and contribution—along with the specific techniques and decisions required to achieve objectives such as unit efficiency, equity toward employees, and compliance with regulations. We have also examined in the preceding two chapters the role of government in design of pay systems and pay discrimination. Now we take up the fourth, and last, basic policy decision shown in the pay model, the nature of the administration of the system. Many facets of pay administration have already been examined. Yet several important issues remain. These are covered in this final part of the book.

The most important remaining issue concerns managing costs. In fact, one of the key reasons for being systematic about pay decisions is to control costs. Some basic questions that need to be answered include: What are the labor costs associated with recommended pay decisions? How can the labor costs be contained? How are these costs to be budgeted and managed?

In addition to these questions, there are other administration issues that also need to be considered. The best-designed system in the world will founder if it is ineffectively implemented and managed. Should line managers participate in administering the system? To what extent? What should line managers and employees be told about the system? Why? Can the effectiveness of the pay system be evaluated? How are compensation departments structured and staffed in different organizations?

The objective of Part 6 is to answer these questions and discuss the techniques involved in administering the pay system. Techniques for managing costs, budgeting and administration are discussed in Chapter 15. Chapter 16 examines compensation systems designed for employee groups working in special circumstances. These include executives, international employees, sales personnel, scientists and engineers, and first-level supervisors. As noted throughout the book, unions often play a significant role in the pay determination process. The book therefore concludes with a separate chapter, 17, devoted to the role of unions in compensation management.

Managing the System

EXHIBIT VI.1
The Pay Model

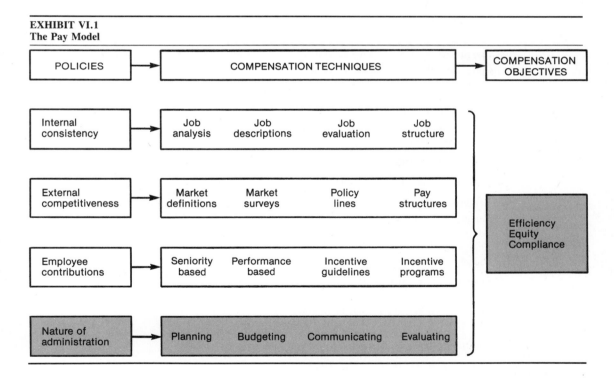

POLICIES	COMPENSATION TECHNIQUES	COMPENSATION OBJECTIVES
Internal consistency	Job analysis — Job descriptions — Job evaluation — Job structure	
External competitiveness	Market definitions — Market surveys — Policy lines — Pay structures	Efficiency Equity Compliance
Employee contributions	Seniority based — Performance based — Incentive guidelines — Incentive programs	
Nature of administration	Planning — Budgeting — Communicating — Evaluating	

493

15 Budgets and Administration

J ohn Russell, former American Compensation Association Board member recently retired, was approached by his Missouri community to develop a salary plan for the city. John worked on it diligently and submitted the plan.

Subsequently, he decided to run for the position of alderman on the city council and was elected. His salary program was then brought before the council for a vote. Russell voted against his own program. He explained his behavior by commenting, "I never realized how tight the budget was!"

Today, managers of compensation should not share John's dilemma. The financial status of the organization, the competitive pressures it faces, and budgeting are integral to managing compensation. The cost implications of decisions such as updating the pay structure, merit increases, or gainsharing proposals are critical for making sound decisions. Consequently budgets are an important part of the administration of compensation; they are also part of managing human resources and the total organization. Creating a compensation budget involves trade-offs among the basic pay policies—how much of the increase in external market rates should be budgeted according to employee contributions to the organization's success compared to automatic across-the-board increases. Trade-offs also occur over short- versus long-term incentives, over pay increases contingent on performance versus seniority, and over direct pay (cash) compared to benefits. Budgeting also involves trade-offs between how much to emphasize compensation compared to other aspects of human resource management. In such cases managers must decide the financial resources to deploy toward compensation compared to staffing (e.g., work force size and job security) compared to training (e.g., work force skills) and so on. The human resource budget implicitly reflects the organization's human resource strategies; it becomes an important part of the human resource plan. Finally, budgeting in the total organization involves allocating financial resources to human resources and/or technology, capital improvements, and the like. So from the perspective of a member of the city council, John Russell ended up making different resource allocation decisions than he might have made from the perspective of the compensation manager. Today managers of compensation need to be much more closely attuned to the overall perspective.[1]

The four basic pay policies dealing with consistency, competiveness, contribution, and administration serve to guide and regulate pay decisions. In turn, the compensation systems (techniques) are designed to be consistent with these policies and to achieve specific pay objectives. Pay systems are intended to serve as mechanisms that assist managers to make better decisions about pay. How the pay systems are used by managers involves the administration of pay.

ADMINISTRATION AND THE PAY MODEL

Consider making pay decisions without a formal system. Under such an arrangement each manager would have total flexibility to pay whatever seemed to work at the moment.

---

[1]Harry J. Holzer, "Wages, Employer Costs, and Employee Performance in the Firm," paper presented at ILR-Cornell Research Conference on "Do Compensation Policies Matter?" (Ithaca, NY: 1989).

Total decentralization of compensation decision making, carried to a ridiculous extreme, would result in a chaotic array of rates. Employees would be treated inconsistently and unfairly. The objectives of individual managers and some employees may be served, but the overall fair treatment of employees and the organization's objectives may be ignored. This may seem like textbook hyperbole to make a point, but it is not. Bethlehem Steel, in the 1920s and 1930s, operated under a "decentralized" pay system—foremen and plant captains had wide discretion; pay inconsistencies for the same work were common. Some foremen even demanded kickbacks from employees' pay checks. Dissatisfaction and grievances were widespread, resulting in legislation and increased interests in unions.[2]

Ideally, any management system, including the compensation system, implies goal-directed behavior. Compensation is managed to achieve the three pay model objectives: efficiency, equity, and compliance. Properly designed pay techniques help managers achieve these objectives. Rather than goal-directed tools, however, pay systems often degenerate into bureaucratic burdens. Techniques become ends in themselves rather than focusing on objectives. Operating managers may complain that pay techniques are more a hindrance than a help, and these managers are frequently correct. So any discussion of the nature of pay administration must again raise the questions: What does this technique do for us? How does it help managers better achieve their objectives? Are employees fairly treated? While it is possible to design a system that includes internal consistency, external competitiveness, and employee contributions, the system will not achieve its objectives without competent administration.

While many pay administration issues have been discussed throughout the book, a few remain to be called out explicitly. Therefore, this chapter covers a variety of compensation administration issues, including (1) managing labor costs, (2) inherent controls, (3) forecasting and budgeting, (4) communication and appeals, (5) structuring the compensation function, and (6) auditing and evaluating the pay system.

MANAGING LABOR COSTS

You already know many of the factors that affect labor costs. As shown in Exhibit 15.1:

$$\text{Labor Cost} = \text{Employment} \times \left(\begin{array}{c} \text{Average Cash} \\ \text{Compensation} \end{array} + \begin{array}{c} \text{Average Benefit} \\ \text{Cost} \end{array} \right)$$

Using this model, there are three main factors to control in order to manage labor costs: employees (i.e., employee numbers, hours worked), average cash compensation (i.e., wages, bonuses, etc.), and average benefit costs (i.e., health and life insurance, pensions, etc.). The cash and benefits factors are this book's focus. However, if our objective is to better manage labor costs it should be clear that all three factors need attention. Controlling benefit costs are discussed at length in Chapters 11 and 12. Here we concentrate on controlling employment and the average salary.

---

[2]Sanford M. Jacoby, "Industrial Labor Mobility in Historical Perspective," *Industrial Relations,* Spring 1983, pp. 261-82.

EXHIBIT 15.1
Managing Labor Costs

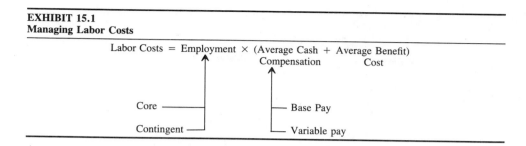

Controlling Employment: Head Count and Hours

Reducing or freezing the number of employees (head count) or the hours worked is the most obvious and perhaps most common approach to managing labor costs. Obviously paying the same to fewer employees is less expensive. Employers who reduce their work forces get headlines. There is even some evidence that announcements of layoffs and plant closings have favorable effects on stock prices because the stock market reacts positively to events designed to improve cash flow and control costs. Obviously, the adverse effects of work force reduction, such as loss of trained and talented employees, and loss of unrealized potential productivity, need to be factored into decisions to reduce staff.

To better manage labor costs, many employers attempt to buffer themselves and employees by establishing different relationships with different groups of employees. As Exhibit 15.2 depicts, the two groups are commonly referred to as core employees, with whom a strong and long term relationship is desired, and contingent workers, whose employment agreements may cover only short, specific time periods.[3] Rather than expand/contract the core work force, many employers achieve flexibility and control labor costs by expanding/contracting the contingent work force.

The pay for core employees has been the main focus of this book. What is known about the compensation of contingent employees? Not enough. Contingent workers are not a homogenous group; their ranks include part time, full time, temporaries, consultants, "life-of-project" workers, leased employees, and subcontracts. One fourth of the U.S. work force is estimated to be contingent and this group is growing twice as fast as the overall civilian labor force. The Bureau of Labor Statistics reports that part-time workers earn less per hour and often do not receive employee benefits such as health insurance. However, given the wide mix of employees classified as contingent, we need to be cautious in generalizing. Nevertheless, contingent workers appear to be cheaper than core employees, all things considered.

Rather than defining employment in terms of number of workers, hours of work is

---

[3]Richard S. Belous, "How Human Resource Systems Adjust to the Shift Toward Contingent Workers," *Monthly Labor Review*, March 1989, pp. 7–12.

EXHIBIT 15.2
Core and Contingent Employees

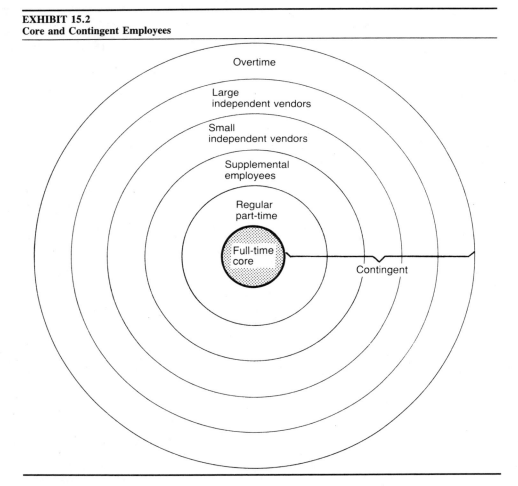

often used. For nonexempt employees, hours over 40 per week are more expensive (1.5 × regular wage). Hence, another approach to managing labor costs is to examine overtime hours versus adding to the work force.

Note that the three factors—employment, cash compensation and benefits cost—are not independent. Overtime hours require higher wages, for example. Other examples are the apparent lower wages (and lack of benefits) for some contingent workers, or a program that sweetens retirement packages to make early retirement more attractive. Sweetened retirements not only drive head count down, but usually the most expensive head count—older, more experienced employees. Hence the average wage and health care costs for the remaining (younger) work force will probably be lowered too.

Controlling Average Cash Compensation

Controlling the average cash compensation, as shown in Exhibit 15.1, includes managing the adjustment in average salary level for the jobs performed and in variable compensation such as annual bonuses, gain sharing, and the like.

Average salary level. A wide variety of approaches are used to manage adjustments to average salary level. Here we discuss two basic approaches: (1) "top down," in which upper management determines pay and allocates it "down" to each sub unit and to individual employees for the plan year; (2) "bottom up," in which individual employees' pay for the next plan year is forecasted and summed up to create an organization salary budget.

CONTROL SALARY LEVEL: TOP DOWN

Top down, unit level budgeting involves estimating the pay increase budget for an entire organization unit. Once the total budget is determined, it is then allocated to each manager, who plans how to distribute it among subordinates. There are many approaches to unit level budgeting in use. A typical one, controlling to planned pay level rise, will be considered. A planned pay level rise is simply the percentage increase in average pay for the unit which is planned to occur.

As shown in Exhibit 15.3, the decision about how much to increase the average pay level planned for the next period is influenced by several factors; how much the average level was increased this period, ability to pay, competitive market pressures, turnover effects, cost-of-living, and so on.

Current Year's Rise

This is the percent by which the average wage changed in the past year; mathematically:

$$\text{Percent level rise} = 100 \times \frac{\text{Average pay year end} - \text{Average pay year beginning}}{\text{Average pay at the beginning of the year}}$$

Ability to Pay

Obviously, the employer's financial circumstances affect the decision regarding how much to increase the average pay level. Financially healthy employers may wish to maintain

---

EXHIBIT 15.3
Planned Level Rise

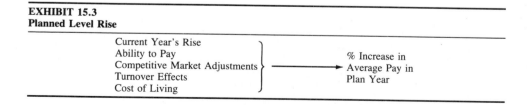

their competitive positions in the labor market, and some may even share outstanding financial success through bonuses and profitsharing.

Conversely, financially troubled employers will be constrained and may not be able to maintain competitive market positions. Note that the conventional response in these circumstances has been to reduce employment [labor costs = employment × (cash compensation + benefits)]. However, other options are to reduce the rate of increase in average pay by controlling adjustments in base pay and/or variable pay.

Competitive Market Adjustments

In Chapter 7, we discussed how managers determine an organization's pay level and how to competitively position it in relation to labor product market competitors. Recall that a distribution of market rates for benchmark jobs were collected and analyzed into a single "average" wage for each benchmark. This "average market wage" became the "going market rate" and was compared to the average wage paid by the organization for its benchmark jobs.[4] The market rates adjust differently each year in response to a variety of pressures.

Turnover Effects

Variously referred to as "churn" or "slippage," the turnover effect recognizes the fact that when people leave (through layoffs, quitting, retiring), they typically are replaced by workers earning a lower wage.[5] Depending on the degree of turnover, the effect can be substantial. Turnover effect can be calculated as Annual Turnover × Planned Average Increase. For example, let us assume that an organization's labor cost equals $1 million a year. If the turnover rate is 15 percent and the planned average increase is 6 percent, the turnover effect is .9 percent, or $9,000 (.009 × $1,000,000). So instead of budgeting $60,000 to fund a 6 percent increase, only $51,000 is needed. Note that from a total labor cost perspective, the lower average pay unit will also reduce those benefit costs linked to base pay, such as pensions. So the turnover effect influences both average pay and benefits costs in the total labor cost equation.

Cost of Living

While there is little research to support it, employees undoubtedly compare their pay increases to changes in their costs of living, and unions consistently argue that increasing living costs justify adjustments in pay.[6]

---

[4]Mark Lerner, "Measuring Pay Costs in your Organization against Pay in Other Organizations," *Personnel,* August 1988, pp. 70-73.

[5]Martin G. Wolf, "A Model to Improve Cashflow Payroll Cost Forecasting," *Compensation and Benefits Review,* January-February 1988, pp. 50-57.

[6]Daniel J. B. Mitchell, "Should the Consumer Price Index Determine Wages?" *California Management Review,* Fall 1982, pp. 5-19.

A distinction. It is important to distinguish among three related concepts: the cost of living, changes in prices in product and service markets, and changes in wages in labor markets. As Exhibit 15.4 shows, changes in wages in labor markets are measured through wage surveys. These changes are incorporated into the system through market adjustments in the budget and updating the policy line and range structure. The second concept, price changes of goods and services in product and service markets, is measured by several government indexes, one of which is the consumer price index. The third concept, the cost of living, is more difficult to measure. Employees' expenditures on goods and services depend on many things: marital status, number of dependents, and ages, personal preferences, and so on. Different employees probably experience different costs of living, and the only accurate way to measure them is to examine the personal financial expenditures of each employee.

The three concepts are interrelated. Wages from the labor market are costs of producing goods and services, and changes in wages create pressures on prices. Similarly, changes in the prices of goods and services create needs for increased wages in order to

EXHIBIT 15.4
Three Distinct but Related Concepts and Their Measures

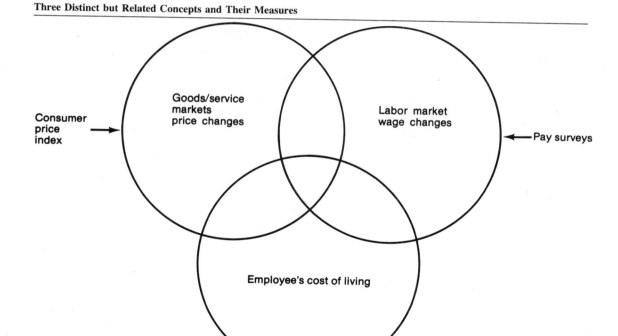

maintain the same lifestyle. Many people refer to the consumer price index (CPI) as a "cost of living" index, and many employers choose, as a matter of pay policy or in response to union pressures to tie wages to it. But in doing so, employers are confounding the concepts of living costs and labor market costs. The CPI does not necessarily reflect an individual employee's cost of living.

What is the CPI? The consumer price index (CPI) measures changes over time in prices of a hypothetical market basket of goods and services. The present index is based on a 1972-73 study of the actual buying habits of 38,000 individuals. From this study, 265 categories of major expenditures were derived, and weights were assigned based on each category's percentage of total expenditures. For example, the index gives a weighting of 5.02 percent to auto purchases. This means that of the total money spent by all 38,000 people in the 1972-73 study, 5.02 percent of it was spent to buy new cars. This weighting plan measures both the price of cars and the frequency of new car purchases. To determine the new car component for today's CPI, today's price of a new car identically equipped to the one purchased in 1972-73 is multiplied by the factor weight of 5.02 percent. The result is called today's *market basket price* of a new car.

There is even an index for those readers who plan to lead the "good life." The annual Moet index tracks price changes for a dozen "upper crust" items. In 1989, the biggest increase was for Beluga caviar, now $47 for a 30-gram jar—up 41 percent from 1988. Other items include Rolex watches for $11,700, up 12 percent, and Rolls Royce Cornich, up 12 percent to $205,500.[7]

The CPI is the subject of public interest because changes in it trigger changes in employer's pay budgets, labor contracts, social security payments, federal and military pensions, and food stamp eligibility. One source estimates that over one half of the U.S. population is affected by payout changes tied to the CPI.[8] Tying budgets or payouts to the CPI is called indexing. Note that the cost of living is one of the factors, shown in Exhibit 15.3, that influences what percent increase average salary level should rise. It also may affect cost of benefits faced by employers either through health insurance coverage or pension costs.

Geographical differences in the CPI. In addition to the national CPI, separate indexes are calculated monthly for five metropolitan areas and bimonthly for 23 other metropolitan areas and various regions. These local CPIs typically are more variable than the national indexes. They do not, as some mistakenly believe, indicate whether prices are absolutely higher in a particular area. Changes in the CPI only indicate whether prices have increased more or less rapidly in an area since the base period. For example, a CPI of 210 in Chicago and 240 in Atlanta does not necessarily mean that it costs more to live in Atlanta. It does mean that prices have risen faster in Atlanta since the base year than they have in Chicago, since both cities started with bases of 100.

---

[7]Randall Poe and Emily L. Baker, "Fast Forward," *Across the Board,* May 1989, pp. 5-6.

[8]Jerry Newman, "The Consumer Price Index: Issues and Understanding," Paper presented at the American Compensation Association, National Conference, Scottsdale, Ariz., October 22, 1981.

An example. Let us assume that the managers take into account all these factors—current year's rise, ability to pay, market adjustments, turnover effects, and changes in the cost of living—and decide that the planned rise in average salary for the next period is 6.3 percent. This means that the organization has set a target of 6.3 percent as the increase in average salary that will occur in the next budget period. It does not mean that everyone's increase will be 6.3 percent. It means that at the end of the budget year, the average salary calculated to include all employees will be 6.3 percent greater than it is now.

The next question is how do we hand out that 6.3 percent budget in a way that is best designed to accomplish managers' objectives for the pay system and thus the organization?

Distributing the budget to subunits. Once the unit budget is estimated, it is distributed down to subunit managers. A variety of methods to determine what percent of the salary budget each manager should receive exists. Some use a uniform percentage, in which each manager gets an equal percentage of the budget based on the salaries of each subunit's employees. Others vary the percentage allocated to each manager based on pay-related problems, such as turnover or performance, which have been identified in that subunit.

Once salary budgets are allocated to each subunit manager, they become a constraint: a limited fund of money that each manager has to allocate to subordinates. Typically, merit increase guidelines are used to help managers make these allocation decisions.

Merit Increase Guidelines

Merit increase guidelines go under many labels: Grids, matrix, and guides are examples. The basic purpose is to guide each manager in determining the pay increase for each employee. As shown in Exhibit 15.5, the grid operates so that the pay increase for each employee is determined by 3 factors: (1) the employee's performance evaluation (horizontal axis: low, medium, or high), the employees' current pay position within the established pay range for that position (vertical axis: maximum to minimum), and the specific percentage amounts within each cell of the grid.

The matrix operates so that if a range position (vertical axis) is the same for two employees, the higher performer will receive a greater merit increase. Similarly, if two employees have equivalent performance evaluations, but Employee *A* is low in the range while Employee *B* is high, then Employee *A* will be eligible for a larger percentage increase.

These grids act as control devices. First, they control the reward schedules to help insure that different managers grant consistent increases to employees with similar performance ratings and in the same position in their salary ranges. Second, grids help control costs. In our example we need to design a grid that will yield a 6.3 percent rise in average salary. To design such a grid depends on the performance distribution of all employees (horizontal axis), their distribution within their ranges (vertical axis), and the percentage increases in the cells of the grid. Once a grid to deliver the 6.3 percent budget

EXHIBIT 15.5
Merit Matrix

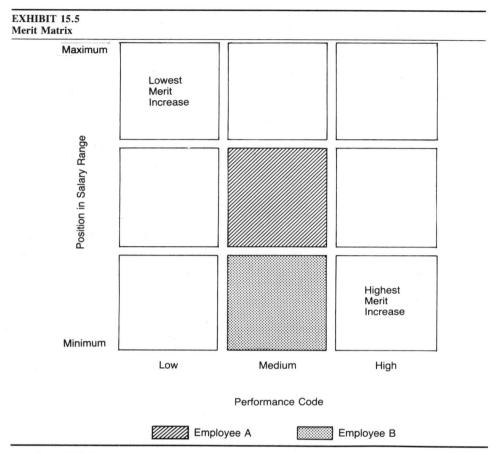

Source: NCR Corporation.

is determined, it is used by managers to plan each employee's increase. (The logic and calculations for alternative merit grids are available in the Appendix to this chapter.)

CONTROL SALARY LEVEL: BOTTOM UP

Bottom-up budgeting requires managers to forecast the pay increase they will recommend for each of their subordinates during the upcoming plan year. Exhibit 15.6 shows an example of the process involved. Each of the steps within this compensation forecasting cycle is described here.

1. *Instruct managers in compensation policies and techniques.* Train managers in the concepts of a sound pay-for-performance policy and in standard company compensation techniques such as the use of pay increase guidelines and budgeting techniques. Also communicate the salary ranges and market data.

EXHIBIT 15.6
Compensation Forecasting and Budgeting Cycle

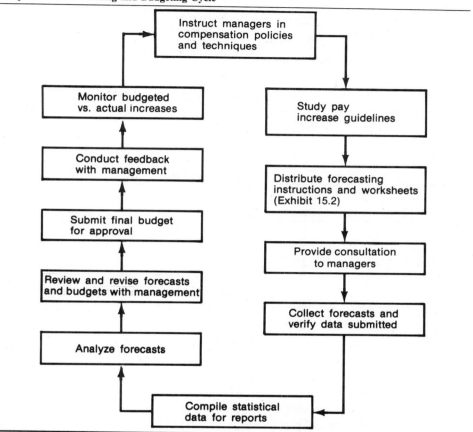

2. *Study pay increase guidelines.* Review with the managers the purpose of increase guidelines and how to use them.
3. *Distribute forecasting instructions and worksheets.* Furnish managers with the forms and instructions necessary to preplan increases.

Exhibit 15.7 is an example of the forecasting worksheets that might be provided. In this exhibit, we see the pay history for an individual employee, Sarah Ross. Her performance rating history, past raises, and timing of these raises are included. Some compensation professionals argue that providing such detailed data and recommendations to operating managers makes the system too mechanical. The result, they argue, is to remove the manager from planning and making judgments about individual employee pay. On the other hand, such histories ensure that managers are at least aware of this information and that pay increases for any one period should be part of a continuing message to individual employees, not some ad hoc response to short-term changes. On the bottom

EXHIBIT 15.7
A Pay History

NAME		YEAR END EXPERIENCE	EMPLOYMENT DATE	YEAR AND SERVICE	YEAR FIRST DEGREE	HIGHEST DEGREE	HIGHEST DISCIPLINE	SOC SEC NO
	Sarah Ross	2	08-22-89	21/04	89	BS	Acctg.	458-56-5332

POSITION		CLASSIF LEVEL	EMPL MO LEVEL	DATE ASSIGNED TO POSITION	DATE ASSIGNED TO CLASS LEVEL OF POSITION		
	Accountant	26		08-22-89	08-22-89		

Previous Salary Change

DATE	PERFORMANCE RATING	AMOUNT	%	MONTHS INTERVAL	ANNUAL VALUE	FIC	SALARY	UPPER BAND OR RANGE MAX	BAND MIDPOINT	LOWER BAND OR RANGE MIN
02 01 90	2.0						23040			
12 01 90	3.0	1920	8.3	10	10		24960			

Forecast Salary Change

DATE	PERFORMANCE RATING	AMOUNT	%	MONTHS INTERVAL	ANNUAL VALUE	FIC	SALARY	UPPER BAND OR RANGE MAX	BAND MIDPOINT	LOWER BAND OR RANGE MIN
09 01 91		2496	10.0	10	12		27456	30018	28016	25214

line of Exhibit 15.7, Ms. Ross's supervisor has recommended a raise of $2,496, to be given in September 1991, 10 months after her last raise. This increase amounts to 10 percent of her base salary ($24,960) and converts to 12 percent on an annualized (12-month) basis. The range maximums, minimums, and midpoints for Ms. Ross's job are shown on the right of the bottom line.

4. *Provide consultation to managers.* Offer advice and salary information services to manager upon request.
5. *Collect forecasts and verify data submitted.* Audit the increases forecasted to ensure they do not exceed the pay guidelines and are consistent with appropriate ranges.
6. *Compile statistical data for reports.* Prepare statistical data in order to feed back the outcomes of pay forecasts and budgets.
7. *Analyze forecasts.* Examine each manager's forecast and recommend changes based on noted inequities among different managers.
8. *Review and revise forecasts and budgets with management.* Consult with managers regarding the analysis and recommended changes.
9. *Submit final budget for approval.* Obtain top management approval of forecasts.
10. *Conduct feedback with management.* Present statistical summaries of the forecasting data by department and establish unit goals.
11. *Monitor budgeted versus actual increases.* Control the forecasted increases versus the actual increases by tracking and reporting periodic status to management.

The result of the forecasting cycle is a budget for the upcoming plan year for each organization's unit as well as estimated pay treatment for each employee. The budget does not lock in the manager to the exact pay change recommended for each employee. Rather, it represents a plan, and deviations due to unforeseen changes such as performance improvements, unanticipated promotions, and the like are common.

This approach to pay budgeting requires managers to plan the pay treatment for each of their employees. It places the responsibility for pay management on the managers. The compensation professional takes on the role of adviser to operating management's use of the system.

VARIABLE PAY AS A COST CONTROL

Variable pay depends on performance and is *not* "rolled into" (added to) employees' base pay. As discussed in Chapter 10, variable pay takes many forms: annual bonuses, spot awards, gain sharing, and so forth. The essence of variable pay is that it must be reearned each period, in contrast to conventional merit pay increases or across-the-board increases that are added to base pay each year and that increase the base on which the following year's increase is calculated.

From a labor cost perspective, conventional increases increase not only the average pay level, but also the costs of all benefits contingent on base pay (e.g., pension). Consequently, the greater the ratio of variable pay to base pay, the more variable (flexible) the organization's labor costs. Reconsider the general labor cost model in Exhibit 15.1; note that the greater the ratio of contingent to core workers and variable to base pay, the greater the variable component of labor costs, and the greater the options available to managers to control these costs. While variability in pay and employment may be an advantage for managing labor costs, it is less appealing from the standpoint of managing equitable treatment of employees. The inherent financial insecurity built into variable plans may adversely affect employees' financial well-being and subsequently their attitudes toward their work and their employers. All to say, managing labor costs is only one objective for managing compensation; others in the pay model include efficiency (productivity and costs) and equitable treatment of employees.

INHERENT CONTROLS

Pay systems have two basic processes that serve to control pay decision making: (1) those inherent in the design of the techniques and (2) the formal budgeting process.

Think back to the several techniques already discussed: job analysis and evaluation, policy lines, range minimums and maximums, performance evaluation, gain sharing, and salary increase guidelines. In addition to their primary purposes, they also regulate managers' pay decisions by limiting what managers may do. Controls are imbedded in the design of these techniques to ensure that decisions are directed toward the pay system's objectives. A few of these controls are examined below.

Range Maximums and Minimums

These ranges set the maximum and minimum dollars to be paid for specific work. The maximum is an important cost control: It represents the highest value the organization places on the output of the work. The individual skills and abilities possessed by employees may be more valuable in another job, but the range maximum represents what all the work produced in a particular job is worth to the organization. For example, the job of airline flight attendant is in a pay range with a maximum that is the highest an airline will pay a flight attendant, no matter how well the attendant performs the job. Pressures to pay over the range maximum occur for a number of reasons—for example, when employees with high seniority reach the maximum or when promotion opportunities are scarce. If employees are paid over the range maximum, these rates are called *red circle rates*. Most employers "freeze" red circle rates until the ranges are shifted upward by market update adjustments so that the rate is back within the range again. If red circle rates become common throughout an organization, then the design of the ranges and the evaluation of the jobs need to be reexamined.

Range minimums are just that: the minimum value placed on the work. Often rates below the minimum are used for trainees. Below minimum payment may also occur for outstanding employees who receive a number of rapid promotions.

Compa-Ratios

Range midpoints reflect the pay policy line of the employer in relationship to external competition. To assess how managers actually pay employees in relation to the midpoint, an index called a *compa-ratio* is often calculated.

$$\text{Compa-Ratio} = \frac{\text{Average rates actually paid}}{\text{Range midpoint}}$$

A compa-ratio of less than 1.00 means that, on average, employees in that range are paid below the midpoint. Translated, this means that managers are paying less than the intended policy. There may be several valid reasons for such a situation. The majority of employees may be new or recent hires; they may be poor performers; or promotion may be so rapid that few employees stay in the job long enough to get into the high end of the range.

A compa-ratio greater than 1.00 means that, on average, the rates exceed the intended policy. The reasons for this are the reverse of those mentioned above: A majority of workers with high seniority; high performance; low turnover; few new hires; or low promotion rates. Compa-ratios may be calculated for individual employees, for each range, for organization units, or for functions.

Other examples of controls designed into the pay techniques include the mutual sign offs on job analysis and job descriptions required of supervisors and subordinates. Another is slotting new jobs into the pay structure via job evaluation, which helps ensure that jobs are compared on the same factors.

Similarly, a performance evaluation system used organization-wide is intended to ensure that all employees are evaluated on similar factors.

Analyzing Costs

Costing out wage proposals is commonly done prior to recommending pay increases. It is also used in preparation for collective bargaining. For example, it is useful to bear in mind the dollar impact of a 1 cent per hour wage change, or a 1 percent change in payroll as one goes into bargaining.[9] Knowing these figures, negotiators can quickly compute the impact of a request for a 9 percent wage increase.

Use of Computers

If you've been thinking to yourself during these various budgetary calculations, "there's got to be an easier way," you're right. Computer software is commercially available to analyze almost any aspect of compensation information you can think of.

Computers can provide analysis and data that will improve the administration of the pay system. For example, computers can easily check the accuracy of past estimates in comparison to what actually occurred (e.g., the percent of employees that actually did receive a merit increase, and the amount). Alternate wage proposals can be quickly simulated and their potential effects compared, using spreadsheet programs.

But computers have wider applications to compensation administration besides costing. In fact, every aspect of compensation may benefit from computer applications. For example, we discussed computerized job analysis and job evaluation and its advantages over conventional methods. Software is also available to evaluate salary survey data and incentive and gain-sharing results.

COMMUNICATION AND APPEALS

Earlier in this book, we stressed that employees must feel that the pay system is fair.[10] Employees' perceptions about the pay system are shaped through the treatment they receive by managers, through the formal communication programs about pay and their performance evaluations (Chapter 8), and through employee participation in various aspects of the design of the system. Additionally, there should be some way for employees to appeal the results of their treatment by the system. Communication and appeals procedures or "speak ups" are our next topics.

Communication or Marketing?

Salaries of the executives in publicly held corporations are published in annual financial reports. Similarly, collective bargaining agreements spell out in detail pay rates for covered employees. And if you know which budget books to examine, you can even find the

---

[9]Stephen Holoviak, *Costing Labor Contracts,* (New York: Praeger Publishing, 1984); Myron Gable and Stephen Holoviak, "Determining the Cost of Supplemental Benefits," *Compensation and Benefits Review,* September-October 1985, pp. 22-23; and Robert E. Allen and Timothy J. Keaveny, "Costing Out a Wage and Benefit Package," *Compensation Review,* Second Quarter 1983, pp. 27-39.

[10]R. Folger and M.A. Konovsky, "Effects of Procedural and Distributive Justice on Reactions to Pay Raise Decisions," *Academy of Management Journal* (in press); J. Greenberg, "Reactions to Procedural Injustice in Payment Distributions: Do the Ends Justify the Means?" *Journal of Applied Psychology,* 72, 1987, pp. 55-61; and R. Folger and J. Greenberg, "Procedural Justice: An Interpretive Analysis of Personnel Systems," in K.M. Rowland and G.R. Ferris, ed., *Human Resources Management,* vol. 3, pp. 141-83 (Greenwich, CT: JAI Press, 1985).

salaries of most public officials. But these groups constitute only a fraction of all employees. Most employees are not told what their coworkers are being paid. The literature on compensation management usually exhorts employers to communicate pay information; however, there is no standard approach on what to communicate to individuals about their own pay or that of their colleagues.

Some organizations have adopted a marketing approach. Similar to selling products to consumers, the pay system is a product, and employees and managers are the customers. Consumer marketing approaches are being applied. This includes consumer attitude surveys about the product, snappy advertising about the pay policies, and elaborate video tapes expounding its policies and strengths. The marketing approach aims to directly manage expectations and attitudes about pay. In contrast, the communication approach tends to provide technical details. The market approach focuses on the quality and advantages of overall policies and is silent on specifics such as range maximums, increase guides, and the like.

The research on pay communication is dated and lags behind current practices. A variety of approaches exist; unfortunately little is known about their effects.

Two reasons are usually given for communicating pay information. The first is that considerable resources have been devoted to design a fair and equitable system that is intended to motivate effective performance and encourage productivity. For managers and employees to gain an accurate view of the pay system and perhaps influence their attitudes about it, they need to be informed.

The second reason is that, according to some research, employees seem to misperceive the pay system.[11] For example, they tend to overestimate the pay of those with lower level jobs and to underestimate the pay of those in higher level jobs. In other words, they tend to think that the pay structure is more compressed than it actually is. If differentials are underestimated, their motivational value in encouraging employees is diminished.[12]

Further, there is some evidence to suggest that the goodwill engendered by the act of being open about pay may also affect perceptions of pay equity.[13] Interestingly, the research also shows that employees in companies with open pay communication policies are as inaccurate in estimating pay differentials as those in companies where pay secrecy prevails. However, employees under open pay policies tend to express greater satisfaction with their pay and with the pay system.

---

[11]Thomas A. Mahoney and William Weitzel, "Secrecy and Managerial Compensation," *Industrial Relations* 17, no. 2 (1978), pp. 245-51; "Administering Pay Programs . . . An Interview with Edward E. Lawler III," *Compensation Review,* First Quarter 1977, pp. 8-16; and Julio D. Burroughs, "Pay Secrecy and Performance: The Psychological Research," *Compensation Review,* Third Quarter 1982, pp. 44-54.

[12]David M. Hegedus and E. Alan Hartman, "The Effects of Intra- and Inter-Organizational Movement on Rate of Movement and Salary," paper presented at 1989 Annual Meeting Academy of Management, Washington, D.C.

[13]Ed Lawler III, "The New Pay," in *Current Issues in Human Resource Management,* eds. Sara L. Rynes and George T. Milkovich (Plano, Tex.: Business Publications, 1986), pp. 404-12.

What to communicate. The first point to be made about pay communication is that if the pay system is not based on work-related or business-related logic, then the wisest course is probably to avoid formal communication until the system is put in order. However, avoiding *formal* communication is not synonymous with avoiding communication. Employees are constantly getting intended and unintended messages through the pay treatment they receive.

The second point is that achieving a fair and equitable pay system requires active involvement and feedback from managers and employees. An open policy helps ensure that employees understand how their pay is determined. The third point is that providing accurate pay information may cause some initial short-term concerns among employees. Over the years, employees probably have rationalized a set of relationships between their pay and the perceived pay and efforts of others. Receiving accurate data may require those perceptions to be adjusted.

Exhibit 15.8 is one major employer's communications policy. Many employers communicate the range for an incumbent's present job and for all the jobs in a typical career path or progression that employees can logically aspire to.

In addition to ranges, some employers communicate the typical pay increases that can be expected for poor, satisfactory, and top performance. The rationale given is that employees exchange data (not always factual) and/or guess at normal treatment, and the rumor mills are probably incorrect. Providing accurate data may have a positive effect on employee work attitudes and behaviors. One potential danger in divulging increase schedule data is the inability to maintain that schedule in the future, for reasons outside the control of the compensation department (e.g., economic or product market conditions). Nevertheless, pay increase data, coupled with performance expectations, should enhance employee motivation, which is a prime objective of the pay system.

Perhaps the most important information to be communicated is the work-related and business-related rationale on which the system is based. Some employees may not agree with these rationales or the results, but at least it will be clear that pay is determined by something other than the whims or biases of their supervisors.

EXHIBIT 15.8
Typical Communications Policy

Program Communications

A. To supervisors. New ranges and guides should be published to affected supervisors upon approval together with a memo explaining the change and outlining the program review, the changes made, the effective date, the new ranges and guides, and any instructions for communication to employees.

B. Supervisors should communicate to affected employees. Employees should understand that our salary ranges are reviewed periodically and that they are competitive with the market. They should be told the dollar value for their salary range and the A–B–C performance definitions. They should know the supervisor's evaluation of their performance—the reasons for his position in the range. Guides are not discussed.

Communication and Pay Satisfaction

Managers who prefer to limit pay communication with employees implicitly assume that employees will become dissatisfied with their own pay if they obtain more information.[14] But this assumption raises two issues. First, it indicates that managers believe their pay system treats employees inequitably or that the present system is not based on work-related logic. Second, research is not clear on how employees make pay comparisons. Most theories indicate that employees compare their pay with that of others around them. Their perceptions about what other employees are actually paid may or may not be accurate, but perceptions affect how employees feel about their own pay.

Most of the research on pay satisfaction and secrecy has concentrated on the accuracy of employees' judgments about the pay of their subordinates and superiors, and the correlation between this accuracy and pay satisfaction. The argument is that reduced secrecy will contribute to improved satisfaction. Not all researchers have found a consistent relationship between communication, accuracy of compensation perceptions, and pay satisfaction.[15] So communication by itself may not measurably contribute to pay satisfaction. Clearly, communicating cannot overcome indefensible pay practices. Pay satisfaction, as noted in various places in this book, is very complex. But if managers believe their pay system to be equitable and can demonstrate its work-related logic to employees, there is a strong likelihood of gaining employee acceptance and confidence by being open about it.

Appeals

Despite an organization's best attempts to help employees understand how their pay is set, employees sometimes feel they have been unjustly treated, either in assessing their own performance, in evaluating their job, or even in considering external competition. Disagreements over pay, or any part of the pay delivery system, can and do occur. Many organizations have designed procedures for handling these disagreements. These procedures provide a mechanism for employees and managers to voice their disagreements and receive a hearing. They help ensure that pay communication is a two-way process.

Employees who belong to a union collectively bargain some of their disagreements and take others through a formal grievance procedure.[16] "Voice" procedures designed for managerial, professional, and other nonunionized employees, especially for compensation questions, are typically less formal.

---

[14]Robert McCaffery, *Managing the Employee Benefits Program* (New York: AMACOM, 1983); and Chris Berger, "The Effects of Pay Level, Pay Values and Fringe Benefits on Pay Satisfaction," Working paper, Krannert School of Management, Purdue University, Lafayette, Indiana, 1983.

[15]E. E. Lawler, *Pay and Organization Development* (Reading, Mass.: Addison-Wesley Publishing, 1981); and G. Douglas Jenkins, Jr., and Edward E. Lawler, "Impact of Employee Participation in Pay Plan Development," *Organizational Behavior and Human Performance 28* (1981), pp. 111-28.

[16]Robert T. Boisseau and Harvey Caras, "A Radical Experiment Cuts Deep into the Attractiveness of Unions," *Personnel Administrator*, October 1983, pp. 76-79.

STRUCTURING THE COMPENSATION FUNCTION

Compensation professionals seem to be constantly reevaluating where within the organization the responsibility for the design and administration of pay systems should be located. The organizational arrangements of the compensation function vary widely.[17]

An important issue related to structuring the function revolves around the degree of decentralization (or centralization) in the overall organization structure. *Decentralized* refers to a management strategy of giving separate organization units the responsibility to design and administer their own systems. This contrasts with a centralized strategy, which locates the design and administration responsibility in a single corporate unit. Some firms, such as Citibank and Pacific Gas and Electric, have relatively large corporate staffs whose responsibility it is to formulate pay policies and design the systems. Administration of these policies and systems falls to those working in various units, often personnel generalists. Such an arrangement runs the risk of formulating policies and practices that are well tuned to overall corporate needs but less well tuned to each unit's particular needs and circumstances. The use of task forces, with members drawn from the generalists in the affected units, to design new policies and techniques helps diminish this potential problem.

Other highly decentralized organizations, such as TRW and Honeywell, have relatively small corporate compensation staffs (two or three professionals). Their primary responsibility is to manage the systems by which executives and the corporate staff are paid. These professionals operate in a purely advisory capacity to other organization subunits. The subunits, in turn, may employ compensation specialists. Or the subunits may choose to employ only personnel generalists rather than compensation specialists, and may turn to outside compensation consultants to purchase the expertise required on specific compensation issues.

Decentralizing certain aspects of pay design and administration has considerable appeal. Pushing these responsibilities (and expenses) closer to the units and managers affected by them may help ensure that decisions are business related. However, decentralization is not without dilemmas. For example, it may be difficult to transfer employees from one business unit to another. Problems adhere to policies which emphasize internal consistency and concerns for potential pay discrimination crop up. So, too, do problems of designing pay systems that support a subunit's objectives but run counter to the overall corporate objectives.

The answer to these and related problems of decentralization can be found in developing a set of corporatewide principles or guidelines which all must meet. These principles probably differ for each major pay technique. For example, a decentralized employer would permit different job evaluation approaches to be adopted by the units, as long as the principles of work relatedness, business relatedness, acceptability to managers and employees, cost effectiveness, and ability to withstand legal challenge were satisfied by the various unit plans.

---

[17]J. R. Galbraith and D. A. Nathanson, *Strategy Implementation: The Role of Structure and Process* (St. Paul, Minn.: West Publishing, 1978).

Keep in mind that the pay system is one of many management systems used in the organization. Consequently, it must be congruent with these other systems. For example, it may be appealing, on paper at least, to decentralize some of the compensation functions. However, if financial data and other management systems are not also decentralized, the pay system will not fit and may even be at odds with other systems.

A final issue related to structuring the responsibility for pay design and administration involves the skills and abilities required in compensation professionals. The grandest strategy and structure may seem well designed, well thought out in the abstract, but could be a disaster if people qualified to carry it out are not part of the staff. Our earlier example in which the business subunits were staffed by personnel generalists who were not trained or prepared to design pay systems tailored to the unit's needs illustrates the point. So all three aspects of management—strategy, structure, and staffing—must be considered.

In view of the importance of a well-trained staff, both the American Compensation Association and the American Society of Personnel Administrators have professional development programs in order to entice readers into the compensation field.[18]

AUDITING AND EVALUATING THE SYSTEM

No management system can maintain itself indefinitely. Constant monitoring is required to be sure techniques remain goal directed. Throughout the book, we have discussed indexes that may identify problems. Typically, the concerns have been with the pay objectives of equity and efficiency. In this section, we add monitoring the system for legal compliance.

As you recall from the previous chapter, two basic standards of discrimination exist: disparate treatment and disparate impact. The disparate treatment standard outlaws the application of different standards to different classes of employees. Disparate impact outlaws practices that may appear to be neutral but have a negative effect on females or minorities, unless those practices can be shown to be business related. We can apply these two standards to our audit, also. Practices can be examined to ascertain any disparate treatment. Results can be examined for disparate impact.

Unequal Treatment

Auditing a pay system for unequal treatment is fairly straightforward. The criteria are outlined in the Equal Pay Act.

Each geographic location constitutes a separate "establishment." Analysis must be done for all protected groups and for all those jobs that the EPA defines as equal. Because disparate treatment affects *individual* employees rather than *classes* of employees, analysis should be done for all females and minorities. Cohort analysis involves comparing treatment of individual employees who belong to protected groups to treatment of white males

---

[18]Schedules and course registration information are available from American Compensation Association, 14040 N. Northsight Blvd., Scottsdale, Arizona 85260, and from American Society of Personnel Administrators, 606 N. Washington Street, Alexandria, Virginia 22314.

EXHIBIT 15.9
IBM Equity Analysis

Individual Minority/Female Data Sheet

- Minority/female comparison versus peers
  Same EEO job category
  Same IBM salary level
  Same appraisal
  Same time in IBM salary level (six months)
- Primary comparisons
  Current salary comparison
  Percent of last increase
  Timing of increase
- Additional analysis
  Length of service
  Time in previous level
  Level jump factor
  Appraisal history
  Leave of absence in level

Salary Equity Measurement Criteria

When comparing individual minority/female salaries to those of peer groups, we must demonstrate:
1. An equitable relationship—minorities' and females' salary equal to or greater than the average salary of peers.
2. An understanding of the reason(s) for a relationship less than stated in 1 above.
3. Action is taken where warranted.

hired at the same time into the same jobs.[19] If differences in pay exist, is there a legitimate reason (e.g., differences in seniority, merit, quantity or quality or production) or legally acceptable factors other than sex?

Exhibit 15.9 shows IBM's Salary Equity Analysis, carried out every six months for all minorities and females. While each facility is responsible for its own analysis, each division reviews the facility data, and corporate headquarters reviews division data. The exhibit shows the criteria IBM uses to define a peer for cohort analysis and the various comparisons that are examined (e.g., current salary, percent of last pay increase, and the timing of that increase).

IBM defines an equitable pay relationship as one in which the salary of minorities and females is *equal to or greater than* the average salary of their peers. If no such equity exists, IBM wants to know why, and what action, if warranted, will be taken to correct the relationship.

Unequal Impact

Elements of a pay system that have unequal impact on protected classes of employees must be business related. Although the notion of disparate impact has been promulgated

---

[19]Frederick S. Hills and Thomas J. Bergmann, "Conducting an Equal Pay for Equal Work Audit," in *Perspectives on Compensation*, eds. L. Gomez-Mejia and D. Balkin (Englewood Cliffs, N.J.: Prentice-Hall, 1987).

by the courts in other personnel areas (testing, hiring, etc.), they have been slower to address compensation applications. Cases have tended to focus on job evaluation and have ignored other elements of the pay system. It would seem logical that employers, and perhaps eventually the courts, would examine all aspects of pay setting for any disparate impact. An unresolved difficulty is separating the effects of one pay practice from those of another. While this difficulty may make the disparate impact standards impossible to satisfy in a court of law, the notion of disparate impact can still guide compensation professionals in analyzing the results of their decisions.

Overall Evaluation

Beyond legal compliance, evaluation serves to assess how well the pay system and its policies achieve specified pay objectives. Evaluation also serves to provide feedback by identifying problem areas and directing future development and design efforts. While most professionals and researchers advocate evaluating pay systems, very little attention has been devoted to how to do it.

The effectiveness of the pay system depends on a variety of factors. Perhaps the most obvious are measures of the specific pay objectives such as those suggested in the pay model used in this book. We have already discussed the objective of regulatory compliance. Equity and efficiency are the other two broad objectives in the pay model. Obtaining measures of these two requires developing an information system that generates such indexes as turnover rates of high performers (retention), job acceptance to job offer ratios (attraction), promotion offers to promotion acceptances (willingness to take on more responsibility), unit productivity, unit labor costs, support staff salaries to total sales ratios, and so on. Similarly, it means comparing such indexes as a unit's compa-ratio to the turnover rates of employees rated satisfactory or better, and the rate of change in salaries to the rate of change in earnings, or return on investments.

Another factor to assess in evaluating the pay system is the reactions of the clients or users of the system. In her research on organization effectiveness, Tsui has designed a process for evaluating the personnel function in terms of its various constituencies.[20] Operating managers' appraisals of the various pay techniques as tools to aid their decision making is often revealing feedback. This is done informally in most organizations, although Tsui advocates a more systematic approach.

Another constituency of the pay system is the work force. Employees' acceptance of their pay and the pay system is vital for pay effectiveness. Surveys of employees' work attitudes are common, and usually a few items in the survey are related to pay. However, employers frequently use surveys the way a drunk uses a lamppost: for support, rather than illumination. Most surveys of pay satisfaction miss the mark as diagnostic devices. To be useful, the questions need to focus on specific pay techniques and on perceptions of various aspects of equity rather than satisfaction. Some employers use

---

[20]Ann S. Tsui and Debbie Hirsch, *Research on Personnel/Human Resources Department Effectiveness: A Review and an Approach,* Fuqua School of Business, Duke University, Durham, N.C., working paper, September 1982.

"sensing sessions" in which small groups of employees are regularly interviewed on a wide range of issues. Pay administrators need to be involved in this process also.

SUMMARY

We have now completed the discussion of the pay administration process. Administration includes control: control of the way managers decide individual employees' pay as well as control of overall costs of labor. As we noted, some controls are designed into the fabric of the pay system (inherent controls, range maximums and minimums, etc.). The salary budgeting and forecasting processes impose additional controls. The formal budgeting process focuses on controlling labor costs and generating the financial plan for the pay system. The budget sets the limits within which the rest of the system operates.

Other aspects of administration we examined in this chapter included the fair treatment of employees in communications and appeals processes. The basic point was that pay systems are tools, and like any tools, they need to be evaluated in terms of usefulness in achieving an organization's objectives.

REVIEW QUESTIONS

1. How does the nature of the administration of the pay system affect the pay objectives?
2. What difference does it make how a compensation function is structured?
3. Give some examples of uses of inherent controls.
4. Why is it important to manage labor costs?
5. Merit increase guidelines have been discussed in this book as both a technique for recognizing performance and a cost control technique. Explain this dual nature.
6. In the EEO auditing section of this chapter, it is stated that IBM defines an equitable pay relationship as one in which the salary of minorities and females is equal to or greater than the average salary of their peers. Do you agree with this standard? Why or why not? What might be some other standards?

Appendix Merit Grids

Merit grids combine 3 variables: level of performance, distribution of employees within their job's pay range, and merit increase percentages.

Example:

1. Assume a performance rating scale of A through D; 30 percent of employees get A, 35 percent get B, 20 percent get C and 15 percent get D. Change to decimals.

A	B	C	D
.30	.35	.20	.15

2. Assume a range distribution as follows: 10 percent of all employees are in the top (fourth) quartile of the pay range for their job, 35 percent are in the third quartile, 30 percent in second quartile, and 25 percent in lowest quartile. Change to decimals.

1	.10
2	.35
3	.30
4	.25

3. Multiply the performance distribution by the range distribution to obtain the percent of employees in each cell. Cell entries = Performance × Range.

	A	*B*	*C*	*D*
1	.30 × .10 = .03	.35 × .10 = .035	.20 × .10 = .02	.15 × .10 = .015
2	.30 × .35 = .105	.35 × .35 = .1225	.20 × .35 = .07	.15 × .35 = .0525
3	.30 × .30 = .09	.35 × .30 = .105	.20 × .30 = .06	.15 × .30 = .045
4	.30 × .25 = .075	.35 × .25 = .1225	.20 × .25 = .05	.15 × .25 = .0375

    Cell entries tell us that 3% of employees are in top quartile of pay range AND received an A performance rating, 10.5 percent of employees are in second quartile of pay range AND received an A performance rating, etc.

4. Distribute increase percentage among cells, varying the percentages according to performance and range distribution, for example, 6 percent to those employees in cell A1, 5 percent to those employees in B1.

5. Multiply increase percentages by the employee distribution for each cell. Sum of all cells should equal the total merit increase percentage.

Example: $6\% \times$ cell A1 $= .06 \times .03 = .0018$

              $5\% \times$ cell B1 $= .05 \times .035 = .00175$

                    etc.

Targeted Merit Increase Percentage $= \overline{\text{Sum}}$

6. Adjust increase percentage among cells if needed in order to stay within budgeted increase.

Compensation Application
EEO at Sun State

You are a new personnel generalist at Sun State. You worked there last summer as an intern, and your boss, Georgia Santos, was very pleased with the job analysis and job descriptions you did during the summer. In fact, those job descriptions provided the basis for a complete job evaluation done this past year. As your first assignment, Georgia has asked you to assess Sun State's vulnerability to charges of pay discrimination. She says they do not discriminate against women, yet she has heard rumors that someone intends to file charges against them. Lisa Johnson was in complaining about her most recent raise. Lisa has a good performance record and received a generous raise based on her performance. However, Lisa said her pay was still below that of the males in her group, and that Sun State is notorious for its poor treatment of women.

EXHIBIT 1
Sun State Personnel Inventory Sheet

Employee	Job Evaluation Points	Age	Sex	Years at Sun	Years on Present Job	Performance Rating*	Monthly Salary
1. Jim	350	24	M	2	2	5	$1,000
2. Henry	350	30	M	5	5	5	1,400
3. Patsy	350	34	F	4	4	4	1,200
4. Don	350	50	M	20	20	1	1,800
5. Jane	425	32	F	10	2	3	2,800
6. Bruce	425	45	M	15	10	3	4,000
7. Joan	425	24	F	1	1	4	2,500
8. Bill	425	34	M	5	5	4	3,000
9. Phil	600	35	M	10	5	2	3,500
10. Katie	600	36	F	8	8	3	2,800
11. Patricia	600	25	F	4	3	4	2,900
12. Jason	600	45	M	20	10	2	3,800
13. Patrick	600	30	M	7	7	5	4,200
14. John	700	38	M	8	8	1	4,600
15. Vera	700	52	F	25	15	5	5,000
16. Dennis	700	45	M	19	16	4	4,600
17. Susan	700	49	F	20	14	5	4,700
18. Laura	400	28	F	6	4	3	1,800
19. Tom	400	50	M	20	8	3	3,400
20. Carol	400	30	F	5	3	5	2,000
21. Richard	500	52	M	22	12	3	3,200
22. Mark	500	66	M	25	10	3	3,200
23. Ann	500	38	F	8	3	4	2,800
24. Janet	500	25	F	2	1	5	2,400
25. Sam	800	47	M	10	10	3	5,200
26. Charles	475	32	M	10	4	3	2,400
27. Lisa	475	35	F	3	3	4	2,400
28. Matthew	475	40	M	8	8	2	3,000
29. Michael	475	35	M	6	6	4	2,800
30. Sharon	475	42	F	12	4	3	2,500
31. Mary	475	29	F	4	2	5	2,100

*1 = Unsatisfactory performance; 5 = Outstanding performance.

EXHIBIT 2

	Male n = 17	Female n = 14	Female:Male Ratio
Age	41.1	34.2	
Tenure at Sun	12.5	8.0	
Tenure at Job	8.6	4.8	
Performance Rating	3.1	4.1	
Monthly Salary	$3,241	$2,707	83.5%
Job Evaluation Points	513.2	501.8	
(Monthly Salary/Job Evaluation Points)	$6.32	$5.39	85.2%
Tenure/Age	.30	.23	

Georgia has provided you the data in Exhibit 1. She has asked you for a report on the state's pay practices from an EEO perspective. She wants you to identify differences in treatment between males and females and decide if these differences are a result of discrimination or if they can be explained by some other factors. You have decided to begin your analysis by calculating separate means for males and females for the variables given in Exhibit 1. These results are shown in Exhibit 2.

1. Based on your analysis, what conclusions can be made about the state's pay system?
2. If you identify any problems, what recommendations would you make for remedying them?
3. You may also recommend further data collection. If you do, specify the data to be collected and why you feel it is needed.
4. You finished your report to Georgia Santos last week. Thus far, you have not met with her to get her reaction to it. You are in the employee cafeteria when Lisa Johnson approaches.

   Lisa asks how you like working for the state. She's heard you've done some EEO analysis and asks you point blank, "Do you think Sun State's pay system is fair?" You remember that your boss mentioned Lisa's complaints about possible sex discrimination. What will you tell Lisa?
5. Following this incident, you decide to write a memo to your boss regarding communication about the pay system. What pay communication policy do you recommend for the state?

Chapter

16

Compensation of Special Groups

After attending a job-enrichment seminar, a sales supervisor decided that some of the suggested techniques could help combat the productivity problem in his sales force. He invited one of his salespeople to his office and told him that he now would be allowed to plan, carry out, and control his own job. The wanted "satisfiers" would be introduced into the man's job.

The salesman asked if he would get more money. The supervisor replied, "No. Money is not a motivator, and you will not be satisfied if I give you more pay."

Once again the employee asked, "Well, if I do what you want, will I get more pay?"

The supervisor answered, "No. You need to understand the motivation theory. Take this book home and read it. Tomorrow we'll get together and I'll explain once again what will really motivate you."

As the man was leaving, he turned back and said, "Well, if I read this book, will I get more money?"

As the story goes, there are some employees for whom "newfangled" sources of job rewards are inappropriate. In contrast to these employees are special groups for whom compensation practices diverge from typical company procedures. In all cases, these special practices have been strategically developed to meet unique compensation needs. This does not suggest that the compensation model becomes inoperative, however. Rather, one or more of the internal, external, or individual dimensions stressed in this book must be specially "tuned" for the groups discussed in this section. This chapter is designed to outline the foundations of, and techniques for, compensating these special groups. Exhibit 16.1 identifies the special groups that will be covered and illustrates the compensation challenges that must be met. The following sections discuss compensation practices designed by companies to meet the special needs of these groups.

As Exhibit 16.1 illustrates, special groups appear to have more divided loyalties or built-in role conflicts than typical groups within an organization. For example, foreign service personnel must carry out corporate directives in a foreign environment that may

---

EXHIBIT 16.1
Compensation Challenges for Special Groups

Supervisors	"In-the-middle" position with often conflicting duties of meeting employee needs and satisfying upper management directives. Exempt status of job may result in no overtime pay. This inequity must be recognized by developing salary differentials with subordinates.
Middle and upper management	Organizational profits presumed to be highly dependent upon quality of performance of these key decision makers. Incentive systems designed to increase motivation viewed as highly important.
Nonsupervisory professional employees	Viewed as highly mobile group with allegiances more to their profession than to any organization. Special emphasis on compensation strategies that will help to retain these employees. Payment also based on special knowledge acquired through extensive education. Compensation relative to that of managers and relative to that of younger peers with more timely (less obsolete) knowledge are particularly important concerns.
Sales personnel	Jobs often unsupervised and especially dependent upon compensation strategies designed to develop and maintain high motivational levels.
Foreign service personnel	Work in foreign countries subject to different cultural, legal, and compensation customs. Geographic distance from domestic operations requires employees capable of exercising greater independence. Equity between foreign and U.S. employees must be balanced against "normal" pay scales in area surrounding foreign subsidiary.

not be at all amenable to U.S. interference. The challenge in foreign service compensation is to identify strategies which encourage flexible and independent decision making.

This chapter argues that special groups share two characteristics.[1] Like Foreign Service personnel, other special groups tend to have major responsibilities on the organization's environmental boundaries. For example, sales people deal with customers outside the organization. Scientists and engineers monitor the knowledge frontier, looking for clues that will generate new paths of technological exploration. Executives are the ambassadors who must interact equally well with politicians, top level competitors, and irate shareholders. Second, these groups become special, that is, receive special treatment, because the tasks they perform in these environments are strategically important to the organization at that time. As an example consider the contrast in compensation treatment for engineers in two different organizations; a high technology firm with a strong research and development component, and an organization where a few engineers are employed, but whose role is not central to the mission of the organization. A survey of just such differences in employee composition and organizational strategy found that research and development organizations with heavy concentrations of engineers had evolved compensation systems that were responsive to the special needs of the engineering contingent. Organizations with a different focus and with fewer engineers merged this group's compensation with the standard package offered other employees.[2]

COMPENSATION STRATEGY FOR SPECIAL GROUPS

Different compensation treatment for special groups does not appear to evolve unless the problem persists for some time. For example, computer and MIS specialists have presented a compensation headache to organizations since computers became an essential tool over two decades ago. The initial response to this problem was to raise wages. Red circle rates, or paying above a grade maximum, were accepted only because the problem was expected to resolve itself. As turnover in this group persisted, though, even despite wages that were much higher than traditionally paid relative to other occupations, organizations began to develop special "market sensitive" grades that maintained the internal differential between different levels of MIS jobs, but which abandoned some of the long-standing relationships to other jobs. Companies depended heavily on the external market rate for pricing level. Since the compensation problem continues to persist, it is likely that even more evidence of special treatment will begin to surface in future years.

A second short-term strategy used by employers is based on recognition of key contributors and providing rewards from an existing program set up for that explicit purpose.[3] Key contributor programs evolved first in high technology firms to reward

---

[1]E.C. Miller, "Supervisory Overtime, Incentive, and Bonus Practices," *Compensation Review,* 1978, 10 (4), pp. 12–25.

[2]J.W. Crim, *Compensating Non-Supervisory Professional Employees* (Research Press, 1978).

[3]M. Spratt and B. Steele, "Rewarding Key Contributors," *Compensation and Benefits Review,* 1985, 17 (3), pp. 24–37.

engineers and scientists who were instrumental in discovering or developing important new technologies. Awards are generally granted after the major task is completed (74 percent of companies surveyed) and usually involve a lump sum cash award ranging between $500 to $100,000. Companies also like to offer special perquisites ("perks") to key contributors (67 percent of companies surveyed) such as company cars, special research funding, sabbaticals, public recognition, and general work life improvements.

When the strategic importance of a group extends for longer periods, though, special compensation programs are developed and endure as a separate branch of the company compensation system. The groups discussed here under that category include supervisors, outside directors of corporate boards, executives, scientific/engineering employees, sales personnel, and foreign service personnel.

SUPERVISORS

Supervisors, as has been noted many times, are caught in the classic "middle" position. On one hand they must respond to the needs and distinct personalities/skills of their subordinates. In doing this, however, they must satisfy the overriding goals of higher level management. Balancing these (at times) conflicting objectives effectively is essential to any organization.

Compensation of supervisory personnel takes on special importance largely because of a need to preserve equity. Attraction and retention of supervisory personnel depend heavily on a compensation system that recognizes the value differential between a sub-ordinate line position and that of a supervisor. Identifying an appropriate wage differential that rewards workers for assuming supervisory responsibilities, yet does not lead to compression with middle manager salary levels, is the key to this problem.

For many years, the strategy was to treat supervisors like lower level managers. Remember, though, both groups are exempt from the overtime provisions of the Fair Labor Standards Act. Imagine a nonexempt employee collecting time and one-half for a long stretch of overtime, being asked if she would like to be a supervisor. The typical response used to be "Why should I take a pay cut for a job that's nothing but a headache."

Organizations now handle this problem in one of three ways. First, the most popular method is to key base salary of supervisors to some amount above the top paid subordinate in the unit (5 percent to 30 percent differential with a mean across organizations of 15 percent).[4]

A second method to maintain equitable differentials is simply to pay supervisors scheduled overtime. Overtime is subject to some stipulated maximum and is not paid for extra hours that are self-scheduled.[5]

Finally, some organizations develop special supervisory incentive and bonus plans, with payouts varying between 0 to 25 percent of salary.[6]

---

[4]Miller (1978).

[5]Ibid.

[6]Ibid.

CORPORATE DIRECTORS

A Board of Directors is comprised of from 10 to 20 individuals who meet on a regular basis to serve a variety of roles (e.g., strategic planning, executive compensation, and evaluation) in the interest of the corporation and its shareholders. Historically, the function of directors was frequently to "rubber stamp" decisions made by top management. Towards this end, directors were chosen from the ranks of people affiliated in some way with the organization (e.g., retired corporate officers, suppliers, attorneys). Today's corporate board is *markedly* different, with members chosen primarily from the outside. Two-thirds of the typical Board are outside directors, taken from the ranks of unaffiliated business executives, representatives from important segments of society, and major shareholders. Along with this shift in membership to unaffiliated members has come increased responsibility for decision making and increased responsibility for the success of the firm. The increased responsibility also brings increased risks that disgruntled shareholders may bring suit for unprofitable or unpopular corporate decisions. It also means a harder time finding competent individuals willing to serve. One survey reported 20 percent of all companies were turned down by a prospective board member.[7] Given these changes, it is not surprising that compensation of directors is a "hot" topic today. Exhibit 16.2 outlines the compensation components for directors.

Generally, the package includes an ever-increasing base pay ($10,000 to $30,000), with incentives for attending Board meetings. The packages are not very sophisticated on such other components as long-term incentives, employee benefits, or perquisites ("perks").

EXHIBIT 16.2
Compensating the Board of Directors

Type of Compensation	Amount	Special Characteristics
Base Compensation ("Retainer Fee")	Generally $10,000–$30,000	Varies with: 1) Board member status 2) Time required to complete duties 3) CEO Compensation 4) Industry
Incentives	Generally $150–$1,000 for in-person meetings, slightly less ($712) for teleconferences	Average 6 meetings/year
Benefits	Liability insurance for shareholder legal cases (10 million–1 billion dollars) Life insurance $50,000–$100,000	Much narrower in scope than for typical employee
Perks	Overseas tours of facilities. Board meetings at prominent vacation resorts.	

Total Financial Compensation $21,675

Source: Y. Tauber, "Trends in Compensation for Outside Directors," *Compensation and Benefits Review*, 1986, 18(1), pp. 43–52.
"Directors Compensation Continues to Rise," *CompFlash* 88(6), 1988, p. 2.

---

[7]*Wall Street Journal*, "Liability Fears," December 16, 1986, p. 1.

MIDDLE AND TOP MANAGEMENT

Middle and top management employees may be classified as special groups for the purposes of compensation to the extent the organization devises special compensation programs to attract, retain, and motivate this relatively scarce human resource. By this definition, not all managers above the supervisory level would qualify for consideration as special groups. It is not at all unusual to find middle managers' salaries determined on the basis of a company-wide job evaluation system or on the basis of a job evaluation system for all exempt employees. However, at some level in the organization hierarchy pay practices for managers/executives typically deviate from traditional company practices. Generally these special practices incorporate the top 1 to 10 percent of the exempt work force.[8]

The major point of deviation in pay practices for this group is tied to the role of the competitive market.[9] Because the performance of these executives plays a major role in the performance of the organization, retention (avoidance of loss to a competitor being not the least of the retention issues) and motivation become particularly important. One requirement for achieving these goals is a salary that is competitive externally. Consequently, many compensation experts agree that executive compensation, in contrast to compensation for lower level jobs, is less likely to be based on maintenance of internal relationships/equity (e.g., based on job evaluation) and more likely to be based on a market competitive rate. It would be foolish, however, to conclude that executive pay should be derived blindly from competitive salary survey data without first understanding the mechanisms and decisions that led to the final dollar figure.

Conceptual/Empirical Perspectives on Executive Pay

There are at least two dominant theoretical explanations for the level of executive pay, one coming from the sociological literature and the other from neoclassical economic theory. From a sociological perspective, Simon argues that executive salaries can be explained by a unique blending of market forces and social comparisons regarding appropriate salary differentials between organizational levels.[10] Simon hypothesizes that salaries of low-level executives are determined by competitive market forces. In turn, salaries of higher level executives are "pegged" from these benchmarks, following widespread norms about appropriate salary differentials between organization levels.

In fact, there have been numerous studies documenting Simon's contention that there is a relatively stable relation among the salaries at different organizational levels.[11] Finkin,

---

[8]Thomas H. Patten, Jr., *Pay: Employee Compensation and Incentive Plans* (New York: Free Press, 1977).

[9]Ernest C. Miller, "How Companies Set Top and Middle Management Salaries . . . A Compensation Review Symposium," *Compensation Review 10* (First Quarter 1977), pp. 15–29.

[10]Herbert A. Simon, *Administrative Behavior*, 2nd ed. (New York: Macmillan, 1957).

[11]Eugene F. Finkin, "How to Figure Our Executive Compensation," *Personnel Journal 57* (July 1978), pp. 371–75; Thomas A. Mahoney, "Organizational Hierarchy and Position Worth," *Academy of Management Journal 22*, no. 4 (1979), pp. 726–37.

EXHIBIT 16.3
Pay Relationships in Organizations

Level	Salary as Percentage of CEO Salary
CEO	100
Executive vice president	72
Group vice president	52
Managers	35

for example, argues that Exhibit 16.3 illustrates a good rule-of-thumb estimate of subordinate salaries in relation to the chief executive officer (CEO) of industrial corporations.

A more systematic description of this relationship also appears in the Conference Board's report on executive compensation.[12] Exhibit 16.4 indicates the ratio of subordinate salary to CEO salary for the top three organizational levels in various types of industries.

The second explanation of executive salaries comes from neoclassical economic theory, and actually complements the sociological explanation rather than contradicting it. The focus here is on explaining the level of executive salaries rather than the differential among salaries at different organizational levels. The premise is that the marginal productivity of the chief executive officer varies directly with some measure of company size (e.g., profitability, sales, number of employees).[13] Intuitively, this explanation makes sense. Presumably CEOs in larger companies are paid more because their jobs are more difficult and demanding.

Numerous studies have been done in the past 20 years demonstrating the relationship between company size and the pay of top executives with direct responsibility for or-

EXHIBIT 16.4
Ratio of Subordinate Salaries to CEO Salary in Six Industries

	Retail Trade	Manufacturing	Banking	Construction	Gas and Electric	Insurance
CEO salary	100	100	100	100	100	100
Second highest-paid executive	72	68	68	77	58	67
Third highest-paid executive	59	53	52	61	54	54

Note: Chairman of the board and president are separate positions.

[12]Harland Fox and Charles Peck, *Top Executive Compensation: 1986* (New York: The Conference Board, 1985), report no. 875.

[13]D. Roberts, *Executive Compensation* (New York: Free Press, 1958); J.R. Deckop and T.A. Mahoney, "The Economics of Executive Compensation," Paper presented at the 42nd National Academy of Management Meetings, New York, 1982; and John R. Deckop, "Determinants of Chief Executive Officer Compensation," *Industrial and Labor Relations Review*, 41(2), 1988, pp. 215–226.

ganizational effectiveness.[14] (Note: the key here is the prediction of salaries for top executives who have *direct responsibility* for organizational performance, whether it be control of a total organization or an independent profit center.) The approach is not particularly effective for prediction of salaries for lower executives who do not have control over decision making. Hence, the sociological model discussed earlier may be more appropriate for identification of differentials in salaries for subordinates once CEO salaries have been identified. For example, the Conference Board regressed CEO salary against company sales and found between 12 and 15 percent of the variance in CEO pay accounted for by company size (measured in sales) in different industries.

One recent study tested the relative importance of economic variables and social comparisons in explaining executive compensation.[15] The social comparison here, though, is not between vice presidents and the CEO, but between the Board of Directors and the CEO. The Board of Directors, it is argued, determines the wages of the CEO. In setting CEO wages the Directors, particularly those who are CEOs in other organizations, use their own salaries as an anchor. Both economic and social comparison variables were significant. Size and profitability affected compensation; so did compensation of outside directors. For every $100,000 more made by these directors, CEOs were paid $51,000 more.

A third group of studies argue that CEO salary isn't solely determined by economic or social comparison processes. Other variables cloud the picture. Generally these studies focus on the type of controls and pressures exerted on the chief executive. For example, one study distinguished between firms with a dominant stockholder and those with control spread among a large number of investors.[16] Where dominant stockholders prevailed there was significantly more emphasis on paying for executive performance and less compensation for the scale of operations (e.g., number of employees or dollar sales). Reasoning that dominant stockholders view the firm primarily as an investment, this view suggests that a dominant shareholder commands both the power and incentive to force direct ties of executive compensation and organizational performance.

Current variants on this research suggest that chief executive officers (CEOs) don't always act functionally rational, that political considerations sometimes dominate over purely economic motives. According to this argument, CEOs have a diversity of goals for the firm, some of which conflict with the profit motive.[17] For example, CEOs perform

---

[14]Marc J. Wallace, "Type of Control, Industrial Concentration, and Executive Pay," *Academy of Management Proceedings*, 1976, pp. 284–88; W. Lewellan and B. Huntsman, "Managerial Pay and Corporate Performance," *American Economic Review* 60 (1970), pp. 710–20; and "More Proof Positive: Top Executive Pay is Tied to Performance," *CompFlash* 84(8) (1984), p. 1.

[15]Charles O'Reilly, Brian Main, and Graef Crystal, "CEO Compensation as Tournament and Social Comparison: A Tale of Two Theories," *Administrative Science Quarterly*, 33, 1988, pp. 257–274.

[16] Gomez-Mejia, Tosi, and Hinkin, "Effect of Managerial Control and Performance on Executive Compensation."

[17]J. Pfeffer, *Power in Organizations* (Marshfield, Mass.: Pitman Publishing, 1981); Gerardo Rivera Ungson and Richard Steers, "Motivation and Politics in Executive Compensation," *Academy of Management Review* 9, no. 2 (1984), pp. 313–23.

political/symbolic roles in their interactions with the external environment.[18] Managing political coalitions within and outside the organization may have short-term and even long-term effects on traditional performance measures. To the extent political roles of CEOs don't converge with profit maximization responsibilities, it may be inappropriate to measure CEO performance on exclusively economic variables.

The stakes are not small in this effort to document and potentially strengthen the linkage between executive pay and performance. Recent evidence indicates stockholder and general public criticism of executive compensation levels is rising.[19] Some individuals arm their arsenal of complaints with such spectacular data as the salaries of the top paid executives in the United States: Michael Eisner (Chairman of Walt Disney) received over 40 million in 1988.[20] E.A. Harrigan (RJR Nabisco former Vice-Chairman) received 21 million dollars.[21] In fact, the average of total compensation for top executives exceeded $2,000,000 in 1988.[22]

It is difficult to determine whether criticisms of CEO salaries are justified. Opponents point out that the Teacher of the Year in 1988 made only $34,800; or that Owen Bieber (President of the Giant United Auto Workers) made only $85,651 in 1987.[23] Whether or not this criticism is justified may be irrelevant. There have already been ramifications. In early 1985 the Reagan Administration lifted import restraints on Japanese cars. The administration reasoned that the large prevailing executive bonuses could be interpreted only as evidence that the auto industry no longer needed special assistance to compete internationally. The next section examines the elements of an executive compensation package, one component of which is the annual bonus.

Components of an Executive Compensation Package

There are five basic elements of most executive compensation packages: (1) base salary, (2) short-term (annual) incentives or bonuses, (3) long-term incentives and capital appreciation plans, (4) employee benefits, and (5) perquisites. Because of the changing nature of tax legislation, each of these at one time or another has received considerable attention in designing executive compensation packages. Exhibit 16.5 traces the trend in the first three of these components over time.

One obvious trend is apparent from these data. Companies are placing more and more emphasis on long-term incentives at the expense of base salary. Such a change in emphasis signals the growing importance attached to making decisions that ensure the long-run growth and survival of a company.

---

[18]Ungson and Steers, "Motivation and Politics in Executive Compensation."

[19]"Big Executive Bonuses Now Come With a Catch: Lots of Criticism," *The Wall Street Journal*, May 15, 1985, p. 35.

[20]Business Week, "Is the Boss Getting Paid Too Much?" *Business Week*, May 1, 1989, 46–62.

[21]Ibid.

[22]Ibid.

[23]Ibid.

EXHIBIT 16.5
Components of Executive Compensation

	Percentage of Total Compensation in			
	1975	*1978*	*1986*	*1988*
Salary	60	60	46	40
Annual bonus	25	25	26	18
Long-term incentive	15	15	28	42

Source: Adapted from assorted issues of *The Wall Street Journal* based on data provided by Sibson & Co.; Towers, Perrin, Forster and Crosby; Wyatt Co.

Base salary. As noted earlier, market competitive salary levels become increasingly more important in determining executive base salary at the top levels of the managerial hierarchy in an organization. This does not eliminate the role of formalized job evaluation systems or the importance of maintaining an internally equitable structure, but in reality these inputs become less important.

What becomes more important, at least for the chief executive officer, is the opinion of a compensation committee, comprised usually of the company's board of directors (or a subset of the board). Frequently this compensation committee will take over some of the data analysis tasks previously performed by the chief personnel officer, even going so far as to analyze salary survey data and performance records for executives of comparably sized firms.[24]

Bonuses. Annual bonuses typically play a major role in executive compensation and are primarily designed to increase performance motivation. For example, 92 percent of all executives in manufacturing, and 81 percent of those in banking, receive bonuses that are a function of their base salary.[25]

There are two constraints on the use of bonuses to compensate executives above base salary levels. First, there are several industries that make relatively little use of bonuses, either because of legal or company policy prohibitions. The types of organizations relying almost exclusively on base salary for total direct compensation typically have one or more of the following characteristics:[26] (1) tight control of stock ownership, (2) not-for-profit institutions, or (3) firms operating in regulated industries.

The second constraint on bonus systems is usually tied to organization level of the executives. Eligibility is typically limited to those executives whose performance is judged to have potentially significant impacts on overall company performance.

---

[24]Ernest C. Miller, "How Companies Set the Base Salary and Incentive Bonus Opportunity for Chief Executive and Chief Operating Officers . . . A Compensation Review Symposium," *Compensation Review* 9 (Fourth Quarter 1976), pp. 30–44; Monci Jo Williams, "Why Chief Executives' Pay Keeps Rising," *Fortune* (April 1, 1985), pp. 66–72, 76.

[25]Fox and Peck, *Top Executive Compensation: 1986*.

[26]William H. Cash, "Executive Compensation," *Personnel Administrator 22*, no. 7 (1977), pp. 11–19.

Typically, executives in companies with bonus plans receive higher total direct compensation (base salary + bonus) than those in nonbonus companies. This is, however, highly dependent upon performance of the particular organization in a particular year. Most companies paying bonuses pay base salaries somewhat lower than nonbonus companies (for example, base pay for bonus-paying companies in the manufacturing sector generally runs about 15 percent below base pay in nonbonus-companies). Consequently when a company has an unprofitable year and bonuses are not granted, direct salary will be somewhat lower than in nonbonus companies, and probably considerably lower than in highly profitable years. The tendency toward use of bonus systems and the proportion of salary they entail places a strong financial incentive on executives to perform well.

Long-term incentive and capital appreciation plans. Exhibit 16.6 dramatically illustrates the increased popularity of long-term incentives. Boards of directors are shifting their focus for executive compensation to long-term achievements, sometimes even at the expense of short-run profits. Exhibit 16.6 outlines the different types of long-run incentive plans and their relative popularity 1986 versus 1981.

The Tax Reform Act (TRA) of 1986 had a serious impact on plans involving actual stock options (Incentive Stock Options). Prior to 1987 (when the law went into effect) Incentive Stock Options were popular because gains resulting from stock price increases were taxed at a capital gains rate rather than the much higher personal income tax rate. The TRA repealed the capital gains deduction and lowered personal income tax ceilings. This, combined with other new rules affecting Incentive stock options, leaves them with few comparative advantages over other options noted in Exhibit 16.6.[27]

Executive benefits. Since many benefits are tied to income level (e.g., life insurance, disability insurance, pension plans), executives typically receive higher benefits than most other exempt employees. Beyond the typical benefits outlined in Chapter 12, however, many executives also receive additional life insurance, exclusions from deductibles for health-related costs, and supplementary pension income exceeding the maximum limits permissible under ERISA guidelines for qualified pension plans.

Of course, various sections of the Employee Retirement Income Security Act and the tax code restrict employer ability to provide benefits for executives that are too far above those of other workers. The assorted clauses require that a plan: (1) cover a broad cross section of employees (generally 80 percent), (2) provide definitely determinable benefits, and (3) meet specific vesting (see Chapter 12) and nondiscrimination requirements. The nondiscrimination requirement specifies that the average value of benefits for low-paid employees must be at least 75 percent of the average value for highly-paid employees.[28]

---

[27]Other tax reform issues are discussed in Gregory Wiber, "After Tax Reform, Part I: Planning Employee Benefit Programs," *Compensation and Benefits Review*, 19(2), 1987, 16–25; and Irwin Rubin, "After Tax Reform, Part 2," *Compensation and Benefits Review*, 20(1), 1988, pp. 26–32.

EXHIBIT 16.6
Usage of Long-Term Incentives (%) for Top Executives

Type of Long-Term Incentive	1981	1986	Comments
Incentive Stock Option (ISO) Executive receives right to purchase stock at stipulated price over specific period of time, in conformance with Internal Revenue Code.	0	85	Relative advantage hurt by 1986 Tax Reform Act (TRA).
Nonqualified Stock Option (NQSO) Similar to incentive stock option, but without conformance with Internal Revenue Code.	87	97	Company receives tax deduction and no charge to earnings. More attractive under TRA (1986).
Stock Appreciation Rights (SARs) Company grants executive the right to appreciation in underlying stock over time.	73	80	Hurt by other accounting rules. Executives receive appreciation without tying up personal wealth.
Phantom Stock Plans Executive receives units analogous to company shares and, at some point in the future, receives the value of the stock appreciation plus dividends.	4	3	No comment
Restricted Stock Awards Executive receives outright grant of shares free or with discount, but is restricted from transferring stock until certain conditions are met; if conditions are not met, stock is forfeited.	19	38	No comment
Performance Unit plan Executive earns specially valued units at no cost, based on achievement of predetermined performance targets.	32	55	No tax or accounting advantages to company.
Performance Share Plan	14	28	Quite expensive.

Source: Adapted from Towers, Perrin, Forster and Crosby, "1986 Top 100 Industrial Executive Compensation Study," TPFC: New York, 1986.

Other amenities that might normally be classified under executive benefits are included in a special category: executive perquisites.

Executive perquisites. Perquisites, or "perks," probably have the same genesis as the expression "rank has its privileges." Indeed, life at the top has its rewards, designed to satisfy several types of executive needs. One type of perk could be classified as "internal," providing that something extra while the executive is inside the company:

---

[28]Dennis Blair and Mark Kimble, "Walking Through the Discrimination Testing Wage for Welfare Plans," *Benefits Quarterly,* 3(2), 1987, pp. 18–26. Author's note: At press time Section 89 of the Tax Code was under serious attack. If repealed, the nondiscrimination laws would change again.

luxury offices, executive dining rooms, special parking. A second category also is designed to be company related, but for business conducted externally: company-paid membership in clubs/associations, payment of hotel, resort, airplane, and auto expenses.

The final category of perquisites should be totally isolated from the first two because of the differential tax status. This category, called "personal perks," includes such things as low-cost loans, personal and legal counseling, free home repairs and improvements, personal use of company property, and expenses for vacation homes.[29] Since 1978, various tax and regulatory agency rulings have slowly been requiring companies to place a value on perks.[30] If this trend continues, the taxable income of executives with creative perk packages may increase considerably.

NONSUPERVISORY PROFESSIONAL EMPLOYEES

Following closely the Fair Labor Standards Act of 1938, a professional is defined here as a person who must have specialized training of a scientific or intellectual nature and whose major duties do not entail the supervision of people. In part, the special distinction of this group is their performance for compensation systems that recognize personal attributes rather than job characteristics. According to a survey of 100 large firms, this leads to two distinct types of compensation systems for professional employees.[31] The first type of system is characterized by relatively few professional employees. The small proportion of professionals precludes a separate compensation mechanism. Rather, professionals are incorporated into the existing job evaluation system for exempt employees. In contrast, slightly less than one-half (44 percent) of the surveyed firms reported some use of what is called a dual-track system.

A dual-track system is defined as:[32]

> A distinct framework within the formal compensation policy of a given organization whereby at least two general tracks of ascending compensation steps are available to exempt employees: (1) a "managerial" track to be ascended through increasing responsibility for supervision or direction of people, and (2) a "professional track" to be ascended through increasing contributions of a professional nature which do not mainly entail the supervision or direction of people.

With few exceptions, a dual-track system seems to be confined to organizations that have large numbers of professional employees.[33]

---

[29]Michael F. Klein, "Executive Perquisites," *Compensation Review* 12 (Fourth Quarter, 1979), pp. 46–50.

[30]R.L. VanKirk and L.S. Schenger, "Executive Compensation: The Trend is Back to Cash," *Financial Executive,* May 1978, pp. 83–91.

[31]John W. Crim, *Compensating Nonsupervisory Professional Employees* (Ann Arbor, Mich.: UMI Research Press, 1978).

[32]Analog Devices, *Parallel Ladder Program and New Products Bonus Program* (Norwood, Mass.: Analog Devices, 1985); Crim, *Compensating Nonsupervisory Professional Employees.*

[33]Crim's research shows that all but one company with a dual-track system had 800 or more professional employees.

EXHIBIT 16.7
IBM Dual Ladder

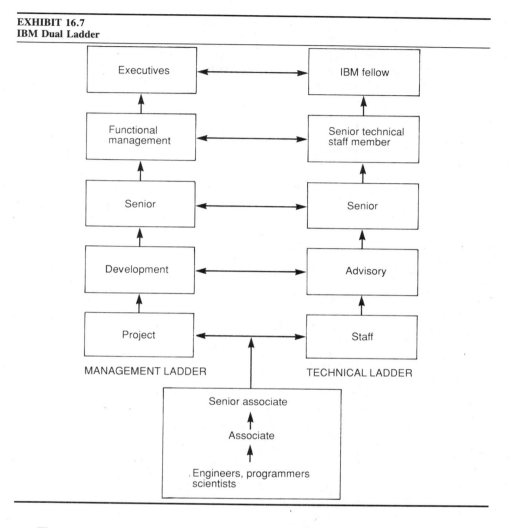

The compensation mechanism in a dual-track system recognizes an inherent distinction in the type of contribution made by professionals versus other exempt employees. For example, consider the dual-track system used at IBM and shown in Exhibit 16.7. Two distinct career ladders emerge for professionals beyond the second level: a managerial track and a professional track. Efforts are made to continue salary equivalencies across tracks at the same level, but there are apparent limitations on the maximum advancement of a professional without movement into a management position. In fact the maximum salary of a professional typically peaks at about 30 percent (range: 10 percent to 65 percent) of the chief executive officer's salary.[34]

---

[34]Crim, *Compensating Nonsupervisory Professional Employees.*

Up to this point little mention has been made of how professional salaries are actually derived. The key lies in the unique nature of scientific and engineering jobs. These so-called knowledge workers have valuable information that has a very short half-life unless updated by new educational infusions. The jobs are also nonrepetitive, reflecting the dynamic nature of the high-tech product market. The dynamism does not lend itself well to standard job analysis and job evaluation methods, both of which work best in stable job environments. Rather, job descriptions tend to be written more generically, reflecting broad level differences in responsibilities without outlining specific duties.

Because the jobs are so variable over time, standard job evaluation also is inappropriate. Instead, organizations tend to rely heavily on external market data in pricing scientist/engineer jobs. Specifically, organizations collect salary information for scientific/engineering jobs categorized by years since the incumbent last received a degree. Because the value of these jobs rests in the knowledge of the incumbents, the degree

EXHIBIT 16.8
Engineering Employees by Years since Last Degree and Weekly Base Salary

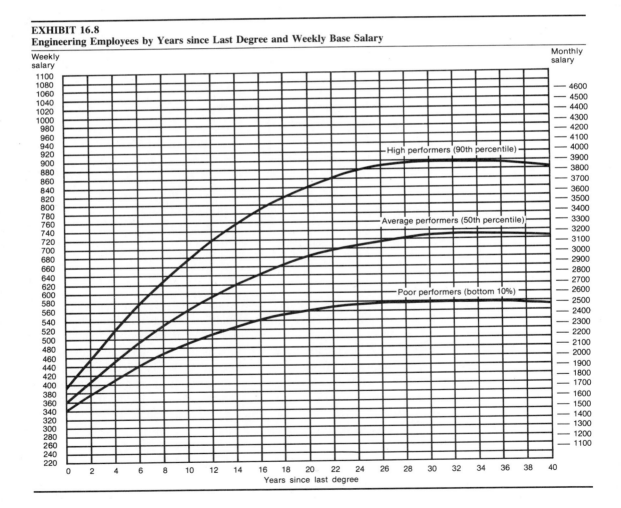

measure is intended to incorporate the half-life of technical obsolescence. In fact, a plot of these data with appropriate smoothing to eliminate aberrations typically shows salary progressions (curves) that are steep for the first five to seven years but which moderate in the magnitude of increase as technical obsolescence erodes the value of jobs. Exhibit 16.8 illustrates such a graph with somewhat greater sophistication built into it (different graphs are constructed for different levels of performance). To collect data in this form the surveying organization must also ask for a breakdown by broad performance levels. Given the Maturity Curve, determining base pay of an incumbent is straightforward. For example, according to the graph in Exhibit 16.8, an incumbent out 22 years since last degree would receive about $3,750 per month as a high performer, but only $2,450 per month if the annual performance review is poor.

Scientists and engineers also receive compensation beyond base pay. Increasingly, profit sharing and stock ownership are provided as incentives.[35] Other financial incentives link payment of specific cash amounts to completion of specific projects within deadline. Post hoc bonuses are also given for patents, publications, elections to professional societies and attainment of professional licenses.[36]

Finally, organizations have devoted considerable creative energy to development of "perks" that satisfy the unique needs of SEs. Included in this grouping are flexible work schedules, large offices, campus-like environments, and lavish athletic facilities.

SALES FORCE AND SALES EXECUTIVES

As indicated at the beginning of this chapter, sales positions provide special challenges to compensation administrators. Because a large part of a salesperson's job is unsupervised, it becomes essential to use compensation to direct sales activities, thus substituting for the absence of close supervision. Fortunately, most sales positions lend themselves well to some form of incentive system, making a salesperson's compensation highly dependent on units sold (or some measure of quantity). Because of this potential for great variability in compensation based on sales volume, mean salary figures reported in Exhibit 16.9 should be interpreted with caution. It is equally important to look at the variability in compensation paid to good and poor salespersons to determine competitiveness.[37]

Factors Explaining Pay Differences Among Salespersons

Over the years a number of factors have been identified to explain pay differentials among salespeople.[38] In large part these factors can be linked to external markets, particularly product markets. These factors include:[39]

---

[35]G. Milkovich, "Compensation Systems in High Technology Companies," *New Perspectives on Compensation* (Englewood Cliffs, N.J.: Prentice-Hall, 1987), pp. 269–277.

[36]Northrum and Malin, 1985.

[37]Charles F. Schultz, "Compensating the Sales Professional," unpublished manuscript, Tower, Perrin, Forster and Crosby, 1985.

[38]The Conference Board, *Compensating Salesmen and Sales Executives 1972* (New York: The Conference Board, 1972); Schultz, "Compensating the Sales Professional."

[39]The Conference Board, *Compensating Salesmen and Sales Executives*.

EXHIBIT 16.9
How Salespeople's Total Compensation is Growing

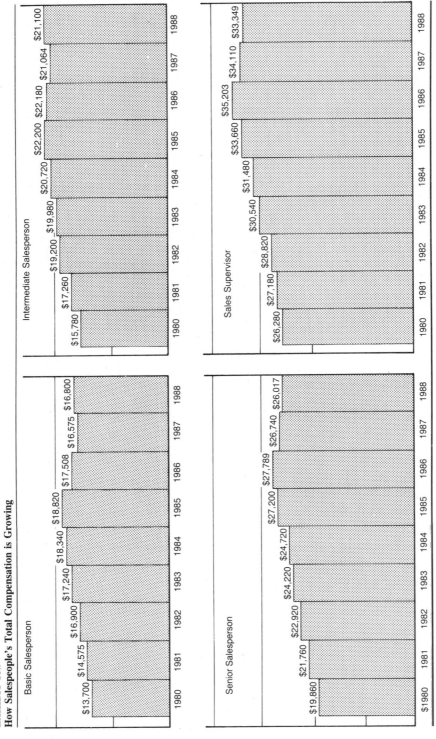

Notes: Sales-support personnel include sales analysts, customer service representatives, sales correspondents, sales training reps, exhibit and display coordinators, etc. Figures for 1980–85 represent medians as calculated by Executive Compensation Service, a subsidiary of the Wyatt Co. Figures for 1986–88 represent averages compiled by Sales & Marketing Management in a survey of consumer, industrial, and service companies. CAUTION: Due to this new benchmark, comparisons between 1986–88 figures and those from previous years should not be made, since the methods involved in gathering these data differ.

Source: "1988 Survey of Selling Costs," *Sales & Marketing Management Magazine*, February 20, 1989, p. 19. ©. Reproduced by permission.

538

1. *The kind of product sold.* In higher sales positions, executives in consumer goods industries earn approximately 10 percent more than in their counterparts in industrial goods industries. This trend reverses, however, at the bottom of the organizational hierarchy with field sales personnel in consumer goods industries earning approximately 10 percent less than industrial goods sales personnel.
2. *Sales volume.* Not surprisingly, there is some relationship between sales volume and earnings. Among sales executives, earnings are 40 to 70 percent higher for those with high sales volume in comparison to those with low sales volume. Unfortunately this positive relationship does not hold up for lower level sales positions.
3. *Type of market.* For high-level sales staff, selling a finished good to intermediaries (e.g., wholesalers, retailers) is more often associated with higher earnings than selling either directly to the consumer or selling goods that require further processing or assembly. Again, this relationship is directly reversed at lower organizational levels for sales personnel.
4. *Selling situation.* A distinction can be made between selling of technical goods versus nontechnical goods. The sale of technical goods frequently involves a team-selling approach, with technical personnel assisting the sales representative in the selling situation. Executive sales personnel in these technical markets earn about 15 percent less than executives in nontechnical fields where a team-selling approach is not necessary. Again, this earnings differential is reversed at lower sales levels, with technical products salespeople earning about 10 percent more than nontechnical sales force.

It probably would be inappropriate for an organization to design a sales compensation plan that conforms to these empirical relationships. No doubt there is a rational foundation for differentiating earnings that would lead to the types of differences just noted. However, the factors to consider in designing a sales compensation plan are much more complex and follow the line of reasoning discussed in the next section.

Factors in Designing a Sales Compensation Plan

The sales environment for many organizations is best characterized as rapidly changing. There are five basic features of this environment to be considered in designing a new sales compensation plan or modifying an existing one.[40]

1. *Customers*
   a. Centralized buying—sales staff may no longer have a direct impact on buying decisions, requiring a compensation plan reflecting this.
   b. Centralized merchandising—if merchandising decisions are not made at the local

---

[40]Gerry Phillips, "Matching the Compensation Plan to the Sales Role," *Canadian Business Review*, Spring 1977, pp. 14–19. For other excellent discussions of issues in designing a sales compensation plan, see Bruce Ellig, "Sales Compensation: A Systematic Approach," *Compensation Review* 15 (First Quarter 1982), pp. 21–45; Lesley Barnes, "Finding the Best Sales Compensation Plan," *Sales and Marketing Management*, August 1989, 46–49.

store level, salespeople may not have much influence on how a product is shelved in the store. This also reduces the control a sales force has over sales volume.

   c. More sophisticated buying decisions—greater awareness of costs, turnover, and profit margins coupled with fewer but more prominent customers leads to a changing sales role and a need for adaptive compensation packages.

2. *Corporate trends*—how the corporation plans to change over time can have important consequences for the sales role. Will the product line become more technical? Will growth come from existing customers and products or expansion along new horizons? These corporate projections must be complemented by a sales compensation package that accounts for desired changes in the sales role.

3. *The sales force*

   a. What are current and projected sales costs if the current compensation package is retained?

   b. Will sales jobs become more routine, with increases in the daily routine calls? Or will increased centralization of buying decisions mandate more individualized sales calls at the central office? The nature of this change will have an impact on the sales manager to salesperson ratio (e.g., routine calls can be handled by sales personnel while tailored sales calls at a central office may require more experienced sales personnel).[41]

   c. Earnings are often based on some measure of sales volume. Compensation plans are going to have to adopt better performance measures as more sales jobs are typified by centralized buying and fewer but larger customers. These trends make it more difficult to identify a salesperson's performance based on gross sales.

4. *Competition*—quite obviously an important factor in designing your sales compensation plan is the practices of your competition. Data on your competitor's type of compensation package, level of compensation, and degree of success should be obtained. Once your competitor has captured a marked or attracted important sales representatives away from your company, it is too late to begin analyzing where your compensation plan has gone awry.

5. *Compensation plan objective*—answers to the previous questions provide the foundation for a set of compensation objectives. For example:

   a. What is to be the trade-off between sales volume and customer service?

   b. What is the future role of building existing business versus opening new accounts?

   c. Do difficulties arise in recruiting new salespeople, or in retaining experienced sales representatives?

   d. To what extent should the compensation plan be designed to reduce sales costs as a percentage of sales?

Answers to these questions and others will play a vital role in designing a sales compensation plan.

---

[41]Kathleen Eisenhardt, "Agency- and Institutional-Theory Explanations: The Case of Retail Sales Compensation," *Academy of Management Journal*, 31(3), 1988, pp. 488–511.

Designing a Sales Compensation Plan—the Options

Basic sales compensation plans come in one of three forms: salary, commission, and a combination (salary and commission) plan. Each of these three strategies for paying sales personnel is designed to focus pay incentives on one or more sales objectives. Consequently, the type of plan appropriate for an organization depends on what it wants to pay for (i.e., the answers to questions in the last section). Exhibit 16.10 indicates the variations on plans and their relative popularity in industry.

In a salary plan the sales force is paid a fixed income not dependent on sales volume. There is an obvious rationale for this kind of strategy; if the major function of a salesperson is to provide customer service or spend disproportionate amounts of time "prospecting for new accounts under low success conditions," then a straight salary plan is appropriate.[42] Any temporary shifts in emphasis to increase sales volume typically are handled with a short-term special incentive plan.

Another situation where salary plans are appropriate involves sales jobs where individual sales performance is difficult to measure; either sales volume is based on group effort with individual contributions difficult to separate, or sales volume in traditional quantified terms is a completely inappropriate index of individual sales effort. An example of a job fitting this latter description would be a position description for a field engineer with an industrial equipment manufacturer. Duties of this job would include:[43]

- Developing and executing sales and product training programs for distributor's sales forces.
- Doing missionary work with selected manufacturers and major oil companies to encourage them to recommend his products to their dealers and mention them in their service and installation manuals.
- Participating in national and local trade shows; conducting occasional training programs for trade groups and associations.

EXHIBIT 16.10
Popularity of Different Sales Compensaiton Plans

Method	All Industries		
	1986 (Percent)	*1984 (Percent)*	*1983 (Percent)*
Straight salary	4.6	17.1	20.4
Draw against commission	3.5	6.8	5.4
Salary + commission	46	29.0	30.9
Salary plus other forms of incentives	46	47	43

Source: Executive Compensation Service, Inc.: *Sales Personnel Report,* Fort Lee: a subsidiary of the Wyatt Company, 1985/1986, 30th edition. 1986 data are based on Lesley Barnes, "Finding the Best Sales Compensation Plan," *Sales and Marketing Management,* August 1986, pp. 46–49.

---

[42]Ibid.

[43]John P. Steinbrink, "How to Pay Your Sales Force," *Harvard Business Review* 56 (July–August 1978), p. 12.

EXHIBIT 16.11
Advantages and Disadvantages of Three Basic Sales Compensation Plans

Straight Salary		Commission		Combination (commission and salary)	
Advantages	*Disadvantages*	*Advantages*	*Disadvantages*	*Advantages*	*Disadvantages*
Assures regular income.	Little financial incentive to increase effort.	Pay tied directly to performance.	High variance in income between salesmen may occur, and income over time (boom versus recession).	Offers benefits of both salary and commission plans. Greater security due to stable base income.	Complex or difficult to communicate.
Develops high degree of company loyalty.	Favors least productive sales personnel.	Easy to communicate and compute.	Generates low loyalty to company.	Allows greater latitude of motivation possibilities	
Simplifies reassignment of salesmen or territories.	Leads to overemphasis on sales or easiest items to sell.		Emphasis on volume sales rather than profits.		
Ensures performance of nonselling activities.	Increases potential of sales compression between veteran and new recruit.		May lead to neglect of nonselling activities.	Compensates salesmen for all selling activities.	
Facilitates administration.					Sometimes costly to administer.
Provides relatively fixed sales costs.	Typically higher direct selling costs than other plans.	Unit sales costs are proportional to net sales.	Problems arise in changing territories or reassigning salespersons.		

- Suggesting ideas for new products and promotional programs; recommending changes or improvements in existing products.

If you can visualize the anger of someone performing this job and being paid on a commission, you can understand why a salary plan is most appropriate for this type of position.

At the opposite extreme in terms of objectives is a sales compensation plan based on straight commission. Salary based on volume of sales exclusively may be appropriate (1) where the market possibilities are broad and sales boundaries vague, yielding high administrative costs for other types of compensation; (2) where company objectives are strongly geared to motivating sales volume through incentives; or (3) where cost accounting procedures stress the importance of strict controls over sales cost to sales volume ratios.

The final type of plan is a potpourri combination of salary and commission payment schemes. Recognize that most sales jobs do not fit the ideal specifications for either salary or commission payment.[44] In fact, they combine features of both types of jobs in such a way that a straight salary floor permits a salesperson to perform functions with no immediate sales-volume payoff (e.g., customer service), while a commission for sales-volume yields the necessary sales incentive. Exhibit 16.11 outlines some of the advantages and disadvantages of the three basic plans. Consider, as a strategy for selecting a sales compensation plan, the following scenario. First, design of the sales plan must be consistent, indeed must enhance, the strategic plan of the organization.[45] Allocation of sales duties should reinforce this organizational thrust. Second, there should be an evaluation of how important the salesperson's role actually is in a particular product/service line. Some products, because of a brand name prominence, literally "sell themselves." When this isn't the case, and the sales effort may play a crucial role, incentive components of

EXHIBIT 16.12
Designing a Sales Compensation Package

		Importance of "Sales" Ability in Closing Sale	
		High	*Low*
Probability that job has highly technical dimension requiring skills not readily available in population.	*High*	High starting salary to attract, large incentive to motivate.	High salary to attract, no incentive necessary.
	Low	Lower starting salary, but large incentive.	Salary only, and not at high level.

---

[44]Ibid.

[45]Donald Nemorov, "Managing the Sales Compensation Program: Integrating Factors for Success," in *New Perspectives on Compensation*, David Balkin and Louis Gomez-Mejia, eds. (Englewood Cliffs, N.J.: Prentice-Hall, 1987), pp. 258–68.

pay become increasingly important.[46] Third, an assessment should be made of the skill level required for a particular line of sales. Consider a product that has highly technical components and requires a sales presentation highly steeped in technical detail. The supply of qualified sales personnel in such a situation is likely to be much smaller than, for example, the number of individuals capable of selling shoes in a local mall. The appropriate compensation package suited to this constellation of scarce skills would be more likely to emphasize a large initial salary component to attract the necessary sales talent.[47] The interaction of these latter two factors would yield compensation strategies such as those shown in Exhibit 16.12.

EMPLOYEES IN U.S. FOREIGN SUBSIDIARIES

The rapid movement of U.S. corporations into foreign markets over the past 20 years has compounded a serious compensation problem that has probably existed for centuries. The nature of this compensation problem is best hinted at in a somewhat apocryphal story told by Teague:[48]

> Based on excavations at Ur it was determined that at least one foreign subsidiary was located there by the Dilmun Empire some 5,000 to 6,000 years ago. The problems of compensating such employees in a foreign country are suggested by the following fictitious exchange initiated by the employees: "The increase in temple taxes and barbarian incursions on the border has raised the cost of living here by 20 percent. Please adjust my stipend accordingly." And the reply may well have gone: "Thanks for the confirmation of border warfare. Rumors of war here have depreciated Urian currency by 30 percent. This rate of exchange gives you a 10 percent margin neither of us foresaw. Therefore, your allowance is hereby cut by 10 percent."

The problems in compensating foreign service personnel falls into two categories. First, it is very expensive to send a U.S. executive overseas, raising costs to 3 to 4 times base salary of the employee targeted for relocation.[49] Second, in part to hold costs down, multinational organizations hire three distinct employee groups: U.S. Expatriates (USEs), Local Country Nationals (LCNs), and Third Country Nationals (TCNs). Problems arise in preserving equity among these three groups. U.S. expatriates are American citizens working for a U.S. subsidiary in a foreign country. Equity for USEs becomes an issue both in "keeping the expatriates whole" relative to salary of their American-based counterparts and also in providing an incentive wage for accepting employment in an unfamiliar, and perhaps less comfortable, environment. Local country nationals present similar challenges in maintaining equity. As citizens of the country in which the U.S. foreign subsidiary is located, LCNs' compensation could be tied to either local wage rates or to

[46]Stephan Motowidlo, "Predicting Sales Turnover from Pay Satisfaction and Expectation," *Journal of Applied Psychology 68*, no. 3 (1983), pp. 484–89.

[47]Schultz, "Compensating the Sales Professional."

[48]Burton W. Teague, *Compensating Key Personnel Overseas* (New York: The Conference Board, 1972), p. 2.

[49]*Wall Street Journal*, "It's Expensive to Station an Executive Overseas," October 10, 1987, p.1.

the rates of USEs performing the same job. Either practice brings up equity problems that will be discussed shortly.

Finally, third country nationals are employees of a U.S. foreign subsidiary who maintain citizenship in a country other than the United States or the country housing the U.S. subsidiary (e.g., an Italian working for a U.S. subsidiary located in Germany). For TCNs three different standards could be used to set wages: comparative wages in the United States, the local country, or the country of citizenship. As noted in the following discussion, each standard presents unique equity problems.

Expatriate Compensation

Maintaining equity for expatriates while serving in a foreign country typically translates into a three-component compensation package.[50]

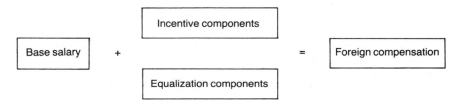

Base salary of expatriates is a function of job worth. Job worth, in turn, is typically determined by using the same job evaluation plan that is applied to domestic employees. Use of the same job evaluation plan for both domestic and foreign employees assumes that job responsibilities are roughly comparable in the two settings and, consequently, that the same compensable factors are appropriate. In many cases this assumption is correct. Granted there may be substantial environmental differences between two (otherwise) identical jobs in different countries, but the incentive and equalization pay components are designed to compensate for these differences. Exhibit 16.13 shows the percentage of firms offering each of four foreign service pay components.

EXHIBIT 16.13
Popularity of Four Foreign Service Pay Components

Component	*1972* (N = 134 firms)	*1982* (N = 123 firms)
Foreign service premium	89%	74%
Cost-of-living allowance	96	97
Tax equalization allowance	90	98
Housing plan	86	94

Source: Burton Teague, *Compensating Foreign Service Personnel* (New York: The Conference Board, 1982), no. 818.

---

[50]International Compensation, *Expatriate Compensation: An Overview* (Boston: International Compensation, 1978), pp. 2–3.

Equalization is one form of equity, in this case designed to "keep the worker whole" (i.e., maintain real income or purchasing power of base pay). This equalization typically comes in the form of four types of allowances:

1. *Taxation component.* Income earned in foreign countries has two potential sources of income tax liability. With few exceptions (Saudia Arabia is one) foreign income tax liabilities are incurred on foreign-earned income. In contrast, most home countries do not impose tax liabilities on foreign-earned income. The major exception, of course, is the United States. To counter this double tax liability most major firms— say the Fortune 150—use some form of taxation adjustment. The most common of these tax equalization plans are designed to have employees pay no more and no less in U.S. and foreign taxes than they would have paid had they remained in the United States. As a result, whether the individual works in a high or low tax country is a neutral factor. Hence, employees do not base the decision to accept foreign assignments on such factors as foreign income tax rates or foreign cost-of-living variances.

   Smaller firms are more likely to let employees fend for themselves. If foreign tax rates are high and cannot be translated into foreign tax credits, such companies may make up the difference with incremental salary dollars. Small firms are likely to negotiate the terms of an overseas assignment with individual employees. Larger firms are more likely to proceduralize overseas conditions of employment.

   Under the Tax Reform Act of 1986 USEs have $70,000 of foreign income excluded from U.S. tax. This tends to increase employer tax reimbursement costs for highly compensated expatriates located in relatively low tax foreign countries. This occurs because greater income is subject to U.S. tax.

2. *Housing allowances.* Despite a wide variety of formulas, housing allowances are designed to compensate the expatriate for the difference between U.S. housing costs and comparable foreign housing. In some instances the multinational company will provide housing for the expatriate cadre, thereby eliminating the need for a housing allowance. Generally an international employee is expected to contribute 10 to 20 percent of base salary toward housing. The excess is paid by the company.[51]

3. *Education and language training allowance.* Many organizations pay for language training of expatriates and their families. They also attempt to ensure educational training for children comparable to U.S. standards. If public schools do not meet these standards the company will typically provide an allowance for private school training.

4. *Cost-of-living allowance (COLA).* As in the illustration at the beginning of this section, COLA adjustments prove to be the major source of complaints, and hence problems, in expatriate compensation. High quality and readily available goods in the United States may be unavailable in a foreign subsidiary. Problems of this nature make it difficult to compensate expatriates for the differences in "cost of living." Despite the

---

[51]Arvind Phatak, Rajan Chandran, and Richard Ajayi, "International Executive Compensation," in *New Perspectives in Compensation,* David Balkin and Luis Gomez-Mejia, eds. (Englewood Cliffs, N.J.: Prentice-Hall, 1987).

inherent difficulties of comparing apples and oranges, most companies use some index of living costs abroad (e.g., State Department "Indexes of Living Costs Abroad").

The final component of expatriate compensation is an incentive for accepting a foreign assignment that requires the expatriate to (1) work with less supervision than an American counterpart; (2) live and work in strange and, in some cases, uncongenial surroundings; and (3) represent the U.S. employer in the host country.[52] Using what is called a *foreign service premium,* companies either pay a flat percentage (typically 15 percent) of base pay as an incentive, or vary the amount as a function of the perceived hardships in the foreign subsidiary. In the latter case an assignment in Brussels would yield little or no foreign service premium. In contrast, Khartoum, Sudan warrants the maximum State Department hardship rating, worth a 25 percent premium. A description of conditions in Khartoum explains the nature of this hardship:

"Many phones in the capital city of Khartoum haven't rung for years. On the street outside, one of Khartoum's main arteries, potholes are big enough to swallow pedestrians. Power lines droop on broken sidewalks, a hazard when there is power, which there often isn't. During a typical week this month electricians were on strike, as were bank workers, bus drivers, pilots, postal workers, doctors, pharmacists, engineers, and university staff"[53]

Local and Third Country Nationals

If anything, developing a compensation package for LCNs and TCNs that is equitable is an even greater challenge than it is for U.S. expatriates. The problem focuses on determining what the standard for equity should be. As an illustration consider the case where three managers—one a USE, another a TCN, and the third an LCN—all perform essentially the same work for a U.S. foreign subsidiary. If the job performed is used as the basis for judging equitable pay, arguably all three employees should receive the same pay, given essentially similar work. If, however, use is made of an equity standard, such as keeping the worker whole, it is likely that income of the three managers will vary considerably as a function of home country economic conditions and past individual salaries.

Most studies show that companies typically resolve this dilemma in favor of the home country balance-sheet approach (i.e., keeping the worker whole).[54] Between 75 to 80 percent of multinational organizations design compensation packages for foreign-service personnel so that the balance sheet neither favors nor penalizes the employee for employment in the firm.[55] As might be expected, then, these companies who favor keeping the worker whole make more extensive use of allowances designed to equalize the real

---

[52]Burton Teague, *Compensating Foreign Service Personnel* (New York: The Conference Board, 1982), report no. 818.

[53]*Wall Street Journal,* "How Khartoum Won No. 1 Ranking as a Hardship Post," April 26, 1989, p. 1.

[54]Teague, *Compensation Key Personnel Overseas;* M.R. Foote, "Controlling the Cost of International Compensation," *Harvard Business Review* 55 (November-December 1977), p. 123; and Murphy and Salter, "Should CEO Pay Be Linked to Results?"

[55]Teague, *Compensating Key Personnel Overseas.*

income effects of employment as foreign-service personnel (e.g., cost-of-living, tax equalization, and housing allowances).

In contrast, companies that prefer an "equal pay for equal work" equity eliminate pay differences. Not surprisingly, these companies tend less frequently to adopt the allowances that are so prevalent under a balance-sheet policy.[56]

Historically, the balance-sheet approach to compensation has been less costly. Salaries were pegged to home country standards rather than to U.S. standards (thus yielding a lower cost as long as salary levels in the United States were among the highest in the world). These cost savings could yield some rather predictable problems, however. If salary differences among these foreign-service personnel became known, complaints about unequal pay for equal work emerged. To minimize this problem, organizations adopted one of two strategies. Either they attempted to make compensation practices secret, or they structured the USE job (typically the source of any large salary differential) as a relatively short-term consulting assignment charged with training LCNs and TCNs and then moving to another assignment before job responsibilities equalized. The USE salary advantage was less noticeable and, perhaps, more justifiable.[57]

As the trend toward internationalization of business spreads in the 1990s, it would be expected that the compensation of foreign-service personnel will assume a greater importance in strategy sessions. The apparent "fire-fighting" and nonsystematic practices currently in vogue are particularly dismaying. Coherent policies and systematic practices must evolve as foreign operations mature and assume greater shares of corporate profits.

SUMMARY

Note that these special groups are special in a second sense, beyond the fact that their compensation has some unique design features. These groups also are special because they are strategically important for organizational success. It is unlikely that such care and attention to system design would arise if the stakes were not so important. As a consequence, the compensation of special groups provides an early forecast of system-wide future compensation changes. Incentive systems, stock ownership plans, and legal insurance, to name but a few compensation components, all originated with one or another special groups. When the special advantages of these "tools" become apparent, organizations begin to assess their value for other employee groups. The end result is more effective compensation systems.

REVIEW QUESTIONS

1. Why is external equity particularly important in the compensation of special groups?
2. Why is a maturity curve approach uniquely appropriate for compensation of scientists and engineers?

---

[56]Ibid.

[57]*Wall Street Journal,* "When in Rome," May 3, 1988, p. 1.

3. What internal equity issues are important in the compensation of supervisors?
4. Assume you want to set up a sales compensation plan for encyclopedia salesmen (door-to-door). What issues would be important, and why?
5. Why is equity such an important concept in the compensation of foreign service personnel?

Compensation Application
Remtol Corporation: The Reluctant Foreman

Remtol Corporation is the world's largest privately owned construction company. Founded in 1927 by James Remington, Remtol had worldwide revenues last year of $3.5 billion. About 55 percent of this revenue was earned in foreign markets. The largest of these foreign markets is currently Saudi Arabia, where oil revenues finance the construction of an entire modern city designed to support 3 million inhabitants. The budget for Remtol's portion of this project is $8.7 billion over a 15-year-period.

Remtol employs 87,000 people worldwide. The breakdown is roughly:

Occupational Group	Employment
Labor	44,000
Clerical	8,800
Semiskilled	1,750
Skilled	2,250
Service (guards, etc.)	1,000
Sales	1,200
Technical	9,000
Professional	13,000
Managerial	6,000

Remtol Corporation has an opening for a new construction foreman to help renovate a Ford Motor Plant in Wixom, Michigan. Because of his past performance as a laborer, Bill Cook has been recommended for the job by the Human Resources Department. Andy White, the general superintendent on the project, has the pleasure of telling Bill about the promotion. Bill is working outside Andy's office right now.

Role for Andy White, General Superintendent

Bill Cook has been with Remtol Corporation for six years as a construction laborer. During that time, he has only missed 11 days of work for illness. Your records show he is a hard worker, and you have heard from a number of sources that Bill is a natural leader. The other laborers respect him and his opinions.

You have been asked by the Human Resources Department to inform Bill that he has been chosen as the new laborer foreman in charge of 25 construction laborers. Along with the promotion comes a raise from $10/hour to $12/hour for all hours worked. The opportunity is an excellent one and you are looking forward to telling Bill the good news.

Role for Bill Cook, Construction Laborer

Andy White, General Superintendent of the Wixom Project, has asked you to come into his office. You are a bit leery of going in. After all, no one wants to be caught snuggling up to management. You don't need a razzing from the other guys or from the construction local in Pontiac.

You hope they do not think anything is wrong with your work. You like the hard physical effort; it keeps you in shape. You also like the interactions with the other laborers. They are a good bunch of guys and they seem to respect you. Their friendship and trust is important to you. Almost as important, though, the job really pays. Overtime during the past three years has always been good. That double-time pay for an average of 500 hours a year sure has helped. Things look equally good in the business for the next year. You wonder what the problem is.

Questions

The following questions should be addressed in the meeting between Bill and Andy.

1. Why is Bill Cook reluctant to take the foreman position?
2. What is the wage differential for Bill between the position of laborer and foreman, assuming a 2,000 hour normal work year and continued overtime equaling past averages?
3. What would you recommend as an appropriate differential? What steps should you take to derive that figure?

Compensation Application
Remtol Corporation: Compensating Engineers

You have obtained the following summary information from market competitors for engineers:

N	Years since Last Degree	Performance Level	Monthly Salary
800	2	Bottom 10 percent	$1,640
		Average (50th percentile)	1,770
		Top 10 percent	2,000
325	4	Bottom 10 percent	1,780
		Average	1,960
		Top 10 percent	2,270
525	8	Bottom 10 percent	2,020
		Average	2,300
		Top 10 percent	2,710
460	12	Bottom 10 percent	2,220
		Average	2,580
		Top 10 percent	3,130
280	20	Bottom 10 percent	2,440
		Average	2,960
		Top 10 percent	3,650
240	28	Bottom 10 percent	2,510
		Average	3,130
		Top 10 percent	3,880
200	36	Bottom 10 percent	2,510
		Average	3,130
		Top 10 percent	3,880

Tasks

1. Plot the maturity curves for the three performance levels expressing the relationship between monthly salary and years since last degree.
2. What should be the approximate salary for the 10 Remtol engineers whose pertinent employment data is outlined in Exhibits 1 and 2?
3. What, if any, changes would you recommend in data collection and construction of future maturity curves? Why?

EXHIBIT 1
Employment Data on Ten Engineers

Employee Code Number	Years since Last Degree	Performance Rating
E 7856	6	9
E 4216	2	7
E 13307	8	10
E 5912	12	4
E 6081	15	10
E 2222	4	10
E 1346	28	4
E 5021	12	2
E 9002	16	7
E 8146	30	9

EXHIBIT 2
Distribution of Engineers' Performance Ratings

Overall Evaluation	Position in Performance Distribution
9–10	Top 10 percent
8	Top 25 percent
7	Median
5–6	Top 75 percent
0–4	Bottom 10 percent

Compensation Application
Remtol Corporation: Costing Out a Compensation Package for Expatriates

Remtol has just successfully bid on construction of a hydroelectric power plant in Zimbabwe, Africa. Eventually the project will employ 1,300 expats (expatriates) and 4,000 local nationals. Normally, you would determine expat salaries by surveying other multinational corporations in the local area. Zimbabwe is so underdeveloped, though, that you represent the first foreign corporation of any substance to undertake a major project. To determine what pay is necessary to attract workers to Zimbabwe, you have decided to use Roger Pewter as a test case for costing. Roger is married and has two children in their early teens. Since the project will require four years to complete, and Roger's contract would have to be a two-year minimum, it is likely that he will want to take his family.

Identify the basic components that you think would have to be included in Roger's compensation package. Now determine specific elements for each basic category. Your choices should be guided by the basic philosophy of "keeping the worker whole." A worker should not be punished either financially or psychically for accepting a foreign subsidiary position.

How would you go about determining if the package is equitable?

17 Union Role In Wage and Salary Administration

Many experts believe that unions are facing their most critical challenge of the last 50 years.[1] Between 1954 and 1987 union membership fell 50 percent.[2] Today only 17 percent of the labor force is unionized.[3] Part of the explanation for this decline is an increasingly hard stance by management. Domestic and international competition are making it increasingly difficult for unions to extract wage concessions from employers.

[1]Thomas A. Kochan, Harry C. Katz, and Robert B. McKersie, *The Transformation of American Industrial Relations* (New York: Basic Books, 1986), pp. 221–23.

[2]Kirkland Ropp, "State of the Unions," *Personnel Administrator* 32(7) (1987), pp. 36–41.

[3]Daniel Quinn Mills, *Labor Management Relations* (New York: McGraw-Hill, 1989).

Indeed, the 1980s have been characterized by an unprecedented number of wage concessions made by unions to preserve employment for their membership. It shouldn't be surprising, then, that a recent survey shows a continued deterioration for unions in the Labor-Management power relationship. Exhibit 17.1 illustrates this fact.

The exhibit indicates that unions and management alike believe that management currently dominates the power relationship between the two groups, and this advantage is only expected to get stronger if estimates of continued membership decline are borne out. Despite these pessimistic statistics, though, it would be a mistake to conclude that the impact of unions on wage and salary administration is minor. Even in a nonunion firm, the actions taken by wage and salary administrators are influenced by external union activity. This chapter outlines factors affecting wages in unionized firms and then illustrates the impact of unions in wage determination. Four specific areas of impact are discussed: (1) impact on general wage and benefit levels, (2) impact on the structure of

EXHIBIT 17.1
Labor-Management Power 1983–1984

| | Percentage yes | | | |
| | Union | | Management | |
Question	1983	1984	1983	1984
1. Does management have the upper hand in negotiations?	82	84	79	83
2. Will management gain more negotiating power in the future?	74	86	89	91
3. Can management force their terms on unions?	84	86	88	90
4. Is there any connection between strikes and layoffs?	63	68	23	26
5. Would union members make wage concessions rather than be laid off?	86	87	83	89
6. In the last three years, has union pressure adversely affected the company?	32	39	88	92
7. Are unions necessary for equitable labor representation?	53	41	3	3
8. Is the current administration against organized labor?	97	97	68	97

| | | Union Response | | | Mgmt Response | |
	Decline	1983	1984	Decline	1983	1984
9. What percentage decline in union membership do you expect in the next 5 years?	20	38%	20%	20	4%	2%
	40	33%	39%	40	26%	28%
	60	19%	31%	60	48%	51%
	80	7%	5%	80	19%	3%
	100	3%	2%	100	3%	3%

Source: R. Wayne Mondy and Shane Preameaux, "The Labor Management Power Relationship Revisited," *Personnel Administrator*, May 1985, pp. 51–54.

wages, (3) spillover to nonunion firms, and (4) impact on wage and salary policies and practices in unionized firms. The final discussion focuses on union response to the changing economic environment of the 1980s and the alternative compensation systems which have evolved in response to these changes.

FACTORS AFFECTING WAGES IN UNIONIZED FIRMS

Some interesting economic realities have made compensation decision making a crucial factor in organizational success for the 1980s. First, it is increasingly apparent that international competition has a significant impact on the profitability of American enterprises. Our ability to compete, in both domestic and foreign markets, continues to decline.[4] As our product prices become noncompetitive in the international market, the result, as any executive in the auto industry during the 1980s can attest, can be catastrophic.

The United States is also experiencing significant changes in the composition of industries. Less manufacturing and more service jobs are being created. Most of these jobs are being created in small firms. In fact, between 1980–1986, 63 percent of all new positions were generated in small firms.[5] Both these small firms fighting to survive and larger firms striving to combat foreign competition seek ways to control labor costs. To understand the direction these efforts take in unionized settings, it would help to first understand the factors affecting wage determination in unionized organizations. These factors include: 1) productivity, 2) changes in the cost of living, 3) ability of an employer to pay, and 4) comparability among wage rates (equity).[6] Not surprisingly, all four of these issues have received considerable attention lately, and the outcome of this attention may well be dramatic changes in compensation of unionized employees.

Productivity

Although the United States has the highest per worker productivity of any country in the world, yearly increases in productivity have lagged far behind most other industrial countries over the past decade. While this decline is undoubtedly due to a host of factors, including slow modernization rates in key manufacturing sectors, a portion of the blame for lower productivity continues to be directed at unions. The sources of these complaints are twofold. First, union contracts establish staffing practices or other work rules that artificially reduce output. Examples of such practices include minimum crew size requirements and provisions limiting subcontracting. Second, union initiated strikes obviously restrict output during the term of the strike.

Alternatively, some experts suggest that output is enhanced by unions. This argument suggests that unions negotiate higher wages and provide an outlet to vent grievances

---

[4]Bureau of National Affairs, *Changing Pay Practices: New Developments in Employee Compensation,* BNA, Washington, D.C., 1988.

[5]Ibid.

[6]Mills, *Labor Management Relations.*

against management. By improving satisfaction and lowering turnover, the net productivity impact of unions is argued to be positive.[7]

No matter the outcome of these debates. Management is acting as if unions result in lower productivity. The result has been an increasingly tougher stand in negotiations and more agreements to tie wage increases to productivity increases. A whole host of compensation changes have resulted, including incentive systems, profit-sharing plans, and merit-based pay plans. The final section of this chapter will discuss the nature of these changes and the role of unions in this process.

Cost of Living

Unions made a strong drive for wage escalator clauses during the 1970s. Cost of living adjustments (COLAs) are designed to increase wages automatically during the life of the contract as a function of changes in the consumer price index. By 1978 COLA clauses had made broad inroads on the labor management scene, despite evidence that such contract clauses fail to keep workers "whole" with respect to inflation.[8] More recently, though, a declining interest in COLAs can be traced to deceleration of the Consumer Price Index during the mid and late 1980s. Historically, unions have clamored for COLAs during periods of high inflation and deemphasized them when inflation rates were more tolerable. Now that the inflation rate has moderated in the past several years, fewer unions consider COLA clauses a vital element of a total package. The number of workers covered by COLA clauses in negotiated contracts declined from 59 percent in 1980 to 49 percent in 1985.[9] This decrease continues into the late 1980s, with COLA clauses included for 40 percent of all workers with contracts negotiated in the first nine months of 1988.[10]

Despite the lessened current interest, escalator clauses deserve discussion, if only in anticipation of future bouts with inflation and renewed interest in this contractual safeguard. All COLAs have two common elements: some measure of change in living costs, and a formula to adjust wages as a function of these changes in living costs. The most common measure of change in living costs is the consumer price index (CPI), prepared by the Bureau of Labor Statistics. Recall from Chapter 15 that the CPI provides an estimate of the change in cost of a market basket of goods (as many as 4,000 individual items may be priced every month to determine changes in the cost patterns). The cost of this market basket is compared against a base period cost to determine change.

The second element of an escalator clause is the formula for adjusting wages as the

---

[7]Richard Freeman, "Individual Mobility and Union Voice in the Labor Market," *American Economic Review* 66 (May 1976), pp. 361–68.

[8]Victor J. Sheifer, "Collective Bargaining and the CPI: Escalation v. Catch-up," *Proceedings of the 31st Annual Meeting, Industrial Relations Research Association Series*, 1978, pp. 257–63.

[9]Richard Henderson, "Contract Concessions: Is the Past Prologue?" *Compensation and Benefits Review* 18(5) (1986), pp. 17–30.

[10]U.S. Department of Labor, "Current Wage Developments," Bureau of Labor Statistics, 40(11), 1988.

CPI changes. The most common formula is to adjust wages 1 cent for each .3 percent rise in the consumer price index.[11]

Ability to Pay and Wage Comparability within Industries

The third factor affecting wage levels in unionized organizations is an employer's ability to pay. In profitable years unions reason that part of the profits should accrue to the work force responsible for much of the organization's success. This argument plays a role in the eventual determination of bargained wage levels. What then follows is well known by the American consumer. Product prices are raised, and labor cost increases are cited as a major reason. In the past this has usually worked. Consumers continued to purchase what remained a competitively priced product. In large part this phenomenon can be explained by introducing the fourth factor affecting wage levels: comparability among wage rates. As one group of workers received wage increases, product competitors acceded to similar demands of their work force. The result was labor cost and product price increases that rose relatively uniformly. As long as unions were able to control wage increase within an industry (usually by organizing the whole industry) no employer suffered a disproportionate wage increase or the resulting noncompetitive product price! Employers were content to go along with this situation as long as they received a reasonable return on investment and their market share remained unaffected. What they failed to realize, and what must be considered in future wage negotiations, is the rapid internationalization of product markets. A classic example is the auto industry. Japanese autoworkers receive compensation worth approximately one half their American counterparts. As long as Japan assumed a small role in the auto market, American auto manufacturers were concerned about wages relative to other domestic manufacturers. As Japan increased its market share due to competitive price/quality differentials, however, the comparative wage differential loomed larger and larger. This differential played a large role in United Auto Worker concessions to both Ford and General Motors in 1982.

Is the auto industry unique, or are wage concessions a new, and potentially permanent, feature of the industrial relations scene? One view argues that wage concessions really are not an important element of the drive for increased competitiveness.[12] During the Depression (1929–1933) average hourly earnings fell 22 percent. In contrast, the height of the "wage concession" period was marked by a 22 percent rise in average hourly earnings (1981–1986).[13] A second view argues that wage concessions are real and have been a fixture of the industrial relations scene at different times during the entire twentieth century.[14] In 1908 the glass bottle blowers accepted a 20 percent wage cut in the hopes of fighting automation. During the 1930s concessions were a regular feature in the

---

[11]Sheifer, "Collective Bargaining and the CPI: Escalation v. Catch-up."

[12]John Dunlop, "Have the 1980's Changed U.S. Industrial Relations," *Monthly Labor Review*, 1988(5), pp. 29–34.

[13]Ibid.

[14]Richard Freeman and James Medoff, *What Do Unions Do?* (N.Y.: Basic Books, 1984.)

construction, printing, and shoe industries. Concessions were also made in the apparel and textile industries during the 1950s. In the 1980s, major contract concessions have occurred in eight industries: air transport, food stores, shoe manufacturing, primary metals, metal cans, transportation equipment, textiles, and trucking.[15] While some of these concessions have followed the traditional form of wage decreases or wage freezes (69 percent of all contract agreements negotiated in 1985 either had a freeze or wage decrease),[16] other concession strategies exist. Because these concession strategies are likely to be a continuing feature of labor-management negotiations, we will discuss each briefly.

A second type of concession comes in the form of lump sum awards. Although not traditionally cast as a concession, lump sum awards do fit this category. Workers receive a lump sum of money at a specified time. The dollar amount is not factored into the base salary of employees. For example, Revlon and the UAW began working under a contract in September of 1988 that awarded workers a lump sum equal to 100 hours of pay rather than a 5 percent increase in base salary. This saves companies money in two ways. Consider a worker with an initial salary of $10,000 dollars. A 5 percent increase would raise base wages to $10,500. Employee benefits tied to base wages (e.g., life insurance is typically provided as some percentage of base wages) would rise correspondingly. During the next year of the contract any percent increase is applied to the new base of $10,500. Contrast this with a lump sum award equal to 5 percent. Employees still receive $500, but it is given as a separate check and not added to base wages. Benefit costs are not affected and any future percentage raises are applied to a base of $10,000 and not $10,500. The difference may be small for one worker during one year, but over many workers and years the savings can be substantial. In the first nine months of 1988, 26 percent of all contracts provided for lump sum payouts.[17]

The third form of concession consists of a back-loaded wage clause. Approximately 33 percent of all workers covered by contracts negotiated in 1985 had "back-loaded" clauses included. These contracts specify low increases during the early years of the contract and larger increases at the back end. Given the time value of money (a fixed dollar amount is worth more now than later), this reduces the overall cost of the wage packages for employers.

A final type of concession centers on reductions in benefit costs. Reductions in paid holidays and vacations (e.g., General Motors Stamping plant workers in Fairfield, Ohio agreed to a 50 percent cut in paid vacations during the last contract negotiation) are exchanged for greater job security and other forms of management trade-offs. Pension and health care costs also have been the target of concession talks. For example, the International Brotherhood of Electrical workers were asked to begin contributing to their health care costs in the most recent contract negotiation with Potomac Electric and Power

---

[15]Robert Gay, "Union Contract Concessions and Their Implications for Union Wage Determination," working paper no. 38, Division of Research and Statistics, Board of Governors of the Federal Reserve System, 1984.

[16]Henderson, "Contract Concessions: Is the Past Prologue?"

[17]U.S. Department of Labor, "Current Wage Developments."

EXHIBIT 17.2
Distribution of Workers By First Year Wage Adjustments In
Major Private Sector Collective Bargaining Settlements

Wage adjustment (% change)	1980	1983	1988[1]
Decreases	0[2]	15	2
No wage change	0	22	12
Increases			
0–4 %	3	14	59
4% and over	97	49	27

[1]first 9 month's data only
[2]percentage of union workers receiving that decrease or increase
Source: Selected Issues from "Current Wage Developments," U.S. Department of Labor, Bureau of Labor Statistics, 1982–1988.

Company.[18] Workers with families now pay $30 per month for coverage, while their single counterparts contribute $10 per month.[19]

The combined impact of these concessions has weakened the relative bargaining power of unions. For example, the impact on wage adjustments has been predictable, as evidenced in Exhibit 17.2.

Notice union wage settlements declined markedly in the early 1980s. In 1983, for example, a large number of contracts were negotiated with wage reductions. Current wage increases have fewer wage reductions, but are still marked by low overall levels of increases. In part, this is obviously due to the declining inflation rate over this period.

THE IMPACT OF UNIONS IN WAGE DETERMINATION

Union Impact on Wage and Benefit Levels

Does the presence of a union in an organization raise the level of wages and benefits of workers above what they would be if the company was not unionized? The commonly held belief among workers is that unions do have a wage impact. Over 80% of the respondents to a quality of employment survey conducted by the Survey Research Center of the University of Michigan believed that unions improved the wages of workers.[20] Efforts to determine if this perception is accurate have been a source of research focus for at least 40 years.

Part of the reason for the continuing interest in this area is that the question of union impact on wages and benefits has been difficult to resolve. Efforts to determine union

---

[18]"A Sign of the Times: Unionized Employees to Pay Part of Their Health Care Costs," *CompFlash,* Dec. 1988, p. 3.

[19]Ibid.

[20]Thomas A. Kochan, "How American Workers View Labor Unions," *Monthly Labor Review,* April 1979, pp. 23–31.

impacts run into several measurement problems. The ideal situation would compare numerous organizations that were identical except for the presence or absence of a union.[21] Any wage differences among these organizations could then be attributed to unionization. Unfortunately, few such situations exist. One alternative strategy adopted has been to identify organizations within the same industry that differ in level of unionization. For example, consider Company A, which is unionized, and Company B, which is not. It is difficult to argue with assurance that wage differences between the two firms are attributable to the presence or absence of a union. First, the fact that the union has not organized the entire industry weakens its power base (e.g., strike efforts to shut down the entire industry could be thwarted by nonunion firms). Consequently, any union impact in this example might underestimate the role of unions in an industry where percentage of unionization is greater. A second problem in measuring union impact is apparent from this example. What if Company B grants concessions to employees as a strategy to avoid unionization? These concessions, indirectly attributable to the presence of a union, would lead to underestimation of union impact on wages.

A second strategy in estimating union impact on wages is to compare two different industries that differ dramatically in the level of unionization.[22] This strategy suffers because nonunionized industries (e.g., agriculture, service) are markedly different from unionized industries in the types of labor employed and their general availability. Such differences have a major impact on wages independent of the level of unionization, and make any statements about union impact difficult to substantiate.

Such difficulties make the now classic work of Gregg Lewis even more impressive.[23] In a review and analysis of 12 studies dealing with union impact on wages, Lewis made a number of insightful observations.[24]

1. The union impact on wages is dependent on the time period.
2. During recessionary periods, the presence of a union has a larger impact on wages. For example, during the 1932–1933 period, union presence may have meant more than 25 percent higher wages for union versus nonunion workers. As the depression receded, union impact reached a low: something less than 5 percent in the late 1940s.
3. Current union impact on wages is estimated somewhere between +10 and +15 percent.[25]

It appears that unions do make a positive difference in wage levels, and this difference is greatest during recessionary periods and least during inflationary periods.[26] Part of the

---

[21]Allan M. Carter and F. Ray Marshall, *Labor Economics* (Homewood, Ill.: Richard D. Irwin, 1982).

[22]Ibid.

[23]H. Gregg Lewis, *Unionism and Relative Wages in the United States* (Chicago: University of Chicago Press, 1963).

[24]Ibid.

[25]Orley Ashenfelter, "Union Relative Wage Effects: New Evidence and a Survey of Their Implications for Wage Inflation," in *Econometric Contributions to Public Policy,* ed. R. Stone and W. Peterson (New York: St. Martin's Press, 1979), pp. 82–113.

[26]Robert Flanagan, Robert Smith, and Ronald Ehrenberg, *Labor Economics and Labor Relations* (Glenview, Ill.: Scott Foresman, 1984).

explanation for this time-based phenomenon is related to union resistance to wage cuts during recessions and the relatively slow responses of unions to wage increases during inflationary periods (because of rigidities or lags introduced by the presence of multi-year labor contracts).

More recent studies support these findings.[27] In addition, research indicates that the presence of a union adds about 20–30 percent to employee benefits. Unions also have an impact on the difference between wages for selected groups. Wage differentials between workers who are different in terms of race, age, service, skill level, and education appear to be lower under collective bargaining.[28]

Corresponding to Lewis's work in the private sector is Lewin's summary of union wage impacts in the public sector.[29] In a summary of 13 public-sector union studies, Lewin concludes that the average wage effect of public-sector unions is approximately +5 percent. As Lewin notes, this wage differential is smaller than typically assumed, and certainly smaller than is estimated for the private sector. Of course, this 5 percent average masks some large variations in wage increases for different occupational groups in the public sector. The largest gains for public-sector employees are reported for fire-fighters, with some studies reporting as much as an 18 percent wage differential attributable to the presence of a union. At the other extreme, however, teachers' unions (primarily affiliates of the National Education Association and the American Federation of Teachers) have not fared as well, with reported impacts generally in the range of 1–4 percent.[30]

The Structure of Wage Packages and the Impact of Two-Tier Pay

The second compensation issue involves the structuring of wage packages. One dimension of this issue concerns the division between direct wages and employee benefits. There is evidence that union employees have employee benefit packages that are about 20–30 percent higher than nonunion employees. While unions have an impact on the relative size of the benefits package, particularly for pensions, employers have become increasingly more sophisticated in controlling total package costs.[31] Most organizations now

---

[27]John Pencavel, "A Reconsideration of the Effects of Unionism on Relative Wages and Employment in the United States: 1920–1980," *Journal of Labor Economics* 2 (1984), pp. 193–204; Harry C. Bentiam, "Union-Nonunion Wage Differential Revisited," *Journal of Labor Research* 8(4) (1987), p. 381; and Richard B. Freeman and James L. Medoff, "The Impact of Collective Bargaining: Illusion or Reality?" in *U.S. Industrial Relations, 1950–1980: A Critical Assessment*, eds. Jack Stieber, Robert B. McKersie, and D. Quinn Mills (Madison: Industrial Relations Research Association, 1981), pp. 47–98.

[28]Freeman, "The Impact of Collective Bargaining: Illusion or Reality?"

[29]David Lewin, "Public Sector Labor Relations: A Review Essay," in *Public Sector Labor Relations: An Analysis and Readings*, eds. David Lewin, Peter Feuille, and Thomas Kochan (Glen Ridge, N.J.: Thomas Horton and Daughters, 1977), pp. 116–44.

[30]For a discussion of the reasons for this smaller public-sector union impact see Lewin et al., *Public Sector Labor Relations: An Analysis and Readings*.

[31]Steven Allen and Robert Clark, "Unions, Pension Wealth, and Age-Compensation Profiles," *Industrial and Labor Relations Review* 39(4) (1986), pp. 502–17; and Augustin Kwasi Fosu, "Impact of Unionism on Pension Fringes," *Industrial Relations* 22, no. 3 (1983), pp. 419–25.

realize that cost control mechanisms must be established when a new benefit is first provided. It would be far better, for example, to negotiate a dollar contribution by the company. Then, as costs rose in subsequent years, the dollar amount either could be renegotiated or the union could determine if the benefit was sufficiently attractive to justify having employees bear the added cost.

A second dimension of the wage structure issue is a relatively new phenomenon. Along with the concession bargaining movement has come two-tier pay plans. Basically a phenomenon of the union sector, two-tier wage structures differentiate pay based upon hiring date. A contract is negotiated which specifies that employees hired after a specified date will receive lower wages than their higher seniority peers working on the same or similar jobs. Two-tier pay plans initially spread because unions viewed them as less painful than wage freezes and staff cuts among existing employees. The trade-off was to bargain away equivalent wage treatment for future employees! Remember, this is a radical departure from the most basic precepts of unionization. Unions evolved and continue to endure, in part, based on the belief that all members are equal. Two-tier plans are obviously at odds with this principle. Lower tier employees, those hired after the contract is ratified, receive wages 50–80 percent lower than employees in the higher tier.[32] The contract may specify that the wage differential may be permanent or the lower tier may be scheduled ultimately to catch up with the upper tier. Eventually the inequity from

---

EXHIBIT 17.3
Experiences with Two-Tier Systems*

Have two tiers	28%
No two tiers	72%
Reasons for not adopting two-tier system	
1. Labor unrest	14%
2. Morale	10%
3. Productivity	2.3%
4. Insufficient benefit from system	26%
5. Other	27%
Concessions granted by management to obtain two-tier system	
1. None	72%
2. Increased employee security	7%
3. Restricted subcontracting	2%
4. Bonus	4%
4. Reframe from shifting operations overseas	0%
5. Increased salary to incumbents	10%
6. Other	10%

*Based on a sample of 434 companies in 1986.
Source: Towers, Perrin, Forster and Crosby, "Survey of Company Experiences with Two Tier Wage Systems." Towers, Perrin, Forster & Crosby: Washington, D.C., 1986.

---

[32]Mollie Bowers and Roger Roderick, "Two-Tier Pay Systems: The Good, the Bad and the Debatable," *Personnel Administrator* 32(6) (1987), pp. 101–12.

receiving different pay for the same level of inputs may cause employee dissatisfaction.[33] Consider the Roman Emperor who implemented a two-tier system for his army in 217 A.D.[34] He was assassinated by his troops shortly thereafter. Although such expressions of dissatisfaction are unlikely today, Exhibit 17.3 indicates two-tier programs may yield a number of problems.

One other feature of these two-tier systems is interesting: There has been a trend towards coupling wage concessions with implementation of profit-sharing plans. Employers reason that profit-sharing plans permit better control over labor costs, with costs varying directly with the ability to pay: highly profitable years trigger higher payments to workers and poor years yield correspondingly smaller incentive costs.

Union Impact: The Spillover Effect

Although union wage settlements have declined in recent years, the impact of unions in general would be understated if only the statistics from Exhibit 17.2 were reported. Unions also have an indirect impact on wages, called the spillover effect, for nonunion employees. Specifically, employers seek to avoid unionization by offering workers the wages, benefits, and working conditions won in rival unionized firms. The nonunion management continues to enjoy the freedom from union "interference" in decision making, and the workers receive the "spillover" of rewards already obtained by their unionized counterparts. Several studies document the existence and importance of this phenomenon, providing further evidence of the continuing role played by unions in wage determination.[35]

Role of Unions in Wage and Salary Administration

Unions increase wage levels in unionized firms relative to nonunionized firms. This tells us little, however, about the specific compensation roles unions play in organizations. The structure of wage demands (i.e., the components of the total wage package that are emphasized most by unions) is largely dependent on union's evaluation of three factors:[36] (1) equity, (2) ability to pay, and (3) cost of living. The fourth factor mentioned earlier that affects wages—productivity—has traditionally been of greater concern to management than union.

On the equity issue, unions structure wage demands to ensure that workers within

[33]James Martin and Melanie Peterson, "Two-Tier Wage Structures: Implications for Equity Theory," *Academy of Management Journal* 30(2) (1987), pp. 297–315; and Mollie Bowers and Roger Roderick, "Two-Tier Pay Systems: The Good, the Bad and the Debatable," Personnel Administrator, June 1987, pp. 101–12.

[34]Wall Street Journal, "Two-Tier Wage Systems Falter as Companies Sense Worker's Resentment," June 16, 1987, p. 1.

[35]Loren Solnick, "The Effect of Blue Collar Unions on White Collar Wages and Fringe Benefits," *Industrial and Labor Relations Review* 38, no. 2 (1985), pp. 23–35; and Lawrence Kahn, "The Effect of Unions on the Earnings of Nonunion Workers," *Industrial and Labor Relations Review* 31, no. 1 (1978), pp. 205–16.

[36]John A. Fossum, *Labor Relations: Development, Structure, Process* (Plano, Tex.: Business Publications, 1982).

an organization are equitably treated relative to each other, and externally relative to the treatment of similar workers in other firms. As a consequence wage and/or benefits changes obtained by nonunion employees in a firm are monitored by the union and form part of the basis for contract demands. Similarly, unions seek to obtain wage packages that can be favorably compared to the settlements received in other industries. For example, the rubber workers may pay particular attention to the terms of a contract worked out between the United Auto Workers and Ford Motor Company. The level of wage increases obtained by the UAW becomes a target for the rubber workers to meet or exceed.

In part, the level of these demands based on the concept of equity is tempered by a second factor: ability to pay. When an organization has highly profitable years, its ability to pay larger wage increases also rises. For example, the United Steel Workers (USW) may feel that equitable or fair treatment requires that they obtain wage concessions equal to those in the auto industry. However, these demands would be tempered somewhat if the steel industry suffered an unprofitable year relative to the auto industry.

Four classic examples of this type of behavior have occurred within the automobile industry during the period 1970–1985. Because of American Motor's profit picture, the UAW agreed to extend the 1973 contract beyond the 1976 expiration date rather than demand a settlement consistent with the Big Three automakers. Operating off an old contract with a considerably lower wage bill gave American Motors the competitive edge it needed to garner a better ability-to-pay position in the subsequent 1979 negotiations. Similarly, the 1979 wage and benefit concessions made by the UAW to avert bankruptcy by Chrysler, and the 1982 concessions for Ford and General Motors, are further examples of wage demands (concessions!) based on ability to pay.

A third factor influential in determining union wage demands centers on the standard of living for union members. Large cost-of-living increases during the 1970s and early 1980s resulted in several years where worker purchasing power (real wages) actually declined. This runs contrary to the union goal of improving member standards of living. Historically, inflation has triggered tougher stands on wage issues at the bargaining table. More recently, the union response has been to negotiate for more liberal cost of living adjustment clauses. Currently though, with union power eroding and inflation rates moderating, standard of living has taken a secondary role for union negotiators to the task of preserving union jobs.

Contractual Wage and Salary Issues

There are basically three characteristics that can be used to describe the role of a union contract in wage and salary administration. The first characteristic is the negotiated magnitude of the economic package. The presence of a union, as already noted, has a + 10–15 percentage impact on the magnitude of the economic package. Unions also play a role in determining two other characteristics of an economic package: 1) form of pay, and 2) administration of pay.

Form of pay deals basically with the question of how the economic package is to be allocated between wages and benefits. Whether because of reduced management control, strong union-worker preference for benefits, or other reasons, unionized employees have a greater percentage of their total wage bill allocated to employee benefits.[37] Typically, this shows up in the form of higher pension expenditures or higher insurance benefits.[38] One particularly well controlled study found unionization associated with 24 percent higher levels of pension expenditures and 46 percent higher insurance expenditures.[39]

Perhaps of the greatest interest to current and future compensation administrators is the role unions play in administering wages. This role is outlined primarily in the contract. The following illustrations of this role are taken from a summary of 1,711 major (1,000 workers or more) collective bargaining agreements, the majority of which were in effect between 1977 and 1986.[40]

Basis of pay. The vast majority of contracts specify that one or more jobs are to be compensated on an hourly basis. Alternatively, agreements may specify a fixed daily, weekly, biweekly, or monthly rate. In addition, agreements often indicate a specific day of the week as payday, and sometimes require payment on or before a certain hour. The following contract clause illustrates this requirement.

> The company will continue to pay wages earned on a weekly basis. The first shift will be paid on/or before 7:30 a.m. Friday; the second shift will be paid on/or before 3:30 p.m. Friday; and the third shift will be paid on/or before 11:30 p.m. Thursday.[41]

Much less frequently, contracts specify some form of incentive system as the basis for pay. The vast majority of clauses specifying incentive pay occur in manufacturing (as opposed to nonmanufacturing) industries. Many of these clauses provide for union-management discussion of incentives:

> It is agreed that all matters pertaining to piecework, incentive pay, and bonus are subject to discussion between the company and the union. . . .
> All work being performed on incentive basis shall have the allowance established prior to the start of the job; and this allowance and description of the job shall be furnished to the men performing the work at the beginning of the shift or job, except in cases where the

---

[37]Bevars Mabry, "The Economics of Fringe Benefits," *Industrial Relations* 12 (1973), pp. 95–106.

[38]Robert Rice, "Skill, Earnings and the Growth of Wage Supplements," *American Economic Review* 56 (1966), pp. 583–93; George Kalamotousakis, "Statistical Analysis of the Determinants of Employee Benefits by Type," *American Economist,* Fall 1972, pp. 139–47; and William Bailey and Albert Schwenk, "Employer Expenditures for Private Retirement and Insurance Plans," *Monthly Labor Review* 95 (1972), pp. 15–19; Fosu, "Impact of Unionism on Pension Fringes."

[39]Loren Solnick, "Unionism and Fringe Benefits Expenditures," *Industrial Relations* 17, no. 1 (1978), pp. 102–7.

[40]U.S. Department of Labor, *Major Collective Bargaining Agreements: Wage Administration Provisions* (Washington, D.C.: Bureau of Labor Statistics, Bulletin 1425–17, 1978); General Motors-UAW, "Agreement between General Motors Corporation and the UAW," 1987; and Bureau of National Affairs, "Wage Patterns and Wage Data," in *Collective Bargaining Negotiations and Contracts* 18.10-18.993 (Washington, D.C.: Bureau of National Affairs, 1984).

[41]General Motors—UAW, "Agreement between General Motors Corporation and the UAW"; Bureau of National Affairs, "Wage Patterns and Wage Data," 1987.

allowance for the work to be performed is to be divided between individuals or groups, in which case the allowance shall be given to the individual or group prior to the end of the shift. If the allowance and the description are not furnished as required above, the job shall be considered day work.

Incentive allowance rates will not be reduced after work has been started upon the particular job or after the completion of the particular job covered by the allowance, except when some reduction is made in the quantity of work originally specified or where the method of performing the work has been revised.[42]

Occupation-wage differentials. Most contracts recognize that different occupations should receive different wage rates. Within occupations, though, a single wage rate prevails.[43]

	Effective date of this agreement
Journeyman brewers and utility men	$7.75
Apprentice brewers	7.75
Brewery workers	7.70
Freight handlers	7.615

Although rare, there are some contracts that do not recognize occupational/skill differentials. These contracts specify a single standard rate for all jobs covered by the agreements. Usually such contracts cover a narrow range of skilled groups.

Experience/merit differentials. Single rates are usually specified for workers within a particular job classification. Single-rate agreements do not differentiate wages on the basis of either seniority or merit. Workers with varying years of experience and output receive the same single rate. Alternatively agreements may specify wage ranges, including all or the top and bottom steps in the range. The following example is fairly typical:[44]

Labor-grade	Minimum							Maximum
A-2	$7.18	$7.23	$7.28	$7.33	$7.38	$7.43	$7.48	$7.53
A-1	6.82	6.87	6.92	6.97	7.02	7.07	$7.12	$7.17
1	6.45	6.50	6.59	6.60	6.65	6.70	6.75	6.80
2	6.11	6.16	6.21	6.26	6.31	6.36	6.41	6.46
3	5.81	5.86	5.91	5.96	6.01	6.06		6.11
4	5.56	5.61	5.66	5.71	5.76			5.81
5	5.36	5.41	5.46					5.51
6	5.15	5.20						5.25
7	4.87	4.92						4.97
8	4.72							4.77
9	4.56							4.61
10	4.51							4.56

---

[42]Ibid.

[43]Ibid.

[44]Ibid.

The vast majority of contracts requiring wage ranges specify seniority as the basis for movement through the range. Automatic progression is an appropriate name for this type of movement through the wage range, with the contract frequently specifying the time interval between movements. This type of progression is most appropriate when the necessary job skills are within the grasp of most employees. Denial of a raise is a significant exception, and frequently is accompanied by the right of the union to submit any wage denial to the grievance procedure.

At the other extreme of management intervention, some agreements permit management to shorten the time between automatic progressions for workers with outstanding performance records. For example:[45]

> Nothing in this provision shall prevent the employer from granting individual increases more frequently than each 16 weeks if, in its judgment, they are merited.

A second strategy for moving employees through wage ranges is based exclusively on merit. Employees who are evaluated more highly receive larger or more rapid increments than average or poor performers. Within these contracts, it is common to specify that disputed merit appraisals may be submitted to grievance. If the right to grieve is not explicitly *excluded,* the union also has the implicit right to grieve.

The third strategy for movement through a range combines automatic and merit progression in some manner. A frequent strategy is to grant automatic increases up to the midpoint of the range and permit subsequent increases only when merited on the basis of performance appraisal.

Other differentials. There are a number of remaining contractual provisions that deal with differentials for reasons not yet covered. A first example deals with differentials for new and probationary employees. About one-half of major agreements refer to differentials for these employees. The most common rate designation is below or at the minimum of the rate range. For example:[46]

> New employees hired on or after the effective date of this Agreement, who do not hold a seniority date in any General Motors plant and are not covered by the provisions of Paragraph (98b) below, shall be hired at a rate equal to eighty five (85) percent of the maximum base rate of the job classification. Such employees shall receive an automatic increase to: 1) ninety (90) percent of the job classification at the expiration of one hundred and eighty (180) days. 2) ninety five (95) percent of the maximum base rate of the job classification at the expiration of three hundred and sixty-five (365) days. 3) the maximum base rate of the job classification at the expiration of five hundred and forty five (545) days.[47]

A second example of contractual differentials deals with different pay to unionized employees who are employed by a firm in different geographic areas. Very few contracts provide for different wages under these circumstances, despite the problems that can arise in paying uniform wages across regions with markedly different costs of living.

---

[45]Ibid.

[46]General Motors—UAW, "Agreement between General Motors Corporation and the UAW."

[47]Ibid.

A final category where differentials are mentioned in contracts deals with part-time and temporary employees. Few contracts specify special rates for these employees. Those that do, however, are about equally split between giving part-time/temporary employees wages above full-time workers (because they have been excluded from the employee benefits program) or below full-time workers.

Wage adjustment provisions. Frequently in multiyear contracts some provision is made for wage adjustment during the term of the contract. There are three major ways these adjustments might be specified: 1) deferred wage increases, 2) cost-of-living adjustments (COLA) or escalator clauses, and 3) reopener clauses. A deferred wage increase is negotiated at the time of initial contract negotiations with the timing and amount specified in the contract. A COLA clause, as noted earlier, involves periodic adjustment based typically on changes in the consumer price index. Finally, a reopener clause specifies that wages, and sometimes such nonwage items as pension/benefits, will be renegotiated at a specified time or under certain conditions.

UNIONS AND ALTERNATIVE REWARD SYSTEMS

It is unlikely that the internationalization of business and the increased cost pressures that organizations face signal the death of traditional long-term labor contracts. Rather, union response is likely to center on insuring that industries buffeted by deregulation and intense competition are able to control labor costs. This signals continued moderation in annual wage increase demands, increased willingness to consider work rule changes, renewed interest in cooperative labor-management relations and further experimentation with profit sharing and other wage proposals that increase cost competitiveness. This section covers the likely union response to these alternative compensation systems.

Lump Sum Awards

Lump sum awards are one-time cash payments to employees that are not added to an employee's base wages. These awards are typically given in lieu of merit increases, which are more costly to the employer. This higher cost results both because merit increases are added on to base wages and because several employee benefits (e.g., life insurance and vacation pay) are figured as a percentage of base wages.

One indication that lump sum payments are popular is the increased negotiation of major settlements that include lump sum clauses. For example, the 1987 UAW agreement included a lump sum payment equal to 3 percent of pay in the second and third years of the three-year contract. These increases were in lieu of the traditional annual improvement factor. The Oil, Chemical and Atomic Workers also accepted a lump sum award in their 1988 agreement. Their contract included a $900 lump sum bonus and a 30-cent-per-hour increase in the first year of a two-year agreement with the major oil companies. Other major companies negotiating lump sum bonuses include Boeing, Lockheed, General Electric Corporation, Westinghouse, General Dynamics, and John Hancock Mutual Life Insurance.

Unions typically dislike lump sum awards for the same reason employers favor them: base wages fall behind and benefit levels are less generous. On the positive side, though, receiving a large cash outlay can be an effective consolation for what is basically a wage concession.

Employee Stock Ownership Plans (ESOP)

An alternative strategy for organizations hurt by intense competition is to obtain wage concessions in exchange for giving employees part ownership in the company. For example, the teamsters negotiated in both the 1988 and previous contract a provision permitting local trucking companies and teamster employees to set up ESOP plans.[48] The National Master Freight agreement specifies that employees will receive 49 percent ownership in a trucking company in exchange for wage concessions of no more than 15 percent over 5 years. So far, these plans have not been very effective in keeping marginal firms from eventually declaring bankruptcy. Approximately 20 such contracts have been negotiated and only three still exist. Most of the remaining firms went out of business.[49]

ESOPs have been more successful in the airline industry where soaring fuel costs and fare wars have severely damaged several companies. Three firms (Western, Republic, and PSA) turned around heavy loss years and became profitable after negotiating ESOPs. These plans specify that employees get 12–32 percent of the airlines stock in exchange for 10–20 percent wage concession. In 1987, the ESOP meant $33 million in payment to Republic employees.[50] Although unions typically only agree to stock ownership plans to keep organizations afloat, occasionally such programs result in considerable rewards for union employees.

Pay-for-Knowledge Plans

Pay-for-knowledge plans do just that: pay employees more for learning a variety of different jobs or skills. For example, the 1986 Chrysler agreement with the UAW specifies that journeymen will get up to 50 cents per hour extra for learning new trades. By coupling this new wage system with drastic cuts in the number of job classifications, organizations have greater flexibility in moving employees quickly into high demand areas. Unions also may favor pay-for-knowledge plans because they make each individual worker more valuable to the firm. In turn, this also lessens the probability that work can be subcontracted out to nonunion organizations.

Gain-Sharing Plans

In the 1970s and early 1980s gain-sharing plans were viewed as very effective ways to align workers and management in efforts to streamline operations and cut costs. Any cost savings resulting from employees working smarter were split according to some formula

---

[48]*Changing Pay Practices: New Developments in Employee Compensation,* BNA: Washington, D.C., 1988.

[49]Ibid.

[50]Ibid.

between the organization and the workers. In the past few years, though, several companies have become disenchanted by gain-sharing plans. Parker Pen, Gould Battery, and Ingersol Rand all recently terminated gain-sharing plans.[51] One of the main problems centers on early productivity improvement plateaus. Payouts are sometimes tied to continued increases in saving. When savings level off, the "gains" shared with workers drop correspondingly.[52] Not surprisingly, unions are not enthusiastic about making changes that continue to benefit the organization but which result in wage gains for employees only in the short run.

Profit-Sharing Plans

Unions have debated the advantages of profit-sharing plans for at least 80 years.[53] Walter Reuther, then President of the CIO in 1948 (soon to become the AFL-CIO in 1955), championed the cause of profit sharing in the auto industry. The goal of unions is to secure sound, stable income levels for the membership. When this is achieved, subsequent introduction of a profit-sharing plan allows union members to share the wealth with more profitable firms while still maintaining employment levels in marginal organizations. We should note, though, that not all unions favor profit-sharing plans. As indicated by recent grumblings of employees at General Motors, inequality in profits between firms in the same industry can lead to wage differentials for workers performing the same work. Payouts to Ford employees on the profit-sharing plan have totaled $9,400 between 1984 and 1988. During the same period General Motors employees received less than $1500.[54] Most General Motors employees would argue the difference in payout cannot be traced to the fact that Ford employees work harder or smarter. In fact, the difference in profitability, the UAW argues, is due to management decision making. Therefore the argument runs, workers should not be penalized for factors beyond their control.

SUMMARY

The United States no longer can view itself as the dominant economic power in the world. Other countries continue to make inroads in product areas traditionally the sole domain of American companies. The impact of this increased competition has been most pronounced in the compensation area. Labor costs must be cut to improve our competitive stance. Alternative compensation systems to achieve this end are regularly being devised. Unions face a difficult situation. How should they respond to these attacks on traditional compensation systems? Many unions believe that crisis demands changing attitudes from both management and unions. Labor and management identify compensation packages

---

[51]John Zalusky, "Labor's Collective Bargaining Experience With Gainsharing and Profit-Sharing," IRRA 39th Annual Meeting, December, 1986, 175–82.

[52]*Changing Pay Practices: New Developments in Employee Compensation*, 1988.

[53]Zalusky, "Labor's Collective Bargaining Experience with Gainsharing and Profit-Sharing"; and William Shaw, "Can Labor be Capitalized?" *American Federationist* 17 (June 1910), p. 517.

[54]*Organized Labor and the New Pay*, BNA.

which both parties can abide. Sometimes these packages include cuts in traditional forms of wages in exchange for compensation tied more closely to the success of the firm. We expect the 1990s will be dominated by more innovation in compensation design and increased exploration between unions and management for ways to improve the competitive stance of American business.

REVIEW QUESTIONS

1. Identify and explain the different types of wage concessions that unions might make. Which of these types of concessions are most likely to create internal equity problems within the union? Why?
2. Why is it difficult to assess the impact that unions have on the general level of wages within firms? How does the concept of spillover contribute to this difficulty?
3. Unions agree to alternative reward systems in response to severe financial problems within organizations. What are some of the current causes of these financial problems, and how do the alternative reward systems deal with these problems? Give specific examples of alternative reward systems and how they help solve financial problems within companies.
4. In what ways do unions affect the day-to-day administration of compensation programs? Give specific examples.
5. Under what economic circumstances do unions favor COLA clauses? Why do fewer contracts specify COLA clauses today than 10 years ago?

Appendix A

The Hay Guide Chart—Profile Method of Position Evaluation (next five pages)

THE HAY GUIDE CHART

ILLUSTRATIVE

HAY GUIDE CHART–PROFILE METHOD
OF POSITION EVALUATION

INDUSTRIAL

Know-How
DEFINITIONS

DEFINITION: Know-How is the sum total to every kind of skill, however acquired, required for acceptable job performance. This sum total which comprises the overall "savvy" has 3 dimensions — the requirements for:

1 Practical procedures, specialized techniques, and scientific disciplines.

2 Know-How of integrating and harmonizing the diversified functions involved in managerial situations occurring in operating, supporting, and administrative fields. This Know-How may be exercised consultatively (about management) as well as executively and involves in some combination the areas of organizing, planning, executing, controlling and evaluating.

3 Active, practicing, face-to-face skills in the area of human relationships (as defined at right).

MEASURING KNOW-HOW: Know-How has both scope (variety) and depth (thoroughness). Thus, a job may require some knowledge about a lot of things, or a lot of knowledge about a few things. The total Know-How is the combination of scope and depth. This comcept makes practical the comparison and weighing of the total Know-How content of different jobs in terms of: "**How much knowledge about how many things.**"

3 HUMAN RELATIONS SKILLS

1. BASIC: Ordinary courtesy and effectiveness in dealing with others.

2. IMPORTANT: Understanding, influencing, and/ or serving people are important, but not critical considerations.

3. CRITICAL: Alternative or combined skills in understanding, selecting, developing and motivating people are important in the highest degree.

KNOW-HOW

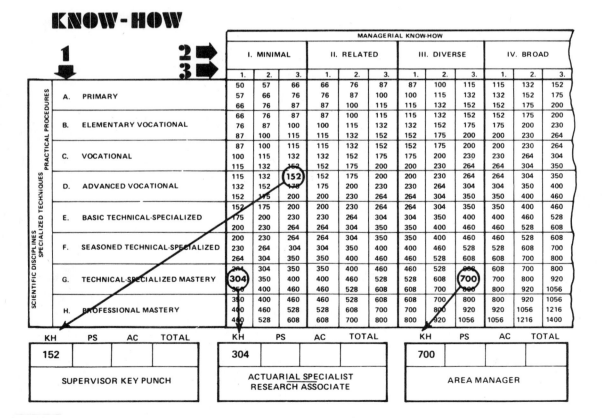

Problem Solving
DEFINITIONS

DEFINITION: Problem Solving is the original, "self-starting" thinking required by the job for analyzing, evaluating, creating, reasoning, arriving at and making conclusions. To the extent that thinking is circumscribed by standards, covered by precedents, or referred to others, Problem Solving is diminished, and the emphasis correspondingly is on Know-How.

Problem Solving has two dimensions:

1 The thinking environment in which the problems are solved.

2 The thinking challenge presented by the problem to be solved.

MEASURING PROBLEM SOLVING: Problem Solving measures the intensity of the mental process which employs Know-How to (1) identify, (2) define, and (3) resolve a problem. "You think with what you know." This is true of even the most creative work. The raw material of any thinking is knowledge of facts, principles and means; ideas are put together from something already there. Therefore, Problem Solving is treated as a percentage utilization of Know-How.

PROBLEM SOLVING

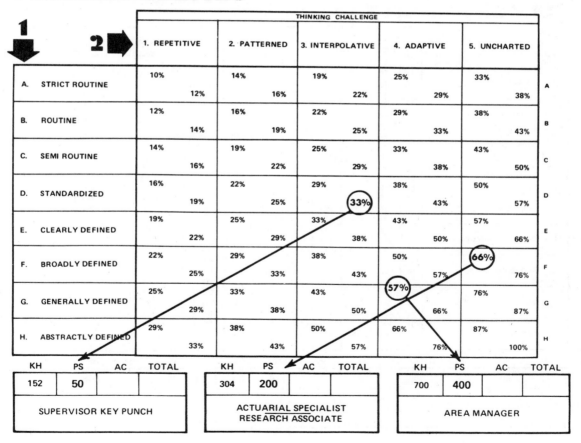

1 **2**		THINKING CHALLENGE									
		1. REPETITIVE		**2. PATTERNED**		**3. INTERPOLATIVE**		**4. ADAPTIVE**		**5. UNCHARTED**	
A. STRICT ROUTINE		10%	12%	14%	16%	19%	22%	25%	29%	33%	38%	A
B. ROUTINE		12%	14%	16%	19%	22%	25%	29%	33%	38%	43%	B
C. SEMI ROUTINE		14%	16%	19%	22%	25%	29%	33%	38%	43%	50%	C
D. STANDARDIZED		16%	19%	22%	25%	29%	(33%)	38%	43%	50%	57%	D
E. CLEARLY DEFINED		19%	22%	25%	29%	33%	38%	43%	50%	57%	66%	E
F. BROADLY DEFINED		22%	25%	29%	33%	38%	43%	50%	57%	(66%)	76%	F
G. GENERALLY DEFINED		25%	29%	33%	38%	43%	50%	(57%)	66%	76%	87%	G
H. ABSTRACTLY DEFINED		29%	33%	38%	43%	50%	57%	66%	76%	87%	100%	H

KH	PS	AC	TOTAL
152	50		

SUPERVISOR KEY PUNCH

KH	PS	AC	TOTAL
304	200		

ACTUARIAL SPECIALIST
RESEARCH ASSOCIATE

KH	PS	AC	TOTAL
700	400		

AREA MANAGER

Accountability
DEFINITIONS

DEFINITION: Accountability is the answerability for action and for the consequences thereof. It is the measured effect of the job on end results. It has three dimensions in the following order of importance.

1 FREEDOM TO ACT — the degree of personal or procedural control and guidance as defined in the left-hand column of the chart.

2 JOB IMPACT ON END RESULTS — as defined at right.

3 MAGNITUDE — indicated by the general dollar size of the area(s) most clearly or primarily affected by the job.

2 IMPACT OF JOB ON END RESULTS

Indirect:

REMOTE: Informational, recording, or incidental services for use by others in relation to some important end result.

CONTRIBUTORY: Interpretive, advisory, or facilitating services for use by others in taking action.

Direct:

SHARED: Participating with others (except own subordinates and superiors), within or outside the organizational unit, in taking action.

PRIMARY: Controlling impact on end results, where shared accountability of others is subordinate.

ACCOUNTABILITY

	1 →					**3** → **2** →										
		(1) VERY SMALL OR INDETERMINATE				(2) SMALL				(3) MEDIUM				(4) L		
		R	C	S	P	R	C	S	P	R	C	S	P	R	C	
A.	PRESCRIBED	10	14	19	25	14	19	25	33	19	25	33	43	25	33	
		12	16	22	29	16	22	29	38	22	29	38	50	29	38	
		14	19	25	33	19	25	33	.43	25	33	43	57	33	43	
B.	CONTROLLED	16	22	29	38	22	29	38	50	29	38	50	66	38	50	
		19	25	33	43	25	33	43	57	33	43	57	76	43	57	
		22	29	38	50	29	38	50	66	38	50	66	87	50	66	
C.	STANDARDIZED	25	33	43	57	33	43	57	76	43	57	76	100	57	76	
		29	38	50	(66)	38	50	66	87	50	66	87	115	66	87	
		33	43	57	76	43	57	76	100	57	76	100	132	76	100	
D.	GENERALLY REGULATED	38	50	66	87	50	66	87	115	66	87	115	152	87	115	
		43	57	76	100	57	76	100	132	76	100	132	175	100	132	
		50	66	87	115	66	87	115	152	87	(115)	152	200	115	152	
E.	DIRECTED	57	76	100	132	76	100	132	175	100	132	175	230	132	175	
		66	87	115	152	87	115	152	200	115	152	200	264	152	200	
		76	100	132	175	100	132	175	230	132	175	230	304	175	230	
F.	ORIENTED DIRECTION	87	115	152	200	115	152	200	264	152	200	264	350	200	264	
		100	132	175	230	132	175	230	304	175	230	304	400	230	304	
		115	152	200	264	152	200	264	350	200	264	350	460	264	350	
G.	BROAD GUIDANCE	132	175	230	304	175	230	304	400	230	304	400	528	304	400	
		152	200	264	350	200	264	350	460	264	350	460	(608)	350	460	
		175	230	304	400	230	304	400	528	304	400	528	700	400	528	
H.	STRATEGIC GUIDANCE	200	264	350	460	264	350	460	608	350	460	608	800	460	608	
		230	304	400	528	304	400	528	700	400	528	700	920	528	700	
		264	350	460	608	350	460	608	800	460	608	800	1056	608	800	
I.	GENERALLY UNGUIDED	304	400	528	700	400	528	700	920	528	700	920	1216	700	920	
		350	460	608	800	460	608	800	1056	608	800	1056	1400	800	1056	
		400	528	700	920	528	700	920	1216	700	920	1216	1690	920	1216	

KH	PS	AC	TOTAL
152	50	**66**	268

SUPERVISOR KEY PUNCH

KH	PS	AC	TOTAL
304	200	**115**	619

ACTUARIAL SPECIALIST RESEARCH ASSOCIATE

KH	PS	AC	TOTAL
700	400	**608**	1708

AREA MANAGER

PROFILES CHECK EVALUATION JUDGEMENT

POINTS

KH	PS	AC	TOTAL
152	50	66	**268**
SUPERVISOR KEY PUNCH			

PERCENTAGES

KH	PS	AC

KH 56%
PS 19%
AC 25%

56-19-25
= 100%

KH	PS	AC	TOTAL
304	200	115	**619**
ACTUARIAL SPECIALIST RESEARCH ASSOCIATE			

KH 49%
PS 32%
AC 19%

49-32-19
=100%

KH	PS	AC	TOTAL
700	400	608	**1708**
AREA MANAGER			

PS 23%
KH 41%
AC 36%

41-23-36
=100%

Appendix B

A Skill-Based Job Evaluation Plan for Manufacturing Jobs:
Factor Definitions and Points

FACTOR 1: BASIC KNOWLEDGE

1st Degree (22 points)

Ability to read, write, add and subtract basic mathematics, interpret and complete simple instructions.

2nd Degree (47 points)

Knowledge of higher mathematical calculations such as basic decimal and fractional equations, ability to read and follow semicomplicated written instructions and to use basic measuring equipment.

3rd Degree (72 points)

Knowledge of a variety of manufacturing skills, specific training, work experience equivalent to trade school or high school, ability to read semicomplicated measuring equipment, graphics, technical or written reports.

4th Degree (111 points)

Extensive specific skills training in a specialized field; equivalent to one–two years of college or vocational (technical) training or master trade certificate.

FACTOR 2: ELECTRICAL/ELECTRONIC SKILLS

Application of the principles of electricity, electronics, electronic logic, and integrated transmission technologies such as lasers. This includes understanding of circuits, their component parts, and how they work together.

1st Degree (7 points)

Operational knowledge of electrical/electronic equipment without understanding the electrical/electronic principles on which the equipment operates.

2nd Degree (15 points)

Operational knowledge of electrical/electronic equipment with understanding the electrical/electronic principles on which the equipment operates.

3rd Degree (23 points)

Application of principles of electronic circuitry and appropriate wiring procedures.

4th Degree (37 points)

Application of principles of miniaturized electronic circuits and digital and analog transmission concepts.

FACTOR 3: MECHANICAL SKILLS

The application of mechanical knowledge of how/why mechanical equipment works. It includes the operation, repair, or maintenance of machinery/mechanical systems.

1st Degree (5 points)

This includes the use of basic mechanical ability to operate/adjust single or multiple pieces of mechanical or electromechanical equipment. It includes, but is not limited to, such elements as clearing jams and setting feed speeds and/or pressure changes.

2nd Degree (12 points)

This includes all elements of 1st Degree basic mechanical ability, with the exceptions that the incumbent is required to have the skills to perform preventive maintenance, disassemble/reassemble specific components, change tools, and the like.

3rd Degree (25 points)

Perform servicing and procedural repair activities on mechanical systems/machinery as the primary function.

4th Degree (31 points)

Apply advanced principles of mechanical skills to repair, rebuild, service to a close tolerance level of fit.

5th Degree (37 points)

Perform sophisticated diagnostic and repair activities on complex mechanical or electro-mechanical machinery/systems.

FACTOR 4: GRAPHICS

Reading, interpreting, and/or preparing graphic representations of information, such as maps, plans, drawings, blueprints, diagrams, schematics, and timing/flowcharts.

1st Degree (5 points)

Understand basic blueprints and/or prepare rough sketches.

2nd Degree (12 points)

Understand more complex blueprints and/or prepare simple graphic information.

3rd Degree (25 points)

Understand complex, technical graphic representations of information and/or prepare technical graphics.

4th Degree (31 points)

Prepare and/or interpret complex, technical graphic representations of a wide range of information.

5th Degree (37 points)

Develop, prepare, and/or interpret highly complex, sophisticated graphic representations.

FACTOR 5: MATHEMATICAL SKILLS

The selection and application of mathematical methods or procedures to solve problems or to achieve desired results.

1st Degree (8 points)

Simple arithmetic computations involving addition, subtraction, multiplication, or division.

2nd Degree (15 points)

Computations involving decimals, percentages, fractions, and/or basic statistics.

3rd Degree (23 points)

Computations involving algebra (e.g., solving for an unknown) or geometry (e.g., areas, volumes).

4th Degree (38 points)

Computations involving the use of trigonometry (properties of triangles and circles including sine, cosine, and tangent functions), logarithms and exponents, and advanced statistics.

FACTOR 6: COMMUNICATION/INTERPERSONAL SKILLS

This factor measures the scope and nature of relationships with others.

1st Degree (28 points)

Little or no contact with others. Relationships involve providing and/or receiving information or documents.

2nd Degree (56 points)

Some contact with others. Relationships often require explanation or interpretation of information.

3rd Degree (84 points)

Substantial contact with others. Relationships usually involve discussions with stakeholders or recommendations on issues regarding policies, programs, and so on. Impact is considerable and may be limited to individual departments/programs.

4th Degree (140 points)

Extensive contact with others. Relationships usually include decisions in a broad sense and will affect several areas within the manufacturing unit.

FACTOR 7: SAFETY SKILLS

This factor measures the requirements for adherence to prescribed safety and personal security practices in the performance of required tasks. These safety and personal security practices are generally required to minimize exposure to hazard or risk in the work environment.

1st Degree (10 points)

Perform work in accordance with a few simple safety procedures to minimize potential for injury.

2nd Degree (40 points)

Perform work in accordance with several specific safety procedures to minimize potential for injury.

3rd Degree (80 points)

Perform work in accordance with a wide range of safety procedures to minimize some potential for injury.

4th Degree (100 points)

Perform work in a highly variable environment where safety principles and procedures need to be tailored to deal with unforeseen hazards to minimize high potential for serious injury.

FACTOR 8: DECISION MAKING/SUPERVISION REQUIRED

This factor measures the degree of decision making required without being checked by others, and the degree to which immediate supervisor is required to outline the procedures to be followed and/or the results to be attained on the job.

1st Degree (36 points)

Limited decision making by the incumbent. Progress of work is checked by others most of the time, and/or 60–90 percent of activities are defined by other than the incumbent.

2nd Degree (89 points)

Routine decision making based on specific criteria. Progress of work is often checked by others, and/or 40–60 percent of activities are defined by other than the incumbent.

3rd Degree (112 points)

Significant decision making based on established guidelines and experience. Progress of work is checked by others some of the time, and/or 25–40 percent of activities are defined by other than the incumbent.

4th Degree (180 points)

Extensive decision making based on broad policies, procedures, and guidelines. Progress of work is seldom checked by others, and/or less than 25 percent of activities are defined by other than the incumbent.

Glossary of Terms

Ability   Refers to the individual's capability to engage in a specific behavior.

Ability to Pay   The ability of a firm to meet employee wage demands while remaining profitable; a frequent issue in contract negotiations with unions. A firm's ability to pay is constrained by its ability to compete in its product market.

Access Discrimination   Focuses on the staffing and allocation decisions made by employers. It denies particular jobs, promotions, or training opportunities to qualified women or minorities. This type of discrimination is illegal under Title VII of the Civil Rights Act of 1964.

Across-the-Board Increases   A general adjustment that provides equal increases to all employees.

Adjective Checklist   An individual (or job) rating technique. In its simplest form, a set of adjectives or descriptive statements. If the employee (job) possesses a trait listed, the item is checked. A rating score from the checklist equals the number of statements checked.

Age Discrimination in Employment Act (ADEA) of 1967 (Amended 1978 and 1986)   It makes nonfederal employees age 40 and over a protected class relative to their treatment in pay, benefits, and other personnel actions.

All-Salaried Work Force   A concept whose objective is to increase employee commitment to the work by adopting a more egalitarian approach to pay practices. It involves equalizing benefits for all employees and converting hourly pay rates to biweekly rates.

Alternation Ranking   A job evaluation method that involves ordering the job descriptions alternately at each extreme. All the jobs are considered. Agreement is reached on which is the most valuable, then the least valuable. Evaluators alternate between the next most valued and next least valued and so on until all the jobs have been ordered.

American Compensation Association (ACA)   A nonprofit organization for training compensation professionals.

Appeals Procedures   Mechanism created to handle pay disagreements. They provide a forum for employees and managers to voice their complaints and receive a hearing.

Base Pay   *See* Base Wage.

586

Base Wage The basic cash compensation that an employee pays for the work performed. Tends to reflect the value of the work itself and ignore differences in contribution attributable to individual employees.

Basic Pay Policies They include decisions on the relative importance of (1) internal consistency, (2) external competitiveness, (3) employee contributions, and (4) the nature of the administration of the pay system. These policies form the foundation on which pay systems are designed and administered and serve as guidelines within which pay is managed to accomplish the system's objectives.

Behaviorally Anchored Rating Scales (BARS) Are a variant on standard rating scales, in which the various scale levels are anchored with behavioral descriptions directly applicable to jobs being evaluated.

Benchmark (or Key) Jobs A prototypical job, or group of jobs, used as reference points for making pay comparisons within or without the organization. Benchmark jobs have well-known and stable contents; their current pay rates are generally acceptable and the pay differentials among them are relatively stable. A group of benchmark jobs, taken together, contains the entire range of compensable factors and is accepted in the external labor market for setting wages.

Bendeaux Plan Individual incentive plan that provides a variation on straight piecework and standard hour plans. Instead of timing an entire task, a Bendeaux plan requires determination of the time required to complete each simple action of a task. Workers receive a wage incentive for completing a task in less than a standard time.

BLS *See* Bureau of Labor Statistics.

Bonus A bonus is a lump-sum payment to an employee in recognition of goal achievement.

"Bottom Up" Approach to Pay Budgeting Under this approach individual employees' pay rates for the next plan year are forecasted and summed to create an organization's total budget.

Budget A plan within which managers operate and a standard against which managers' actual expenditures are evaluated.

Bureau of Labor Statistics A major source of publicly available pay data. It also publishes the Consumer Price Index.

Cafeteria (Flexible) Benefit Programs A benefit plan in which employees have a choice as to the benefits they receive within some dollar limit. Usually a common core benefit package is required (e.g., specific minimum levels of health, disability, retirement, and death benefit) plus elective programs from which the employee may select a set dollar amount. Additional coverage may be available through employee contributions.

Capital Appreciation Plans *See* Long-Term Incentive and Capital Appreciation.

Career Paths Refers to the progression of jobs within an organization.

Central Tendency Error A rating error that occurs when a rater consistently rates a group of employees at or close to the midpoint of a scale irrespective of true score performance of ratees.

Churn *See* turnover effect.

Civil Rights Act Title VII of the Civil Rights Act of 1964 prohibits discrimination in terms and conditions of employment (including benefits) that is based on race, color, religion, sex, or national origin.

Classification   Job evaluation method that involves slotting job descriptions into a series of classes or grades that cover the range of jobs and that serve as a standard against which the job descriptions are compared.

Coinsurance   Employees share in the cost of a benefit provided to them.

Commission   Payment tied directly to achievement of performance standards. Commissions are directly tied to a profit index (sales, production level) and employee costs; thus, they rise and fall in line with revenues.

Comparable Worth   A doctrine that maintains that women performing jobs judged to be equal on some measure of inherent worth should be paid the same as men, excepting allowable differences, such as seniority, merit, and production-based pay plans, and other non-sex-related factors.

Compa-Ratio   An index that helps assess how managers actually pay employees in relation to the midpoint of the pay range established for jobs. It estimates how well actual practices correspond to intended policy. Calculated as the following ratio:

$$\text{Compa-Ratio} = \frac{\text{Average rates actually paid}}{\text{Range midpoint}}$$

Compensable Factors   Job attributes that provide the basis for evaluating the relative worth of jobs inside an organization. A compensable factor must be work related, business related, and acceptable to the parties involved.

Compensation   All forms of financial returns and tangible services and benefits employees receive as part of an employment relationship.

Compensation Budgeting   A part of the organization's planning process; helps to ensure that future financial expenditures are coordinated and controlled. It involves forecasting the total expenditures required by the pay system during the next period as well as the amount of the pay increases. "Bottom up" and "top down" are the two typical approaches to the process.

Compensation Differentials   Differentials in pay among jobs across and within organizations, and among individuals in the same job in an organization.

Compensation Objectives   The desired results of the pay system. The basic pay objectives include efficiency, equity, and compliance with laws and regulations. Objectives shape the design of the pay system and serve as the standard against which the success of the pay system is evaluated.

Compensation System Controls   Basic processes that serve to control pay decision making. They include (1) controls inherent in the design of the pay techniques (e.g., increase guidelines, range maximums and minimums), and (2) budgetary controls.

Competitive Objective   The midpoints for each pay range. The pay policy line that connects the midpoints becomes a control device: compensation must be managed to conform to these midpoints if the organization is to maintain the pay policy it has specified.

Compliance Pay Objective   It involves conforming to various federal and state laws and regulations. To ensure continuous compliance, pay objectives need to be adjusted as these laws and regulations change.

Comprehensive Occupational Data Analysis Program (CODAP)   The earliest attempt to quantify job analysis using task-oriented data.

Compression   Very narrow pay differentials among jobs at different organization levels as a result of wages for jobs filled from the outside (frequently these are entry level jobs) increasing faster than the internal pay structure.

Congruency   The degree of consistency or "fit" between the compensation system and other organizational components such as the strategy, product-market stage, culture and values, employee needs, union status.

Consumer Price Index (CPI)   Published by the Bureau of Labor Statistics, U.S. Department of Labor, it measures the changes in prices of a fixed market basket of goods and services purchased by a hypothetical average family.

Content Theories   Motivation theories that focus on *what* motivates people rather than on *how* people are motivated. Maslow's need hierarchy theory and Herzberg's two-factor theory fall in this category.

Contingent employees   Workers whose employment is of a limited duration (part-time or temporary).

Contributory Benefit Financing Plans   Costs shared between employer and employee.

Conventional Job Analysis Methods   These methods (e.g., functional job analysis) typically involve an analyst using a questionnaire in conjunction with structured interviews of job incumbents and supervisors. They place considerable reliance on analysts' ability to understand the work performed and to accurately describe it.

Cooperative Wage Study (CWS)   A study undertaken by 12 steel companies and the United Steel Workers to design an industrywide point plan (the Steel Plan) for clerical and technical personnel.

Coordination of Benefits   Efforts to ensure that employer coverage of an employee does not "double pay" because of identical protection offered by the government (private pension and social security coordination) or a spouse's employer.

Core Employees   Workers with whom a long-term, full-time work relationship is anticipated.

Cost of Living   Actual individual expenditures on goods and services. The only way to measure it accurately is to examine the expense budget of each employee.

Cost of Living Adjustments (COLAs)   Across-the-board wage and salary increases or supplemental payments based on changes in some index of prices, usually the consumer price index (CPI). If included in a union contract, COLAs are designed to increase wages automatically during the life of the contract as a function of changes in the consumer price index (CPI).

Cost Saving Plans   Group incentive plans that focus on cost savings rather than on profit increases as the standard of group incentive (e.g., Scanlon, Rucker, Improshare).

CPI   *See* Consumer Price Index.

Culture   The informal rules, rituals, and value system of an organization which influence the way employees behave.

Davis-Bacon Act of 1931   Requires most federal contractors to pay wage rates prevailing in the area.

Deductibles   Employer cost-saving tool where the first X dollars of cost when a benefit is used (e.g., hospitalization) are borne by the employee. Subsequent costs up to some maximum are covered by the employer.

Deferred Compensation Program   Provide income to an employee at some future time as compensation for work performed now. Types of deferred compensation programs include stock option plans and pension plans.

Defined Benefits Plan   A benefits option or package in which the employer agrees to give the specified benefit without regard to cost maximums. Contrast to defined contribution plan.

Defined Contribution Plan   A benefits option or package in which the employer negotiates a dollar maximum payout. Any change in benefit costs over time reduces the amount of coverage unless new dollar limits are negotiated.

Direct Compensation   Pay received directly in the form of cash (e.g., wages, bonuses, incentives).

Direct Pay   *See* Direct Compensation.

Disparate (Unequal) Impact Standard   Outlaws the application of pay practices that may appear to be neutral but have a negative effect on females or minorities, unless those practices can be shown to be business related.

Disparate (Unequal) Treatment Standard   Outlaws the application of different standards to different classes of employees, unless they can be shown to be business related.

Distributive Justice   Fairness in the amount of reward distributed to employees.

DOLs   Original Department of Labor Methodology of job analysis. It categorized data to be collected as (1) actual work performed and (2) work traits or characteristics. Actual work performed is further refined into three categories: worker functions (what the worker does), work fields (the methods and techniques employed), and products and services (output).

Double-Track System   A framework for professional employees in an organization whereby at least two general tracks of ascending compensation steps are available: (1) a "managerial" track to be ascended through increasing responsibility for supervision of people and (2) a "professional" track to be ascended through increasing contributions of a professional nature.

Drive Theory   A motivational theory that assumes that all behavior is induced by drives (i.e., energizers such as thirst, hunger, sex), and that present behavior is based in large part on the consequences or rewards of past behavior.

Efficiency Pay Objective   Involves (1) improving productivity and (2) controlling labor costs.

Efficiency Wage Theory   A theory to explain why firms are rational in offering higher than necessary wages.

Employee Benefits   That part of the total compensation package, other than pay for time worked, provided to employees in whole or in part by employer payments (e.g., life insurance, pension, workers' compensation, vacation).

Employee Contributions   Refers to comparisons among individuals doing the same job for the same organization.

Employee Equity   *See* Employee Contributions.

Employee Retirement Income Security Act of 1974 (ERISA)   An act regulating private employer pension and welfare programs. The act has provisions that cover eligibility for participation, reporting, and disclosure requirements, establish fiduciary standards for the financial management of retirement funds, set up tax incentives for funding pension plans, and establish the Pension Benefit Guaranty Corporation to insure pension plans against financial failures.

Employee Services and Benefits Programs that include a wide array of alternative pay forms ranging from payments for time not worked (vacations, jury duty) through services (drug counseling, financial planning, cafeteria support) to protection (medical care, life insurance, and pensions).

Employer of Choice The view that a firm's external wage competitiveness is just one facet of its overall human resource policy, and competitiveness is more properly judged on overall policies. So challenging work, high calibre colleagues, or an organization's prestige must be factored in to an overall consideration of attractiveness.

Entry Jobs Jobs which are filled from the external labor market and whose pay tends to reflect external economic factors rather than an organization's culture and traditions.

Equal Employment Opportunity Commission (EEOC) A commission of the federal government charged with enforcing the provisions of the Civil Rights Act of 1964 and the EPA of 1963 as it pertains to sex discrimination in pay.

Equal Pay Act (EPA) of 1963 An amendment to the Fair Labor Standards Act of 1938, prohibiting pay differentials on jobs which are substantially equal in terms of skills, effort, responsibility, and working conditions, except when they are the result of bona fide seniority, merit, or production-based systems, or any other job-related factor other than sex.

Equalization Component As a part of an expatriate compensation package, equalization is one form of equity designed to "keep the worker whole" (i.e., maintain real income or purchasing power of base pay). This equalization typically comes in the form of four types of allowances: tax equalization, housing, education and language training, and cost-of-living (COLA) allowances.

Equity Absolute or relative justice or "fairness" in an exchange such as the employment contract. Absolute fairness is evaluated against a universally accepted criterion of equity, while relative fairness is assessed against a criterion that may vary according to the individuals involved in the exchange, the nature of what is exchanged, and the context of the exchange.

Equity Pay Objective Fair pay treatment for all the participants in the employment relationship. Focuses attention on pay systems that recognize employee contributions as well as employee needs.

Equity Theory A theory proposing that in an exchange relationship (such as employment) the equality of outcome/input ratios between a person and a comparison other (a standard or relevant person/group) will determine fairness or equity. If the ratios diverge from each other, the person will experience reactions of unfairness and inequity.

ESOP (Employee Stock Ownership Plan) A plan in which a company borrows money from a financial institution using its stock as a collateral for the loan. Principal and interest loan repayment are tax deductible. With each loan repayment, the lending institution releases a certain amount of stock being held as security. The stock is then placed into an Employee Stock Ownership Trust (ESOT) for distribution at no cost to all employees. The employees receive the stock upon retirement or separation from the company. TRASOPs and PAYSOPs are variants of ESOPs.

Essay   An open-ended performance appraisal format. The descriptors used could range from comparisons with other employees through adjectives, behaviors, and goal accomplishment.

Exchange Value   The price of labor (the wage) determined in a competitive market; in other words, labor's worth (the price) is whatever the buyer, and seller agree upon.

Executive Perquisites (Perks)   They are special benefits made available to top executives (and sometimes other managerial employees). May be taxable income to the receiver. Company-related perks may include luxury office, special parking, and company-paid membership in clubs/associations, hotels, resorts. Personal perks include such things as low-cost loans, personal and legal counseling, free home repairs and improvements, and so on. Since 1978 various tax and agency rulings have slowly been requiring companies to place a value on perks, thus increasing the taxable income of executives.

Exempt Jobs   Jobs not subject to the provisions of the Fair Labor Standards Act with respect to minimum wage and overtime. Exempt employees include most executives, administrators, professionals, and outside sales representatives.

Expatriates   Employees assigned outside their base country for any period of time in excess of one year.

Expectancies   Beliefs (or subjective probability estimates) individuals have that particular actions on their part will lead to certain outcomes or goals.

Expectancy (VIE) Theory   A motivation theory that proposes that individuals will select an alternative based on how this choice relates to outcomes such as rewards. The choice made is based on the strength or value of the outcome and on the perceived probability that this choice will lead to the desired outcome.

External Competitiveness   Refers to the pay relationships among organizations and focuses attention on the competitive positions reflected in these relationships.

Extrinsic Rewards   Rewards that a person receives from sources other than the job itself. They include compensation, supervision, promotions, vacations, friendships, and all other important outcomes apart from the job itself.

Face Validity   The determination of the relevance of a measuring device on "appearance" only.

Factor Comparison   A job evaluation method in which jobs are assessed on the bases of two criteria: (1) a set of compensable factors and (2) wages for a selected set of jobs.

Factor Scales   Reflect different degrees within each compensable factor. Most commonly five to seven degrees are defined. Each degree may also be anchored by the typical skills, tasks and behaviors, or key job titles.

Factor Weights   Indicate the importance of each compensable factor in a job evaluation system. Weights can be derived either through committee judgment or statistical analysis.

Fair Labor Standards Act of 1938 (FLSA)   A federal law governing minimum wage, overtime pay, equal pay for men and women in the same types of jobs, child labor, and recordkeeping requirements.

Federal Insurance Contributions Act (FICA)   The source of Social Security contribution withholding requirements. The FICA deduction is paid by both employer and employee.

Flat Rates　A single rate, rather than a range of rates, for all individuals performing each job. Ignores seniority and performance differences.

Flexible Benefits　*See* Cafeteria (Flexible) Benefit Programs.

Flexible Benefits Plan　Benefits package in which employees are given a core of critical benefits (necessary for minimum security) and permitted to expend the remainder of their benefits allotment on options that they find most attractive.

Forms of Compensation　Pay may be received directly in the form of cash (e.g., wages, bonuses, incentives) or indirectly through services and benefits (e.g., pensions, health insurance, vacations). This definition excludes other forms of rewards or returns that employees may receive, such as promotion, recognition for outstanding work behavior, and the like.

Forms of Pay　*See* Forms of Compensation.

Functional Job Analysis (FJA)　A conventional approach to job analysis which is followed by the U.S. Department of Labor. Five categories of data are collected: what the worker does; the methodologies and techniques employed; the machines, tools, and equipment used; the products and services that result; and the traits required of the worker. FJA constitutes a modification of the DOLs methodology and is widely used in the public sector.

Gain-Sharing or Group Incentive Plans　Incentive plans that are based on some measure of group performance rather than individual performance. Taking data on a past year as a base, group incentive plans may focus on cost savings (e.g., the Scanlon, Rucker, and Improshare plans) or on profit increases (profit-sharing plans) as the standard to distribute a portion of the accrued funds among relevant employees.

Gantt Plan　Individual incentive plan that provides for variable incentives as a function of a standard expressed as time period per unit of production. Under this plan a standard time for a task is purposely set at a level requiring high effort to complete.

General Schedule (GS)　A job evaluation plan used by the U.S. Office of Personnel Management for white collar employees. It has 18 "grades" (classes). Most jobs are in 15 grades; the top three are combined into a "supergrade" which covers senior executives.

Generic Job Analysis　Generalized, less detailed data collection at a job level used to write a broad job description that covers a large number of related tasks. The result is that 2 people doing the same broadly defined job could be doing entirely different, yet related, tasks.

Geographic Differentials　*See* locality pay.

Group Incentive Plans　*See* Gain-Sharing or Group Incentive Plans.

Halo Error　A positive or negative rating error in which rating in one performance dimension strongly influences ratings on other performance dimensions, irrespective of true score relationship across dimensions.

Halsey 50–50 Method　Individual incentive plan that provides for variable incentives as a function of a standard expressed as time period per unit of production. This plan derives its name from the shared split between worker and employer of any savings in direct costs.

Hay System　A point factor system that evaluates jobs with respect to know-how, problem solving, and accountability. It is used primarily for exempt (managerial/professional) jobs.

Health Maintenance Organization (HMO)   A nontraditional health care delivery system. HMOs offer comprehensive benefits, outpatient services as well as hospital coverages, for a fixed monthly prepaid fee.

Hierarchies (or job structures)   Jobs ordered according to their relative content and/or value.

Hit Rate   The ability of a job evaluation plan to replicate a predetermined, agreed-upon job structure.

Human Capital Theory   A branch of labor economics proposing that the investment one is willing to make to enter an occupation is related to the returns one expects to earn over time in the form of compensation.

Improshare (IMproved PROductivity through SHARing)   A gain-sharing plan in which a standard is developed which identifies the expected hours required to produce an acceptable level of output. Any savings arising from production of agreed-upon output in fewer than expected hours are shared by the firm and the worker.

Incentive   Inducement offered in advance to influence future performance (e.g., sales commissions).

Incentive Stock Options (ISOs)   A form of deferred compensation designed to influence long-term performance. Gives an executive a right to pay today's market price for a block of shares in the company at a future time. No tax is due until the shares are sold.

Increase Guidelines   Inherent compensation system controls. They specify amount and timing of pay increases on an organization-wide basis.

Indirect Compensation   Pay received through services and benefits (e.g., pensions, health insurance, vacations).

Individual-Based Systems   They focus on employee rather than job characteristics. Pay is based on the highest work-related skills employees possess rather than on the specific job performed.

Instrumentality   The perceived contingency that an outcome (performing well) has for another outcome (a reward such as pay).

Internal Consistency   Refers to the pay relationships among jobs or skill levels within a single organization and focuses attention on employee and management acceptance of those relationships. It involves establishing equal pay for jobs of equal worth and acceptable pay differentials for jobs of unequal worth.

Internal Equity   *See* Internal Consistency.

Internal Labor Markets   The rules or procedures that serve to regulate the allocation of employees among different jobs within a single organization.

Internal Pricing   Pricing jobs in relationship to what other jobs within the organization are paid.

Interrater Reliability   The extent of agreement among raters rating the same individual, group, or phenomena.

Inventories   Questionnaires in which tasks, behaviors, and abilities are listed. The core of all quantitative job analysis.

Job Analysis   The systematic process of collecting and making certain judgments about all of the important information related to the nature of a specific job. It provides the knowledge needed to define jobs and conduct job evaluation.

Job Based Systems Focus on jobs as the basic unit of analysis to determine the pay structure; hence, job analysis is required.

Job Classes or Grades Each represents a grouping of jobs which are considered substantially similar for pay purposes.

Job Cluster A series of jobs grouped for job evaluation and wage and salary administration purposes on the basis of common skills, occupational qualifications, technology, licensing, working conditions, union jurisdiction, workplace, career paths, and organizational tradition.

Job Content Information that describes a job. May include responsibility assumed and/or the tasks performed.

Job Description A summary of the most important features of the job as it is performed. It identifies the job and describes the general nature of the work, specific task responsibilities, outcomes, and employee characteristics required to perform the job.

Job Evaluation A systematic procedure designed to aid in establishing pay differentials among jobs within a single employer. It includes classification, comparison of the relative worth of jobs, blending internal and external market forces, measurement, negotiation, and judgment.

Job Evaluation Committee Usually having a membership representing all important constituencies within the organization. It may be charged with the responsibility of (1) selecting a job evaluation system, (2) carrying out or at least supervising the process of job evaluation, and (3) evaluating the success with which the job evaluation has been conducted. Its role may vary among organizations.

Job Evaluation Manual Contains information on the job evaluation plan and is used as a "yardstick" to evaluate jobs. It includes a description of the job evaluation method used, descriptions of all jobs, and if relevant, a description of compensable factors, numerical degree scales, and weights. May also contain a description of available review or appeals procedure.

Job Family Jobs involving work of the same nature but requiring different skill and responsibility levels (e.g., computing and account-recording is a job family; bookkeeper, accounting clerk, teller are jobs within that family).

Job Grade *See* Pay Grade.

Job Hierarchy A grouping of jobs based on their job-related similarities and differences, and on their value to the organization's objectives.

Job Structure Relationships among jobs inside an organization, based on work content and the job's relative contribution to achieving organization's objectives.

Job Value Approach to Pay Survey Under this approach the employer uses its internal job evaluation plan to assess the benchmark jobs provided in the survey.

Just Wage Doctrine A theory of job value that posited a "just" or equitable wage for any occupation based on that occupation's place in the larger social hierarchy. According to this doctrine, pay structures should be designed and justified on the basis of societal norms, custom, and tradition, not on the basis of economic and market forces.

Key Jobs *See* Benchmark (or Key) Jobs.

Knowledge Systems Link pay to additional (depth) knowledge related to the same job, (scientists and teachers).

Labor Demand   In economic models the demand for labor is a curve that indicates how the desired level of employment varies with changes in the price of labor when other factors are held constant. The shape of the labor demand curve is downward sloping. Thus, an increase in the wage rate will reduce the demand for labor in both the short and long run.

Labor Supply   In economic models the supply of labor is a curve or schedule representing the average pay required to attract different numbers of employees. The shape of the labor supply curve varies depending on the assumptions. In perfectly competitive markets, an individual firm faces a horizontal (elastic) supply of labor curve.

Lag Pay Level Policy   Setting a wage structure to match market rates at beginning of plan year only. The rest of the plan year, internal rates will lag behind market rates. Its objective is to offset labor costs, but it may hinder a firm's ability to attract and retain quality employees.

Lead Pay Level Policy   Setting a wage structure to lead the market throughout the plan year. Its aim is to maximize a firm's ability to attract and retain quality employees and to minimize employee dissatisfaction with pay.

Least Squares Line   In regression analysis, the line fitted to a scatterplot of coordinates that minimizes the squared deviations of coordinates around the line. This line is known as the "best fit" line.

Legally Required Benefits   Benefits that are required by statutory law: workers' compensation, social security, and unemployment compensation.

Leniency Error   A rating error in which rated performance consistently exceeds true score performance of ratees.

Leveling   Weighing market survey data according to the closeness of the job matches.

Level of Aggregation   The size of the work unit for which performance is measured (e.g., individual, work group, department, plant, organization) and to which rewards are distributed.

Level Rise   The percentage increase in the average wage rate paid.

$$\text{Percent level rise} = 100 \times \frac{\text{Average pay year end} - \text{Average pay year beginning}}{\text{Average pay at the beginning of the year}}$$

Linear Regression   A statistical technique which allows an analyst to build a model of a relationship between variables that are assumed to be linearly related.

Local Country Nationals (LCNs)   Citizens of a country in which a U.S. foreign subsidiary is located. LCNs' compensation is tied either to local wage rates or to the rates of U.S. expatriates performing the same job. Each practice has different equity implications.

Locality Pay   Adjusting pay rates for employees in a specific geographic area to account for local conditions such as labor shortages, housing cost differentials, etc.

Long-Term Disability (LTD) Plans   An insurance plan that provides payments to replace income lost through an inability to work that is not covered by other legally required disability income plans.

Long-Term Incentives   Inducements offered in advance to influence longer range (multiyear) results. Usually offered to top managers and professionals to focus on long-term organization objectives.

Lump Sum Award Payment of entire increase (typically merit increase) at one time. Amount is not factored into base pay so any benefits tied to base pay also don't increase.

Management by Objectives (MBO) An employee planning, development, and appraisal procedure in which a supervisor and a subordinate, or group of subordinates, jointly identify and establish common performance goals. Employee performance on the absolute standards is evaluated at the end of the specified period.

Marginal Product of Labor The additional output associated with the employment of one additional human resources unit, with other factors held constant.

Marginal Productivity Theory (MPT) By contrast with Marxist "surplus value" theory, MPT focuses on labor demand rather than supply and argues that employers will pay a wage to a unit of labor that equals that unit's use (not exchange) value. That is, work is compensated in proportion to its contribution to the organization's production objectives.

Marginal Revenue of Labor The additional revenue generated when the firm employs one additional unit of human resources, with other factors held constant.

Market Pay Lines Summarize the distributions of market rates for the benchmark jobs under consideration. Several methods to construct the lines can be used: a single line connecting the distributions' midpoints (means or medians), or the 25th, 50th, and 75th percentiles. Often the lines are fitted to the data through a statistical procedure, such as regression analysis.

Market Pricing Setting pay structures almost exclusively through matching pay for a very large percentage of jobs with rates paid in the external market.

Maturity Curves A plot of the empirical relationship between current pay and years since a professional has last received a degree (YSLD), thus allowing organizations to determine a competitive wage level for specific professional employees with varying levels of experience.

Merit Pay A reward that recognizes outstanding past performance. It can be given in the form of lump-sum payments or as increments to the base pay. Merit programs are commonly designed to pay different amounts (often at different times) depending on the level of performance.

Merit Pay Increase Guidelines Ties pay increases to performance. They may take one of two forms: The simplest version specifies pay increases permissible for different levels of performance. More complex guidelines tie pay not only to performance but also to position in the pay range.

Merrick Plan Individual incentive plan that provides for variable incentives as a function of units of production per time period. It works like the Taylor plan, but three piecework rates are set: (1) high—for production exceeding 100 percent of standard; (2) medium—for production between 83 percent and 100 percent of standard; and (3) low—for production less than 83 percent of standard.

Middle and Top Management Employees, above the supervisory level, who have technical and administrative training and whose major duties entail the direction of people and the organization. They can be classified as special groups to the extent the organization devises special compensation programs to attract and retain these relatively scarce human resources. By this definition, not all managers above the supervisory level qualify for consideration as a special group.

Minimum Wage   A minimum wage level for most Americans established by Congress as part of the FLSA of 1938.

Motivation   An individual's willingness to engage in some behavior. Primarily concerned with: (1) what energizes human behavior; (2) what directs or channels such behavior; and (3) how this behavior is maintained or sustained.

Multi-Skill Systems   Link pay to the number of *different jobs* (breadth) an employee is certified to do, regardless of the specific job he or she is doing.

National Electrical Manufacturing Association (NEMA)   A point factor job evaluation system that evolved into the National Position Evaluation Plan sponsored by NMTA associates.

National Metal Trades Association Plan (NMTA)   A point factor job evaluation plan for production, maintenance, and service personnel.

National Position Evaluation Plan   A point factor job evaluation system that evolved from the former NEMA plan. Today, the plan is sponsored by 11 management/manufacturing associations and is offered under the umbrella group known as NMTA associates.

Need Theories   Motivation theories that focus on internally generated needs which induce behaviors designed to reduce these needs.

Nonexempt Employees   Employees who are subject to the provisions of the Fair Labor Standards Act.

Nonqualified Deferred Compensation Plans   A plan does not qualify for tax exemption if an employer who pays high levels of deferred compensation to executives does not make proportionate contributions to lower level employees.

Objective Performance-Based Pay Systems   Focus on objective performance standards (e.g., counting output) derived from organizational objectives and a thorough analysis of the job (e.g., incentive and gain-sharing plans).

Organizational Culture   The composite of shared values, symbols, and cognitive schemes which ties people together in the organization.

Organizational Values   Shared norms and beliefs regarding what is socially, organizationally, and individually right, worthy, or desirable. The composite of values contributes to form a common organizational culture.

Paired Comparison   A ranking job evaluation method that involves comparing all possible pairs of jobs under study.

Pay Bands   Combining separate job classifications into a smaller number of divisions, called bands. Created in order to increase flexibility.

Pay Discrimination   It is usually defined to include: (1) access discrimination which occurs when qualified women and minorities are denied access to particular jobs, promotions, or training opportunities; and (2) valuation discrimination which takes place when minorities or women are paid less than white males for performing substantially equal work. Both types of discrimination are illegal under Title VII of the Civil Rights Act of 1964. Others argue that valuation discrimination can also occur when men and women hold entirely different jobs (in content or results) which are of comparable worth to the employer. Existing federal laws do not support the "equal pay for work of comparable worth" standard.

Pay Equity   *See* comparable worth.

Pay-for-Knowledge System   A compensation practice whereby employees are paid for the number of different jobs they can adequately perform or the amount of knowledge they possess.

Pay Grade   One of the classes, levels, or groups into which jobs of the same or similar values are grouped for compensation purposes. All jobs in a pay grade have the same pay range—maximum, minimum, and midpoint.

Pay Increase Guidelines   The mechanism through which performance levels are translated into pay increases and, therefore, dictate the size and time of the pay reward for good performance.

Pay Level   An average of the array of rates paid by an employer.

Pay Level Policies   Decisions concerning a firm's level of pay vis-à-vis product and labor market competitors. There are three classes of pay level policies: to lead, to match, or to follow competition.

Pay Mix   Relative emphasis among compensation components such as base pay, merit, incentives, and benefits.

Pay Objectives   *See* Compensation Objectives.

Pay Plan Design   A process to identify pay levels, components, and timing which best match individual needs and organizational requirements.

Pay Policy Line   Represents the organization's pay level policy relative to what competitors pay for similar jobs.

Pay Ranges   The range of pay rates from minimum to maximum set for a pay grade or class. They put limits on the rates an employer will pay for a particular job.

Pay Satisfaction   A function of the discrepancy between employee perceptions of how much pay they *should* receive and how much pay they *do* receive. If these perceptions are equal an employee is said to experience pay satisfaction.

Pay Structures   The array of pay rates for different jobs within a single organization; they focus attention on differential compensation paid for work of unequal worth.

Pay Techniques   Mechanisms or technologies of compensation management, such as job analysis, job descriptions, market surveys, job evaluation, and the like, that tie the four basic pay policies to the pay objectives.

Pay with Competition Policy   This policy tries to ensure that a firm's labor costs are approximately equal to those of its competitors. It seeks to avoid placing an employer at a disadvantage in pricing products or in maintaining a qualified work force.

PAYSOPs (Payroll-Based Tax Credit Employee Stock Ownership Plans)   A new form of TRASOPs beginning in 1983 in which the tax credit allotted to plan sponsors who permit and match voluntary employee contributions is payroll based, not investment based.

Pension Plan   A form of deferred compensation. All pension plans usually have four common characteristics: (1) they involve deferred payments to a former employee (or surviving spouse) for past services rendered; and they all specify (2) a normal retirement age at which time benefits begin to accrue to the employee; (3) the formula employed to calculate benefits; and (4) integration with social security benefits.

Percentage Pay Range Overlap   The degree to which adjacent pay ranges in a structure overlap is usually calculated in terms of the following percentage:

$$\text{Percentage overlap} = 100 \times \frac{\text{Maximum rate for lower pay grade} - \text{Minimum rate for higher pay grade}}{\text{Maximum rate for lower pay grade} - \text{Minimum rate for lower pay grade}}$$

Performance Evaluation (or performance appraisal)   A process to determine the correspondence between worker behavior/task outcomes and employer expectations (performance standards).

Performance Ranking   The simplest, fastest, easiest to understand, and least expensive performance appraisal technique. Orders employees from highest to lowest in performance.

Performance Standards   An explicit statement of what work output is expected from employees in exchange for compensation.

Planned Compa-Ratio Budgeting   A form of top down budgeting in which a planned compa-ratio rather than a planned level rise is established to control pay costs.

Planned Level Rise   The percentage increase in average pay that is planned to occur after considering such factors as anticipated rates of change in market data, changes in cost of living, the employer's ability to pay, and the effects of turnover and promotions. This index may be used in top down budgeting to control compensation costs.

Planned Level Rise Budgeting   A form of top down budgeting under which a planned level rise rather than a planned compa-ratio is established as the target to control pay costs.

Point (Factor) Method   A job evaluation method that employs (1) compensable factors, (2) factor degrees numerically scaled, and (3) weights reflecting the relative importance of each factor. Once scaled degrees and weights are established for each factor, each job is measured against each compensable factor and a total score is calculated for each job. The total points assigned to a job determine the job's relative value and hence its location in the pay structure.

Policy Capturing Approach to Factor Selection   *See* Statistical Approach to Factor Selection.

Portability   Transferability of pension benefits for employees moving to a new organization; ERISA does not require mandatory portability of private pensions. On a voluntary basis, the employer may agree to let an employee's pension benefits transfer to an individual retirement account (IRA) or, in a reciprocating arrangement, to the new employer.

Portal-to-Portal Act of 1947   Defines compensable working time to include only the "principal activity" unless the custom is otherwise.

Position Analysis Questionnaire (PAQ)   A structured job analysis technique that classifies job information into seven basic factors: information input, mental processes, work output, relationships with other persons, job context, other job characteristics, and general dimensions. The PAQ analyzes jobs in terms of worker-oriented data.

Position Description Questionnaire (PDQ)   A quantitative job analysis technique.

Pregnancy Discrimination Act of 1978   An amendment to Title VII of the Civil Rights Act. It requires employers to extend to pregnant employees or spouses of employees the same disability and medical benefits provided other employees or spouses of employees.

Prevailing Wage Laws   A government-defined prevailing wage is the minimum wage that must be paid for work done on covered government projects or purchases. In practice these prevailing rates have been union rates paid in various geographic areas. The main prevailing wage laws are: (1) Davis-Bacon (1931), (2) Walsh-Healey Public Contracts Act (1936), and (3) McNamara-O'Hara Service Contract Act of 1965.

Procedural Equity   Concerned with the process used to make and implement decisions about pay. It suggests that the way pay decisions are made and implemented may be as important to employees as the results of the decisions.

Procedural Justice   Fairness in the procedures used to determine the amount of reward employees will receive.

Process Theories   Motivation theories that focus on *how* people are motivated rather than on what motivates people (e.g., drive, expectancy and equity theories).

Product Market   The market (or market segments) in which a firm competes to sell products or services.

Professional Employee   An employee who has specialized training of a scientific or intellectual nature and whose major duties do not entail the supervision of people.

Profit-Sharing Plans   Focus on profitability as the standard for group incentive. These plans typically can be found in one of three distributions: (1) cash or current distribution plans provide full payment to participants soon after profits have been determined (quarterly or annually); (2) deferred plans have a portion of current profits credited to employee accounts, with cash payment made at time of retirement, disability, severance, or death; and (3) combination plans incorporate aspects of both current and deferred options.

Progression through the Pay Ranges   There are three strategies to move employees through the pay ranges: (1) automatic or seniority-based progression, which is most appropriate when the necessary job skills are within the grasp of most employees; (2) merit progression, which is more appropriate when jobs allow variations in performance; and (3) a combination of automatic and merit progression. For example, employers may grant automatic increases up to the midpoint of the range and permit subsequent increases only when merited on the basis of performance appraisal.

Qualified Deferred Compensation Plan   To qualify for tax exemption, a deferred compensation program must provide contributions or benefits for employees other than executives that are proportionate in compensation terms to contributions provided to executives.

Quantitative Job Analysis (QJA)   Job analysis method that relies on scaled questionnaires and inventories that produce job-related data which are documentable, can be statistically analyzed, and may be more objective.

Range Maximums   The maximum values to be paid for a job grade, representing the top value the organization places on the output of the work.

Range Midpoint   The salary midway between the minimum and maximum rates of a salary range. The midpoint rate for each range is usually set to correspond to the pay policy line and represents the rate paid for satisfactory performance on the job.

Range Minimums   The minimum values to be paid for a job grade, representing the minimum value the organization places on the work. Often rates below the minimum are used for trainees.

Range Overlap   The degree of overlap between adjoining grade ranges is determined by the differences in midpoints among ranges and the range spread. A high degree of overlap and narrow midpoint differentials indicate small differences in the value of jobs in the adjoining grades, and permit promotions without much change in the rates paid. By contrast, a small degree of overlap and wide midpoint differentials allow the manager to reinforce a promotion with a large salary increase. Usually calculated as

$$\text{Percentage overlap} = 100 \times \frac{\text{Maximum rate for lower pay grade} - \text{Minimum rate for higher pay grade}}{\text{Maximum rate for lower pay grade} - \text{Minimum rate for lower pay grade}}$$

Range Width or Spread   The range maximum and minimum are usually based on what other employers are doing and some judgment about how the range spread fits the organization, including the amount of individual discretion in the work. Usually calculated as

$$\frac{[\text{Range Maximum} - \text{Range Minimum}]}{\text{Range Minimum}}$$

Ranges   *See* Pay Ranges.

Ranking   A simple job evaluation method that involves ordering the job descriptions from highest to lowest in value.

Rating Errors   Errors in judgment that occur in a systematic manner when an individual observes and evaluates a person, group, or phenomenon. The most frequently described rating errors include halo, leniency, severity, and central tendency errors.

Red Circle Rates   Pay rates that are above the maximum rate for a job or pay range for a grade.

Regression   A statistical technique for relating present pay differentials to some criterion, that is, pay rates in the external market, rates for jobs held predominantly by men, or factor weights that duplicate present rates for all jobs in the organization.

Reinforcement Theories   Such as expectancy and operant conditioning theory grant a prominent role to rewards (e.g., compensation) in motivating behavior. They argue that pay motivates behavior to the extent merit increases and other work-related rewards are allocated on the basis of performance.

Relative Value of Jobs   Refers to their relative contribution to organizational goals, to their external market rates, or to some other agreed-upon rates.

Relevant Markets   Those employers with whom an organization competes for skills and products/services. Three factors commonly used to determine the relevant markets are: the occupation or skills required, the geography (willingness to relocate and/or commute), and the other employers involved (particularly those who compete in the product market).

Reliability   The consistency of the results obtained. That is, the extent to which any measuring procedure yields the same results on repeated trials. Reliable job information does not mean that it is accurate (valid), comprehensive, or free from bias.

Reopener Clause   A provision in an employment contract that specifies that wages, and sometimes such nonwage items as pension/benefits, will be renegotiated under certain conditions (changes in cost of living, organization profitability, and so on).

Revenue Act of 1978   It primarily simplified pension plans, added tax incentives for individual retirement accounts (IRAs), and adjusted requirements for ESOPs. The act also provided that cafeteria benefit plans need not be included in gross income, and reaffirmed the legality of deferring compensation and taxes due on it for an employee.

Reward System   The composite of all organizational mechanisms and strategies used to formally acknowledge employee behaviors and performance. It includes all forms of compensation, promotions, and assignments; nonmonetary awards and recognitions; training opportunities; job design and analysis; organizational design and working conditions; the supervisor; social networks; performance standards and reward criteria; performance evaluation; and the like.

Rowan Plan   Individual incentive plan that provides for variable incentives as a function of a standard expressed as time period per unit of production. It is similar to the Halsey plan, but in this plan a worker's bonus increases as the time required to complete the task decreases.

Rucker Plan   A group cost savings plan in which cost reductions due to employee efforts are shared with the employees. It involves a somewhat more complex formula than a Scanlon plan for determining employee incentive bonuses.

Salary   Pay given to employees who are exempt from regulations of the Fair Labor Standards Act, and hence do not receive overtime pay (e.g., managers and professionals). "Exempts" pay is calculated at an annual or monthly rate rather than hourly.

Salary Continuation Plans   Benefit options that provide some form of protection for disability. Some are legally required, such as workers' compensation provisions for work-related disability, and Social Security disability income provisions for those who qualify.

Salary Sales Compensation Plan   Under this plan the sales force is paid a fixed income not dependent on sales volume.

Sales Compensation   Any form of compensation paid to sales representatives. Sales compensation formulas usually attempt to establish direct incentives for sales outcomes.

Scaling   Determining the intervals on a measurement instrument.

Scanlon Plan   A group cost savings plan designed to lower labor costs without lowering the level of a firm's activity. Incentives are derived as the ratio between labor costs and sales values of production (SVOP).

Seniority Increases   These tie pay increases to a progression pattern based on seniority. To the extent performance improves with time on the job, this method has the rudiments of paying for performance.

Severity Error   A rating error in which rated performance is consistently lower than the true score performance of ratees.

Short-Term Disability   *See* Workers' Compensation.

Short-Term Incentives   Inducements offered in advance to influence future short-range (annual) results. Usually very specific performance standards are established.

Short-Term Income Protection   *See* Unemployment Insurance.

Sick Leave   Paid time when not working due to illness or injury.

Simplified Employee Pension (SEP)   A retirement income arrangement intended to markedly reduce the paperwork for regular pension plans.

Single Rate Pay System   A compensation policy under which all employees in a given job are paid at the same rate instead of being placed in a pay grade. Generally applies to situations in which there is little room for variation in job performance, such as an assembly line.

Skill-Based/Global Approach to Wage Survey   This approach does not emphasize comparison of pay for specific jobs. Instead, it recognizes that employers usually tailor jobs to the organization or individual employee. Therefore, the rates paid to every individual employee in an entire skill group or function are included in the salary survey and become the reference point to design pay levels and structures.

Skill Based Pay System   *See* Pay-for-Knowledge System.

Skill Requirement   Includes experience, training, and ability as measured by the performance requirements of a particular job.

Slippage   *See* turnover effect.

Social Information Processing Theory (SIP)   Counters need theory by focusing on external factors that motivate performance. According to SIP theorists, workers pay attention to environmental cues (e.g., inputs/outputs of coworkers) and process this information in a way that may alter personal work goals, expectancies, and perceptions of equity. In turn this influences job attitudes, behavior, and performance.

Social Security   The Social Security Act of 1935 established what has become the federal old-age, survivors, disability, and health insurance system. The beneficiaries are workers that participate in the Social Security program, their spouses, dependent parents, and dependent children. Benefits vary according to: (1) earnings of the worker, (2) length of time in the program, (3) age when benefits start, (4) age and number of recipients other than the worker, and (5) state of health of recipients other than the worker.

Special Groups   Employee groups for whom compensation practices diverge from typical company procedures (e.g., supervisors, middle and upper management, nonsupervisory professionals, sales, and foreign service personnel).

Spillover Effect   This phenomenon refers to the fact that improvements obtained in unionized firms "spill over" to nonunion firms seeking ways to lessen workers' incentives for organizing a union.

Standard Hour Plan   Individual incentive plan in which rate determination is based on time period per unit of production, and wages vary directly as a constant function of production level. In this context, the incentive rate in standard hour plans is set based on completion of a task in some expected time period.

Standard Rating Scales   Characterized by: (1) one or more performance standards being developed and defined for the appraiser; and (2) each performance standard having a measurement scale indicating varying levels of performance on that dimension. Appraisers rate the appraisee by checking the point on the scale that best represents the appraisee's performance level. Rating scales vary in the extent to which anchors along the scale are defined.

Statistical Approach to Factor Selection This method uses a variety of statistical procedures to derive factors from data collected through quantitative job analysis from a sample of jobs that represent the range of the work employees (or an employee group) perform in the company. It is often labeled as "policy capturing" to contrast it with the committee judgment approach.

Stock Appreciation Rights (SARs) An SAR permits an executive all the potential capital gain of a stock incentive option (ISO) without requiring the purchase of stock and, thus, reduces an executive's cash commitment. Payment is provided on demand for the difference between the stock option price and current market price.

Stock Purchase Plan (Nonqualified) A plan that is, in effect, a management stock purchase plan. It allows senior management or other key personnel to buy stock in the business. This plan has certain restrictions: (1) the stockholder must be employed for a certain period of time; (2) the business has the right to buy back the stock; and (3) stockholders cannot sell the stock for a defined period.

Stock Purchase Plan (Qualified) A program under which employees buy shares in the company's stock, with the company contributing a specific amount for each unit of employee contribution. Also, stock may be offered at a fixed price (usually below market) and paid for in full by the employees.

Straight Piecework System Individual incentive plan in which rate determination is based on units of production per time period, and wages vary directly as a constant function of production level.

Strategic Issues Critical considerations in compensation design such as congruency between the pay system and the strategy, the organization's culture and values, employee needs, and the nature of the union relationships.

Strategy The fundamental direction of the organization. It guides the deployment of all resources, including compensation.

Subjective Performance-Based Pay Systems Focus on subjective performance standards (e.g., achievement of agreed-upon objectives) derived from organizational objectives and a thorough analysis of the job.

Substantive Equity In contrast with procedural equity, substantive equity refers to the equity of the outcomes (results such as pay level, structure, and employee differentials) of the pay system.

Supplemental Unemployment Benefits (SUB) Plan Employer-funded plan which supplements state unemployment insurance payments to workers during temporary periods of layoffs. Largely concentrated in the automobile, steel, and related industries.

Surplus Value The difference between labor's use and exchange value. According to Marx, under capitalism wages are based on labor's exchange value—which is lower than its use value—and, thus, provide only a subsistent wage.

SVOP (Sales Value of Production) This concept includes sales revenue and the value of goods in inventory.

Tax Equalization Allowances A method whereby an expatriate pays neither more nor less tax than the assumed home-country tax on base remuneration. The employer usually deducts the assumed home-country tax from monthly salary and reimburses the employee for all taxes paid in the country of assignment and any actual home-country tax on company remuneration only.

Taylor Plan   Individual incentive plan that provides for variable incentives as a function of units of production per time period. It provides two piecework rates that are established for production above (or below) standard, and these rates are higher (or lower) than the regular wage incentive level.

Third Country Nationals (TCNs)   Employees of a U.S. foreign subsidiary who maintain citizenship in a country other than the United States or the host country. TCNs' compensation is tied to comparative wages in the local country, the United States, or the country of citizenship. Each approach has different equity implications.

Thrift Savings Plans   The typical thrift plan is designed to help American workers in meeting savings goals. The most common plan involves a 50 percent employer match on employee contributions up to a maximum of 6 percent of pay.

Title VII of the Civil Rights Act of 1964   A major piece of legislation prohibiting pay discrimination. It is much broader in intent than the EPA, forbidding discrimination on the basis of race, color, religion, sex, pregnancy, or national origin.

"Top Down" Approach to Pay Budgeting   Also known as unit-level budgeting. Under this approach a total pay budget for the organization (or unit) is determined and allocated "down" to individual employees during the plan year. There are many approaches to unit-level budgeting. They differ in the type of financial index used as a control measure. Controlling to planned level rise and controlling to a planned compa-ratio are two typical approaches.

Total Compensation   The complete pay package for employees including all forms of money, benefits, services, and in-kind payments.

TRASOP (Tax Reduction Act Employee Stock Ownership Plan)   A form of Employee Stock Ownership Plan (ESOP) that meets specific requirements of the Tax Reform Act of 1975, as amended.

Two-Tier Pay Plans   Wage structures that differentiate pay for the same jobs based on hiring date. A contract is negotiated that specifies that employees hired after a specified date will receive lower wages than their higher seniority peers working on the same or similar jobs.

Turnover Effect   The downward pressure on average wage that results from the replacement of high-wage-earning employees with workers earning a lower wage.

Unemployment Benefits   *See* Unemployment Insurance.

Unemployment Compensation   *See* Unemployment Insurance.

Unemployment Insurance (UI)   State-administered programs that provide financial security for workers during periods of joblessness. These plans are wholly financed by employers except in Alabama, Alaska, and New Jersey, where there are provisions for relatively small employee contributions.

Unequal Impact   *See* Disparate (Unequal) Impact Standard.

Unequal Treatment   *See* Disparate (Unequal) Treatment Standard.

United States Expatriates (USEs)   American citizens working for a U.S. subsidiary in a foreign country. Main compensation concerns are "to keep the expatriates whole" relative to American-based counterparts and, also, to provide them with an incentive wage for accepting the assignment in a foreign country.

Universal Job Factors   Factors that could theoretically be used to evaluate all jobs in all organizations.

Use Value   The value or price ascribed to the use or consumption of labor in the production of goods or services.

Valence   The amount of positive or negative value placed on specific outcomes by an individual.

Validity   The accuracy of the results obtained. That is, the extent to which any measuring device measures what it purports to measure.

Valuation Discrimination   Focuses on the pay women and minorities receive for the work they perform. Discrimination occurs when members of these groups are paid less than white males for performing substantially equal work. This definition of pay discrimination is based on the standard of "equal pay for equal work." Many believe that this definition is limited. In their view, valuation discrimination can also occur when men and women hold entirely different jobs (in content or results) which are of comparable worth to the employer. Existing federal laws do not support the "equal pay for work of comparable worth" standard.

Variable Pay   Tying pay to productivity or some measure that can vary with the firm's profitability.

Vesting   A benefit plan provision that guarantees that participants will, after meeting certain requirements, retain a right to the benefits they have accrued, or some portion of them, even if employment under their plan terminates before retirement.

VIE Theory   *See* Expectancy Theory.

Wage   Pay given to employees who are covered by overtime and reporting provisions of the Fair Labor Standards Act. "Nonexempts" usually have their pay calculated at an hourly rate rather than a monthly or annual rate.

Wage Adjustment Provisions   Clauses in a multiyear union contract which specify the types of wage adjustments that have to be implemented during the life of the contract. These adjustments might be specified in three major ways: (1) deferred wage increases—negotiated at the time of contract negotiation with the time and amount specified in the contract; (2) cost-of-living adjustments (COLAs) or escalator clauses; and (3) reopener clauses.

Wage and Price Controls   Government regulations that aim at maintaining low inflation and low levels of unemployment. They frequently focus on "cost push" inflation, limiting the size of the pay raises and the rate of increases in the prices charged for goods and services. Used for limited time periods only.

Wage Survey   The systematic process of collecting information and making judgments about the compensation paid by other employers. Wage survey data are useful to design pay levels and structures.

Walsh-Healey Public Contracts Act of 1936   A federal law requiring certain employers holding federal contracts for the manufacture or provision of materials, supplies, and equipment to pay industry-prevailing wage rates.

Work or Task Data   Involve the elemental units of work (tasks), with emphasis on the purpose of each task, collected for job analysis. Work data describe the job in terms of actual tasks performed and their output.

Worker or Behavioral Data   Include the behaviors required by the job. Used in job analysis.

Workers' Compensation   An insurance program, paid for by the employer, designed to protect employees from expenses incurred for a work-related injury or disease. Each state has its own workers' compensation law.

YSLD   Years since a professional has last received a degree.

Name Index

A

Abraham, L. M., 152
Abrami, Philip, 289
Adams, J. S., 43, 256, 257
Ahern, E., 398
Ajayi, Richard, 546
Aldag, Ramon J., 54, 58
Aldrich, Mark, 487
Alexander, R. A., 152, 466
Alexander, S., 266
Allen, Robert E., 509
Allen, Steven, 563
Allport, Karin, 105
Alvares, Kim, 286
Alvord, W. G., 77
Anderson, C. H., 152
Anderson, C. S., 173
Anderson, Gary, 77
Anderson, R. C., 290
Andrisiani, P. J., 180
Arvey, R. D., 75, 129, 152, 157, 158, 485
Ash, P., 152
Ash, R. A., 53, 57, 70, 75, 77, 370
Ashenfelter, Orley, 472, 562
Atchinson, Thomas J., 113, 130

B

Bailey, William, 567
Baird, Lloyd, 289
Baker, George P., 6, 187
Baker, Helen, 125
Bakerman, Theodore, 384
Balkin, David, 13, 14, 173, 234, 270, 331, 387, 445, 486, 515, 543
Bandura, A., 255
Barber, Alison E., 197

Barnard, C. L., 323
Barnes, J., 269
Barnes, Lesley, 539, 541
Barr, Steven, H., 54, 58
Barrett, Gerald, 152, 158, 159, 297, 451, 466
Barron, Frank, 281
Barron, John M., 170
Barry, Dave, 463
Bates, Marsh W., 160
Baumann, Phyllis Tropper, 459
Baylos, L. M., 376
Beadle, Carson E., 368
Beatty, James R., 480
Beatty, Richard, 289, 290, 480
Becker, Brian, 182, 185
Becker, Gary S., 180
Beebe, T., 269
Belcher, David W., 34, 100, 110, 126, 216
Belcher, John, 344
Belenky, Ann Holt, 52
Belitsky, A. H., 249
Bellak, Alvin O., 100, 480
Belous, Richard S., 497
Bemis, Stephen E., 52
Bencoe, Allyn, 74
Benge, Eugene J., 100, 114, 128
Bennett, N., 77
Bentiam, Harry C., 563
Berger, Brigette, 475
Berger, Chris, 257, 512
Berger, P. K., 58
Bergmann, Barbara R., 472
Bergmann, Thomas J., 233, 474, 515
Berkowitz, L., 43, 256
Bernardin, H. J., 286, 289, 290, 293, 294, 296
Beyer, Janice M., 17
Bieber, Owen, 530
Bigoness, William, 289
Billet, Thomas, 411

Birnbaum, M. H., 70
Bishop, John, 170
Blair, Dennis, 533
Blau, Francine, 463
Blencoe, Allyn, 75
Blencoe, W. A., 294
Blum, J., 75
Blumrosen, Ruth G., 157, 480
Bognanno, Michael L., 36
Boisseau, Robert T., 512
Borman, Martin, 269
Boudreau, John, 53, 257
Bowers, Mollie, 564
Brandt, Alfred R., 73
Bretz, Robert, 370
Brief, Arthur P., 54, 58
Briggs, Vernon M., Jr., 175, 183
Brinks, James T., 105
Broderick, Renae, 3
Bronson, J. S., 16
Brown, C., 179
Brown, Judith Olans, 459
Bryan, J., 251
Buchele, Robert, 487
Buckley, M. R., 293, 294, 296
Bullock, R. J., 350
Burk, Samuel L. H., 114
Burnaska, R. F., 269
Burnett, John H., 70, 75
Burns, Mike, 104 ,148
Burroughs, Julio D., 510
Byrne, John A., 32

C

Cafferty, T. P., 288
Caldwell, David F., 75
Callahan, Thomas, 262
Cambell, Donald J., 259
Camp, C., 75

Subject Index